Street by Stre

SHEFFIELD

BARNSLEY, CHESTERFIELD, DONCASTER, ROTHERHAM

Chapeltown, Conisbrough, Dronfield, Mexborough, Mosborough, Rawmarsh, Stocksbridge, Thurnscoe, Wath upon Dearne, Wombwell

1st edition May 2001

© Automobile Association Developments Limited 2001

This product includes map data licensed from Ordnance Survey® with the permission of the Controller of Her Majesty's Stationery Office. © Crown copyright 2000. All rights reserved. Licence No: 399221.

Published by AA Publishing (a trading name of Automobile Association Developments Limited, whose registered office is Norfolk House, Priestley Road, Basingstoke, Hampshire, RG24 9NY. Registered number 1878835).

Mapping produced by the Cartographic Department of The Automobile Association.

A CIP Catalogue record for this book is available from the British Library.

Printed by G. Canale & C. s.p.a., Torino, Italy

The contents of this atlas are believed to be correct at the time of the latest revision. However, the publishers cannot be held responsible for loss occasioned to any person acting or refraining from action as a result of any material in this atlas, nor for any errors, omissions or changes in such material. The publishers would welcome information to correct any errors or omissions and to keep this atlas up to date. Please write to Publishing, The Automobile Association, Fanum House, Basing View, Basingstoke, Hampshire, RG21 4EA.

Ref: MD072

Key to map pages ii-iii

Key to map symbols iv-1

Enlarged scale pages 2-11

Street by Street 12-191

Index – towns & villages 192-193

Index – streets 194-237

Index – featured places 238-244

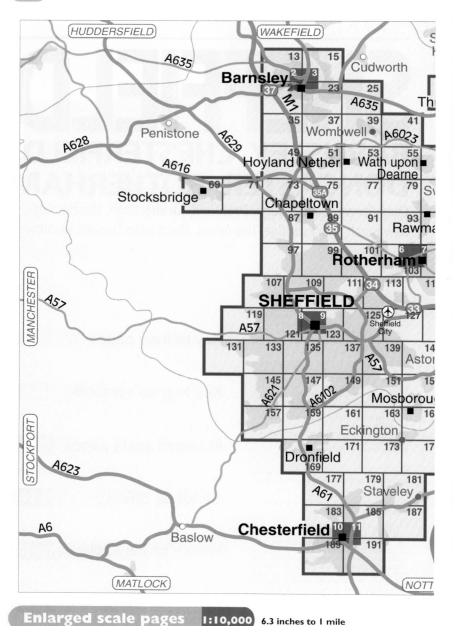

HUDDERSFIELD   WAKEFIELD

A635

Barnsley

Cudworth

13   15

2   3

37   21   23   25

A635   Th

M1

A628   Penistone

A629

35   37   39   41

Wombwell   A6023

A616

49   51   53   55

Hoyland Nether   Wath upon Dearne

69   71   73   75   77   79

Stocksbridge

Chapeltown

35A

87   89   91   93

35   Rawma

97   99   101   6   7

Rotherham

103

MANCHESTER

A57

107   109   111   34   113   11

SHEFFIELD

119   125   33

A57   8   9   127

121   123   Sheffield City

131   133   135   137   139   14

A57   Aston

145   147   149   151   15

A621   A6102   Mosborou

157   159   161   163   16

STOCKPORT

Eckington

171   173   17

A623

Dronfield

169

177   179   181

A61   Staveley

A6   Baslow

183   185   187

Chesterfield 10   11

189   191

MATLOCK   NOTT

Enlarged scale pages   **1:10,000**   6.3 inches to 1 mile

0   1/4   miles   1/2

0   1/4   1/2   kilometres   3/4   1

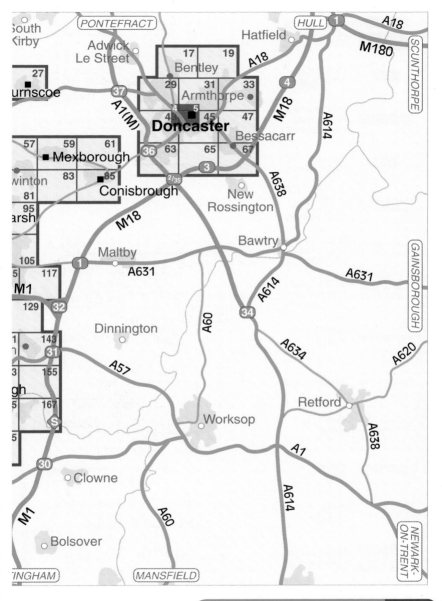

4.2 inches to 1 mile **Scale of main map pages** **1:15,000**

miles

0   1/4   1/2   3/4   1

kilometres

0   1/4   1/2   3/4   1   1 1/4   1 1/2

iv

Junction 9	Motorway & junction
Services	Motorway service area
	Primary road single/dual carriageway
Services	Primary road service area
	A road single/dual carriageway
	B road single/dual carriageway
	Other road single/dual carriageway
	Restricted road
	Private road
← ←	One way street
	Pedestrian street
	Track/ footpath
	Road under construction
[= = =]	Road tunnel
P	Parking

P+🚌	Park & Ride
🚌	Bus/coach station
⇌	Railway & main railway station
⇌	Railway & minor railway station
⊖	Underground station
⊖	Light railway & station
+++++++++	Preserved private railway
LC	Level crossing
●—●—●	Tramway
- - - - - -	Ferry route
··············	Airport runway
— · — · — ·	Boundaries- borough/ district
▼▼▼▼▼▼▼	Mounds
93	Page continuation 1:15,000
7	Page continuation to enlarged scale 1:10,000

River/canal lake, pier

Toilet with disabled facilities

Aqueduct lock, weir

Petrol station

465
▲
Winter Hill
Peak (with height in metres)

PH Public house

Beach

PO Post Office

Coniferous woodland

Public library

Broadleaved woodland

Tourist Information Centre

Mixed woodland

Castle

Park

Historic house/ building

Cemetery

Wakehurst Place NT National Trust property

Built-up area

Museum/ art gallery

Featured building

✝ Church/chapel

City wall

Country park

A&E Accident & Emergency hospital

Theatre/ performing arts

Toilet

Cinema

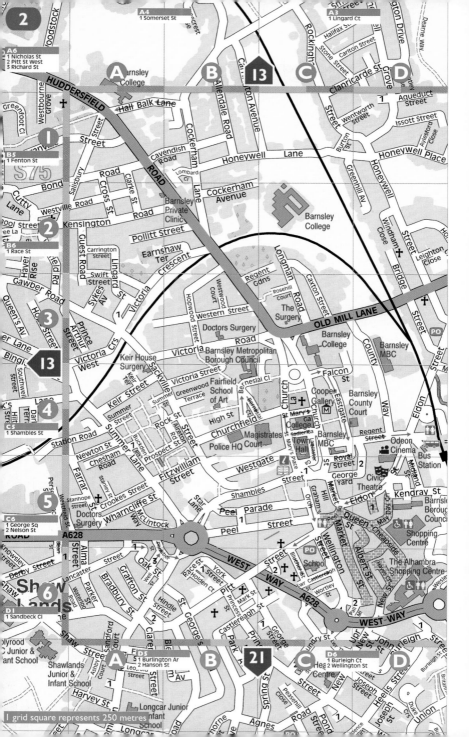

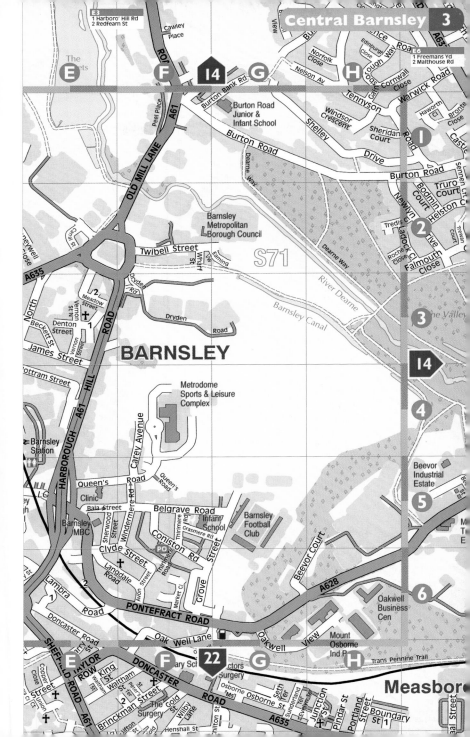

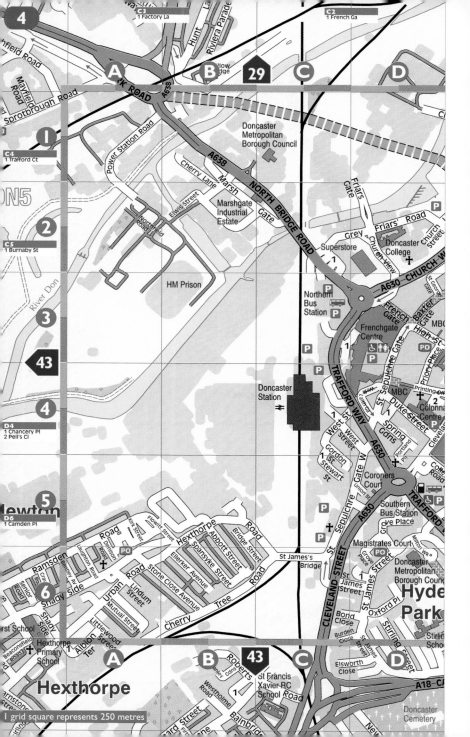

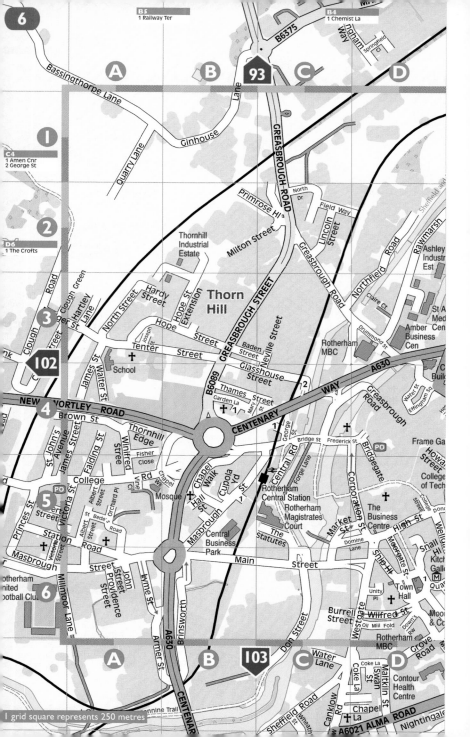

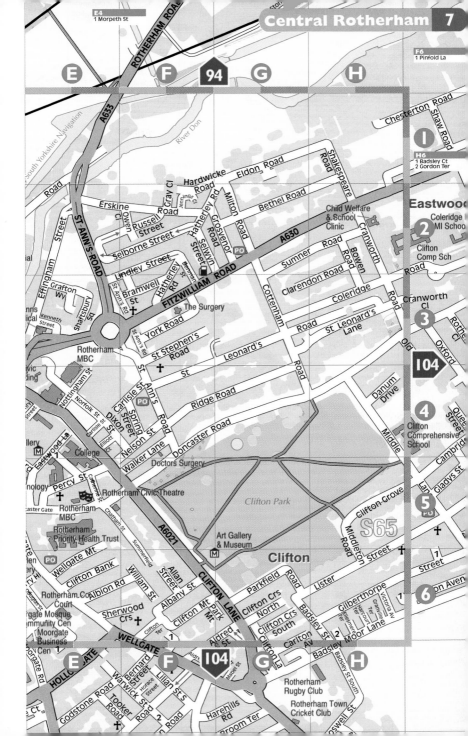

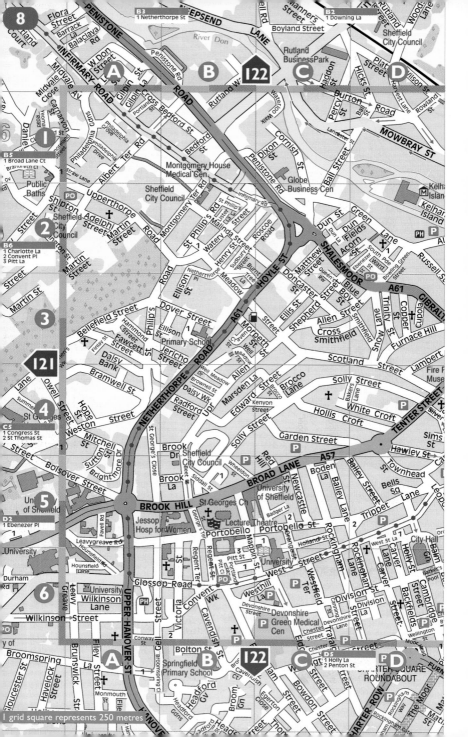

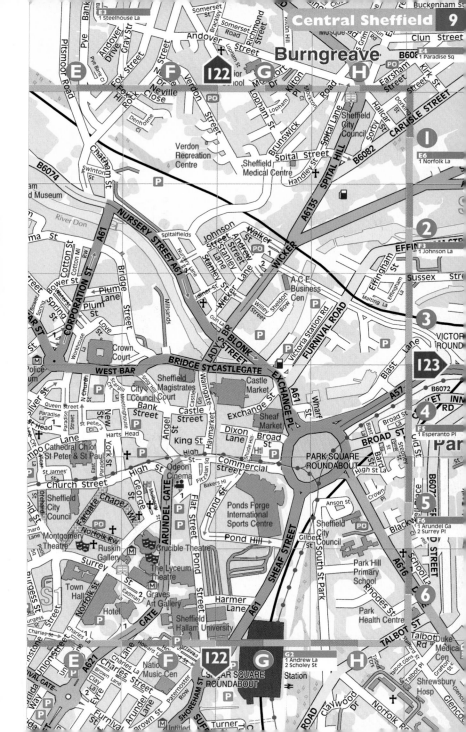

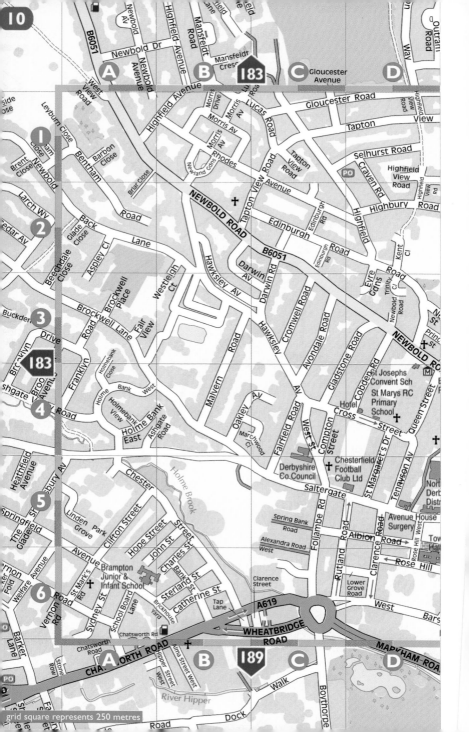

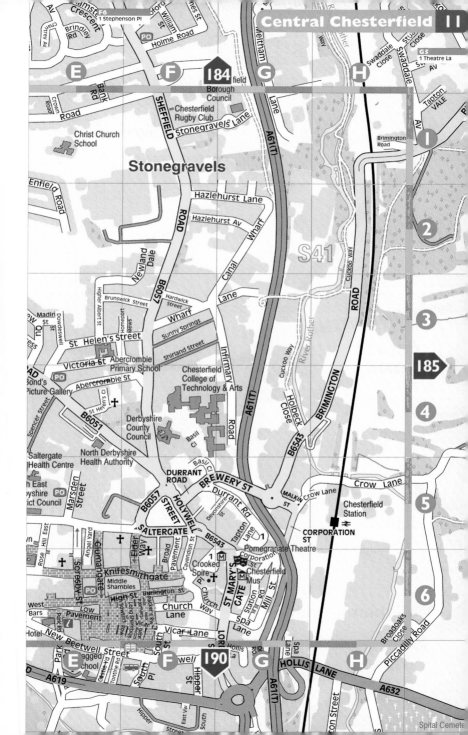

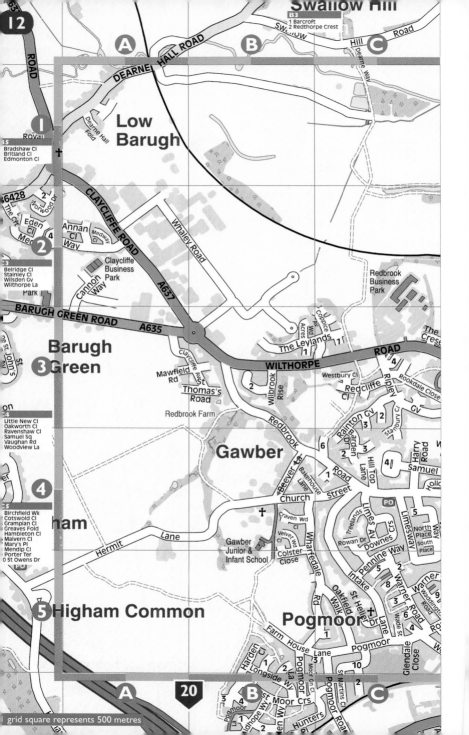

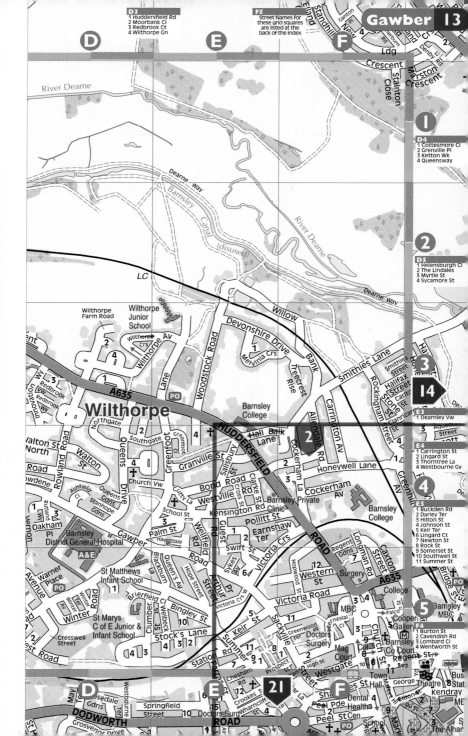

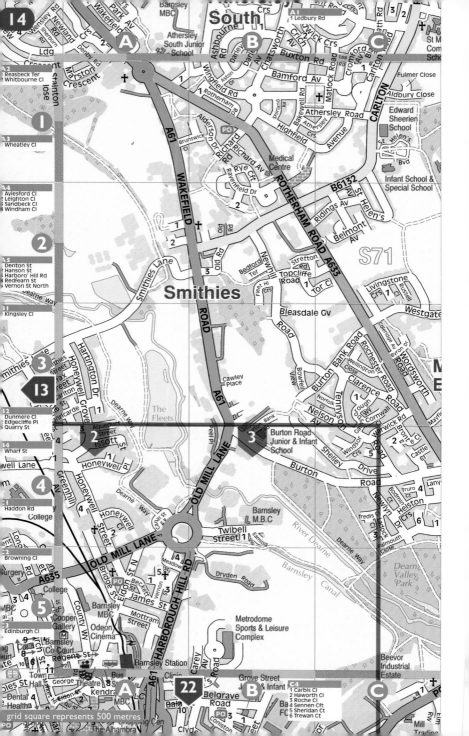

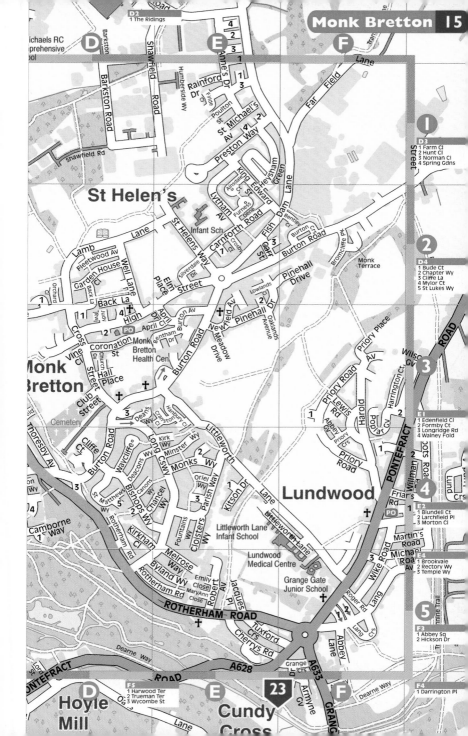

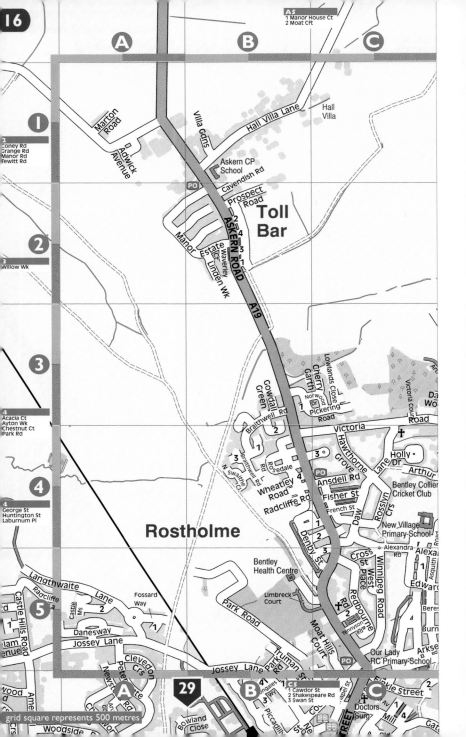

16

A5
1 Manor House Ct
2 Moat Cft

A   B   C

1

2
Coney Rd
Grange Rd
Manor Rd
Hewitt Rd

Marton Road

Adwick Avenue

Villa Gdns

Hall Villa Lane

Hall Villa

Askern CP School

PO

Cavendish Rd

Prospect Road

Toll Bar

2

3
Willow Wk

Manor Estate

ASKERN ROAD

Waverley Cl

Linden Wk

4
3
1

3

Gowdall Green

Braithwell Rd

Cherry Garth

Lowlands Close

Norwood Dr

Pickering Road

Victoria Court

Da Wo

Road

4
Acacia Ct
Ayton Wk
Chestnut Ct
Park Rd

Braithwell Rd

N swathe

Rosedale

Victoria

Hawthorne Grove

Holly Dr

Arthur

4

4
George St
Huntington St
Laburnum Pl

Wheatley Road

Radcliffe Rd

PO

Ansdell Rd

Fisher St

French St

Roslyn Crs

Bentley Collier Cricket Club

New Village Primary School

Rostholme

Denby St

Cross St

West Place

Winnipeg Road

Alexandra Rd

Alexa

Edwa

Bentley Health Centre

Limbreck Court

Redbourne Road

Beres

5

Langthwaite Lane

Radcliffe La

Castle Ms

Danesway

Jossey Lane

Fossard Way

Park Road

Moat Hills Court

Tennyson Rd

Arkse

Burn

Castle Hills Road

lam enue

Clevedon Crs

Jossey Lane

Truman St

Park Rd

Our Lady RC Primary School

PO

Finkle Street

A   29   B

C5
1 Cawdor St
2 Shakespeare Rd
3 Swan St

Piccadill

Doctors Surg

STREET

Gate

Woodside

Bowland Close

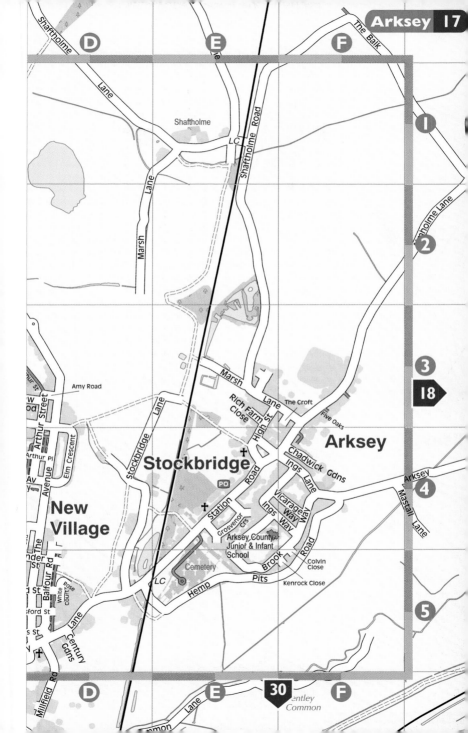

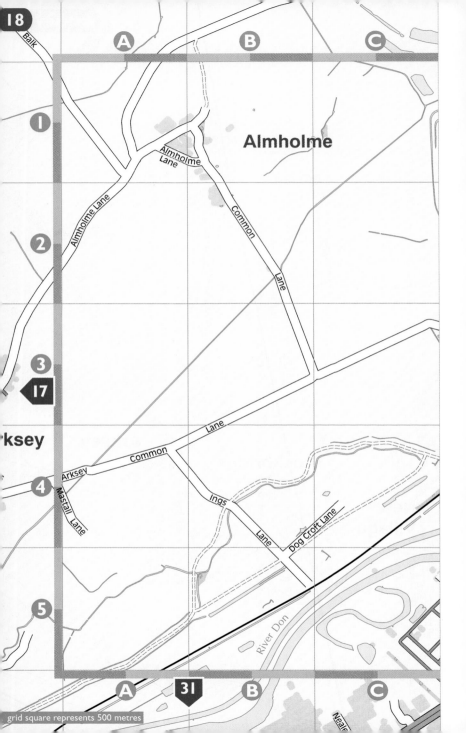

Almholme

18

Balk

A
B
C

I

Almholme Lane

Almholme Lane

Common Lane

2

3

17

rksey

Lane

Common

Arksey

4

Ings

Mastall Lane

Lane

Dog Croft Lane

5

River Don

A
31
B
C

grid square represents 500 metres

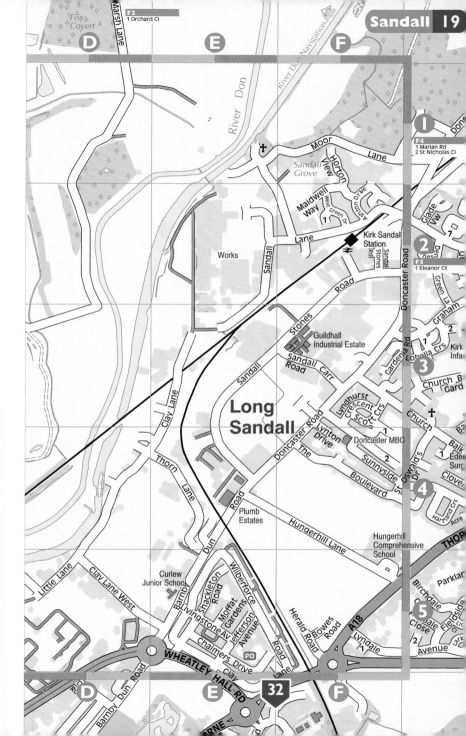

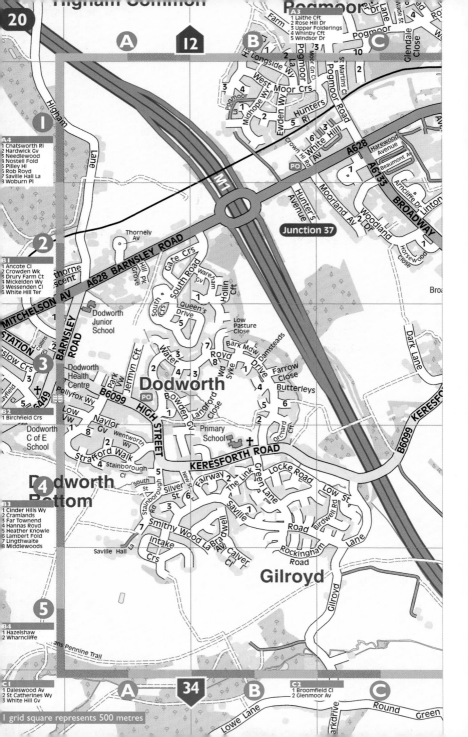

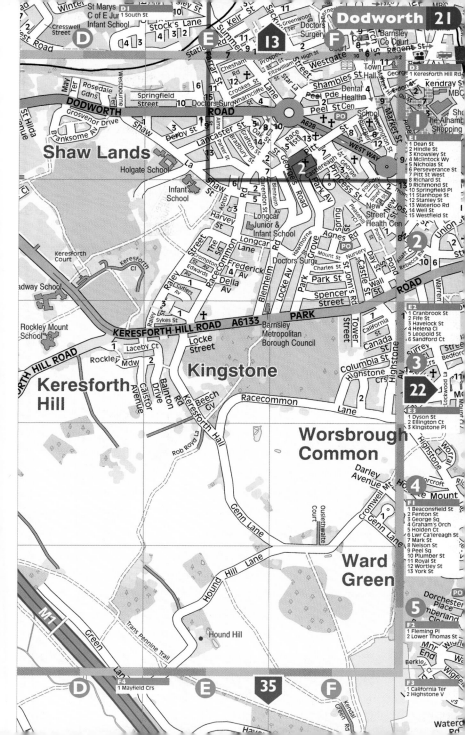

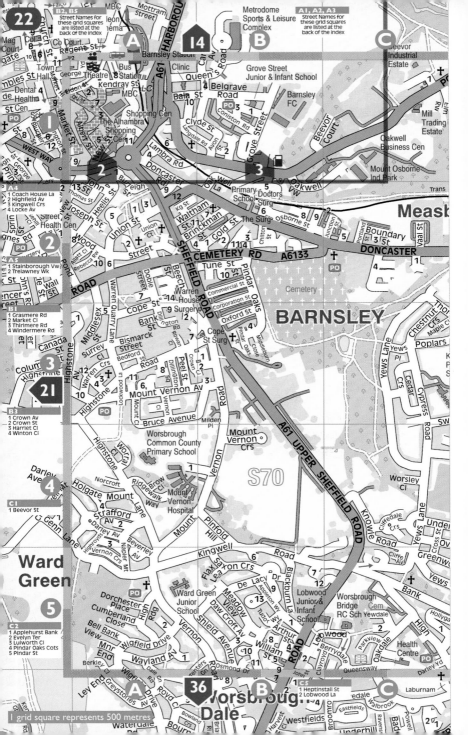

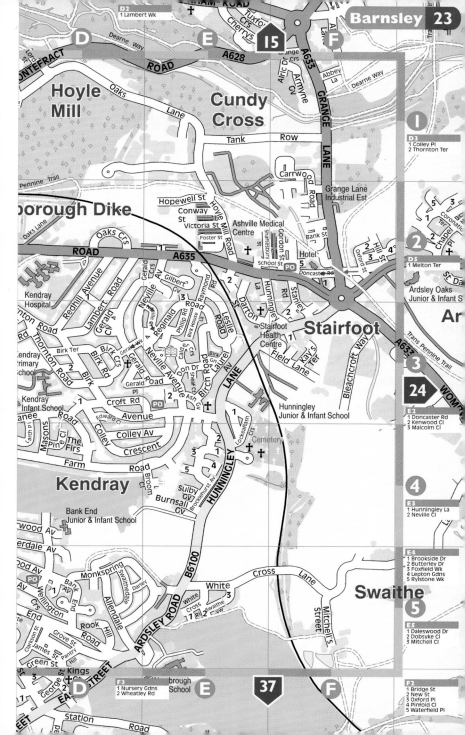

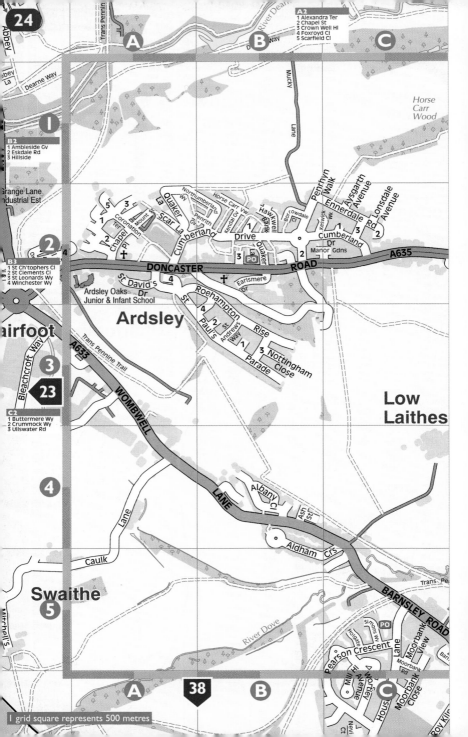

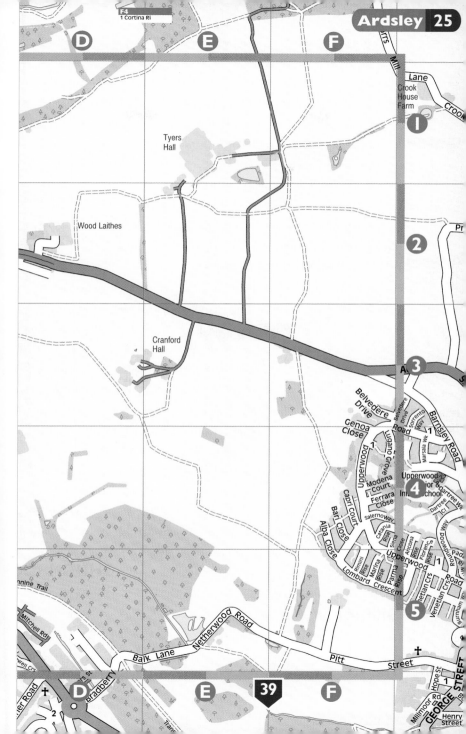

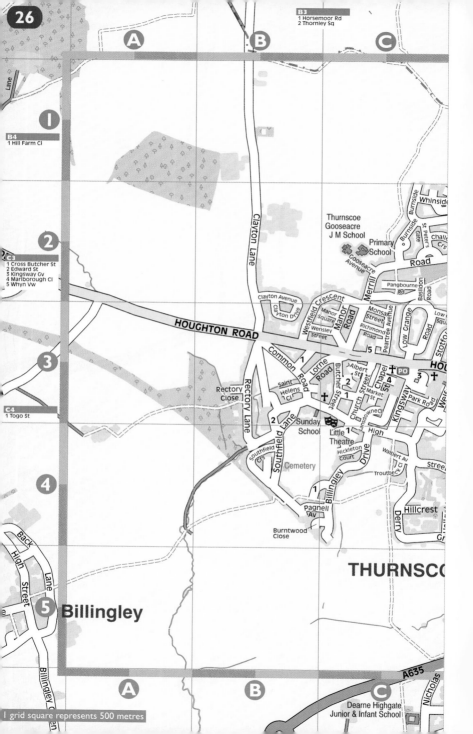

B3
1 Horsemoor Rd
2 Thornley Sq

A
B
C

1

B4
1 Hill Farm Cl

2

C3
1 Cross Butcher St
2 Edward St
3 Kingsway Gv
4 Marlborough Cl
5 Whyn Vw

Clayton Lane

Thurnscoe
Gooseacre
J M School

Primary
School

Gooseacre
Avenue

Merrill Road

Pangbourne
Rd

Basilon
Road

Burnside
Whinside

St Peter's
Gate

Challa

Low
Squa

Clayton Avenue

Clayton Drive

Westfield Crescent

Manor
Square

Wensley
Street

Manor Road

Monsal
Street

Richmond
Road

Peartree Avenue

Low Grange
Road

Stotfo

HOUGHTON ROAD

3

C4
1 Togo St

Common Road

Lorne Road

Butcher Street

Albert
St

Chapel St

PO

3

HO

Rectory
Close

Rectory Lane

Saint
Helens
Cl

Church Street

Market
St

Kingsway

Park Road

Wel

We

1

5

Southfield Lane

2

Sunday
School

Little
Theatre

Hickleton
Court

Billingley Drive

Drive

High

Jandowns...ll

1

Walbert Av

Troutbeck

Derry

street

Hillcrest

Gr

Southfield
Crs

Cemetery

4

1

Pagnell
Av

Burntwood
Close

THURNSC

Back
Lane

High
Street

5
Billingley

Billingley C...

A
B
C

A635

Nicholas

Dearne Highgate
Junior & Infant School

D3
1 Ashberry Cl

I
D4
1 Barley Vw
2 Hall Farm Ri
3 Wheatfield Dr

Stotfold

2
E3
1 Chapman St
2 Clarke St

Thurnscoe Eas

3

E5
1 West St

4

5

Doncaster
Barnsley

Whin Gardens

Lingamore
Leys

Willow
Road

School
Street

Oak
Road

Orchard
Way

Garden
Street

John Street

Holly Bush Drive

Chapel Lane

Brunswick
Street

Cromwell Street

Briton
Street

Hanover
Street

St Hilda's

J Cl

Lancaster Street

York Street

Brunswick
Street

Delahton by
Windsor

Roman St

Briton
Square

Grange
Crs

Grange

Hill
Primary
School

Hanover
Square

Windsor Square

Stuart Street

Norman
St

Dane
St

Dane
Lane

Street
North

Windsor
Street

Street

George Street

Albion Drive

Thurnscoe Station

STATION ROAD

PO

1

2

Thurnscoe
Business
Centre

Phoenix Lane

Dane
Street
South

Saxon Street

Coronation

Tudor
Street

The
Windings

LIDGET LANE B64

Shepherd Lane

1   3
Drive

2

Hall   Farm

King St

Queen St

Princess St

Barrowfield   Road

Chestnut

Crossgate

Lindley
Crescent

Thurnscoe Bridge Lane

Lane

Colliery
Lane

A635

Goldthorpe
RC JMI
School

Lockwood
Road

Gosling Gate Road

B6098

King   Street

Queen
Street

Kathleen
Grove

Nora Street

St Mary's Road

Central St

Hamilton Rd

East St

Doncaster

The Surgery

Picknills Avenue

Garden Street

De**F**ne

Goldthorpe
Station

St Michael's

D

1

BARNSLEY   ROAD

Dearne

Saltersbrook

Road

Queen
Street

4

9

Elizabeth St

Main Street

E

Infant
School

PO

Market St

Co Operative St

Victoria St

Cross St

3   2

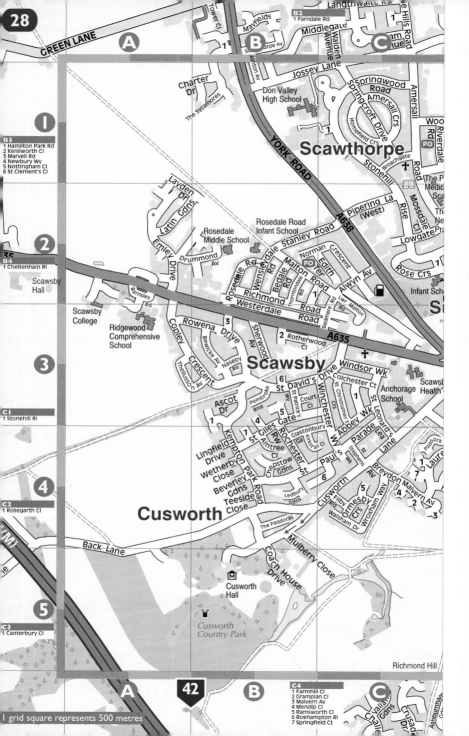

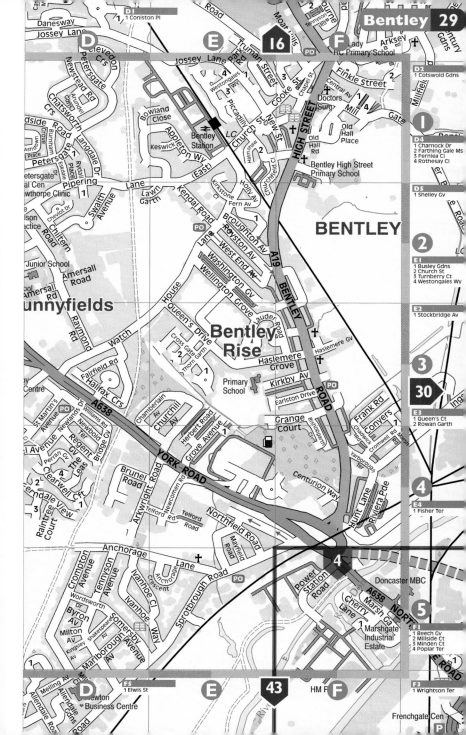

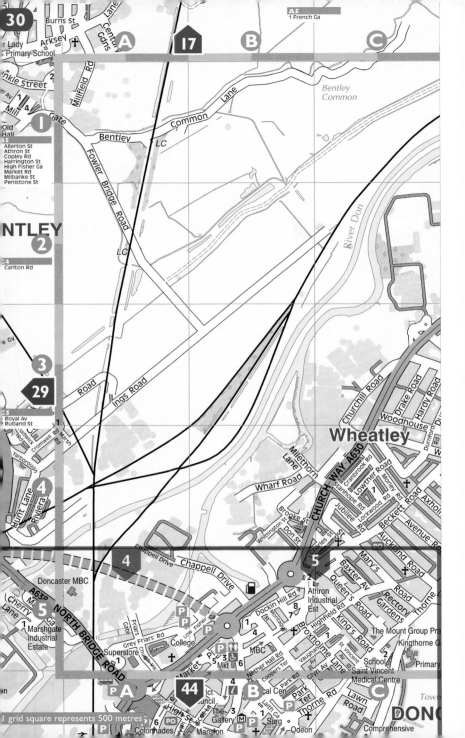

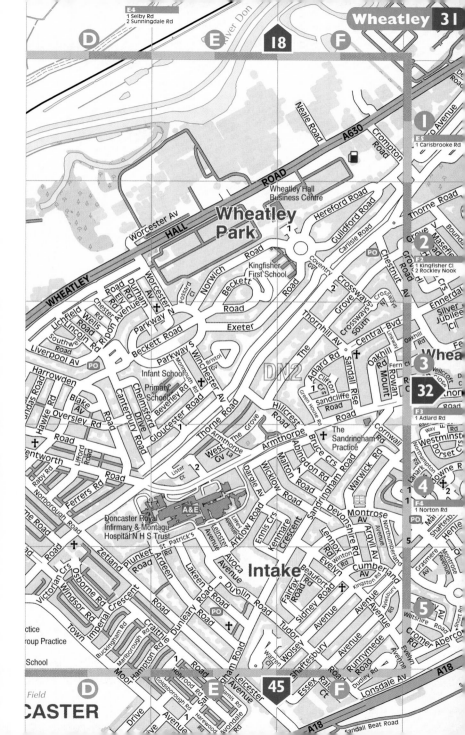

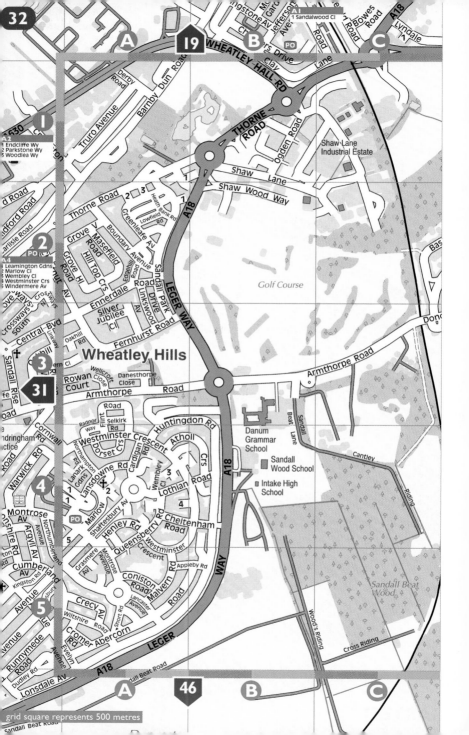

A **B** **C**

19 WHEATLEY HALL RD

1 Sandalwood Cl

Bowes Road

A18

Lyndale

Jefferson Av

Clay Lane

Cardd

Jeferson

Clay

Lane

Kingstone Av

Madstone Av

Drive

PO

A630

I

1 Endcliffe Wy
2 Parkstone Wy
3 Woodlea Wy

A2

Truro Avenue

Derby Road

Barnby Dun Road

THORNE ROAD

Ogden Road

Shaw Lane Industrial Estate

Thorne Road

2 3

Heath Bank Rd

Lowfield Rd

Shaw Lane

Shaw Wood Way

2

PO

A14

1 Leamington Gdns
2 Marlow Cl
3 Wembley Cl
4 Westminster Crs
5 Windermere Av

Carlisle Road

Grove Road

Grove Hill

Nut Av

Masefield Road

Boundary Avenue

Greenleafe Av

Edgehill

Hill Top Crs

A18

Sandall Park DRIVE

LEGER WAY

Golf Course

Ove Way

Crossways South

Central Bvd

Oakhill Rd

Ennerdale Road

Silver Jubilee Cl

Linkswood Av

Fernhurst Road

Wheatley Hills

+

3

31

Sandall Rise

fe Road

Rowan Court

Wellcroft Close

Danesthorpe Close

Armthorpe Road

Armthorpe Road

Don

Armthorpe Road

ndringham Rd

actice

Cornwall Road

Road

Warwick Rd

4

Montrose Av

shire Av

Argyll Av

ton

Cumberland Av

Kingston Rd

sbury

Avenue

Northumberland

5

Runnymede Road

Dudley Rd

Avenue

Radnor Road

Flint Selkirk Rd

Way Rd

Lanark Gdns

Northampton

Dorset Crs

Westminster Crescent

Lansdowne Road

Cardigan

Shaftesbury Av

Marlow

1

PO

Grasmere Av

Montrose Avenue

Henley Rd

Queensberry Rd

5

Crecy Av

Wiltshire Road

Cromer

Abercorn

Evelyn

A18

Huntingdon Rd

Atholl Crs

Wembley Av

Lothian Road

3

4

Cheltenham Road

Westminster Crescent

Coniston Road

Malvern Road

Lancaster Avenue

Appleby Rd

Wood's Riding

LEGER

WAY

A18

Danum Grammar School

Sandall Wood School

Intake High School

Beat Lane

Sandall

Cantley

Riding

Sandall Beat Wood

Cross Riding

Sandall Beat Road

Lonsdale Av

A 46 **B** **C**

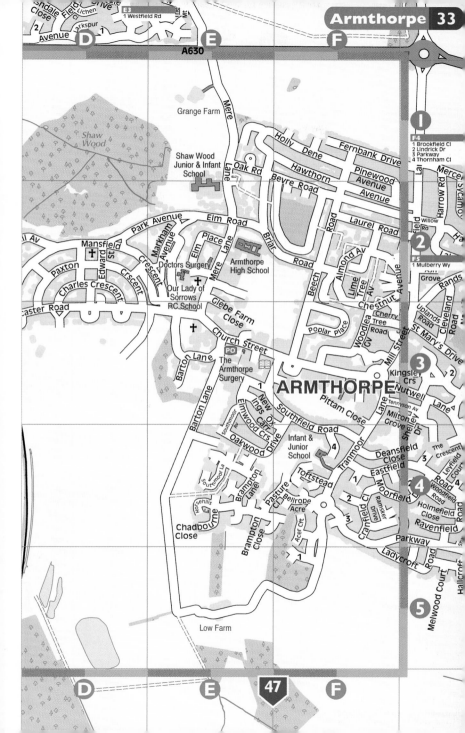

D E F

A630

Grange Farm

Shaw Wood

Shaw Wood Junior & Infant School

Holly Dene
Fernbank Drive
Hawthorn
Pinewood Avenue
Avenue
Oak Rd
Bevre Road
Mere Lane
Laurel Road

Willow

2
F5
1 Mulberry Wy

Park Avenue
Elm Road
Elm Place
Mere Lane
Mansfield
Markham Avenue
Edward St
Crescent
Doctors Surgery
Our Lady of Sorrows RC School
Paxton
Crescent
Briar Road
Beech Road
Almond Av
Lime Tree Av
Ash Grove
Rands

Armthorpe High School

Charles Crescent
caster Road

Chestnut Avenue
Cherry Tree
Poplar Place
Woodlea Tree Road
Cleveland Road
Uplands Road
St Mary's Drive

Glebe Farm Close
Church Street

PO
The Armthorpe Surgery

ARMTHORPE

Barton Lane
New Oak Ings Carr
Southmoor
Elmwood Crs
Oakwood Drive

Southfield Road
Pittam Close
Mill Street
Tennyson Av
Kingsley Crs
Nutwell Lane

3
Milton Grove
Shelley Dr
The Crescent
Leyfield Court

Infant & Junior School

Tranmoor Lane
Deansfield Close
Eastfield Road
Moorfield
Woodfield Road

4

Brampton Lane
Pasture Cl
Bellrope Acre
Toftstead
Cranfield Cl
Ramsker Drive
Holmefield Close
Ravenfield

Chadbourne
Close
Brampton Close
Southmoor La
Rosehills

Acer Crt

Parkway
Ladycroft Road
Melwood Court
Hallcroft

5

Low Farm

D E F

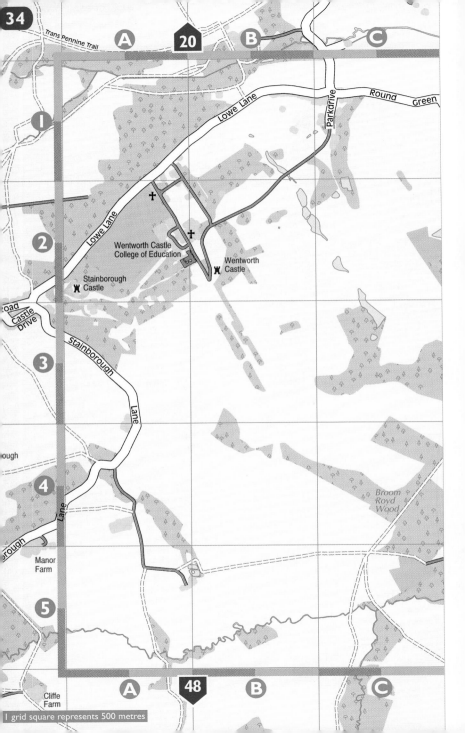

M1

Green Lane

D

Trans Pennine Trail

Hound Hill

E

21

F

Mnr End

Wig

Berkle

Ley End

Greystones

Wig

Kendal

Green Rd

Haverlands Lane

I

Wate Rd

Have

Lane

Trans Pennine

Worsbr
Reserve

Roundgreen

Worsbrough
Mill Country
Park

2

Rockley Lane

Stampers Hill

M1

3

36

SHEFFI

A61

4

Colfield

1

Rockley Abbey
Farm

Balk Lane

Rockley Av

Castle Vw

Hill Top Rd

Worsbrough

Winste

Woo

Perc

Mer

swa

Gree

5

Falcon Drive

Ospre

1

The
Old
Park

D

E

49

F

Ro

Lane

Birdwell

A61

SHEFFIELD

Birdwell
Primary S

Hay

Chapel
Court

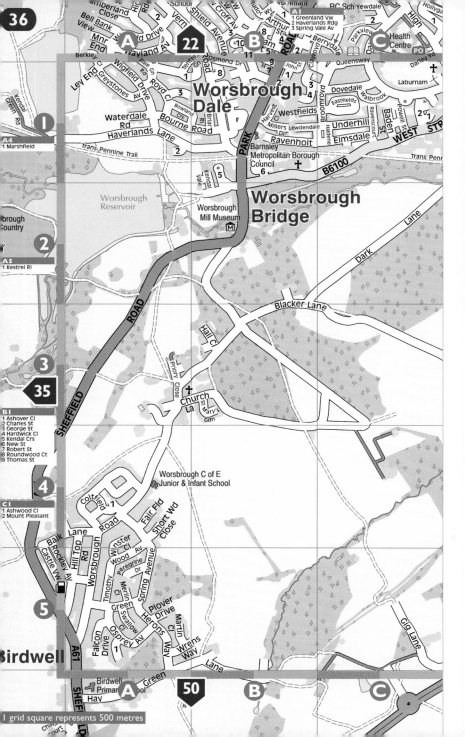

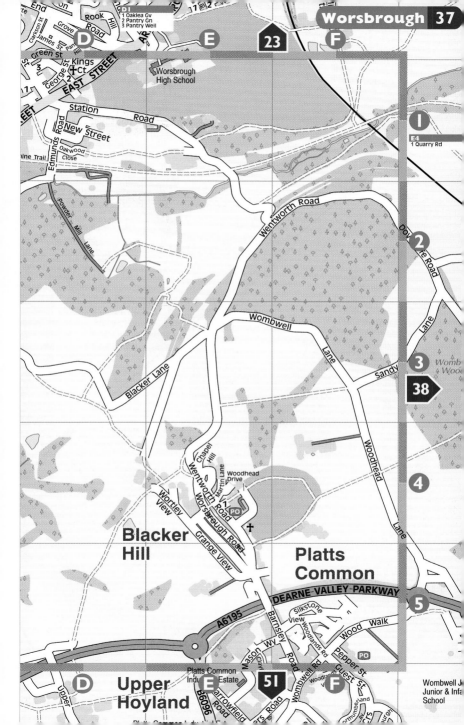

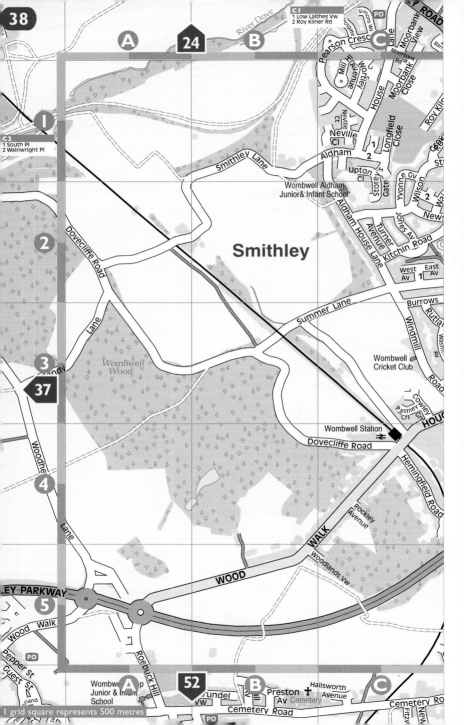

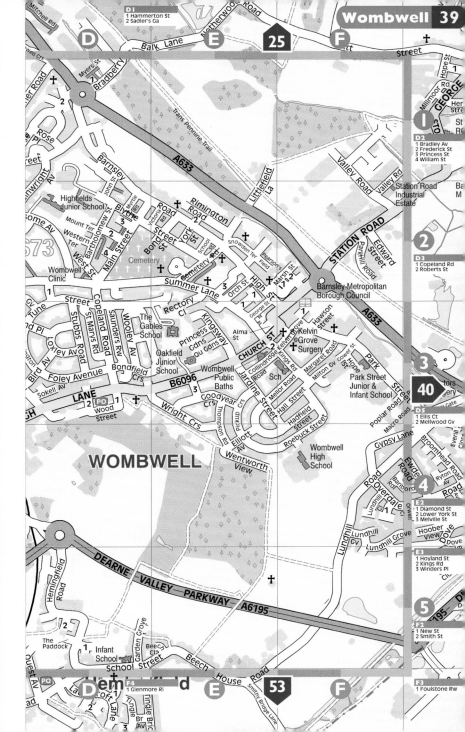

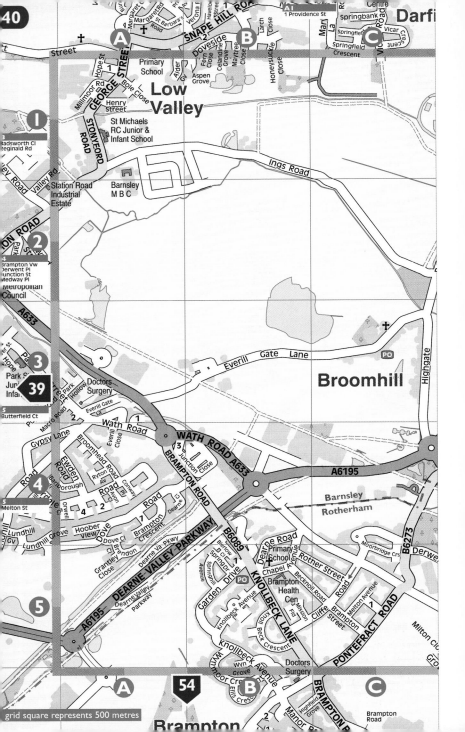

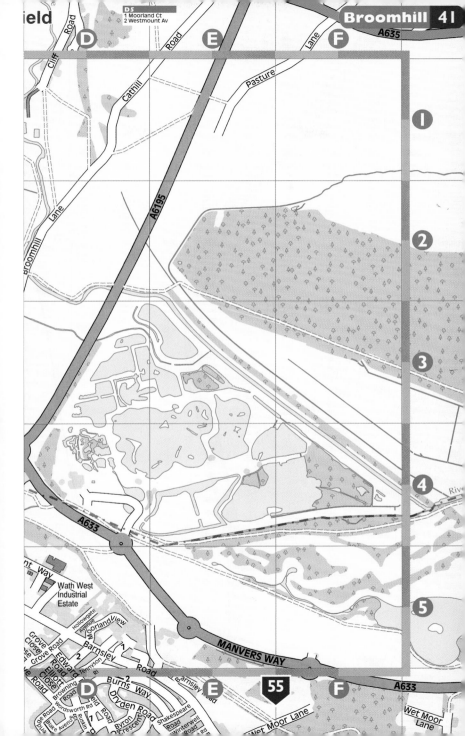

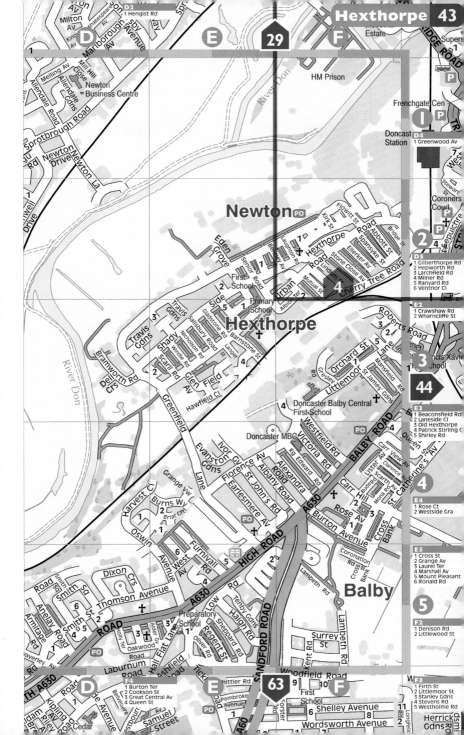

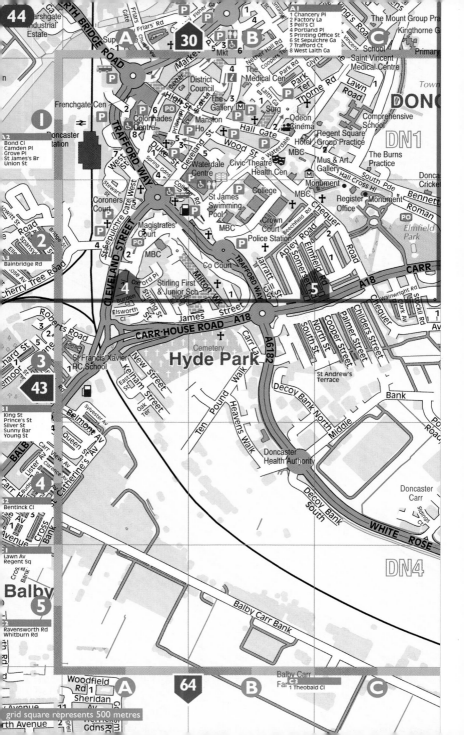

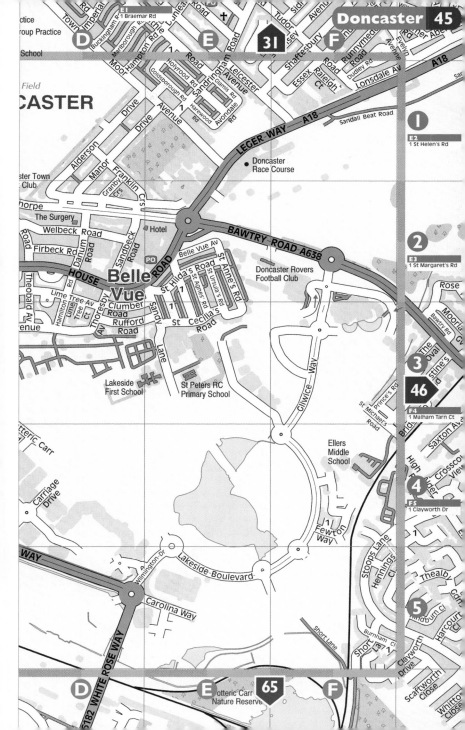

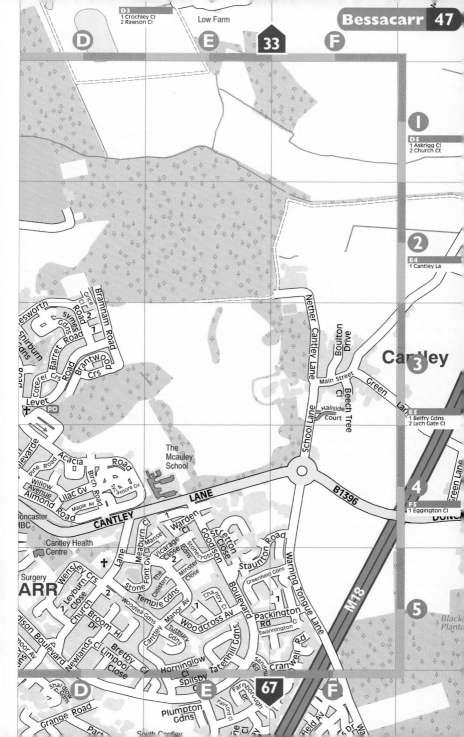

D3
1 Crochley Cl
2 Rawson Cl

Low Farm

33

D

E

F

I

D5
1 Askrigg Cl
2 Church Ct

2

E4
1 Cantley La

Cree Road
symes Gdns
2
7

Bramham Road

Barret Road

Brantwood Crs

Coterel Crs

esworth

Shirburn Gdns

Road

Levet

PO

Nether Cantley Lane

Boulton Drive

Cantley

3

Main Street

Beech Tree Cl

Green Lane

Hallside Court

School Lane

E5
1 Belfry Gdns
2 Lych Gate Cl

evarde

Pine Road

Acacia

Road

The Mcauley School

B1396

4

Green Lane

Willow

Avenue

Almond

Road

Lilac Gv

Birch Road

Sycamore Gv

Maple Av

E5
1 Eggington Cl

DONCA

CANTLEY

LANE

Doncaster MBC

Cantley Health Centre

Meaburn Cl

Lane

Mansel

Font Gv

Vicarage Cl

The Cloisters

Warden Cl

Stonecross Cl

Minster Close

Goodison

Seton Close

Staunton Road

Warning Tongue Lane

M18

5

Black Planta

Surgery

ARR

Wensley Crs

Leyburn Close

Church

2

Stone

Temple Gdns

Woodlea Gdns

Manor Av

Cha.. ry Cl

Woodcross Av

Greenfield Gdns

Boulevard

7

Packington Rd

Swannington

Cranwell Rd

Sandhu Rd

Broom Hl Dr

Newlands Cl

Bretby Cl

Limpool Close

Cantley

Tutbury Gdns

Horninglow Cl

Tatenhill Gdns

Spilsby

shardlow Gdns

D

Grange Road

E

Plumpton Gdns

Fairford Cl

67

Farnborough

F

field Av

Wa

South Cantley

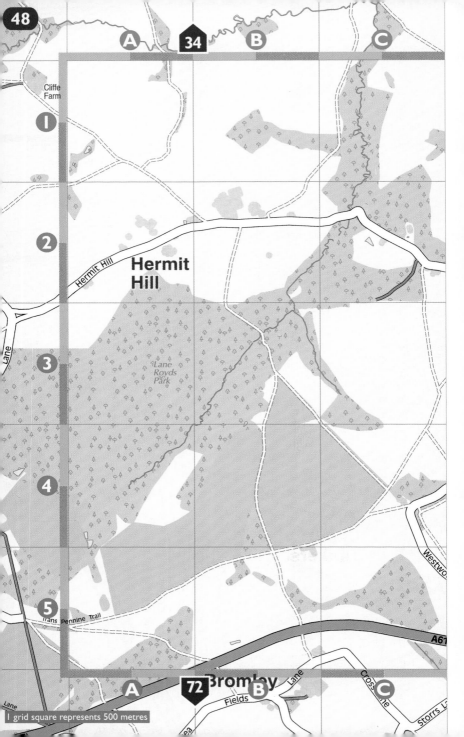

A
34
B
C

Cliffe
Farm

1

2

Hermit Hill

Hermit Hill

Lane

3

Lane Royds Park

4

5

Trans Pennine Trail

Westwo

A61

A
72
B
Bromley
Fields

Lane

Cross le

C

Storrs L

Lane

ea

1 grid square represents 500 metres

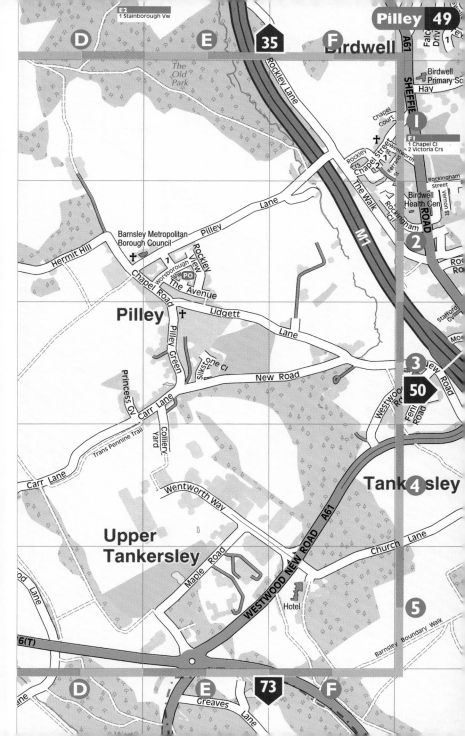

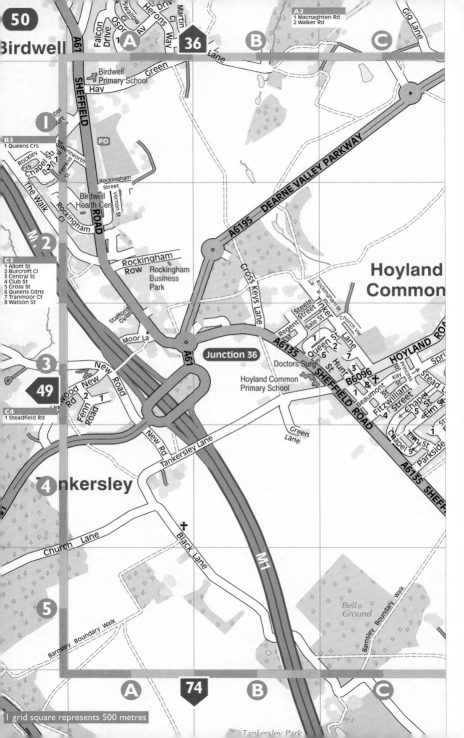

36

A
1 Macnaghten Rd
2 Walker Rd

A
B
C

Gig Lane

SHEFFIELD

Birdwell
Primary School

Hay

Green

Martin Lane

PO

B3
1 Queens Crs

Rockley
Crs

Chapel St

The Walk

Rockingham
Street

Birdwell
Health Cen

Vernon St

ROCKINGHAM ROAD

Rockingham Ct

M1

C3
1 Allott St
2 Burcroft Cl
3 Central St
4 Club St
5 Cross St
6 Queens Gdns
7 Tranmoor Ct
8 Watson St

Stafford Gv

Moor La

Rockingham
Row

Rockingham
Business
Park

DEARNE VALLEY PARKWAY

A6195

Cross Keys Lane

Rockingham St

Steele
Street

Timber
Lane

Church Vw

**Hoyland
Common**

Regent
Street

Sale St

Queen St

Hunt St

HOYLAND ROAD

Princess

Spri

A6135

7

6

2

1

3

X

B6096

Kay
St

Stead L

Beaumont
St

Fitzwilliam
Street

4

Chapel St

5

Elm St

Parkside

A6135 SHEFF

Elm St

1 St

3

New Road

Newwood Rd

New

Fenn
Road

2

7

49

C4
1 Steadfield Rd

A61

Junction 36

Doctors Surg

Hoyland Common
Primary School

SHEFFIELD ROAD

Green
Lane

New Rd

Tankersley Lane

4

Tankersley

Church   Lane

Black Lane

M1

*Bell
Ground*

Barnsley   Boundary   Walk

Barnsley Boundary Walk

5

A
74
B
C

Tankersley Park

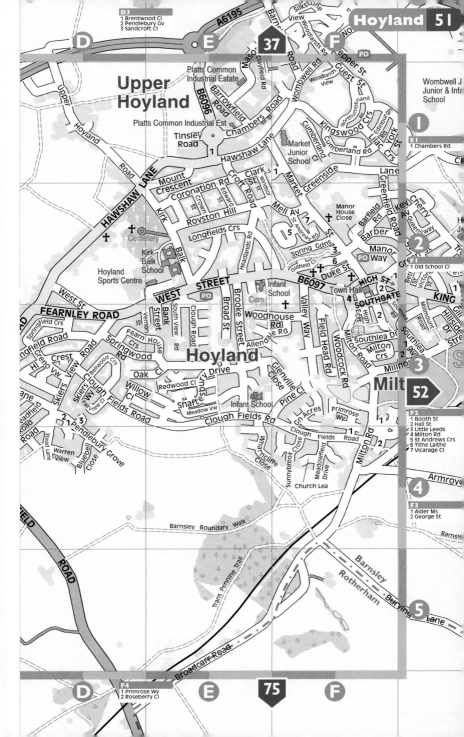

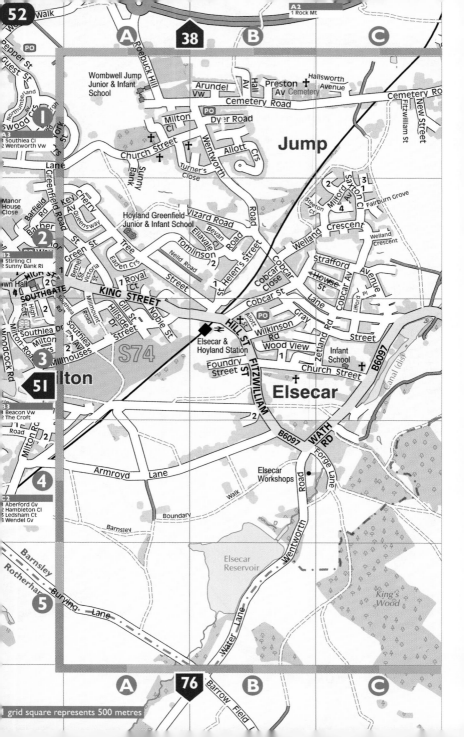

grid square represents 500 metres

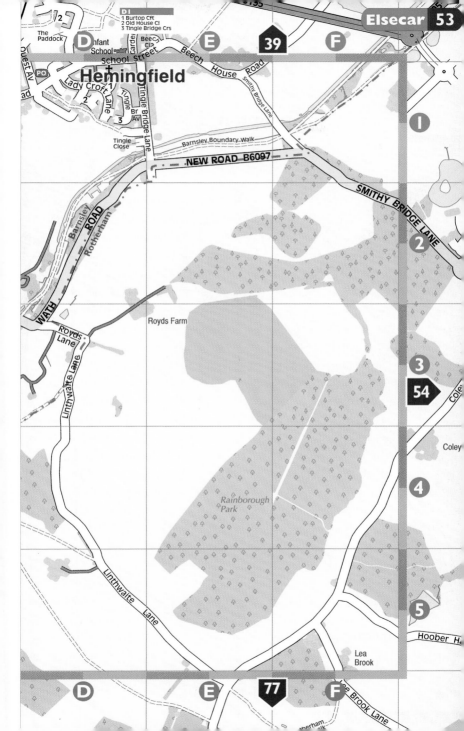

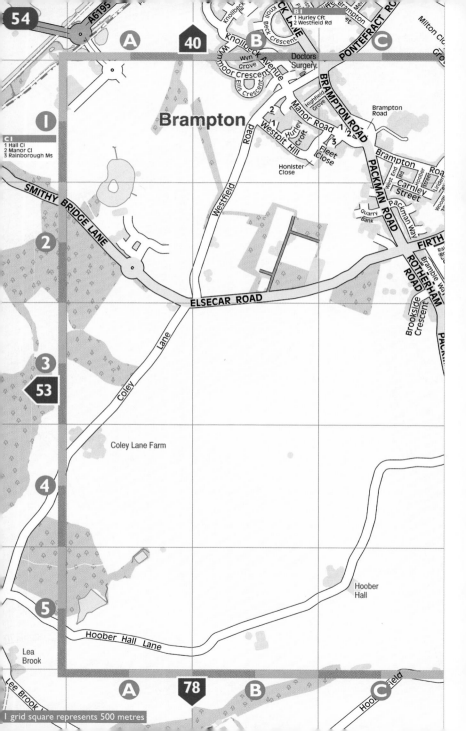

54

A6195

40

A

B

KNOLLBECK LANE

B1
1 Hurley Cft
2 Westfield Rd

PONTEFRACT RD

C

Milton clo

Knollbeck Crescent

Beck Crescent

cliffe brampton

st

Knollbeck Avenue

Wyn moor Crescent

Wyn Grove

Doctors Surgery

BRAMPTON ROAD

Brampton Road

Ellis Crescent

I

CI
1 Hall Cl
2 Manor Cl
3 Rainborough Ms

Brampton

Westfield Road

2
1

Westpit Hill

Hurley Croft

Manor Road

Highfield Grove

3

Fleet Close

1/2

Brampton Road

Packman Road

Brampton Road

Carnley Street

Hoober Street

Linden

Wood

Honister Close

Quarry Bank

Packman Way

2

SMITHY BRIDGE LANE

FIRTH

ROTHERHAM ROAD

Bramble Way

Ra

Rd

PACK

Brookside Crescent

ELSECAR ROAD

3

53

Coley Lane

Coley Lane Farm

4

5

Hoober Hall

Hoober Hall Lane

Lea Brook

Lee Brook

Hoo field

Hoo

A

78

B

C

1 grid square represents 500 metres

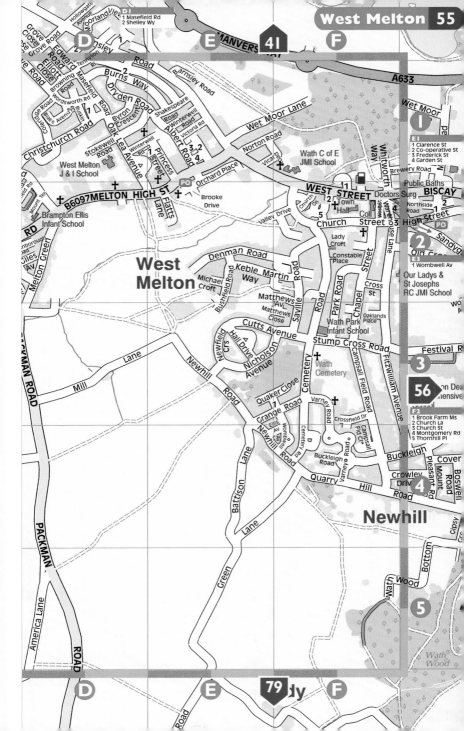

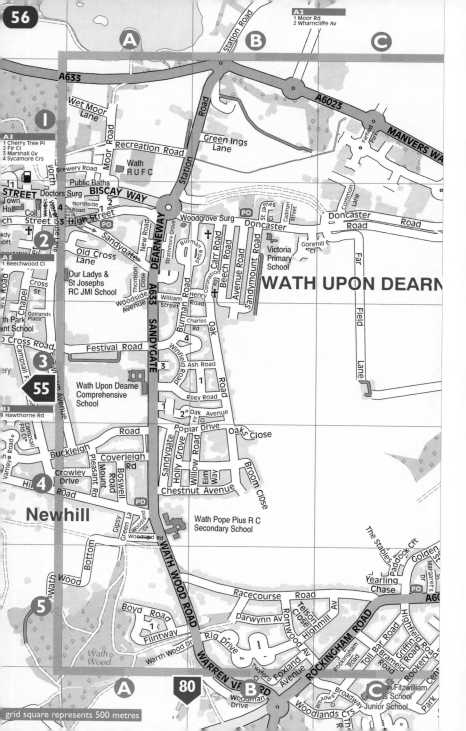

A633

WATH UPON DEARN

A6023

MANVERS WA

Wet Moor Lane

Green Ings Lane

Recreation Road

Wath RUFC

Brewery Road

Public Baths

Doctors Surg

Northside Road

BISCAY WAY

High Street

PO

Woodgrove Surg

Doncaster Road

Common Lane

Doncaster Road

St James

Cadman Street

Victoria Primary School

Gorehill Cl

DEARNEWAY

Strathmore Grove

New Road

Old Cross Lane

Sandygate

Burman Road

Carr Road

Beech Road

Avenue Road

Sandymount

Our Ladys & St Josephs RC JMI School

Woodside Avenue

Thomson Close

A633 SANDYGATE

William Street

Coronation Street

Henry Road

Charles Rd

Oak Road

Far Field Lane

Festival Road

Winfield Road

Ash Road

Wath Upon Dearne Comprehensive School

Riley Road

Oak Avenue

Fir Tree

Poplar Drive

Oaks Close

Buckleigh Road

Coverleigh Rd

Sandygate

Holly Grove

Willow Road

Broom Close

Crowley Drive

Boswell Road

Pleasant Mount Rd

Chestnut Avenue

Elm Way

Varney Road

Campsall Fld Cl

Hill Road

Newhill

Gipsy Green La

Woodland Gv

Woodland Rd

PO

Wath Pope Pius R C Secondary School

WATH WOOD ROAD

The Stables

Paddock Ct

Golden St

Margarets Dr

Yearling Chase

PO

A60

Wath Wood

Bottom Wood

Boyd Road

Flintway

Warth Wood Dr

Rig Drive

Racecourse Road

Darwynn Av

Romwood Av

Telson Close

Highmill Av

ROCKINGHAM ROAD

Toll Bar Road

Highfield Road

Griffin Road

Brameld Road

Rookery Road

Cent

WARREN VA RD

Twyford Close

Foxland Avenue

Rockingham Road

Broadway

Broadway

Woodlands Crs

n Fitzwilliam s School

Junior School

Park

Woodman Drive

A3
1 Cherry Tree Pl
2 Fir Cl
3 Marshall Gv
4 Sycamore Crs

A2
1 Moor Rd
2 Wharncliffe Av

1 Beechwood Cl

1 Hawthorne Rd

55

grid square represents 500 metres

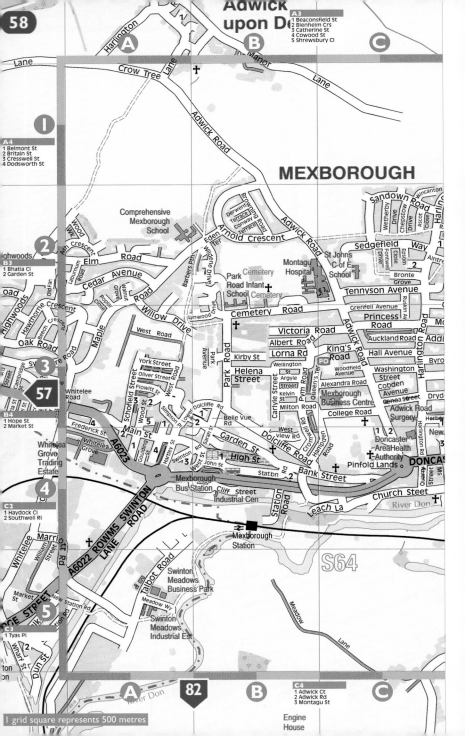

Windhill

Old Denaby

Denaby Main

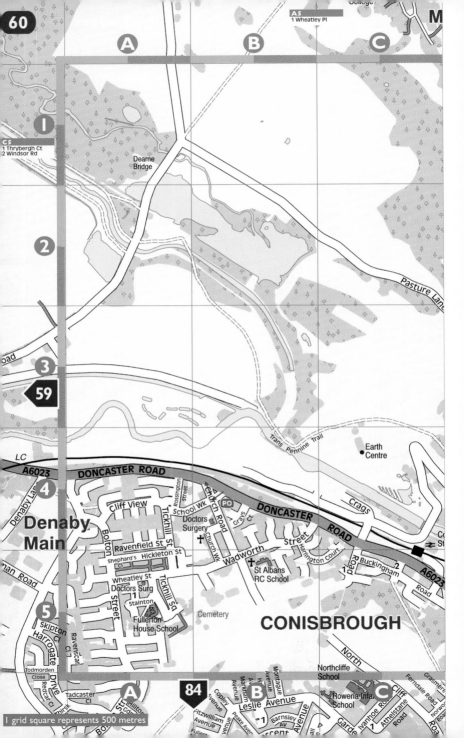

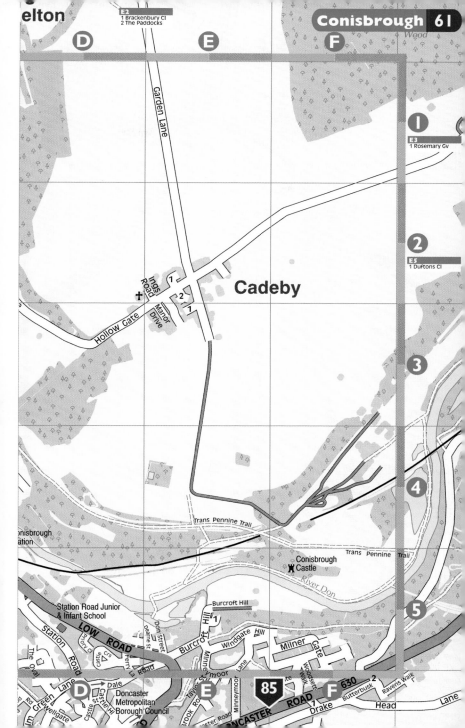

Wood

E2
1 Brackenbury Cl
2 The Paddocks

Garden Lane

I

E3
1 Rosemary Gv

2

E5
1 Duftons Cl

Ings Road

Manor Drive

7

2

7

Cadeby

Hollow Gate

3

4

Trans Pennine Trail

Trans Pennine Trail

onisbrough
ation

Conisbrough
Castle

River Don

5

Burcroft Hill
1

Station Road Junior
& Infant School

Don Street

dearne St

Burcroft Hill

Windgate Hill

Milner Gate

LOW ROAD

Station Road

Priory Cl

Crs

Ferry La

Minneymoor Lane

Wooseat Walk

Ravens Walk

The Oval

Green Lane

Wellgate

Castle H

Castle Cl

Dale

D **E** **F**

85

630 2

Doncaster
Metropolitan
Borough Council

Taylor Road

Minneymoor Lane

Butterbusk

Head Lane

DONCASTER ROAD

Drake

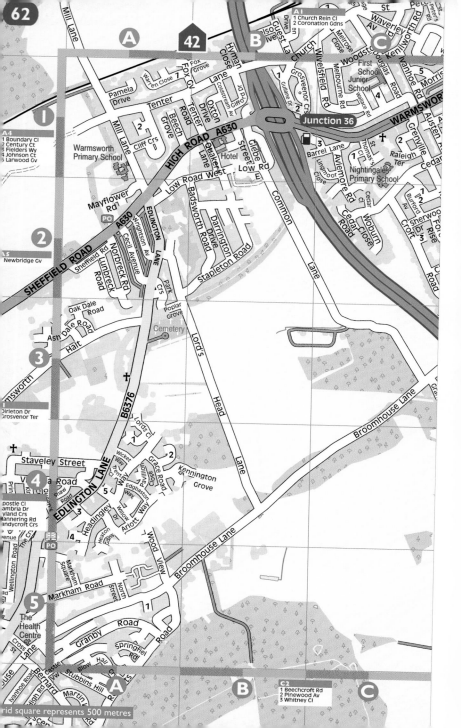

A1
1 Church Rein Cl
2 Coronation Gdns

A4
1 Boundary Cl
2 Century Ct
3 Fielders Wy
4 Johnson Ct
5 Larwood Gv

A5
Newbridge Gv

C2
1 Beechcroft Rd
2 Pinewood Av
3 Whitney Cl

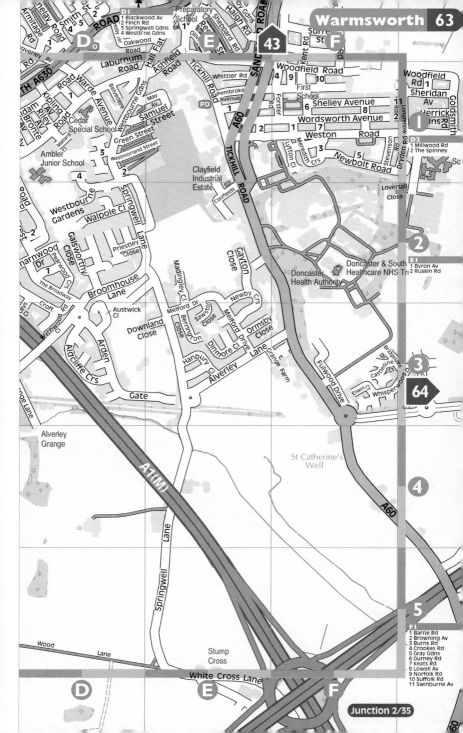

64

A **44** B C

Woodfield Rd **1**
Sheridan Av
Herrick Gdns

Goldsmith Rd

Longfellow Rd

Dryden Rd

Stevenson Rd

11
2
8

ly Avenue
rth Ave
Road

5
Newbolt Road

Loversall Close

Balby Carr School

Weston Road

ly Carr Bank

A1
1 Chesterton Rd

Balby Carr Farm

2

Doncaster & South Humber
Healthcare NHS Trust

Bridgegate Drive Ct

Orwood Dr

Coppicewood Court

Whisingwood

Whisingwood Drive

3

63

Drive

Hall Balk Lane

Hall Balk Lane

M18

4

A60

Skipwith Close

Dudup Hill

Wadworth Hill

5

✝

Loversall

The Surgery

Rake's Lane

A B C

D   **E**   **45**   **F**

I

2

3

66

4

5

Potteric Carr
Nature Reserve

A6182 WHITE ROSE WAY

Short

Claworth Drive

Scaftworth Close

Whitto Close

Beeston
Plantation

Loversal
Carr

Potteric
Carr

Junction 3

Rake's
Lane

St Catherine's Well Stream

D   **E**   **F**

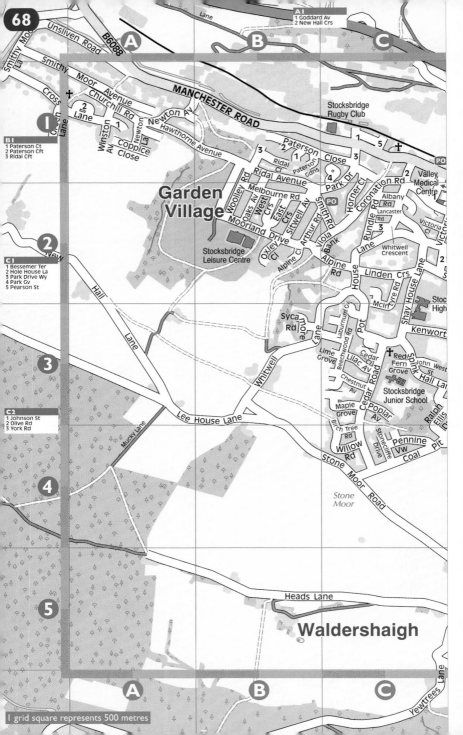

Garden Village

Stocksbridge Rugby Club

Stocksbridge Leisure Centre

Stocksbridge Junior School

Stocksbridge High

Valley Medical Centre

MANCHESTER ROAD

B6088

Unsliven Road

Smithy Moor Avenue

Smithy Moor La

Cross La

Churchill Rd

Winston Av

Coppice Close

Newton La

Newton Av

Hawthorne Avenue

Paterson Close

Paterson Gdns

Ridal Cl

Ridal Avenue

Woolley Rd

Melbourne Rd

Oaks Av

West Crs

East Crs

Sitwell Av

Smith Rd

Arthur Rd

Viola Bank

Park Dr

Horner Cl

Coronation Rd

Rundle Rd

Albany Rd

Lancaster Rd

Victoria Cl

Whitwell Crescent

Moorland Drive

Oxley Cl

Alpine Cl

Alpine Rd

House Lane

Linden Crs

Tyre Rd

Shay House Lane

McInt

Kenwort

Sycamore Rd

Laburnum Gv

Pot

Lime Grove

Beechwood Rd

Lilac Av

Cedar Cl

Cedar Road

Redi Fern Grove

Spink

John West St

Hall Lan

Chestnut Av

Maple Grove

Poplar Av

Birch Tree Rd

Stonecliffe

Willow Rd

Pennine Vw

Coal Pit

Ralph

Ellis

Hall Lane

New

Whitwell Lane

Mucky Lane

Lee House Lane

Stone Moor Road

Stone Moor

Heads Lane

Waldershaigh

Yewtrees Lane

PO

1 grid square represents 500 metres

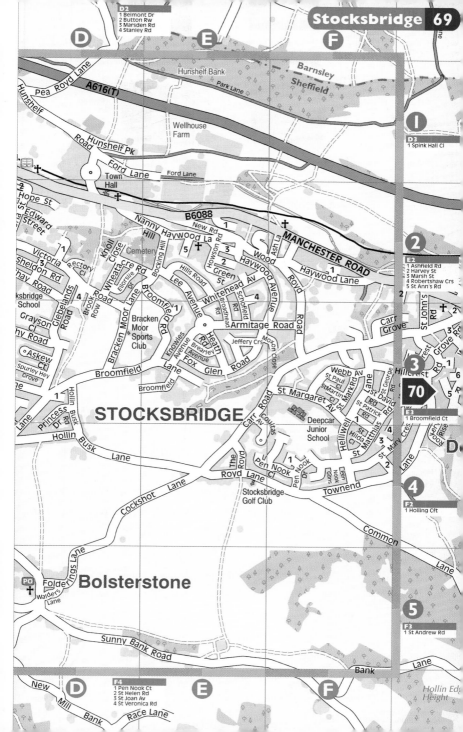

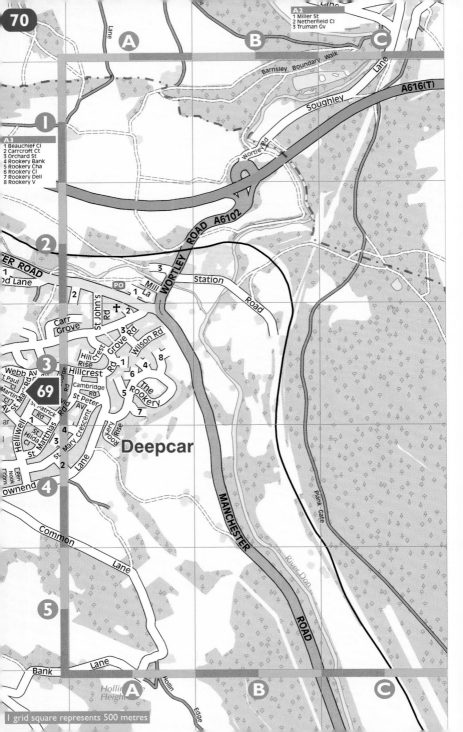

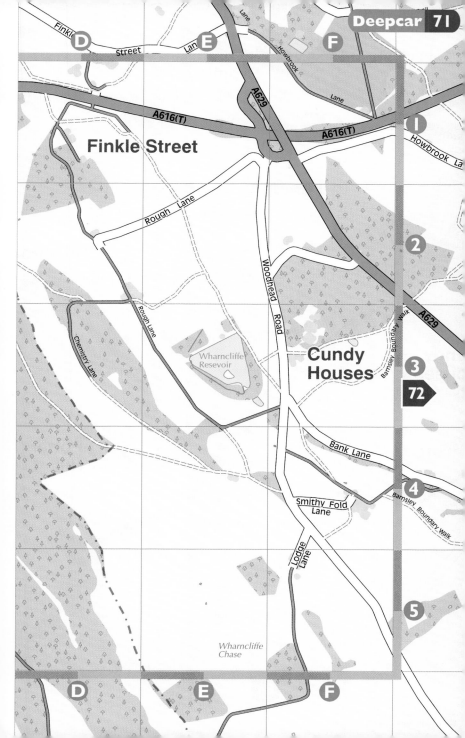

Finkl... Street

D

Lan E

Lane

Howbrook

Lane

F

A629

A616(T)

A616(T)

Finkle Street

I

Howbrook La

Rough Lane

2

Woodhead Road

A629

Rough Lane

Chemistry Lane

Wharncliffe Resevoir

Cundy Houses

Barnsley Boundary Walk

3

72

Bank Lane

4

Smithy Fold Lane

Barnsley Boundary Walk

Lodge Lane

5

Wharncliffe Chase

D

E

F

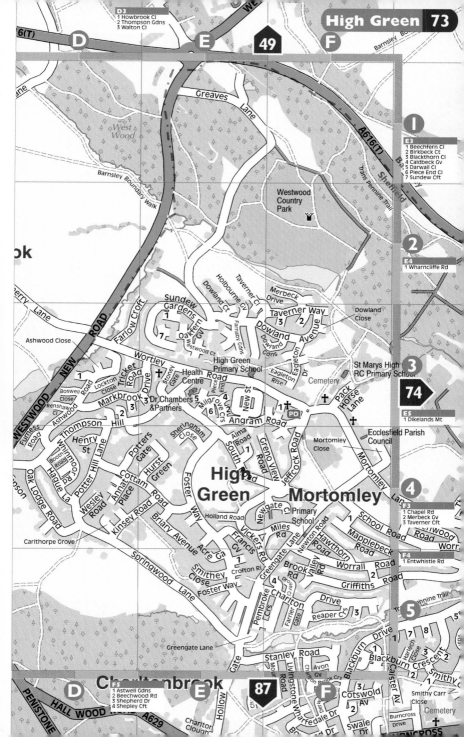

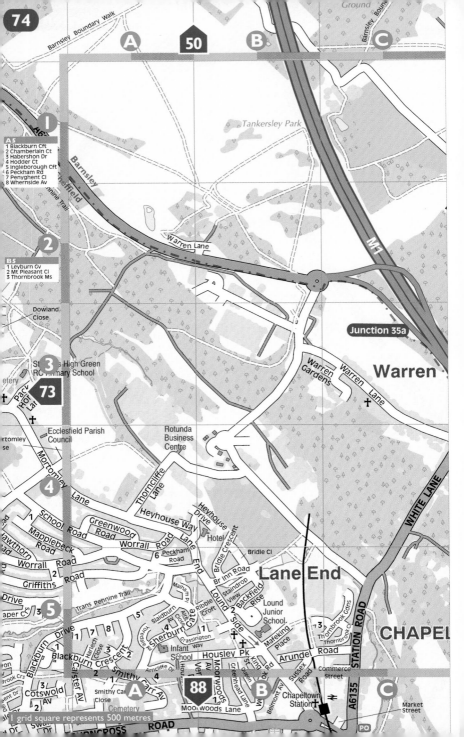

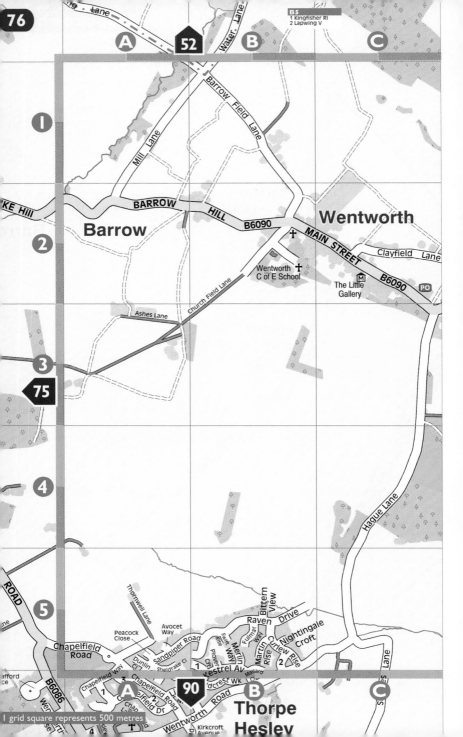

53

D

E

F

Lea Brook

Lee Brook Lane

I

Coley Lane

Rotherham Roundwalk

Street

Street Lane

2

CORTWORTH LANE

Cortworth

Rotherham

3

78

Roundwalk

4

Wentworth Park

5

Morley Pond

D

E

91

F

Dog Kennel Pond

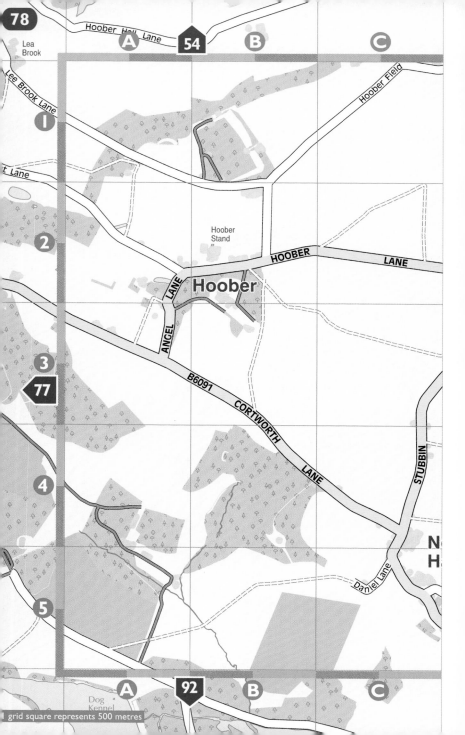

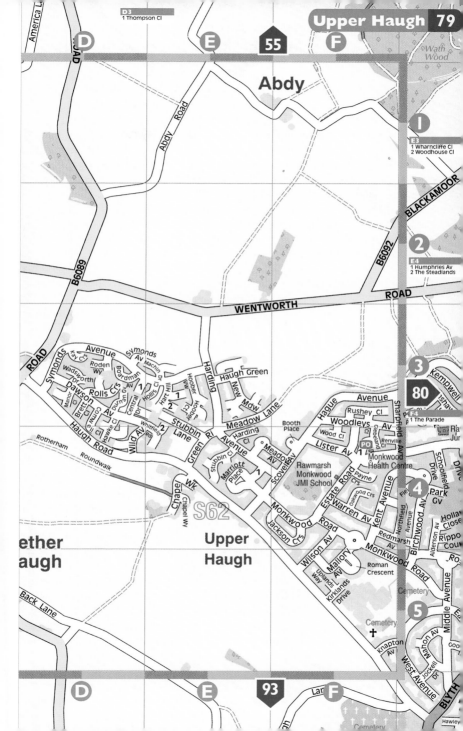

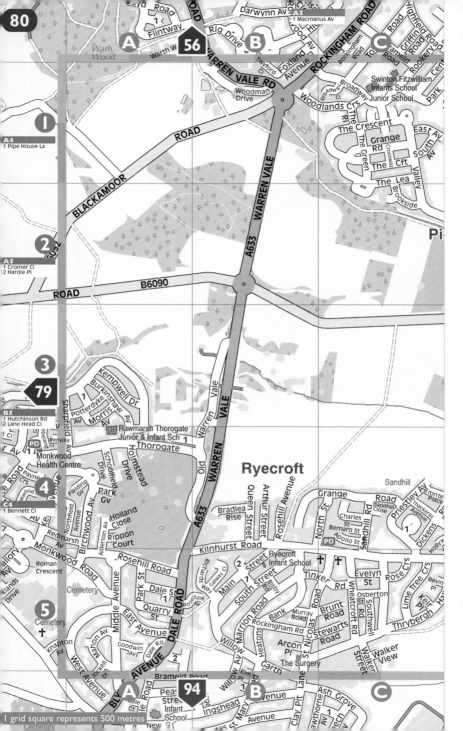

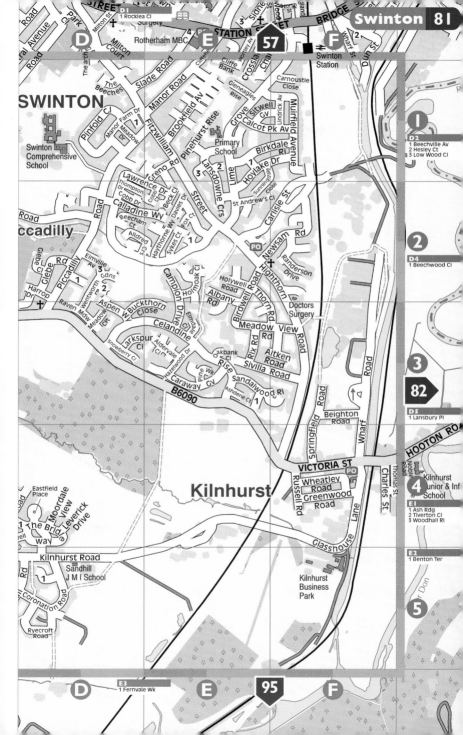

82

58

A B C

1

River Don

Swinton
Meadows
Industrial E

Engine
House
Farm

Denaby
Common

Denaby Lane

2

Doncaster
Rotherham

Hooton
Common

Holmes Lane

3

81

ighton
Road

Wharf

HOOTON ROAD

B6090

A ST
PO

Charles St

Nobelthorpe
Road

Thomas St

Kilnhurst
Junior & Infants
School

KILNHURST

ROAD

Howdike Lane

4

ey
wood

house Lane

5

River Don

Carr Lane

A

A

B

B

A630

C

C

1 grid square represents 500 metres

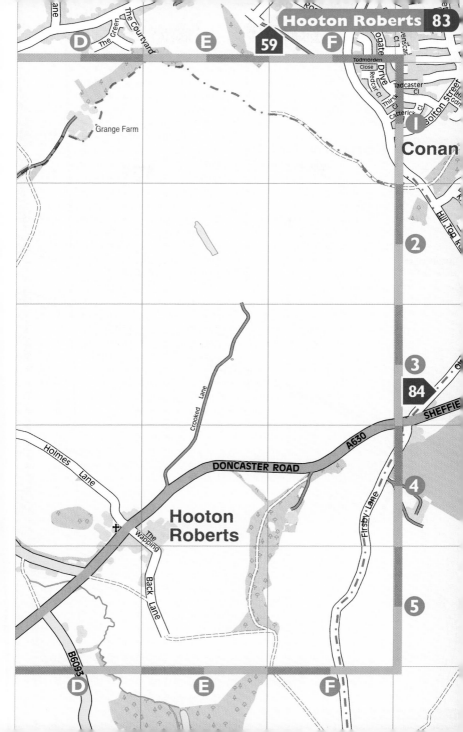

D

The Green

The Courtyard

E

59

F

ogate

Todmorden
Close

Drive

Redcar Cl

Thirsk
Cl

Tadcaster
Cl

Catterick

Bolton Street

Grange Farm

I

Conan

2

Hill Top Rd

3

84

SHEFFIE

Crooked Lane

DONCASTER ROAD

A630

4

Holmes Lane

Hooton
Roberts

The
Wapping

Back Lane

Firsby Lane

5

B6093

D

E

F

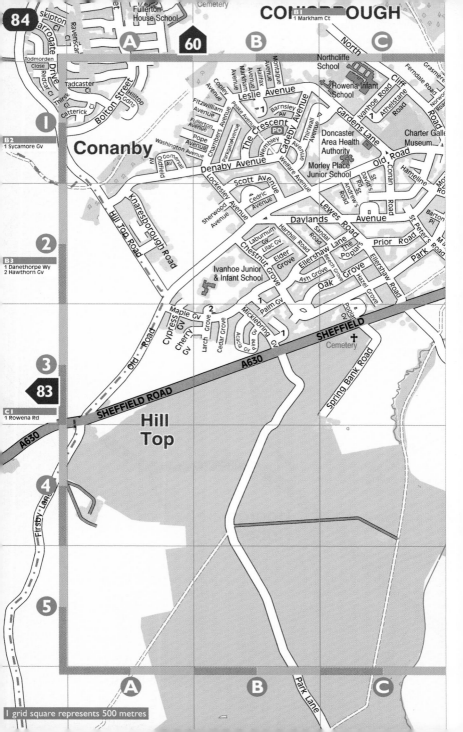

I grid square represents 500 metres

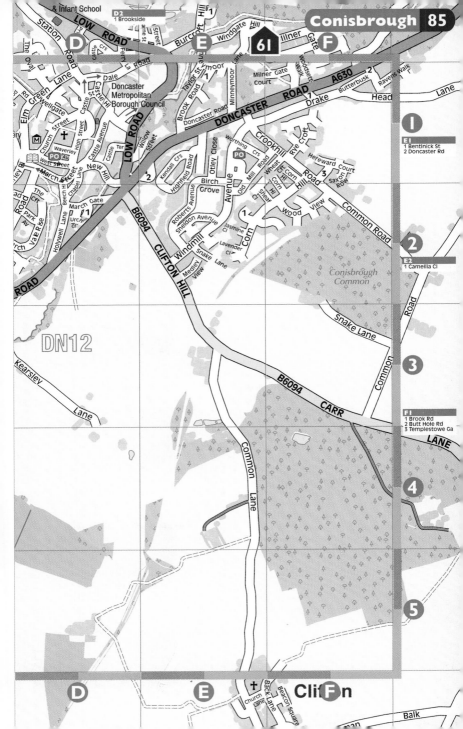

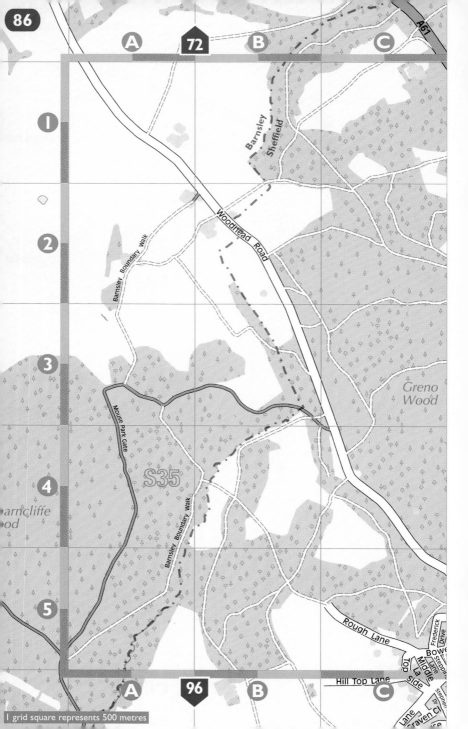

A **72** B C

A61

1

2

Barnsley
Sheffield

Woodhead Road

Barnsley Boundary Walk

3

Greno
Wood

Mouse Park Gate

S35

4

Barnsley Boundary Walk

arncliffe
od

5

Rough Lane

Frederick Drive

Bow

Middle

La

side

Hill Top Lane

A **96** B C

Stephen

Lane

Craven Cl

1 grid square represents 500 metres

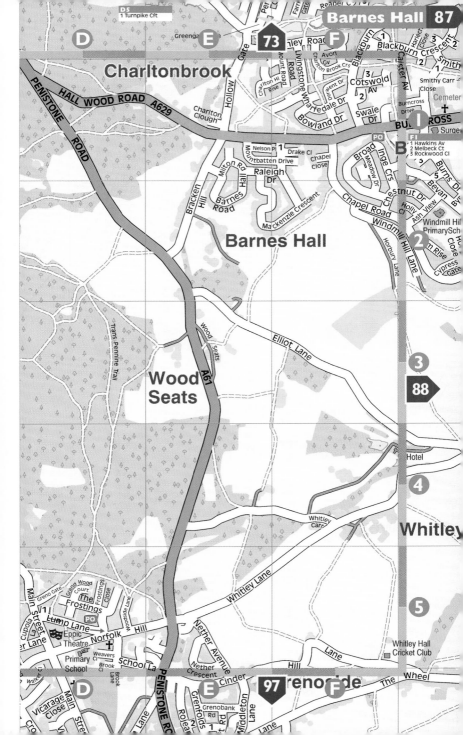

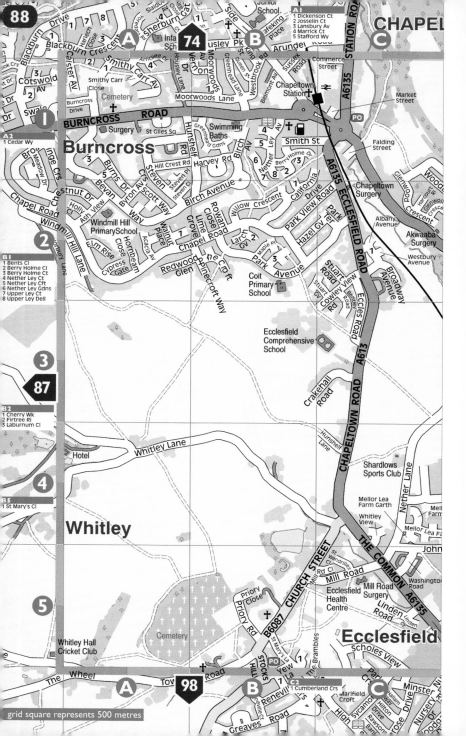

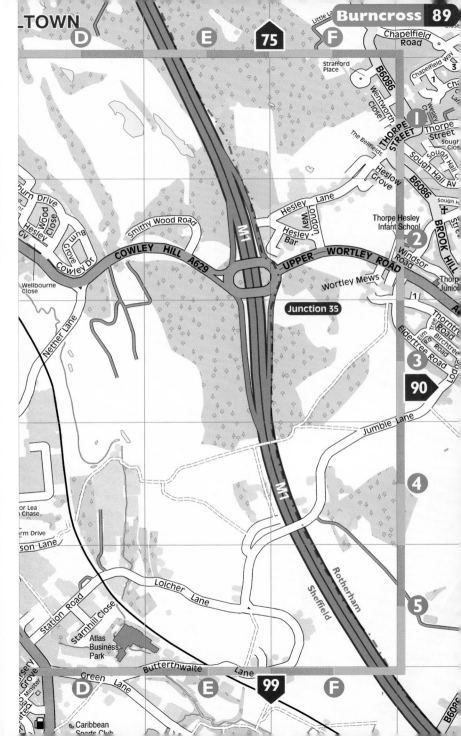

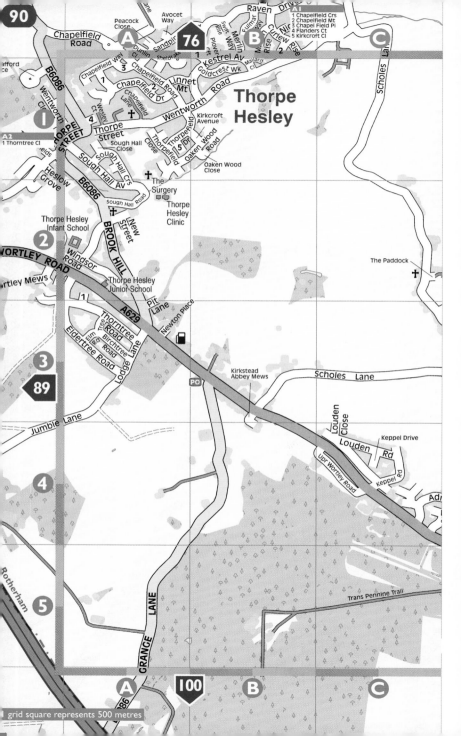

grid square represents 500 metres

D **E** **77** **F**

E4
1 Remount Wy

Morley
Pond

Roundwalk

Rotherham

Scholes

Scholes
Green

Dog
Kennel
Pond

I

E5
1 Dropp'well Fm Cl

2

F4
1 Sidons Cl

Scholes
Coppice

S61

Lapwater Rd

Rock
& Infa

Wingfield

3

92

Wingfi
Rd

Town

Lane

F5
1 Burgen Rd
2 Kent Rd

Roughwood   Road

Pepper
Close

The
Willows

The
Coppice

Monks
Close

Becket Crs

Crumwell Rd

Town Lane

Oaks La

Studmoor Road

Beevers Rd

Fox
Close

Maycock

Avenue

Remount Rd

Clover
Grn

Strafford
Rd

Ash
Worth
Dr

Infant School

Roughwood
Junior School

Jewitt

Crane

Rd

Road

Sandbergh
Road

Lovetot
Rd

Hudson
Road

Woodcock

Elliott Dr

4

imberw
Park

Keppel's
Column

mirals Crest

Hesley Grange

The
Grange

Wentworth
Place

Oaks Lane

UPPER WORTLEY ROAD

A629

Dropping Well

Shea   man Av

Rhodes Av

Abdy Road

Redscope Cts

Wellfield Rd

Cinderhill Rd

Kimberworth

Hungerhill
Road

Grange

Webster
Crs

Hill Vw Rd

Carr Vw Rd

Upper Wortley Road

West
Vw Rd

Redscope
Road

Redscope
Junior &
Infant School

Warris Cl

Clifford

Road

Binders
Rd

Wheatley Rd

Duke
St

Sellars Rd

Birks

Bower

Park

William Pl

Kimberworth Park
Clinic

Kimberworth Park

5

Gloucester Rd

ille Av

Beauchamp
Road

Bents

Chamb

PO

St Anns
Surg

Leybourne

Byrley Road

Morley

Langdon Rd

Grea

Park

Ellam Road

Hutton Road

Warren
Hill

Ellam Cl

Kimberworth Park
Medical Centre

PO

D **E** **101** **F**

Watson
Glen

Farm

Ox
Close

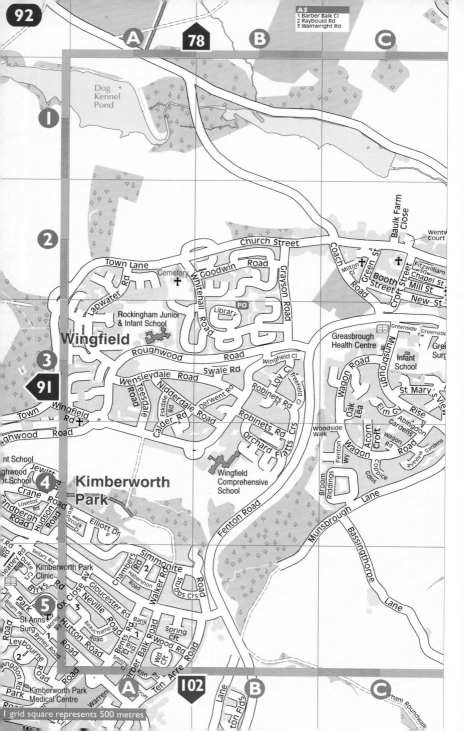

A **78** **B** **C**

A5
1 Barber Balk Cl
2 Raybould Rd
3 Wainwright Rd

I

Dog
Kennel
Pond

Baulk Farm
Close

Wentw
Court

2

Church Street

Town Lane

Goodwin Road

Grayson Road

Coach Road

Milton

Green St

Booth Street

Fitzwilliam Sq

Chapel St

Mill St

New St

Cemetery

Whitehall Road

Lapwater Rd

Library

PO

Rockingham Junior
& Infant School

Greasbrough
Health Centre

Greenside

Greenside

Gre
Sur

Wingfield

Roughwood Road

Wingfield Cl

Infant
School

Munsbrough

3

91

Wensleydale Road

Swale Rd

Toy Cl

Treefield Cl

St Mary's

St Mary's View

Teesdale Road

Nidderdale Road

Robinets Rd

Wagon Road

Oak Lea

Elm Gv

Abingdon Gardens

Rise

Town

Wingfield Rd

Calder Rd

Eskdale Rd

Derwent Rd

Robinets Rd

Flatts Crs

Woodside Walk

Fenton Wy

Acorn Croft

Coppice Gdns

Wagon Road

Pyeview Gardens

ghwood Road

Orchard

Wingfield
Comprehensive
School

**Kimberworth
Park**

nt School

ghwood
r School

Jewitt

Crane Road

Lovetot Rd

Hudson Road

Pocock

Elliott Dr

Broom Riddings

Fenton Road

Wagon Gdns

Munsbrough Lane

Bassingthorpe Lane

andbergh Road

Sellars Rd

Simmonite

Chambers

Habershon Road

Walker Road

bbs Crs

Kimberworth Park
Clinic

Duke

Gloucester Rd

Sirius

Road

Rd

heatley Rd

Birks

Close

Neville Rd

Beauchamp Rd

Bank

Spring Cft

5

St Anns
Surg

Morley

Bents Rig Cl

Wood Rd

Smithy

Wd Cft

Ten Acre Road

Hutton Road

Byrley Road

Barber Balk Road

Lane

A **102** **B** **C**

Kimberworth Park
Medical Centre

Warren

ton Flds

rham Roundwalk

1 grid square represents 500 metres

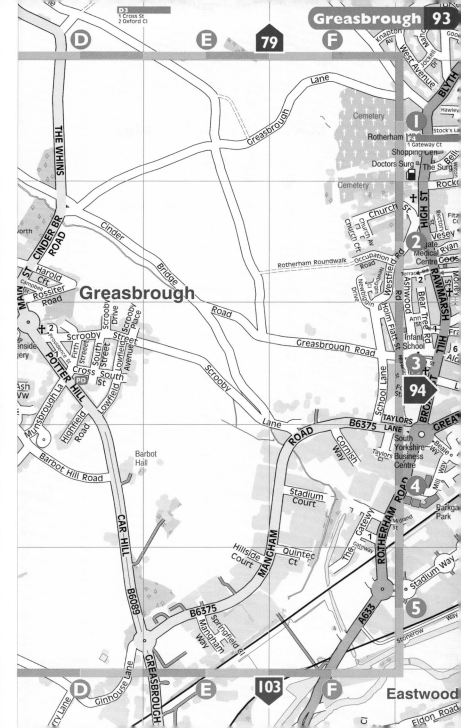

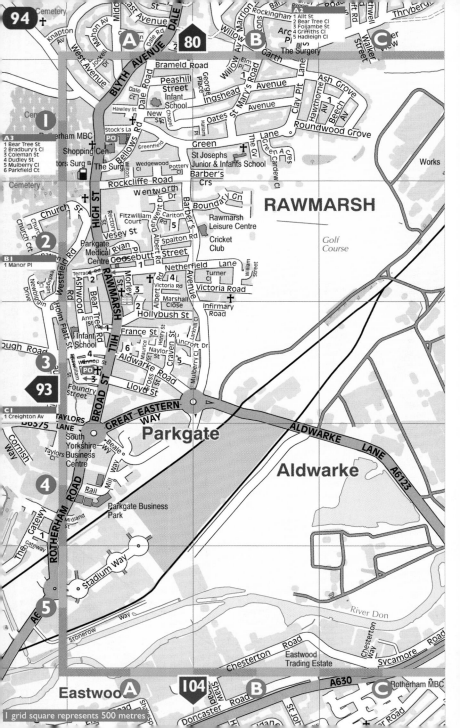

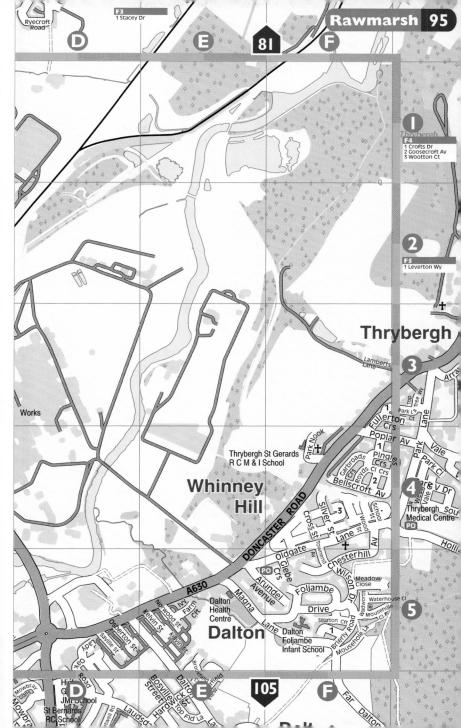

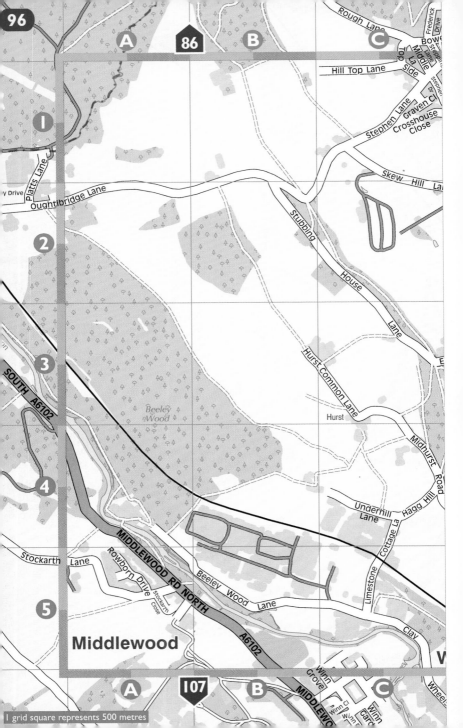

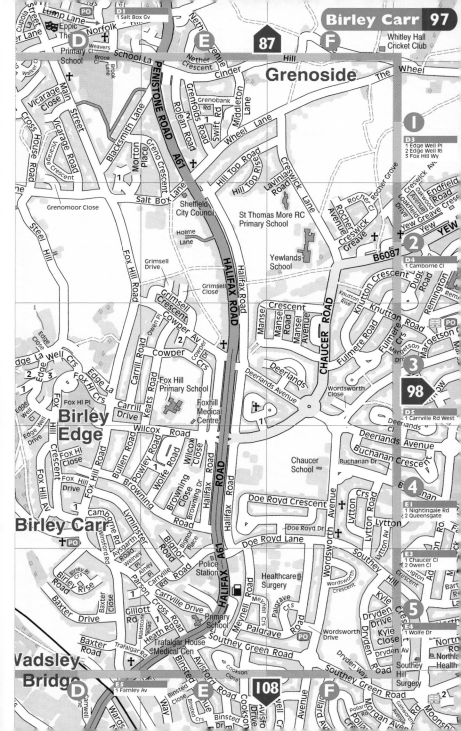

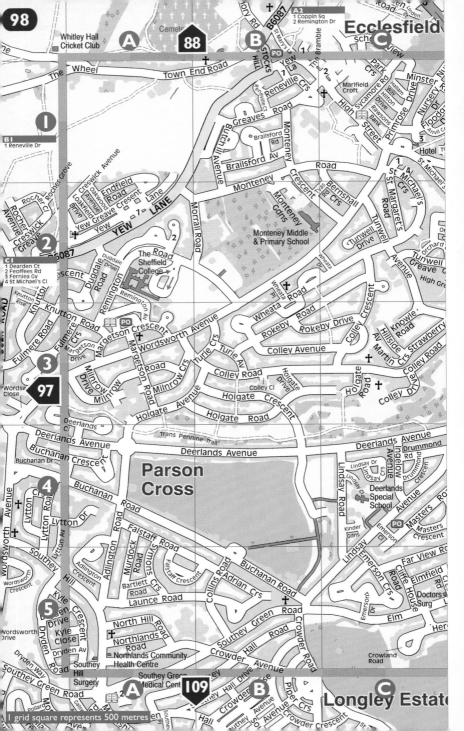

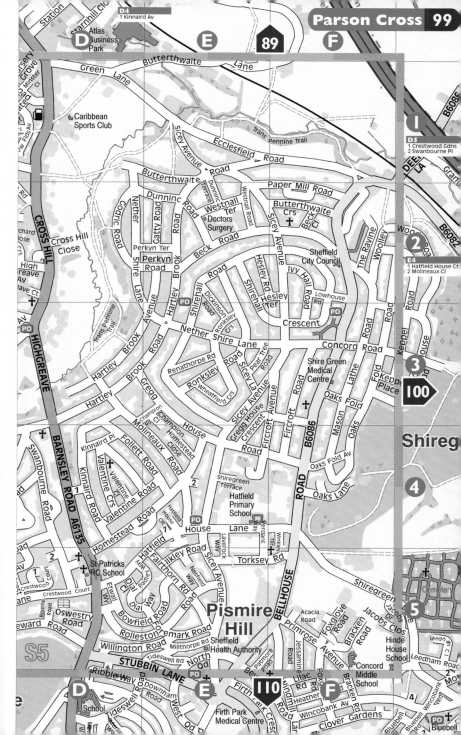

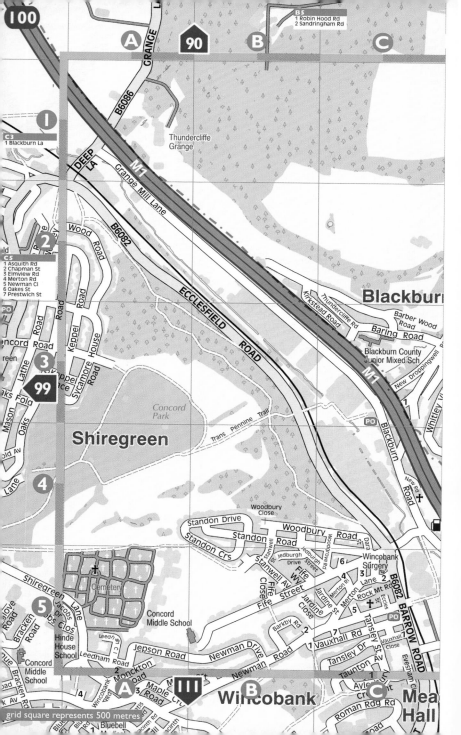

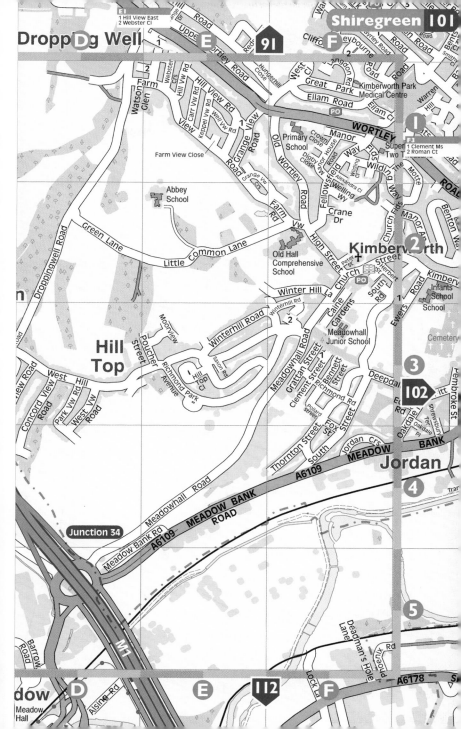

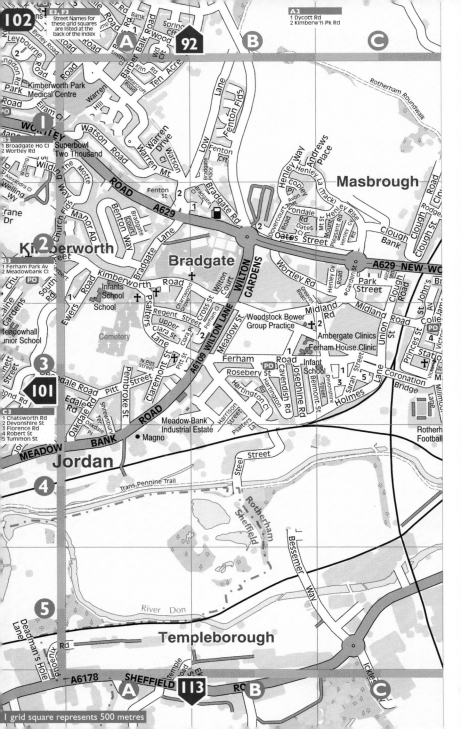

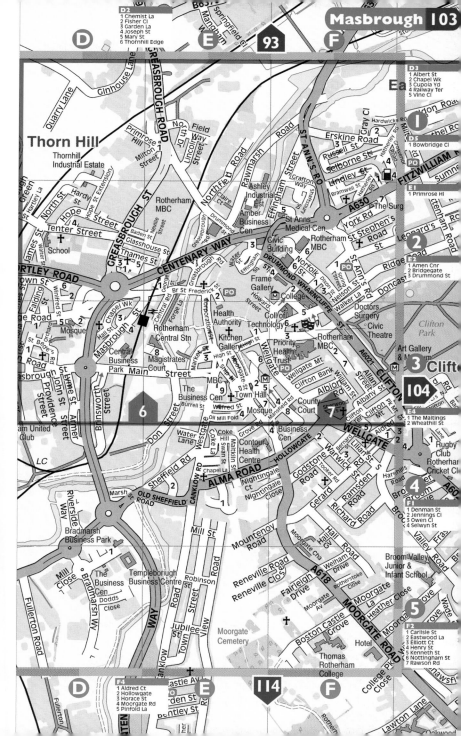

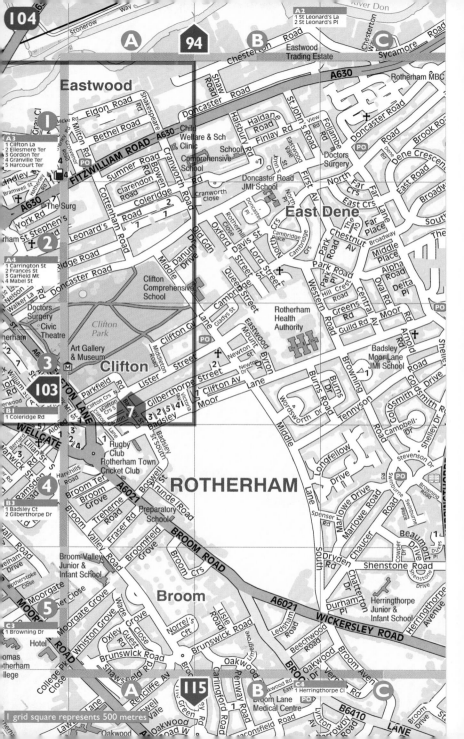

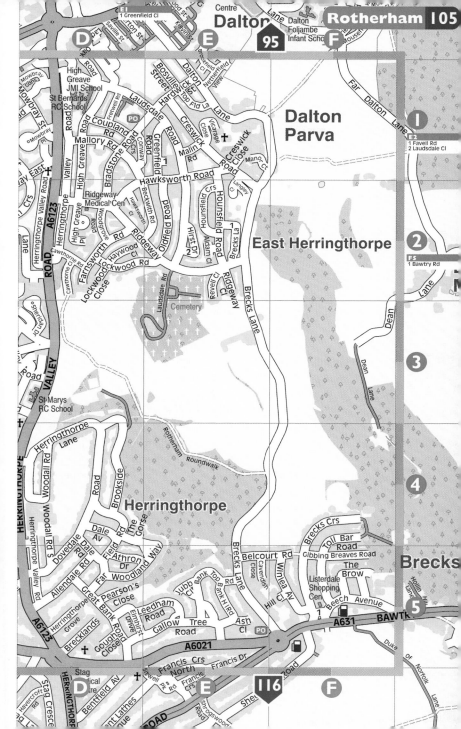

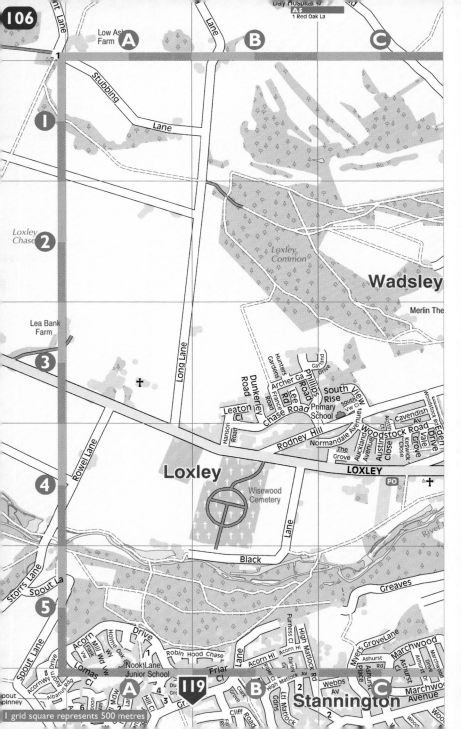

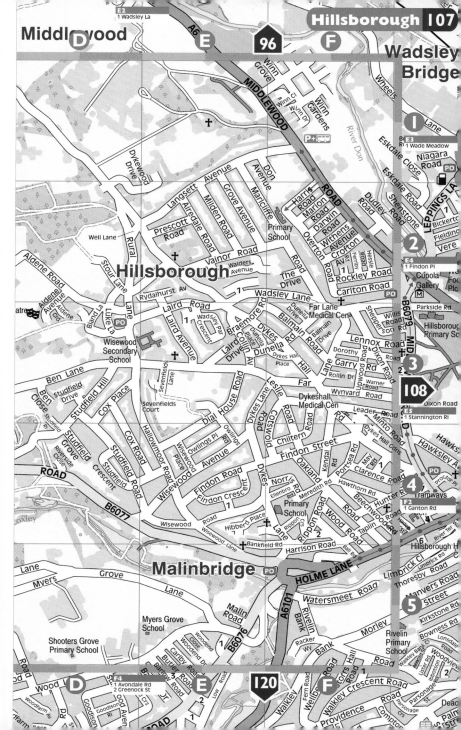

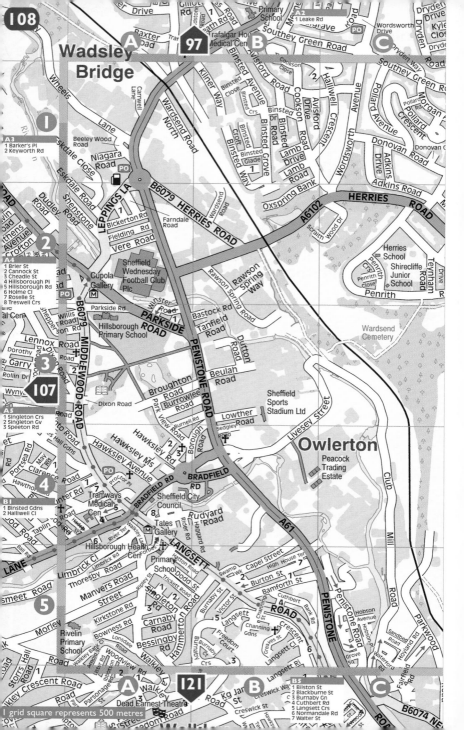

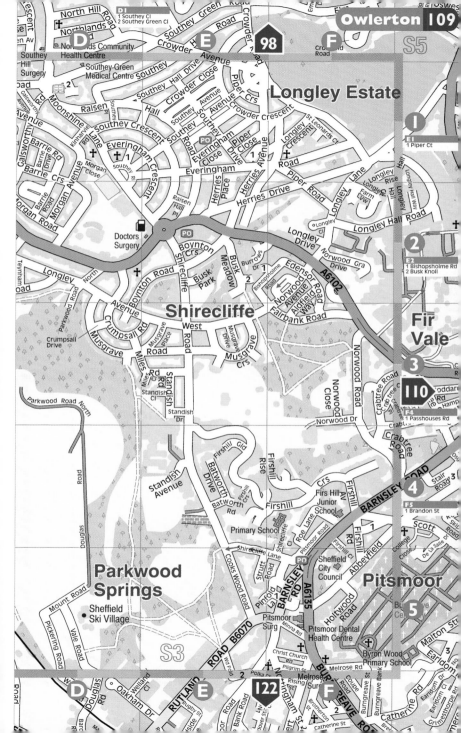

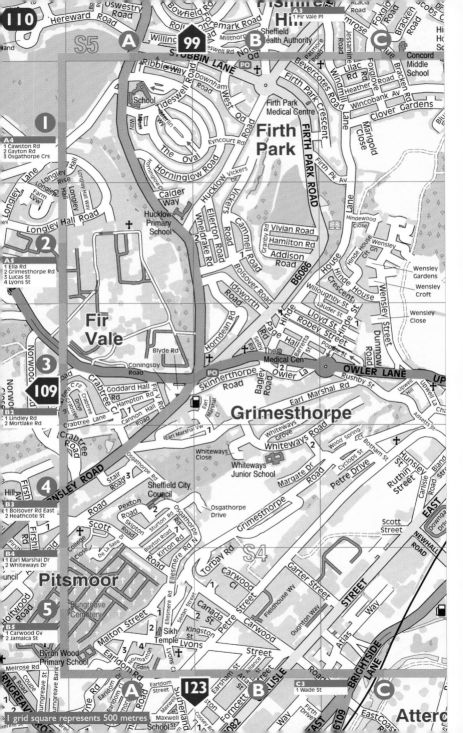

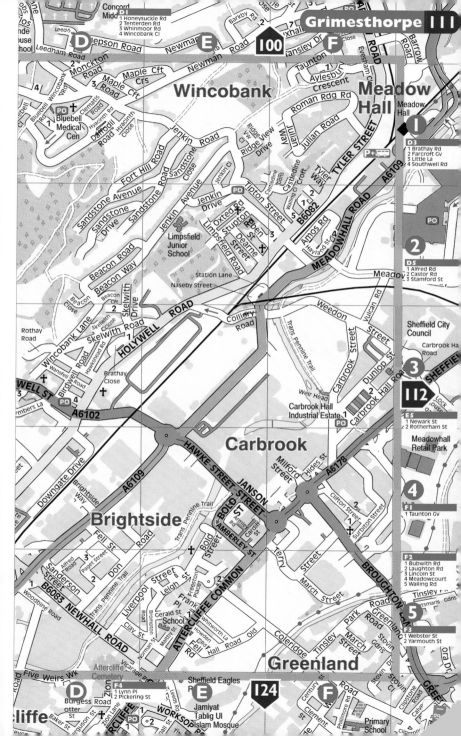

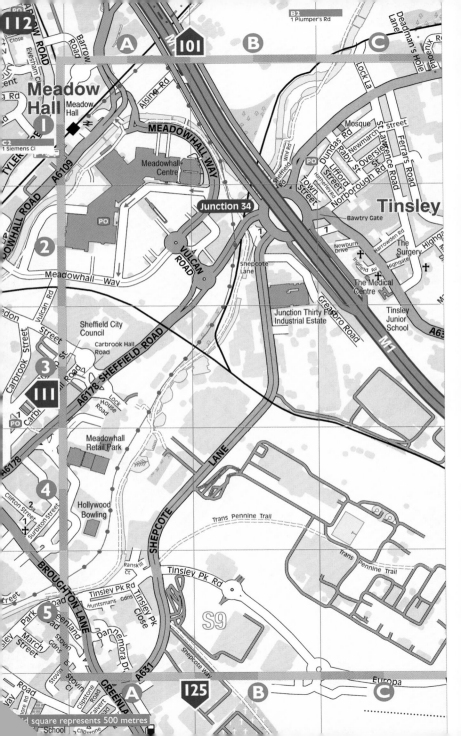

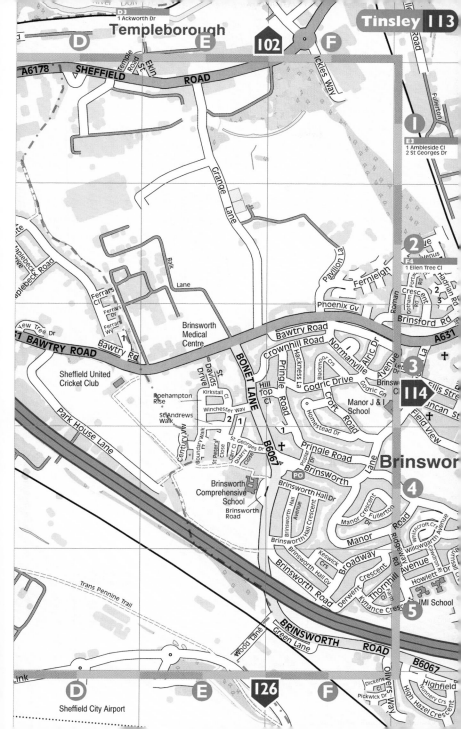

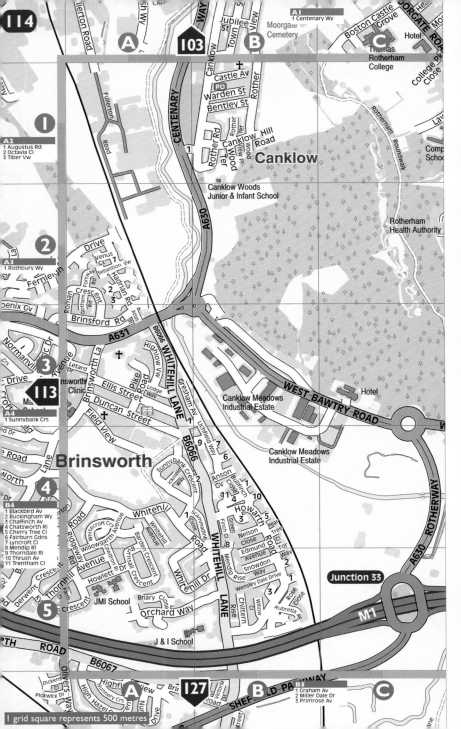

114

A **103** B **A1** 1 Centenary Wy **C**

Moorgate
Cemetery

Boston Castle Grove

DORGATE ROAD

Hotel

Thomas
Rotherham
College

College P
Close

1

A2
1 Augustus Rd
2 Octavia Cl
3 Tiber Vw

Jubilee St

Castle Av

PO

Warden St

Bentley St

Canklow Hill
Road

Canklow

Canklow Woods
Junior & Infant School

Rotherham
Roundwalk

Comp
Scho

Rotherham
Health Authority

2

A3
1 Rothbury Wy

Drive

Venus
Ct

Fernleigh

enix Gv

Fortway

Sebastion Vw

Hadrian Rd

Roman

Crescent

Brinsford Rd

A631

B6066 WHITEHILL LANE

Gresham Av

3

113

A4
1 Sunnybank Crs

Normanvil

Drive

Ma
School

nsworth
Clinic

Highlow Vw

Road

Ellis Street

Duncan Street

Field View

Lodge
Way

Brinsworth

Lane

orth

Road

Sunnybank Crescent

ckriield
Way

Lichfield Way

B6066

4

B4
1 Blackbird Av
2 Buckingham Wy
3 Chaffinch Av
4 Chatsworth Ri
5 Cherry Tree Cl
6 Fairburn Gdns
7 Lyncroft Cl
8 Mendip Ri
9 Thorndale Ri
10 Thrush Av
11 Trentham Cl

Whitehill Avenue

Willowgarth Avenue

Barden Crescent

Scannadine
Close

WHITEHILL LANE

Anson
Gv

Bulfinch
Close

Howarth
Road

Green

Nelson
Close

Edmund
Avenue

Snowdon
Way

Wensley Dale Drive

Finch Close

Mendip
Rise

Chiltern
Rise

Willow

Tor
Way

Pear
Tree

Rose
Close

Aubretia

5

JMI School

Orchard Way

Briary Close

Whitehill Dr

J & I School

127

A B SHEF LD PA WAY C

B5
1 Graham Av
2 Miller Dale Dr
3 Primrose Av

Canklow Meadows
Industrial Estate

Canklow Meadows
Industrial Estate

WEST BAWTRY ROAD

Hotel

ROTHERWAY

A630

Junction 33

M1

A630

Olivers La

B6067

Dickens

Pickwick Dr

Highfi

High Hazel

Nur

View

Bri

Victoria
Road

1 grid square represents 500 metres

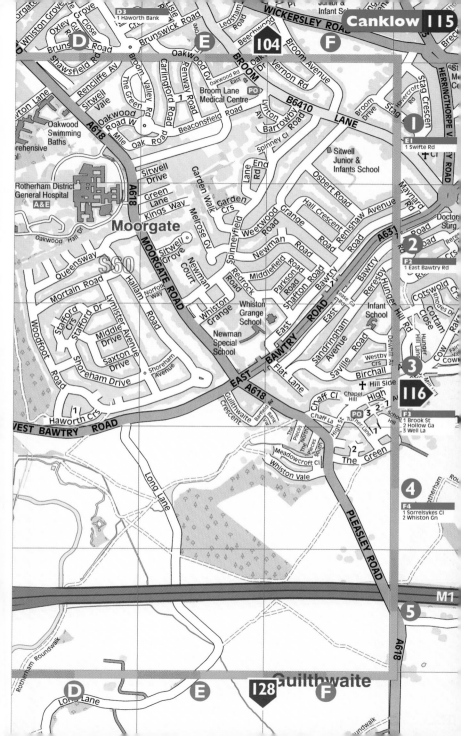

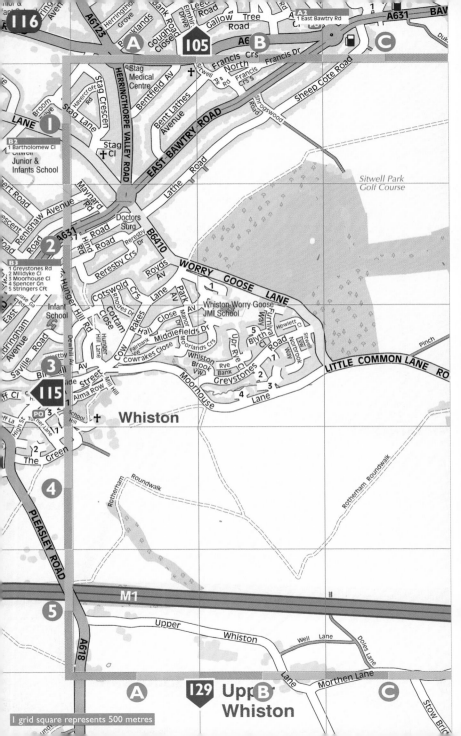

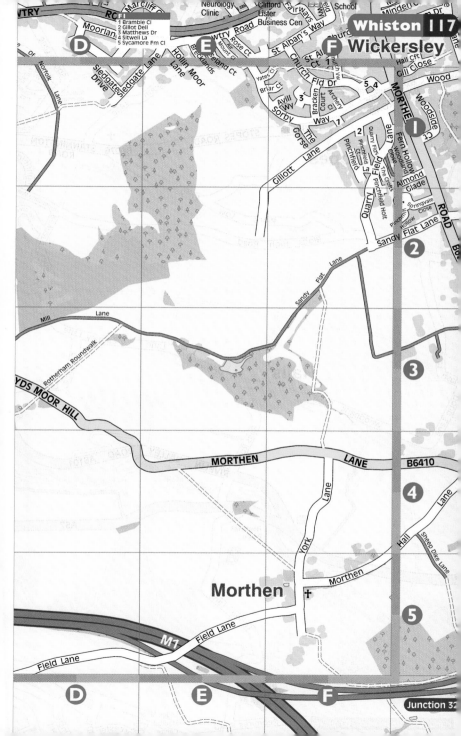

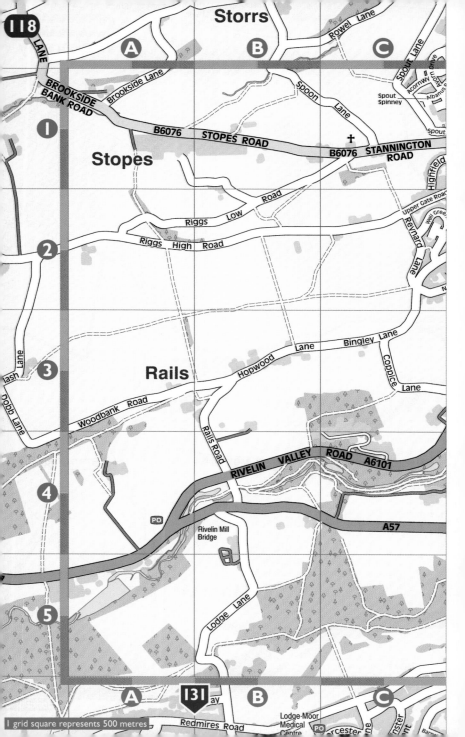

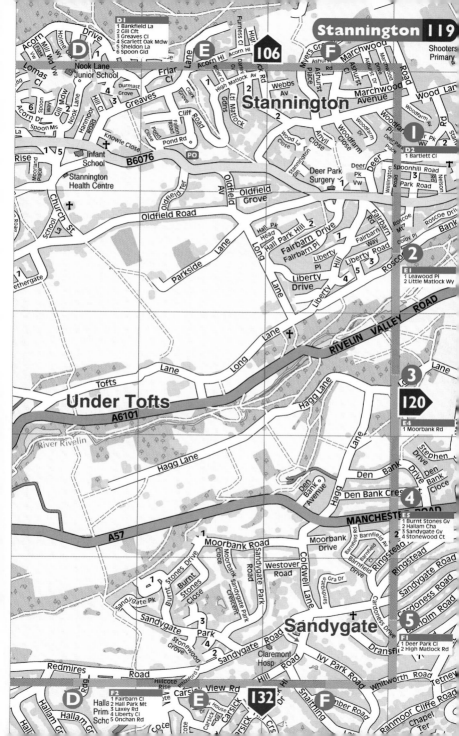

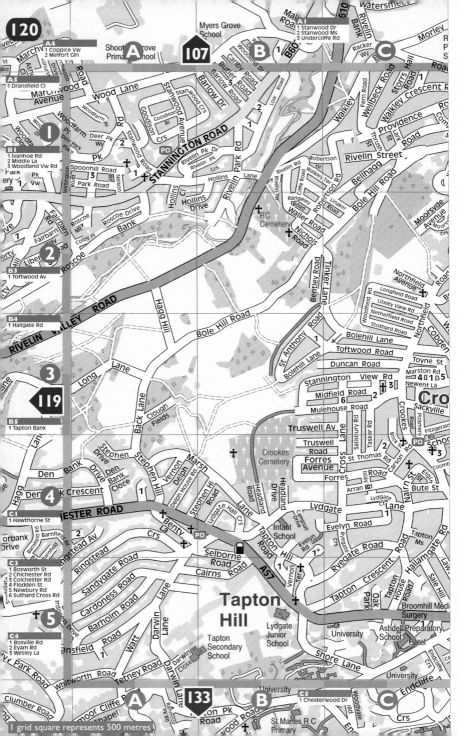

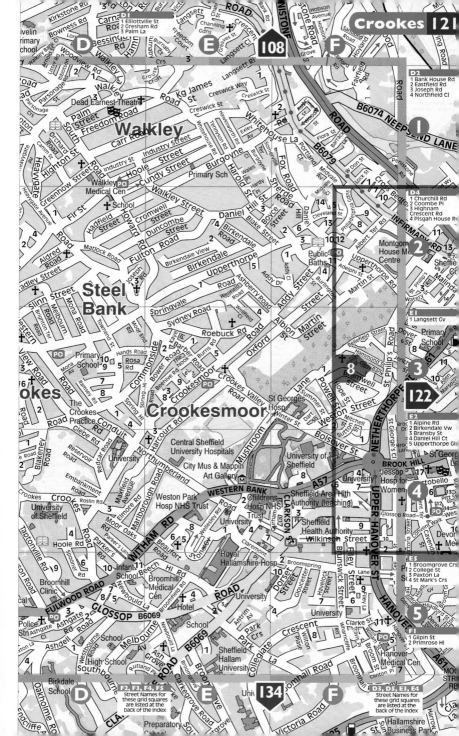

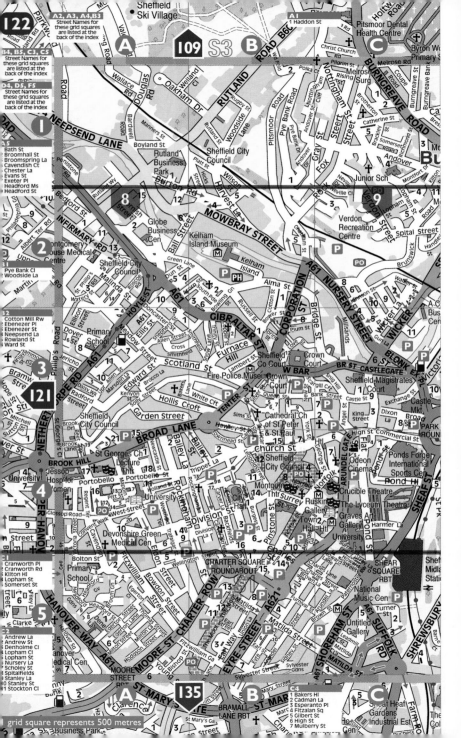

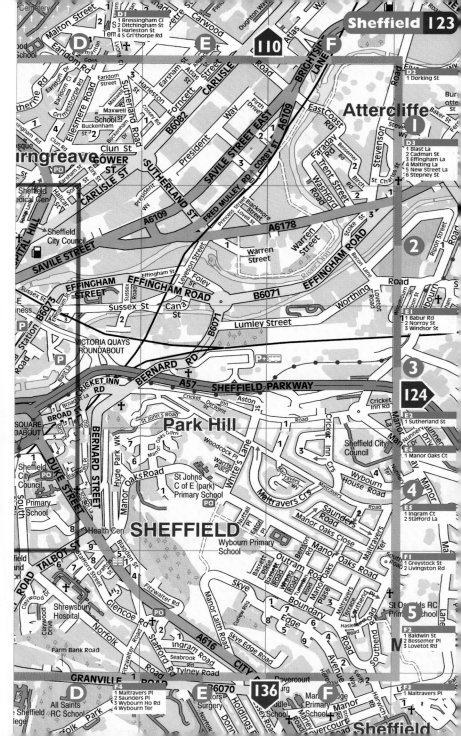

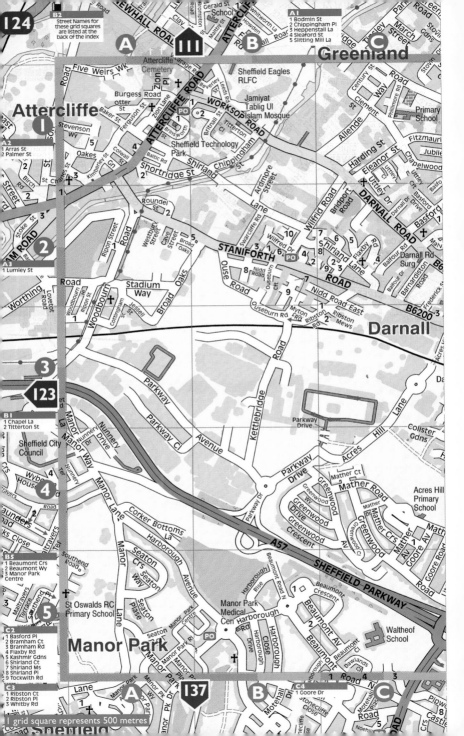

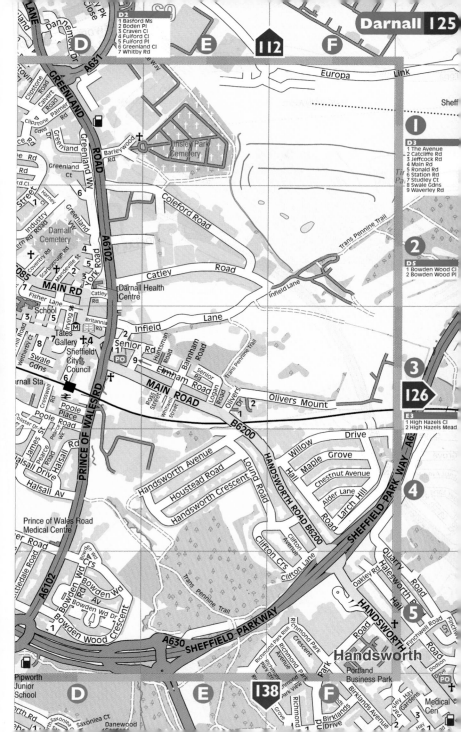

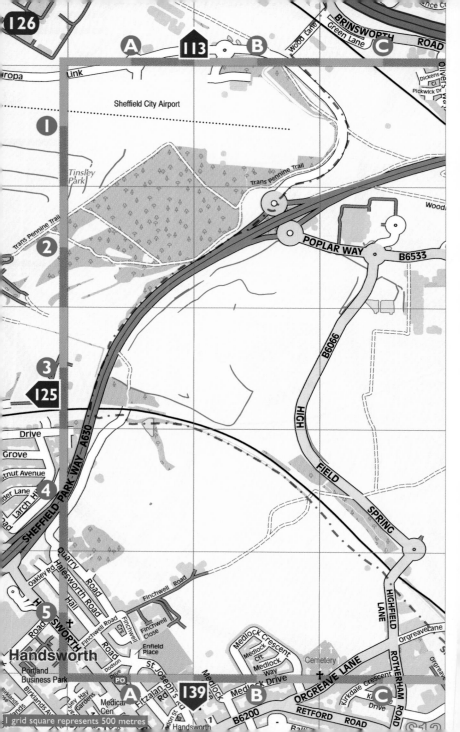

A
113
B
C

BRINSWORTH ROAD
Green Lane
Wood Lane
Dickens
Pickwick Dr

Link
Europa

Sheffield City Airport

I

Tinsley Park

Trans Pennine Trail

Trans Pennine Trail

Wood

POPLAR WAY

B6533

2

Trans Pennine Trail

B6066

3

125

High

Field

B6066

Spring

Drive

Grove

tnut Avenue

der Lane

Larch H

4

SHEFFIELD PARK WAY – A630

Quarry Road

Oakley Rd

Hall

Halesworth Road

Finchwell Road

Finchwell Road

Finchwell Close

Highfield Lane

Orgreave Lane

5

H SWORTH Road

Finchwell Road

Dodson Drive

Finchwell Cl

Enfield Place

Medlock Crescent

Medlock Cft

Medlock Way

Cemetery

orgreav

Handsworth

Portland Business Park

St Joseph's Rd

Medlock Drive

ROTHERHAM ROAD

A

Fitzalan Rd

139

B

ORGREAVE LANE

C

Kirkdale Crescent

K Drive

PO

Medical Cen

Birkianoft St

ley Hay Gardens

Birmingham Av

nds

St

Handsworth

B6200

RETFORD ROAD

ail

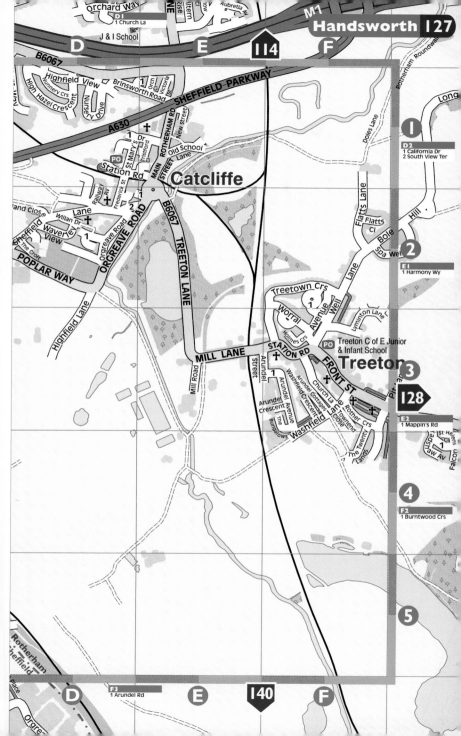

128

A

115

B

C

Guilthwaite

A4
1 Bradshaw Wy

Rotherham Roundwalk

Long Lane

1

Rotherham Roundwalk

Flatts Lane

Flatts Cl

Hill

Bole

Spa Well Crs

Rotherham Roundwalk

Spa House

2

Lane

Well

Lyminton Lane

Burnt Wood

Treeton C of E Junior & Infant School

PO

Treeton

3

Pit Lane

127

FRONT S

urch La

Rother Crs

Townend

WOOD

St Helens

Bradshaw Av

1

Falcon Drive

The Twenty

Spans

Close

4

LANE

B6067

5

AUG

A

141

B

C

West

1 grid square represents 500 metres

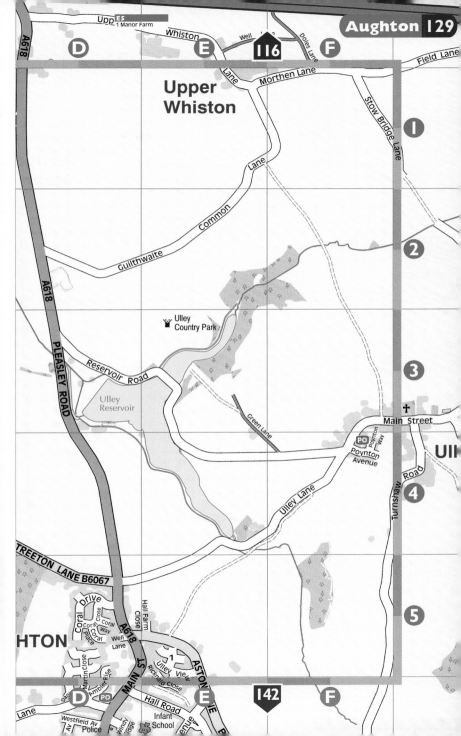

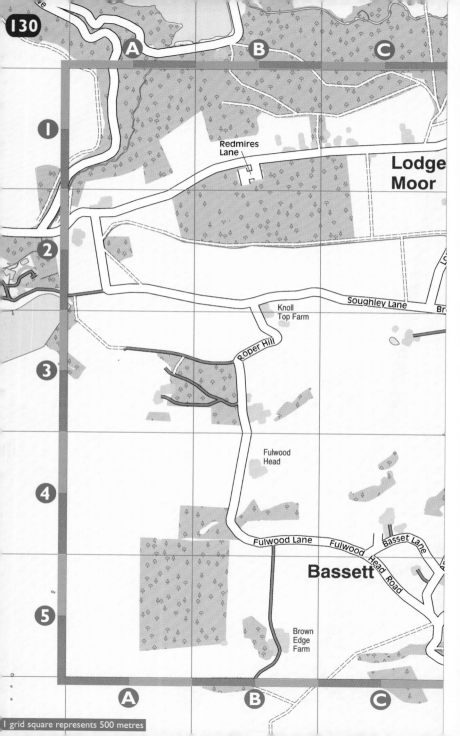

A B C

1

Redmires
Lane

Lodge
Moor

2

Soughley Lane

Br

Knoll
Top Farm

Roper Hill

3

Fulwood
Head

4

Fulwood Lane Fulwood Head Road Basset Lane

Bassett

5

Brown
Edge
Farm

A B C

1 grid square represents 500 metres

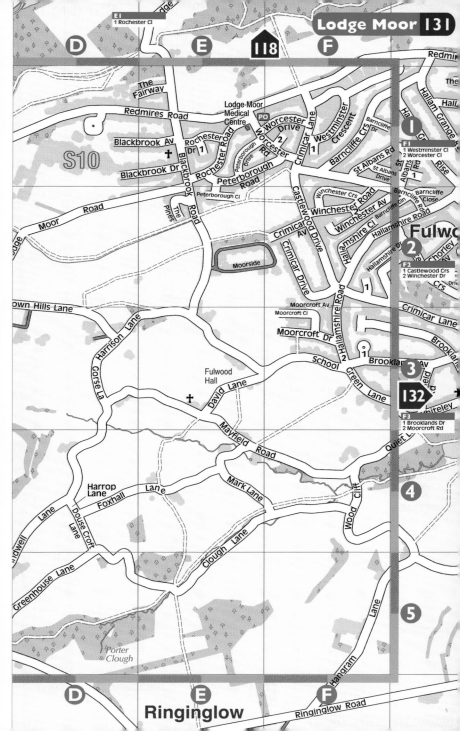

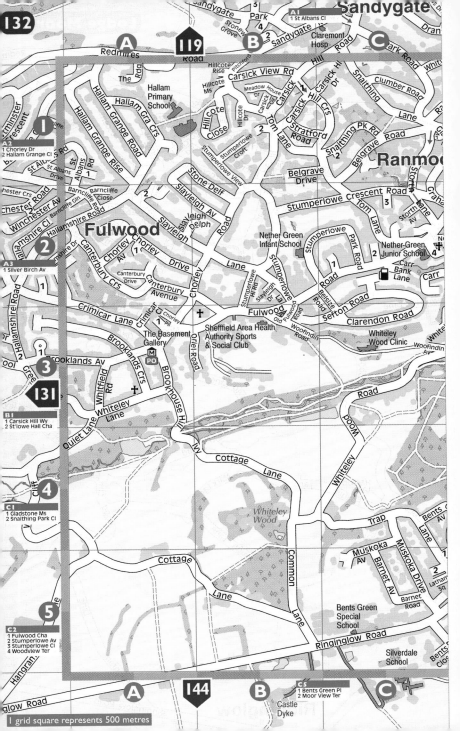

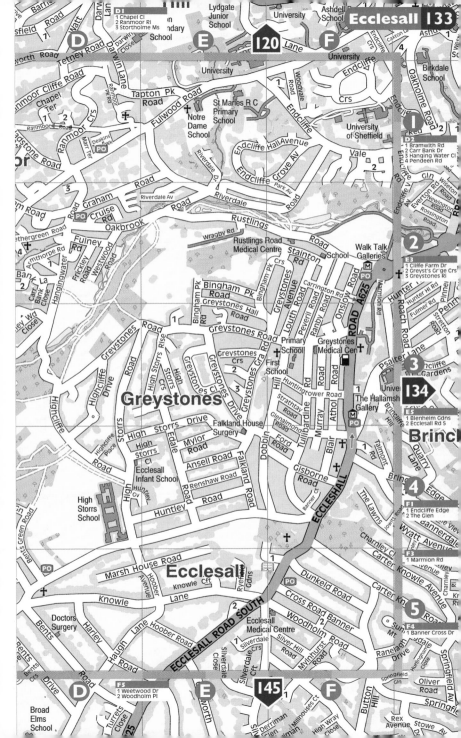

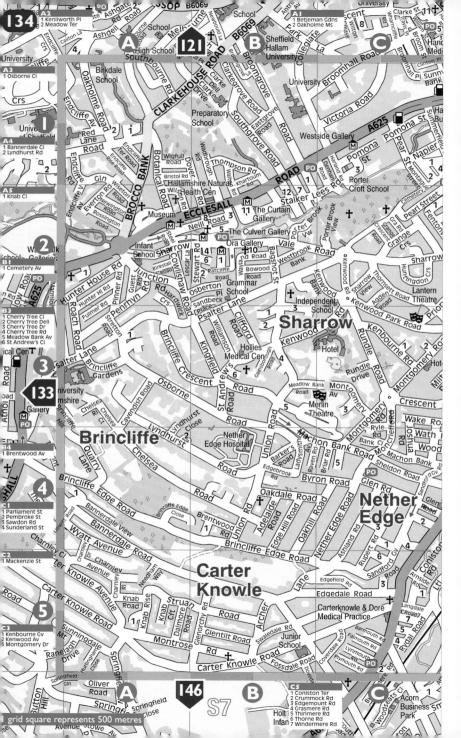

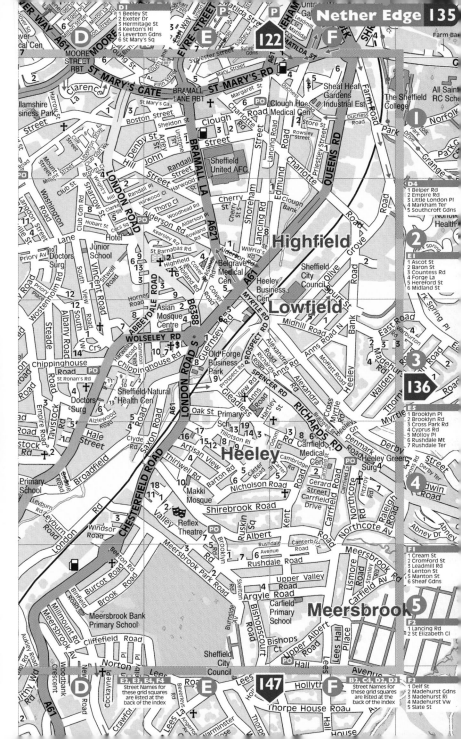

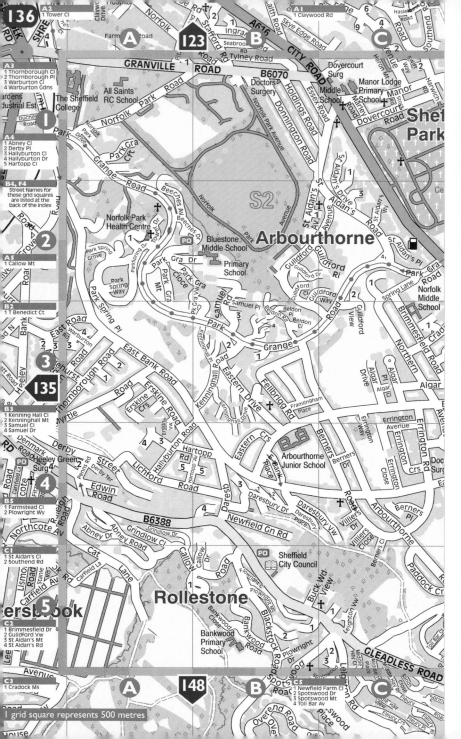

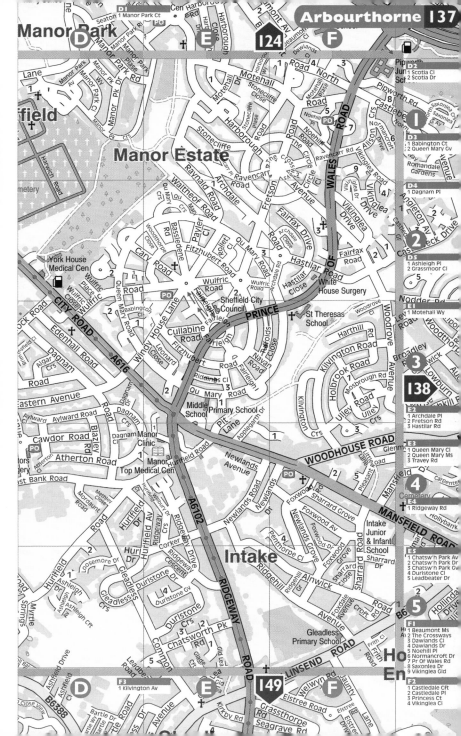

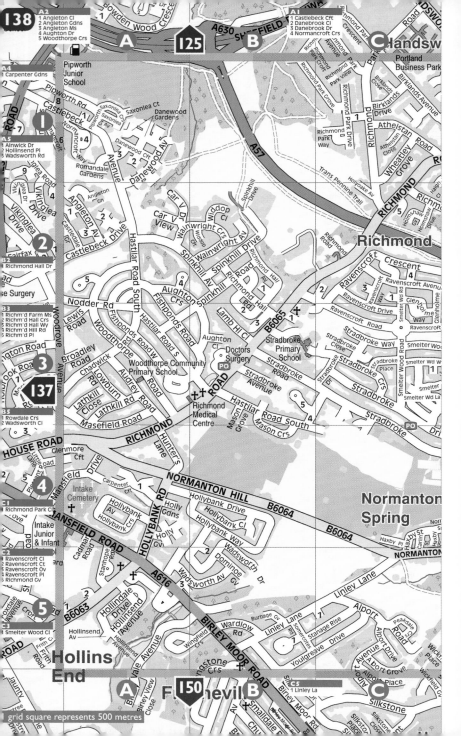

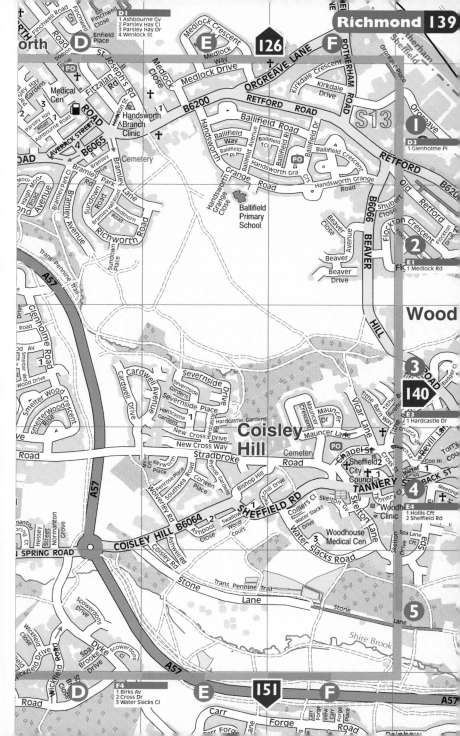

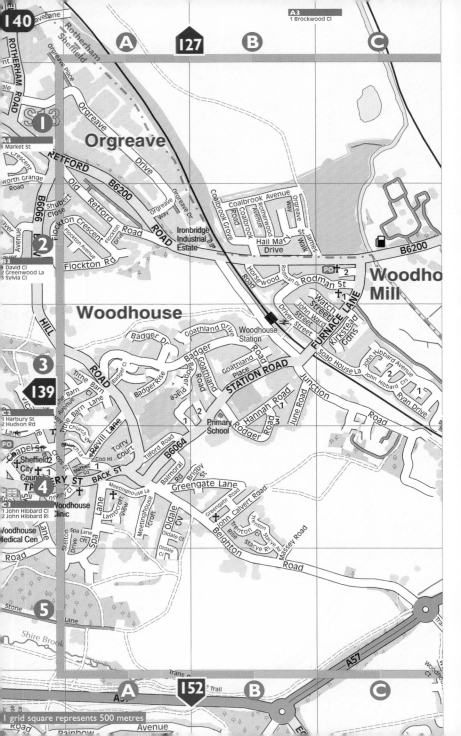

D3
1 John Hibbard Av

D

E

128

F

West Lane

I

Falconer Lane

Smallage Lane

West Lane

Springwood Av

Hall Clo

Aston Comprehensive School

Augh
Aven

Aysgarth Rise

RETFORD ROAD SHEFFIELD ROAD

Chestnut Rd

Holly
Ter

Oak
Ter

Becch Way

A618 AUGH

2

King
Stre

Fence

Aston Fence Junior & Infant School

Sheffield Road

Aston Swallownest Junior & Infant School

Nursery Road

HIGH STRE

ROTHERHAM ROAD

School Street

Park St

Main Street

use

Park Hill

Sorby Road

West Park Drive

3

142

Park Dr

CHESTERFIELD RD

Sw

B6200

Chesterfield Rd

Pickering Crs

Ilkley Cls

Sherby Drive

Ilkley Crs

1

Wetherby Drive

Collingham Rd

2

Soap House

River Rother

Lane

4

Chesterfield Road

CHESTERFIELD ROAD

5

A57

A57

Rotherham Sheffield

Wragg Lane

Rotherham Road

s Pennine Trail

Woodhouse

Poplar Avenue

Chestnut Avenue

Tulip Tree Close

Woodlands Avenue

Cairns Road

Woodhouse Lane

Woodhouse Av

Woodho use Crs

D

Rosemary Road

The Av

Lime St

Rotherva
Close

E

153

F

Queen's Road

Beighton

Oak Rd

Elm Rd

High

Manvers Road

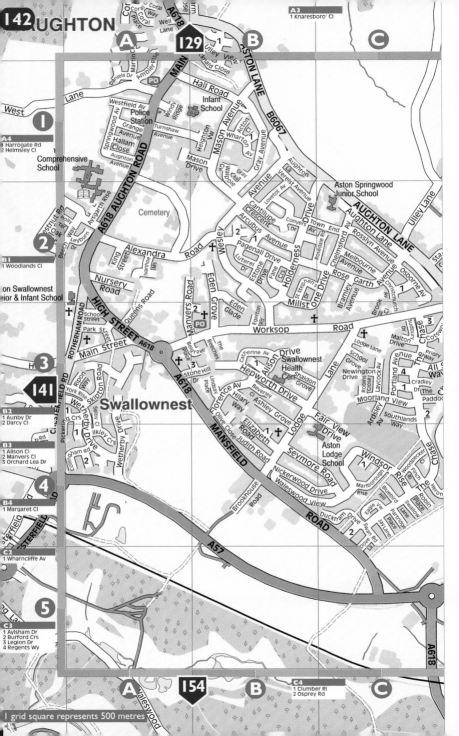

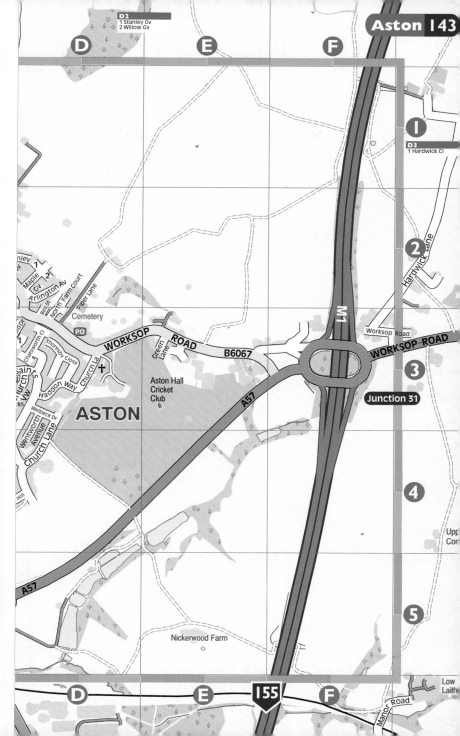

D2
1 Stanley Gv
2 Willow Gv

D   **E**   **F**

I

D3
1 Hardwick Cl

2

Hardwick Lane

Stanley
Maple
Gv
Arlington Av
Bell St
North Farm Court
Piper Lane
Cemetery
PO

Worksop Road

3

WORKSOP   ROAD

Green Lane

B6067

Thoresby Close
Chatsworth Cl
Haddon Way
Church La
Church
Welbeck Dr
Wentworth Avenue
Church Lane
HILL

ASTON

Aston Hall
Cricket
Club

Junction 31

A57

4

Upp
Cor

5

A57

Nickerwood Farm

D   **E**   **155**   **F**

Manor Road

Low
Laith

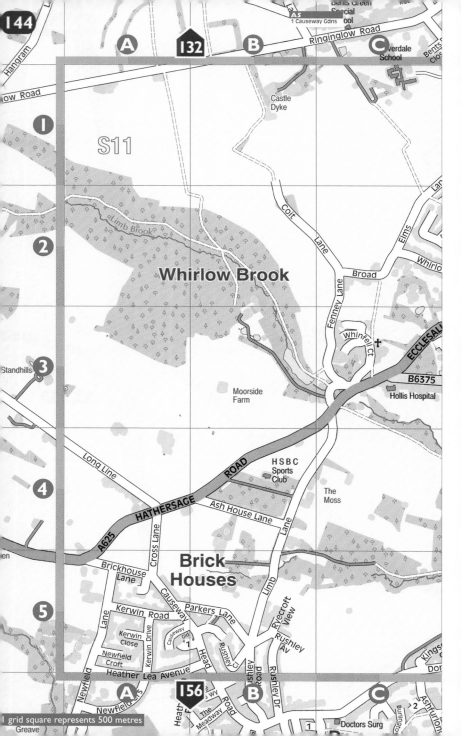

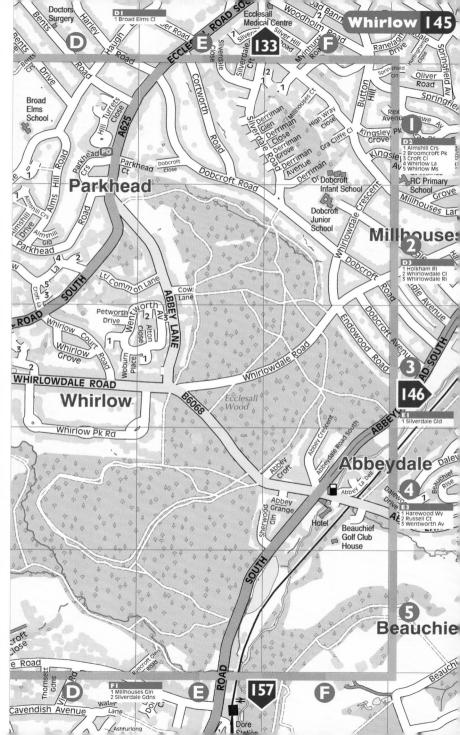

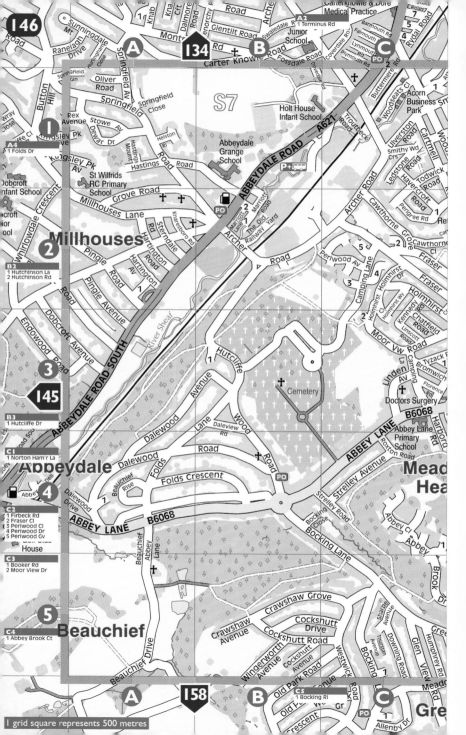

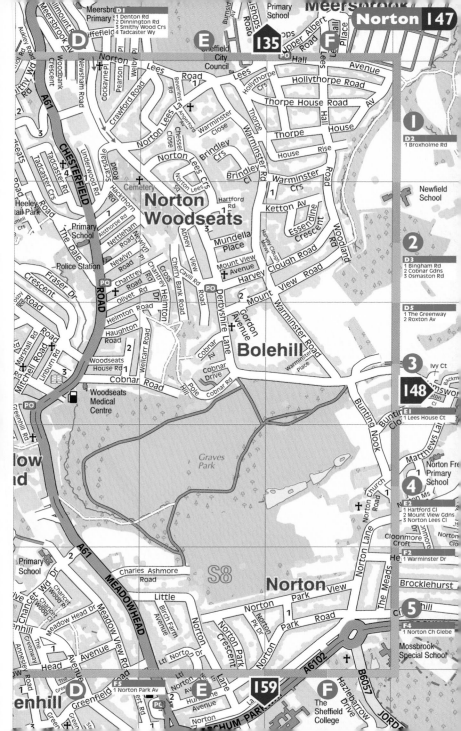

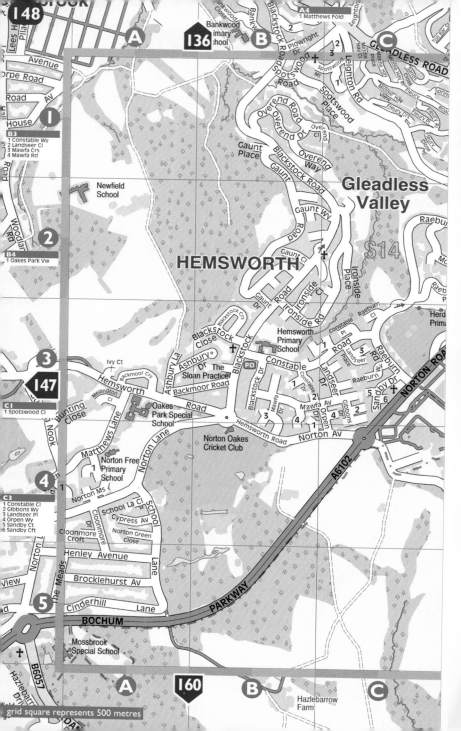

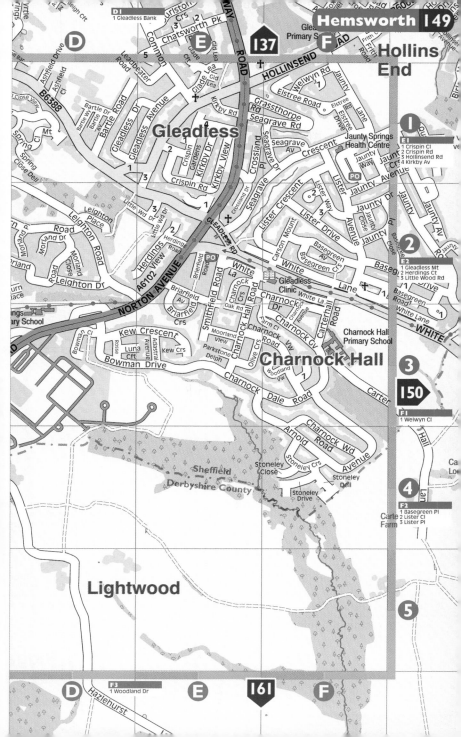

Hollins End

D1
1 Gleadless Bank

137

Gleadless
Primary S...

F

Gleadless

HOLLINSEND

Hollinsend Road

Frith

Welwyn Rd

Elstree Road

Grassthorpe
Rd

Seagrave Rd

Seagrave
Av

Jaunty Springs
Health Centre

Jaunty
Way

PO

Jaunty Avenue

I
E1
1 Crispin Cl
2 Crispin Rd
3 Hollinsend Rd
4 Kirkby Av

Ashfield Drive

B6388

Bartle Dr Road

Bartle

Spring
Close Dell

Gleadless Avenue

Gleadless Dr

Crispin
Gardens

Kirkby Dr

Kirkby View

Crispin Rd

Crossland Dr

Crossland

Seagrave
Crescent

Seagrave Dr

Lister Crescent

Lister Way

Lister Drive

Jaunty
Crescent

Jaunty

Jaunty Avenue

Jaunty
Close

Jaunty Av

Leighton
Road

Leighton
place

Moorland Dr

Morland
Close

Leighton Dr

Little Wd Dr

Herdings
View

Herdings
Road

Carson Mount

Basegreen
Av

Basegreen Cl

White
Lane

Basegreen Road

White Lane

2
E2
1 Gleadless Mt
2 Herdings Ct
3 Little Wood Rd

Basegreen
Road

WHITE

A6102 NORTON AVENUE

PO

Brierfield
Road

Smithfield Road

White La

Charnock
Crs

Oak Rd

Gleadless
Clinic

Charnock Hall Road

White La

Charnock
Dr

Charnock
Avenue

Charnock Gv

Carterhall
Road

Charnock Hall
Primary School

Briarfield
Av

Briarfield
Crs

Farm Cl

Charnock
Road

Charnock Vw

Moorland
View

Charnock Hall

3

150
F1
1 Welwyn Cl

Kew Crescent

Luna
Cft

Rosse

Adastral
Avenue

Kew Crs

Bowman
Cl

Bowman Drive

Olive Grove

Parkstone
Delph

Woodland
Vw

Charnock
Dale Road

Charnock Wd

Arnold
Road

Carter...

Charnock Wd
Avenue

Stoneley
Close

Stoneley Crs

Stoneley
Dell

Carte...
Farm

4
F2
1 Basegreen Pl
2 Lister Cl
3 Lister Pl

Sheffield
Derbyshire County

Stoneley
Drive

5

Lightwood

D
Hazlehurst

F3
1 Woodland Dr

E

161

F

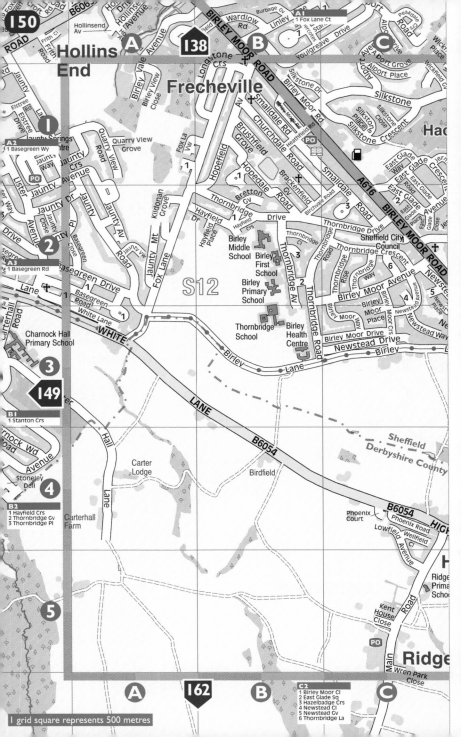

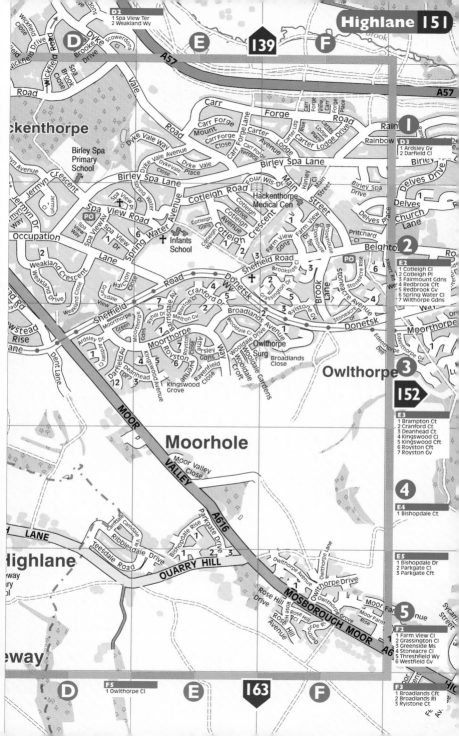

Hackenthorpe

Birley Spa Primary School

Moorhole

Owlthorpe

Highlane

139

152

163

D2
1 Spa View Ter
2 Weakland Wy

D3
1 Ardsley Gv
2 Darfield Cl

E2
1 Cotleigh Cl
2 Cotleigh Pl
3 Fairmount Gdns
4 Redbrook Cft
5 Redbrook Gv
6 Spring Water Cl
7 Wilthorpe Gdns

E3
1 Brampton Ct
2 Cranford Ct
3 Deanhead Ct
4 Kingswood Cl
5 Kingswood Cft
6 Royston Cft
7 Royston Gv

E4
1 Bishopdale Ct

E5
1 Bishopdale Dr
2 Parkgate Cl
3 Parkgate Cft

F2
1 Farm View Cl
2 Grassington Cl
3 Greenside Ms
4 Stoneacre Cl
5 Threshfield Wy
6 Westfield Gv

F3
1 Broadlands Cft
2 Broadlands Ri
3 Rylstone Ct

F5
1 Owlthorpe Cl

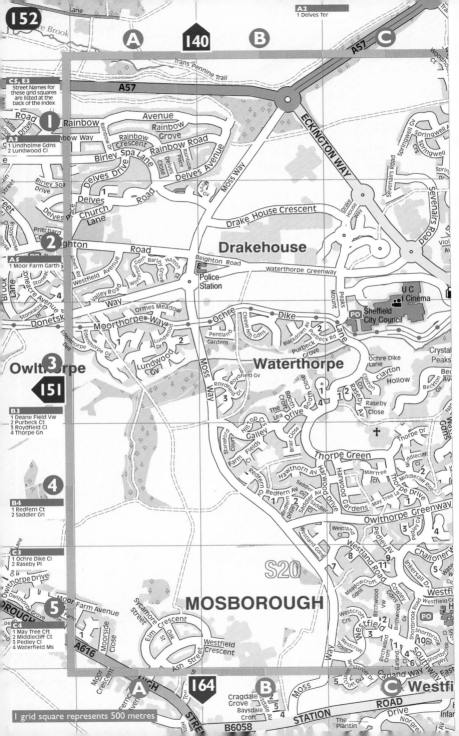

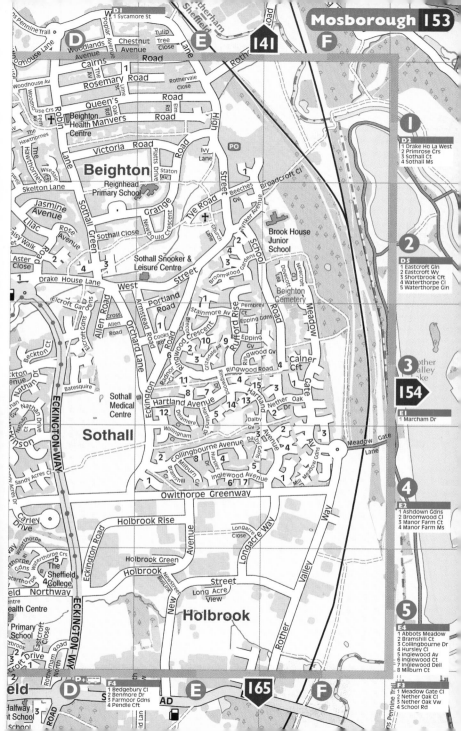

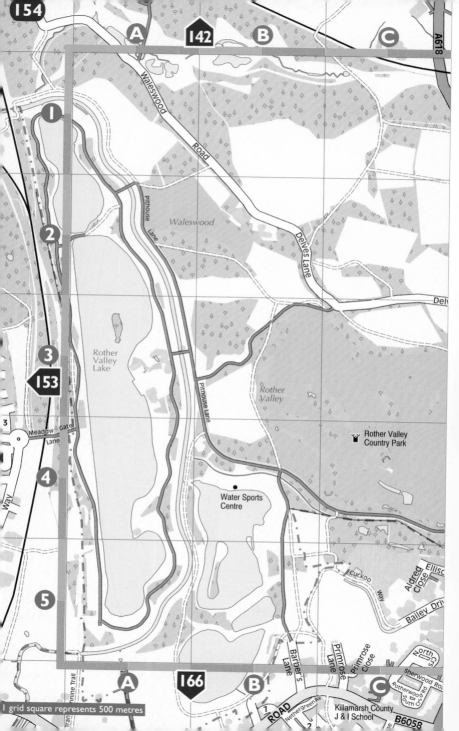

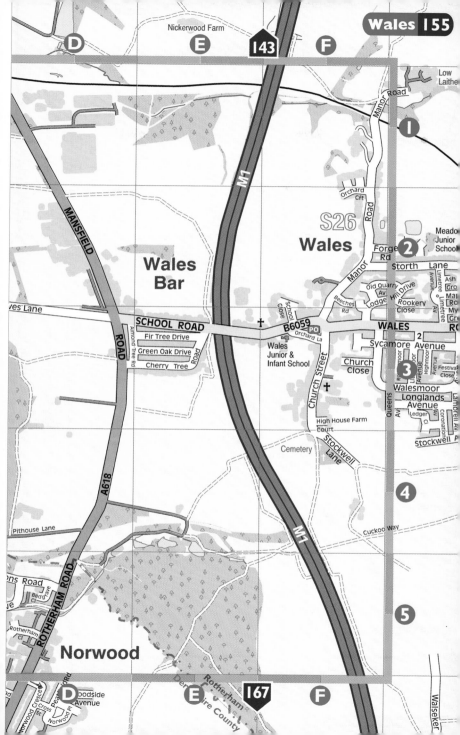

Nickerwood Farm

D **E** 143 **F**

Low Laithe

Manor Road

I

Orchard Cft

S26
Wales

Meado
Junior
School

Forge Rd **2**

Storth Lane

Ash
Gro
Ma
Ro
My
Gre

Manor Road

Old Quarry Av
Lodge

Hill Drive

Limetree Avenue

Rookery Close

Limetree

MANSFIELD

**Wales
Bar**

ves Lane

SCHOOL ROAD

Fir Tree Drive

Green Oak Drive

Cherry Tree

Almond Tree Rd

ROAD

School Close

Beeches Rd

B6059

† PO

Orchard La

WALES

2

Sycamore Avenue

WALES RC

Wales
Junior &
Infant School

Church Street

Church
Close

Walesmoor **3**

Moor Avenue

Highmoor

Avenue

Festival
Clos

Longlands
Avenue

Lamorell Av

†

Queens Av

Ledger
Cl

Coronation

Stockwell

High House Farm
Court

Cemetery

Stockwell
Lane

A618

4

Cuckoo Way

Pithouse Lane

M1

ons Road

Beda
Cl

Bedgrave

ROTHERHAM ROAD

5

Rotherham
Cl

Norwood Crescent
Cross St

Pearl St

Pearson Pl

Norwood

oodside
Avenue

Norwood Pl

Rotherham
Derbyshire County

Walseker

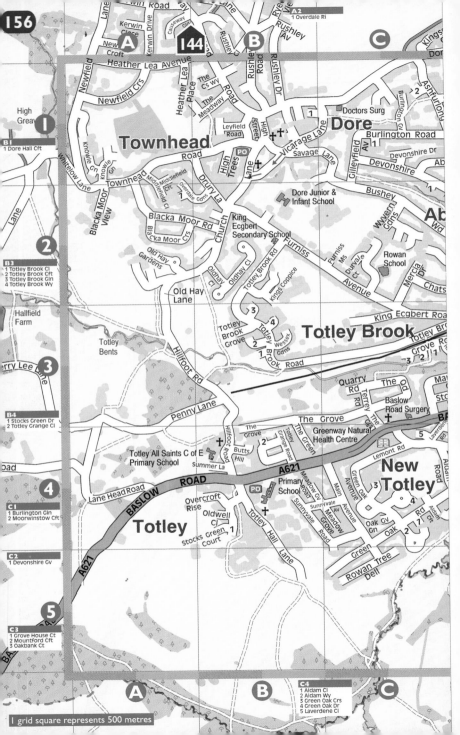

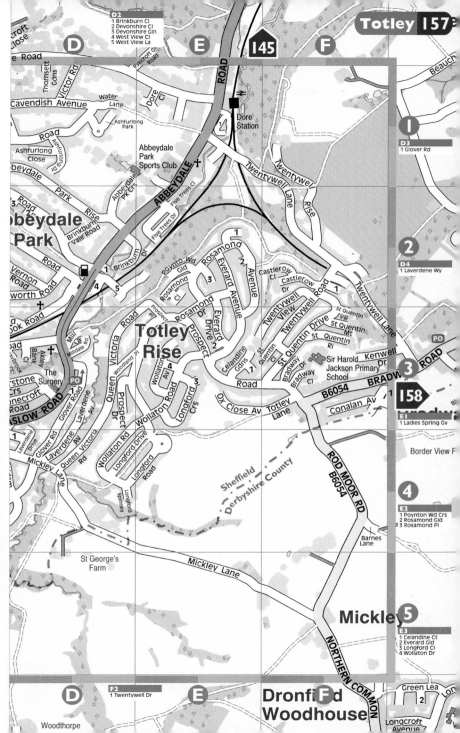

145

D2
1 Brinkburn Cl
2 Devonshire Cl
3 Devonshire Gln
4 West View Cl
5 West View La

D E F

Beauch

Thornsett Gdns

Cavendish Avenue

Victor Rd

Water Lane

Dore Rd

ROAD

Dore Station

I

D3
1 Glover Rd

Ashfurlong Park

Road

Ashfurlong Close

Ashfurlong Dr

Abbeydale Park Sports Club

Abbeydale Pk Crs

ABBEYDALE

Five Trees Cl

Five Trees Dr

Twentywell Lane

Twentywell Rise

Abbeydale Park

Road

Rise

Brinkburne Vale Road

Brinkburn Dr

Brinkburn

Poynto Wd Gld

Rosamond Gld

Rosamond Cl

Rosamond Dr

Everard Avenue

Avenue

Castlerow Cl

Castlerow Dr

Twentywell View

Twentywell Road

St Quentin Vw

St Quentin Mt

St Quentin Ri

2

D4
1 Laverdene Wy

Vernon Road

worth Road

ook Road

Prospect Rd

Queen Victoria Road

Woodland Rd

Wollaton Av

Rosamond Dr

Everard Dr

Prospect

Celandine Gdns

St Quentin Cl

St Quentin Dr

St Harold Jackson Primary School

Bradway Dr

Bradway Cl

Kenwell Dr

PO

ROAD

3

BRADW

The Surgery

Mill Milldale Rd

Akley Bank Cl

onecroft rs

PO

Glover Road

Laverdene Av

ASLOW ROAD

Longford Crs

Wollaton Road

Longford Rd

Ox Close Av

Totley Lane

Road

B6054

BRADWAY

Conalan Av

158

E1
1 Ladies Spring Gv

Border View F

Laverdene Drive

Glover Rd

Laverdene Av

Queen Victoria Rd

Prospect Dr

Wollaton Rd

Longford Drive

Longford Road

Longford Spinney

Mickley Lane

Sheffield Derbyshire County

ROD MOOR RD

B6054

Barnes Lane

4

E2
1 Poynton Wd Crs
2 Rosamond Gld
3 Rosamond Pl

St George's Farm

Mickley Lane

Mickley

5

E3
1 Celandine Ct
2 Everard Gld
3 Longford Cl
4 Wollaton Dr

D

F2
1 Twentywell Dr

E

Dronfield Woodhouse

NORTHERN COMMON

Green Lea

2

F

Woodthorpe

Longcroft Avenue

Totley Rise

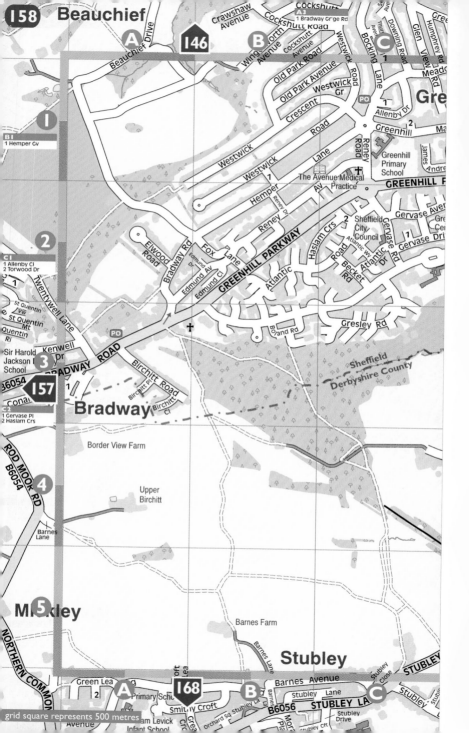

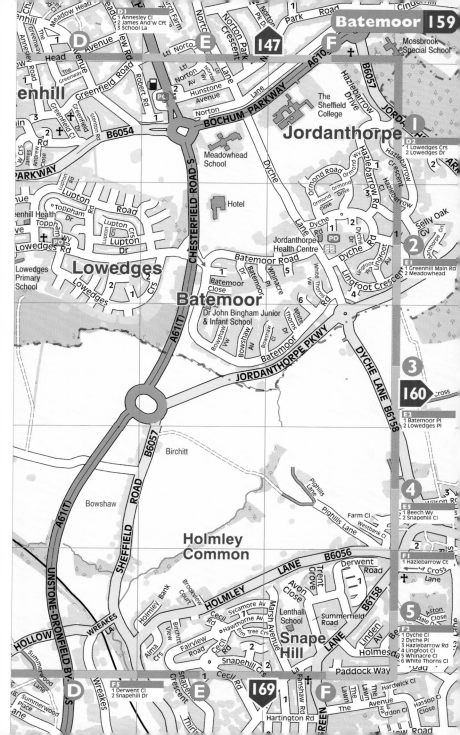

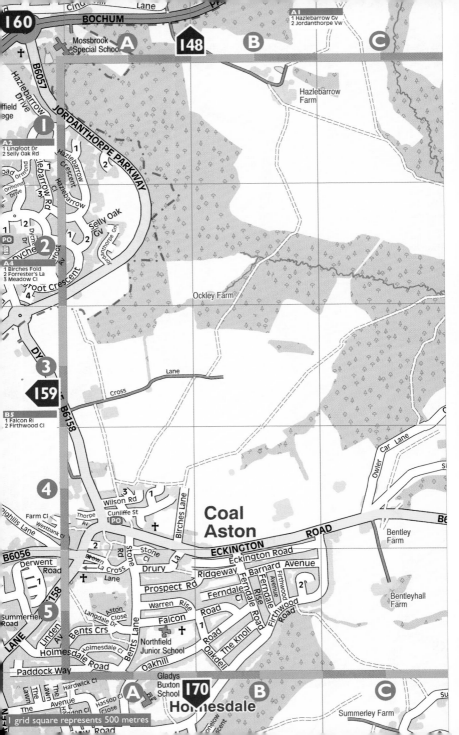

160

Cinder Lane

A **148** **B** **C**

A1
1 Hazlebarrow Gv
2 Jordanthorpe Vw

Mossbrook
Special School

Hazlebarrow
Farm

B6057

Hazlebarrow Drive

ffield
ege

JORDANTHORPE PARKWAY

I

A2
1 Lingfoot Dr
2 Selly Oak Rd

Hazlebarrow Crescent

Hazlebarrow Rd

Hazlebarrow Cl

Ormond

Ormond Drive

Selly Oak Gv

Ockley Farm

Lingfoot Av

PO

Dyche

2

A4
1 Birches Fold
2 Forrester's La
3 Meadow Cl

Lingfoot Crescent

DY

3

159

B6158

Cross Lane

B5
1 Falcon Rl
2 Firthwood Cl

4

Farm Cl

Pighills Lane

Westbank Cl

Wilson Rd

Thorpe Av

Cunliffe St

PO

Coal Aston

Birches Lane

Owler Car Lane

Bentley Farm

ECKINGTON ROAD

Eckington Road

B6056

Derwent Road

B6158

Stone Rd

Stone Cl

Brown La

Cross Lane

Drury La

Prospect Rd

Ridgeway

Ferndale Cl

Barnard Avenue

Ferndale Road

Ferndale Rise

Firthwood Avenue

Firthwood Road

2

Bentleyhall Farm

Summerfiel
Road

5

Linden Av

Aston Close

Langdale Dr

Bents Lane

Bents Crs

Warren Rise

Falcon Road

Road

The Knoll

Oakdell

Northfield Junior School

LANE

Holmesdale Road

Holmesdale Cl

Oakhill

Paddock Way

Hardwick Cl

Hassop Cl

The Lawn

The Lawn Avenue

Gladys Buxton School

170

A **Holmesdale** **B** **C**

Summerley Farm

Road

1 grid square represents 500 metres

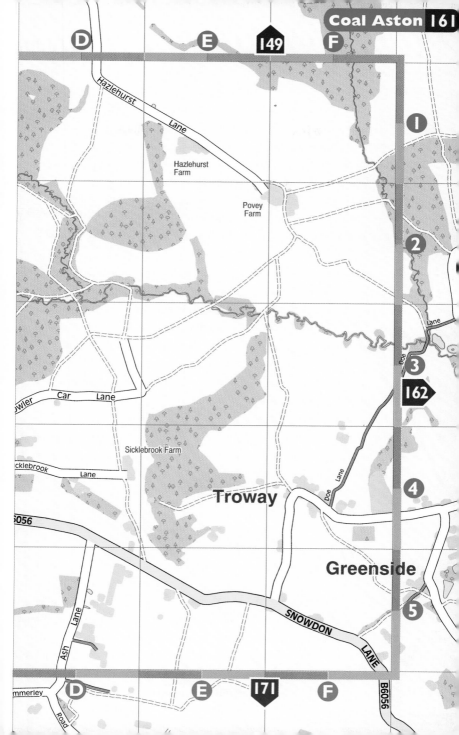

D

E

149

F

Hazlehurst Lane

Hazlehurst Farm

Povey Farm

1

Lane

2

Doe

Lane

3

162

owler Car Lane

Sicklebrook Farm

icklebrook Lane

Doe Lane

4

Doe

Troway

Greenside

6056

5

Ash Lane

SNOWDON LANE

mmerley

D

E

171

F

B6056

Road

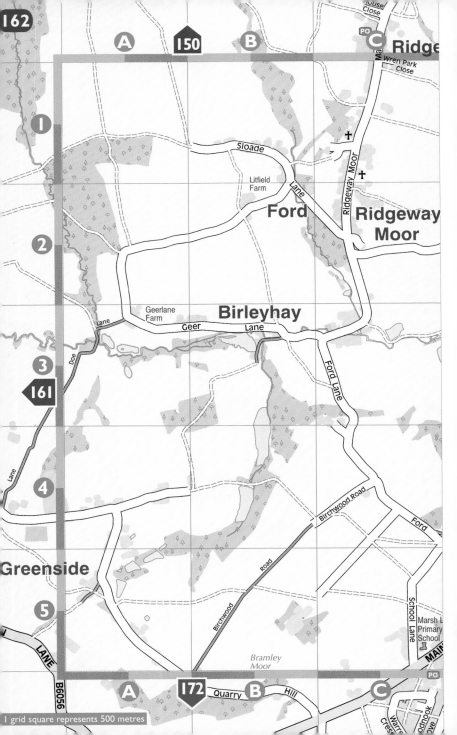

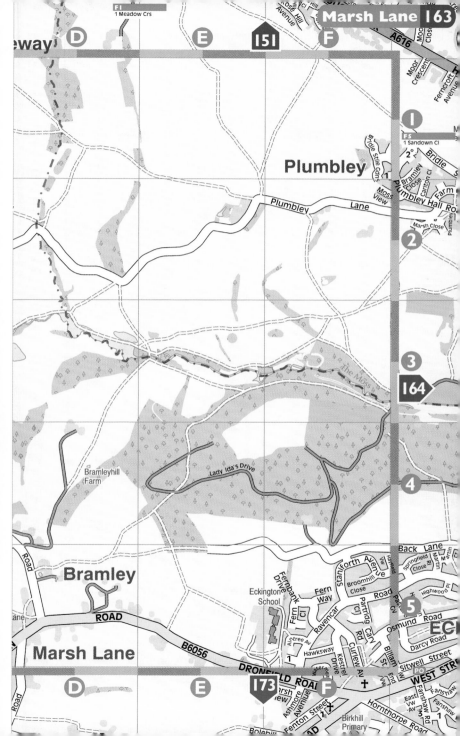

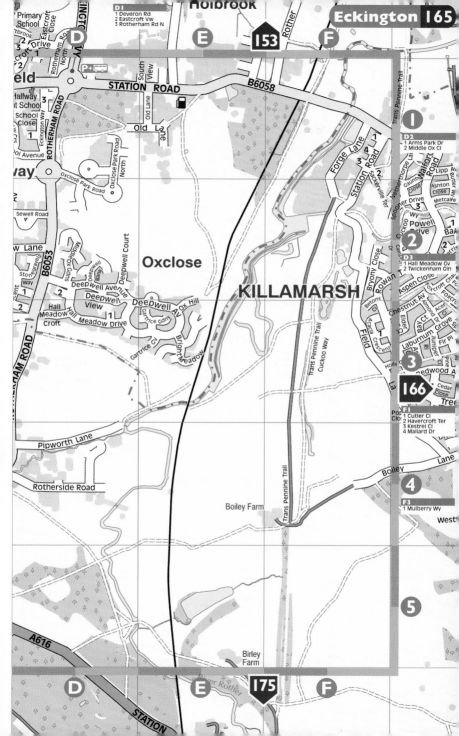

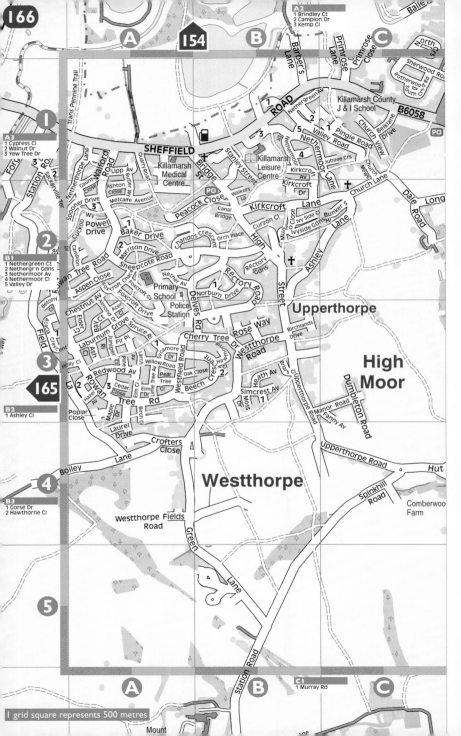

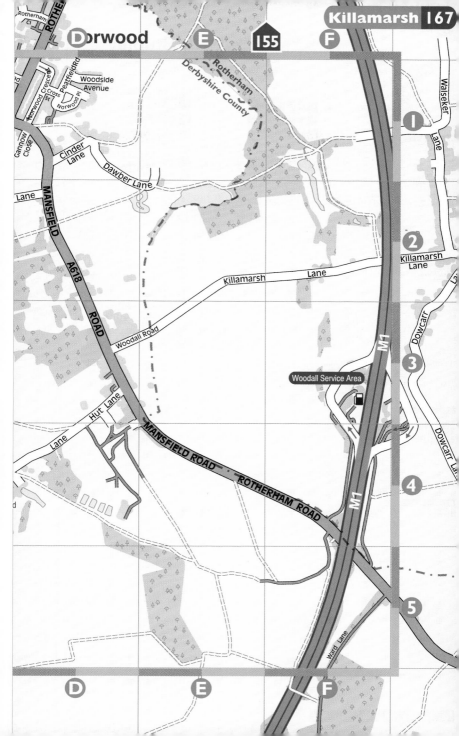

rwood

D

E

155

F

Rotherham

Derbyshire County

Woodside Avenue

Norwood Crescent
Cross St
Norwood Pl
Pextfield

Rotherham Cl

ROTHE

Norwood

Cannow Close

Cinder Lane

Dawber Lane

Lane

MANSFIELD

A618

ROAD

Killamarsh Lane

Woodall Road

Hut Lane

Lane

MANSFIELD ROAD

ROTHERHAM ROAD

Woodall Service Area

Walseker Lane

1

2

Killamarsh Lane

Dowcarr

M1

3

Dowcarr Lane

4

M1

5

Ward Lane

D

E

F

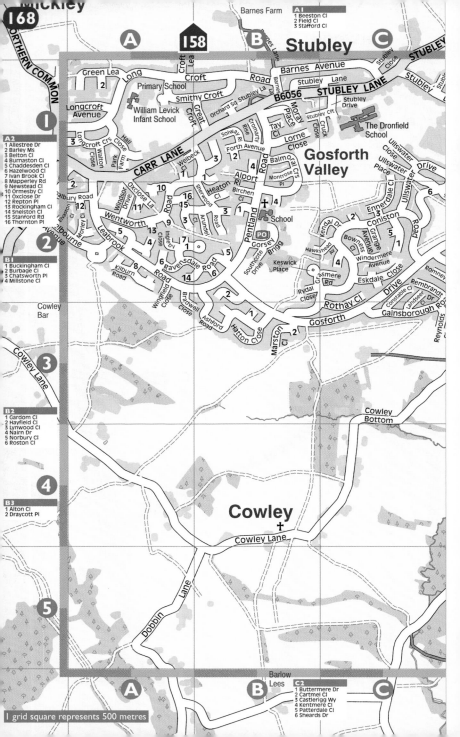

Mickley

168

NORTHERN COMMON

158

A
B
C

Barnes Farm

A1
1 Beeston Cl
2 Field Cl
3 Stafford Cl

Stubley

STUBLEY LANE

Green Lea

Long Croft

Croft Lea

Barnes Avenue

Stubley Close

Longcroft Avenue

Primary School

Smithy Croft

Great Croft

Orchard Sq

Stubley La

B6056

Stubley Lane

STUBLEY LANE

Stubley

Stubley Drive

William Levick Infant School

Hall Farm

Longcroft Crs

Close

Walton

Park Farm

CARR LANE

Welbeck

Cromarty Rise

Solway

Forth Avenue

Moray Place

Tay Cl

Stubley Cft

Cruck Close

Lorne Close

The Dronfield School

Ullswater Close

A2
1 Allestree Dr
2 Barley Ms
3 Belton Cl
4 Burnaston Cl
5 Chaddesden Cl
6 Hazelwood Cl
7 Ivan Brook Cl
8 Mapperley Rd
9 Newstead Cl
10 Ormesby Cl
11 Oxclose Dr
12 Repton Pl
13 Rockingham Cl
14 Sneiston Cl
15 Stanford Rd
16 Thornton Pl

Dalbury Road

Windsor Drive

Oxclose La

10

Heaton Cl

3

Alport Rl

4

Balmoral Crs

Montrose Pl

Birchen Cl

Road

4

Ullswater Place

Ullswater Drive

6

Gosforth Valley

12

Wentworth

11

Road

16

Sherwood

15

School

Ennerdale Cl

2

Coniston

3

Kendal Dr

Grange Avenue

5

B1
1 Buckingham Cl
2 Burbage Cl
3 Chatsworth Pl
4 Millstone Cl

Leabrook

5

13

9

3

Arundel

Road

Pentland

PO

Gorse

Brigg

Hawkshead Rd

Bowness Rd

Windermere Avenue

1

Kilburn Road

8

6

Ravensdale

Road

Southcote Drive

Keswick Place

Gasmere Rd

Eskdale Close

Romney

14

6

Gosforth

Gainsborough Rd

Constable Cl

Rembrandt

Larkdeer Dr

Cowley Bar

Morley Cl

Ingley

7

1

Bradwell Close

Wingfield Close

Ashford Road

2

Hatton Close

Marston Cl

2

Rothay Cl

Rydal Close

Reynolds

Cowley Lane

B2
1 Gardom Cl
2 Hayfield Cl
3 Lynwood Cl
4 Nairn Dr
5 Norbury Cl
6 Roston Cl

Cowley Bottom

B3
1 Alton Cl
2 Draycott Pl

Cowley

Cowley Lane

Dobbin Lane

Barlow Lees

C2
1 Buttermere Dr
2 Cartmel Cl
3 Castlerigg Wy
4 Kentmere Cl
5 Patterdale Cl
6 Sheards Dr

A
B
C

1 grid square represents 500 metres

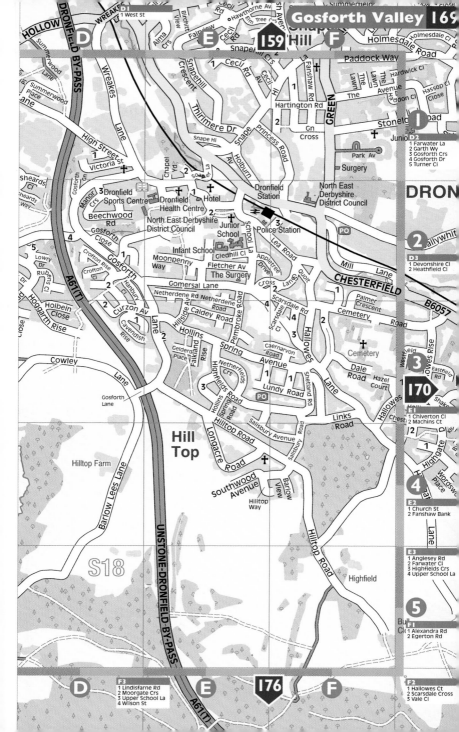

159

DRON

170

176

D2
1 Farwater La
2 Garth Wy
3 Gosforth Crs
4 Gosforth Dr
5 Turner Cl

D3
1 Devonshire Cl
2 Heathfield Cl

E1
1 Chiverton Cl
2 Machins Ct

E2
1 Church St
2 Fanshaw Bank

E3
1 Anglesey Rd
2 Farwater Cl
3 Highfields Crs
4 Upper School La

F1
1 Alexandra Rd
2 Egerton Rd

F2
1 Hallowes Ct
2 Scarsdale Cross
3 Vale Cl

F3
1 Lindisfarne Rd
2 Moorgate Crs
3 Upper School La
4 Wilson St

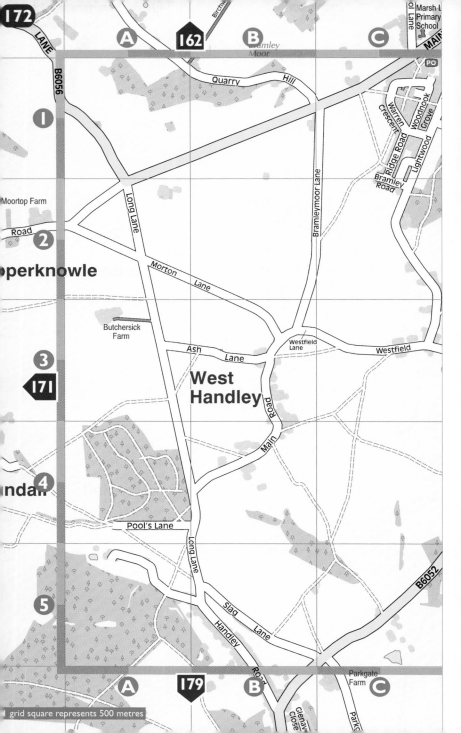

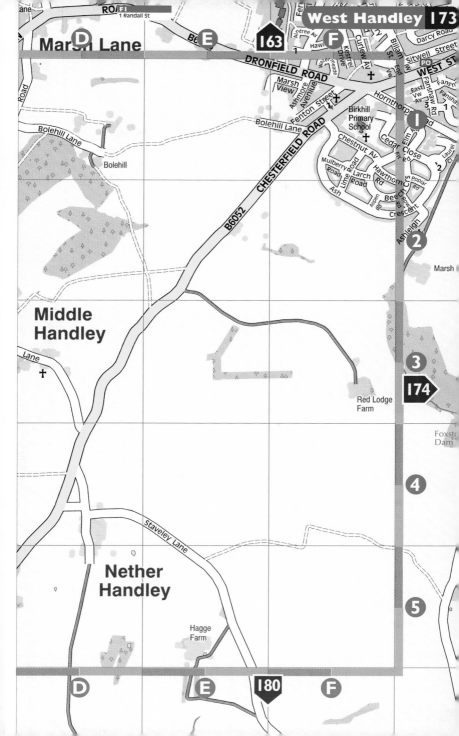

RO/**F1**
1 Randall St

Marsh Lane **D**

E

163

F

Alntree Av
Hawk

Fenr

Curlew Av

Billam St

Darcy Road

Sitwell Street

WEST ST

PO

Fanshaw Rd

East Vw
Av

Fansh

Fansh
1

DRONFIELD ROAD

Watermeade

Kestrel Drive

Hornthorp

Marsh
View

Ashmore Avenue

Fenton Street

Bolehill Lane

Birkhill
Primary
School

Cedar R

Elm Av

Laurel

I

Bolehill Lane

Chestnut Av

Hawthorn

Bee Ch Road
Road

Poplar
Rd

Bolehill

CHESTERFIELD ROAD

Mulberry
Road

Lime Road

Larch
Road

Aspen

Crescent

Ash

B6052

Ashleigh

2

Marsh

**Middle
Handley**

Lane

†

3

174

Red Lodge
Farm

Foxsto
Dam

4

Staveley Lane

**Nether
Handley**

5

Hagge
Farm

D

E

180

F

ECKINGTON

Osmund Road

Darcy Road

HIGH STREET

Welfare
street

1 Fanshaw Dr
2 Hazel Rd
3 Valley View Cl

Eckington
Health Cen.
Derbyshire
County Council

PARK
HILL

Sitwell Street

A

WEST STREET

B

Lansbury Rd

Tertia
lege

Mar

John Street
Edw

William
Street

cksett La.

C

SOUTHGATE

Billam
End

Hornthorpe Road

Fanshaw Av

Fanshaw Wy

East
Vw

3

Fanshaw Rd

1

Pitt Street

Pipeyard Lane

Henry
St

Joseph
Street

Hardle
Street

Barratt
Rd

Albert
Lane

Street

S21

Birkhill
Prima
Schoo

1

Chestnut Av

Cedar Close

Elm Rd

Laurel
Cl

Setcup

Hawthorn Rd

Larch
Road

Poplar
Rd

Beech
Crescent

Aspen

Rowan

Ashleigh
Court

2

Marsh Farm

B6053

STAVELEY

Breck   Lane

3

◄ **173**

F.   e
Farm

Breck Lane

Foxstone
Dam

LANE

4

Slittingmil

5

White
Lodge

A

B

River Rother

C

1 grid square represents 500 metres

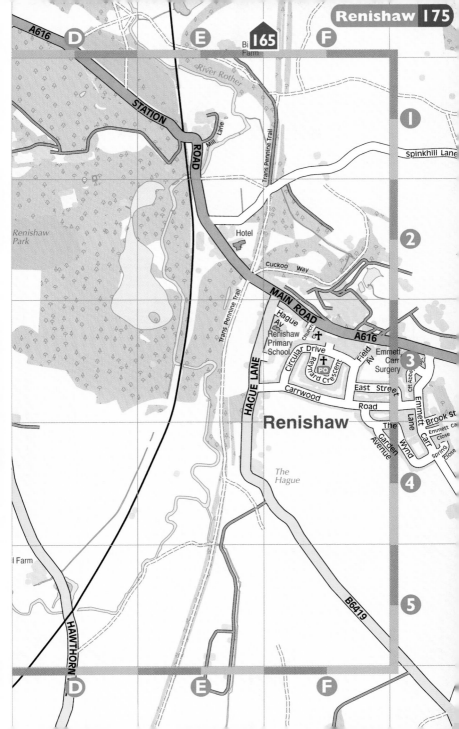

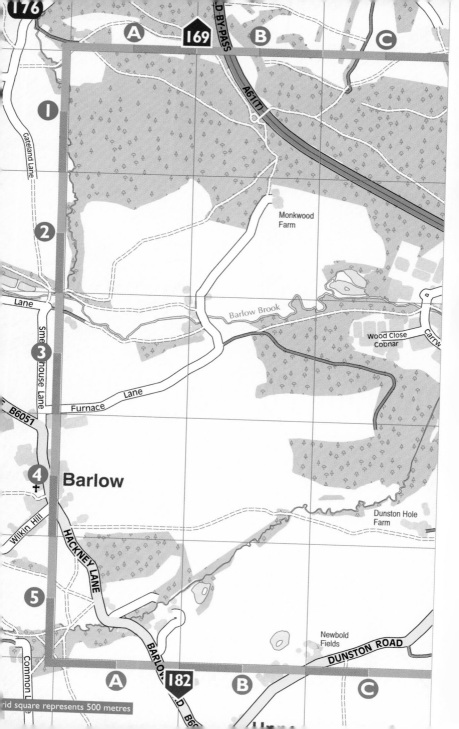

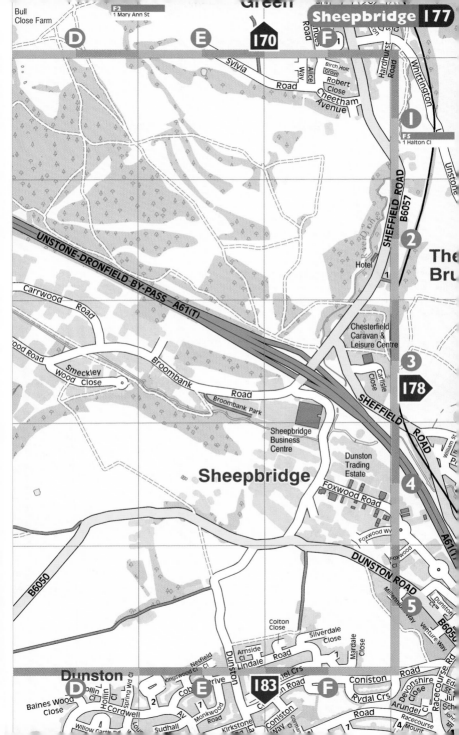

Bull
Close Farm

F2
1 Mary Ann St

D

E

170

F 1

Green

Sylvia

Road

Alice
Way

Birch Holt
Grove

Robert
Close

Cheetham
Avenue

Hardhurst
Road

Whittington

I

F5
1 Halton Cl

Unstone

SHEFFIELD ROAD

B6057

2

The
Bru

Hotel

1

Chesterfield
Caravan &
Leisure Centre

Carlisle
Close

3

178

SHEFFIELD ROAD

Carrwood   Road

UNSTONE-DRONFIELD BY-PASS   A61(T)

ood Road

Smeckley
Wood   Close

Broombank

Road

Broombank Park

Sheepbridge
Business
Centre

Dunston
Trading
Estate

Foxwood Road

William St

4

A61(T)

Sheepbridge

Foxwood Wy

Foxwood

DUNSTON ROAD

Millennium Way

Venture Way

Dunston
Ct

5

B605C

B6050

Colton
Close

Arnside
Cl

Nesfield
Cl

Kingswood Cl

Dunston

Lindale

Silverdale
Close

Road

Mardale
Close

1

Dunston

ollin
Cl

Hollin
Cordwell

Baines Wood
Close

Spring Wd

Cob

Drive

Av

Monkwood
Road

E

Kirkstone

183

n Road

Coniston

Rydal Crs

F

Coniston
Way

Road

Racecourse Rd

Devonshire
Close

Arundel

Racecourse

Jur

Ed
St
Sch

John

4

Sudhall

Willow Garth Rd

Lou

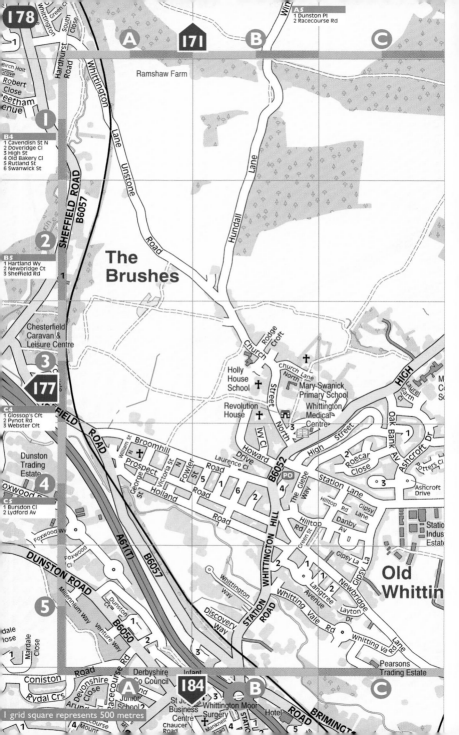

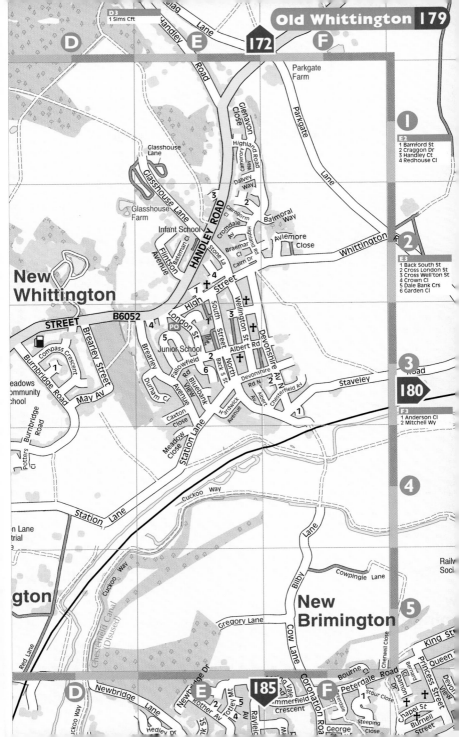

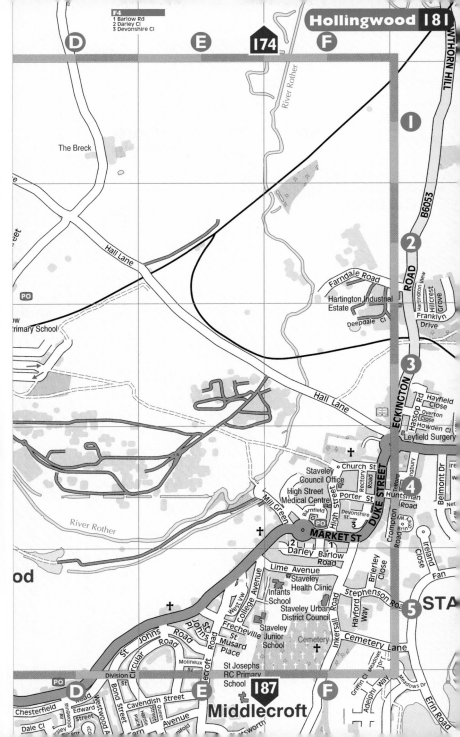

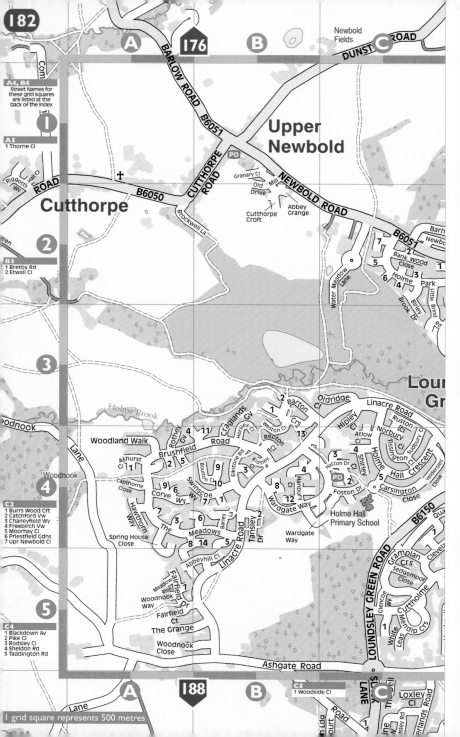

176

A   B   C

Newbold
Fields

DUNSTON ROAD

1

Com

BARLOW ROAD

B6051

PO

Granary Cl
Old
Drive
Mill

**Upper
Newbold**

NEWBOLD ROAD

B6051

Barh
Newbc

7
Bank_wood
Close
2
1

5   3
Holme

6   4

Park
Little
Brook Dr

Birley

Rd

†

ROAD

Riggotts
Wy
Hall Cl

CUTTHORPE ROAD

B6050

Cutthorpe

Brockwell La

Cutthorpe
Croft

Abbey
Grange

Water Meadow Lane

2

3

Holme Brook

Lou...
Gr...

oodnook

Woodnook

Lane

Woodland Walk

Rothley

Craglands
Road

Horsley Cl

Gv

Repton

Weston Cl

4   11

Brushfield

Ashurst
Cl   1

2   5

Capthorne
Close

9   6

Corve
Wy

7

The
Meadows

Barton
Cl

1

13

Oldridge
Cl

Linacre Road

Hipley
Cl

Atlow

Ruston
Cl

Norbury

Tissington

Sudbury Cl

3

Hatton Dr

Shirley

Holme
Hall
Crescent

Yeldersley

Carsington
Close

Hawthorn
Way

Swinscoe
Wy

9
7

10

Elkstone Rd

Kirsley
Cl

4

8
Hanbury
Cl

12

Foston Dr

PO
2

B6150

Qua

4

The

7

3

6

8   14

Spring House
Close

Barley La

Tansley
Dr

2

Wardgate Way

Wardgate
Way

Holme Hall
Primary School

LOUNSLEY GREEN ROAD

Grampian
Crs

Cleve

Sedgemoor
Close

Cuttholme

Clwe

5

Abbeyhill Cl

Fairfield Dr

Meadow
Rise
Woodnook
Way
7

Fairfield
Ct

The Grange

Woodnook
Close

Ashgate Road

Glencoe

White
Leas

Mendip Crs

1

SLO...
LANE

Loxley
Cl

Loxley Road

Isley Rd

ne
erlands Rd

Lane

188

A   B   C

dg
Road
court

1 grid square represents 500 metres

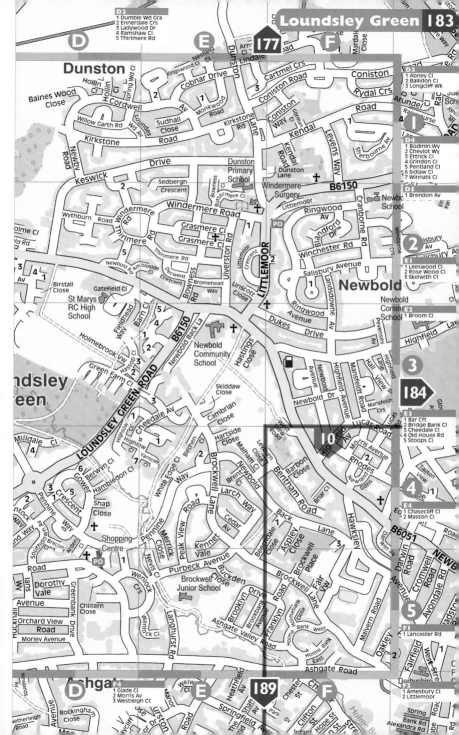

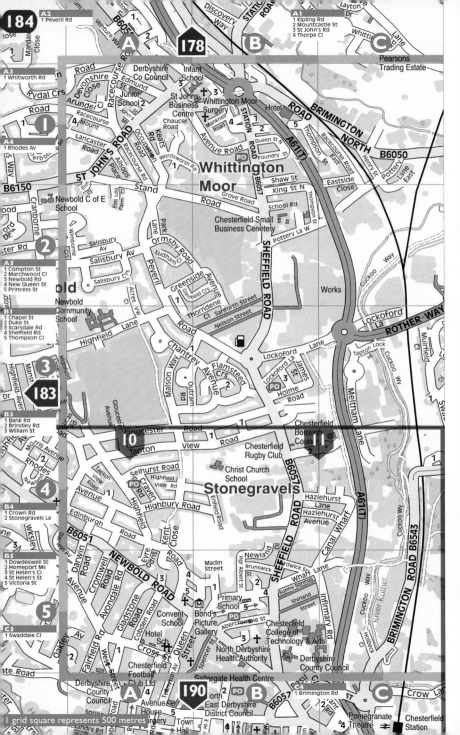

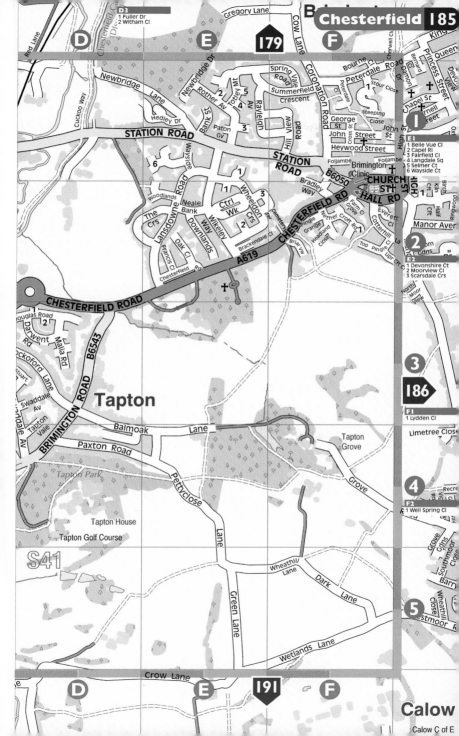

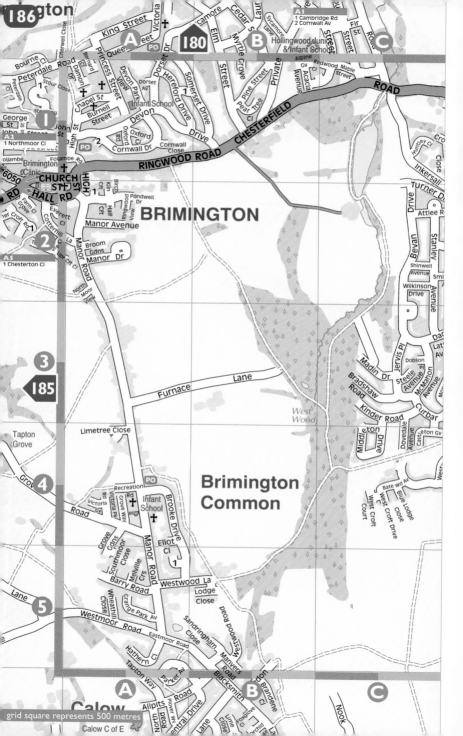

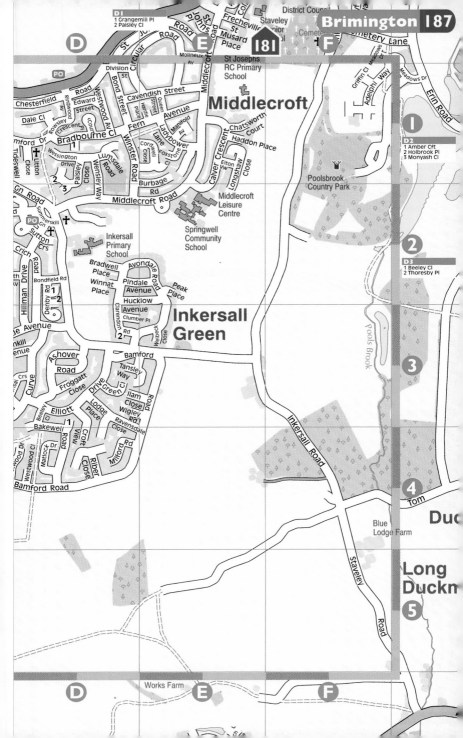

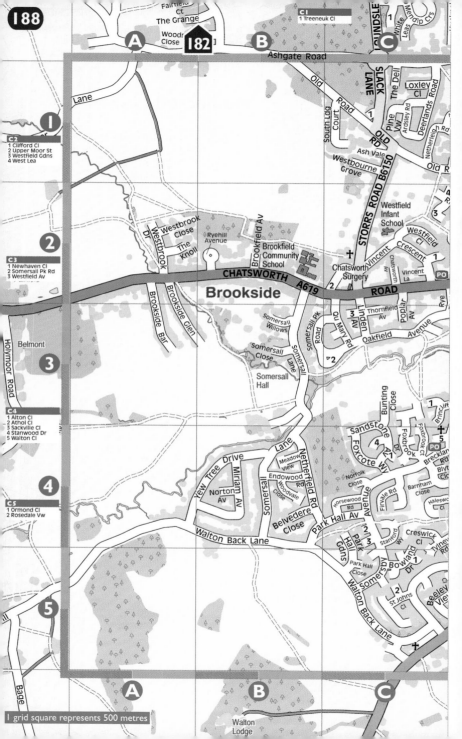

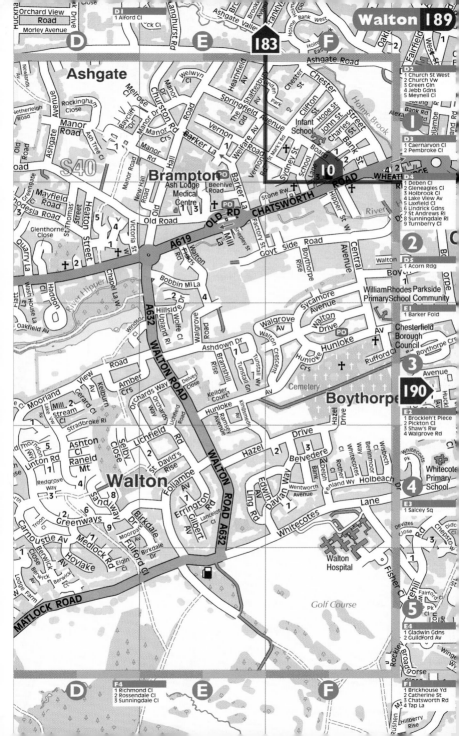

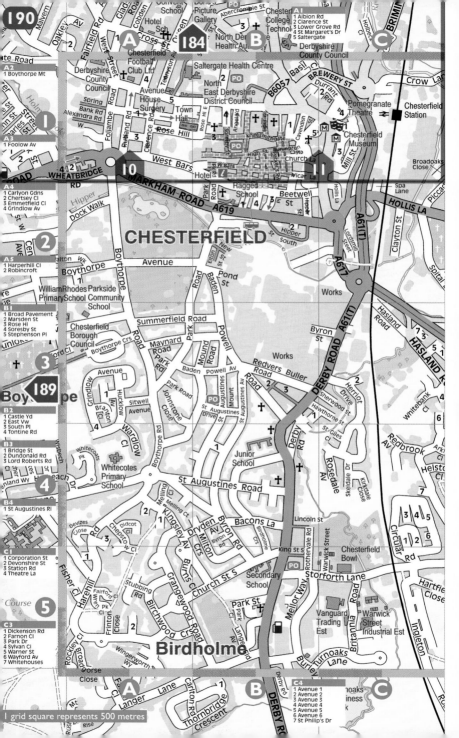

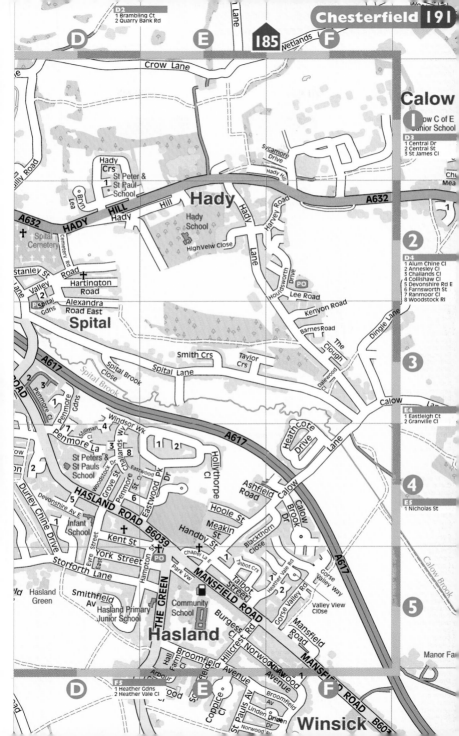

Abbeydale	145 F4
Abbeydale Park	156 C2
Abdy	79 E1
Aldwarke	94 B4
Almholme	18 B1
Apperknowle	171 F2
Arbourthorne	136 B2
Ardsley	24 A3
Arksey	17 F4
Armthorpe	33 F3
Ashgate	189 D1
Aston	143 D3
Attercliffe	123 F1
Aughton	128 C5
Balby	43 F5
Barlow	176 A4
Barnes Hall	87 E2
Barnsley	3 F3
Barnsley	22 B3
Barrow	76 A2
Barrow Hill	180 B2
Bassett	130 B5
Batemoor	159 E3
Beauchief	145 F5
Beighton	153 D1
Belle Vue	45 D2
Bentley	29 F2
Bentley Rise	29 E3
Bessacarr	46 C5
Birdholme	190 A5
Birdwell	35 F5
Birley Carr	96 C4
Birley Edge	97 D3
Birleyhay	162 A3
Blackburn	100 C2
Blacker Hill	37 D4
Bolehill	147 E3
Bolsterstone	69 D5
Bow Broom	57 D4
Boythorpe	189 F3
Bradgate	102 A2
Bradway	158 A3
Bramley	163 D5
Brampton	54 A1
Brampton	189 E1
Brick Houses	144 A5
Brightside	111 D4
Brimington	186 A2
Brimington Common	186 B4
Brincliffe	134 A4
Bromley	72 B1
Brookside	188 B2
Broom	104 A5
Broomhill	40 C3
The Brushes	178 A2
Burncross	87 F1
Burngreave	122 C1
Cadeby	61 E2
Canklow	114 B1
Cantley	47 F3
Carbrook	111 E4
Carter Knowle	134 B5
Catcliffe	127 E1
Chapeltown	74 C5
Charltonbrook	87 D1
Charnock Hall	149 E3
Chesterfield	190 A2
Clifton	7 G6
Coal Aston	160 B4
Coisley Hill	139 E4
Conanby	84 A1
Conisbrough	60 B5
Cortworth	77 F2
Cowley	168 B4
Crookes	120 C3
Crookesmoor	121 E3
Cundy Cross	23 E1
Cundy Hos	71 F3
Cusworth	28 A4
Dalton	95 E5
Dalton Parva	105 F1
Darnall	124 C3
Deepcar	70 A4
Denaby Main	59 F4
Dodworth	20 A3
Doncaster	5 H3
Dore	156 C1
Drakehouse	152 B2
Dronfield	170 A2
Dropping Well	90 C5
Dunston	183 D1
East Dene	104 B2
East Herringthorpe	105 E2
Ecclesall	133 E5

Ecclesfield	88 C5
Eckington	164 A5
Elscar	52 B3
Finkle Street	71 D1
Firth Park	110 B1
Fir Vale	110 A3
Ford	162 B2
Frecheville	150 A1
Fulwood	132 A2
Garden Village	68 A2
Gawber	12 B4
Gilroyd	20 B5
Gleadless	149 E1
Gleadless Valley	148 C2
Gosforth Valley	168 B1
Greasbrough	93 D2
Greenhill	158 C1
Greenland	111 F5
Greenside	161 F5
Grenoside	97 E1
Greystones	133 D3
Grimesthorpe	110 B3
Guilthwaite	128 C1
Hackenthorpe	150 C1
Hady	191 E2
Halfway	164 C1
Hallowes	170 A3
Handsworth	125 F5
Harley	75 E2
Hasland	191 E5
Heeley	135 E4
Hemingfield	53 D1
Hemsworth	148 A2
Hermit Hill	48 A2
Herringthorpe	105 D4
Hexthorpe	43 E3
Highfield	135 F2
High Green	73 E4
Highlane	150 C5
High Moor	166 C3
Hillsborough	107 D2
Hill Top	84 A4
Hill Top	101 D3
Hill Top	169 E4
Holbrook	153 E5
Hollingwood	180 C5
Hollins End	137 F5
Holmesdale	170 A1
Holmley Common	159 E4
Hoober	78 B2
Hood Hill	75 E3
Hooton Roberts	83 E4
Howbrook	72 C2
Hoyland	51 E3
Hoyland Common	50 C2
Hoyle Mill	23 D1
Hundall	171 F4
Hyde Park	4 D6
Inkersall Green	187 E3
Intake	31 E5
Intake	137 E5
Jordanthorpe	159 F1
Jordon	101 F4
Jump	52 B1
Kendray	23 D4
Keresforth Hill	21 D3
Killamarsh	165 E2
Kilnhurst	81 E4
Kimberworth	101 F2
Kimberworth Park	92 A4
Kingstone	21 E3
Lane End	74 B5
Lightwood	149 D5
Lodge Moor	130 C1
Longley Estate	109 F1
Long Sandall	19 E3
Loundsley Green	182 C3
Loversall	64 B5
Low Barugh	12 A1
Lowedges	159 D2
Lowfield	135 E3
Low Laithes	24 C3
Low Valley	40 A1
Loxley	106 A4
Lundwood	15 F4
Malinbridge	107 E5
Manor Estate	137 D1
Manor Park	123 F5
Marsh Lane	163 D5
Masbrough	102 C2
Meadow Hall	111 F1
Meadow Head	146 C4
Measborough Dike	22 C2
Meersbrook	135 F5

Mexborough	58 B1
Mickley	157 F5
Middlecroft	187 E1
Middle Handley	173 D3
Middlewood	96 A5
Millhouses	145 F2
Milton	51 F3
Monk Bretton	14 C3
Moorgate	115 D2
Moorhole	151 E4
Morthen	117 E5
Mortomley	73 F4
Mosborough	152 A5
Nether Edge	134 C4
Nether Handley	173 D5
Nether Haugh	78 C4
Newbold	183 F2
New Brimington	179 F5
Newhill	55 F4
Newton	43 E2
New Totley	156 C4
New Village	17 D4
New Whittington	179 D2
Normanton Spring	138 C4
Norton	147 F5
Norton Woodseats	147 E2
Norwood	155 D5
Old Denaby	59 D5
Old Whittington	179 D5
Orgreave	140 A1
Owlerton	108 B4
Owlthorpe	151 F3
Oxclose	165 E2
Parkgate	94 A4
Parkhead	145 D2
Park Hill	123 E4
Parkwood Springs	109 D5
Parson Cross	98 A4
Piccadilly	80 C2
Pilley	49 D3
Pismire Hill	99 E5
Pitsmoor	109 F5
Platts Common	37 F5
Plumbley	163 F1
Pogmoor	12 B5
Potter Hill	72 C4
Rails	118 A3
Ranmoor	132 C1
Rawmarsh	94 B2
Renishaw	175 E4
Richmond	138 C2
Ridgeway	150 C5
Ridgeway Moor	162 C2
Rollestone	136 A5
Rostholme	16 A4
Rotherham	104 A4
Ryecroft	80 B4
St Helen's	15 D2
Sandygate	119 F5
Scawsby	28 B3
Scawthorpe	28 B1
Scholes	91 D2
Sharrow	134 B3
Shaw Lands	21 D1
Sheepbridge	177 E4
Sheffield	123 D4
Sheffield Park	136 C1
Shirecliffe	109 E3
Shiregreen	100 A4
Smithies	14 A2
Smithley	38 B2
Snape Hill	159 F5
Sothall	153 D4
Spital	191 D3
Sprotbrough	42 A3
Stairfoot	23 F3
Stannington	119 E1
Steel Bank	121 D2
Stocksbridge	17 D4
Stocksbridge	69 D3
Stonegravels	11 F1
Stopes	118 A1
Stubbley	158 B5
Sunnyfields	28 C3
Swaithe	23 F5
Swallownest	142 A3
Swinton	80 C1
Swinton Bridge	57 F4
Tankersley	49 F4
Tapton	185 D3
Tapton Hill	120 B5
Templeborough	102 A5
Thorn Hill	6 B3
Thorpe Hesley	90 B1

Thrybergh	95	F3
Thurnscoe	26	C5
Thurnscoe East	27	F3
Tinsley	112	C2
Toll Bar	16	B2
Totley	156	A4
Totley Brook	156	B3
Totley Rise	157	D3
Townhead	156	A1
Treeton	127	F3
Troway	161	E4
Under Tofts	119	D3
Unstone	170	C4
Unstone Green	170	B5
Upper Haugh	79	E4
Upper Hoyland	51	D1
Upper Newbold	182	B1
Upper Tankersley	49	D4
Upperthorpe	166	B3
Upper Whiston	129	E1
Wadsley	106	C2
Wadsley Bridge	96	C5
Waldershaigh	68	B5
Wales	155	F2
Wales Bar	155	E2
Walkley	121	D1
Walton	189	D4
Ward Green	21	F5
Warren	74	C3
Waterthorpe	152	B3
Wath upon Dearne	56	B2
Wentworth	76	C2
Westfield	164	C1
West Handley	172	A3
West Melton	55	D2
Westthorpe	166	B4
Wheatley	30	C4
Wheatley Hills	32	A3
Wheatley Park	31	E2
Whinney Hill	95	E4
Whirlow	145	D3
Whirlow Brook	144	A2
Whiston	116	A3
Whitley	88	A4
Whittington Moor	184	B1
Wilthorpe	13	D3
Wincobank	111	E1
Windhill	59	D2
Wingfield	91	F3
Wombwell	39	D4
Woodhouse	140	A3
Woodhouse Mill	140	C2
Wood Seats	87	E3
Worsbrough Bridge	36	B2
Worsbrough Common	21	F4
Worsbrough Dale	36	B1

USING THE STREET INDEX

Street names are listed alphabetically. Each street name is followed by its postal town or area locality, the Postcode District, the page number, and the reference to the square in which the name is found.

Abbey Brook Ct *SHEFS* S8 .... 146 C4 🔟

Some entries are followed by a number in a blue box. This number indicates the location of the street within the referenced grid square. The full street name is listed at the side of the map page.

GENERAL ABBREVIATIONS

ACC	ACCESS	E	EAST	LDG	LODGE
ALY	ALLEY	EMB	EMBANKMENT	LGT	LIGHT
AP	APPROACH	EMBY	EMBASSY	LK	LOCK
AR	ARCADE	ESP	ESPLANADE	LKS	LAKES
ASS	ASSOCIATION	EST	ESTATE	LNDG	LANDING
AV	AVENUE	EX	EXCHANGE	LTL	LITTLE
BCH	BEACH	EXPY	EXPRESSWAY	LWR	LOWER
BLDS	BUILDINGS	EXT	EXTENSION	MAG	MAGISTRATE
BND	BEND	F/O	FLYOVER	MAN	MANSIONS
BNK	BANK	FC	FOOTBALL CLUB	MD	MEAD
BR	BRIDGE	FK	FORK	MDW	MEADOWS
BRK	BROOK	FLD	FIELD	MEM	MEMORIAL
BTM	BOTTOM	FLDS	FIELDS	MKT	MARKET
BUS	BUSINESS	FLS	FALLS	MKTS	MARKETS
BVD	BOULEVARD	FLS	FLATS	ML	MALL
BY	BYPASS	FM	FARM	ML	MILL
CATH	CATHEDRAL	FT	FORT	MNR	MANOR
CEM	CEMETERY	FWY	FREEWAY	MS	MEWS
CEN	CENTRE	FY	FERRY	MSN	MISSION
CFT	CROFT	GA	GATE	MT	MOUNT
CH	CHURCH	GAL	GALLERY	MTN	MOUNTAIN
CHA	CHASE	GDN	GARDEN	MTS	MOUNTAINS
CHYD	CHURCHYARD	GDNS	GARDENS	MUS	MUSEUM
CIR	CIRCLE	GLD	GLADE	MWY	MOTORWAY
CIRC	CIRCUS	GLN	GLEN	N	NORTH
CL	CLOSE	GN	GREEN	NE	NORTH EAST
CLFS	CLIFFS	GND	GROUND	NW	NORTH WEST
CMP	CAMP	GRA	GRANGE	O/P	OVERPASS
CNR	CORNER	GRG	GARAGE	OFF	OFFICE
CO	COUNTY	GT	GREAT	ORCH	ORCHARD
COLL	COLLEGE	GTWY	GATEWAY	OV	OVAL
COM	COMMON	GV	GROVE	PAL	PALACE
COMM	COMMISSION	HGR	HIGHER	PAS	PASSAGE
CON	CONVENT	HL	HILL	PAV	PAVILION
COT	COTTAGE	HLS	HILLS	PDE	PARADE
COTS	COTTAGES	HO	HOUSE	PH	PUBLIC HOUSE
CP	CAPE	HOL	HOLLOW	PK	PARK
CPS	COPSE	HOSP	HOSPITAL	PKWY	PARKWAY
CR	CREEK	HRB	HARBOUR	PL	PLACE
CREM	CREMATORIUM	HTH	HEATH	PLN	PLAIN
CRS	CRESCENT	HTS	HEIGHTS	PLNS	PLAINS
CSWY	CAUSEWAY	HVN	HAVEN	PLZ	PLAZA
CT	COURT	HWY	HIGHWAY	POL	POLICE STATION
CTRL	CENTRAL	IMP	IMPERIAL	PR	PRINCE
CTS	COURTS	IN	INLET	PREC	PRECINCT
CTYD	COURTYARD	IND EST	INDUSTRIAL ESTATE	PREP	PREPARATORY
CUTT	CUTTINGS	INF	INFIRMARY	PRIM	PRIMARY
CV	COVE	INFO	INFORMATION	PROM	PROMENADE
CYN	CANYON	INT	INTERCHANGE	PRS	PRINCESS
DEPT	DEPARTMENT	IS	ISLAND	PRT	PORT
DL	DALE	JCT	JUNCTION	PT	POINT
DM	DAM	JTY	JETTY	PTH	PATH
DR	DRIVE	KG	KING	PZ	PIAZZA
DRO	DROVE	KNL	KNOLL	QD	QUADRANT
DRY	DRIVEWAY	L	LAKE	QU	QUEEN
DWGS	DWELLINGS	LA	LANE	QY	QUAY

R	RIVER
RBT	ROUNDABOUT
RD	ROAD
RDG	RIDGE
REP	REPUBLIC
RES	RESERVOIR
RFC	RUGBY FOOTBALL CLUB
RI	RISE
RP	RAMP
RW	ROW
S	SOUTH
SCH	SCHOOL
SE	SOUTH EAST
SER	SERVICE AREA
SH	SHORE
SHOP	SHOPPING
SKWY	SKYWAY
SMT	SUMMIT
SOC	SOCIETY

SP	SPUR
SPR	SPRING
SQ	SQUARE
ST	STREET
STN	STATION
STR	STREAM
STRD	STRAND
SW	SOUTH WEST
TDG	TRADING
TER	TERRACE
THWY	THROUGHWAY
TNL	TUNNEL
TOLL	TOLLWAY
TPK	TURNPIKE
TR	TRACK
TRL	TRAIL
TWR	TOWER
U/P	UNDERPASS
UNI	UNIVERSITY

UPR	UPPER
V	VALE
VA	VALLEY
VIAD	VIADUCT
VIL	VILLA
VIS	VISTA
VLG	VILLAGE
VLS	VILLAS
VW	VIEW
W	WEST
WD	WOOD
WHF	WHARF
WK	WALK
WKS	WALKS
WLS	WELLS
WY	WAY
YD	YARD
YHA	YOUTH HOSTEL

POSTCODE TOWNS AND AREA ABBREVIATIONS

ABRD	Abbeydale Road
ARMTH	Armthorpe
ATT	Attercliffe
AU/AST/KP	Aughton/Aston/Kiveton Park
BSLY	Barnsley
BSLYN/ROY	Barnsley north/Royston
BSVR	Bolsover
BTLY	Bentley
CHNE	Chesterfield north & east
CHPT/GREN	Chapeltown/Grenoside
CHSW	Chesterfield south & west
CONI	Conisbrough
CUD/GR	Cudworth/Grimethorpe
DARN/MH	Darnall/Meadowhall
DEARNE	Wath upon Dearne/Bolton upon Dearne

DOD/DAR	Dodworth/Darton
DON	Doncaster
DONS/BSCR	Doncaster south/Bessacarr
DRON	Dronfield
ECC	Ecclesall
ECK/KIL	Eckington/Killamarsh
FUL	Fulwood
GLV	Gleadless Valley
HACK//IN	Hackenthorpe/Intake
HAN/WDH	Handsworth/Woodhouse
HOY	Hoyland
KIMB	Kimberworth
MALT	Maltby
MEX/SWTN	Mexborough/Swinton
MOS	Mosborough
NROS/TKH	New Rossington/Tickhill

OWL	Owlerton
RAW	Rawmarsh
RCH	Rural Chesterfield
RHAM	Rotherham
RHAM/THRY	Rotherham/Thrybergh
SHEF	Sheffield
SHEFN	Sheffield north
SHEFP/MNR	Sheffield Park/Manor
SHEFS	Sheffield south
ST/HB/BR	Stannington/Hillsborough/Bradfield
STKB/PEN	Stocksbridge/Penistone
STV/CWN	Staveley/Clowne
TOT/DORE	Totley/Dore
WHHL	Wheatley Hills
WMB/DAR	Wombwell/Darfield

A

Abbey Brook Ct *SHEFS* S8	146 C4
Abbey Brook Dr *SHEFS* S8	146 C4
Abbey Cl *SHEFS* S8	146 C4
Abbey Crs *ABRD* S7	145 F4
Abbey Cft *ABRD* S7	145 F4
Abbeydale Park Crs *TOT/DORE* S17	157 D2
Abbeydale Park Ri *TOT/DORE* S17	156 C1
Abbeydale Rd *SHEFS* S8	135 D3
Abbeydale Rd South *SHEFS* S8	145 F4
	TOT/DORE S17	157 E2
Abbeyfield Rd *ATT* S4	109 F5
Abbey Gra *ABRD* S7	145 F4
	RCH S42	182 B2
Abbey Gv *BSLYN/ROY* S71	15 F3
Abbeyhill Cl *CHSW* S40	182 A5
Abbey La *BSLYN/ROY* S71	15 F5
	BSLYN/ROY S71	23 F1
	ECC S11	145 E2
	SHEFS S8	146 C4
Abbey Lane Dell *SHEFS* S8	145 F4
Abbey Sq *BSLYN/ROY* S71	15 F3
Abbey View Rd *SHEFS* S8	147 E2
Abbey Wk *BTLY* DN5	28 C4
Abbots Meadow *MOS* S20	153 E4
Abbott St *DONS/BSCR* DN4	4 B5
Abdy Rd *KIMB* S61	91 E4
	RAW S62	79 E1
Abercorn Rd *WHHL* DN2	32 A5
Abercrombie St *CHNE* S41	11 E4
Aberford Gv *HOY* S74	52 C2
Abingdon Gdns *KIMB* S61	92 C3
Abingdon Rd *WHHL* DN2	31 F4
Abney Cl *CHSW* S40	183 D3
	SHEFS S8	136 A4
Abney Dr *SHEFS* S8	136 A4
Abney Rd *SHEFS* S8	136 A4
Acacia Av *CHPT/GREN* S35	88 A2
	STV/CWN S43	186 B1
Acacia Ct *BTLY* DN5	16 B4
Acacia Crs *ECK/KIL* S21	165 F3
Acacia Gv *CONI* DN12	84 B3
Acacia Rd *DONS/BSCR* DN4	47 D4
	SHEFS S5	99 F5
Acer Cl *ECK/KIL* S21	166 A3
Acer Cft *ARMTH* DN3	33 F4
Ackworth Dr *DARN/MH* S9	113 D3
Acorn Cft *KIMB* S61	92 C4
Acorn Dr *ST/HB/BR* S6	106 A5

	ST/HB/BR S6	118 C1
	ST/HB/BR S6	119 D1
Acorn Hl *ST/HB/BR* S6	106 B5
Acorn Rdg *CHSW* S40	189 D5
Acorn St *OWL* S3	8 C2
Acorn Wy *ST/HB/BR* S6	118 C1
Acre Ga *CHPT/GREN* S35	73 E4
Acres Hill La *DARN/MH* S9	124 C4
Acres Hill Rd *DARN/MH* S9	124 C3
Acres View Cl *CHNE* S41	184 A2
Acton Cl *AU/AST/KP* S26	142 B1
Adastral Av *HACK//IN* S12	149 E3
Addison Rd *MEX/SWTN* S64	58 C3
	SHEFN S5	110 B2
Addy Cl *ST/HB/BR* S6	121 F2
Addy Dr *ST/HB/BR* S6	121 F2
Addy St *ST/HB/BR* S6	121 F3
Adelaide Rd *ECC* S11	134 B4
Adelphi St *ST/HB/BR* S6	8 A2
Adelphi Wy *STV/CWN* S43	187 F1
Adkins Dr *SHEFN* S5	108 C1
Adkins Rd *SHEFN* S5	108 C1
Adlard Rd *WHHL* DN2	31 F3
Adlington Crs *SHEFN* S5	98 A5
Adlington Rd *SHEFN* S5	98 A5
Admirals Crest *KIMB* S61	90 C4
Adrian Crs *SHEFN* S5	98 B5
Adsetts St *ATT* S4	110 C3
Adwick Av *BTLY* DN5	16 A1
Adwick Ct *MEX/SWTN* S64	58 C4
Adwick Pk *DEARNE* S63	57 E2
Adwick Rd *MEX/SWTN* S64	58 C4
	MEX/SWTN S64	58 C4
Agden Rd *ABRD* S7	134 C2
Agnes Rd *BSLY* S70	21 F2
Ainsdale Ct *BSLYN/ROY* S71	15 E2
Ainsley Rd *FUL* S10	121 D3
Ainsty Rd *ABRD* S7	135 D3
Aintree Av *DONS/BSCR* DN4	46 B2
	ECK/KIL S21	163 F5
Aintree Cl *BTLY* DN5	28 B4
Aintree Dr *MEX/SWTN* S64	58 C2
Aire Cl *CHPT/GREN* S35	74 A5
Airedale Rd *ST/HB/BR* S6	107 F2
Aireton Rd *BSLY* S70	2 B4
Aisby Dr *NROS/TKH* DN11	67 E5
Aisthorpe Rd *SHEFS* S8	147 D2
Aitken Rd *MEX/SWTN* S64	81 E3
Aizlewood Rd *SHEFS* S8	135 D3
Akley Bank Cl *TOT/DORE* S17	157 D3
Alba Cl *WMB/DAR* S73	25 E4
Albanus Rdg *ST/HB/BR* S6	118 C1
Albany Av *CHPT/GREN* S35	88 C3
Albany Cl *WMB/DAR* S73	24 B4

Albany Rd *ABRD* S7	135 D3
	DONS/BSCR DN4	43 E4
	MEX/SWTN S64	81 E2
	STKB/PEN S36	68 C2
Albany St *RHAM/THRY* S65	7 F6
Albert Av *STV/CWN* S43	179 E5
Albert Rd *DEARNE* S63	55 E1
	HACK//IN S12	151 F2
	MEX/SWTN S64	58 B3
	RAW S62	94 A2
	SHEFS S8	135 E4
	STV/CWN S43	179 E3
Albert St *BSLY* S70	2 D5
	DEARNE S63	26 C3
	ECK/KIL S21	174 B1
	MEX/SWTN S64	57 E4
	RHAM S60	6 A5
Albert Terrace Rd *ST/HB/BR* S6	8 A2
Albion Dr *DEARNE* S63	27 F3
Albion Rd *CHSW* S40	10 D5
	RHAM/THRY S65	7 E6
Albion St *ST/HB/BR* S6	121 F3
Albion Ter *DONS/BSCR* DN4	43 F3
Alcester Rd *ABRD* S7	135 D3
Aldam Cl *RHAM/THRY* S65	105 E2
	TOT/DORE S17	156 C4
Aldam Cft *TOT/DORE* S17	156 C4
Aldam Rd *DONS/BSCR* DN4	62 C1
	TOT/DORE S17	156 C4
Aldam Wy *TOT/DORE* S17	156 C4
Aldbury Cl *BSLYN/ROY* S71	14 C1
Aldcliffe Crs *DONS/BSCR* DN4	63 D3
Aldene Av *ST/HB/BR* S6	107 D3
Aldene Gld *ST/HB/BR* S6	107 D3
Aldene Rd *ST/HB/BR* S6	107 D2
Alder Gv *DONS/BSCR* DN4	43 E5
	WMB/DAR S73	40 A1
Alder La *DARN/MH* S9	125 F4
Alder Ms *HOY* S74	51 F3
Alderney Rd *SHEFP/MNR* S2	135 E3
Alderson Av *RAW* S62	80 A5
Alderson Dr *BSLYN/ROY* S71	14 B1
	WHHL DN2	45 D1
Alderson Pl *SHEFP/MNR* S2	135 E2
Alderson Rd *SHEFP/MNR* S2	135 D2
Alderson Rd North *SHEFP/MNR* S2	135 E2
Aldervale Cl *MEX/SWTN* S64	81 E5
Aldesworth Rd *DONS/BSCR* DN4	46 C3
Aldfield Wy *SHEFN* S5	109 F3
Aldham Crs *WMB/DAR* S73	24 B4
Aldham House La *WMB/DAR* S73	38 C2
Aldred Cl *ECK/KIL* S21	154 C5
Aldred Ct *RHAM/THRY* S65	103 F4

Aldred Rd *FUL* S10 .... **121** D2
Aldred St *RHAM/THRY* S65 .... **103** F4
Aldwarke La *RHAM/THRY* S65 ..... **94** B4
   RHAM/THRY S65 .... **105** D2
Aldwarke Rd *RAW* S62 .... **94** A3
Alexander St *BTLY* DN5 .... **16** C5
Alexandra Cl *KIMB* S61 .... **101** F1
Alexandra Rd *AU/AST/KP* S26 ..... **142** A2
   BTLY DN5 .... **16** C5
   DONS/BSCR DN4 .... **43** F4
   DRON S18 .... **169** F1 🗓
   MEX/SWTN S64 .... **58** C3
   SHEFP/MNR S2 .... **135** E5
Alexandra Rd East *CHNE* S41 .... **191** D5
Alexandra Rd West *CHSW* S40 ... **10** C5
Alexandra Ter *BSLYN/ROY* S71 ... **24** A2 🗓
Alford Cl *CHSW* S40 .... **189** D1 🗓
Alfred St *DARN/MH* S9 .... **111** D5 🗓
Algar Cl *SHEFP/MNR* S2 .... **136** C3
Algar Crs *SHEFP/MNR* S2 .... **137** D3
Algar Dr *SHEFP/MNR* S2 .... **136** C3
Algar Pl *SHEFP/MNR* S2 .... **136** C3
Algar Rd *SHEFP/MNR* S2 .... **136** C3
Alice Rd *KIMB* S61 .... **102** C2
Alice Wy *DRON* S18 .... **177** F1
Alison Cl *AU/AST/KP* S26 .... **142** B3 🗓
Alison Crs *SHEFP/MNR* S2 .... **137** F1
Alison Dr *AU/AST/KP* S26 .... **142** B3
Allan St *RHAM/THRY* S65 .... **7** F6
Allatt Cl *BSLY* S70 .... **22** A2
Alldred Crs *MEX/SWTN* S64 .... **81** D2
Allendale *BSLY* S70 .... **23** D5
Allenby Cl *SHEFS* S8 .... **158** C1 🗓
Allenby Dr *SHEFS* S8 .... **158** C1
Allendale Gdns *BTLY* DN5 .... **43** D1
Allendale Rd *BTLY* DN5 .... **43** D1
   DOD/DAR S75 .... **13** F3
   HOY S74 .... **51** E3
   RHAM/THRY S65 .... **105** D5
Allende Wy *DARN/MH* S9 .... **124** C1
Allestree Dr *DRON* S18 .... **168** A2 🗓
Alliance St *ATT* S4 .... **123** E1
Allott Crs *HOY* S74 .... **52** B1
Allott St *HOY* S74 .... **50** C3 🗓
   HOY S74 .... **52** B3
All Saints Wy *AU/AST/KP* S26 ..... **142** C3
Allsops Pl *CHNE* S41 .... **184** A1
Allt St *RAW* S62 .... **94** A2 🗓
Alma Crs *DRON* S18 .... **159** E5
Alma Rd *CHPT/GREN* S35 .... **73** E4
   RHAM S60 .... **103** E4
Alma Rw *RHAM* S60 .... **116** A3
Alma St *BSLY* S70 .... **2** A5
   OWL S3 .... **8** D2
   WMB/DAR S73 .... **39** E3
Almholme La *BTLY* DN5 .... **18** A1
Almond Av *ARMTH* DN3 .... **33** F2
Almond Dr *ECK/KIL* S21 .... **166** A3
Almond Rd *DONS/BSCR* DN4 ...... **47** D4
Almond Tree Rd *AU/AST/KP* S26 .. **155** D3
Almshill Crs *ECC* S11 .... **145** D2 🗓
Almshill Gld *ECC* S11 .... **145** D2
Almshill Rd *ECC* S11 .... **145** D2
Alney Pl *ST/HB/BR* S6 .... **97** E5
Alnwick Cl *HACK/IN* S12 .... **138** A5 🗓
Alnwick Rd *HACK/IN* S12 .... **137** F5
Alpha Rd *RHAM/THRY* S65 .... **104** C2
Alpine Cl *STKB/PEN* S36 .... **68** B2
Alpine Gv *STV/CWN* S43 .... **180** B5
Alpine Rd *ST/HB/BR* S6 .... **121** E2 🗓
   STKB/PEN S36 .... **68** B2
Alport Av *HACK/IN* S12 .... **150** C1
Alport Dr *HACK/IN* S12 .... **138** C5
Alport Gv *HACK/IN* S12 .... **138** C5
Alport Pl *HACK/IN* S12 .... **150** C1
Alport Ri *DRON* S18 .... **168** B1
Alport Rd *HACK/IN* S12 .... **138** C5
Alric Dr *BSLYN/ROY* S71 .... **23** F1
   RHAM S60 .... **113** F3
Alsing Rd *DARN/MH* S9 .... **112** A1
Alston Cl *DONS/BSCR* DN4 .... **46** B5
Alston Rd *DONS/BSCR* DN4 .... **66** B1
Alton Cl *CHSW* S40 .... **188** C4 🗓
   DRON S18 .... **168** B3 🗓
   ECC S11 .... **145** E3
Alum Chine Cl *CHNE* S41 .... **191** D4 🗓
Alverley La *DONS/BSCR* DN4 ..... **63** E3
Alwyn Av *BTLY* DN5 .... **28** C2
Amber Crs *CHSW* S40 .... **189** D3
Amber Cft *STV/CWN* S43 .... **187** D2 🗓
Amberley St *DARN/MH* S9 .... **111** E4
Ambler Ri *AU/AST/KP* S26 .... **142** A1
Ambleside Cl *CHNE* S41 .... **183** D2
   MOS S20 .... **164** C2 🗓
   RHAM S60 .... **113** E3 🗓
Ambleside Gv *BSLYN/ROY* S71 ... **24** B2 🗓
Amen Cnr *RHAM* S60 .... **6** C4 🗓
America La *DEARNE* S63 .... **55** D5
Amersall Crs *BTLY* DN5 .... **28** C1
Amersall Rd *BTLY* DN5 .... **28** C1
Amesbury Cl *CHNE* S41 .... **183** F2 🗓

Amos Rd *DARN/MH* S9 .... **111** F2
Amy Rd *BTLY* DN5 .... **17** D3
Anchorage Crs *BTLY* DN5 .... **29** E5
Anchorage La *BTLY* DN5 .... **29** D5
Ancote Cl *DOD/DAR* S75 .... **20** B1 🗓
Anderson Cl *STV/CWN* S43 .... **179** F3 🗓
Andover Dr *OWL* S3 .... **122** B1
Andover St *OWL* S3 .... **122** B1
Andrew La *OWL* S3 .... **9** G2 🗓
Andrews Pl *KIMB* S61 .... **102** B1
Andrew St *OWL* S3 .... **9** G2
Andwell La *FUL* S10 .... **130** C5
Anelay Rd *DONS/BSCR* DN4 ...... **43** D5
Anfield Rd *DONS/BSCR* DN4 ...... **46** C5
Angel La *RAW* S62 .... **78** A2
Angel St *SHEF* S1 .... **9** F4
Angerford Av *SHEFS* S8 .... **147** E1
Anglesey Rd *DRON* S18 .... **169** E3 🗓
Angleton Av *SHEFP/MNR* S2 ...... **138** A2
Angleton Cl *SHEFP/MNR* S2 ...... **138** A2 🗓
Angleton Gdns *SHEFP/MNR* S2 .. **138** A2
Angleton Gn *SHEFP/MNR* S2 ..... **138** A2
Angleton Ms *SHEFP/MNR* S2 ..... **138** A2 🗓
Angram Rd *CHPT/GREN* S35 ...... **73** E3
Annat Pl *CHPT/GREN* S35 .... **73** D4
Annesley Cl *CHNE* S41 .... **191** D4 🗓
   SHEFS S8 .... **159** D1 🗓
Annesley Rd *SHEFS* S8 .... **147** D5
Anns Rd *SHEFP/MNR* S2 .... **135** E3
Anns Rd North *SHEFP/MNR* S2 .. **135** F3
Ann St *RAW* S62 .... **94** A3
Ansdell Rd *BTLY* DN5 .... **16** C4
Ansell Rd *ECC* S11 .... **133** E4
Anson Gv *RHAM* S60 .... **114** B4
Anson St *SHEFP/MNR* S2 .... **9** H5
Ansten Crs *DONS/BSCR* DN4 ..... **46** C3
Antrim Av *FUL* S10 .... **121** E5
Anvil Cl *ST/HB/BR* S6 .... **119** F1
Anvil Crs *CHPT/GREN* S35 .... **98** C1
Apley Rd *DON* DN1 .... **5** F6
Apollo St *RAW* S62 .... **80** C4
Apostle Cl *DONS/BSCR* DN4 ...... **62** C1 🗓
Appleby Rd *WHHL* DN2 .... **32** A5
Applegarth Cl *HAN/WDH* S13 ..... **137** F4 🗓
Applegarth Dr *HACK/IN* S12 ...... **137** E4
Applehurst Bank *BSLY* S70 .... **22** C2 🗓
Appleton Wy *BSLY* S70 .... **22** B5
   BTLY DN5 .... **29** E5
Appletree Dr *DRON* S18 .... **169** E2
April Cl *BSLYN/ROY* S71 .... **15** D3
April Dr *BSLYN/ROY* S71 .... **15** E3
Aqueduct St *BSLYN/ROY* S71 .... **2** D1
Arbourthorne Rd *SHEFP/MNR* S2 **136** C4
Archdale Cl *SHEFP/MNR* S2 ...... **137** F2
Archdale Pl *SHEFP/MNR* S2 ...... **137** E2 🗓
Archdale Rd *SHEFP/MNR* S2 ..... **137** E1
Archer Ga *ST/HB/BR* S6 .... **106** B3
Archer La *ABRD* S7 .... **134** B5
Archer Rd *SHEFS* S8 .... **146** B2
Archery Cl *MALT* S66 .... **117** F1
Archibald Rd *ABRD* S7 .... **134** C4 🗓
Arcon Pl *RAW* S62 .... **80** B5
Arcubus Av *AU/AST/KP* S26 ...... **142** B2
Ardeen Rd *WHHL* DN2 .... **31** E5
Arden Cl *CHSW* S40 .... **183** D5
Arden Ga *DONS/BSCR* DN4 .... **63** D3
Ardmore St *DARN/MH* S9 .... **124** B2
Ardsley Av *AU/AST/KP* S26 .... **142** C4
Ardsley Cl *MOS* S20 .... **151** D3
Ardsley Dr *MOS* S20 .... **151** D3
Ardsley Gv *MOS* S20 .... **151** D3 🗓
Ardsley Rd *BSLY* S70 .... **23** D5
   CHSW S40 .... **188** C1
Argyle Rd *SHEFS* S8 .... **135** E5
Argyle St *MEX/SWTN* S64 .... **58** B3
Argyll Av *WHHL* DN2 .... **31** F4
Arklow Cl *CHNE* S41 .... **190** C4
Arklow Rd *WHHL* DN2 .... **31** E5
Arksey Common La *BTLY* DN5 .... **17** F4
Arksey La *BTLY* DN5 .... **16** C5
Arkwright Rd *BTLY* DN5 .... **29** D4
Arley St *SHEFP/MNR* S2 .... **135** E1
Arlington Av *AU/AST/KP* S26 ..... **143** D3
Arlott Wy *CONI* DN12 .... **62** A4
Armer St *RHAM* S60 .... **6** A6
Armitage Rd *DONS/BSCR* DN4 ... **43** D5
   STKB/PEN S36 .... **69** E3
Armley Rd *DARN/MH* S9 .... **111** E4
Armroyd La *HOY* S74 .... **52** A4
Arms Park Dr *MOS* S20 .... **165** D2 🗓
Armstead Rd *MOS* S20 .... **153** D2
Armthorpe La *WHHL* DN2 .... **31** E4
Armthorpe Rd *ECC* S11 .... **133** D2
   WHHL DN2 .... **31** E4
Armyne Gv *BSLYN/ROY* S71 ...... **23** F1
Arncliffe Dr *BSLY* S70 .... **20** C1
   CHPT/GREN S35 .... **88** A1
Arnold Av *HACK/IN* S12 .... **149** F4
Arnold Crs *MEX/SWTN* S64 .... **58** B2
Arnold Rd *RHAM/THRY* S65 .... **104** C3
Arnold St *ST/HB/BR* S6 .... **121** D1
Arnside Cl *CHNE* S41 .... **177** E5
Arnside Rd *SHEFS* S8 .... **134** C5
Arran Rd *FUL* S10 .... **120** C4

Arras St *DARN/MH* S9 .... **124** A2 🗓
Arthington St *SHEFS* S8 .... **135** E4 🗓
Arthur Av *BTLY* DN5 .... **16** C4
Arthur Pl *BTLY* DN5 .... **16** C4
Arthur Rd *STKB/PEN* S36 .... **68** B2
Arthur St *BSLY* S70 .... **22** B5
   BTLY DN5 .... **16** C5
   RAW S62 .... **80** B4
Artisan Vw *SHEFS* S8 .... **135** E4
Arundel Av *RHAM* S60 .... **127** F3
   RHAM/THRY S65 .... **95** E5
Arundel Cl *CHNE* S41 .... **184** A1
   DRON S18 .... **168** B2
Arundel Cottages *RHAM* S60 .... **127** F3 🗓
Arundel Crs *RHAM* S60 .... **127** E5
Arundel Gdns *BTLY* DN5 .... **29** D1
Arundel Ga *SHEF* S1 .... **9** F5
   SHEF S1 .... **9** F6 🗓
Arundel La *SHEF* S1 .... **122** C5
Arundel Rd *CHPT/GREN* S35 ..... **74** B5
   RHAM/THRY S65 .... **127** F3 🗓
   RHAM/THRY S65 .... **104** A4
Arundel St *RHAM* S60 .... **127** E3
   SHEF S1 .... **122** B5
Arundel Vw *HOY* S74 .... **52** B5
Ascot Av *DONS/BSCR* DN4 .... **46** B3
Ascot Cl *MEX/SWTN* S64 .... **58** C2
Ascot Dr *BTLY* DN5 .... **28** B3
Ascot St *SHEFP/MNR* S2 .... **135** E1 🗓
Ashberry Cl *DEARNE* S63 .... **27** D3 🗓
Ashberry Rd *ST/HB/BR* S6 .... **121** E2
Ashbourne Cl *CHSW* S40 .... **182** B4 🗓
Ashbourne Gv *HAN/WDH* S13 .... **139** D1 🗓
Ashbourne Rd *HAN/WDH* S13 .... **139** D1
Ashburnham Gdns *BTLY* DN5 ..... **42** C1
Ashbury Dr *SHEFS* S8 .... **148** A3
Ashbury La *SHEFS* S8 .... **148** A3
Ashby Ct *BSLY* S70 .... **21** E2
Ash Cl *ECK/KIL* S21 .... **166** A3
   RHAM/THRY S65 .... **105** E5
Ash Ct *BTLY* DN5 .... **42** B3
Ash Crs *ECK/KIL* S21 .... **173** F2
   MEX/SWTN S64 .... **57** F2
Ashcroft Dr *CHNE* S41 .... **178** C4
Ashdell *ECC* S11 .... **121** D5 🗓
Ashdell La *ECC* S11 .... **121** D5 🗓
Ashdell Rd *ECC* S11 .... **121** D5
Ashdene Ct *MEX/SWTN* S64 ...... **81** E3
Ashdown Dr *CHSW* S40 .... **189** E3
Ashdown Gdns *MOS* S20 .... **153** E2 🗓
Ashdown Pl *BTLY* DN5 .... **28** C2
Asher Rd *ABRD* S7 .... **135** D2 🗓
Ashes La *RAW* S62 .... **76** A3
Ashfield Cl *DOD/DAR* S75 .... **13** D4
   HACK/IN S12 .... **149** D1
Ashfield Dr *HACK/IN* S12 .... **149** D1
Ashfield Rd *CHNE* S41 .... **191** E4
   DONS/BSCR DN4 .... **63** E1
   STKB/PEN S36 .... **69** E2 🗓
Ashford Rd *DRON* S18 .... **168** B3
   ECC S11 .... **134** B2 🗓
Ashfurlong Cl *TOT/DORE* S17 .... **157** D1
Ashfurlong Dr *TOT/DORE* S17 ... **157** D1
Ashfurlong Pk *TOT/DORE* S17 ... **157** D1
Ashfurlong Rd *TOT/DORE* S17 ... **156** C1
Ashgate Av *CHSW* S40 .... **189** D1
Ashgate Cl *ECC* S11 .... **121** D5
Ashgate La *FUL* S10 .... **121** D5 🗓
Ashgate Rd *CHSW* S40 .... **10** A4
   ECC S11 .... **121** D5
Ashgate Valley Rd *CHSW* S40 ... **183** E5
Ash Gv *BSLY* S70 .... **23** E3
   CONI DN12 .... **84** B2
   FUL S10 .... **121** E5
   RAW S62 .... **94** B1
Ash House La *TOT/DORE* S17 .... **144** B4
Ashland Rd *ABRD* S7 .... **134** C5
   ECK/KIL S21 .... **164** C5
Ash La *DRON* S18 .... **161** D5
   ECK/KIL S21 .... **172** A3
   STKB/PEN S36 .... **69** F2
Ashleigh Av *HACK/IN* S12 .... **137** D5
Ashleigh Ct *ECK/KIL* S21 .... **174** A2
Ashleigh Cft *HACK/IN* S12 .... **137** D5
Ashleigh Dr *HACK/IN* S12 .... **137** D5
Ashleigh Pl *HACK/IN* S12 .... **137** D5 🗓
Ashley Cl *ECK/KIL* S21 .... **166** B2 🗓
Ashley Gv *AU/AST/KP* S26 .... **142** B3
Ashley La *ECK/KIL* S21 .... **166** B2
Ashmore Av *ECK/KIL* S21 .... **173** F4
Ashover Cl *BSLY* S70 .... **36** B1 🗓
Ashover Rd *STV/CWN* S43 .... **187** D3
Ashpool Cl *HAN/WDH* S13 .... **139** C4
Ash Rdg *MEX/SWTN* S64 .... **81** E1 🗓
Ash Rd *DEARNE* S63 .... **56** A3
Ash St *MOS* S20 .... **164** A1
   ST/HB/BR S6 .... **121** F1
   WMB/DAR S73 .... **24** B4
Ashton Cl *CHSW* S40 .... **189** D4
   ECK/KIL S21 .... **166** A2
Ashton Dr *ARMTH* DN3 .... **19** F2
Ash Tree Cl *CHSW* S40 .... **189** D1
Ashurst Cl *RCH* S42 .... **182** A4
   ST/HB/BR S6 .... **106** C5
Ashurst Dr *ST/HB/BR* S6 .... **106** C5

Ashurst Pl *ST/HB/BR* S6 .... 106 C5
Ashurst Rd *ST/HB/BR* S6 .... 106 C5
Ash V *CHSW* S40 .... 188 C5
Ashwell Rd *HAN/WDH* S13 .... 139 E4
Ashwood Av *BSLY* S70 .... 36 C1 🔟
CHPT/GREN S35 .... 73 D3
Ashwood Rd *CHPT/GREN* S35 .... 73 D3
RAW S62 .... 94 A2
Ashworth Dr *KIMB* S61 .... 91 E4
Askern Rd *BTLY* DN5 .... 16 B2
Askew Ct *STKB/PEN* S36 .... 69 D3
Askrigg Cl *DONS/BSCR* DN4 .... 47 D5 🔟
Asline Rd *SHEF/MNR* S2 .... 135 E2
Aspen Cl *ECK/KIL* S21 .... 166 A2
Aspen Gv *WMB/DAR* S73 .... 40 B1
Aspen Rd *ECK/KIL* S21 .... 173 F2
Aspen Wy *MEX/SWTN* S64 .... 81 D3
Aspley Cl *CHSW* S40 .... 10 A3
DARN/MH S9 .... 100 C5 🔟
Asquith Rd *BTLY* DN5 .... 16 C3
Aster Cl *MOS* S20 .... 153 D2
Aston Cl *DRON* S18 .... 160 A5
Aston Dr *BSLYN/ROY* S71 .... 14 B1
Aston La *AU/AST/KP* S26 .... 129 E5
Aston St *SHEF/MNR* S2 .... 123 E3
Astwell Gdns *CHPT/GREN* S35 .... 73 F5 🔟
Athelstan Cl *HAN/WDH* S13 .... 138 C1
Athelstan Rd *CONI* DN12 .... 84 C1
Athelstan Rd *HAN/WDH* S13 .... 138 C1
Athersley Crs *BSLYN/ROY* S71 .... 14 B1
Athersley Gdns *MOS* S20 .... 151 E3
Athersley Rd *BSLYN/ROY* S71 .... 14 B1
Atherton Cl *SHEF/MNR* S2 .... 137 D4
Atherton Rd *SHEF/MNR* S2 .... 137 D4
Athol Cl *CHSW* S40 .... 188 C4 🔟
Atholl Crs *WHHL* DN2 .... 32 A4
Athron St *RHAM/THRY* S65 .... 105 D5
Atkin Pl *SHEF/MNR* S2 .... 135 E2 🔟
Atlantic Dr *SHEFS* S8 .... 158 C2
Atlantic Rd *SHEFS* S8 .... 158 B2
Atlantic Wy *SHEFS* S8 .... 158 C2
Atlas St *ATT* S4 .... 123 E1
RHAM S60 .... 114 A3
Atlas Wy *ATT* S4 .... 110 C5
Atlow Cl *MOS* S20 .... 182 C4
Atterby Dr *NROS/TKH* DN11 .... 67 E5
Attercliffe Common *DARN/MH* S9 .... 111 E5
Attercliffe Rd *DARN/MH* S9 .... 124 A1
Attlee Rd *STV/CWN* S43 .... 186 C2
Aubretia Av *RHAM* S60 .... 114 B5
Auckland Av *ST/HB/BR* S6 .... 106 C4
Auckland Dr *MOS* S20 .... 164 B2
Auckland Ri *MOS* S20 .... 164 C2
Auckland Rd *DON* DN1 .... 30 C4
MEX/SWTN S64 .... 58 C5
Auckland Wy *MOS* S20 .... 164 C2
Audrey Rd *HAN/WDH* S13 .... 138 A3
Aughton Av *AU/AST/KP* S26 .... 142 A1
Aughton Cl *HAN/WDH* S13 .... 138 B3
Aughton Crs *HAN/WDH* S13 .... 138 A2
Aughton Dr *HAN/WDH* S13 .... 138 A2 🔟
Aughton Rd *AU/AST/KP* S26 .... 142 A2
Augustus Rd *RHAM* S60 .... 114 A2 🔟
Aukley Rd *SHEFS* S8 .... 135 D5
Aunby Dr *AU/AST/KP* S26 .... 142 B2 🔟
Austen Av *DONS/BSCR* DN4 .... 62 C1
Austin Cl *ST/HB/BR* S6 .... 106 C4
Austin St *ST/HB/BR* S6 .... 106 C3
Austwick Cl *DONS/BSCR* DN4 .... 63 D3
Avenue 1 *CHNE* S41 .... 190 C4 🔟
Avenue 2 *CHNE* S41 .... 190 C4 🔟
Avenue 3 *CHNE* S41 .... 190 C4 🔟
Avenue 4 *CHNE* S41 .... 190 C4 🔟
Avenue 5 *CHNE* S41 .... 190 C4 🔟
Avenue 6 *CHNE* S41 .... 190 C4 🔟
Avenue Rd *CHNE* S41 .... 184 B1
DEARNE S63 .... 56 B2
WHHL DN2 .... 30 C4
The Avenue *BTLY* DN5 .... 17 D5
DARN/MH S9 .... 125 D3 🔟
DOD/DAR S75 .... 49 E2
DONS/BSCR DN4 .... 46 A3
DRON S18 .... 169 F1
MOS S20 .... 153 D1
Aviemore Cl *STV/CWN* S43 .... 179 F2
Aviemore Rd *DONS/BSCR* DN4 .... 62 C1
Avill Wy *MALT* S66 .... 117 F1
Avisford Dr *SHEFN* S5 .... 108 B3
Avisford Rd *SHEFN* S5 .... 97 E5
Avoca Av *WHHL* DN2 .... 31 E5
Avocet Wy *KIMB* S61 .... 76 A5
Avon Cl *DRON* S18 .... 159 F5
WMB/DAR S73 .... 40 A4
Avondale Rd *CHSW* S40 .... 10 C4
KIMB S61 .... 102 B3
ST/HB/BR S6 .... 107 F4 🔟
STV/CWN S43 .... 187 D2
WHHL DN2 .... 45 E1
Avon Gv *CHPT/GREN* S35 .... 73 F5
Avon Mt *KIMB* S61 .... 102 B3
Avon St *BSLYN/ROY* S71 .... 3 F6

Axholme Rd *WHHL* DN2 .... 30 C4
Aylesbury Crs *DARN/MH* S9 .... 111 F1
Aylesbury Rd *WHHL* DN2 .... 31 F5
Aylesford Cl *BSLYN/ROY* S71 .... 2 D1
Aylsham Dr *AU/AST/KP* S26 .... 142 C5 🔟
Aylward Cl *SHEF/MNR* S2 .... 137 D3
Aylward Rd *SHEF/MNR* S2 .... 137 D3
Aysgarth Av *BSLYN/ROY* S71 .... 24 C2
Aysgarth Ri *AU/AST/KP* S26 .... 142 A2
Aysgarth Rd *ST/HB/BR* S6 .... 97 D5
Ayton Wk *BTLY* DN5 .... 16 B4 🔟

B

Babington Cl *SHEF/MNR* S2 .... 137 D3
Babington Ct *SHEF/MNR* S2 .... 137 D3 🔟
Babur Rd *ATT* S4 .... 123 E1 🔟
Backfield Ri *CHPT/GREN* S35 .... 74 B5
Backfields *SHEF* S1 .... 8 D6
Back La *BSLYN/ROY* S71 .... 15 D2
BTLY DN5 .... 28 A4
DRON S18 .... 171 D2
ECK/KIL S21 .... 164 A5
FUL S10 .... 120 A3
RAW S62 .... 79 D5
RHAM/THRY S65 .... 83 E5
Backmoor Crs *SHEFS* S8 .... 148 A3
Backmoor Rd *SHEFS* S8 .... 148 A3
Back Rd *DRON* S18 .... 171 D2
Back South St *STV/CWN* S43 .... 179 E3 🔟
Back St *HAN/WDH* S13 .... 140 A4
Bacon La *DARN/MH* S9 .... 123 F2
Bacons La *CHSW* S40 .... 190 B4
Baden Powell Av *CHSW* S40 .... 190 A3
Baden Powell Rd *CHSW* S40 .... 190 B2
Baden St *BSLY* S70 .... 36 C1
RHAM S60 .... 6 B3
Badger Cl *HAN/WDH* S13 .... 140 A3
Badger Dr *HAN/WDH* S13 .... 140 A3
Badger La *SHEF* S1 .... 8 C5
Badger Pl *HAN/WDH* S13 .... 140 A3
Badger Ri *HAN/WDH* S13 .... 140 A3
Badger Rd *HAN/WDH* S13 .... 140 A3
Badsley Ct *RHAM/THRY* S65 .... 7 H6 🔟
RHAM/THRY S65 .... 104 B3 🔟
Badsley Moor La *RHAM/THRY* S65 .... 104 A4
Badsley St *RHAM/THRY* S65 .... 7 G6
Badsley St South *RHAM/THRY* S65 .... 104 A4
Badsworth Cl *WMB/DAR* S73 .... 40 A3 🔟
Badsworth Rd *DONS/BSCR* DN4 .... 62 A2
Bagley Rd *ATT* S4 .... 110 B3
Bagshaw's Rd *HACK/IN* S12 .... 137 F4 🔟
Bagshot St *FUL* S10 .... 134 B2
Bahram Rd *DONS/BSCR* DN4 .... 46 A4 🔟
Bailey La *ECK/KIL* S21 .... 154 C3
Bailey La *SHEF* S1 .... 8 C5
Bailey St *SHEF* S1 .... 8 C5
Bainbridge Rd *DONS/BSCR* DN4 .... 44 A3 🔟
Baines Wood Cl *CHNE* S41 .... 183 D1
Bainton Dr *BSLY* S70 .... 21 E3
Bakehouse La *DOD/DAR* S75 .... 12 C4
Baker Dr *ECK/KIL* S21 .... 166 A2
Bakers Hl *SHEF* S1 .... 9 F5
Bakers La *SHEF* S1 .... 9 F5
Baker St *DARN/MH* S9 .... 124 A1
Bakewell Rd *BSLYN/ROY* S71 .... 14 B1
STV/CWN S43 .... 187 D4
Bala St *BSLYN/ROY* S71 .... 3 E5
Balby Carr Bank *DONS/BSCR* DN4 .... 44 B5
Balby Rd *DONS/BSCR* DN4 .... 43 F5
Baldwin St *DARN/MH* S9 .... 123 F2 🔟
Balfour Dr *DARN/MH* S9 .... 124 C2
Balfour Rd *DARN/MH* S9 .... 124 C2
DARN/MH S9 .... 17 D5
Balk La *BSLY* S70 .... 35 F4
RHAM S60 .... 113 E2
Ballidon Cl *CHSW* S40 .... 183 D5 🔟
Ballfield Av *HAN/WDH* S13 .... 139 E1
Ballfield Cl *HAN/WDH* S13 .... 139 E1
Ballfield Crs *HAN/WDH* S13 .... 139 E1
Ballfield Dr *HAN/WDH* S13 .... 139 E1
Ballfield Pl *HAN/WDH* S13 .... 139 E1
Ballfield Ri *HAN/WDH* S13 .... 139 E1
Ballfield Rd *HAN/WDH* S13 .... 139 E1
Ballfield Wy *HAN/WDH* S13 .... 139 E1
Ball Rd *ST/HB/BR* S6 .... 107 F5
Ball St *OWL* S3 .... 8 C2
Balmain Dr *ST/HB/BR* S6 .... 107 F3
Balmain Rd *ST/HB/BR* S6 .... 107 F3
Balm Gn *SHEF* S1 .... 8 D5
Balmoak La *CHNE* S41 .... 185 D4
Balmoral Crs *DRON* S18 .... 168 B1
Balmoral Rd *HAN/WDH* S13 .... 140 A4
Balmoral Wy *STV/CWN* S43 .... 179 F2
Baltic Rd *DARN/MH* S9 .... 124 A1
Bamford Av *BSLYN/ROY* S71 .... 14 B1
Bamford Rd *STV/CWN* S43 .... 187 D3
Bamford St *STV/CWN* S43 .... 179 E2 🔟
Bamforth St *ST/HB/BR* S6 .... 108 B5
Bank Cl *ABRD* S7 .... 134 C4
KIMB S61 .... 92 A5

Bank End Av *BSLY* S70 .... 23 D5
Bank End Rd *BSLY* S70 .... 22 C5
Bankfield La *ST/HB/BR* S6 .... 119 D1 🔟
Bankfield Rd *ST/HB/BR* S6 .... 107 E5
Bank House Rd *FUL* S10 .... 121 D2 🔟
Bank La *CHPT/GREN* S35 .... 71 F4
Bank Rd *CHNE* S41 .... 184 B3 🔟
Bank St *BSLY* S70 .... 22 A3
BSLYN/ROY S71 .... 23 F2
CHSW S40 .... 10 D6
HOY S74 .... 51 E3
MEX/SWTN S64 .... 58 B4
SHEF S1 .... 9 F4
STV/CWN S43 .... 185 E1
Bank Top Rd *RHAM/THRY* S65 .... 105 E5
Bank Vw *RHAM* S60 .... 115 F3
Bank Wood Cl *CHSW* S40 .... 182 C2
Bankwood Cl *SHEFS* S8 .... 136 B5
Bankwood Crs *NROS/TKH* DN11 .... 66 B5
Bankwood La *NROS/TKH* DN11 .... 66 B4
Bankwood Rd *SHEF/MNR* S2 .... 136 B5
Banner Ct *ECC* S11 .... 133 F4
Banner Cross Dr *ECC* S11 .... 133 F4 🔟
Bannerdale Cl *ECC* S11 .... 134 A4
Bannerdale Rd *ECC* S11 .... 134 A4
Bannerdale Vw *ECC* S11 .... 134 A4
Bannham Rd *DARN/MH* S9 .... 125 E3
Barber Balk Cl *KIMB* S61 .... 92 A5 🔟
Barber Balk Rd *KIMB* S61 .... 102 A1
Barber Crs *ST/HB/BR* S6 .... 121 E3 🔟
Barber Rd *FUL* S10 .... 121 E3 🔟
Barber's Av *RAW* S62 .... 94 A2
Barber's Crs *RAW* S62 .... 94 A1
Barber's La *ECK/KIL* S21 .... 154 B5
Barber Pth *MEX/SWTN* S64 .... 58 A2
Barber St *HOY* S74 .... 51 F2
Barber Wood Rd *KIMB* S61 .... 100 C3
Barbot Hill Rd *KIMB* S61 .... 93 D4
Bar Cft *CHSW* S40 .... 183 E5 🔟
Barcroft *DOD/DAR* S75 .... 12 B3 🔟
Barden Crs *RHAM* S60 .... 114 A4
Barden Dr *DOD/DAR* S75 .... 12 C4
Bardolf Rd *DONS/BSCR* DN4 .... 46 C3
Bard St *SHEF/MNR* S2 .... 9 H4
Bardwell Rd *OWL* S3 .... 122 A1
Barfield Av *RHAM* S60 .... 115 E3
Barfield Rd *HOY* S74 .... 51 F2
Barholme Rd *CHNE* S41 .... 182 C2
Barholm Rd *FUL* S10 .... 120 A5
Bari Cl *WMB/DAR* S73 .... 25 F4
Baring Rd *KIMB* S61 .... 100 C3
Barkby Rd *DARN/MH* S9 .... 100 B3
Barker Fold *CHSW* S40 .... 189 E1 🔟
Barker La *CHSW* S40 .... 189 E1
Barker's Pl *ST/HB/BR* S6 .... 108 A5 🔟
Barker's Pool *SHEF* S1 .... 8 D6
Barker St *ECC* S11 .... 134 B4
Barker St *MEX/SWTN* S64 .... 57 F3
Bark Mdw *DOD/DAR* S75 .... 20 B3
Barkston Rd *BSLYN/ROY* S71 .... 15 D1
Barlborough Rd *WMB/DAR* S73 .... 39 F4
Barlby Gv *HACK/IN* S12 .... 152 A2
Barley La *CHSW* S40 .... 182 B4
Barley Ms *DRON* S18 .... 168 A2 🔟
Barley Vw *DEARNE* S63 .... 27 D4 🔟
Barleywood Rd *DARN/MH* S9 .... 125 D1
Barlow Dr *ST/HB/BR* S6 .... 120 B1
Barlow Lees La *DRON* S18 .... 169 D4
Barlow Rd *CHNE* S41 .... 176 A5
ST/HB/BR S6 .... 107 E5
STV/CWN S43 .... 181 F4 🔟
Barlow Vw *DRON* S18 .... 169 F4
Barmouth Rd *ABRD* S7 .... 134 C5
Barnard Av *DRON* S18 .... 160 B5
Barnardiston Rd *DARN/MH* S9 .... 124 C2
Barnby Dun Rd *WHHL* DN2 .... 32 A1
Barncliffe Cl *FUL* S10 .... 132 A2
Barncliffe Crs *FUL* S10 .... 131 F1
Barncliffe Dr *FUL* S10 .... 131 F1
Barncliffe Gln *FUL* S10 .... 131 F2
Barncliffe Rd *FUL* S10 .... 132 A2
Barn Cl *CHSW* S40 .... 183 D5
Barnes Av *DRON* S18 .... 168 B1
Barnes Cl *SHEFP/MNR* S2 .... 122 C5
Barnes Hall Rd *CHPT/GREN* S35 .... 87 E2
Barnes La *DRON* S18 .... 157 F4
DRON S18 .... 158 B5
DRON S18 .... 168 B1
Barnes Rd *CHNE* S41 .... 191 F3
Barnet Av *ECC* S11 .... 132 C5
Barnet Rd *ECC* S11 .... 132 C5
Barnfield Av *FUL* S10 .... 119 F4
Barnfield Cl *FUL* S10 .... 119 F5
STV/CWN S43 .... 181 F4
Barnfield Dr *FUL* S10 .... 119 F5
Barnfield Rd *FUL* S10 .... 119 F4
Barnham Cl *CHSW* S40 .... 188 C4
Barnsdale Av *MOS* S20 .... 151 E3
Barnsley Av *CONI* DN12 .... 84 B1
Barnsley Boundary Wk
CHPT/GREN S35 .... 70 B1
CHPT/GREN S35 .... 86 A5
HOY S74 .... 52 A4

WMB/DAR S73		53 E1
Barnsley Rd ATT S4		109 F4
BTLY DN5		28 A2
DEARNE S63		41 D5
DEARNE S63		55 E1
DOD/DAR S75		20 A2
HOY S74		37 E5
KIMB S61		75 F4
OWL S3		109 F5
SHEFN S5		99 D4
WMB/DAR S73		24 C5
WMB/DAR S73		39 D1
Barnstone St DONS/BSCR DN4		43 E3
Barnwell Crs WMB/DAR S73		24 C5
Baron St SHEF S1		135 E1 🔟
Barrack Rd DRON S18		171 E2
Barratt Rd ECK/KIL S21		174 B1
Barrel La DONS/BSCR DN4		62 B1
Barret Rd DONS/BSCR DN4		47 D3
Barretta St ATT S4		110 B3
Barrie Crs CHSW S40		109 D1
Barrie Dr SHEFN S5		109 D1
Barrie Rd DONS/BSCR DN4		63 F1 🔟
SHEFN S5		109 D2
Barrowby Rd RHAM S60		115 E1
Barrow Field La RAW S62		76 B1
Barrowfield Rd DEARNE S63		27 E4
HOY S74		51 E1
Barrow Hl RAW S62		76 A2
Barrow Rd DARN/MH S9		100 C5
DARN/MH S9		101 D5
Barry Rd STV/CWN S43		186 A5
Bartholomew Cl RHAM S60		116 B2 🔟
Bartholomew St WMB/DAR S73		39 D2
Bartle Av HACK/IN S12		149 D1
Bartle Dr HACK/IN S12		149 D1
Bartle Rd HACK/IN S12		149 D1
Bartlett Cl ST/HB/BR S6		119 D2 🔟
Bartle Wy HACK/IN S12		149 D1
Barton Crs CHSW S40		182 B3
Barton La ARMTH DN3		33 E3
Barton Pl CONI DN12		84 C2
Barton Rd SHEFS S8		135 E4
Basegreen Av HACK/IN S12		149 F2
Basegreen Cl HACK/IN S12		150 A2
Basegreen Crs HACK/IN S12		149 F2
Basegreen Dr HACK/IN S12		149 F2
Basegreen Pl HACK/IN S12		149 F2 🔟
Basegreen Rd HACK/IN S12		150 A3 🔟
Basegreen Wy HACK/IN S12		150 A2 🔟
Basford Av DARN/MH S9		124 C2
Basford Dr DARN/MH S9		124 C2
Basford Ms DARN/MH S9		125 D2 🔟
Basford Pl DARN/MH S9		124 C2 🔟
Basford St DARN/MH S9		124 C3
Basil Av ARMTH DN3		32 C2
Basil Cl CHNE S41		11 F4
Basildon Rd DEARNE S63		26 C2
Baslow Rd TOT/DORE S17		156 A4
Bassett La FUL S10		130 C4
Bassett Pl SHEFP/MNR S2		123 E5
Bassett Rd SHEFP/MNR S2		123 F5
Bassingthorpe La KIMB S61		92 C4
Bassledene Rd SHEFP/MNR S2		137 D2 🔟
Bastock Rd ST/HB/BR S6		108 B3
Bateman Cl STV/CWN S43		179 E2
Batemoor Cl SHEFS S8		159 E2
Batemoor Dr SHEFS S8		159 E2
Batemoor Pl SHEFS S8		159 E2 🔟
Batemoor Rd SHEFS S8		159 E2
Batesquire MOS S20		153 D3
Bate Wood Av STV/CWN S43		186 C4
Bath St OWL S3		122 A5 🔟
Battison La DEARNE S63		55 E4
Batt St SHEFP/MNR S2		135 E1 🔟
Batworth Dr ATT S4		109 E4
Batworth Rd SHEFN S5		109 E4
Baulk Farm Cl RAW S62		92 C2
Bawtry Ga DARN/MH S9		112 C2
Bawtry Rd DARN/MH S9		113 D3
DONS/BSCR DN4		45 E3
DONS/BSCR DN4		67 D2
RHAM S60		113 F3
RHAM/THRY S65		105 F5 🔟
Baxter Av DON DN1		5 G1
Baxter Cl ST/HB/BR S6		97 D5
Baxter Dr ST/HB/BR S6		97 D5
Baxter Ga DON DN1		4 D3
Baxter Rd ST/HB/BR S6		97 D5
Baycliff Dr CHSW S40		189 D1
Bay Cl ECK/KIL S21		166 A3
Baysdale Cft MOS S20		164 B1
Beacon Cl DARN/MH S9		111 D2
Beacon Cft DARN/MH S9		111 D2
Beacon Rd DARN/MH S9		111 D2
Beaconsfield Rd		
DONS/BSCR DN4		43 E3 🔟
RHAM S60		115 E1
Beaconsfield St MEX/SWTN S64		58 A3 🔟
Beacon Vw HOY S74		52 B5 🔟
Beacon Wy DARN/MH S9		111 D2
Beale Wy RAW S62		94 A4
Bear Tree Cl RAW S62		94 A2 🔟
Bear Tree Rd RAW S62		94 A2
Bear Tree St RAW S62		94 A3 🔟
Beauchamp Rd KIMB S61		92 A5
Beauchief Abbey La SHEFS S8		146 A5
Beauchief Cl STKB/PEN S36		70 A3 🔟
Beauchief Dr SHEFS S8		158 A1
Beauchief Ri SHEFS S8		146 A4
Beaufort Rd FUL S10		121 E4
WHHL DN2		31 F5
Beaumont Av BSLY S70		20 C1
Beaumont Cl SHEFP/MNR S2		124 C5
Beaumont Crs SHEFP/MNR S2		124 B5 🔟
Beaumont Dr RHAM/THRY S65		104 C4
Beaumont Ms SHEFP/MNR S2		137 F1 🔟
Beaumont Rd North		
SHEFP/MNR S2		124 B5
Beaumont Wy HOY S74		50 C3
Beaumont Wy SHEFP/MNR S2		124 B5 🔟
Beaver Av HAN/WDH S13		139 F2
Beaver Cl HAN/WDH S13		139 F2
Beaver Dr HAN/WDH S13		139 F2
Beaver Hill Rd HAN/WDH S13		139 F2
Beck Cl MEX/SWTN S64		81 E2
SHEFN S5		99 F2
Becket Crs KIMB S61		91 E4
Becket Rd SHEFS S8		158 C1
Beckett Rd DON DN1		30 C4
WHHL DN2		31 E2
Beckett St BSLYN/ROY S71		3 E3
Becknoll La WMB/DAR S73		40 B5
Beck Rd SHEFN S5		99 E2
Beckton Av MOS S20		152 C5
Beckton Ct MOS S20		153 D3
Beckton Gv MOS S20		152 C5
Beckwith Rd RHAM/THRY S65		105 D2
Bedale Rd BTLY DN5		28 B2
SHEFS S8		135 D4
Bedford St BSLY S70		22 A3
ST/HB/BR S6		8 B1
Bedford Ter BSLYN/ROY S71		14 B2
Bedgebury Cl MOS S20		153 F4 🔟
Bedgrave Cl ECK/KIL S21		155 D5
Beecham Cl RAW S62		94 C1
Beech Av RAW S62		94 C1
RHAM/THRY S65		105 F5
Beech Cl WMB/DAR S73		39 D5
Beech Crs ECK/KIL S21		166 A3
ECK/KIL S21		173 F2
MEX/SWTN S64		57 F3
Beechcroft Rd DONS/BSCR DN4		62 C2 🔟
Beechdale Cl CHSW S40		183 E5
Beeches Dr SHEFP/MNR S2		136 A2
Beeches Dr SHEFP/MNR S2		136 A2
Beeches Gv MOS S20		153 E2
Beeches Rd AU/AST/KP S26		155 F2
The Beeches AU/AST/KP S26		142 B3
MEX/SWTN S64		81 D3
Beechfern Cl CHPT/GREN S35		73 E3 🔟
Beechfield Rd DON DN1		5 F6
Beech Gv BSLY S70		21 E5
BTLY DN5		29 F1 🔟
CONI DN12		84 C2
DONS/BSCR DN4		62 A1
Beech Hill CONI DN12		85 D2
Beech Hill Rd FUL S10		121 D5
Beech House Rd WMB/DAR S73		39 E5
Beech St ARMTH DN3		33 F2
DEARNE S63		56 B2
Beech St BSLY S70		22 A3
STV/CWN S43		180 B5
Beech Tree Cl ARMTH DN3		47 F3
Beechville Av MEX/SWTN S64		81 D2 🔟
Beech Wy AU/AST/KP S26		141 F2
DRON S18		159 E5 🔟
Beechwood Cl DEARNE S63		56 A5 🔟
RAW S62		81 D4 🔟
Beechwood Rd CHPT/GREN S35		73 F5 🔟
DRON S18		169 D2
RHAM/THRY S65		104 B5
ST/HB/BR S6		107 F3
STKB/PEN S36		68 C3
Beehive Rd CHSW S40		189 E2
FUL S10		121 E3
Beeley Cl STV/CWN S43		187 D3 🔟
Beeley St SHEFP/MNR S2		135 D1 🔟
Beeley Vw CHSW S40		188 C5
Beeley Wood La ST/HB/BR S6		96 B5
Beeley Wood Rd ST/HB/BR S6		108 A1 🔟
Beeston Cl DRON S18		168 A1 🔟
Beeton Rd SHEFS S8		135 D5
Beet St OWL S3		8 B5
Beetwell St CHSW S40		190 B2
Beever La DOD/DAR S75		12 B4
Beevers Rd KIMB S61		91 E4
Beevor Ct BSLYN/ROY S71		3 G6
Beevor St BSLYN/ROY S71		22 C1 🔟
Beighton Rd HACK/IN S12		151 F2
HAN/WDH S13		140 B4
MEX/SWTN S64		81 F3
Beighton Rd East MOS S20		152 A2
Belcourt Rd RHAM/THRY S65		105 E5
Beldon Cl SHEFP/MNR S2		136 B3
Beldon Pl SHEFP/MNR S2		136 B3
Beldon Rd SHEFP/MNR S2		136 B3
Belfry Gdns DONS/BSCR DN4		47 E5 🔟
Belgrave Dr FUL S10		132 B1 🔟
Belgrave Pl AU/AST/KP S26		142 A3
Belgrave Rd BSLYN/ROY S71		3 F5
FUL S10		132 C1 🔟
Belgrave Sq SHEFP/MNR S2		135 E2 🔟
Belklane Dr ECK/KIL S21		166 C1
Bell Bank Vw BSLY S70		22 A5
Bellefield St OWL S3		8 A3
Belle Vue Av DONS/BSCR DN4		45 E2
Belle Vue Cl STV/CWN S43		185 E1 🔟
Belle Vue Rd MEX/SWTN S64		58 B4
The Bellfields KIMB S61		89 F1
Bellhagg Rd ST/HB/BR S6		120 C1
Bellhouse Rd SHEFN S5		99 F5
Bellows Rd RAW S62		94 A1
Bellrope Acre ARMTH DN3		33 F4
Bellscroft Av RHAM/THRY S65		95 F4
Bells Sq SHEF S1		8 D5
Bell St AU/AST/KP S26		143 D3
Bellwood Crs HOY S74		51 D3
Belmont Av BSLYN/ROY S71		14 C2
CHPT/GREN S35		88 B3
DONS/BSCR DN4		44 A3
Belmont Dr STKB/PEN S36		69 D2 🔟
Belmont St KIMB S61		102 B3
MEX/SWTN S64		58 A4 🔟
Belper Rd SHEFS S8		135 D4 🔟
Belridge Cl DOD/DAR S75		12 C3 🔟
Belsize Rd ECC S11		132 B2
Belton Cl DRON S18		168 A2 🔟
Belvedere DONS/BSCR DN4		63 D1
Belvedere Av CHSW S40		189 F4
Belvedere Cl RCH S42		188 B4
Belvedere Dr WMB/DAR S73		25 F3
Ben Cl ST/HB/BR S6		107 D3
Beninmoor Wy CHSW S40		189 F4
Benita Av MEX/SWTN S64		59 D4
Ben La ST/HB/BR S6		107 D5
Benmore Dr MOS S20		153 F4 🔟
Bennett Cl RAW S62		80 C4 🔟
Bennett St KIMB S61		101 F3
SHEFP/MNR S2		135 D2 🔟
Benson Rd SHEFP/MNR S2		123 F5
Bentfield Av RHAM/THRY S65		116 A1
Bentham Dr BSLYN/ROY S71		15 E3
Bentham Rd CHSW S40		10 A1
Bentinck Cl DON DN12		5 E6
Bentinck St CONI DN12		85 E1 🔟
Bent Lathes Av RHAM S60		115 F2
Bentley Av DONS/BSCR DN4		43 E2
Bentley Cl BSLYN/ROY S71		15 F2
Bentley Common La BTLY DN5		30 A1
Bentley Rd BTLY DN5		29 F2
CHPT/GREN S35		88 C2
FUL S10		120 B2
Bentley St RHAM S60		114 B1
Benton Ter MEX/SWTN S64		81 E2 🔟
Benton Wy KIMB S61		102 A2
Bents Cl CHPT/GREN S35		88 B1 🔟
ECC S11		132 C5
Bents Crs DRON S18		160 A5
ECC S11		145 D1
Bents Green Av ECC S11		132 C5
Bents Green Cl ECC S11		132 C4
Bents Green Pl ECC S11		132 C5 🔟
Bents La DRON S18		160 A5
Bents Rd ECC S11		133 D5
KIMB S61		92 A5
Benty La FUL S10		120 A4
Beresford Rd BTLY DN5		16 C5
Berkley Cl BSLY S70		22 A5
Bernard St STV/CWN S43		180 A5
Bernard Rd ATT S4		123 E3
SHEFP/MNR S2		123 D3
Bernard St RAW S62		80 C4
RHAM/THRY S65		105 F4
SHEFP/MNR S2		123 D3
Berners Cl SHEFP/MNR S2		136 C5
Berners Dr SHEFP/MNR S2		136 C4
Berners Pl SHEFP/MNR S2		136 C4
Berners Rd SHEFP/MNR S2		136 B4
Berneslai Cl BSLY S70		2 B4
Berneslai Ct BSLY S70		2 B4
Bernshall Crs SHEFN S5		98 C2
Berresford Rd ECC S11		134 B2 🔟
Berrington Rd DONS/BSCR DN4		63 E3
Berry Av ECK/KIL S21		164 A5
Berrydale BSLY S70		22 B5
Berry Holme Cl CHPT/GREN S35		88 B1 🔟
Berry Holme Dr CHPT/GREN S35		88 B1 🔟
Berry Holme Ter CHPT/GREN S35		88 B1
Berry La CHPT/GREN S35		72 B3
Berwick Av CHSW S40		189 D5
Berwick Cl CHSW S40		189 D4
Berwick Ct CHSW S40		189 D5
Berwyn Cl CHSW S40		183 G4
Bessacarr La DONS/BSCR DN4		66 C1
Bessemer Pl DARN/MH S9		123 F2 🔟
Bessemer Rd DARN/MH S9		123 F1
Bessemer Ter STKB/PEN S36		6 C1 🔟
Bessemer Wy RHAM S60		102 B4
Bessingby Rd ST/HB/BR S6		108 A5
Bethel Rd RHAM/THRY S65		7 G2
Bethel St HOY S74		52 A2

Betjeman Gdns *ECC* S11 .... **134** A1 🄰
Betony Cl *ECK/KIL* S21 .... **165** F3
Beulah Rd *ST/HB/BR* S6 .... **108** B3
Bevan Cl *HOY* S74 .... **52** B2
Bevan Dr *STV/CWN* S43 .... **186** C2
Bevan Wy *CHPT/GREN* S35 .... **88** A2
Bevercotes Rd *SHEFN* S5 .... **110** B1
Beverley Av *BSLY* S70 .... **22** A4
Beverley Cl *AU/AST/KP* S26 ...... **142** B3
Beverley Gdns *BTLY* DN5 .... **28** B4
Beverley Rd *WHHL* DN2 .... **31** E3
Beverleys Rd *SHEFS* S8 .... **147** E1
Beverley St *DARN/MH* S9 .... **124** B1
Bevin Pl *RAW* S62 .... **80** C5
Bevre Rd *ARMTH* DN3 .... **33** E1
Bewicke Av *BTLY* DN5 .... **28** B3
Bhatia Cl *MEX/SWTN* S64 .... **58** B3 🄰
Bickerton Rd *ST/HB/BR* S6 ...... **108** A2
Bierlow Cl *WMB/DAR* S73 .... **40** C4
Bignor Pl *ST/HB/BR* S6 .... **97** E5
Bignor Rd *ST/HB/BR* S6 .... **97** E4
Bilby La *STV/CWN* S43 .... **179** F5
Billam Pl *KIMB* S61 .... **91** F5
Billam St *ECK/KIL* S21 .... **165** F5
Billingley Dr *DEARNE* S63 .... **26** C4
Bilston St *ST/HB/BR* S6 .... **108** B5 🄰
Binders Rd *KIMB* S61 .... **91** F5
Binfield Rd *SHEFS* S8 .... **135** D5
Bingham Park Crs *ECC* S11 ...... **133** E2
Bingham Park Rd *ECC* S11 .... **133** E3
Bingham Rd *SHEFS* S8 .... **147** D3 🄰
Bingley La *ST/HB/BR* S6............ **118** C3
Bingley Rd *DOD/DAR* S75 .... **13** D5
Binsted Av *SHEFN* S5 .... **97** E5
Binsted Cl *SHEFN* S5 .... **108** B1
Binsted Crs *SHEFN* S5 .... **108** B1
Binsted Cft *SHEFN* S5 .... **108** B1
Binsted Dr *SHEFN* S5 .... **108** B1
Binsted Gdns *SHEFN* S5 .... **108** B1 🄰
Binsted Gld *SHEFN* S5 .... **108** B1
Binsted Gv *SHEFN* S5 .... **108** B1
Binsted Rd *SHEFN* S5 .... **108** B1
Binsted Wy *SHEFN* S5 .... **108** B1
Birchall Av *RHAM* S60 .... **115** F3
Birch Av *CHPT/GREN* S35 .... **88** A2
Birch Cl *BTLY* DN5 .... **42** B3
 ECK/KIL S21 .... **166** A3
Birchen Cl *CHSW* S40 .... **183** E4
 DONS/BSCR DN4 .... **66** C2
 DRON S18 .... **168** B2
Birches Fold *DRON* S18 .... **160** A4 🄰
Birches La *DRON* S18 .... **160** A4
Birch Farm Av *SHEFS* S8 .... **147** E5
Birchfield Crs *DOD/DAR* S75 ...... **20** B2 🄰
Birchfield Wk *DOD/DAR* S75 ...... **12** C5 🄰
Birch Gv *CONI* DN12 .... **85** E1
Birch Holt Gv *DRON* S18 .... **177** F1
Birchitt Cl *TOT/DORE* S17 .... **158** A3
Birchitt Pl *TOT/DORE* S17 .... **158** A3
Birchitt Rd *TOT/DORE* S17 .... **158** A3
Birchitt Vw *DRON* S18 .... **159** E5
Birch Kiln Cft *STV/CWN* S43 .... **186** A1
Birchlands Dr *ECK/KIL* S21 .... **166** B3
Birch La *STV/CWN* S43 .... **180** B5
Birch Rd *BSLY* S70 .... **23** E3
 DARN/MH S9 .... **123** F1
 DONS/BSCR DN4 .... **47** D4
Birchtree Rd *KIMB* S61 .... **90** A3
Birch Tree Rd *STKB/PEN* S36 .... **68** C3
Birchvale Rd *HACK/IN* S12 .... **150** B2
Birchwood Av *RAW* S62 .... **80** A5
Birchwood Cl *MOS* S20 .... **152** C5 🄰
Birchwood Crs *CHSW* S40 .... **190** A5
Birchwood Cft *MOS* S20 .... **152** C5
Birchwood Dell *DONS/BSCR* DN4... **67** F2
Birchwood Gdns *MOS* S20 .... **152** C5 🄰
Birchwood Gv *MOS* S20 .... **152** C5
Birchwood Ri *MOS* S20 .... **152** C5 🄰
Birchwood Rd *ECK/KIL* S21 ...... **162** B5
Birchwood Vw *MOS* S20 .... **152** C5
Birchwood Wy *MOS* S20 .... **152** C5 🄰
Bird Av *WMB/DAR* S73 .... **39** D3
Birdholme Crs *CHSW* S40 .... **190** B4
Birdwell Rd *ATT* S4 .... **111** D3
 DOD/DAR S75 .... **20** B4
 MEX/SWTN S64 .... **81** E3
Birk Av *BSLY* S70 .... **23** D3
Birkbeck Ct *CHPT/GREN* S35 ...... **73** E3 🄰
Birk Crs *BSLY* S70 .... **23** D3
Birkdale Cl *DONS/BSCR* DN4 ...... **67** F1
Birkdale Dr *CHSW* S40 .... **189** D4
Birkdale Ri *MEX/SWTN* S64 .... **81** E1
Birkendale *ST/HB/BR* S6 .... **121** E2
Birkendale Rd *ST/HB/BR* S6 ..... **121** E2
Birkendale Vw *ST/HB/BR* S6 .... **121** E2 🄰
Birk Gn *BSLY* S70 .... **23** E3
Birk House La *BSLY* S70 .... **23** E3
Birklands Av *HAN/WDH* S13 ..... **138** C1
Birklands Cl *HAN/WDH* S13 ...... **138** C1
Birklands Dr *HAN/WDH* S13 ..... **138** C1
Birk Rd *BSLY* S70 .... **23** D3
Birks Av *HAN/WDH* S13 .... **139** F4 🄰
Birks Rd *KIMB* S61 .... **91** F5
Birk Ter *BSLY* S70 .... **23** D3
Birley Brook Dr *CHSW* S40 .... **182** C2

Birley La *HACK/IN* S12 .... **150** B3
Birley Moor Av *HACK/IN* S12 .... **150** C2
Birley Moor Cl *HACK/IN* S12 .... **150** C2 🄰
Birley Moor Dr *HACK/IN* S12 .... **150** C2
Birley Moor Pl *HACK/IN* S12 .... **150** C3
Birley Moor Rd *HACK/IN* S12 ... **150** C2
Birley Moor Wy *HACK/IN* S12 .. **138** B5
Birley Moor Wy *HACK/IN* S12 .. **150** C2
Birley Rise Crs *ST/HB/BR* S6 .... **97** D5
Birley Rise Rd *ST/HB/BR* S6 ..... **97** D5
Birley Spa Dr *HACK/IN* S12 ...... **151** F1
Birley Spa La *HACK/IN* S12 ...... **151** D1
Birley Vale Av *HACK/IN* S12 ..... **150** A1
Birley Vale Cl *HACK/IN* S12 ...... **150** A1
Birstall Cl *CHSW* S40 .... **183** D2
Bisby Rd *RAW* S62 .... **80** B5
Biscay Wy *DEARNE* S63 .... **56** A2
Bishopdale Ct *MOS* S20 .... **151** E4 🄰
Bishopdale Dr *HACK/IN* S12 ..... **151** E5 🄰
Bishopdale Ri *HACK/IN* S12 ...... **151** E5
Bishop Hl *HAN/WDH* S13 .... **139** E4
Bishopgarth Cl *BTLY* DN5 .... **29** F3
Bishop Hl *HAN/WDH* S13 .... **139** E4
Bishops Ct *SHEFS* S8 .... **135** E5
Bishopscourt Rd *SHEFS* S8 ...... **135** E5
Bishopsholme Rd *SHEFN* S5 .... **109** E2 🄰
Bishop St *SHEF* S1 .... **122** A5
Bishops Wy *BSLY/ROY* S71 .... **15** D4
Bittern Vw *KIMB* S61 .... **76** B5
Blacka Moor Crs *TOT/DORE* S17 ... **156** A2
Blackamoor Rd *RAW* S62 .... **80** A2
Blacka Moor Rd *TOT/DORE* S17 ... **156** A2
Blacka Moor Vw *TOT/DORE* S17 . **156** A2
Blackbird Av *RHAM* S60 .... **114** B4 🄰
Blackbrook Av *FUL* S10 .... **131** D1
Blackbrook Dr *FUL* S10 .... **131** D1
Blackbrook Rd *FUL* S10 .... **131** E1
Blackburn Cfs *CHPT/GREN* S35 .. **73** F5
Blackburn Cft *CHPT/GREN* S35 . **74** A5 🄰
Blackburn Dr *CHPT/GREN* S35 ... **87** F1
Blackburne St *ST/HB/BR* S6 ..... **108** B5 🄰
Blackburn La *BSLY* S70 .... **22** B5
 DOD/DAR S75 .... **13** E5
 KIMB S61 .... **100** C3 🄰
Blackburn Rd *KIMB* S61 .... **100** C3 🄰
Blackburn Rd *BSLY* S70 .... **22** B5 🄰
Blackdown Av *CHSW* S40 .... **182** C4 🄰
 MOS S20 .... **152** B3
Blacker La *BSLY* S70 .... **36** B3
Black Hill Rd *RHAM/THRY* S65 .. **105** E5
Black La *HOY* S74 .... **50** A4
 ST/HB/BR S6........................ **106** B5
Blackmoor Ct *RHAM* S60 .... **113** F3
Blackmore St *ATT* S4 .... **123** E2
Blacksmith La *CHPT/GREN* S35 .. **97** D1
Blackstock Cl *SHEFS* S8 .... **148** B3
Blackstock Crs *GLV* S14 .... **148** B3
Blackstock Dr *SHEFS* S8 .... **148** B3
Blackstock Rd *SHEFP/MNR* S2 .. **136** B5
 SHEFS S8 .... **148** B3
Blackthorn Cl *CHNE* S41 .... **191** E5
 CHPT/GREN S35 .... **73** E3 🄰
Blackwell Cl *SHEFP/MNR* S2 .... **123** D4 🄰
Blackwell Pl *SHEFP/MNR* S2 .... **9** H5
Blackwood Av *DONS/BSCR* DN4 .. **63** D1 🄰
Blagden St *SHEFP/MNR* S2 ...... **123** D4
Blair Athol Rd *ECC* S11 .... **133** F4
Blake Av *DEARNE* S63 .... **55** D3
 WHHL DN2 .... **31** D3
Blake Grove Rd *ST/HB/BR* S6 .. **121** F2 🄰
Blakeney Rd *FUL* S10 .... **121** D4
Blake St *ST/HB/BR* S6 .... **121** E2
Blandford Cl *CHNE* S41 .... **187** F2
Bland La *ST/HB/BR* S6 .... **107** D3
Bland St *ATT* S4 .... **110** C4
Blast La *ATT* S4 .... **9** H4
 SHEFP/MNR S2 .... **9** H4
Blaxton Cl *MOS* S20 .... **151** E3 🄰
Blayton Rd *ATT* S4 .... **110** A5
Blazley Rd *DARN/MH* S9 .... **137** D4
Bleachcroft Wy *BSLY* S70 .... **23** F3
Bleasdale Gv *BSLY/ROY* S71 ...... **14** B3
Blenheim Av *BSLY* S70 .... **21** F2
Blenheim Crs *MEX/SWTN* S64 .... **58** A3 🄰
Blenheim Gdns *ECC* S11 .... **133** E5 🄰
Blenheim Rd *BSLY* S70 .... **21** E3
Blonk St *OWL* S3 .... **9** G3
Blucher St *BSLY* S70 .... **2** C6
Bluebank Vw *CHNE* S41 .... **179** E3
Bluebell Cl *HOY* S74 .... **51** D4
 SHEFN S5 .... **110** C1
Bluebell Rd *SHEFN* S5 .... **111** D1
Bluebird Rd *AU/AST/KP* S26 ..... **142** C4
Blue Boy St *OWL* S3 .... **8** C3
Blue Lodge Cl *STV/CWN* S43 ... **186** C4
Blundell Cl *BSLY/ROY* S71 .... **15** E2 🄰
Blyde Rd *SHEFN* S5 .... **110** A3
Blyth Av *RAW* S62 .... **94** A1
Blyth Cl *CHSW* S40 .... **188** C4
 RHAM S60 .... **116** B3
Blythe St *WMB/DAR* S73 .... **39** D2
Boardman Av *RAW* S62 .... **79** D3
Bobbin Mill La *CHSW* S40 .... **189** E2
Bochum Pkwy *SHEFS* S8 .... **148** A5

Bocking Cl *SHEFS* S8 .... **146** B4
Bocking Hl *STKB/PEN* S36 .... **69** E2
Bocking La *SHEFS* S8 .... **146** B4
Bocking Ri *SHEFS* S8 .... **146** C5 🄰
Boden La *SHEF* S1 .... **8** C5
Boden Pl *DARN/MH* S9 .... **125** D2 🄰
Bodmin Ct *BSLYN/ROY* S71 .... **14** C4
Bodmin St *DARN/MH* S9 .... **124** A1 🄰
Bodmin Wy *CHSW* S40 .... **183** D4 🄰
Boiley La *ECK/KIL* S21 .... **165** F4
Boland Rd *TOT/DORE* S17 .... **158** B3
Bold St *DARN/MH* S9 .... **111** E4
Bole Cl *WMB/DAR* S73 .... **40** A1
Bole Hl *RHAM* S60 .... **127** F2
Bolehill La *ECK/KIL* S21 .... **173** D1
 FUL S10 .... **120** B3
Bole Hill Rd *FUL* S10 .... **120** A3
Bolsover Rd *SHEFS* S8 .... **110** B2
Bolsover Rd East *ATT* S4 .... **110** B3 🄰
Bolsover St *OWL* S3 .... **121** F4
Bonet La *RHAM* S60 .... **113** C3
Booker Rd *SHEFS* S8 .... **146** C5 🄰
Booth Cl *MOS* S20 .... **152** B3
Booth Cft *MOS* S20 .... **152** B3
Booth Pl *RAW* S62 .... **79** F3
Booth Rd *CHPT/GREN* S35 .... **73** D4
Booth St *HOY* S74 .... **51** F2 🄰
 KIMB S61 .... **92** C2
Borough Rd *ST/HB/BR* S6 .... **108** B4
Borrowdale Av *MOS* S20 .... **164** C2 🄰
Borrowdale Cl *BSLYN/ROY* S71 .. **24** C1 🄰
 MOS S20 .... **164** C2 🄰
Borrowdale Dr *MOS* S20 .... **164** C1
Borrowdale Rd *MOS* S20 .... **164** C2
Bosville Rd *FUL* S10 .... **120** C4 🄰
Bosville St *RHAM/THRY* S65 ..... **105** E1
Boswell Cl *CHPT/GREN* S35 ...... **73** D5
Boswell Rd *DEARNE* S63 .... **56** A4
 DONS/BSCR DN4 .... **46** A5
Boswell St *RHAM/THRY* S65 ..... **104** A4
Bosworth St *FUL* S10 .... **120** C3 🄰
Botanical Rd *FUL* S10 .... **134** A3
Botham St *ATT* S4 .... **110** C4
The Boulevard *ARMTH* DN3 .... **19** F4
Boulton Cl *RCH* S42 .... **182** B4
Boulton Dr *ARMTH* DN3 .... **47** F3
Boundary Av *WHHL* DN2 .... **32** A2
Boundary Gn *RAW* S62 .... **94** A2
Boundary Rd *SHEFP/MNR* S2 ... **123** F5
Boundary St *BSLY* S70 .... **22** C2
Boundary Wk *RHAM* S60 .... **113** E4
Bourne Cl *STV/CWN* S43 .... **185** F1
Bourne Rd *BSLY* S70 .... **21** E3
 SHEFN S5 .... **99** D5
Bowbridge Cl *RHAM* S60 .... **103** D5 🄰
Bowden Gv *DOD/DAR* S75 .... **20** A3
Bowden Wood Av *DARN/MH* S9 . **125** D5 🄰
Bowden Wood Cl *DARN/MH* S9 . **125** D5 🄰
Bowden Wood Crs *DARN/MH* S9 **125** D5
Bowden Wood Dr *DARN/MH* S9 . **125** D5
Bowden Wood Pl *DARN/MH* S9 . **125** D5 🄰
Bowden Wood Rd *DARN/MH* S9 . **125** D5
Bowdon St *SHEF* S1 .... **122** A5
Bowen Rd *RHAM/THRY* S65 .... **7** H2
Bower Cl *KIMB* S61 .... **91** F5
Bower La *CHPT/GREN* S35 .... **86** C5
Bower Rd *FUL* S10 .... **121** E3
 MEX/SWTN S64 .... **57** E4
Bower Spring *OWL* S3 .... **9** F3
Bower St *OWL* S3 .... **9** E3
Bowes Rd *ARMTH* DN3 .... **19** F5
Bowfield Vw *BSLYN/ROY* S71 ..... **14** B3
Bowfield Rd *SHEFN* S5 .... **99** D5
Bowland Crs *BSLY* S70 .... **36** A1
Bowland Dr *CHPT/GREN* S35 ..... **87** F1
 CHSW S40 .... **183** E5
Bowlease Gdns *DONS/BSCR* DN4 . **46** C4
Bowling Green St *OWL* S3 .... **8** D3
Bowman Cl *HACK/IN* S12 .... **149** D5
Bowman Dr *HACK/IN* S12 .... **149** D3
Bowness Cl *CHNE* S41 .... **183** E2
 DRON S18 .... **168** C2
Bowness Dr *CHNE* S41 .... **183** E2
Bowness Rd *CHNE* S41 .... **183** E2
 ST/HB/BR S6 .... **108** A5
Bowood Rd *ECC* S11 .... **134** B2
Bowshaw Av *SHEFS* S8 .... **159** E3
Bowshaw Cl *SHEFS* S8 .... **159** E3
Bowshaw Vw *SHEFS* S8 .... **159** E3
Boyce St *ST/HB/BR* S6 .... **108** C3
Boyd Rd *DEARNE* S63 .... **56** A5
Boyland St *OWL* S3 .... **122** A1

Boynton Crs *SHEFN* S5 .... 109 E2
Boynton Rd *SHEFN* S5 .... 109 D3
Boythorpe Av *CHSW* S40 .... 189 F2
Boythorpe Crs *CHSW* S40 .... 190 A3
Boythorpe Mt *CHSW* S40 .... 190 A2 ⑤
Boythorpe Ri *CHSW* S40 .... 189 F2
Boythorpe Rd *CHSW* S40 .... 190 A2
Brackenbury Cl *BTLY* DN5 .... 61 E2 ⑤
Bracken Ct *MALT* S66 .... 117 F1
Brackendale Cl *STV/CWN* S43 ..... 185 E2
Brackenfield Gv *HACK/IN* S12 ..... 150 B1
Bracken Hl *CHPT/GREN* S35 .... 87 E2
Bracken Moor La *STKB/PEN* S36 ... 69 D3
Bracken Rd *SHEFN* S5 .... 99 F5
    SHEFN S5 .... 110 E3
Brackley St *OWL* S3 .... 122 C1
Bradberry Balk La *WMB/DAR* S73 .. 39 D1
Bradbourne Cl *STV/CWN* S43 ...... 187 D1
Bradbury's Cl *RAW* S62 .... 94 A3 ⑤
Bradbury St *S70* 2 A6
    SHEFS S70 .... 135 E4 ⑤
Bradfield Rd *ST/HB/BR* S6 .... 108 A4
Bradgate Cl *KIMB* S61 .... 102 B2
Bradgate Ct *KIMB* S61 .... 102 A2
Bradgate La *KIMB* S61 .... 102 A2
Bradgate Pl *KIMB* S61 .... 102 B1
Bradgate Rd *KIMB* S61 .... 102 B2
Bradlea Ri *RAW* S62 .... 80 B4
Bradley Av *WMB/DAR* S73 .... 39 D2 ⑤
Bradley St *FUL* S10 .... 120 C2
Bradley Wy *STV/CWN* S43 .... 185 F2
Bradmarsh Wy *RHAM* S60 .... 103 D5
Bradshaw Av *RHAM* S60 .... 128 A3
Bradshaw Cl *DOD/DAR* S75 ...... 12 B5 ⑤
Bradshaw Rd *STV/CWN* S43 .... 186 C3
Bradshaw Wy *RHAM* S60 .... 128 A4 ⑤
Bradway Cl *TOT/DORE* S17 .... 157 F3
Bradway Dr *TOT/DORE* S17 .... 157 F3
Bradway Grange Rd
    TOT/DORE S17 .... 158 A3 ⑤
Bradway Rd *TOT/DORE* S17 .... 157 F3
Bradwell Av *DOD/DAR* S75 .... 20 B5
Bradwell Cl *DRON* S18 .... 168 A2
Bradwell Pl *STV/CWN* S43 .... 135 F3
Bradwell St *SHEFP/MNR* S2 ...... 135 F3
Braemar Cl *STV/CWN* S43 .... 179 E2
Braemore Rd *ST/HB/BR* S6 .... 107 E3
Brailsford Av *SHEFN* S5 .... 98 E1
Brailsford Rd *SHEFN* S5 .... 98 E1
Braithwell Rd *BTLY* DN5 .... 16 B4
Bramall La *SHEFP/MNR* S2 .... 135 E1
Bramble Cl *MALT* S66 .... 117 F1 ⑤
The Brambles *CHPT/GREN* S35 .... 98 B1
Bramble Wy *DEARNE* S63 .... 54 C2
Brambling Ct *CHNE* S41 .... 191 D2 ⑤
The Bramblings *DONS/BSCR* DN4 .. 67 E2
Brameld Rd *MEX/SWTN* S64 .... 56 C5
    RAW S62 .... 94 A1
Bramham Ct *DARN/MH* S9 .... 124 C2 ⑤
Bramham Rd *DARN/MH* S9 .... 124 C2 ⑤
    DONS/BSCR DN4 .... 47 D3
Bramley Av *AU/AST/KP* S26 ...... 142 C5 ⑤
    HAN/WDH S13 .... 139 D3
Bramley Cl *MOS* S20 .... 164 A2
Bramley Dr *HAN/WDH* S13 .... 139 D3
Bramley Hall Rd *HAN/WDH* S13 .. 139 D2
Bramley La *HAN/WDH* S13 .... 139 D1
Bramleymoor La *ECK/KIL* S21 .... 172 C2
Bramley Park Cl *HAN/WDH* S13 ... 139 D2
Bramley Park Rd *HAN/WDH* S13 .. 139 D1
Bramley Rd *ECK/KIL* S21 .... 172 C2
Brampton Cl *ARMTH* DN3 .... 33 E5
Brampton Ct *MOS* S20 .... 151 E3 ⑤
Brampton Crs *WMB/DAR* S73 ...... 40 A4
Brampton La *ARMTH* DN3 .... 33 E4
Brampton Rd *DEARNE* S63 .... 54 C1
    WMB/DAR S73 .... 40 A4
Brampton St *WMB/DAR* S73 .... 40 A5
Brampton Vw *WMB/DAR* S73 .... 40 A4 ⑤
Bramshill Cl *MOS* S20 .... 153 E4 ⑤
Bramshill Ct *MOS* S20 .... 153 E4 ⑤
Bramshill Ri *CHSW* S40 .... 189 D3
Bramwell Cl *OWL* S3 .... 8 A4
    RHAM/THRY S65 .... 7 F3
Bramwith Rd *ECC* S11 .... 133 D2 ⑤
Bramworth Rd *DONS/BSCR* DN4 .... 63 F3
Brandeth Rd *ST/HB/BR* S6 .... 121 F2 ⑤
Brandon St *OWL* S3 .... 109 F5 ⑤
Brandreth Rd *ST/HB/BR* S6 .... 121 E2 ⑤
Branton Cl *CHSW* S40 .... 190 A3
Brantwood Crs *DONS/BSCR* DN4 ... 47 D3
Brathay Cl *ATT* S4 .... 111 D3
Brathay Rd *ATT* S4 .... 111 D3 ⑤
Bray St *CHNE* S41 .... 179 E3 ⑤
Brearley Av *CHNE* S41 .... 179 D5
    STKB/PEN S36 .... 69 E3
Brearley St *CHNE* S41 .... 179 D5
Breckland Rd *CHSW* S40 .... 188 C4
Brecklands *RHAM/THRY* S65 ...... 105 D5
Breck La *ECK/KIL* S21 .... 174 A3
Brecks Crs *RHAM/THRY* S65 ...... 105 F4

Brecks La *RHAM/THRY* S65 .... 105 E2
Brecon Cl *CHSW* S40 .... 183 D4
    MOS S20 .... 153 E3
Brendon Av *CHSW* S40 .... 183 D5 ⑤
Brendon Cl *WMB/DAR* S73 .... 40 A4
Brent Cl *CHSW* S40 .... 183 D4
Brentwood Av *ECC* S11 .... 134 B4 ⑤
Brentwood Cl *HOY* S74 .... 51 D3 ⑤
Brentwood Rd *ECC* S11 .... 134 B4
Bressingham Cl *ATT* S4 .... 123 D1 ⑤
Bressingham Rd *ATT* S4 .... 122 C1
Bretby Cl *DONS/BSCR* DN4 .... 47 D5
Bretby Rd *CHSW* S40 .... 182 B5 ⑤
Brett Cl *RAW* S62 .... 79 D3
Bretton Cl *CHSW* S40 .... 182 B4 ⑤
Bretton Gv *HACK/IN* S12 .... 150 B2 ⑤
Brewery Cl *DEARNE* S63 .... 55 F1
Brewery St *CHNE* S41 .... 11 F5
Breydon Av *BTLY* DN5 .... 28 C4
Briar Cft *MALT* S66 .... 117 E1
Briar Ct *RCH* S42 .... 182 A4 ⑤
Briarfield Av *HACK/IN* S12 .... 149 E2
Briarfield Crs *HACK/IN* S12 .... 149 E3
Briar Ri *BSLY* S70 .... 36 B1
Briar Rd *ABRD* S7 .... 134 C4
    ARMTH DN3 .... 33 E2
Briars Cl *ECK/KIL* S21 .... 166 B3
Briar Vw *STV/CWN* S43 .... 185 F2
Briary Av *CHPT/GREN* S35 .... 73 E4
Briary Cl *RHAM* S60 .... 114 A5
Brickhouse La *TOT/DORE* S17 ..... 144 A5
Brickhouse Yd *CHNE* S41 .... 10 A6
Brick St *FUL* S10 .... 120 C3
Bridby St *HAN/WDH* S13 .... 140 A4
Bridge Bank Cl *CHSW* S40 .... 183 E3 ⑤
Bridge Gv *BTLY* DN5 .... 29 D4
Bridge Inn Rd *CHPT/GREN* S35 .... 74 B5
Bridgegate *RHAM* S60 .... 6 D4
Bridgehalgh La *DONS/BSCR* DN4 .. 4 B5
Bridge Rd *DONS/BSCR* DN4 .... 46 A4
Bridge St *BSLY* S70 .... 23 F2 ⑤
    BSLYN/ROY S71 .... 2 D2
    CHSW S40 .... 190 B3 ⑤
    DONS/BSCR DN4 .... 4 B5
    ECK/KIL S21 .... 166 B1
    MEX/SWTN S64 .... 57 F5
    OWL S3 .... 9 E2
    RHAM S60 .... 6 D4
Bridle Cl *CHPT/GREN* S35 .... 74 B5
Bridle Crs *CHPT/GREN* S35 .... 74 B5
Bridle Stile *MOS* S20 .... 164 A1
Bridle Stile Gdns *MOS* S20 ...... 163 F1
The Bridleway *RAW* S62 .... 81 D4
Bridport Rd *DARN/MH* S9 .... 124 C2
Brier Cl *MOS* S20 .... 152 B4
Brierfield Cl *DOD/DAR* S75 .... 13 D5
Brierfield Rd *HACK/IN* S12 .... 149 E2
Brierley Cl *STV/CWN* S43 .... 181 F5
Brierley Rd *DEARNE* S63 .... 46 B5
    DRON S18 .... 170 C5
Brierly Rd *RHAM/THRY* S65 .... 95 F5
Brier St *ST/HB/BR* S6 .... 108 A4 ⑤
Bright Meadow *MOS* S20 .... 165 E3
Brightmore Dr *OWL* S3 .... 8 A5
Brighton Terrace Rd *FUL* S10 .... 121 D3
Brightside La *DARN/MH* S9 ...... 123 F1
Brightside Wy *ATT* S4 .... 111 D4
Brimington Rd *CHNE* S41 .... 11 H4
Brimington Rd North *CHNE* S41 .. 184 B1
Brimmesfield Dr
    pjSHEFP/MNR S2 .... 136 C2 ⑤
Brimmesfield Rd *SHEFP/MNR* S2 . 136 C3
Brimmsfield Cl *SHEFP/MNR* S2 ... 137 D3
Brinckman St *BSLY* S70 .... 188 C3
Brincliffe Crs *ECC* S11 .... 134 A3
Brincliffe Edge Cl *ECC* S11 .... 134 A4
Brincliffe Edge Rd *ECC* S11 ...... 133 F4
Brincliffe Gdns *ECC* S11 .... 134 A3
Brincliffe Hl *ECC* S11 .... 133 F3
Brindley Ct *ECK/KIL* S21 .... 166 A2 ⑤
Brindley Crs *SHEFS* S8 .... 147 E1
Brindley Rd *CHNE* S41 .... 184 B3 ⑤
Brinkburn Ct *TOT/DORE* S17 ..... 157 D2 ⑤
Brinkburn Dr *TOT/DORE* S17 ..... 157 D2
Brinkburn Vale Rd *TOT/DORE* S17 . 157 D2
Brinsford Rd *RHAM* S60 .... 114 A3
Brinsworth Hall Av *RHAM* S60 .. 113 F4
Brinsworth Hall Crs *RHAM* S60 .. 113 F4
Brinsworth Hall Dr *RHAM* S60 .. 113 F5
Brinsworth Hall Gv *RHAM* S60 .. 113 F4
Brinsworth La *RHAM* S60 .... 113 F4
Brinsworth Rd *RHAM* S60 .... 113 E4
    RHAM S60 .... 113 F5
Brinsworth St *DARN/MH* S9 ...... 124 A1
    RHAM S60 .... 127 D1
Bristol Av *WHHL* DN2 .... 31 E3
Bristol Gv *ECC* S11 .... 134 A1
Britain St *MEX/SWTN* S64 .... 58 A4 ⑤
Britannia Cl *BSLY* S70 .... 22 A2
Britannia Rd *CHSW* S40 .... 190 C5

Britland Cl *DOD/DAR* S75 .... 12 B5 ⑤
Britnall St *DARN/MH* S9 .... 124 B1
Briton Sq *DEARNE* S63 .... 27 E2
Briton St *DEARNE* S63 .... 27 E2
Brittain St *SHEF* S1 .... 122 C5 ⑤
Broachgate *BTLY* DN5 .... 28 C1
Broadcarr Rd *HOY* S74 .... 75 E1
Broadcroft Cl *MOS* S20 .... 153 E2
Broad Elms Cl *ECC* S11 .... 145 D1 ⑤
Broad Elms La *ECC* S11 .... 144 C2
Broadfield Rd *SHEFS* S8 .... 135 D4
Broadgate House Cl *KIMB* S61 .. 102 B2 ⑤
Broadgorse Cl *CHSW* S40 .... 190 A5
Broadhead Rd *STKB/PEN* S36 .... 58 A2
Broad Inge Crs *CHPT/GREN* S35 .. 87 F1
Broadlands Av *MOS* S20 .... 151 E3
Broadlands Cl *MOS* S20 .... 151 F3
Broadlands Cft *MOS* S20 .... 151 F3 ⑤
Broadlands Ri *HACK/IN* S12 ..... 151 F3 ⑤
Broad La *SHEF* S1 .... 8 B5
Broad Lane Ct *SHEF* S1 .... 8 B5 ⑤
Broadley Rd *HAN/WDH* S13 ...... 137 F3
Broad Oaks *DARN/MH* S9 .... 124 A2
Broad Pavement *CHSW* S40 ...... 11 F6
Broad St *HOY* S74 .... 51 E2
    RAW S62 .... 94 A3
    SHEF S1 .... 9 G4
    SHEFP/MNR S2 .... 9 H4
Broad Street La *SHEFP/MNR* S2 ... 9 H4
Broadway *BSLY* S70 .... 20 C2
    MEX/SWTN S64 .... 80 C1
    RHAM S60 .... 113 F5
    RHAM/THRY S65 .... 104 C2
Broadway Av *CHPT/GREN* S35 .... 88 C2
Broadway Cl *MEX/SWTN* S64 ..... 80 C1
Broadway East *RHAM/THRY* S65 . 104 C2
The Broadway *DONS/BSCR* DN4 .. 63 D2
Brocco Bank *ECC* S11 .... 134 A2
Brocco La *OWL* S3 .... 8 C4
Brocco St *OWL* S3 .... 8 C4
Brockfield Cl *BSLY* S70 .... 22 B5 ⑤
Brocklehurst Av *BSLY* S70 .... 23 E4
    SHEFS S8 .... 148 A5
Brocklehurst Piece *CHSW* S40 ... 189 D2 ⑤
Brockwell La *CHSW* S40 .... 183 E4
    RCH S42 .... 182 A2
Brockwell Pl *CHSW* S40 .... 10 A3
Brockwood Cl *HAN/WDH* S13 .... 140 A3 ⑤
Bromcliffe Pk *BSLYN/ROY* S71 .... 15 F2
Bromehead Wy *CHNE* S41 .... 183 E2
Bromley Carr Rd *CHPT/GREN* S35 . 72 C2
Brompton Rd *BTLY* DN5 .... 42 A3
    DARN/MH S9 .... 111 E5
Bromwich Rd *SHEFS* S8 .... 146 C3
Bronte Av *DONS/BSCR* DN4 ...... 63 D1
Bronte Cl *BSLYN/ROY* S71 .... 14 C4
Bronte Gv *MEX/SWTN* S64 .... 58 C2
Bronte Pl *RAW* S62 .... 80 C4
Brookbank Av *CHSW* S40 .... 183 E5
Brook Cl *AU/AST/KP* S26 .... 142 C5
    CHPT/GREN S35 .... 87 D5
Brook Dr *OWL* S3 .... 8 B4
Brooke Dr *DEARNE* S63 .... 55 E2
    STV/CWN S43 .... 186 A4
Brooke St *DON* S1 .... 30 B4
    HOY S74 .... 51 E2
Brook Farm Ms *DEARNE* S63 ... 55 F2 ⑤
Brookfield Av *CHSW* S40 .... 188 B2
    MEX/SWTN S64 .... 81 E1
Brookfield Cl *ARMTH* DN3 .... 33 F4 ⑤
    RHAM/THRY S65 .... 95 E5
Brookfield Rd *SHEFS* S8 .... 135 D5 ⑤
Brook Hl *KIMB* S61 .... 90 A2
    OWL S3 .... 8 A5
Brookhouse Cl *HACK/IN* S12 ..... 151 F2
Brookhouse Dr *HACK/IN* S12 .... 151 F2
Brookhouse Hl *ECC* S11 .... 132 A3
Brookhouse Rd *AU/AST/KP* S26 . 142 B4
Brooklands Av *FUL* S10 .... 131 F3
Brooklands Crs *FUL* S10 .... 132 A3
Brooklands Dr *FUL* S10 .... 131 F3 ⑤
Brook La *CHPT/GREN* S35 .... 97 D1
    HACK/IN S12 .... 151 F2
    OWL S3 .... 8 A5
Brooklyn Dr *CHSW* S40 .... 183 E5
Brooklyn Pl *SHEFS* S8 .... 135 E5 ⑤
Brooklyn Rd *SHEFS* S8 .... 135 E5 ⑤
Brook Rd *CHPT/GREN* S35 .... 73 F5
    CONI DN12 .... 85 F1 ⑤
    RHAM/THRY S65 .... 104 C1
    SHEFS S8 .... 135 D5
Brook Rw *STKB/PEN* S36 .... 69 D3
Brookside *CONI* DN12 .... 85 D2 ⑤
    MEX/SWTN S64 .... 80 C2
    RHAM/THRY S65 .... 105 D4
Brookside Bar *CHSW* S40 .... 188 A2
Brookside Cl *HACK/IN* S12 ...... 151 F2
Brookside Crs *DEARNE* S63 .... 54 C3
Brookside Dr *BSLY* S70 .... 23 E4 ⑤
Brookside Gln *CHSW* S40 .... 188 A2
Brookside La *ST/HB/BR* S6 ...... 118 A1
Brooks Rd *STV/CWN* S43 .... 180 C2
Brook St *RHAM* S60 .... 115 F3 ⑤
Brookvale *BSLYN/ROY* S71 .... 15 E4 ⑤

Brookview Ct *DRON* S18 .... 159 E5
Brook Wy *BTLY* DN5 .... 17 E5
Broom Av *RHAM/THRY* S65 .... 104 C5
Broombank Pk *DRON* S18 .... 177 E3
Broombank Rd *DRON* S18 .... 177 E3
Broom Cl *BSLY* S70 .... 23 E4
  CHNE S41 .... 183 E2 🄳
  DEARNE S63 .... 56 B4
  ECC S11 .... 135 D1
Broom Crs *RHAM/THRY* S65 .... 104 A5
Broomcroft Pk *ECC* S11 .... 145 D2 🄳
Broom Dr *RHAM* S60 .... 115 F1
Broome Av *MEX/SWTN* S64 .... 57 E5
Broomfield Av *CHNE* S41 .... 191 C5
Broomfield Cl *BSLY* S70 .... 20 C2 🄳
Broomfield Ct *STKB/PEN* S36 .... 69 E5 🄳
Broomfield Gv *RHAM/THRY* S65 .. 104 A5
  STKB/PEN S36 .... 69 D3
Broomfield La *STKB/PEN* S36 .... 69 D3
Broomfield Rd *FUL* S10 .... 121 E5
  STKB/PEN S36 .... 69 E2
Broom Gdns *STV/CWN* S43 .... 186 A2
Broom Gn *OWL* S3 .... 122 A5
Broom Gv *RHAM/THRY* S65 .... 104 A4
Broomgrove Crs *FUL* S10 .... 121 E5 🄳
Broomgrove La *FUL* S10 .... 121 E5
Broomgrove Rd *FUL* S10 .... 121 E5
Broomhall Pl *FUL* S10 .... 121 F5
Broomhall St *OWL* S3 .... 134 C1
Broomhead Rd *WMB/DAR* S73 ...... 40 A4
Broom Hill *DONS/BSCR* DN4 .... 47 D5
Broomhill La *DEARNE* S63 .... 41 D2
Broomhill Rd *CHNE* S41 .... 178 A4
Broomhouse La *CONI* DN12 .... 62 A5
  DONS/BSCR DN4 .... 63 D2
Broom La *RHAM/THRY* S65 .... 104 B5
Broom Ter *RHAM/THRY* S65 .... 103 F4
Broom Valley Rd *RHAM* S60 .... 104 A5
  RHAM/THRY S65 .... 103 F4
Broomville St *MEX/SWTN* S64 ...... 57 F5 🄳
Broomwood Cl *MOS* S20 .... 153 E2 🄳
Broomwood Gdns *MOS* S20 .... 153 E2
Brotherton St *OWL* S3 .... 122 C1
Broughton Av *BTLY* DN5 .... 29 E2
Broughton La *DARN/MH* S9 .... 111 F5
Broughton Rd *DONS/BSCR* DN4 .... 66 C1 🄳
  ST/HB/BR S6 .... 108 A3
Brow Cl *BSLY* S70 .... 22 A4
Brow Crs *MOS* S20 .... 164 C1
Brownell St *OWL* S3 .... 8 B3
Brown Hills La *FUL* S10 .... 130 C2
Browning Av *DONS/BSCR* DN4 ...... 63 F1 🄳
Browning Cl *BSLYN/ROY* S71 .... 14 C2 🄳
  ST/HB/BR S6 .... 97 E4
Browning Dr *RHAM/THRY* S65 ... 104 C3 🄳
  MEX/SWTN S64 .... 58 B2
  RHAM/THRY S65 .... 104 C3
  ST/HB/BR S6 .... 97 D4
Brown La *DRON* S18 .... 160 A5
  SHEF S1 .... 122 B5
Brown St *RHAM* S60 .... 102 C2
  SHEF S1 .... 122 B5
The Brow *RHAM/THRY* S65 .... 105 F5
Broxholme La *DON* DN1 .... 5 F2
Broxholme Rd *SHEFS* S8 .... 147 D2 🄳
Bruce Av *BSLY* S70 .... 22 A4
Bruce Crs *WHHL* DN2 .... 31 F4
Bruce Rd *ECC* S11 .... 134 B2 🄳
Brunel Rd *BTLY* DN5 .... 29 D4
Brunswick Cl *BSLYN/ROY* S71 ...... 14 A1
Brunswick Rd *OWL* S3 .... 9 G1
  RHAM S60 .... 104 A5
Brunswick St *CHNE* S41 .... 11 E3
  DEARNE S63 .... 27 E2
Brunt Rd *RAW* S62 .... 80 C5
Bryan Rd *DARN/MH* S9 .... 111 F2 🄳
Bryn Lea *CHNE* S41 .... 191 D2
Bryony Cl *ECK/KIL* S21 .... 165 F2
Bubup Hl *NROS/TKH* DN11 .... 64 A5
Bubwith Rd *DARN/MH* S9 .... 111 F2 🄳
Buchanan Crs *SHEFN* S5 .... 97 F4
Buchanan Dr *SHEFN* S5 .... 97 F4
Buchanan Rd *SHEFN* S5 .... 98 A4
Buckden Cl *CHSW* S40 .... 183 E5
Buckden Rd *BSLY* S70 .... 2 A4
Buckenham St *ATT* S4 .... 123 D1
Buckingham Cl *DRON* S18 .... 168 B1 🄳
Buckingham Rd *CONI* DN12 .... 60 C5
  WHHL DN2 .... 31 D5
Buckingham Wy *RHAM* S60 .... 114 B4 🄳
Buckleigh Rd *DEARNE* S63 .... 55 F2
Buckley Ct *BSLY* S70 .... 22 A2 🄳
Buckthorn Cl *MEX/SWTN* S64 .... 81 D3

Buck Wood Vw *SHEFP/MNR* S2 .... 136 B5
Bude Ct *BSLYN/ROY* S71 .... 15 D4 🄳
Bude Rd *DONS/BSCR* DN4 .... 43 F4
Bullen Rd *ST/HB/BR* S6 .... 97 D4
Bullfinch Cl *RHAM* S60 .... 114 B4
The Bungalows *RHAM* S60 .... 127 F3
Bunker S Hl *ECK/KIL* S21 .... 166 C2
Bunting Cl *CHSW* S40 .... 188 C3
  SHEFS S8 .... 147 F4
Bunting Nook *SHEFS* S8 .... 147 F3
Burbage Cl *DRON* S18 .... 168 B1 🄳
Burbage Gv *HACK/IN* S12 .... 138 B5
Burbage Rd *STV/CWN* S43 .... 187 D2
Burcot Rd *SHEF* S1 .... 135 D5
Burcroft Cl *HOY* S74 .... 50 C5 🄳
Burcroft Hl *CONI* DN12 .... 61 E5
Burden Cl *DON* DN1 .... 4 C6
Burford Av *DONS/BSCR* DN4 .... 62 C2
Burford Crs *AU/AST/KP* S26 .... 142 C3 🄳
Burgen Rd *KIMB* S61 .... 91 F5 🄳
Burgess Cl *CHNE* S41 .... 191 E5
Burgess Rd *DARN/MH* S9 .... 124 A1
Burgess St *SHEF* S1 .... 8 D6
Burgoyne Cl *ST/HB/BR* S6 .... 121 E1
Burgoyne Rd *ST/HB/BR* S6 .... 121 F1
Burkinshaw Av *RAW* S62 .... 80 A3
Burleigh Ct *BSLY* S70 .... 2 D6 🄳
Burley Cl *CHSW* S40 .... 190 B5
Burlington Ar *BSLY* S70 .... 2 D5 🄳
Burlington Ct *ST/HB/BR* S6 .... 121 F2 🄳
Burlington Gln *TOT/DORE* S17 .... 156 C1 🄳
Burlington Gv *TOT/DORE* S17 ..... 156 C1
Burlington Rd *TOT/DORE* S17 ..... 156 C1
Burlington St *CHSW* S40 .... 11 F6
  ST/HB/BR S6 .... 121 F2
Burman Rd *DEARNE* S63 .... 56 A2
Burnaby Ct *ST/HB/BR* S6 .... 108 B5
Burnaby Crs *ST/HB/BR* S6 .... 108 B5
Burnaby Gn *ST/HB/BR* S6 .... 108 B5 🄳
Burnaby St *DON* DN1 .... 4 C5 🄳
  ST/HB/BR S6 .... 108 B5
Burnaston Cl *DRON* S18 .... 168 A2 🄳
Burnbridge Rd *CHNE* S41 .... 179 D3
Burncross Dr *CHPT/GREN* S35 ...... 88 A1
Burncross Rd *CHPT/GREN* S35 ..... 87 F1
Burnell Rd *ST/HB/BR* S6 .... 108 A4
Burnell St *STV/CWN* S43 .... 186 A1
Burngreave Bank *ATT* S4 .... 122 C1
Burngreave Rd *ATT* S4 .... 109 F5
Burn Gv *CHPT/GREN* S35 .... 89 D2
Burnham Av *DONS/BSCR* DN4 .... 45 D3
Burnham Gv *BTLY* DN5 .... 29 D1
Burnsall Crs *RHAM* S60 .... 114 A4
Burnsall Rd *BSLY* S70 .... 23 E4
Burns Cl *CHSW* S40 .... 190 A5
Burns Dr *CHPT/GREN* S35 .... 88 A1
  DRON S18 .... 170 A3
  RHAM/THRY S65 .... 104 C3
Burnside *DEARNE* S63 .... 26 C2
Burnside Av *SHEFS* S8 .... 135 E5
Burns Rd *DONS/BSCR* DN4 .... 63 F1 🄳
  RHAM/THRY S65 .... 104 B3
  ST/HB/BR S6 .... 121 E3
Burns St *BTLY* DN5 .... 16 C5
Burns Wy *DEARNE* S63 .... 55 D1
  DONS/BSCR DN4 .... 43 E4
Burnt Stones Cl *FUL* S10 .... 119 E5
Burnt Stones Dr *FUL* S10 .... 119 E5
Burnt Stones Gv *FUL* S10 .... 119 E5 🄳
Burnt Tree La *OWL* S3 .... 8 B2
Burntwood Cl *DEARNE* S63 .... 26 B4
Burntwood Crs *RHAM* S60 .... 127 F2 🄳
Burrell St *RHAM* S60 .... 6 C6
Burrowlee Rd *ST/HB/BR* S6 .... 108 A3
Burrows Dr *SHEFN* S5 .... 109 F4
Burrows Gv *WMB/DAR* S73 .... 38 C3
Burrs Wood Cft *CHSW* S40 .... 182 C2 🄳
Bursdon Cl *CHNE* S41 .... 178 C5 🄳
Burton Av *BSLYN/ROY* S71 .... 15 E3
  DONS/BSCR DN4 .... 43 F4
Burton Bank Rd *BSLYN/ROY* S71 .... 3 F1
Burton Crs *BSLYN/ROY* S71 .... 15 F2
Burtonlees Ct *DONS/BSCR* DN4 .... 46 C5 🄳
Burton Rd *BSLYN/ROY* S71 .... 15 D4
  OWL S3 .... 8 C1
Burton St *BSLYN/ROY* S71 .... 2 C1
  ST/HB/BR S6 .... 108 B5
Burton Ter *DONS/BSCR* DN4 .... 43 F4 🄳
Burtop Cft *WMB/DAR* S73 .... 53 D1 🄳
Burying La *RAW* S62 .... 51 F5
Bushey Wood Rd *TOT/DORE* S17 156 C2
Bushfield Rd *DEARNE* S63 .... 55 E3
Busk Knoll *SHEFN* S5 .... 109 E2 🄳
Busk Meadow *SHEFN* S5 .... 109 E2
Busk Pk *SHEFN* S5 .... 109 E2
Busley Gdns *BTLY* DN5 .... 29 E1 🄳
Butcher St *DEARNE* S63 .... 26 C3
Butchill Av *SHEFN* S5 .... 98 B1
Bute St *FUL* S10 .... 120 C4
Butler Rd *ST/HB/BR* S6 .... 107 E5
Butler Wy *ECK/KIL* S21 .... 166 A1
Butterbusk *CONI* DN12 .... 85 F1
Butterfield Ct *WMB/DAR* S73 .... 40 B5 🄳
Butterley Dr *BSLY* S70 .... 23 E4 🄳

Butterleys *DOD/DAR* S75 .... 20 B3
Buttermere Cl *CHNE* S41 .... 183 E2
Buttermere Dr *DRON* S18 .... 168 C2 🄳
Buttermere Rd *SHEFS* S8 .... 146 C1
Buttermere Wy *BSLYN/ROY* S71 ... 24 C2 🄳
Butterthwaite Crs *SHEFN* S5 .... 99 F2
Butterthwaite La *CHPT/GREN* S35 .. 99 D1
Butterthwaite Rd *SHEFN* S5 .... 99 D1
Butterton Dr *CHSW* S40 .... 182 B4 🄳
Butt Hole Rd *CONI* DN12 .... 82 C5
Button Hl *ECC* S11 .... 145 F1
Button Rw *STKB/PEN* S36 .... 69 D2 🄳
Butts Hl *TOT/DORE* S17 .... 156 B4
Byland Wy *BSLYN/ROY* S71 .... 15 D5
Byrley Rd *KIMB* S61 .... 91 F5
Byron Av *BTLY* DN5 .... 29 D5
  CHPT/GREN S35 .... 88 A2
  DONS/BSCR DN4 .... 63 E1 🄳
Byron Cl *DRON* S18 .... 170 A4
Byron Crs *DEARNE* S63 .... 55 D1
Byron Dr *BSLYN/ROY* S71 .... 14 C3
  RHAM/THRY S65 .... 104 B3
Byron Rd *ABRD* S7 .... 134 B4
  CHSW S40 .... 190 B4
  MEX/SWTN S64 .... 58 C3
  MOS S20 .... 153 E3 🄳
Byron St *CHSW* S40 .... 190 B3

C

Cadeby Av *CONI* DN12 .... 84 B1
Cadman Ct *MOS* S20 .... 164 B2
Cadman La *SHEF* S1 .... 9 E6
Cadman Rd *HACK/IN* S12 .... 138 A5
Cadman St *ATT* S4 .... 123 D3 🄳
  DEARNE S63 .... 56 B2
  MOS S20 .... 164 A2
Caernarvon Cl *CHSW* S40 .... 189 D3 🄳
Caernarvon Rd *DRON* S18 .... 169 E3
Caine Gdns *KIMB* S61 .... 101 F3
Cairn Dr *STV/CWN* S43 .... 179 E2
Cairngorm Cl *STV/CWN* S43 .... 179 E2
Cairns Rd *FUL* S10 .... 120 A5
  MOS S20 .... 153 D1
Caister Av *CHPT/GREN* S35 .... 74 A5
Caistor Av *BSLY* S70 .... 21 D3
Calcot Park Av *MEX/SWTN* S64 .... 81 E1
Caldbeck Gv *CHPT/GREN* S35 ...... 73 E3 🄳
Calder Crs *BSLY* S70 .... 21 E5
Calder Rd *KIMB* S61 .... 92 A4
Calder Wy *SHEFN* S5 .... 110 A2
Caldey Rd *DRON* S18 .... 169 E3
California Crs *BSLY* S70 .... 22 A3 🄳
California Dr *CHPT/GREN* S35 .... 88 A2
  RHAM S60 .... 127 D2 🄳
California St *BSLY* S70 .... 21 F3
California Ter *BSLY* S70 .... 21 F3 🄳
Calladine Wy *MEX/SWTN* S64 ...... 81 D2
Callow Dr *SHEFP/MNR* S2 .... 136 B5
Callow Mt *SHEFP/MNR* S2 .... 136 A5
Callow Rd *SHEFP/MNR* S2 .... 136 A5 🄳
Callywhite La *DRON* S18 .... 170 A2
Calner Cft *MOS* S20 .... 153 F3
Calow Brook Dr *CHNE* S41 .... 191 F4
Calow La *BSVR* S44 .... 191 F3
  CHNE S41 .... 191 F4
Calver Cl *DOD/DAR* S75 .... 20 B3
Calver Crs *STV/CWN* S43 .... 187 E2
Calvert Rd *DARN/MH* S9 .... 125 D1
Camborne Cl *ST/HB/BR* S6 .... 97 D4 🄳
Camborne Rd *ST/HB/BR* S6 .... 97 D4
Camborne Wy *BSLYN/ROY* S71 .... 15 D4
Cambria Dr *DONS/BSCR* DN4 .... 62 C1 🄳
Cambrian Cl *CHSW* S40 .... 183 E3
Cambridge Crs *RHAM/THRY* S65 104 B2
Cambridge Pl *RHAM/THRY* S65 .. 104 B2
Cambridge Rd *SHEFS* S8 .... 135 F4
  STKB/PEN S36 .... 70 A3
  STV/CWN S43 .... 186 A1 🄳
Cambridge St *MEX/SWTN* S64 ...... 57 F5
  NROS/TKH DN11 .... 66 C5
  RHAM/THRY S65 .... 104 B3
  SHEF S1 .... 8 D6
  SHEF S1 .... 122 B5 🄳
Camdale Ri *HACK/IN* S12 .... 151 D4
Camdale Vw *HACK/IN* S12 .... 151 D4
Camden Pl *DON* DN1 .... 4 D6 🄳
Camellia Cl *CONI* DN12 .... 85 E2 🄳
Camerory Wy *STV/CWN* S43 .... 179 E1
Cammell Rd *SHEFN* S5 .... 110 B2
Camms Cl *ECK/KIL* S21 .... 164 D4 🄳
Camm St *ST/HB/BR* S6 .... 121 D1
Campbell Dr *RHAM/THRY* S65 ... 104 C4
  STV/CWN S43 .... 180 C2
Campbell St *RAW* S62 .... 93 D2
Camping La *SHEFS* S8 .... 146 C2
Campion Dr *ECK/KIL* S21 .... 166 A2 🄳
  MEX/SWTN S64 .... 81 E2
Campo La *SHEF* S1 .... 8 D5
Campsall Dr *FUL* S10 .... 120 B4
Campsall Field Cl *DEARNE* S63 ..... 55 F4
Campsall Field Rd *DEARNE* S63 .... 55 F4
Canada St *ATT* S4 .... 110 B5

BSLY S70 .... 21 F3
Canal Br *ECK/KIL* S21 .... 166 B2
Canal St *ATT* S4 .... 123 E3
    BSLYN/ROY S71 .... 3 E2
Canal Whf *CHNE* S41 .... 11 C3
Canklow Hill Rd *RHAM* S60 ...... 114 B1
Canklow Rd *RHAM* S60 .... 103 E4
Canning St *SHEF* S1 .... 8 C6
Cannock St *ST/HB/BR* S6 .... 108 A4 🖪
Cannon Hall Rd *SHEFN* S5 .... 110 A4
Cannon Wy *DOD/DAR* S75 .... 12 A2
Canons Wy *BSLYN/ROY* S71 ...... 15 D4
Canterbury Av *FUL* S10 .... 132 A2
Canterbury Cl *BTLY* DN5 .... 28 C3 🖪
Canterbury Crs *FUL* S10 .... 132 A2
Canterbury Dr *FUL* S10 .... 132 A2
Canterbury Rd *SHEFS* S8 .... 135 F5
    WHHL DN2 .... 31 D3
Cantilupe Crs *AU/AST/KP* S26 .. 142 D2
Cantley La *DONS/BSCR* DN4 ...... 46 B3
Cantley Riding *WHHL* DN2 .... 32 C4
    DONS/BSCR DN4 .... 47 E4 🖪
Capel Ri *STV/CWN* S43 .... 185 E1 🖪
Capel St *ST/HB/BR* S6 .... 108 B5
Capri Ct *WMB/DAR* S73 .... 25 F4
Capthorne Rd *RCH* S42 .... 182 A4
Caraway Gv *MEX/SWTN* S64 ...... 81 E3
Carbis Cl *BSLYN/ROY* S71 .... 14 C4 🖪
Carbrook Hall Rd *DARN/MH* S9 .. 111 F3
Carbrook St *DARN/MH* S9 .... 111 F3
Cardew Cl *RAW* S62 .... 94 B1
Cardiff St *DARN/MH* S9 .... 111 E4
Cardigan Rd *WHHL* DN2 .... 32 A4
Cardoness Dr *FUL* S10 .... 119 F5
Cardoness Rd *FUL* S10 .... 119 F5
Cardwell Av *HAN/WDH* S13 ...... 139 D5
Cardwell Dr *HAN/WDH* S13 ...... 139 D5
Carey Av *BSLYN/ROY* S71 .... 3 F5
Carfield Av *SHEFS* S8 .... 135 F5
Carfield La *SHEFS* S8 .... 136 A5
Car Hl *KIMB* S61 .... 93 D4
Carisbrooke Rd *WHHL* DN2 ...... 31 E5 🖪
Carlby Rd *ST/HB/BR* S6 .... 107 E5
Carley Dr *MOS* S20 .... 153 D4
Carlinford Rd *RHAM* S60 .... 104 B5
Carlin St *HAN/WDH* S13 .... 138 C5
Carlisle Cl *CHNE* S41 .... 177 F3
Carlisle Rd *ATT* S4 .... 110 C4
    WHHL DN2 .... 9 H1
Carlisle St *ATT* S4 .... 110 C4
    MEX/SWTN S64 .... 81 E2
    RHAM/THRY S65 .... 7 E4
Carlisle St East *ATT* S4 .... 123 E1
Carlthorpe Gv *CHPT/GREN* S35 .. 73 D4
Carlton Av *RHAM/THRY* S65 .... 104 A5
Carlton Cl *MOS* S20 .... 164 A2
Carlton Rd *BSLYN/ROY* S71 ...... 14 C1
    RAW S62 .... 94 A2
    ST/HB/BR S6 .... 107 F2
    WHHL DN2 .... 30 C4 🖪
Carlton St *BSLYN/ROY* S71 .... 13 F5
Carlyle St *MEX/SWTN* S64 .... 58 B3
Carlyon Gdns *CHSW* S40 .... 190 A4 🖪
Carnaby Rd *ST/HB/BR* S6 .... 108 A5
Carnarvon St *ST/HB/BR* S6 ...... 121 F2 🖪
Carnforth Rd *BSLYN/ROY* S71 .. 15 E2
Carnley St *DEARNE* S63 .... 54 C2
Carnoustie Av *CHSW* S40 .... 189 D4
Carnoustie Cl *MEX/SWTN* S64 .. 81 F1
Carolina Wy *DONS/BSCR* DN4 .. 45 D3
Carpenter Cl *HACK/IN* S12 ...... 138 A4 🖪
Carpenter Gdns *HACK/IN* S12 .. 138 A4 🖪
Carr Bank Cl *ECC* S11 .... 133 D2
Carr Bank Dr *ECC* S11 .... 133 D2 🖪
Carr Bank La *ECC* S11 .... 132 C2
Carr Cl *RHAM* S60 .... 113 E4
Carrcroft Ct *STKB/PEN* S36 ...... 70 A3 🖪
Carrfield Dr *SHEFS* S8 .... 135 F4
Carrfield La *SHEFP/MNR* S2 .... 135 F4
Carrfield Rd *SHEFS* S8 .... 135 F4
Carrfield St *SHEFP/MNR* S2 .... 135 F4
Carr Forge Cl *HACK/IN* S12 ...... 151 E1
Carr Forge La *HACK/IN* S12 .... 151 E1
Carr Forge Mt *HACK/IN* S12 .... 151 E1
Carr Forge Pl *HACK/IN* S12 ...... 151 E1
Carr Forge Rd *HACK/IN* S12 .... 151 E1
Carr Forge Ter *HACK/IN* S12 .... 151 E1
Carr Forge Vw *HACK/IN* S12 .... 151 F1
Carr Gv *STKB/PEN* S36 .... 69 F3
Carr Head Rd *CHPT/GREN* S35 .. 72 C2
Carr Hl *DONS/BSCR* DN4 .... 43 F4
Carr House Rd *DON* DN1 .... 44 A3
    DONS/BSCR DN4 .... 5 H6
Carriage Dr *DONS/BSCR* DN4 .. 45 D4
Carrill Dr *ST/HB/BR* S6 .... 97 D3
Carrill Rd *ST/HB/BR* S6 .... 97 D3
Carrington Av *DOD/DAR* S75 .... 13 F3
Carrington Rd *ECC* S11 .... 133 F2
Carrington St *DOD/DAR* S75 ...... 2 A2
    RHAM/THRY S65 .... 104 A3 🖪
Carr La *CHPT/GREN* S35 .... 49 D4
    CONI DN12 .... 85 F3
    DOD/DAR S75 .... 49 D3
    DON DN1 .... 44 B3

DONS/BSCR DN4 .... 66 C2
DRON S18 .... 168 A1
RHAM/THRY S65 .... 82 B5
Carr Rd *DEARNE* S63 .... 56 B2
    ST/HB/BR S6 .... 121 D1
    STKB/PEN S36 .... 69 E4
Carr St *BSLYN/ROY* S71 .... 15 E2
Carr View Av *DONS/BSCR* DN4 .. 43 F4
Carr View Rd *KIMB* S61 .... 101 E1
Carrville Dr *ST/HB/BR* S6 .... 97 E5
Carrville Rd *ST/HB/BR* S6 .... 97 E5
Carrville Rd West *ST/HB/BR* S6 .. 97 D5 🖪
Carrwell La *ST/HB/BR* S6 .... 108 A1
Carrwood Rd *BSLY* S70 .... 23 F1
    DRON S18 .... 176 C3
    ECK/KIL S21 .... 175 F3
Carsick Gv *FUL* S10 .... 132 C1
Carsick Hill Crs *FUL* S10 .... 132 B1
Carsick Hill Cr *FUL* S10 .... 132 C1
Carsick Hill Rd *FUL* S10 .... 132 B1
Carsick Hill Wy *FUL* S10 .... 132 B1 🖪
Carsick View Rd *FUL* S10 .... 132 B1
Carsington Cl *CHSW* S40 .... 182 C4
Carson Mt *HACK/IN* S12 .... 149 F2
Carson Rd *FUL* S10 .... 120 C4
Carter Hall La *HACK/IN* S12 .... 149 F3
Carterhall Rd *HACK/IN* S12 .... 149 F3
Carter Knowle Av *ECC* S11 ...... 133 F5
Carter Knowle Rd *ECC* S11 ...... 133 F5
Carter Lodge Av *HACK/IN* S12 .. 151 E1
Carter Lodge Dr *HACK/IN* S12 .. 151 F1
Carter Lodge Pl *HACK/IN* S12 .. 151 F1
Carter Lodge Ri *HACK/IN* S12 .. 151 F1
Carter Lodge Wy *HACK/IN* S12 . 151 F1
Carter Pl *SHEFS* S8 .... 135 F4
Carter Rd *SHEFS* S8 .... 135 E4
Cartmel Cl *DRON* S18 .... 168 C2 🖪
Cartmel Crs *CHNE* S41 .... 183 E1
Cartmel Crs *SHEFS* S8 .... 146 C2
Cartmel Rd *SHEFS* S8 .... 146 C1
Car Vale Dr *SHEFP/MNR* S2 .... 138 A2
Car Vale Vw *SHEFP/MNR* S2 .... 138 A2
Carver La *SHEF* S1 .... 8 D5
Carver St *SHEF* S1 .... 8 D6
Carwood Cl *ATT* S4 .... 110 B5
Carwood Gv *ATT* S4 .... 110 B5 🖪
Carwood Rd *ATT* S4 .... 110 B5
Cary Rd *ECK/KIL* S21 .... 163 F5
    SHEFP/MNR S2 .... 137 D2
Castell Crs *DONS/BSCR* DN4 .... 46 C5
Castle Av *CONI* DN12 .... 85 D1
    RHAM S60 .... 114 B1
Castlebeck Av *SHEFP/MNR* S2 .. 137 F1
Castlebeck Cft *SHEFP/MNR* S2 . 138 A1 🖪
Castlebeck Dr *SHEFP/MNR* S2 .. 138 A1
Castle Cl *BSLYN/ROY* S71 .... 14 C4
    BTLY DN5 .... 42 C2
Castle Crs *CONI* DN12 .... 61 D5
Castledale Cft *SHEFP/MNR* S2 .. 137 F2 🖪
Castledale Gv *SHEFP/MNR* S2 .. 137 F2
Castledale Pl *SHEFP/MNR* S2 .. 137 F2 🖪
Castledine Ct *DONS/BSCR* DN4 .. 63 F3
Castledine Cft *DARN/MH* S9 .... 111 F2
Castledine Gdns *DARN/MH* S9 .. 111 E2
Castlegate *OWL* S3 .... 9 F4
Castle Gn *SHEF* S1 .... 9 F4
Castle Hl *CONI* DN12 .... 85 D1
    ECK/KIL S21 .... 164 B4
Castle Hill Av *MEX/SWTN* S64 .. 59 D4
Castle Hill Cl *ECK/KIL* S21 ...... 164 B4
Castle Ms *BTLY* DN5 .... 16 A5
Castlereagh St *BSLY* S70 .... 2 B6
Castlerigg Wy *DRON* S18 .... 168 C2 🖪
Castlerow Cl *TOT/DORE* S17 .... 157 F2
Castlerow Dr *TOT/DORE* S17 .... 157 F2
Castle St *BSLY* S70 .... 21 F2
    CONI DN12 .... 85 D1
    SHEF S1 .... 9 F4
Castle Ter *CONI* DN12 .... 85 D1
Castleton Gv *STV/CWN* S43 .... 186 C4
Castle Vw *BSLY* S70 .... 35 F5
    ECK/KIL S21 .... 164 B5
Castlewood Crs *FUL* S10 .... 131 F2 🖪
Castlewood Dr *FUL* S10 .... 131 F2
Castle Yd *CHSW* S40 .... 190 B2 🖪
Castor Rd *DARN/MH* S9 .... 111 D3 🖪
Catania Ri *WMB/DAR* S73 .... 25 F4
Catchford Vw *WMB/DAR* S73 .. 182 C2 🖪
Catcliffe Rd *DARN/MH* S9 ...... 125 D3 🖪
Catherine Av *AU/AST/KP* S26 .. 142 B3
Catherine Rd *ATT* S4 .... 122 C1
Catherine St *CHSW* S40 .... 10 B6
    DON DN1 .... 5 E5
    MEX/SWTN S64 .... 58 A3 🖪
    OWL S3 .... 122 C1
    RHAM/THRY S65 .... 7 E5
Cathill Rd *WMB/DAR* S73 .... 41 D1
Cat La *SHEFS* S8 .... 136 A5
Catley Rd *DARN/MH* S9 .... 125 D2
Cattal St *DARN/MH* S9 .... 124 B2 🖪
Catterick Cl *CONI* DN12 .... 83 F1
Cauldon Dr *CHSW* S40 .... 182 A4 🖪
Caulk La *BSLY* S70 .... 24 A5
Causeway Gdns *TOT/DORE* S17 .. 144 A5 🖪
Causeway Gld *TOT/DORE* S17 .. 144 A5

Causeway Head Rd
    TOT/DORE S17 .... 144 A5
The Causeway *TOT/DORE* S17 .. 156 B1
Cavendish Av *ST/HB/BR* S6 .... 106 C3
    TOT/DORE S17 .... 156 C1
Cavendish Cl *RHAM/THRY* S65 .. 105 E5
Cavendish Ct *OWL* S3 .... 122 A5 🖪
Cavendish Pl *STV/CWN* S43 .... 180 C3
Cavendish Ri *DRON* S18 .... 169 D3
Cavendish Rd *BTLY* DN5 .... 16 B2
    DOD/DAR S75 .... 2 A1
    ECC S11 .... 134 A3
    KIMB S61 .... 102 B3
Cavendish St *CHSW* S40 .... 11 F6
    OWL S3 .... 8 B6
    STV/CWN S43 .... 187 D1
Cavendish St North *CHNE* S41 .. 178 B4 🖪
Cave St *DARN/MH* S9 .... 124 A2
Cavill Rd *SHEFS* S8 .... 147 E2
Cawdor Rd *SHEFP/MNR* S2 .... 137 E4
Cawdor St *BTLY* DN5 .... 16 C5 🖪
Cawdron Ri *RHAM* S60 .... 114 A4
Cawley Pl *BSLYN/ROY* S71 .... 14 B3
Cawston Rd *ATT* S4 .... 110 A4 🖪
Cawthorne Cl *RHAM/THRY* S65 .. 105 D2
    SHEFS S8 .... 146 C2
Cawthorne Gv *SHEFS* S8 .... 146 C2
Cawthorne Rd *RHAM/THRY* S65. 105 D2
Caxton Cl *CHNE* S41 .... 179 E3
Caxton La *ECC* S11 .... 120 C5
Caxton Rd *ECC* S11 .... 121 D5 🖪
Caxton St *BSLY* S70 .... 2 C5
Cecil Av *DONS/BSCR* DN4 .... 62 A2
    DRON S18 .... 169 E1
Cecil Rd *DRON* S18 .... 159 E5
    DRON S18 .... 169 E1
Cecil Sq *SHEFP/MNR* S2 .... 135 D2
Cedar Av *CHSW* S40 .... 183 E4
    MEX/SWTN S64 .... 58 A2
Cedar Cl *DONS/BSCR* DN4 .... 62 C2
    ECK/KIL S21 .... 166 A3
    ECK/KIL S21 .... 173 F1
    STKB/PEN S36 .... 68 C3
Cedar Crs *BSLY* S70 .... 22 C3
Cedar Gv *CONI* DN12 .... 84 B3
Cedar Rd *DONS/BSCR* DN4 ...... 62 C1
    STKB/PEN S36 .... 68 C3
Cedar St *STV/CWN* S43 .... 180 B5
Cedar Wy *CHPT/GREN* S35 ...... 88 A2 🖪
Cedric Av *CONI* DN12 .... 84 B2
Celandine Ct *TOT/DORE* S17 .. 157 E5 🖪
Celandine Gdns *TOT/DORE* S17 . 157 E3
Celandine Gv *WMB/DAR* S73 .... 40 B1
Celandine Ri *MEX/SWTN* S64 .... 81 E3
Cemetery Av *ECC* S11 .... 134 B1 🖪
Cemetery La *STV/CWN* S43 .... 181 F5
Cemetery Rd *BSLY* S70 .... 22 A2
    CHNE S41 .... 191 D2
    DEARNE S63 .... 55 F3
    DRON S18 .... 169 F3
    ECC S11 .... 134 C2
    HOY S74 .... 52 B1
    MEX/SWTN S64 .... 58 B3
    WMB/DAR S73 .... 39 E2
Cemetery Ter *STV/CWN* S43 .... 185 F2
Centenary Wy *RHAM* S60 .... 6 B4
    RHAM S60 .... 114 A1 🖪
Central Av *BTLY* DN5 .... 29 F1
    CHSW S40 .... 189 F2
    MEX/SWTN S64 .... 80 C1
    RHAM/THRY S65 .... 104 C2
Central Bvd *WHHL* DN2 .... 31 F3
Central Cl *DRON* S18 .... 170 C5
Central Dr *CHNE* S41 .... 191 D3 🖪
    RAW S62 .... 79 D3
Central Rd *RHAM* S60 .... 6 C5
Central St *CHNE* S41 .... 191 D3 🖪
    DEARNE S63 .... 27 E5
Central Wk *STV/CWN* S43 ...... 185 E2
Centurion Wy *BTLY* DN5 .... 29 F4
Century Ct *CONI* DN12 .... 62 A4 🖪
Century Gdns *BTLY* DN5 .... 17 D5
Century St *DARN/MH* S9 .... 124 C1
Century Vw *RHAM* S60 .... 113 E4
Chadbourne Cl *ARMTH* DN3 .... 33 E4
Chaddesden Cl *DRON* S18 ...... 168 A2 🖪
Chadwick Gdns *BTLY* DN5 .... 17 F4
Chadwick Rd *BTLY* DN5 .... 29 F4
    HAN/WDH S13 .... 138 A3
Chaff Cl *RHAM* S60 .... 115 F3
Chaffinch Av *RHAM* S60 .... 114 B4 🖪
Chaff La *RHAM* S60 .... 115 F3
Challands Cl *CHNE* S41 .... 191 D4 🖪
Challands Wy *CHNE* S41 .... 191 D4 🖪
Challenger Crs *DEARNE* S63 ...... 26 C2
Challenger Dr *BTLY* DN5 .... 42 C1
Challoner Gn *MOS* S20 .... 152 C5 🖪
Challoner Wy *MOS* S20 .... 152 C5
Chalmers Dr *MOS* S20 .... 19 E5
Chamberlain Av *BTLY* DN5 .... 29 D3
Chamberlain Ct *CHPT/GREN* S35 . 74 A5 🖪
Chambers Av *CONI* DN12 .... 84 B1
Chambers La *ATT* S4 .... 110 C3
Chambers Rd *HOY* S74 .... 51 E1 🖪

Church St South *CHSW* S40 .... **190** B5
Church St West *CHSW* S40 .... **189** D2 🗓
Church Vw *AU/AST/KP* S26 .... **142** C5
  CHSW S40 .... **189** D2 🗓
  DOD/DAR S75 .... **13** D4
  DON DN1 .... **4** D2
  ECK/KIL S21 .... **166** C1
  HAN/WDH S13 .... **140** A4
  HOY S74 .... **50** C3
Church Wk *CONI* DN12 .... **60** B4
Church Wy *CHNE* S41 .... **11** F6
  DON DN1 .... **30** C4
Churston Rd *CHSW* S40 .... **189** E1
Cinder Bridge Rd *RAW* S62 .... **93** D2
Cinder Hill La *CHPT/GREN* S35 .... **97** E1
Cinderhill La *SHEFS* S8 .... **148** A5
Cinderhill Rd *KIMB* S61 .... **91** F4
Cinder Hills Wy *DOD/DAR* S75 .... **20** B3 🗓
Cinder La *ECK/KIL* S21 .... **167** D1
Circle *SHEFP/MNR* S2 .... **137** F2
The Circle *SHEFP/MNR* S2 .... **137** F1
Circular Dr *ECK/KIL* S21 .... **175** F3
Circular Rd *CHNE* S41 .... **190** C4
  STV/CWN S43 .... **187** D1
City Rd *SHEFP/MNR* S2 .... **125** E5
Claire Ct *RHAM* S60 .... **6** D5
Clanricarde St *BSLYN/ROY* S71 .... **2** C1
Clara Pl *KIMB* S61 .... **102** A3
Clarell Gdns *DONS/BSCR* DN4 .... **46** C3
Claremont Crs *FUL* S10 .... **121** E4 🗓
Claremont Pl *FUL* S10 .... **121** E4
Claremont St *KIMB* S61 .... **102** A3
Clarence Av *DONS/BSCR* DN4 .... **43** F4
Clarence La *SHEFP/MNR* S2 .... **135** D2
Clarence Rd *BSLYN/ROY* S71 .... **14** C3
  CHSW S40 .... **10** D6
  ST/HB/BR S6 .... **107** F4
Clarence St *CHSW* S40 .... **10** C6
  DEARNE S63 .... **55** E1 🗓
Clarendon Rd *ECC* S11 .... **132** C3
  RHAM/THRY S65 .... **7** C3
  STV/CWN S43 .... **187** D2
Clarendon St *BSLY* S70 .... **2** A6
Clark Av *DONS/BSCR* DN4 .... **5** H6
Clarke Dell *FUL* S10 .... **134** B1
Clarke Dr *FUL* S10 .... **134** B1
Clarkegrove Rd *FUL* S10 .... **121** E5
Clarkehouse Rd *FUL* S10 .... **134** A1
Clarke Sq *SHEFP/MNR* S2 .... **135** D2
Clarke St *DEARNE* S63 .... **27** E5 🗓
  DOD/DAR S75 .... **2** A1
  FUL S10 .... **121** F5
Clark Gv *ST/HB/BR* S6 .... **119** E1
Clarkson St *BSLY* S70 .... **23** D5
  FUL S10 .... **121** F4
Clark St *HOY* S74 .... **51** E1
Claycliffe Av *DOD/DAR* S75 .... **12** A3
Claycliffe La *DOD/DAR* S75 .... **12** A2
Clayfield La *MEX/SWTN* S64 .... **59** E3
Clayfield Rd *MEX/SWTN* S64 .... **59** E3
Clayfields *DONS/BSCR* DN4 .... **63** E2
Clayfield Vw *MEX/SWTN* S64 .... **59** E3
Clay La *WHHL* DN2 .... **122** B5 🗓
  WHHL DN2 .... **19** E4
  WHHL DN2 .... **32** B1
Clay La West *WHHL* DN2 .... **19** D5
Clay Pit La *RAW* S62 .... **94** B1
Clayroyd *BSLY* S70 .... **36** B1
Clay St *DARN/MH* S9 .... **111** D5
Clayton Av *DEARNE* S63 .... **26** B2
Clayton Crs *MOS* S20 .... **152** C3
Clayton Dr *DEARNE* S63 .... **26** B3
Clayton Hollow *MOS* S20 .... **152** C3
Clayton La *DEARNE* S63 .... **26** B3
Clay Wheels La *ST/HB/BR* S6 .... **96** C5
Claywood Dr *SHEFP/MNR* S2 .... **123** C5
Claywood Rd *SHEFP/MNR* S2 .... **136** A1 🗓
Clayworth Dr *DONS/BSCR* DN4 .... **45** F5 🗓
Clearwell Cft *BTLY* DN5 .... **29** D4
Cleeve Hill Gdns *MOS* S20 .... **152** B3
Clematis Rd *SHEFS* S8 .... **111** D1
Clement Ms *KIMB* S61 .... **101** F3 🗓
Clementson Rd *FUL* S10 .... **121** D3 🗓
Clement St *DARN/MH* S9 .... **124** C1
  KIMB S61 .... **101** F3
Clevedon Crs *BTLY* DN5 .... **28** A5
Cleveland St *DON* DN1 .... **4** C6
  ST/HB/BR S6 .... **121** F2
Cleveland Wy *CHSW* S40 .... **182** C5
Cliff Av *BSLY* S70 .... **22** C5
Cliff Crs *DONS/BSCR* DN4 .... **62** A1
Cliffe Av *BSLY* S70 .... **22** C5
Cliffe Bank *MEX/SWTN* S64 .... **81** E1
Cliffe Ct *BSLYN/ROY* S71 .... **15** D4
Cliffedale Crs *BSLY* S70 .... **22** C5
Cliffe Farm Dr *ECC* S11 .... **133** E3 🗓
Cliffefield Rd *MEX/SWTN* S64 .... **81** E1
  SHEFS S8 .... **135** D5
Cliffe House Rd *SHEFS* S8 .... **98** C5
Cliffe La *BSLYN/ROY* S71 .... **15** D4 🗓
Cliffe Rd *ST/HB/BR* S6 .... **120** B2
  WMB/DAR S73 .... **40** C5
Clifford Cl *CHSW* S40 .... **188** C2 🗓
Clifford Rd *ECC* S11 .... **134** B3

KIMB S61 .... **91** F5
Cliff Rd *ST/HB/BR* S6 .... **119** E1
  WMB/DAR S73 .... **41** D1
Cliff St *ECC* S11 .... **135** D1
  MEX/SWTN S64 .... **58** B4
Cliff Vw *CONI* DN12 .... **60** A4
Clifton Av *DARN/MH* S9 .... **125** F4
  RHAM/THRY S65 .... **104** B3
Clifton Bank *RHAM/THRY* S65 .... **7** F5
Clifton Crs *DARN/MH* S9 .... **125** E4
  WHHL DN2 .... **31** F3
Clifton Crs North *RHAM/THRY* S65 .... **7** G6
Clifton Crs South *RHAM/THRY* S65 .... **7** G6
Clifton Dr *BTLY* DN5 .... **42** B2
Clifton Gv *RHAM/THRY* S65 .... **7** H5
Clifton Hl *CONI* DN12 .... **85** E2
Clifton La *DARN/MH* S9 .... **125** F5
  RHAM/THRY S65 .... **7** F6
Clifton Mt *RHAM/THRY* S65 .... **7** F6
Clifton St *BSLY* S70 .... **22** B2 🗓
  CHSW S40 .... **10** A6
  DARN/MH S9 .... **111** F4
Clifton Ter *RHAM/THRY* S65 .... **7** F6
Clinton Pl *FUL* S10 .... **134** C1
Clipstone Gdns *DARN/MH* S9 .... **125** D1
Clipstone Rd *DARN/MH* S9 .... **125** D1
The Cloisters *DONS/BSCR* DN4 .... **47** E5
Cloisters Wy *BSLYN/ROY* S71 .... **15** E5
Cloonmore Cft *SHEFS* S8 .... **147** F4
Cloonmore Dr *SHEFS* S8 .... **148** A4
Clough Bank *KIMB* S61 .... **102** C2
  SHEFP/MNR S2 .... **135** F2
Clough Flds *FUL* S10 .... **120** A3
Clough Fields Rd *HOY* S74 .... **51** D3
Clough Gn *KIMB* S61 .... **102** C2
Clough La *ECC* S11 .... **131** E5
Clough Rd *HOY* S74 .... **51** E3
  KIMB S61 .... **102** C2
  SHEF S1 .... **135** E1
Clough St *KIMB* S61 .... **102** B2
The Clough *CHNE* S41 .... **191** F3
Clover Gdns *SHEFN* S5 .... **110** C1
Clover Gn *KIMB* S61 .... **91** E4
Club Garden Rd *ECC* S11 .... **135** D2
Club Garden Wk *ECC* S11 .... **135** D1
Club Mill Rd *ST/HB/BR* S6 .... **108** C4
Club St *BSLYN/ROY* S71 .... **15** D3
  ECC S11 .... **135** D2
  HOY S74 .... **50** C3 🗓
Clumber Pl *STV/CWN* S43 .... **187** D5
Clumber Ri *AU/AST/KP* S26 .... **142** C4 🗓
Clumber Rd *DONS/BSCR* DN4 .... **45** D3
  FUL S10 .... **132** C1
Clumber St *DOD/DAR* S75 .... **13** E5
Clun Rd *ATT* S4 .... **123** D1
Clun St *ATT* S4 .... **123** C1
Clyde Rd *SHEFS* S8 .... **135** D4
Clyde St *BSLYN/ROY* S71 .... **3** E6
Coach House Dr *BTLY* DN5 .... **28** B4
Coach House La *BSLY* S70 .... **22** A4 🗓
The Coach Houses *FUL* S10 .... **121** E3 🗓
Coach Rd *KIMB* S61 .... **92** C2
Coalbrook Av *HAN/WDH* S13 .... **140** B2
Coalbrook Gv *HAN/WDH* S13 .... **140** B2
Coalbrook Rd *HAN/WDH* S13 .... **140** B1
Coal Pit La *STKB/PEN* S36 .... **68** C4
Coalpit Rd *CONI* DN12 .... **59** F5
Coates St *SHEFP/MNR* S2 .... **123** D5 🗓
Cobb Ct *MEX/SWTN* S64 .... **81** E2
Cobb Dr *MEX/SWTN* S64 .... **81** D2
Cobcar Av *HOY* S74 .... **52** B2
Cobcar Cl *HOY* S74 .... **52** B2
Cobcar La *HOY* S74 .... **52** B2
Cobcar St *HOY* S74 .... **52** B3
Cobden Av *MEX/SWTN* S64 .... **58** C3
Cobden Pl *FUL* S10 .... **121** D3 🗓
Cobden Rd *CHSW* S40 .... **10** C4
Cobden View Rd *FUL* S10 .... **120** C3
Cobnar Av *SHEFS* S8 .... **147** E5
Cobnar Dr *CHNE* S41 .... **183** E1
  SHEFS S8 .... **147** E5
Cobnar Gdns *SHEFS* S8 .... **147** D3 🗓
Cobnar Rd *SHEFS* S8 .... **147** D3
Cockayne Pl *SHEFS* S8 .... **147** D1
Cockerham Av *DOD/DAR* S75 .... **2** B2
Cockerham La *DOD/DAR* S75 .... **2** B1
Cockshot La *STKB/PEN* S36 .... **69** D4
Cockshutt Av *SHEFS* S8 .... **146** B5
Cockshutt Dr *SHEFS* S8 .... **146** B5
Cockshutt Rd *SHEFS* S8 .... **146** B5
Coisley Hl *HAN/WDH* S13 .... **139** D5
Coisley Rd *HAN/WDH* S13 .... **139** E4
Coit La *ECC* S11 .... **144** B2
Coke Hl *RHAM* S60 .... **103** E4
Coke La *RHAM* S60 .... **103** E4
Colby Pl *ST/HB/BR* S6 .... **120** A2
Colchester Ct *BTLY* DN5 .... **28** C3
Colchester Rd *FUL* S10 .... **120** C3
Coldstream Av *DONS/BSCR* DN4 .... **62** B1
Coldwell La *FUL* S10 .... **119** F4
Coleford Rd *DARN/MH* S9 .... **125** E2
Coleridge Av *BSLYN/ROY* S71 .... **14** C3
Coleridge Rd *DARN/MH* S9 .... **111** F5
  DEARNE S63 .... **55** D1

RHAM/THRY S65 .... **7** H3
  RHAM/THRY S65 .... **104** B1 🗓
Coley La *RAW* S62 .... **77** E1
Colister Dr *DARN/MH* S9 .... **124** C3
Colister Gdns *DARN/MH* S9 .... **124** C4
College Av *STV/CWN* S43 .... **181** E5
College Park Cl *RHAM* S60 .... **114** C1
College Rd *DON* DN1 .... **4** D5
  MEX/SWTN S64 .... **58** C3
  RHAM S60 .... **6** A5
College St *FUL* S10 .... **121** E5 🗓
  RHAM/THRY S65 .... **6** D5
Collegiate Crs *FUL* S10 .... **134** B1
Colley Av *BSLY* S70 .... **23** D4
  SHEFN S5 .... **98** B3
Colley Cl *SHEFN* S5 .... **98** B3
Colley Crs *BSLY* S70 .... **23** D4
  SHEFN S5 .... **98** C3
Colley Dr *SHEFN* S5 .... **98** C3
Colley Pl *BSLY* S70 .... **23** D3 🗓
Colley Rd *SHEFN* S5 .... **98** B3
Colliers Cl *HAN/WDH* S13 .... **139** F4
Colliery La *DEARNE* S63 .... **27** D5
Colliery Rd *ATT* S4 .... **111** E3
Colliery Yd *DOD/DAR* S75 .... **49** E4
Collin Av *ST/HB/BR* S6 .... **107** E3
Collinridge Rd *WMB/DAR* S73 .... **39** E3
Collingbourne Av *MOS* S20 .... **153** E4 🗓
Collingbourne Dr *MOS* S20 .... **153** E4 🗓
Collingham Rd *AU/AST/KP* S26 .... **142** A4
Collins Rd *SHEFN* S5 .... **99** E5
Collishaw Cl *CHNE* S41 .... **191** D4 🗓
Colonel Ward Dr *MEX/SWTN* S64 .... **57** F5
Coister Cl *DOD/DAR* S75 .... **12** B5
Coltfield *BSLY* S70 .... **36** A4
Colton Cl *CHNE* S41 .... **177** F5
Columbia St *BSLY* S70 .... **21** F5
Colver Rd *SHEFP/MNR* S2 .... **135** E2
Colvin Cl *BTLY* DN5 .... **17** F5
Colwall St *DARN/MH* S9 .... **124** A1
Commerce St *CHPT/GREN* S35 .... **88** B1
Commercial St *BSLY* S70 .... **22** B2
  SHEF S1 .... **9** G5
Common La *BTLY* DN5 .... **18** B2
  CONI DN12 .... **85** E4
  DEARNE S63 .... **56** C2
  DONS/BSCR DN4 .... **62** B2
  ECC S11 .... **132** B5
  STKB/PEN S36 .... **69** F4
Common Rd *CONI* DN12 .... **85** F2
  CONI DN12 .... **85** E2
  DEARNE S63 .... **26** B3
Commonside *FUL* S10 .... **121** D3
The Common *CHPT/GREN* S35 .... **88** C4
Compass Crs *CHNE* S41 .... **179** D3
Compton St *CHSW* S40 .... **10** C4
  ST/HB/BR S6 .... **120** C1
Conalan Av *TOT/DORE* S17 .... **157** F3
Conan Rd *CONI* DN12 .... **84** C1
Concord Rd *SHEFN* S5 .... **99** F3
Concord View Rd *KIMB* S61 .... **101** D4
Conduit La *FUL* S10 .... **121** D3 🗓
Conduit Rd *FUL* S10 .... **121** D3
Coney Rd *BTLY* DN5 .... **16** B2 🗓
Congress St *SHEF* S1 .... **8** C5 🗓
Coningsby Rd *SHEFN* S5 .... **110** A3
Coniston Pl *BTLY* DN5 .... **29** D1 🗓
Coniston Rd *BSLYN/ROY* S71 .... **3** F5
  CHNE S41 .... **183** E1
  DRON S18 .... **168** C2
  MEX/SWTN S64 .... **59** D2
  SHEFS S8 .... **134** C5
  WHHL DN2 .... **32** A5
Coniston Ter *SHEFS* S8 .... **134** C5 🗓
Coniston Wy *CHNE* S41 .... **183** F1
Constable Cl *DRON* S18 .... **168** C3
Constable Cl *DRON* S18 .... **148** C3 🗓
Constable Dr *SHEFS* S8 .... **148** B3 🗓
Constable Pl *DEARNE* S63 .... **55** F2
  GLV S14 .... **148** C3
Constable Rd *SHEFS* S8 .... **148** B3
Constable Wy *SHEFS* S8 .... **148** B3 🗓
Convent Gv *DONS/BSCR* DN4 .... **46** B4
Convent Pl *OWL* S3 .... **8** B6 🗓
Convent Wk *OWL* S3 .... **8** B6
Conway Crs *RHAM/THRY* S65 .... **105** D1
Conway Pl *WMB/DAR* S73 .... **40** A4
Conway St *BSLY* S70 .... **23** E2
Conway Ter *MEX/SWTN* S64 .... **58** B2
Conyers Dr *AU/AST/KP* S26 .... **142** B2
Conyers Rd *BTLY* DN5 .... **29** F4
Coo Hl *HAN/WDH* S13 .... **140** A4
Cooke Dr *BTLY* DN5 .... **29** E1
Cookson Cl *SHEFN* S5 .... **97** E5
Cookson Rd *SHEFN* S5 .... **108** B1
Cookson St *DONS/BSCR* DN4 .... **43** F4 🗓
Cooks Rd *MOS* S20 .... **153** E3
Cooks Wood Rd *OWL* S3 .... **109** E5
Coombe Pl *FUL* S10 .... **121** D4 🗓
Coombe Rd *FUL* S10 .... **120** C4
Co-operative St *DEARNE* S63 .... **55** E1 🗓
Coopers Ter *DON* DN1 .... **5** E3
Cooper St *DONS/BSCR* DN4 .... **44** C3
Copeland Rd *WMB/DAR* S73 .... **39** D3 🗓
Cope St *BSLY* S70 .... **22** A3

Copley Av *CONI* DN12 .... 84 B1
Copley Crs *BTLY* DN5 .... 28 A3
Copley Pl *KIMB* S61 .... 102 B2
Copley Rd *DON* DN1 .... 5 E2
Copper Cl *BSLY* S70 .... 22 A2 🔢
Copper St *OWL* S3 .... 8 D3
Coppice Av *DOD/DAR* S75 .... 12 C5
Coppice Cl *STKB/PEN* S36 .... 68 A1
Coppice Gdns *KIMB* S61 .... 92 C4
Coppice La *ST/HB/BR* S6 .... 118 C3
The Coppice *KIMB* S61 .... 91 D4
Coppice Vw *FUL* S10 .... 120 A4 🔢
Copplewood Ct *DONS/BSCR* DN4 .... 64 A3
Coppin Sq *SHEFN* S5 .... 98 A2 🔢
Coral Cl *AU/AST/KP* S26 .... 129 D5
Coral Dr *AU/AST/KP* S26 .... 129 D5
Coral Pl *AU/AST/KP* S26 .... 129 D5
Coral Wy *AU/AST/KP* S26 .... 129 D5
Corby St *ATT* S4 .... 123 E1
Cordwell Av *CHNE* S41 .... 183 D1
Cordwell Cl *STV/CWN* S43 .... 187 E3
Corker Bottoms La
   SHEFP/MNR S2 .... 124 A4
Corker Rd *HACK/IN* S12 .... 137 F4
Cornfield Cl *CHSW* S40 .... 182 B4 🔢
Corn Hl *CONI* DN12 .... 85 E2
Cornish St *OWL* S3 .... 8 B3
Cornish Wy *RAW* S62 .... 93 F4
Cornwall Av *STV/CWN* S43 .... 186 A1 🔢
Cornwall Cl *BSLYN/ROY* S71 .... 14 C1
   STV/CWN S43 .... 186 A1
Cornwall Dr *STV/CWN* S43 .... 186 A1
Cornwall Rd *WHHL* DN2 .... 31 F4
Cornwell Cl *RAW* S62 .... 79 D3
Coronation Br *RHAM* S60 .... 102 C3
Coronation Gdns
   DONS/BSCR DN4 .... 62 A1 🔢
Coronation Rd *DEARNE* S63 .... 56 B2
   DONS/BSCR DN4 .... 45 F5
   HOY S74 .... 51 E2
   MEX/SWTN S64 .... 57 F5
   RAW S62 .... 81 D5
   STKB/PEN S36 .... 68 C2
   STV/CWN S43 .... 185 F1
Coronation St *BSLYN/ROY* S71 .... 15 D3
   DEARNE S63 .... 27 E4
Coronation Ter *BSLYN/ROY* S71 .... 24 A4
Corporation St *BSLY* S70 .... 22 B3
   CHNE S41 .... 11 G5
   OWL S3 .... 9 E3
   RHAM S60 .... 6 C5
Cortina Ri *WMB/DAR* S73 .... 25 F4 🔢
Cortworth La *RAW* S62 .... 77 E2
Cortworth Rd *ECC* S11 .... 145 E5
Corve Wy *RCH* S42 .... 182 A4
Corwen Pl *HAN/WDH* S13 .... 139 E4
Cossey Rd *ATT* S4 .... 123 D1
Cotelgh Av *HACK/IN* S12 .... 151 E2
Cotleigh Cl *HACK/IN* S12 .... 151 E2
Cotleigh Crs *HACK/IN* S12 .... 151 E2
Cotleigh Dr *HACK/IN* S12 .... 151 E2
Cotleigh Gdns *HACK/IN* S12 .... 151 E2
Cotleigh Pl *HACK/IN* S12 .... 151 E2 🔢
Cotleigh Rd *HACK/IN* S12 .... 151 E2
Cotleigh Wy *HACK/IN* S12 .... 151 E2
Cotswold Av *CHPT/GREN* S35 .... 87 F2
Cotswold Crs *RHAM* S60 .... 116 A2
Cotswold Dr *AU/AST/KP* S26 .... 142 C3
Cotswold Gdns *BTLY* DN5 .... 29 D2 🔢
Cotswold Rd *ST/HB/BR* S6 .... 107 F3
Cottage La *ECC* S11 .... 132 A5
Cottam Cl *RHAM* S60 .... 116 A5
Cottam Rd *CHPT/GREN* S35 .... 73 D4
Cottenham Rd *RHAM/THRY* S65 .... 7 G3
Cotterhill La *STV/CWN* S43 .... 185 F2
Cottesmore Cl *DOD/DAR* S75 .... 13 D4 🔢
Cottingham St *DARN/MH* S9 .... 124 A3
Cotton Mill Rw *OWL* S3 .... 9 E3
Cotton St *OWL* S3 .... 9 E3
Coultas Av *STKB/PEN* S36 .... 69 E3
Countess Rd *SHEF* S1 .... 135 E1 🔢
County Wy *BSLY* S70 .... 2 D3
Coupe Rd *ATT* S4 .... 122 C1
Coupland Rd *RHAM/THRY* S65 .... 105 D1
Courey Gv *WHHL* DN2 .... 31 F2
Coventry Rd *DARN/MH* S9 .... 125 D2
Cover Cl *RAW* S62 .... 75 E2
Coverdale Rd *ABRD* S7 .... 134 C5
Coverleigh Rd *DEARNE* S63 .... 56 A4
Cow La *ECC* S11 .... 145 E2
   STV/CWN S43 .... 179 F5
Cowley Bottom *DRON* S18 .... 168 C3
Cowley Dr *CHPT/GREN* S35 .... 89 D2
Cowley Gdns *MOS* S20 .... 152 C5
Cowley Gn *WMB/DAR* S73 .... 38 B3
Cowley Hl *CHPT/GREN* S35 .... 89 D2
Cowley La *DRON* S18 .... 169 D3
Cowley View Rd *CHPT/GREN* S35.... 88 C3
Cowlishaw Rd *ECC* S11 .... 134 A2
Cowood St *MEX/SWTN* S64 .... 58 A3 🔢

Cowper Av *ST/HB/BR* S6 .... 97 E3
Cowper Crs *ST/HB/BR* S6 .... 97 E3
Cowper Dr *RHAM/THRY* S65 .... 104 C5
   ST/HB/BR S6 .... 97 E3
Cowpingle La *STV/CWN* S43 .... 179 F5
Cowrakes Cl *RHAM* S60 .... 116 A3
Cow Rakes La *RHAM* S60 .... 116 A3
Cox Pl *ST/HB/BR* S6 .... 107 D3
Cox Rd *ST/HB/BR* S6 .... 107 D4
Crabtree Cl *SHEFN* S5 .... 110 A3
Crabtree Crs *SHEFN* S5 .... 110 A3
Crabtree Dr *SHEFN* S5 .... 110 A3
Crabtree La *SHEFN* S5 .... 109 F4
Crabtree Pl *SHEFN* S5 .... 109 F4
Crabtree Rd *SHEFN* S5 .... 109 F3
Cradley Dr *AU/AST/KP* S26 .... 142 C3
Cradock Ms *SHEFP/MNR* S2 .... 136 C3 🔢
Cradock Rd *SHEFP/MNR* S2 .... 136 C3
Cragdale Gv *MOS* S20 .... 164 B1
Craggon Dr *STV/CWN* S43 .... 179 E2 🔢
Craglands Gv *RCH* S42 .... 182 B4
Crags Rd *CONI* DN12 .... 60 C4
Craithie Rd *ABRD* S7 .... 31 D5
Crakehall Rd *CHPT/GREN* S35 .... 88 B3
Cramlands *DOD/DAR* S75 .... 20 B5 🔢
Cranborne Rd *CHNE* S41 .... 183 F2
Cranbrook Dr *DON* DN1 .... 30 C4
Cranbrook St *BSLY* S70 .... 21 E2 🔢
Crane Dr *KIMB* S61 .... 101 F2
Crane Rd *KIMB* S61 .... 91 F4
Cranfield Cl *ARMTH* DN3 .... 33 F4
Cranford Ct *MOS* S20 .... 151 E5 🔢
Cranford Dr *HACK/IN* S12 .... 151 E5
Cranston Cl *BSLYN/ROY* S71 .... 15 E3
Cranwell Rd *DONS/BSCR* DN4 .... 67 F1
Cranworth Cl *RHAM/THRY* S65 .... 7 H3
Cranworth Pl *OWL* S3 .... 122 C1 🔢
Cranworth Rd *OWL* S3 .... 122 C1 🔢
   RHAM/THRY S65 .... 7 H2
Craven Cl *DARN/MH* S9 .... 125 D2 🔢
   DONS/BSCR DN4 .... 46 C4 🔢
Craven Rd *CHNE* S41 .... 10 D1
Craven St *OWL* S3 .... 8 B3
   RAW S62 .... 94 A3
Craven Wood Cl *DOD/DAR* S75 .... 12 B4
Crawford Rd *SHEFS* S8 .... 147 D1
Crawshaw Av *SHEFS* S8 .... 146 B5
Crawshaw Gv *SHEFS* S8 .... 146 B5
Crawshaw Rd *DONS/BSCR* DN4 .... 43 E2 🔢
Cream St *SHEFP/MNR* S2 .... 135 F1 🔢
Crecy Av *WHHL* DN2 .... 32 A5
Creighton Av *RAW* S62 .... 94 C1 🔢
Crescent Rd *ABRD* S7 .... 134 C3
The Crescent *CONI* DN12 .... 84 B1
   DOD/DAR S75 .... 12 C5
   MEX/SWTN S64 .... 80 C1
   STV/CWN S43 .... 185 E2
   TOT/DORE S17 .... 156 C3
Cresswell Rd *DARN/MH* S9 .... 125 D3
   MEX/SWTN S64 .... 57 E4
Cresswell St *DOD/DAR* S75 .... 13 D5
   MEX/SWTN S64 .... 58 A4 🔢
Crest Rd *SHEFN* S5 .... 98 C5
Crestwood Ct *SHEFN* S5 .... 99 D5
Crestwood Gdns *SHEFN* S5 .... 99 D5 🔢
Creswick Av *SHEFN* S5 .... 98 A5
Creswick Cl *CHSW* S40 .... 188 C4
   RHAM/THRY S65 .... 105 E1
Creswick Greave *SHEFN* S5 .... 97 F2
Creswick La *CHPT/GREN* S35 .... 97 F1
Creswick Rd *RHAM/THRY* S65 .... 105 E1
Creswick St *ST/HB/BR* S6 .... 121 E1
Creswick Wy *ST/HB/BR* S6 .... 121 E1
Crich Rd *STV/CWN* S43 .... 187 D2
Cricket Inn Crs *SHEFP/MNR* S2 .... 123 F3
Cricket Inn Rd *SHEFP/MNR* S2 .... 123 D3
Cricket View Rd *RAW* S62 .... 75 E2
Crimicar Av *FUL* S10 .... 131 F2
Crimicar Cl *FUL* S10 .... 132 A3
Crimicar Dr *FUL* S10 .... 131 F2
Crimicar La *FUL* S10 .... 131 F1
Crispin Cl *HACK/IN* S12 .... 149 E1 🔢
Crispin Gdns *HACK/IN* S12 .... 149 E1
Crispin Rd *HACK/IN* S12 .... 149 E1 🔢
Crochley Cl *DONS/BSCR* DN4 .... 47 D5
Croft Cl *ECC* S11 .... 145 D2 🔢
Crofters Cl *ECK/KIL* S21 .... 166 A4
Croft La *ECC* S11 .... 145 D2
Croft Lea *DRON* S18 .... 168 A1
Crofton Av *ST/HB/BR* S6 .... 107 D3
Crofton Cl *DRON* S18 .... 169 D2
Crofton Ri *CHPT/GREN* S35 .... 73 E5
   DRON S18 .... 169 D2
Croft Rd *BSLY* S70 .... 23 D3
   DONS/BSCR DN4 .... 62 C2
   HACK/IN S12 .... 137 F5
   HOY S74 .... 51 E1
   RHAM S60 .... 113 F3
Crofts of *RHAM/THRY* S65 .... 95 F4 🔢
The Crofts *MALT* S66 .... 117 F1
   RHAM S60 .... 6 D6 🔢
Croft St *BSLY* S70 .... 22 B5 🔢
   KIMB S61 .... 92 C3
The Croft *BTLY* DN5 .... 17 F3

CONI DN12 .... 85 D2
HOY S74 .... 52 B3 🔢
MEX/SWTN S64 .... 80 C1
RHAM S60 .... 127 D2
Croft Vw *STV/CWN* S43 .... 187 D4
Cromarty Ri *DRON* S18 .... 168 B1
Cromdale Av *STV/CWN* S43 .... 179 E2
Cromer Cl *RAW* S62 .... 80 A5 🔢
Cromer Rd *MOS* S20 .... 32 A5
Cromford Av *BSLYN/ROY* S71 .... 14 C1
Cromford Dr *STV/CWN* S43 .... 186 C1
Cromford St *SHEFP/MNR* S2 .... 135 F1 🔢
Crompton Av *BSLY* S70 .... 21 E2
   BTLY DN5 .... 29 D5
Crompton Rd *WHHL* DN2 .... 31 F1
Cromwell Dr *BTLY* DN5 .... 29 D5
Cromwell Mt *BSLY* S70 .... 21 F4
Cromwell Rd *BTLY* DN5 .... 10 C3
   CHSW S40 .... 10 C3
   MEX/SWTN S64 .... 58 B4
Cromwell St *DEARNE* S63 .... 27 E2
   ST/HB/BR S6 .... 121 D2
Crooked La *CONI* DN12 .... 83 E4
Crookes *FUL* S10 .... 120 C3
Crookesmoor Dr *ST/HB/BR* S6 .... 121 E3 🔢
Crookesmoor Rd *FUL* S10 .... 121 E3
   FUL S10 .... 121 D4
Crookes St *DONS/BSCR* DN4 .... 63 F1 🔢
Crookes Valley Rd *FUL* S10 .... 2 A5
Crookhill Rd *CONI* DN12 .... 121 E3
Crosby Ct *BSLYN/ROY* S71 .... 85 E3
Crosby Rd *SHEFS* S8 .... 15 E2
Cross Allen Rd *MOS* S20 .... 146 C3
Cross Bank *DONS/BSCR* DN4 .... 153 D5
Cross Bedford St *ST/HB/BR* S6 .... 43 F4
Cross Burgess St *SHEF* S1 .... 8 A1
Cross Butcher St *DEARNE* S63 .... 8 D6
Cross Chantrey Rd *SHEFS* S8 .... 26 C3 🔢
Crosscourt Vw *DONS/BSCR* DN4 .... 147 E2
Cross Dr *HAN/WDH* S13 .... 46 A4
Crossfield Dr *DEARNE* S63 .... 139 F4
Cross Ga *BTLY* DN5 .... 55 F3
Crossgate *DEARNE* S63 .... 29 E3
Cross Ga *MEX/SWTN* S64 .... 27 D4
Cross Hl *CHPT/GREN* S35 .... 59 D4
Cross Hill Cl *CHPT/GREN* S35 .... 99 D2
Crosshouse La *CHPT/GREN* S35 .... 99 D2
Cross House Rd *CHPT/GREN* S35 .... 96 C1
Cross Keys La *HOY* S74 .... 97 D1
Crossland Dr *HACK/IN* S12 .... 50 B2
Crossland Pl *HACK/IN* S12 .... 149 E2
Crossland St *MEX/SWTN* S64 .... 149 E1
Cross La *CHPT/GREN* S35 .... 81 E1
   DRON S18 .... 72 C1
   DRON S18 .... 160 A5
   FUL S10 .... 169 E2
   SHEFS S8 .... 120 C4
   TOT/DORE S17 .... 160 A3
Cross London St *STV/CWN* S43 .... 144 A5
Cross Myrtle Rd *SHEFP/MNR* S2 .... 179 E3 🔢
Cross Park Rd *SHEFS* S8 .... 135 F3
Cross Riding *DONS/BSCR* DN4 .... 135 E3 🔢
Cross Road Banner *ECC* S11 .... 32 C5
Cross Smithfield *OWL* S3 .... 133 F5
Cross South St *KIMB* S61 .... 8 C3
Cross St *BSLY* S70 .... 93 D3
   BSLYN/ROY S71 .... 22 C5
   BTLY DN5 .... 15 D3
   CHSW S40 .... 16 C5
   DEARNE S63 .... 10 C4
   DOD/DAR S75 .... 55 F2
   DONS/BSCR DN4 .... 2 A1
   ECK/KIL S21 .... 43 E5 🔢
   HAN/WDH S13 .... 167 D1
   HOY S74 .... 139 F4
   KIMB S61 .... 50 C3 🔢
   KIMB S61 .... 93 D3 🔢
   RAW S62 .... 102 B3
   RHAM/THRY S65 .... 94 A3
   STV/CWN S43 .... 95 F4
   .... 186 A1
Cross Turner St *SHEFP/MNR* S2 .. 122 C5 🔢
Crossway *MEX/SWTN* S64 .... 80 C1
Crossways *WHHL* DN2 .... 31 F2
Crossways North *WHHL* DN2 .... 31 F2
Crossways South *WHHL* DN2 .... 31 F3
The Crossways *SHEFP/MNR* S2 .. 137 F3 🔢
Cross Wellington St
   STV/CWN S43 .... 179 E3 🔢
Crowden Wk *DOD/DAR* S75 .... 20 B1 🔢
Crowder Av *SHEFN* S5 .... 98 B5
Crowder Cl *SHEFN* S5 .... 109 E1
Crowder Crs *SHEFN* S5 .... 109 E1
Crowder Rd *SHEFN* S5 .... 98 B5
Crowland Rd *SHEFN* S5 .... 98 C5
Crow La *CHNE* S41 .... 11 C5
   DRON S18 .... 170 C4
Crowley Dr *DEARNE* S63 .... 55 F4
Crown Av *BSLY* S70 .... 22 B3 🔢
Crown Cl *BSLY* S70 .... 22 A5
   CHNE S41 .... 179 E3 🔢
   KIMB S61 .... 101 F1
Crown Hill Rd *DOD/DAR* S75 .... 20 B1
Crownhill Rd *RHAM* S60 .... 113 E3
Crown Pl *SHEFP/MNR* S2 .... 9 H5

Crown Rd *CHNE* S41 .... 11 E1
Crown St *BSLY* S70 .... 22 B5 🔲
  HOY S74 .... 57 E5
  MEX/SWTN S64 .... 57 E5
Crown Well Hi *BSLYN/ROY* S71 .... 24 A2 🔲
Crowther Pl *SHEFP/MNR* S2 .... 135 D2 🔲
Crow Tree La *MEX/SWTN* S64 .... 58 A1
Croydon St *ECC* S11 .... 135 D2 🔲
Cruck Cl *DRON* S18 .... 168 C1
Cruise Rd *ECC* S11 .... 133 D2
Crummock Rd *CHSW* S40 .... 134 C5 🔲
Crummock Wy *BSLYN/ROY* S71 .... 24 C2 🔲
Crumpsall Dr *ST/HB/BR* S6 .... 109 D3
Crumpsall Rd *SHEFN* S5 .... 109 D3
Crumwell Rd *KIMB* S61 .... 91 E4
Crusader Dr *BTLY* DN5 .... 42 C1
Cuckoo Wy *ECK/KIL* S21 .... 165 F3
  STV/CWN S43 .... 185 D1
Cullabine Rd *SHEFP/MNR* S2 .... 137 D5
Cumberland Dr *DN2* 31 F5
Cumberland Cl *BSLY* S70 .... 22 A5
  HOY S74 .... 51 F1
Cumberland Crs *CHPT/GREN* S35 .... 88 C2 🔲
Cumberland Dr *BSLYN/ROY* S71 .... 24 A2
Cumberland Rd *HOY* S74 .... 51 F1
Cumberland Wy *SHEF* S1 .... 122 B5 🔲
Cundy St *ST/HB/BR* S6 .... 121 D2
Cunliffe St *DRON* S18 .... 160 A4
Cunningham Rd *DON* DN1 .... 5 F6
Cupola *OWL* S3 .... 8 D3
Cupola La *CHPT/GREN* S35 .... 87 D5
Cupola Yd *RHAM* S60 .... 6 B5
Curbar Curve *STV/CWN* S43 .... 186 C3
Curlew Av *ECK/KIL* S21 .... 163 F5
Curlew Rdg *SHEFP/MNR* S2 .... 123 E5
Curlew Ri *KIMB* S61 .... 76 B5
Curzon Av *DRON* S18 .... 169 D3
Curzon Cl *ECK/KIL* S21 .... 166 B2
Cusworth La *BTLY* DN5 .... 28 C4
Cuthbert Bank Rd *ST/HB/BR* S6 .... 108 B5
Cuthbert Rd *ST/HB/BR* S6 .... 108 B5 🔲
Cutler Cl *ECK/KIL* S21 .... 165 F1 🔲
Cutlers Av *BSLY* S70 .... 21 E5
Cutthorne Rd *CHSW* S40 .... 182 C5
Cutthorpe Cft *RCH* S42 .... 182 A3
Cutthorpe Rd *RCH* S42 .... 182 A2
Cutts Av *DEARNE* S63 .... 55 E3
Cutts Ter *SHEFS* S8 .... 135 D3 🔲
Cutty La *DOD/DAR* S75 .... 13 E4
Cyclops St *ATT* S4 .... 110 C4
Cypress Av *SHEFS* S8 .... 148 A4
Cypress Cl *ECK/KIL* S21 .... 166 A3 🔲
Cypress Ga *CONI* DN12 .... 84 A3
Cypress Gv *CHPT/GREN* S35 .... 88 A2
Cypress Rd *BSLY* S70 .... 22 C5
Cyprus Rd *SHEFS* S8 .... 135 E5 🔲

D

Dade Av *STV/CWN* S43 .... 186 C3
Daffodil Rd *SHEFN* S5 .... 111 D1
Dagnam Cl *SHEFP/MNR* S2 .... 137 D4
Dagnam Crs *SHEFP/MNR* S2 .... 137 D3
Dagnam Dr *SHEFP/MNR* S2 .... 137 D3
Dagnam Pl *SHEFP/MNR* S2 .... 137 D4 🔲
Dagnam Rd *SHEFP/MNR* S2 .... 137 D3
Daisy Bank *OWL* S3 .... 8 A3
Daisy Wk *MOS* S20 .... 152 C2
  OWL S3 .... 8 B4
Dalby Gdns *MOS* S20 .... 153 E4
Dalby Gv *MOS* S20 .... 153 E4
Dale Av *RHAM/THRY* S65 .... 105 D4
Dale Bank Crs *CHNE* S41 .... 179 E3 🔲
Dale Cl *STV/CWN* S43 .... 187 D1
Dale Ct *RAW* S62 .... 94 A1
Dale Green Rd *BSLY* S70 .... 22 A5
Dale Rd *CONI* DN12 .... 85 D1
  DRON S18 .... 169 F3
  ECK/KIL S21 .... 166 C2
  RAW S62 .... 80 A5
  RHAM/THRY S65 .... 105 D4
Dale St *RAW* S62 .... 80 A5
Daleswood Av *BSLY* S70 .... 20 C1 🔲
Daleswood Dr *BSLY* S70 .... 23 E5 🔲
The Dale *SHEFS* S8 .... 147 D2
Daleview Rd *SHEFS* S8 .... 146 B3
Dalewood Av *SHEFS* S8 .... 146 A4
Dalewood Cl *CHNE* S41 .... 191 F3
Dalewood Dr *SHEFS* S8 .... 145 F4
Dalewood Dr *SHEFS* S8 .... 146 A4
Dalmore Rd *ECC* S11 .... 134 A5
Dalton Ct *BSLY* S70 .... 135 D3 🔲
Dalton La *RHAM/THRY* S65 .... 105 E1
Dalvey Wy *STV/CWN* S43 .... 179 E2
Damer St *FUL* S10 .... 121 E4 🔲
Damon Dr *STV/CWN* S43 .... 186 A1
Damsteads *DOD/DAR* S75 .... 20 B3
Danby Av *CHNE* S41 .... 178 C4
Danebrook Cl *SHEFP/MNR* S2 .... 138 A1 🔲
Danebrook Dr *SHEFP/MNR* S2 .... 138 A1 🔲
Danesthorpe Cl *WHHL* DN2 .... 32 A3
Dane St *DEARNE* S63 .... 27 E3
Dane St North *DEARNE* S63 .... 27 E3

Dane St South *DEARNE* S63 .... 27 E3
Danesway *BTLY* DN5 .... 16 A5
Danethorpe Wy *CONI* DN12 .... 84 B3 🔲
Danewood Av *SHEFP/MNR* S2 .... 138 A2
Danewood Cft *SHEFP/MNR* S2 .... 138 A1
Danewood Gdns *SHEFP/MNR* S2 .... 138 A1
Daniel Hi *ST/HB/BR* S6 .... 121 F2
Daniel Hill Ct *ST/HB/BR* S6 .... 121 E2 🔲
Daniel Hill St *ST/HB/BR* S6 .... 121 E2 🔲
Daniel Hill Ter *ST/HB/BR* S6 .... 121 F2 🔲
Daniel La *RAW* S62 .... 78 C5
Daniels Dr *AU/AST/KP* S26 .... 142 A1
Dannemora Dr *DARN/MH* S9 .... 112 A5
Danum Dr *RHAM/THRY* S65 .... 7 H4
Danum Rd *DONS/BSCR* DN4 .... 100 C4
Dara St *DARN/MH* S9 .... 124 C4
Darcy Cl *AU/AST/KP* S26 .... 142 B2 🔲
Darcy Rd *ECK/KIL* S21 .... 164 A5
Daresbury Dr *SHEFP/MNR* S2 .... 136 B4
Daresbury Pl *SHEFP/MNR* S2 .... 136 B4
Daresbury Rd *SHEFP/MNR* S2 .... 136 B4
Daresbury Vw *SHEFP/MNR* S2 .... 136 B4
Darfield Av *MOS* S20 .... 151 D3
Darfield Cl *MOS* S20 .... 151 D3 🔲
Dargle Av *WHHL* DN2 .... 31 E4
Dark La *BSLY* S70 .... 20 C5
  BSLY S70 .... 36 C2
  CHNE S41 .... 185 F5
Darley *BSLY* S70 .... 23 D5
Darley Av *BSLY* S70 .... 21 F4
  BSLYN/ROY S71 .... 14 B1
Darley Cl *BSLYN/ROY* S71 .... 14 B1
  STV/CWN S43 .... 181 F4 🔲
Darley Gv *ST/HB/BR* S6 .... 106 B5
Darley Ter *DOD/DAR* S75 .... 13 E5 🔲
Darley Yd *BSLY* S70 .... 36 C1
Darnall Dr *DARN/MH* S9 .... 124 C2
Darnall Rd *DARN/MH* S9 .... 124 B2
Darrington Dr *DONS/BSCR* DN4 .... 62 B2
Darrington Pl *BSLYN/ROY* S71 .... 15 F4 🔲
Darton St *BSLY* S70 .... 23 E2
Dart Sq *OWL* S3 .... 121 F3
Darwall St *CHPT/GREN* S35 .... 73 E5 🔲
Darwent Rd *CHNE* S41 .... 185 D3
Darwin Av *CHSW* S40 .... 10 B2
Darwin Cl *FUL* S10 .... 120 A5
Darwin La *FUL* S10 .... 120 A5
Darwin Rd *CHSW* S40 .... 10 C3
  ST/HB/BR S6 .... 107 F2
Darwynn Av *MEX/SWTN* S64 .... 56 B5
Davian Wy *CHSW* S40 .... 189 F4
David Cl *HAN/WDH* S13 .... 140 B3 🔲
David La *FUL* S10 .... 131 E3
Davies Dr *MEX/SWTN* S64 .... 81 E2
Davis St *RHAM/THRY* S65 .... 104 B2
Davy Rd *CONI* DN12 .... 59 F5
Dawber La *ECK/KIL* S21 .... 167 D1
Daw Croft Av *BSLY* S70 .... 22 B5
Dawlands Cl *SHEFP/MNR* S2 .... 137 F1 🔲
Dawlands Dr *SHEFP/MNR* S2 .... 137 F1 🔲
Daw La *BTLY* DN5 .... 16 C4
Dawson Av *RAW* S62 .... 79 D3
Daw Wd *BTLY* DN5 .... 16 C5
Daylands Av *CONI* DN12 .... 84 B2
Day St *BSLY* S70 .... 21 F2
Deacons Wy *BSLYN/ROY* S71 .... 15 D4
Deadman's Hole La *DARN/MH* S9 .... 101 F5
Deakins Wk *FUL* S10 .... 133 D1
Dean Cl *BTLY* DN5 .... 42 B2
Deane Field Vw *MOS* S20 .... 152 B3 🔲
Deanhead Ct *MOS* S20 .... 151 E3 🔲
Deanhead Dr *MOS* S20 .... 151 D3
Dean La *RHAM/THRY* S65 .... 105 F3
Deansfield Cl *ARMTH* DN3 .... 33 F4
Dean St *BSLY* S70 .... 21 E1 🔲
Deans Wy *BSLYN/ROY* S71 .... 15 D5
Dearden Ct *CHPT/GREN* S35 .... 98 C1 🔲
Dearne Br *BTLY* DN5 .... 60 A1
Dearne Cl *WMB/DAR* S73 .... 40 A4
Dearne Hall Fold *DOD/DAR* S75 .... 12 A1
Dearne Hall Rd *DOD/DAR* S75 .... 12 A1
Dearne Rd *WMB/DAR* S73 .... 40 B5
Dearne St *CONI* DN12 .... 61 D5
  DARN/MH S9 .... 111 E2
Dearne Valley Pkwy
  WMB/DAR S73 .... 39 D5
Dearneway *DEARNE* S63 .... 56 A2
Dearnley Vw *DOD/DAR* S75 .... 13 E3 🔲
Deben Cl *CHSW* S40 .... 189 D3 🔲
Decoy Bank North
  DONS/BSCR DN4 .... 44 B3
Decoy Bank South
  DONS/BSCR DN4 .... 44 B3
Deepdale Cl *STV/CWN* S43 .... 181 F3
Deepdale Rd *KIMB* S61 .... 101 F3
Deep La *SHEFN* S5 .... 100 A1
Deepwell Av *MOS* S20 .... 165 D2
Deepwell Bank *MOS* S20 .... 165 D2
Deepwell Ct *MOS* S20 .... 165 D2
Deepwell Vw *MOS* S20 .... 165 D2
Deerlands Av *SHEFN* S5 .... 97 E3
Deerlands Cl *SHEFN* S5 .... 97 F3
Deerlands Mt *SHEFN* S5 .... 97 F3
Deerlands Rd *CHSW* S40 .... 188 C1
Deer Park Cl *ST/HB/BR* S6 .... 119 F1 🔲

Deer Park Pl *ST/HB/BR* S6 .... 119 F1 🔲
Deer Park Rd *ST/HB/BR* S6 .... 119 F1 🔲
Deer Park Vw *ST/HB/BR* S6 .... 119 F1 🔲
Deer Park Wy *ST/HB/BR* S6 .... 120 A1
Deightonby St *DEARNE* S63 .... 27 E3
De Lacy Dr *BSLY* S70 .... 22 B5
Delamere Cl *MOS* S20 .... 153 E5
De La Salle Dr *ATT* S4 .... 110 A5
Delf St *SHEFP/MNR* S2 .... 135 F3 🔲
Della Av *BSLY* S70 .... 21 E2
Dell Crs *DONS/BSCR* DN4 .... 43 D3
The Dell *CHSW* S40 .... 188 C1
Delph Bank *CHSW* S40 .... 189 F4
Delph House Rd *FUL* S10 .... 120 A4
Delta Pl *RHAM/THRY* S65 .... 104 C2
Delves Av *HACK/IN* S12 .... 152 A2
Delves Cl *CHSW* S40 .... 189 E3
  HACK/IN S12 .... 152 A1
Delves Dr *HACK/IN* S12 .... 152 A2
Delves La *AU/AST/KP* S26 .... 154 B2
Delves Pl *HACK/IN* S12 .... 151 F2
Delves Rd *ECK/KIL* S21 .... 166 A2
  HACK/IN S12 .... 152 A2
Delves Ter *HACK/IN* S12 .... 152 A2 🔲
Denaby Av *CONI* DN12 .... 84 B1
Denaby La *CONI* DN12 .... 82 C2
Den Bank Av *FUL* S10 .... 119 F4
Den Bank Cl *FUL* S10 .... 120 A4
Den Bank Crs *FUL* S10 .... 119 F4
Den Bank Dr *FUL* S10 .... 119 F4
Denby Rd *STV/CWN* S43 .... 187 D3
Denby St *BTLY* DN5 .... 16 B4
  SHEFP/MNR S2 .... 135 D1
Dene Crs *RHAM/THRY* S65 .... 104 C1
Dene La *OWL* S3 .... 122 A5
Dene Rd *RHAM/THRY* S65 .... 104 C1
Denham Rd *FUL* S10 .... 134 C1
Denholme Cl *OWL* S3 .... 9 F1
Denison Ct *BSLY* S70 .... 22 A2 🔲
Denison Rd *DONS/BSCR* DN4 .... 4 A5
Denman Rd *DEARNE* S63 .... 55 E2
Denman St *RHAM/THRY* S65 .... 7 F2
Denmark Rd *SHEFP/MNR* S2 .... 135 F4
Dent La *MOS* S20 .... 151 D3
Denton Rd *SHEFS* S8 .... 147 D1 🔲
Denton St *BSLYN/ROY* S71 .... 3 E3
Derby Pl *SHEFP/MNR* S2 .... 136 A4 🔲
Derby Rd *CHSW* S40 .... 190 B3
  WHHL DN2 .... 32 A1
Derbyshire La *SHEFS* S8 .... 147 E2
Derby St *BSLY* S70 .... 21 E1
  SHEFP/MNR S2 .... 135 F4
Derby Ter *SHEFP/MNR* S2 .... 136 A4
Derriman Av *ECC* S11 .... 145 F1
Derriman Cl *ECC* S11 .... 145 F1
Derriman Dr *ECC* S11 .... 145 F1
Derriman Gln *ECC* S11 .... 145 E1
Derriman Gv *ECC* S11 .... 145 F1
Derry Gv *DEARNE* S63 .... 26 C4
Derwent Cl *DRON* S18 .... 159 F5 🔲
Derwent Crs *CHNE* S41 .... 185 E2
  RHAM S60 .... 113 F5
Derwent Dr *CHPT/GREN* S35 .... 87 F1
  MEX/SWTN S64 .... 59 D2 🔲
  RAW S62 .... 94 A2
Derwent Pl *WMB/DAR* S73 .... 40 A4 🔲
Derwent Rd *DRON* S18 .... 159 F5
  KIMB S61 .... 92 B3
  MEX/SWTN S64 .... 59 D2
Derwent St *SHEFP/MNR* S2 .... 123 E3
Derwent Ter *MEX/SWTN* S64 .... 58 B2
Derwent Wy *DEARNE* S63 .... 40 C5
Deveron Rd *MOS* S20 .... 165 D1 🔲
Devizes Cl *CHSW* S40 .... 190 A4
Devon Dr *STV/CWN* S43 .... 186 A1
Devon Park Vw *STV/CWN* S43 .... 186 A1
Devonshire Av East *CHNE* S41 .... 191 D4
Devonshire Av North
  STV/CWN S43 .... 179 E3
Devonshire Cl *CHNE* S41 .... 184 A1
  DRON S18 .... 169 D3 🔲
  STV/CWN S43 .... 181 F4 🔲
  TOT/DORE S17 .... 157 D2 🔲
Devonshire Ct *STV/CWN* S43 .... 185 E2 🔲
Devonshire Dr *DOD/DAR* S75 .... 13 E3
  TOT/DORE S17 .... 156 C1
Devonshire Gln *TOT/DORE* S17 .... 157 D2 🔲
Devonshire Gv *TOT/DORE* S17 .... 156 C2 🔲
Devonshire La *SHEF* S1 .... 8 C6
Devonshire Rd *TOT/DORE* S17 .... 156 C1
  WHHL DN2 .... 31 F4
Devonshire Rd East *CHNE* S41 .... 191 D4 🔲
Devonshire Rd North
  STV/CWN S43 .... 179 E3
Devonshire St *CHNE* S41 .... 11 F5
  KIMB S61 .... 102 C3 🔲
  SHEF S1 .... 8 B6
  STV/CWN S43 .... 181 F4
Dewar Dr *ABRD* S7 .... 146 A1
Dewhill Av *RHAM* S60 .... 115 F3
Dial Cl *SHEFN* S5 .... 99 D5
Dial House Rd *ST/HB/BR* S6 .... 107 E4
Dial Wy *SHEFN* S5 .... 99 D5
Diamond St *WMB/DAR* S73 .... 39 E2 🔲
Dickens Cl *RHAM* S60 .... 126 C1

Dickenson Ct *CHPT/GREN* S35 ...... 88 A1
Dickenson Rd *CHNE* S41 ...... 190 C3
Dickens Rd *RAW* S62 ...... 80 C4
Dickinson Pl *BSLY* S70 ...... 22 A3
Dickinson Rd *BSLY* S70 ...... 22 A3
SHEFN S5 ...... 99 E2
Didcot Cl *CHSW* S40 ...... 190 A4
Digby Cl *KIMB* S61 ...... 101 F1
Dike Hl *RAW* S62 ...... 75 F2
Dikelands Mt *CHPT/GREN* S35 ...... 73 E5
Dillington Rd *BSLY* S70 ...... 22 A3
Dillington Sq *BSLY* S70 ...... 22 A3
Dingle La *CHNE* S41 ...... 191 F3
Dinmore Cl *DONS/BSCR* DN4 ...... 63 E5
Dinnington Rd *SHEFS* S8 ...... 147 D1
Dirleton Dr *DONS/BSCR* DN4 ...... 62 B1
Discovery Wy *CHNE* S41 ...... 178 B5
Ditchingham St *ATT* S4 ...... 123 D1
Division La *SHEF* S1 ...... 8 C6
Division St *SHEF* S1 ...... 8 D6
STV/CWN S43 ...... 187 D1
Dixon Crs *DONS/BSCR* DN4 ...... 43 D5
Dixon La *SHEF* S1 ...... 9 G4
Dixon Rd *ST/HB/BR* S6 ...... 107 F3
Dixon St *OWL* S3 ...... 8 C1
RHAM S60 ...... 7 F4
Dobbin Hl *ECC* S11 ...... 133 E4
Dobbin La *DRON* S18 ...... 168 A5
Dobcroft Av *ABRD* S7 ...... 145 F3
Dobcroft Cl *ECC* S11 ...... 145 E1
Dobcroft Rd *ECC* S11 ...... 145 E1
Dobie Pl *BSLY* S70 ...... 22 A2
Dobson Pl *STV/CWN* S43 ...... 186 C3
Dobsyke Cl *BSLY* S70 ...... 23 E5
Dockin Hill Rd *DON* DN1 ...... 5 F2
Dock Wk *CHSW* S40 ...... 190 A2
Dodds Cl *RHAM* S60 ...... 103 D5
Dodd St *ST/HB/BR* S6 ...... 108 A5
Dodson Dr *HAN/WDH* S13 ...... 126 A5
Dodsworth St *MEX/SWTN* S64 ...... 58 A4
SHEFS S8 ...... 162 A3
Doe Royd Crs *SHEFN* S5 ...... 97 E4
Doe Royd Dr *SHEFN* S5 ...... 97 F4
Doe Royd La *SHEFN* S5 ...... 97 E5
Dog Croft La *BTLY* DN5 ...... 18 B5
Dolcliffe Rd *MEX/SWTN* S64 ...... 58 B4
Doles La *RHAM* S60 ...... 116 C5
RHAM S60 ...... 127 F1
Domine La *RHAM* S60 ...... 6 C5
Dominoe Gv *HACK/IN* S12 ...... 138 B5
Don Av *ST/HB/BR* S6 ...... 107 E1
Doncaster Ga *RHAM/THRY* S65 ...... 6 D5
Doncaster Pl *RHAM/THRY* S65 ...... 104 B2
Doncaster Rd *ARMTH* DN3 ...... 19 F4
ARMTH DN3 ...... 32 C3
BSLY S70 ...... 3 E6
BSLY S70 ...... 22 C2
BSLY S70 ...... 23 E2
BSLYN/ROY S71 ...... 23 F2
CONI DN12 ...... 60 A4
CONI DN12 ...... 85 E1
DEARNE S63 ...... 27 F5
DEARNE S63 ...... 56 B2
DEARNE S63 ...... 56 C2
MEX/SWTN S64 ...... 58 A4
RHAM/THRY S65 ...... 7 F5
RHAM/THRY S65 ...... 95 E5
Doncaster St *OWL* S3 ...... 8 C2
Don Dr *BSLY* S70 ...... 23 E3
Donetsk Wy *HACK/IN* S12 ...... 151 E2
Donnington Rd *MEX/SWTN* S64 ...... 59 E2
SHEF/MNR S2 ...... 136 B1
Donovan Cl *SHEFN* S5 ...... 108 C1
Donovan Rd *SHEFN* S5 ...... 108 C1
Don Rd *DARN/MH* S9 ...... 111 D5
Don St *CONI* DN12 ...... 61 E5
DON DN1 ...... 30 B4
RHAM S60 ...... 103 E4
Dorchester Pl *BSLY* S70 ...... 22 A5
Dore Cl *TOT/DORE* S17 ...... 157 E1
Dore Hall Cft *TOT/DORE* S17 ...... 156 B1
Dore Rd *TOT/DORE* S17 ...... 144 C5
Dorking St *ATT* S4 ...... 9 H1
Dorothy Rd *ST/HB/BR* S6 ...... 107 F3
Dorothy Vw *CHSW* S40 ...... 183 D5
Dorset Av *STV/CWN* S43 ...... 186 A1
Dorset Crs *WHHL* DN2 ...... 32 A4
Dorset Dr *STV/CWN* S43 ...... 186 A1
Dorset St *FUL* S10 ...... 121 F5
Douglas Rd *STV/CWN* S43 ...... 184 C3
DONS/BSCR DN4 ...... 42 C5
OWL S3 ...... 109 D5
OWL S3 ...... 122 A1
Douglas St *RHAM* S60 ...... 6 D6
Douse Croft La *FUL* S10 ...... 131 D4
Dovecliffe Rd *WMB/DAR* S73 ...... 37 F2
Dove Cl *WMB/DAR* S73 ...... 40 A4
Dovecott Lea *MOS* S20 ...... 153 F2
Dovedale *FUL* S10 ...... 36 C1
Dovedale Av *STV/CWN* S43 ...... 186 A5
Dovedale Rd *ABRD* S7 ...... 138 B5
RHAM/THRY S65 ...... 105 D5
Dove La *AU/AST/KP* S26 ...... 142 C5

Dovercourt Rd *KIMB* S61 ...... 102 B2
SHEF/MNR S2 ...... 136 C1
Doveridge Cl *CHNE* S41 ...... 178 B4
Dove Rd *WMB/DAR* S73 ...... 40 A4
Dover Rd *FUL* S10 ...... 134 A1
Dover St *OWL* S3 ...... 8 A3
Dowdeswell St *CHNE* S41 ...... 11 E3
Dowland Av *CHPT/GREN* S35 ...... 73 E3
Dowland Cl *CHPT/GREN* S35 ...... 73 F3
Dowland Dr *CHPT/GREN* S35 ...... 73 E3
Dowland Gdns *CHPT/GREN* S35 ...... 73 E3
Downes Crs *DOD/DAR* S75 ...... 12 C4
Downgate Dr *ATT* S4 ...... 110 C4
Downham Rd *SHEFN* S5 ...... 110 B1
Downing La *OWL* S3 ...... 8 B2
Downing Rd *SHEFS* S8 ...... 146 C5
Downland Cl *DONS/BSCR* DN4 ...... 63 D3
Downlands *STV/CWN* S43 ...... 185 E2
Down's Rw *RHAM* S60 ...... 6 D6
Drake Cl *CHPT/GREN* S35 ...... 87 F1
Drake Head La *CONI* DN12 ...... 85 F1
Drake House Crs *MOS* S20 ...... 152 B2
Drake House La *MOS* S20 ...... 153 D2
Drake House La West *MOS* S20 ...... 153 D2
Drake House Wy *MOS* S20 ...... 152 C2
Drake Rd *WHHL* DN2 ...... 30 C3
Dransfield Cl *FUL* S10 ...... 120 A5
Dransfield Rd *FUL* S10 ...... 119 F5
Draycott Pl *DRON* S18 ...... 168 B3
Driver Rd *HAN/WDH* S13 ...... 140 B3
The Drive *ST/HB/BR* S6 ...... 107 F2
Dronfield Rd *ECK/KIL* S21 ...... 173 E1
Droppingwell Farm Cl *KIMB* S61 ...... 91 E5
Droppingwell Rd *KIMB* S61 ...... 101 D2
Drover Cl *CHPT/GREN* S35 ...... 73 F5
Drummond Av *BTLY* DN5 ...... 28 A2
Drummond Crs *SHEFN* S5 ...... 98 C4
Drummond Rd *SHEFN* S5 ...... 98 C4
Drummond St *RHAM* S60 ...... 6 D3
Drury Farm Ct *DOD/DAR* S75 ...... 20 B1
Drury La *DRON* S18 ...... 160 A5
TOT/DORE S17 ...... 156 B1
Dryden Av *CHSW* S40 ...... 190 A4
SHEFN S5 ...... 97 F5
Dryden Dr *SHEFN* S5 ...... 97 F5
Dryden Rd *BSLYN/ROY* S71 ...... 3 F1
DEARNE S63 ...... 55 D1
DONS/BSCR DN4 ...... 64 A1
MEX/SWTN S64 ...... 58 C3
RHAM/THRY S65 ...... 104 C5
SHEFN S5 ...... 97 F5
Dryden Wy *SHEFN* S5 ...... 97 F5
Dublin Rd *WHHL* DN2 ...... 31 E5
Duchess Rd *SHEF/MNR* S2 ...... 135 F1
Duckham Dr *AU/AST/KP* S26 ...... 142 C4
Ducksett La *ECK/KIL* S21 ...... 164 B5
Dudley Rd *ST/HB/BR* S6 ...... 107 F2
WHHL DN2 ...... 45 F1
Dudley St *RAW* S62 ...... 94 A3
Duftons Cl *CONI* DN12 ...... 61 E5
Dugdale Dr *SHEFN* S5 ...... 98 A2
Dugdale Rd *SHEFN* S5 ...... 98 A2
Duke Crs *BSLY* S70 ...... 22 A1
KIMB S61 ...... 102 A3
Duke La *SHEF* S1 ...... 122 B5
Duke of Norfolk La *MALT* S66 ...... 105 F5
Dukes Dr *CHNE* S41 ...... 183 F1
Dukes Pl *SHEF/MNR* S2 ...... 104 C5
Duke St *BSLY* S70 ...... 22 A2
CHNE S41 ...... 184 B1
DON DN1 ...... 4 D4
HOY S74 ...... 51 F2
MEX/SWTN S64 ...... 57 E4
MOS S20 ...... 164 B2
STV/CWN S43 ...... 181 F4
Dumbleton Rd *ECK/KIL* S21 ...... 166 C5
Dumble Wood Gra *CHSW* S40 ...... 183 D2
Duncan Rd *FUL* S10 ...... 120 C1
Duncan St *RHAM* S60 ...... 114 A3
Duncombe St *ST/HB/BR* S6 ...... 121 F2
Dundas Rd *DARN/MH* S9 ...... 112 C1
WHHL DN2 ...... 30 C4
Dundonald Rd *CHSW* S40 ...... 190 B3
Dunedin Gln *MOS* S20 ...... 164 C1
Dunedin Gv *MOS* S20 ...... 164 C2
Dunella Dr *ST/HB/BR* S6 ...... 107 E2
Dunella Pl *ST/HB/BR* S6 ...... 107 E3
Dunella Rd *ST/HB/BR* S6 ...... 107 E3
Dun Flds *OWL* S3 ...... 8 C2
Dunkeld Rd *ECC* S11 ...... 133 F5
Dunkerley Rd *ST/HB/BR* S6 ...... 106 B3
Dun La *OWL* S3 ...... 8 C2
Dunleary Rd *WHHL* DN2 ...... 31 E5
Dunlin Cl *KIMB* S61 ...... 76 A5
Dunlop St *DARN/MH* S9 ...... 111 F3
Dunmere Cl *BSLYN/ROY* S71 ...... 14 B2
Dunmow Rd *ATT* S4 ...... 110 C3
Dunninc Rd *SHEFN* S5 ...... 99 E2
Dunninc Ter *SHEFN* S5 ...... 99 E2
Dunniwood Av *DONS/BSCR* DN4 ...... 67 E2
Dunniwood Reach
DONS/BSCR DN4 ...... 67 D1
Dunston Ct *CHNE* S41 ...... 178 A5
Dunston La *CHNE* S41 ...... 183 F1
Dunston Pl *CHNE* S41 ...... 178 A5

Dunston Rd *CHNE* S41 ...... 176 C5
Dun St *MEX/SWTN* S64 ...... 81 F1
OWL S3 ...... 8 C2
Durham Cl *CHNE* S41 ...... 179 E3
Durham La *FUL* S10 ...... 121 F4
Durham Pl *RHAM/THRY* S65 ...... 104 C5
Durham Rd *FUL* S10 ...... 121 F4
WHHL DN2 ...... 31 F2
Durley Chine Dr *CHNE* S41 ...... 191 D4
Durlstone Cl *HACK/IN* S12 ...... 137 E5
Durlstone Crs *HACK/IN* S12 ...... 137 E5
Durlstone Dr *HACK/IN* S12 ...... 137 D5
Durlstone Gv *HACK/IN* S12 ...... 137 E5
Durmast Gv *ST/HB/BR* S6 ...... 119 D1
Durnan Gv *RAW* S62 ...... 79 D3
Durnford Rd *WHHL* DN2 ...... 30 C4
Durrant Rd *CHNE* S41 ...... 11 F5
Durvale Ct *TOT/DORE* S17 ...... 156 C2
Dutton Rd *ST/HB/BR* S6 ...... 108 B3
Dyche Cl *SHEFS* S8 ...... 159 F2
Dyche Dr *SHEFS* S8 ...... 159 F2
Dyche La *SHEFS* S8 ...... 159 E1
Dyche Pl *SHEFS* S8 ...... 159 F2
Dyche Rd *SHEFS* S8 ...... 159 F2
Dycott Rd *KIMB* S61 ...... 102 A2
Dyer Rd *HOY* S74 ...... 52 B1
Dykes Hall Gdns *ST/HB/BR* S6 ...... 107 F4
Dykes Hall Pl *ST/HB/BR* S6 ...... 107 F3
Dykes Hall Rd *ST/HB/BR* S6 ...... 107 E3
Dykes La *ST/HB/BR* S6 ...... 107 E4
Dyke Vale Av *HACK/IN* S12 ...... 151 E1
Dyke Vale Cl *HACK/IN* S12 ...... 151 E1
Dyke Vale Pl *HACK/IN* S12 ...... 151 E1
Dyke Vale Rd *HACK/IN* S12 ...... 139 D5
Dyke Vale Wy *HACK/IN* S12 ...... 151 D1
Dykewood Dr *ST/HB/BR* S6 ...... 107 D1
Dyson Pl *ECC* S11 ...... 134 B2
Dyson St *BSLY* S70 ...... 21 E3

E

Eaden Crs *HOY* S74 ...... 52 A2
Eagleton Dr *CHPT/GREN* S35 ...... 73 F3
Eagleton Ri *CHPT/GREN* S35 ...... 73 F3
Eagle Vw *AU/AST/KP* S26 ...... 142 C4
Eaming Vw *BSLYN/ROY* S71 ...... 3 G2
Earldom Cl *ATT* S4 ...... 123 D1
Earldom Dr *ATT* S4 ...... 123 D1
Earldom Rd *ATT* S4 ...... 110 A5
Earldom St *ATT* S4 ...... 123 D1
Earlesmere Av *DONS/BSCR* DN4 ...... 43 E4
Earl Marshal Cl *ATT* S4 ...... 110 B3
Earl Marshal Dr *ATT* S4 ...... 110 B4
Earl Marshal Rd *ATT* S4 ...... 110 B3
Earl Marshal Vw *ATT* S4 ...... 110 A4
Earlsmere Dr *BSLYN/ROY* S71 ...... 24 B2
Earlston Dr *BTLY* DN5 ...... 29 F3
Earl St *SHEF* S1 ...... 122 B5
Earl Wy *SHEF* S1 ...... 122 B5
Earnshaw Ter *DOD/DAR* S75 ...... 2 A2
Earsham St *ATT* S4 ...... 123 D1
Easedale Cl *RCH* S42 ...... 182 A4
East Av *MEX/SWTN* S64 ...... 80 C1
RAW S62 ...... 80 A5
WMB/DAR S73 ...... 38 C2
East Bank Cl *SHEF/MNR* S2 ...... 136 B4
East Bank Pl *SHEF/MNR* S2 ...... 136 B4
East Bank Rd *SHEF/MNR* S2 ...... 136 A3
East Bank Vw *SHEF/MNR* S2 ...... 136 B4
East Bank Wy *SHEF/MNR* S2 ...... 136 B4
East Bawtry Rd *RHAM* S60 ...... 115 F2
RHAM S60 ...... 116 A1
RHAM S60 ...... 116 A2
East Coast Rd *DARN/MH* S9 ...... 123 F1
East Crs *RHAM/THRY* S65 ...... 104 C2
STKB/PEN S36 ...... 68 B2
Eastcroft Cl *MOS* S20 ...... 153 D5
Eastcroft Dr *MOS* S20 ...... 164 C1
Eastcroft Gln *MOS* S20 ...... 153 D5
Eastcroft Vw *MOS* S20 ...... 165 D1
Eastcroft Wy *MOS* S20 ...... 153 D5
Eastern Av *SHEF/MNR* S2 ...... 136 C3
Eastern Crs *SHEF/MNR* S2 ...... 136 B4
Eastern Dr *SHEF/MNR* S2 ...... 136 B3
Eastfield Pl *RAW* S62 ...... 81 D4
Eastfield Rd *ARMTH* DN3 ...... 33 F4
DRON S18 ...... 170 A3
FUL S10 ...... 121 D2
Eastfields *BSLY* S70 ...... 36 C1
Eastgate *BSLY* S70 ...... 2 C4
East Glade Av *HACK/IN* S12 ...... 150 C2
East Glade Cl *HACK/IN* S12 ...... 150 C2
East Glade Crs *HACK/IN* S12 ...... 150 C1
East Glade Pl *HACK/IN* S12 ...... 150 C1
East Glade Rd *HACK/IN* S12 ...... 150 C1
East Glade Sq *HACK/IN* S12 ...... 150 C2
East Glade Wy *HACK/IN* S12 ...... 150 C1
Eastgrove Rd *FUL* S10 ...... 134 B1
East Laith Ga *DON* DN1 ...... 5 F3
Eastleigh Ct *CHNE* S41 ...... 191 E4
Eastmoor Rd *STV/CWN* S43 ...... 186 A5
East Pde *SHEF* S1 ...... 9 E5
East Rd *RHAM/THRY* S65 ...... 104 C2

SHEFP/MNR S2 ...... **135** F3
Eastside Cl *CHNE* S41 ...... **184** C2
East St *BSLY* S70 ...... **37** D1
 DEARNE S63 ...... **27** F5
 DON DN1 ...... **44** A3
 ECK/KIL S21 ...... **175** F3
East Vw *CHSW* S40 ...... **190** B2 🔲
East View Av *ECK/KIL* S21 ...... **174** A1
Eastwood Cl *CHNE* S41 ...... **191** D4
Eastwood La *RHAM/THRY* S65 ...... **7** E5
Eastwood Mt *RHAM/THRY* S65 ...... **104** B3
Eastwood Park Dr *CHNE* S41 ...... **191** E4
Eastwood Rd *ECC* S11 ...... **134** B2 🔲
Eastwood V *RHAM/THRY* S65 ...... **104** B1
Eaton Pl *SHEFP/MNR* S2 ...... **123** E4
Ebenezer Pl *OWL* S3 ...... **8** D2 🔲
Ebenezer St *OWL* S3 ...... **8** D2
Eben St *DARN/MH* S9 ...... **111** E2
Ecclesall Rd *ECC* S11 ...... **133** F3
Ecclesall Rd South *ECC* S11 ...... **133** E5 🔲
Ecclesfield Rd *CHPT/GREN* S35 ...... **88** C2
 DARN/MH S9 ...... **100** A2
 SHEFN S5 ...... **99** E1
Eccles St *DARN/MH* S9 ...... **100** C5
Eckington Rd *DRON* S18 ...... **160** B5
 MOS S20 ...... **153** D5
Edale Rd *ECC* S11 ...... **133** E4
 KIMB S61 ...... **101** F3
Eden Dr *ST/HB/BR* S6 ...... **106** C4
Edenfield Cl *BSLYN/ROY* S71 ...... **15** E1 🔲
Eden Gld *AU/AST/KP* S26 ...... **142** B3
Eden Gv *AU/AST/KP* S26 ...... **142** B2
 DONS/BSCR DN4 ...... **43** E2
Edenhall Rd *SHEFP/MNR* S2 ...... **137** D3
Edensor Rd *SHEFN* S5 ...... **109** F2
Edenthorpe Dell *HACK/IN* S12 ...... **151** F3
Edenthorpe Gv *MOS* S20 ...... **152** A3
Edgbaston Wy *CONI* DN12 ...... **62** A4
Edgebrook Rd *ECC* S11 ...... **134** B4
Edgecliffe Pl *BSLYN/ROY* S71 ...... **14** B2 🔲
Edge Cl *ST/HB/BR* S6 ...... **97** D3
Edgedale Rd *ABRD* S7 ...... **134** C5
Edgefield Rd *ABRD* S7 ...... **134** C5
Edge Hill Rd *ABRD* S7 ...... **134** B4
Edgehill Rd *WHHL* DN2 ...... **32** A2
Edge La *ST/HB/BR* S6 ...... **96** C3
Egremont Rd *ABRD* S7 ...... **134** C5 🔲
Edge Well Cl *ST/HB/BR* S6 ...... **97** D3
Edge Well Crs *ST/HB/BR* S6 ...... **97** D3
Edge Well Dr *ST/HB/BR* S6 ...... **97** D4
Edge Well Pl *ST/HB/BR* S6 ...... **97** D3 🔲
Edge Well Ri *ST/HB/BR* S6 ...... **97** D3 🔲
Edinburgh Cl *BSLYN/ROY* S71 ...... **14** C3 🔲
Edinburgh Dr *CHNE* S41 ...... **10** C2
 HOY S74 ...... **51** F1
Edith Ter *BTLY* DN5 ...... **28** B2
Edlington La *DONS/BSCR* DN4 ...... **62** A2
Edmonton Cl *DOD/DAR* S75 ...... **12** B5 🔲
Edmund Av *RHAM* S60 ...... **114** B5
 TOT/DORE S17 ...... **158** A2
Edmund Dr *TOT/DORE* S17 ...... **158** A2
Edmund Rd *SHEFP/MNR* S2 ...... **135** F2
Edmunds St *CHNE* S41 ...... **184** A1
Edward Cl *ECC* S11 ...... **23** D3
Edward Rd *DEARNE* S63 ...... **41** D5
Edward St *ARMTH* DN3 ...... **33** D2
 BTLY DN5 ...... **16** C5
 DEARNE S63 ...... **26** C3 🔲
 ECK/KIL S21 ...... **164** B5
 HOY S74 ...... **51** E2
 MEX/SWTN S64 ...... **57** E4
 OWL S3 ...... **8** B4
 STKB/PEN S36 ...... **69** D2
 STV/CWN S43 ...... **187** D1
 WMB/DAR S73 ...... **39** F2
Edwin Av *CHSW* S40 ...... **189** E4
Edwin Rd *SHEFP/MNR* S2 ...... **136** A4
Effingham La *ATT* S4 ...... **9** H3
Effingham Rd *ATT* S4 ...... **123** D2
 DARN/MH S9 ...... **123** F2
Effingham Sq *RHAM* S60 ...... **6** D4
Effingham St *ATT* S4 ...... **9** H2
 RHAM/THRY S65 ...... **7** E3
Egerton Cl *SHEF* S1 ...... **122** A5
Egerton La *OWL* S3 ...... **122** A5 🔲
Egerton Rd *AU/AST/KP* S26 ...... **142** B3
 DRON S18 ...... **169** F1 🔲
Egerton St *OWL* S3 ...... **122** A5
Eggington Cl *ARMTH* DN3 ...... **47** F5 🔲
Eilam Cl *KIMB* S61 ...... **101** F1
Eilam Rd *KIMB* S61 ...... **101** F1
Ekin St *KIMB* S61 ...... **102** B5
Eland Gate Cl *NROS/TKH* DN11 ...... **67** D5
Elcroft Gdns *MOS* S20 ...... **153** D2
Elder Ct *ECK/KIL* S21 ...... **166** A3
Elder Gv *CONI* DN12 ...... **84** B2
Eldertree Rd *KIMB* S61 ...... **90** A3
Elder Wy *CHSW* S40 ...... **11** F6
Eldon Rd *RHAM/THRY* S65 ...... **7** G1
Eldon St *BSLY* S70 ...... **2** C5
 SHEF S1 ...... **8** C6

Eldon St North *BSLY* S70 ...... **2** D4
Eleanor Ct *ARMTH* DN3 ...... **19** F5 🔲
Eleanor St *DARN/MH* S9 ...... **124** C1
Elgin Cl *CHSW* S40 ...... **189** D5
Elgin St *FUL* S10 ...... **120** C4
Eliot Cl *STV/CWN* S43 ...... **186** A4
Elizabeth Rd *AU/AST/KP* S26 ...... **142** B3
Elkstone Rd *CHSW* S40 ...... **182** B4
Ella Rd *ATT* S4 ...... **110** A5 🔲
Ellavale *HOY* S74 ...... **52** B2
Ellenbro Rd *ST/HB/BR* S6 ...... **107** F4
Ellen Tree Cl *RHAM* S60 ...... **113** F4 🔲
Ellerker Av *DONS/BSCR* DN4 ...... **4** B6
Ellers Av *DONS/BSCR* DN4 ...... **46** A4
Ellers Crs *DONS/BSCR* DN4 ...... **46** A4
Ellers Dr *DONS/BSCR* DN4 ...... **46** A4
Ellershaw La *CONI* DN12 ...... **84** B2
Ellershaw Rd *CONI* DN12 ...... **84** C2
Ellers Rd *DONS/BSCR* DN4 ...... **46** A4
Ellerton Gdns *DONS/BSCR* DN4 ...... **46** C3
Ellerton Rd *SHEFN* S5 ...... **110** B3
Ellesmere Rd *ATT* S4 ...... **110** A5
 ATT S4 ...... **123** D1
Ellesmere Rd North *ATT* S4 ...... **110** A5
Ellesmere Ter *RHAM/THRY* S65 ...... **7** H6
Ellington Ct *BSLY* S70 ...... **21** E3 🔲
Ellin St *SHEF* S1 ...... **135** E1
Elliot La *CHPT/GREN* S35 ...... **87** F3
Elliot Rd *ST/HB/BR* S6 ...... **121** E3 🔲
Elliott Av *WMB/DAR* S73 ...... **39** E4
Elliott Cl *DEARNE* S63 ...... **55** D1
Elliott Ct *RHAM/THRY* S65 ...... **7** E4
Elliott Dr *SHEFP/MNR* S2 ...... **92** A4
 STV/CWN S43 ...... **187** D1
Elliottville St *ST/HB/BR* S6 ...... **121** D1 🔲
Ellis Av *DEARNE* S63 ...... **55** E4
Ellis Ct *WMB/DAR* S73 ...... **39** D5 🔲
Ellis Crs *WMB/DAR* S73 ...... **54** B1
Ellisons Rd *ECK/KIL* S21 ...... **154** C5
Ellison St *OWL* S3 ...... **8** A3
 RHAM S60 ...... **114** A3
Ellorslie Dr *STKB/PEN* S36 ...... **69** D2
Elm Cl *CHNE* S41 ...... **184** A2
 ECK/KIL S21 ...... **166** A3
Elm Crs *BTLY* DN5 ...... **17** D4
 MOS S20 ...... **152** A5
Elmdale Cl *MEX/SWTN* S64 ...... **81** E3
Elm Dr *ECK/KIL* S21 ...... **166** A3
Elmfield Av *SHEFN* S5 ...... **98** C5
Elmfield Rd *DON* DN1 ...... **5** F6
Elm Green La *CONI* DN12 ...... **85** D1
Elm Gv *KIMB* S61 ...... **92** C3
Elmham Rd *DARN/MH* S9 ...... **125** E3
 DONS/BSCR DN4 ...... **46** C3
Elmhirst Dr *RHAM/THRY* S65 ...... **105** D5
Elm La *SHEFN* S5 ...... **98** C5
Elm Lodge Farm Cl *CHNE* S41 ...... **184** A2
Elmore Rd *FUL* S10 ...... **121** D4
Elm Pl *ARMTH* DN3 ...... **33** D2
 BSLYN/ROY S71 ...... **15** E2
 RAW S62 ...... **84** B1
Elm Ri *CHPT/GREN* S35 ...... **88** A2
Elm Rd *ARMTH* DN3 ...... **33** E2
 ECK/KIL S21 ...... **174** A1
 MEX/SWTN S64 ...... **58** A2
 MOS S20 ...... **153** E1
Elm Rw *BSLYN/ROY* S71 ...... **22** C1
Elmsdale *BSLY* S70 ...... **36** C1
Elm St *HOY* S74 ...... **51** E3
 STV/CWN S43 ...... **180** B5
Elm Tree Crs *DRON* S18 ...... **159** E5
Elm Tree Rd *KIMB* S61 ...... **90** A3
Elmview Rd *DARN/MH* S9 ...... **100** C5 🔲
Elmville Av *MEX/SWTN* S64 ...... **81** D2
Elm Wy *DEARNE* S63 ...... **56** B4
Elmwood Crs *ARMTH* DN3 ...... **33** E3
Elmwood Dr *MOS* S20 ...... **164** B2
Elsecar Rd *RAW* S62 ...... **54** A3
Elstree Dr *HACK/IN* S12 ...... **149** F1
Elstree Rd *HACK/IN* S12 ...... **149** F1
Elsworth Cl *DON* DN1 ...... **44** A3
Elton St *CHSW* S40 ...... **190** B2
Elton Vw *STV/CWN* S43 ...... **187** E1
Elwin Ct *DONS/BSCR* DN4 ...... **63** F3
Elwis St *BTLY* DN5 ...... **4** B1
Ely Rd *WHHL* DN2 ...... **31** D2
Embankment Rd *FUL* S10 ...... **121** D4
Emerson Cl *SHEFN* S5 ...... **98** C4
Emerson Crs *SHEFN* S5 ...... **98** C5
Emerson Dr *SHEFN* S5 ...... **98** C5
Emily Cl *BSLYN/ROY* S71 ...... **15** E5
Emley Dr *BTLY* DN5 ...... **28** A2
Emmetfield Cl *CHSW* S40 ...... **190** A4 🔲
Empire Rd *ABRD* S7 ...... **135** D3
 SHEFS S8 ...... **135** D4 🔲
Endcliffe Av *ECC* S11 ...... **133** F1
Endcliffe Crs *ECC* S11 ...... **133** F1
Endcliffe Edge *FUL* S10 ...... **133** F1 🔲
Endcliffe Glen Rd *ECC* S11 ...... **134** A1
Endcliffe Grove Av *FUL* S10 ...... **133** E1
Endcliffe Hall Av *FUL* S10 ...... **133** E1
Endcliffe Rise Rd *ECC* S11 ...... **134** A1
Endcliffe Terrace Rd *ECC* S11 ...... **134** A1

Endcliffe Vale Av *ECC* S11 ...... **134** A2 🔲
Endcliffe Vale Rd *FUL* S10 ...... **133** F1
Endcliffe Wy *WHHL* DN2 ...... **32** A2 🔲
Endfield Rd *SHEFN* S5 ...... **98** A2
Endowood Rd *ABRD* S7 ...... **145** F3
 CHSW S40 ...... **188** B4
Enfield Pl *HAN/WDH* S13 ...... **126** A5
Enfield Rd *CHNE* S41 ...... **11** E2
Ennerdale Av *MOS* S20 ...... **164** C2 🔲
Ennerdale Cl *DRON* S18 ...... **168** C2
 MEX/SWTN S64 ...... **59** D2
Ennerdale Crs *CHNE* S41 ...... **183** D2 🔲
Ennerdale Dr *MOS* S20 ...... **164** C2 🔲
Ennerdale Rd *BSLYN/ROY* S71 ...... **24** C2
 WHHL DN2 ...... **32** A3
Ennis Crs *WHHL* DN2 ...... **31** E4
Entwhistle Rd *CHPT/GREN* S35 ...... **73** F4 🔲
Epping Gdns *MOS* S20 ...... **153** E3
Epping Gv *MOS* S20 ...... **153** E3
Epsom Cl *MEX/SWTN* S64 ...... **58** C2
Epsom Rd *DONS/BSCR* DN4 ...... **46** B2
Erington Av *SHEFP/MNR* S2 ...... **136** C3
Erington Crs *SHEFP/MNR* S2 ...... **136** C4
Erington Rd *CHSW* S40 ...... **189** E4
 SHEFP/MNR S2 ...... **136** C3
Erington Wy *SHEFP/MNR* S2 ...... **136** C3
Erskine Crs *SHEFP/MNR* S2 ...... **136** A3
Erskine Rd *RHAM/THRY* S65 ...... **7** E2
 SHEFP/MNR S2 ...... **136** A3
Erskine Vw *SHEFP/MNR* S2 ...... **136** A4
Eskdale Cl *DRON* S18 ...... **168** C2
 ST/HB/BR S6 ...... **107** F1
Eskdale Dr *BTLY* DN5 ...... **29** D1
Eskdale Rd *BSLYN/ROY* S71 ...... **24** B2 🔲
 KIMB S61 ...... **92** A3
 ST/HB/BR S6 ...... **107** F1
Esperanto Pl *SHEF* S1 ...... **9** F5 🔲
Essendine Crs *SHEFS* S8 ...... **147** F2
Essex Av *WHHL* DN2 ...... **45** F1
Essex Rd *BSLY* S70 ...... **22** A3 🔲
 SHEFP/MNR S2 ...... **136** B1
Estate Rd *RAW* S62 ...... **79** F4
Estone Dr *AU/AST/KP* S26 ...... **142** B2
Ettrick Cl *CHSW* S40 ...... **183** D4 🔲
Etwall Cl *CHSW* S40 ...... **182** B3 🔲
Etwall Wy *SHEFN* S5 ...... **99** D5
Europa Link *DARN/MH* S9 ...... **125** F1
Evans St *OWL* S3 ...... **122** A5 🔲
Evanston Gdns *DONS/BSCR* DN4 ...... **43** E4
Evelyn Av *WHHL* DN2 ...... **31** F5
Evelyn Rd *FUL* S10 ...... **120** B4
Evelyn St *RAW* S62 ...... **80** C5
Evelyn Ter *BSLY* S70 ...... **22** C2 🔲
Everard Av *TOT/DORE* S17 ...... **157** E2
Everard Dr *TOT/DORE* S17 ...... **157** E3
Everard Gld *TOT/DORE* S17 ...... **157** E3 🔲
Everett Cl *STV/CWN* S43 ...... **185** F2
Everill Cl *WMB/DAR* S73 ...... **40** A4
Everill Gate La *WMB/DAR* S73 ...... **40** A3
Everingham Cl *SHEFN* S5 ...... **109** E1
Everingham Crs *SHEFN* S5 ...... **109** D1
Everingham Rd *DONS/BSCR* DN4 ...... **46** C3
 SHEFN S5 ...... **109** E1
Everton Rd *ECC* S11 ...... **134** A2
Evesham Cl *DARN/MH* S9 ...... **100** C5
Ewden Rd *WMB/DAR* S73 ...... **40** A4
Ewden Wy *DOD/DAR* S75 ...... **20** B1
Ewers Rd *KIMB* S61 ...... **102** A3
Ewood Dr *DONS/BSCR* DN4 ...... **46** C4
Exchange Pl *ATT* S4 ...... **9** G4
Exchange St *SHEF* S1 ...... **9** G4
Exeter Dr *OWL* S3 ...... **135** D1 🔲
Exeter Pl *OWL* S3 ...... **122** A5 🔲
Exeter Rd *WHHL* DN2 ...... **31** E3
Exeter Wy *OWL* S3 ...... **121** F5 🔲
Exley Av *ST/HB/BR* S6 ...... **121** E1
Eyam Rd *FUL* S10 ...... **120** C4 🔲
Eyncourt Rd *SHEFN* S5 ...... **110** B1
Eyre Gdns *CHNE* S41 ...... **10** D1
Eyre La *SHEF* S1 ...... **122** B5
Eyre St *SHEF* S1 ...... **135** E1
Eyre St East *CHNE* S41 ...... **191** D5

F

Factory La *DON* DN1 ...... **4** C3 🔲
Factory St *CHSW* S40 ...... **189** E2
Fairbank Rd *SHEFN* S5 ...... **109** F3
Fairbank Vw *RHAM* S60 ...... **116** A3
Fairbarn Cl *ST/HB/BR* S6 ...... **119** F2 🔲
Fairbarn Dr *ST/HB/BR* S6 ...... **119** F2
Fairbarn Pl *ST/HB/BR* S6 ...... **119** F2
Fairbarn Rd *ST/HB/BR* S6 ...... **119** F2
Fairbarn Wy *ST/HB/BR* S6 ...... **119** F2
Fairburn Gdns *RHAM* S60 ...... **114** B4 🔲
Fairburn Gv *HOY* S74 ...... **52** C2
Fairfax Dr *SHEFP/MNR* S2 ...... **137** F2
Fairfax Rd *SHEFP/MNR* S2 ...... **137** F2
 WHHL DN2 ...... **31** F5
Fair Fld *BSLY* S70 ...... **36** A4
Fairfield Cl *DONS/BSCR* DN4 ...... **66** B1
 STV/CWN S43 ...... **185** E1 🔲

Fairfield Ct *CHSW* S40 ...... **182** A5
Fairfield Dr *CHSW* S40 ...... **182** A5
Fairfield Rd *BTLY* DN5 ...... **29** D5
  CHSW S40 ...... **10** C5
  OWL S3 ...... **121** F1
Fairford Cl *CHSW* S40 ...... **190** A5
  DONS/BSCR DN4 ...... **67** E1
Fairleigh *SHEFP/MNR* S2 ...... **137** E2
Fairleigh Dr *RHAM* S60 ...... **103** E5
Fairmount Gdns *HACK/IN* S12 ...... **151** E2 🔟
Fairthorn Rd *SHEFN* S5 ...... **99** E5
Fair Vw *CHSW* S40 ...... **10** A3
Fairview Ct *HOY* S74 ...... **51** D3
Fair View Dr *AU/AST/KP* S26 ...... **142** B3
Fairview Rd *DRON* S18 ...... **159** E5
Fairway *DOD/DAR* S75 ...... **20** B4
The Fairway *FUL* S10 ...... **131** E1
Falcon Dr *BSLY* S70 ...... **36** A5
  RHAM S60 ...... **128** A4
Falconer La *HAN/WDH* S13 ...... **141** D1
Falcon Ri *DRON* S18 ...... **160** B5 🔟
Falcon Rd *DRON* S18 ...... **160** A5
Falcon St *BSLY* S70 ...... **2** C4
Falding St *CHPT/GREN* S35 ...... **88** C1
  RHAM S60 ...... **6** A5
Falkland Ri *DRON* S18 ...... **169** E3
Falkland Rd *ECC* S11 ...... **133** E4
Fallon Rd *CHNE* S41 ...... **119** E1
Fallowfield Rd *CHNE* S41 ...... **179** E3
Falmouth Cl *BSLYN/ROY* S71 ...... **14** C5
Falmouth Rd *ABRD* S7 ...... **134** C5
Falstaff Crs *SHEFN* S5 ...... **98** A5
Falstaff Rd *SHEFN* S5 ...... **98** A4
Fane Crs *AU/AST/KP* S26 ...... **142** B2
Fanny Av *ECK/KIL* S21 ...... **166** C3
Fanshaw Av *ECK/KIL* S21 ...... **174** A1
Fanshaw Bank *DRON* S18 ...... **169** E2 🔟
Fanshaw Dr *ECK/KIL* S21 ...... **174** A1 🔟
Fanshaw Rd *DRON* S18 ...... **169** F1
  ECK/KIL S21 ...... **174** A1
Fanshaw Wy *ECK/KIL* S21 ...... **174** A1
Faraday Rd *DARN/MH* S9 ...... **123** F1
Faranden Rd *DARN/MH* S9 ...... **124** B2 🔟
Far Crs *RHAM/THRY* S65 ...... **104** C2
Farcroft Gv *ATT* S4 ...... **111** E3 🔟
Far Dalton La *RHAM/THRY* S65 ...... **105** F1
Far Field La *BSLYN/ROY* S71 ...... **15** F1
  DEARNE S63 ...... **56** C2
Farfield Pk *DEARNE* S63 ...... **56** C1
Far Field Rd *RHAM/THRY* S65 ...... **105** D5
Fargate *SHEF* S1 ...... **9** E5
Far Golden Smithies
  MEX/SWTN S64 ...... **57** D4
Farish Pl *SHEFP/MNR* S2 ...... **135** F4 🔟
Far La *RHAM/THRY* S65 ...... **104** C2
  ST/HB/BR S6 ...... **107** F3
Farlow Cft *CHPT/GREN* S35 ...... **73** D3
Farm Bank Rd *SHEFP/MNR* S2 ...... **123** D5
Farm Cl *BSLYN/ROY* S71 ...... **15** D3 🔟
  DRON S18 ...... **159** F4
  HACK/IN S12 ...... **149** E3
  RHAM S60 ...... **113** F5
Farm Close Gv *STV/CWN* S43 ...... **185** F2
Farm Crs *MOS* S20 ...... **164** A2
Farm Fields Cl *MOS* S20 ...... **152** B4
Farmhill Cl *BTLY* DN5 ...... **28** C4 🔟
Farm House La *DOD/DAR* S75 ...... **12** B5
Farmoor Gdns *MOS* S20 ...... **153** F4 🔟
Farm Rd *BSLY* S70 ...... **23** D4
  SHEFP/MNR S2 ...... **135** F1
Farmstead Cl *SHEFP/MNR* S2 ...... **136** B5 🔟
Farm View Cl *HACK/IN* S12 ...... **151** F2 🔟
  KIMB S61 ...... **101** E1
Farm View Dr *HACK/IN* S12 ...... **151** F2
Farm View Gdns *HACK/IN* S12 ...... **151** F2
Farm View Rd *KIMB* S61 ...... **101** D1
Farnaby Gdns *CHPT/GREN* S35 ...... **73** D3
Farnborough Dr *DONS/BSCR* DN4 ...... **67** E1
Farndale Rd *BTLY* DN5 ...... **28** B2 🔟
  ST/HB/BR S6 ...... **108** A2
  STV/CWN S43 ...... **181** F2
Farnley Av *ST/HB/BR* S6 ...... **97** E5 🔟
Farnon Cl *CHNE* S41 ...... **190** C3 🔟
Farnsworth Rd *RHAM/THRY* S65 ...... **105** D2
Farnsworth St *CHNE* S41 ...... **191** D4 🔟
Far Pl *RHAM/THRY* S65 ...... **104** C2
Farrar Rd *SHEFS* S8 ...... **135** D3 🔟
Farrar St *BSLY* S70 ...... **2** A5
Farrier Ga *CHPT/GREN* S35 ...... **73** F5
Farrow Cl *DOD/DAR* S75 ...... **20** B3
Farthing Gale Ms *BTLY* DN5 ...... **29** D4 🔟
Far Townend *DOD/DAR* S75 ...... **20** B3 🔟
Far View Rd *SHEFN* S5 ...... **98** C5
Farwater Cl *DRON* S18 ...... **169** D2
Farwater La *DRON* S18 ...... **169** D2 🔟
Favell Rd *HACK/IN* S12 ...... **8** A5
  RHAM/THRY S65 ...... **105** E2 🔟
Fawcett St *OWL* S3 ...... **8** A3
Fearnehough St *DARN/MH* S9 ...... **124** B2 🔟
Fearn House Crs *HOY* S74 ...... **51** D3
Fearnley Av *HOY* S74 ...... **51** D3
Fellbrigg Rd *SHEFP/MNR* S2 ...... **136** B3
Fellowsfield Wy *KIMB* S61 ...... **101** F2
Fell Rd *DARN/MH* S9 ...... **111** E5
Fell St *DARN/MH* S9 ...... **111** D4

Fenland Wy *CHSW* S40 ...... **189** F4
Fenney La *ECC* S11 ...... **144** C3
Fenn Rd *DOD/DAR* S75 ...... **50** A3
Fenton Cft *KIMB* S61 ...... **102** B1
Fenton Flds *KIMB* S61 ...... **102** B1
Fenton Rd *KIMB* S61 ...... **92** B4
Fenton St *BSLY* S70 ...... **2** B5 🔟
  ECK/KIL S21 ...... **173** F1
  KIMB S61 ...... **102** A2
Fentonville St *ECC* S11 ...... **134** C2
Fenton Wy *KIMB* S61 ...... **92** C4
Feoffees Rd *CHPT/GREN* S35 ...... **98** C1 🔟
Ferguson St *DARN/MH* S9 ...... **124** A1
Ferham Cl *KIMB* S61 ...... **102** B1
Ferham Park Av *KIMB* S61 ...... **102** B3 🔟
Ferham Rd *KIMB* S61 ...... **102** B3
Fern Av *BTLY* DN5 ...... **29** E2
  MOS S20 ...... **153** D1
  STV/CWN S43 ...... **187** D1
Fernbank Dr *ARMTH* DN3 ...... **33** F1
Fern Cl *ECK/KIL* S21 ...... **163** F5
  WHHL S31 ...... **31** F3
  WMB/DAR S73 ...... **40** B1
Ferncroft Av *MOS* S20 ...... **164** A1
Ferndale Av *DRON* S18 ...... **160** B5
Ferndale Ri *DRON* S18 ...... **160** B5
Ferndale Rd *CONI* DN12 ...... **84** C1
  DRON S18 ...... **160** B5
Fernhurst La *WBTLY* DN5 ...... **28** C4
Fernhurst Rd *WHHL* DN2 ...... **32** A3
Fernlea Ct *BTLY* DN5 ...... **29** D4 🔟
Fernlea Gv *CHPT/GREN* S35 ...... **98** C1 🔟
Fernleigh Dr *RHAM* S60 ...... **113** F2
Fern Rd *ST/HB/BR* S6 ...... **120** C1
Fernvale Wk *MEX/SWTN* S64 ...... **81** E3 🔟
Fern Wy *ECK/KIL* S21 ...... **163** F5
Ferrand St *BSLY* S70 ...... **49** F1
Ferrara Cl *WMB/DAR* S73 ...... **25** F4
Ferrars Cl *DARN/MH* S9 ...... **113** D3
Ferrars Rd *DARN/MH* S9 ...... **113** D3
Ferrars Rd *DARN/MH* S9 ...... **112** C1
Ferrars Wy *DARN/MH* S9 ...... **113** D3
Ferrers Rd *WHHL* DN2 ...... **31** D4
Ferriby Rd *ST/HB/BR* S6 ...... **107** F2
Ferry Boat La *MEX/SWTN* S64 ...... **59** D4
Ferry La *CONI* DN12 ...... **61** D5
Festival Rd *DEARNE* S63 ...... **56** A3
Fewton Wy *DONS/BSCR* DN4 ...... **45** F4
Field Av *ECK/KIL* S21 ...... **175** F3
Field Cl *DRON* S18 ...... **168** A1 🔟
Fielders Wy *CONI* DN12 ...... **62** A4 🔟
Field Ga *NROS/TKH* DN11 ...... **67** E5
Field Head Rd *HOY* S74 ...... **51** F5
Fieldhead Rd *SHEFP/MNR* S2 ...... **135** E3 🔟
Fieldhouse Wy *ATT* S4 ...... **110** B5
Fielding Gv *RAW* S62 ...... **80** A4
Fielding Rd *ST/HB/BR* S6 ...... **108** A2
Field La *BSLY* S70 ...... **23** F3
  ECK/KIL S21 ...... **165** F3
  RHAM S60 ...... **117** D5
Field Vw *RHAM* S60 ...... **114** A3
Field Wy *RHAM* S60 ...... **6** C2
Fife Cl *DARN/MH* S9 ...... **100** B5
Fife Rd *DARN/MH* S9 ...... **100** B5
Fife Wy *DARN/MH* S9 ...... **100** B5
Filby Rd *BTLY* DN5 ...... **28** C4
Filey La *OWL* S3 ...... **121** F5
Finch Ri *AU/AST/KP* S26 ...... **142** F5
Finch Rd *DONS/BSCR* DN4 ...... **63** D1 🔟
Finchwell Cl *HAN/WDH* S13 ...... **126** A5
Finchwell Crs *HAN/WDH* S13 ...... **126** A5
Finchwell Rd *HAN/WDH* S13 ...... **126** A5
Findon Crs *ST/HB/BR* S6 ...... **107** E4
Findon Pl *ST/HB/BR* S6 ...... **107** E4 🔟
Findon Rd *ST/HB/BR* S6 ...... **107** E4
Findon St *ST/HB/BR* S6 ...... **107** E4 🔟
Finkle St *BTLY* DN5 ...... **29** F1
Finlay Rd *RHAM/THRY* S65 ...... **104** B1
Finlay St *OWL* S3 ...... **8** A3
Firbeck Rd *DONS/BSCR* DN4 ...... **45** D2
  SHEFS S8 ...... **146** C2 🔟
Firbeck Wy *NROS/TKH* DN11 ...... **67** E5
Fir Cl *DEARNE* S63 ...... **56** A3 🔟
Fircroft Av *SHEFN* S5 ...... **99** E4
Fircroft Rd *SHEFN* S5 ...... **99** E4
Fir Pl *ECK/KIL* S21 ...... **166** A3
Fir Rd *ECK/KIL* S21 ...... **173** F1
Firsby La *CONI* DN12 ...... **83** F4
Firshill Av *ATT* S4 ...... **109** F4
Firshill Cl *ATT* S4 ...... **109** F4
Firshill Crs *ATT* S4 ...... **109** E4
Firshill Gld *ATT* S4 ...... **109** F4 🔟
Firshill Ri *ATT* S4 ...... **109** F4
Firshill Wk *ATT* S4 ...... **109** F4 🔟
First Av *RHAM/THRY* S65 ...... **104** B1
The Firs *BSLY* S70 ...... **23** D4
Fir St *FUL* S10 ...... **121** D2
  STV/CWN S43 ...... **180** C5
Firth Dr *ATT* S4 ...... **123** E1
Firth Park Av *SHEFN* S5 ...... **110** B1
Firth Park Crs *SHEFN* S5 ...... **110** B1
Firth Park Rd *SHEFN* S5 ...... **110** B1

Firth Rd *DEARNE* S63 ...... **54** C2
Firth St *DONS/BSCR* DN4 ...... **43** F3 🔟
  KIMB S61 ...... **93** D3
Firthwood Av *DRON* S18 ...... **160** B5
Firthwood Cl *DRON* S18 ...... **160** B5 🔟
Firthwood Rd *DRON* S18 ...... **160** B5
Fir Tree Dr *AU/AST/KP* S26 ...... **155** E5
Firtree Ri *CHPT/GREN* S35 ...... **88** B2 🔟
Fir Vale Pl *SHEFN* S5 ...... **110** A3 🔟
Fir Vale Rd *SHEFN* S5 ...... **110** A3
Fisher Cl *CHSW* S40 ...... **188** C4
  RHAM S60 ...... **6** A5
Fisher La *DARN/MH* S9 ...... **125** D2
Fisher St *BTLY* DN5 ...... **16** C4
Fisher Ter *BTLY* DN5 ...... **29** E4 🔟
Fishponds Rd *HAN/WDH* S13 ...... **138** A2
Fishponds Rd West
  HAN/WDH S13 ...... **138** A3
Fitzalan Rd *HAN/WDH* S13 ...... **139** D1
Fitzalan Sq *SHEF* S1 ...... **9** F5
Fitzgerald Rd *FUL* S10 ...... **120** C3
Fitzhubert Rd *SHEFP/MNR* S2 ...... **137** E2
Fitzmaurice Rd *DARN/MH* S9 ...... **124** C1
Fitzroy Rd *SHEFP/MNR* S2 ...... **135** F4
Fitzwalter Rd *SHEFP/MNR* S2 ...... **123** E5
  SHEFP/MNR S2 ...... **136** A1
Fitzwilliam Av *CONI* DN12 ...... **84** A1
  DEARNE S63 ...... **55** F3
Fitzwilliam Ct *RAW* S62 ...... **94** A2
Fitzwilliam Ga *SHEF* S1 ...... **122** A5
Fitzwilliam Rd *RHAM/THRY* S65 ...... **7** F5
Fitzwilliam Sq *RAW* S62 ...... **92** C2
Fitzwilliam St *BSLY* S70 ...... **2** A5
  HOY S74 ...... **50** C3
  HOY S74 ...... **52** B3
  MEX/SWTN S64 ...... **81** D1
  RAW S62 ...... **94** A3
  SHEF S1 ...... **122** A5
  WMB/DAR S73 ...... **52** C1
Five Oaks *BTLY* DN5 ...... **17** F3
Five Trees Cl *TOT/DORE* S17 ...... **157** E2
Five Trees Dr *TOT/DORE* S17 ...... **157** E2
Five Weirs Wk *DARN/MH* S9 ...... **124** A1
Flamsteed Crs *CHNE* S41 ...... **184** B3
Flanders Ct *KIMB* S61 ...... **90** A1 🔟
Flask Vw *ST/HB/BR* S6 ...... **106** A5
Flat La *RHAM* S60 ...... **115** F3
Flat St *SHEF* S1 ...... **9** F5
Flatts Cl *RHAM* S60 ...... **127** F2
Flatts La *DEARNE* S63 ...... **55** E2
  RHAM S60 ...... **127** F2
Flaxby Rd *DARN/MH* S9 ...... **124** C1
Flax Lea *BSLY* S70 ...... **22** B5
Fleet Cl *DEARNE* S63 ...... **54** B1
Fleet Hill Crs *BSLYN/ROY* S71 ...... **14** B2
Fleetwood Av *BSLYN/ROY* S71 ...... **15** D2
Fleming Pl *BSLY* S70 ...... **21** F2 🔟
Fletcher Av *DRON* S18 ...... **169** E2
Fleury Cl *GLV* S14 ...... **148** C1
Fleury Crs *GLV* S14 ...... **148** C1
Fleury Pl *GLV* S14 ...... **148** C1
Fleury Ri *GLV* S14 ...... **148** C1
Fleury Rd *GLV* S14 ...... **148** C1
Flint Rd *WHHL* DN2 ...... **32** A4
Flintson Av *CHNE* S41 ...... **179** E2
Flintway *DEARNE* S63 ...... **56** A5
Flockton Av *HAN/WDH* S13 ...... **139** F2
Flockton Crs *HAN/WDH* S13 ...... **139** F2
Flockton Dr *HAN/WDH* S13 ...... **140** A2
Flockton Rd *HAN/WDH* S13 ...... **140** A2
Flodden St *FUL* S10 ...... **120** C3 🔟
Floodgate Dr *CHPT/GREN* S35 ...... **98** C3
Flora St *ST/HB/BR* S6 ...... **121** F1
Florence Av *AU/AST/KP* S26 ...... **142** B3
  DONS/BSCR DN4 ...... **43** E4
Florence Rd *KIMB* S61 ...... **102** C3 🔟
  SHEFS S8 ...... **146** C3
  MEX/SWTN S64 ...... **58** A5
Flowitt St *DONS/BSCR* DN4 ...... **4** A5
Flowright Cl *SHEFP/MNR* S2 ...... **136** B5
Folderings La *STKB/PEN* S36 ...... **69** D5
Folds Crs *SHEFS* S8 ...... **146** A4
Folds Dr *SHEFS* S8 ...... **146** A4 🔟
Folds La *SHEFS* S8 ...... **146** A4
Foley Av *WMB/DAR* S73 ...... **39** D3
Foley St *ATT* S4 ...... **123** E2
Foljambe Av *CHSW* S40 ...... **189** E4
Foljambe Dr *RHAM/THRY* S65 ...... **95** F5
Foljambe Rd *CHSW* S40 ...... **10** C6
  RHAM/THRY S65 ...... **104** C1
  STV/CWN S43 ...... **185** F1
Foljambe St *RAW* S62 ...... **94** A2 🔟
Follett Rd *SHEFN* S5 ...... **99** D4
Fontwell Dr *MEX/SWTN* S64 ...... **58** C2
Foolow Av *CHSW* S40 ...... **190** A3 🔟
Forbes Rd *ST/HB/BR* S6 ...... **108** A5
Ford La *HACK/IN* S12 ...... **162** C3
  STKB/PEN S36 ...... **69** D1
Ford Rd *ECC* S11 ...... **133** F4
  ECK/KIL S21 ...... **162** C4
Fore Hill Av *DONS/BSCR* DN4 ...... **66** B1
Foremark Rd *SHEFN* S5 ...... **99** E5
Forest Ri *DONS/BSCR* DN4 ...... **62** C2
Forge La *ECK/KIL* S21 ...... **165** F1

HOY S74 .... 52 B4
RHAM S60 .... 6 C5
SHEF S1 .... 135 E1 🔢
Forge Rd AU/AST/KP S26 .... 155 F2
Formby Cl BSLYN/ROY S71 .... 15 E1 🔢
Forncett St ATT S4 .... 123 E1
Fornham St SHEFP/MNR S2 .... 122 C5 🔢
Forres Av FUL S10 .... 120 B4
Forres Rd FUL S10 .... 120 C4
Forrester's La DRON S18 .... 160 A4 🔢
Forster Rd DONS/BSCR DN4 .... 63 F1
Forth Av DRON S18 .... 168 B1
Fort Hill Rd DARN/MH S9 .... 111 D2
Fortway Rd RHAM S60 .... 114 A2
Fossard Cl WHHL DN2 .... 31 E3
Fossard Wy BTLY DN5 .... 16 A5
Fossdale Rd ABRD S7 .... 134 B5
Foster's Cl MEX/SWTN S64 .... 57 D5
Foster St BSLY S70 .... 23 E2
Foster Wy CHPT/GREN S35 .... 73 E4
Foston Dr CHSW S40 .... 182 C4
Foulstone Rw WMB/DAR S73 .... 39 F3 🔢
Foundry St BSLY S70 .... 21 F2
CHNE S41 .... 184 B1
HOY S74 .... 52 B3
RAW S62 .... 94 A3
Fountains Wy BSLYN/ROY S71 .... 15 E4
Four Wells Dr HACK/IN S12 .... 151 E2
Fowler Bridge Rd BTLY DN5 .... 30 A1
Fowler St CHNE S41 .... 178 A4
Foxbrook Cl RCH S42 .... 182 A4 🔢
Foxbrook Ct CHSW S40 .... 188 C3
Foxbrook Dr CHSW S40 .... 188 C4
Fox Cl KIMB S61 .... 91 E4
Foxcote Wy CHSW S40 .... 188 C4
Fox Ct MEX/SWTN S64 .... 81 E2
Foxcroft Cha ECK/KIL S21 .... 166 A2
Foxcroft Dr ECK/KIL S21 .... 166 A2
Foxcroft Gv ECK/KIL S21 .... 166 A2
Foxfield Wk BSLY S70 .... 23 E4 🔢
Fox Glen Rd STKB/PEN S36 .... 69 E3
Foxglove Rd SHEFN S5 .... 99 F5
Fox Gv DONS/BSCR DN4 .... 62 A1
Foxhall La FUL S10 .... 131 D4
Fox Hill Av ST/HB/BR S6 .... 97 D4
Fox Hill Cl ST/HB/BR S6 .... 97 D4
Fox Hill Crs ST/HB/BR S6 .... 97 D4
Fox Hill Dr ST/HB/BR S6 .... 97 D4
Fox Hill Pl ST/HB/BR S6 .... 97 D4
Fox Hill Rd ST/HB/BR S6 .... 97 D2
Fox Hill Wy ST/HB/BR S6 .... 97 D3 🔢
Foxland Av MEX/SWTN S64 .... 80 C3
Fox La HACK/IN S12 .... 150 A2 🔢
Fox Lane Ct HACK/IN S12 .... 150 A1 🔢
Fox Lane Vw HACK/IN S12 .... 150 A1
Fox Rd ST/HB/BR S6 .... 121 F1
Foxroyd Cl BSLYN/ROY S71 .... 24 A2 🔢
Foxstone Cl STV/CWN S43 .... 187 E1
Fox St KIMB S61 .... 101 F3
OWL S3 .... 122 C1
Foxwood Av HACK/IN S12 .... 137 F4
Foxwood Cl CHNE S41 .... 177 F5
Foxwood Dr HACK/IN S12 .... 137 F5
Foxwood Gv HACK/IN S12 .... 137 F5
Foxwood Rd CHNE S41 .... 177 F4
HACK/IN S12 .... 137 F4
Foxwood Wy CHNE S41 .... 177 F5
Framlingham Pl SHEFP/MNR S2 .. 136 B3
France Rd ST/HB/BR S6 .... 106 B3
Frances St DON DN1 .... 5 E3
RHAM/THRY S65 .... 104 A4 🔢
France St RAW S62 .... 94 A3
Francis Cl STV/CWN S43 .... 185 E2
Francis Crs North
RHAM/THRY S65 .... 116 B1
Francis Crs South
RHAM/THRY S65 .... 116 B1
Francis Dr RHAM/THRY S65 .... 116 B1
Francis Gv CHPT/GREN S35 .... 73 E4
Franklin Cl WHHL DN2 .... 45 D1
Franklyn Rd CHSW S40 .... 10 A4
Frank Pl DARN/MH S9 .... 111 E5
Frank Rd BTLY DN5 .... 29 F3
Fraser Cl SHEFS S8 .... 146 C2 🔢
Fraser Crs SHEFS S8 .... 146 C2
Fraser Dr SHEFS S8 .... 147 D2
Fraser Rd RHAM/THRY S65 .... 146 A1
SHEFS S8 .... 146 C2
Frecheville St STV/CWN S43 .... 181 E5
Frederick Av BSLY S70 .... 21 E2
Frederick Dr CHPT/GREN S35 .... 86 C5
Frederick St DARN/MH S9 .... 124 C3
DEARNE S63 .... 55 E1 🔢
MEX/SWTN S64 .... 58 A3
RHAM S60 .... 6 C4
RHAM S60 .... 127 D2
WMB/DAR S73 .... 39 D2 🔢
Frederic Pl BSLY S70 .... 22 A3 🔢
Fred Mulley Rd ATT S4 .... 123 E2
Freebirch Vw CHSW S40 .... 182 C2 🔢
Freedom Ct ST/HB/BR S6 .... 108 B5
Freedom Rd ST/HB/BR S6 .... 121 D1
Freeman Rd BSLY S70 .... 22 A2 🔢
Freemans Yd BSLY S70 .... 3 E6 🔢

Freeston Pl DARN/MH S9 .... 111 E5
French Ga DON DN1 .... 4 C2 🔢
French St BTLY DN5 .... 16 C4
Fretson Rd SHEFP/MNR S2 .... 137 E2 🔢
Fretwell Rd RHAM/THRY S65 ...... 105 D1
Friar Cl ST/HB/BR S6 .... 119 E1
Friars Ga BTLY DN5 .... 4 D1
Frickley Rd ECC S11 .... 133 D2
Frinton Cl CHSW S40 .... 190 A5
Frith Cl HACK/IN S12 .... 137 F5
Frith Rd HACK/IN S12 .... 137 F5
Froggatt Cl STV/CWN S43 .... 187 D3
Froggatt La SHEF S1 .... 122 B5 🔢
Front St RHAM S60 .... 127 F3
Frostings Cl CHPT/GREN S35 .... 87 D5
The Frostings CHPT/GREN S35 ...... 87 D5
Fulford Cl CHSW S40 .... 189 D4
DARN/MH S9 .... 125 D2 🔢
Fulford Pl DARN/MH S9 .... 125 D2 🔢
Fuller Dr CHNE S41 .... 185 D3 🔢
Fullerton Av CONI DN12 .... 84 A1
Fullerton Crs RHAM/THRY S65 ...... 95 F4
Fullerton Dr RHAM S60 .... 113 F4
Fullerton Rd RHAM S60 .... 103 D5
RHAM S60 .... 114 A1
Fulmar Wy KIMB S61 .... 76 B5
Fulmer Cl BSLYN/ROY S71 .... 14 C1
Fulmere Crs SHEFN S5 .... 97 F3
Fulmere Rd SHEFN S5 .... 97 F3
Fulmer Rd ECC S11 .... 134 A3
Fulney Rd ECC S11 .... 133 D2
Fulton Rd FUL S10 .... 121 D2
Fulwood Cha FUL S10 .... 132 C2 🔢
Fulwood Dr DONS/BSCR DN4 .... 63 F3
Fulwood Head Rd FUL S10 .... 130 C4
Fulwood La FUL S10 .... 130 B4
Fulwood Rd ECC S11 .... 121 D5
ECC S11 .... 132 B3
FUL S10 .... 133 E1
Furnace Hl OWL S3 .... 8 D3
Furnace La DRON S18 .... 176 A3
HAN/WDH S13 .... 140 B3
STV/CWN S43 .... 186 A3
Furness Cl ST/HB/BR S6 .... 106 B5
Furness Dene BSLYN/ROY S71 ...... 15 E2
Furness Rd CHPT/GREN S35 .... 73 D4
Furniss Av TOT/DORE S17 .... 156 B2
Furniss Ms TOT/DORE S17 .... 156 C2
Furnival Rd DONS/BSCR DN4 .... 43 E4
Furnival Rd ATT S4 .... 9 G3
Furnival St SHEF S1 .... 122 B5
Furnival Wy RHAM S60 .... 116 B3
Fylde Cl BSLYN/ROY S71 .... 15 E1

G

Gainsborough Rd ABRD S7 .... 134 B3
DRON S18 .... 168 C3
Gainsborough Wy BSLYN/ROY S71 .. 3 H1
Galley Rd MOS S20 .... 152 B4
Gallow Tree Rd RHAM/THRY S65 .. 105 E5
Galsworthy Av SHEFN S5 .... 109 D1
Galsworthy Cl DONS/BSCR DN4 .... 63 D2
Galsworthy Rd SHEFN S5 .... 109 D1
Galway Cl RAW S62 .... 80 B5
Gamston Rd SHEFS S8 .... 135 D3
Gannow Cl ECK/KIL S21 .... 167 D1
Ganton Rd ST/HB/BR S6 .... 107 F2 🔢
Garbroads Crs RHAM/THRY S65 .... 95 F4
Garden Av ECK/KIL S21 .... 175 F4
Garden Cl STV/CWN S43 .... 179 E3 🔢
Garden Crs RHAM S60 .... 115 E2
Garden Dr WMB/DAR S73 .... 40 B5
Garden Gv WMB/DAR S73 .... 39 D5
Garden House Cl BSLYN/ROY S71 .. 15 D2
Gardenia Rd ARMTH DN3 .... 19 F5
Garden La BTLY DN5 .... 61 E1
RHAM S60 .... 6 B4
Gardens La CONI DN12 .... 84 C1
The Gardens DONS/BSCR DN4 .... 46 B5
Garden St DEARNE S63 .... 27 D3
DEARNE S63 .... 55 E1 🔢
KIMB S61 .... 102 C2
MEX/SWTN S64 .... 58 B3 🔢
MEX/SWTN S64 .... 58 B4
SHEF S1 .... 122 B3
Garden Wk RHAM S60 .... 115 E1
Gardom Cl DRON S18 .... 168 B2 🔢
Garfield Mt RHAM/THRY S65 ...... 104 A4 🔢
Garland Cl MOS S20 .... 164 C1
Garland Cft MOS S20 .... 164 C1
Garland Dr ST/HB/BR S6 .... 106 B3
Garland Mt MOS S20 .... 152 C5 🔢
Garland Mt MOS S20 .... 164 C1
Garry Rd ST/HB/BR S6 .... 107 F3
Garter St ATT S4 .... 110 B5
Garth Cl DARN/MH S9 .... 124 B2 🔢
Garth Wy DRON S18 .... 169 D2 🔢
Gartrice Gdns MOS S20 .... 165 E3
Gartrice Gv MOS S20 .... 165 D3
Gashouse La ARMTH DN3 .... 164 B3
Gate Crs DOD/DAR S75 .... 20 A2

Gatefield Cl CHSW S40 .... 183 D2
Gatefield Rd ABRD S7 .... 134 C4 🔢
Gateway Cl RAW S62 .... 93 F4
Gateway Ct RAW S62 .... 93 F4 🔢
The Gateway RAW S62 .... 93 F5
Gatty Rd SHEFN S5 .... 99 F2
Gaunt Cl ECK/KIL S21 .... 166 A2
GLV S14 .... 148 B2
Gaunt Dr GLV S14 .... 148 B2
Gaunt Pl GLV S14 .... 148 B1
Gaunt Rd GLV S14 .... 148 B1
Gaunt Wy GLV S14 .... 148 B2
Gawber Rd DOD/DAR S75 .... 13 D4
Gayton Cl DONS/BSCR DN4 .... 63 E2
Gayton Rd ATT S4 .... 110 A4 🔢
Geer La HACK/IN S12 .... 162 A3
Gelderd Pl DRON S18 .... 169 E3
Gell St OWL S3 .... 122 A5
Genn La BSLY S70 .... 21 E4
Genoa Cl WMB/DAR S73 .... 25 F3
Genoa St MEX/SWTN S64 .... 58 C3
George Pl MEX/SWTN S64 .... 59 D4 🔢
RAW S62 .... 94 B1
George Sq BSLY S70 .... 2 C6 🔢
George St BSLY S70 .... 2 C6
BSLY S70 .... 36 B1 🔢
BSLY S70 .... 37 D1
BTLY DN5 .... 16 C4 🔢
CHNE S41 .... 178 A4
DEARNE S63 .... 27 F4
HOY S74 .... 51 F3 🔢
RHAM S60 .... 6 C4 🔢
SHEF S1 .... 9 F5
STV/CWN S43 .... 187 E3
WMB/DAR S73 .... 39 E3
WMB/DAR S73 .... 40 A1
George Yd BSLY S70 .... 2 C5
Gerald Cl BSLY S70 .... 23 D3
Gerald Crs BSLY S70 .... 23 E2
Gerald Pl BSLY S70 .... 23 D3
Gerald Rd BSLY S70 .... 23 D3
Gerald St DARN/MH S9 .... 111 E5
Gerald Wk BSLY S70 .... 23 D3
Gerard Cl CHSW S40 .... 189 D3
SHEFP/MNR S2 .... 135 F4 🔢
Gerard Rd RHAM S60 .... 105 F4
Gerard St SHEFS S8 .... 135 F4
Gervase Av SHEFS S8 .... 158 C2
Gervase Dr SHEFS S8 .... 158 C2
Gervase Pl SHEFS S8 .... 158 C2 🔢
Gervase Rd SHEFS S8 .... 158 C2
Gibbing Greaves Rd
RHAM/THRY S65 .... 105 F5
Gibbons Dr SHEFS S8 .... 148 C3
Gibbons Wy SHEFS S8 .... 148 C3 🔢
Gibraltar St OWL S3 .... 8 D3
Gifford Dr DONS/BSCR DN4 .... 62 B1
Gifford Rd SHEFP/MNR S2 .... 135 E3 🔢
Gig La HOY S74 .... 36 C5
Gilbert Av CHSW S40 .... 189 E4
Gilbert Gv BSLY S70 .... 23 E2
Gilberthorpe Dr
RHAM/THRY S65 .... 104 B3 🔢
Gilberthorpe Rd
DONS/BSCR DN4 .... 43 D5 🔢
Gilberthorpe St RHAM/THRY S65 ... 7 H6
Gilbert St SHEFP/MNR S2 .... 9 G5
Giles Av DEARNE S63 .... 55 D2
Gill Cft ST/HB/BR S6 .... 119 C1 🔢
Gilleyfield Av TOT/DORE S17 .... 156 C1
Gill Mdw ST/HB/BR S6 .... 119 D1
Gillot Dell MALT S66 .... 117 F1 🔢
Gillott La MALT S66 .... 117 F1
Gillott Rd ST/HB/BR S6 .... 97 D5
Gill St DON DN1 .... 5 F6
HOY S74 .... 52 B3
Gilpin La ST/HB/BR S6 .... 8 A1
Gilpin St ST/HB/BR S6 .... 8 A1
ST/HB/BR S6 .... 121 F1 🔢
Gilroyd La DOD/DAR S75 .... 20 C5
Ginhouse La KIMB S61 .... 6 B1
Gipsy Green La DEARNE S63 .... 56 A4
Gipsy La CHNE S41 .... 178 C4
DRON S18 .... 171 E2
Gisborne Rd ECC S11 .... 133 F4
Glade Cl CHSW S40 .... 10 A2
Glade Cft HACK/IN S12 .... 137 E5
Glade Lea HACK/IN S12 .... 149 E1
The Glade CHSW S40 .... 189 E1
Gladstone Ms FUL S10 .... 132 C1 🔢
Gladstone Rd CHSW S40 .... 10 C4
DONS/BSCR DN4 .... 43 E3
FUL S10 .... 132 C1
Gladwin Gdns CHSW S40 .... 189 E4 🔢
Gladys St RHAM/THRY S65 .... 104 B3
Glamis Rd WHHL DN2 .... 45 E1
Glasshouse La CHNE S41 .... 179 E1
MEX/SWTN S64 .... 58 A4
STV/CWN S43 .... 179 E2
Glasshouse St RHAM S60 .... 6 B4
Glastonbury Ga BTLY DN5 .... 28 B4
Gleadless Av HACK/IN S12 .... 149 D1
Gleadless Bank HACK/IN S12 .... 149 D1 🔢
Gleadless Common HACK/IN S12 .. 137 D5
Gleadless Ct SHEFP/MNR S2 ...... 135 F4 🔢

Gleadless Crs HACK/IN S12 .... 137 D5
Gleadless Dr HACK/IN S12 .... 149 D1
Gleadless Mt HACK/IN S12 .... 149 E2 🔢
Gleadless Rd HACK/IN S12 .... 136 C5
   HACK/IN S12 .... 149 E2
   SHEFP/MNR S2 .... 136 B4 🔢
   SHEFS S8 .... 135 E3
   SHEFS S8 .... 135 E4 🔢
Glebe Cl MEX/SWTN S64 .... 81 D2
Glebe Crs RHAM/THRY S65 .... 95 F5
Glebe Farm La ARMTH DN3 .... 33 E3
Glebeland Cl RAW S62 .... 79 F3
Glebelands Rd STKB/PEN S36 .... 69 D3
Glebe Rd FUL S10 .... 121 D3
   MEX/SWTN S64 .... 81 D2
Glebe St DONS/BSCR DN4 .... 62 B1
Gledhill Cl DRON S18 .... 169 E2
Glenalmond Rd ECC S11 .... 133 F3
Glenavon Cl STV/CWN S43 .... 179 E1
Glencoe Dr SHEFP/MNR S2 .... 123 D5 🔢
Glencoe Pl SHEFP/MNR S2 .... 123 D5 🔢
Glencoe Rd SHEFP/MNR S2 .... 123 D5
Glencoe Wy CHSW S40 .... 182 C5
Glendale Cl DOD/DAR S75 .... 20 C1
Gleneagles Cl CHSW S40 .... 189 D4 🔢
Gleneagles Dr ARMTH DN3 .... 67 F1 🔢
   DONS/BSCR DN4 .... 67 F1
Gleneagles Ri WMB/DAR S73 .... 81 E1
Glen Field La DONS/BSCR DN4 .... 43 E3
Glenfield Crs CHNE S41 .... 184 A2
Glenholme Pl HAN/WDH S13 .... 138 C3
Glenholme Rd HAN/WDH S13 ...... 139 D3 🔢
Glenholme Wy HAN/WDH S13 .... 139 D3 🔢
Glenmoor Av BSLY S70 .... 20 C2 🔢
Glenmore Cft HACK/IN S12 .... 137 F4
Glenmore Ri WMB/DAR S73 .... 39 F4 🔢
Glenorchy Rd ABRD S7 .... 134 B5
Glen Rd ABRD S7 .... 134 C4
The Glen ECC S11 .... 133 F2 🔢
Glenthorne Cl CHSW S40 .... 189 D2
Glentilt Rd ABRD S7 .... 134 B5
Glen View Rd SHEFS S8 .... 146 C5
Glenville Cl HOY S74 .... 51 E3
Glenwood Crs CHPT/GREN S35 .... 88 C1
Gliwice Wy DONS/BSCR DN4 .... 45 F3
Glossop Rd FUL S10 .... 121 D5
   OWL S3 .... 8 A6
Glossop's Cft CHNE S41 .... 178 C4 🔢
Gloucester Av HAN/WDH S13 .... 140 A3
Gloucester Crs FUL S10 .... 121 F5 🔢
Gloucester Rd CHNE S41 .... 10 C1
   KIMB S61 .... 92 A5
   WHHL DN2 .... 31 E4
Gloucester St FUL S10 .... 121 F5
Glover Rd SHEFP/MNR S2 .... 135 E3 🔢
   TOT/DORE S17 .... 157 D3 🔢
Glumangate CHSW S40 .... 11 E5
Glyn Av DON DN1 .... 5 F2
Goathland Cl HAN/WDH S13 .... 140 A3
Goathland Pl HAN/WDH S13 .... 140 A3
Goathland Rd HAN/WDH S13 .... 140 B3
Goddard Av STKB/PEN S36 .... 68 A1 🔢
Goddard Hall Rd SHEFN S5 .... 110 A3
Godric Dr RHAM S60 .... 113 F3
Godric Gn RHAM S60 .... 113 F3
Godric Rd SHEFN S5 .... 99 D2
Godstone Rd RHAM S60 .... 103 F4
Goldcrest Wk KIMB S61 .... 90 B1
Gold Cft BSLY S70 .... 22 B2 🔢
Golden Smithies La
   MEX/SWTN S64 .... 56 C5
Goldsborough Rd WHHL DN2 .... 45 E1
Goldsmith Dr RHAM/THRY S65 .... 104 C3
Goldsmith Rd DONS/BSCR DN4 .... 64 A1
   RHAM/THRY S65 .... 104 C3
Gold St BSLY S70 .... 22 B2
Gomersal La DRON S18 .... 169 E2
Gomersall Av CONI DN12 .... 84 A1
Goodison Bvd DONS/BSCR DN4 .... 46 C5
Goodison Crs ST/HB/BR S6 .... 120 A1
Goodison Ri ST/HB/BR S6 .... 120 A1
Goodwin Av RAW S62 .... 80 A5
Goodwin Crs MEX/SWTN S64 .... 57 E4
Goodwin Rd KIMB S61 .... 92 B2
   SHEFS S8 .... 135 E4 🔢
Goodyear Crs WMB/DAR S73 .... 39 E3
Goore Av DARN/MH S9 .... 124 C5
Goore Dr DARN/MH S9 .... 124 C4 🔢
Goore Rd DARN/MH S9 .... 124 C5
Gooseacre Av DEARNE S63 .... 26 A2
Goosebutt St RAW S62 .... 94 A3
Goosecroft Av RHAM/THRY S65 ...... 95 F4 🔢
Gordon Av SHEFS S8 .... 147 E3
Gordon Rd ECC S11 .... 134 B2 🔢
Gordon St BSLY S70 .... 23 F2
   DON DN1 .... 4 C4
Gordon Ter RHAM/THRY S65 .... 7 H6 🔢
Gorehill Cl DEARNE S63 .... 56 B2
Gorman Cl CHNE S41 .... 183 F1
Gorse Dr ECK/KIL S21 .... 166 E5 🔢
Gorse La FUL S10 .... 131 D3
The Gorse MALT S66 .... 117 F1
   RHAM/THRY S65 .... 105 D4

Gorse Valley Rd CHNE S41 .... 191 F5
Gorse Valley Wy CHNE S41 .... 191 F5
Gorsey Brigg DRON S18 .... 168 A2
Gosber Brig ECK/KIL S21 .... 164 B5
Gosber St ECK/KIL S21 .... 164 B5
Gosforth Cl DRON S18 .... 169 D2
Gosforth Crs DRON S18 .... 169 D2 🔢
Gosforth Dr DRON S18 .... 169 D2 🔢
Gosforth Gn DRON S18 .... 169 D2
Gosforth La DRON S18 .... 169 D2
Gotham Rd RHAM S60 .... 114 A3
Gough Cl RHAM/THRY S65 .... 105 D5
Goulding St MEX/SWTN S64 .... 58 A4
Gowdall Gn BTLY DN5 .... 16 B3
Gower Crs CHSW S40 .... 183 D4
Gower St ATT S4 .... 123 D1
   WMB/DAR S73 .... 39 F3
Goyt Side Rd CHSW S40 .... 189 E2
Grace Rd CONI DN12 .... 62 A4
Grafton St BSLY S70 .... 2 A6
   SHEFP/MNR S2 .... 123 D5
Grafton Wy RHAM/THRY S65 .... 7 E3
Graham Av RHAM S60 .... 114 B5 🔢
Graham Rd ECC S11 .... 133 D2
   FUL S10 .... 132 C2
Graham's Orch BSLY S70 .... 2 C5
Grampian Cl BTLY DN5 .... 28 C4 🔢
   DOD/DAR S75 .... 12 C5 🔢
Grampian Crs CHSW S40 .... 182 C5
Granary Cl RCH S42 .... 182 B1
Granby Crs WHHL DN2 .... 45 D2
Granby Rd CONI DN12 .... 62 A5
   SHEFS S8 .... 110 B2
Grange Av AU/AST/KP S26 .... 142 A1
   DONS/BSCR DN4 .... 43 E5 🔢
   DRON S18 .... 168 C2
Grange Cliffe Cl ECC S11 .... 145 F1
Grange Cl DONS/BSCR DN4 .... 67 D1
Grange Crs BSLYN/ROY S71 .... 15 F5
   DEARNE S63 .... 27 E3
   ECC S11 .... 134 C2
Grange Crescent Rd ECC S11 .... 134 C2
Grange Dr RHAM S60 .... 91 E5
Grange Farm DONS/BSCR DN4 .... 63 E3
Grange La BSLYN/ROY S71 .... 23 F1
   DONS/BSCR DN4 .... 100 A1
   KIMB S61 .... 90 A1
   RHAM S60 .... 113 E1
Grange Mill La SHEFN S5 .... 100 A1
Grangemill Pl STV/CWN S43 .... 187 D1 🔢
Grange Park Av STV/CWN S43 .... 186 A5
Grange Rd BTLY DN5 .... 16 B2 🔢
   DEARNE S63 .... 55 E3
   DONS/BSCR DN4 .... 67 D1
   ECC S11 .... 134 C2
   MEX/SWTN S64 .... 80 C1
   MOS S20 .... 153 E2
   RAW S62 .... 80 B4
   RHAM S60 .... 115 F2
Grange St DEARNE S63 .... 27 E3
The Grange CHSW S40 .... 182 A5
   KIMB S61 .... 91 D4
   HOY S74 .... 37 E4
Grange Vw DONS/BSCR DN4 .... 43 E4
   HOY S74 .... 37 E4
Grange View Crs KIMB S61 .... 101 E1
Grange View Rd KIMB S61 .... 101 E1
Grangewood Rd CHSW S40 .... 190 A5
Grantley Cl WMB/DAR S73 .... 40 A5
Granville Cl CHNE S41 .... 191 E4 🔢
Granville Rd SHEFP/MNR S2 .... 136 A1
Granville St DOD/DAR S75 .... 13 E4
   SHEFP/MNR S2 .... 122 C5 🔢
Granville Ter RHAM/THRY S65 .... 7 H6
Grasmere Av WHHL DN2 .... 32 A5
Grasmere Cl CHNE S41 .... 183 E2
Grasmere Rd BSLYN/ROY S71 .... 3 F5
   CONI DN12 .... 84 C1
   DRON S18 .... 168 C2
   SHEFS S8 .... 134 C5 🔢
Grassdale Vw HACK/IN S12 .... 151 D2
Grassington Dr HACK/IN S12 .... 151 F2 🔢
Grassington Rd HACK/IN S12 .... 151 E2
Grassington Wy CHPT/GREN S35 ..... 74 A3
Grassmoor Cl HACK/IN S12 .... 137 D5
Grassthorpe Rd HACK/IN S12 .... 149 E1
Grattan St KIMB S61 .... 101 F3
Graven Cl CHPT/GREN S35 .... 96 C1
Gray Av AU/AST/KP S26 .... 142 B1
Gray Cl RHAM/THRY S65 .... 7 F2
Gray Gdns DONS/BSCR DN4 .... 63 F1 🔢
Grays Ct CONI DN12 .... 60 B4
Grayson Cl STKB/PEN S36 .... 69 D3
Grayson Rd KIMB S61 .... 92 B2
Gray St HOY S74 .... 52 B3
   MOS S20 .... 164 A1
   OWL S3 .... 122 C1
Greasbro Rd DARN/MH S9 .... 112 B2
Greasbrough La RAW S62 .... 93 E3
Greasbrough Rd KIMB S61 .... 6 C1
   RAW S62 .... 93 F5
   RHAM S60 .... 6 C2
Greasbrough St RHAM S60 .... 6 B3
Great Bank Rd RHAM/THRY S65 .... 105 D5

Great Central Av
   DONS/BSCR DN4 .... 43 F4 🔢
Great Cft DRON S18 .... 168 B1
Great Eastern Wy RAW S62 .... 94 A4
Great Park Rd KIMB S61 .... 101 F1
Greaves Cl ST/HB/BR S6 .... 119 D1 🔢
Greaves Fold DOD/DAR S75 .... 12 C5 🔢
Greaves La CHPT/GREN S35 .... 73 E1
   ST/HB/BR S6 .... 106 C5
   ST/HB/BR S6 .... 119 D1
Greaves Rd KIMB S61 .... 102 B2
   SHEFN S5 .... 98 B1
Greaves St ST/HB/BR S6 .... 108 B5
Green Acres HOY S74 .... 51 F3
   RAW S62 .... 94 B1
Greenacres Cl DRON S18 .... 170 A4 🔢
Greenbank Dr CHSW S40 .... 183 D5
Green Boulevarde
   DONS/BSCR DN4 .... 46 C4
Green Cha ECK/KIL S21 .... 164 A5
Green Cl DRON S18 .... 170 C5
   STV/CWN S43 .... 187 D3
Green Cross DRON S18 .... 169 F1
Green Farm Cl CHSW S40 .... 183 D3
Greenfield RAW S62 .... 94 A1
Greenfield Cl RHAM/THRY S65 ..... 105 E1 🔢
   SHEFS S8 .... 159 D1
Greenfield Dr SHEFS S8 .... 159 D1
Greenfield Gdns DONS/BSCR DN4 ... 47 E5
Greenfield La DONS/BSCR DN4 .... 43 E5
Greenfield Rd HOY S74 .... 51 F1
   RHAM/THRY S65 .... 105 E1
Greenfields ECK/KIL S21 .... 164 A5 🔢
Green Finch Cl RHAM S60 .... 114 B4
Greenfoot Cl DOD/DAR S75 .... 47 E5
Greenfoot La DOD/DAR S75 .... 13 E4
Greengate Cl CHSW S40 .... 189 D2
Greengate La CHPT/GREN S35 .... 73 E5
   HAN/WDH S13 .... 140 A4
Greengate Rd HAN/WDH S13 .... 140 B4
Green Gln CHSW S40 .... 189 D2 🔢
Greenhall Rd ECK/KIL S21 .... 164 A5
Greenhead Gdns CHPT/GREN S35 ... 88 B1
Greenhead La CHPT/GREN S35 .... 74 C5
Greenhill Av BSLYN/ROY S71 .... 2 C1
   SHEFS S8 .... 146 C5
Greenhill Main Rd SHEFS S8 .... 159 E1 🔢
Greenhill Pkwy SHEFS S8 .... 158 C2
   TOT/DORE S17 .... 158 B2
Greenhill Rd SHEFS S8 .... 146 C3
Greenhouse La FUL S10 .... 131 D5
Green House Rd WHHL DN2 .... 31 F3
Greenhow St FUL S10 .... 121 D2
Green Ings La DEARNE S63 .... 56 B1
Greenland Cl DARN/MH S9 .... 125 D2 🔢
Greenland Dr DARN/MH S9 .... 125 D1
Greenland Rd DARN/MH S9 .... 125 D1
Greenlands Av NROS/TKH DN11 ...... 67 E5
Greenland Vw BSLY S70 .... 36 A1 🔢
   DARN/MH S9 .... 125 D2
Greenland Wy DARN/MH S9 .... 125 D1
Green La ARMTH DN3 .... 47 F3
   AU/AST/KP S26 .... 129 E3
   AU/AST/KP S26 .... 143 E3
   CHNE S41 .... 185 E3
   CHPT/GREN S35 .... 99 D1
   DEARNE S63 .... 55 E5
   DOD/DAR S75 .... 20 B4
   DOD/DAR S75 .... 21 D5
   DRON S18 .... 169 F1
   ECK/KIL S21 .... 166 A4
   HOY S74 .... 50 B4
   KIMB S61 .... 101 D2
   OWL S3 .... 8 C2
   RAW S62 .... 94 A1
   RHAM S60 .... 113 F5
   RHAM S60 .... 115 E2
Green Lea DRON S18 .... 168 A1
Greenleafe Av WHHL DN2 .... 32 A2
Green Oak Av TOT/DORE S17 .... 156 C4
Green Oak Crs TOT/DORE S17 ...... 156 C4 🔢
Green Oak Dr AU/AST/KP S26 .... 155 E3
   TOT/DORE S17 .... 156 C4 🔢
Green Oak Rd TOT/DORE S17 .... 156 C5
Greenock St ST/HB/BR S6 .... 107 F4 🔢
Green Ri RAW S62 .... 79 E4
Greenside CHNE S41 .... 184 A2
Greenside Av CHNE S41 .... 184 A2
Greenside La HOY S74 .... 51 F2
Green Side MALT S66 .... 118 A1 🔢
Green Spring Av BSLY S70 .... 36 A5
Greens Rd RHAM/THRY S65 .... 104 C3
Greens Rd BSLY S70 .... 37 D1
   CHNE S41 .... 178 B5
   DONS/BSCR DN4 .... 63 D1
   HOY S74 .... 52 A2
   KIMB S61 .... 92 C2
   STKB/PEN S36 .... 69 E2
The Green CHNE S41 .... 191 E5
   CONI DN12 .... 59 D5
   MEX/SWTN S64 .... 80 C1
   RHAM S60 .... 115 D1
   TOT/DORE S17 .... 156 B4

Greenways *CHSW* S40 .... **189** D4
The Greenway *SHEFS* S8 .... **147** D5 ▣
Greenwood Av *BSLY* S70 .... **22** C5
 DARN/MH S9 .... **124** B4
 DONS/BSCR DN4 .... **43** D4 ▣
Greenwood Cl *DARN/MH* S9 .... **124** C4
Greenwood Crs *DARN/MH* S9 .... **124** B4
Greenwood Dr *DARN/MH* S9 .... **124** B4
Greenwood La *ST/HB/BR* S13 .... **140** B3 ▣
Greenwood Rd *CHPT/GREN* S35 .... **74** A4
 DARN/MH S9 .... **124** C4
 MEX/SWTN S64 .... **81** F4
Greenwood Ter *BSLY* S70 .... **2** B4
Greenwood Wy *DARN/MH* S9 .... **124** B4
Gregg House Crs *SHEFS* S5 .... **99** E4
Gregg House Rd *SHEFS* S5 .... **99** E4
Gregory La *STV/CWN* S43 .... **179** E5
Gregory Rd *SHEFS* S8 .... **135** E4 ▣
Grend Wood Ct *CHPT/GREN* S35 .... **87** D5
Grenfell Av *MEX/SWTN* S64 .... **58** C3
Grenfolds Rd *CHPT/GREN* S35 .... **97** E1
Grenobank Rd *CHPT/GREN* S35 .... **97** E1
Greno Crs *CHPT/GREN* S35 .... **97** E1
Greno Ga *CHPT/GREN* S35 .... **87** D5
Grenomoor Cl *CHPT/GREN* S35 .... **97** D2
Greno Rd *MEX/SWTN* S64 .... **81** D2
Greno Vw *HOY* S74 .... **51** D3
Greno View Rd *CHPT/GREN* S35 .... **73** E3
Grenville Pl *DOD/DAR* S75 .... **13** D4 ▣
Grenville Rd *DONS/BSCR* DN4 .... **62** C1
Gresham Av *RHAM* S60 .... **114** A3
Gresham Rd *ST/HB/BR* S6 .... **121** D1 ▣
Gresley Rd *DONS/BSCR* DN4 .... **43** F3
 SHEFS S8 .... **158** D3
Grey Friars' Rd *DON* DN1 .... **4** C2
Greystock St *ATT* S4 .... **123** F1 ▣
Greystones Av *BSLY* S70 .... **36** A1
 ECC S11 .... **133** F3
Greystones Cl *ECC* S11 .... **133** E3
Greystones Crs *ECC* S11 .... **133** E3
Greystones Dr *ECC* S11 .... **133** E3
Greystones Grange *ECC* S11 .... **133** E3 ▣
Greystones Grange Rd *ECC* S11 .... **133** E3 ▣
Greystones Hall Rd *ECC* S11 .... **133** E3 ▣
Greystones Ri *ECC* S11 .... **133** E3 ▣
Greystones Rd *ECC* S11 .... **133** E3 ▣
 RHAM S60 .... **116** B3 ▣
Grice Cl *DONS/BSCR* DN4 .... **47** D2
Griffin Cl *STV/CWN* S43 .... **187** F1
Griffin Rd *MEX/SWTN* S64 .... **56** C5
Griffiths Cl *RAW* S62 .... **94** A2 ▣
Griffiths Rd *CHPT/GREN* S35 .... **73** F5
Grimesthorpe Rd *ATT* S4 .... **110** A5 ▣
 ATT S4 .... **110** B3 ▣
 ATT S4 .... **123** E1
Grimsell Cl *ST/HB/BR* S6 .... **97** E2
Grimsell Crs *ST/HB/BR* S6 .... **97** E2
Grimsell Dr *ST/HB/BR* S6 .... **97** E2
Grindlow Av *CHSW* S40 .... **190** A4 ▣
Grindlow Cl *SHEFS* S8 .... **136** A4
Grindlow Dr *SHEFP/MNR* S2 .... **136** A4
Grindon Cl *CHSW* S40 .... **183** D4 ▣
Grizedale Av *MOS* S20 .... **153** E3
Grizedale Cl *MOS* S20 .... **153** E5 ▣
Grosvenor Crs *BTLY* DN5 .... **17** E4
 DONS/BSCR DN4 .... **62** B1
Grosvenor Dr *BSLY* S70 .... **21** D1
Grosvenor Rd *RHAM/THRY* S65 .... **7** F2
Grosvenor Sq *SHEFP/MNR* S2 .... **135** D2 ▣
Grosvenor Ter *DONS/BSCR* DN4 .... **62** B1 ▣
Grouse Cft *ST/HB/BR* S6 .... **121** D1
Grove Cl *DEARNE* S63 .... **41** D5
 ST/HB/BR S6 .... **107** E2
Grove Gdns *STV/CWN* S43 .... **186** A5
Grove Hill Rd *WHHL* DN2 .... **31** F2
Grove House Ct *TOT/DORE* S17 .... **156** C3 ▣
Grove Pl *DON* DN1 .... **4** D5
Grove Rd *ABRD* S7 .... **146** A2
 CHNE S41 .... **184** B2
 DEARNE S63 .... **40** C5
 RHAM S60 .... **103** E4
 STKB/PEN S36 .... **70** A3
 STV/CWN S43 .... **185** F4
 TOT/DORE S17 .... **156** C3
Grove Sq *ST/HB/BR* S6 .... **108** C5
Grove St *BSLY* S70 .... **23** D5
 BSLYN/ROY S71 .... **5** F6
 CHNE S41 .... **191** D4
The Grove *RAW* S62 .... **94** B1
 RHAM/THRY S65 .... **104** C2
 ST/HB/BR S6 .... **106** C4
 TOT/DORE S17 .... **156** B3
 WHHL DN2 .... **31** E4
Grove V *WHHL* DN2 .... **32** A2
Grove Wy *STV/CWN* S43 .... **186** A4
Guernsey Rd *SHEFP/MNR* S2 .... **135** E2 ▣
Guest La *DONS/BSCR* DN4 .... **42** B5
Guest Rd *DOD/DAR* S75 .... **2** A1
 ECC S11 .... **134** A2
 RHAM S60 .... **104** A5
Guest St *HOY* S74 .... **51** F1
Guildford Av *CHSW* S40 .... **189** E4 ▣
 SHEFP/MNR S2 .... **136** B2
Guildford Cl *SHEFP/MNR* S2 .... **136** B2

Guildford Dr *SHEFP/MNR* S2 .... **136** B2
Guildford Ri *SHEFP/MNR* S2 .... **136** B2
Guildford Rd *WHHL* DN2 .... **31** F2
Guildford Vw *SHEFP/MNR* S2 .... **136** C2 ▣
Guildford Wy *SHEFP/MNR* S2 .... **136** B3
Guild Rd *RHAM/THRY* S65 .... **104** C3
Guilthwaite Common La
 AU/AST/KP S26 .... **129** D2
Guilthwaite Crs *RHAM* S60 .... **115** E3
Gullane Dr *DONS/BSCR* DN4 .... **62** B1
Gun La *OWL* S3 .... **9** F3
Gurney Rd *DONS/BSCR* DN4 .... **63** F1 ▣
Gypsy La *WMB/DAR* S73 .... **39** F4

H

Habershon Dr *CHPT/GREN* S35 .... **74** A5 ▣
Habershon Rd *KIMB* S61 .... **92** A5
Hackness La *RHAM* S60 .... **113** F3
Hackney La *DRON* S18 .... **176** A4
Hackthorn Rd *SHEFS* S8 .... **147** D2
Haddon Cl *CHSW* S40 .... **189** D2
 DRON S18 .... **169** F1
Haddon Pl *STV/CWN* S43 .... **187** E1
Haddon Ri *MEX/SWTN* S64 .... **59** E1
Haddon Rd *BSLYN/ROY* S71 .... **14** C1 ▣
Haddon St *OWL* S3 .... **122** A1 ▣
Haddon Wy *AU/AST/KP* S26 .... **143** D5
Haden St *ST/HB/BR* S6 .... **108** A4
Hadfield St *FUL* S10 .... **121** D2
 WMB/DAR S73 .... **39** F4
Hadleigh Cl *RAW* S62 .... **94** A2 ▣
Hadrian Rd *RHAM* S60 .... **114** A4
Hady Crs *CHNE* S41 .... **191** D1
Hady Hl *CHNE* S41 .... **191** D2
Hady La *CHNE* S41 .... **191** E2
Haggard Rd *ST/HB/BR* S6 .... **108** B4
Hagg Hl *FUL* S10 .... **120** A2
 ST/HB/BR S6 .... **96** C4
Hagg La *FUL* S10 .... **119** E4
Hague Av *ECK/KIL* S21 .... **175** F3
 RAW S62 .... **79** F3
Hague La *CHPT/GREN* S35 .... **73** D4
 ECK/KIL S21 .... **175** E3
 KIMB S61 .... **76** C4
Haigh Moor Cl *HAN/WDH* S13 .... **138** C2
Haigh Moor Rd *HAN/WDH* S13 .... **139** D2
Haigh Rd *DONS/BSCR* DN4 .... **43** E5
Hail Mary Dr *HAN/WDH* S13 .... **140** B3
Hakehill Cl *DONS/BSCR* DN4 .... **66** B1
Halcyon Cl *HACK/IN* S12 .... **151** E1
Haldane Rd *RHAM/THRY* S65 .... **104** B1
Hale St *SHEFS* S8 .... **135** D4
Halesworth Cl *CHSW* S40 .... **188** C4
Halesworth Rd *HAN/WDH* S13 .... **125** F5
Half Acre La *DRON* S18 .... **170** B3
Half Cft *STV/CWN* S43 .... **186** A5
Halfway Dr *MOS* S20 .... **164** C1
Halfway Gdns *MOS* S20 .... **164** C1
Halifax Av *CONI* DN12 .... **84** B1
Halifax Crs *BTLY* DN5 .... **29** D3
Halifax Rd *CHPT/GREN* S35 .... **97** E2
 SHEFN S5 .... **97** E5
 ST/HB/BR S6 .... **97** E5
Halifax St *BSLYN/ROY* S71 .... **13** F3
Hallam Cha *FUL* S10 .... **119** E5 ▣
Hallam Cl *AU/AST/KP* S26 .... **142** A5
 DONS/BSCR DN4 .... **46** A5
Hallamgate Rd *FUL* S10 .... **120** C5
Hallam Grange Cl *FUL* S10 .... **132** A2 ▣
Hallam Grange Crs *FUL* S10 .... **132** A1
Hallam Grange Ri *FUL* S10 .... **132** A1
Hallam Grange Rd *FUL* S10 .... **132** A1
Hallam La *SHEF* S1 .... **122** B5 ▣
Hallam Pl *RAW* S62 .... **94** B1
Hallam Rd *RHAM* S60 .... **115** D3
Hallamshire Cl *FUL* S10 .... **131** F2
Hallamshire Dr *FUL* S10 .... **131** F2
Hallamshire Rd *FUL* S10 .... **131** F2
Hallam Wy *CHPT/GREN* S35 .... **98** C1
Hall Av *HOY* S74 .... **52** B1
 MEX/SWTN S64 .... **58** C3
Hall Balk La *DOD/DAR* S75 .... **2** A1
 DONS/BSCR DN4 .... **64** B3
 NROS/TKH DN11 .... **64** A4
Hallcar St *ATT* S4 .... **9** H1
Hall Cl *BSLY* S70 .... **36** B3
 DEARNE S63 .... **54** C1 ▣
 DRON S18 .... **168** A1
Hall Close Av *RHAM* S60 .... **116** A3
Hall Cross Hl *DON* DN1 .... **5** G4
Hall Dr *DEARNE* S63 .... **55** E3
Hall Farm Cl *AU/AST/KP* S26 .... **129** E5
 CHNE S41 .... **191** E5
Hall Farm Dr *DEARNE* S63 .... **27** D4
Hall Farm Ri *DEARNE* S63 .... **27** D4 ▣
Hall Flat La *DONS/BSCR* DN4 .... **63** E1
Hallgate *DEARNE* S63 .... **27** D4
Hall Ga *DON* DN1 .... **5** E4
 MEX/SWTN S64 .... **59** D3
Hallgate Rd *FUL* S10 .... **120** B4 ▣

Hall Gv *RHAM* S60 .... **103** F4
Halliwell Cl *SHEFN* S5 .... **108** B1 ▣
Halliwell Crs *SHEFN* S5 .... **108** C1
Hall La *STV/CWN* S43 .... **181** D2
Hall Meadow Cft *MOS* S20 .... **165** D3
Hall Meadow Dr *MOS* S20 .... **165** D3
Hall Meadow Gv *MOS* S20 .... **165** D3 ▣
Hallowes Cl *DRON* S18 .... **169** F2 ▣
Hallowes Dr *DRON* S18 .... **169** F3
Hallowes La *DRON* S18 .... **169** F3
Hallowes Ri *DRON* S18 .... **170** A3
Hallowmoor Rd *ST/HB/BR* S6 .... **107** E4
Hall Park Head *ST/HB/BR* S6 .... **119** E2
Hall Park Hl *ST/HB/BR* S6 .... **119** F2
Hall Park Mt *ST/HB/BR* S6 .... **119** F2 ▣
Hall Pl *BSLYN/ROY* S71 .... **15** D3
Hall Rd *AU/AST/KP* S26 .... **142** B1
 DARN/MH S9 .... **125** F4
 HAN/WDH S13 .... **125** F5
 RHAM S60 .... **103** F4
 STV/CWN S43 .... **185** F2
Hall Road Old *DARN/MH* S9 .... **111** E5
Hallside Ct *ARMTH* DN3 .... **47** F3
Hall St *HOY* S74 .... **51** F2 ▣
 RHAM S60 .... **6** B5
 WMB/DAR S73 .... **39** F5
Hallsworth Av *HOY* S74 .... **52** B1
Hall Vw *CHNE* S41 .... **183** F3
Hall Villa La *BTLY* DN5 .... **16** B1
Hall Wood Rd *CHPT/GREN* S35 .... **87** D1
Hallyburton Cl *SHEFP/MNR* S2 .... **136** A4 ▣
Hallyburton Dr *SHEFP/MNR* S2 .... **136** A4 ▣
Hallyburton Rd *SHEFP/MNR* S2 .... **136** A4
Halmshaw *BTLY* DN5 .... **29** E1
Halsall Av *DARN/MH* S9 .... **125** D4
Halsall Dr *DARN/MH* S9 .... **124** C4
Halsall Rd *DARN/MH* S9 .... **125** D4
Halsbury Rd *RHAM/THRY* S65 .... **104** B1
Halton Cl *CHNE* S41 .... **177** F5 ▣
Halton Ct *HACK/IN* S12 .... **152** A2
Hambledon Cl *CHSW* S40 .... **183** D4
Hambledon Cl *DOD/DAR* S75 .... **12** C5 ▣
 HOY S74 .... **52** C2 ▣
Hameline Rd *CONI* DN12 .... **84** C1
Hamilton Cl *MEX/SWTN* S64 .... **59** D2 ▣
Hamilton Park Rd *BTLY* DN5 .... **28** B3 ▣
Hamilton Rd *DEARNE* S63 .... **27** F5
 DONS/BSCR DN4 .... **62** B2
 SHEFN S5 .... **110** B2
Hammerton Rd *ST/HB/BR* S6 .... **108** A5
Hammerton St *WMB/DAR* S73 .... **39** D1 ▣
Hammond St *OWL* S3 .... **8** A3
Hampden Rd *MEX/SWTN* S64 .... **58** B4
Hampton Rd *SHEFN* S5 .... **110** A3
 WHHL DN2 .... **45** D1
Hampton St *CHNE* S41 .... **191** E5
Hanbury Cl *BSLYN/ROY* S71 .... **15** E3
 CHSW S40 .... **182** B4
 DONS/BSCR DN4 .... **63** E3
 DRON S18 .... **169** D2
Handby St *CHNE* S41 .... **191** E4
Handley Cl *STV/CWN* S43 .... **179** E2 ▣
Handley Rd *ECK/KIL* S21 .... **172** B5
 STV/CWN S43 .... **179** E2
Handley St *OWL* S3 .... **9** G2
Hands Rd *FUL* S10 .... **121** D3
Handsworth Av *DARN/MH* S9 .... **125** E4
Handsworth Crs *DARN/MH* S9 .... **125** E4
Handsworth Grange Cl
 HAN/WDH S13 .... **139** E2
Handsworth Grange Crs
 HAN/WDH S13 .... **139** E1
Handsworth Grange Rd
 HAN/WDH S13 .... **139** E1
Handsworth Rd *DARN/MH* S9 .... **125** E4
Hanging Water Cl *FUL* S10 .... **133** D2 ▣
Hangingwater Rd *ECC* S11 .... **133** D3
Hanley Cl *HACK/IN* S12 .... **151** F2
Hanmoor Rd *ST/HB/BR* S6 .... **119** D1
Hannah Rd *HAN/WDH* S13 .... **140** B3
Hannas Royd *DOD/DAR* S75 .... **20** B3 ▣
Hanover Sq *DEARNE* S63 .... **27** E3
 OWL S3 .... **121** F5
Hanover St *DEARNE* S63 .... **27** E2
 OWL S3 .... **121** F5 ▣
Hanover Wy *OWL* S3 .... **121** F5
Hanson Rd *ST/HB/BR* S6 .... **106** B4
Hanson St *BSLY* S70 .... **2** D5 ▣
Harbord Rd *SHEFS* S8 .... **146** C5
Harborough Av *SHEFP/MNR* S2 .... **124** A4
 SHEFP/MNR S2 .... **137** E1
Harborough Cl *SHEFP/MNR* S2 .... **124** B5
Harborough Dr *SHEFP/MNR* S2 .... **124** B5
Harborough Hill Rd
 BSLYN/ROY S71 .... **3** E3 ▣
Harborough Rd *SHEFP/MNR* S2 .... **124** B5
Harborough Rd *SHEFP/MNR* S2 .... **124** B5
Harborough Wy *SHEFP/MNR* S2 .... **137** E1
Harbury St *HAN/WDH* S13 .... **140** C2 ▣
Harcourt Cl *DONS/BSCR* DN4 .... **46** A5
Harcourt Crs *FUL* S10 .... **121** E4 ▣
Harcourt Ri *CHPT/GREN* S35 .... **88** C2
Harcourt Rd *FUL* S10 .... **121** E4
Harcourt Ter *RHAM/THRY* S65 .... **7** H6
Hardcastle Dr *HAN/WDH* S13 .... **139** E3 ▣

Hardcastle Gdns *HAN/WDH* S13 ...... **139** E3
Hardcastle Rd *HAN/WDH* S13 ...... **139** E4
Harden Cl *DOD/DAR* S75 ...... **12** B5
Hardhurst Rd *DRON* S18 ...... **177** F1
Hardie Pl *RAW* S62 ...... **80** A5 ▪
   STV/CWN S43 ...... **187** E1
Hardie St *ECK/KIL* S21 ...... **174** B1
Harding Av *RAW* S62 ...... **79** E3
Harding Cl *RAW* S62 ...... **79** E4
Harding St *DARN/MH* S9 ...... **124** C1
Hardwick Av *CHNE* S41 ...... **179** E3
Hardwick Cl *AU/AST/KP* S26 ...... **143** D3 ▪
   BSLY S70 ...... **36** B1 ▪
   DRON S18 ...... **169** F1
Hardwick Crs *ECC* S11 ...... **134** A2
Hardwicke Rd *RHAM/THRY* S65 ...... **7** F2
Hardwick Gv *DOD/DAR* S75 ...... **20** A4 ▪
Hardwick St *CHNE* S41 ...... **11** F3
   RHAM/THRY S65 ...... **105** E1
Hardy Pl *ST/HB/BR* S6 ...... **121** E2
Hardy Rd *WHHL* DN2 ...... **30** C3
Hardy St *KIMB* S61 ...... **6** A3
Harefield Rd *ECC* S11 ...... **134** B2 ▪
Harehill Rd *CHSW* S40 ...... **190** A5
Harehills Rd *RHAM/THRY* S65 ...... **7** F2
Harewood Av *BSLY* S70 ...... **20** C1
Harewood Rd *WHHL* DN2 ...... **45** E1
Harewood Wy *ECC* S11 ...... **145** E3 ▪
Harland Rd *FUL* S10 ...... **134** C1
Harlech Cl *CHPT/GREN* S35 ...... **74** A5
Harleston St *ATT* S4 ...... **123** D1 ▪
Harley Rd *ECC* S11 ...... **133** D5
   RAW S62 ...... **75** E2
Harlington Ct *CONI* DN12 ...... **60** B4
Harlington Rd *MEX/SWTN* S64 ...... **58** C3
Harmer La *SHEF* S1 ...... **9** F6
Harmony Wy *RHAM* S60 ...... **127** E1 ▪
Harney Cl *DARN/MH* S9 ...... **125** D2
Harold Av *BSLYN/ROY* S71 ...... **15** F3
Harold Cft *RAW* S62 ...... **93** D2
Harold St *ST/HB/BR* S6 ...... **121** E1
Harperhill Cl *CHSW* S40 ...... **190** A5 ▪
Harriet Cl *BSLY* S70 ...... **22** B3 ▪
Harrington Ct *BSLYN/ROY* S71 ...... **15** F3
Harrington Rd *SHEF/MNR* S2 ...... **135** E2 ▪
Harrington St *DON* DN1 ...... **5** E2
Harrison La *FUL* S10 ...... **131** D3
Harrison Rd *ST/HB/BR* S6 ...... **107** F5
Harrison St *KIMB* S61 ...... **102** B4
Harris Rd *ST/HB/BR* S6 ...... **107** F2
Harrogate Dr *CONI* DN12 ...... **59** F5
Harrogate Rd *AU/AST/KP* S26 ...... **142** D3
   WHHL DN2 ...... **31** D3
Harrop La *FUL* S10 ...... **131** D4
Harrowden Rd *DARN/MH* S9 ...... **112** C2
   WHHL DN2 ...... **31** D3
Harrow St *ECC* S11 ...... **135** D1
Harry Firth Cl *DARN/MH* S9 ...... **124** B2 ▪
Harry Rd *DOD/DAR* S75 ...... **12** C4
Hartfield Cl *CHNE* S41 ...... **190** C5
Hartford Cl *SHEFS* S8 ...... **147** E2 ▪
Hartford Rd *SHEFS* S8 ...... **147** E2
Hart Hl *RAW* S62 ...... **79** E3
Harthill Rd *CONI* DN12 ...... **84** B2
   HAN/WDH S13 ...... **137** F3
Hartington Av *ABRD* S7 ...... **146** A2
Hartington Cl *KIMB* S61 ...... **102** B3
Hartington Dr *BSLYN/ROY* S71 ...... **14** A3
Hartington Rd *ABRD* S7 ...... **146** A2
   CHNE S41 ...... **191** D2
   DRON S18 ...... **169** F1
   KIMB S61 ...... **102** B3
Hartland Av *MOS* S20 ...... **153** E3 ▪
Hartland Cl *MOS* S20 ...... **153** E3 ▪
Hartland Dr *MOS* S20 ...... **153** E3
Hartland Wy *CHNE* S41 ...... **178** B5 ▪
Hartley Brook Av *SHEFN* S5 ...... **99** D3
Hartley Brook Rd *SHEFN* S5 ...... **99** D3
Hartley La *KIMB* S61 ...... **6** A3
Hartley St *MEX/SWTN* S64 ...... **58** A4
   SHEF/MNR S2 ...... **135** E3
Hartopp Av *SHEF/MNR* S2 ...... **136** A4
Hartopp Cl *SHEF/MNR* S2 ...... **136** A4 ▪
Hartopp Dr *SHEF/MNR* S2 ...... **136** B4 ▪
Hartopp Rd *SHEF/MNR* S2 ...... **136** A4
Harts Head *SHEF* S1 ...... **9** E4
Hartside Cl *CHSW* S40 ...... **183** E4
Harvest Cl *BSLY* S70 ...... **38** A5
   DONS/BSCR DN4 ...... **43** D4
Harvest La *OWL* S3 ...... **122** B1
Harvest Wy *CHSW* S40 ...... **182** B4 ▪
Harvey Clough Ms *SHEFS* S8 ...... **147** E2
Harvey Clough Rd *SHEFS* S8 ...... **147** E2
Harvey Rd *CHNE* S41 ...... **191** F2
   CHPT/GREN S35 ...... **88** B1
Harvey St *BSLY* S70 ...... **22** B5 ▪
   STKB/PEN S36 ...... **69** E2 ▪
Harwell Rd *SHEFS* S8 ...... **135** D3
Harwich Rd *SHEF/MNR* S2 ...... **136** C1
Harwood Cl *SHEF/MNR* S2 ...... **135** D2
Harwood Dr *MOS* S20 ...... **152** B4
Harwood Gdns *MOS* S20 ...... **152** C4
Harwood Rd *SHEF/MNR* S2 ...... **135** F2
Harwood Ter *BSLYN/ROY* S71 ...... **15** F5 ▪
Haslam Crs *SHEFS* S8 ...... **158** C2 ▪

Hasland Rd *CHNE* S41 ...... **190** C3
Haslehurst Rd *SHEF/MNR* S2 ...... **123** F5
Haslemere Gv *BTLY* DN5 ...... **29** E3
Hassop Cl *CHSW* S40 ...... **183** D5
   DRON S18 ...... **170** A1
Hastilar Cl *SHEF/MNR* S2 ...... **137** E2 ▪
Hastilar Rd *SHEF/MNR* S2 ...... **137** E2 ▪
Hastilar Rd South *HAN/WDH* S13 ... **138** A3
   SHEF/MNR S2 ...... **138** A2
Hastings Cl *CHSW* S40 ...... **183** E3
Hastings Mt *ABRD* S7 ...... **146** A1
Hastings Rd *ABRD* S7 ...... **146** A1
Hatchell Dr *DONS/BSCR* DN4 ...... **67** E2
Hatchellwood Vw
   DONS/BSCR DN4 ...... **67** F2
Hatfield House Ct *SHEFN* S5 ...... **99** E4 ▪
Hatfield House Cft *SHEFN* S5 ...... **99** E4 ▪
Hatfield House La *SHEFN* S5 ...... **99** D5
Hatherley Rd *DARN/MH* S9 ...... **112** B1
   MEX/SWTN S64 ...... **57** E4
   RHAM/THRY S65 ...... **7** F2
Hathern Cl *STV/CWN* S43 ...... **186** A5
Hathersage Rd *TOT/DORE* S17 ...... **144** A4
Hatton Cl *DRON* S18 ...... **168** B3
Hatton Dr *CHSW* S40 ...... **182** C4
Hatton Rd *ST/HB/BR* S6 ...... **108** A5
Haugh Gn *RAW* S62 ...... **79** E3
Haugh La *ECC* S11 ...... **133** D5
Haugh Rd *RAW* S62 ...... **79** D3
Haughton Rd *SHEFS* S8 ...... **147** D5
Havercroft Rd *RHAM* S60 ...... **116** A1
   SHEFS S8 ...... **146** C1
Havercroft Ter *ECK/KIL* S21 ...... **165** F1 ▪
Haverdale Ri *DOD/DAR* S75 ...... **13** E4
Haverlands La *BSLY* S70 ...... **35** E1 ▪
Haverlands Rdg *BSLY* S70 ...... **35** A1 ▪
Hawes Cl *MEX/SWTN* S64 ...... **59** D2
Hawfield Cl *DONS/BSCR* DN4 ...... **43** E3
Hawke Cl *RAW* S62 ...... **79** D3
Hawke Rd *WHHL* DN2 ...... **31** D4
Hawke St *DARN/MH* S9 ...... **111** E4
Hawkins Av *CHPT/GREN* S35 ...... **87** F1 ▪
Hawkshead Av *DRON* S18 ...... **168** B3
Hawkshead Rd *ATT* S4 ...... **111** D3
Hawksley Av *CHSW* S40 ...... **10** B2
   ST/HB/BR S6 ...... **108** A4
Hawksley Ms *ST/HB/BR* S6 ...... **108** A4
Hawksley Rd *ST/HB/BR* S6 ...... **108** A4
Hawksway *ECK/KIL* S21 ...... **163** F5
Hawksworth Cl *RHAM/THRY* S65 ... **105** E1
Hawksworth Rd *RHAM/THRY* S65 ... **105** D2
   ST/HB/BR S6 ...... **121** E1
Hawkwell Bank *BSLYN/ROY* S71 ..... **24** B2
Hawley Dr *DRON* S18 ...... **171** E2
   RAW S62 ...... **94** A1
   SHEF S1 ...... **8** D4
Haworth Bank *RHAM* S60 ...... **115** D3 ▪
Haworth Cl *BSLYN/ROY* S71 ...... **14** C4 ▪
Haworth Crs *RHAM* S60 ...... **115** D3
Hawshaw La *HOY* S74 ...... **51** D2
Hawson St *WMB/DAR* S73 ...... **39** F3
Hawthorn Av *ARMTH* DN3 ...... **33** F1
   MOS S20 ...... **152** B4
Hawthorne Av *DRON* S18 ...... **159** E5
   RAW S62 ...... **94** B1
   STKB/PEN S36 ...... **68** A1
Hawthorne Cl *ECK/KIL* S21 ...... **166** B3 ▪
Hawthorne Crs *MEX/SWTN* S64 ...... **57** F3
Hawthorne Gv *BTLY* DN5 ...... **16** C4
Hawthorne Rd *DEARNE* S63 ...... **56** B3 ▪
The Hawthornes *MOS* S20 ...... **153** D1
Hawthorne St *BSLY* S70 ...... **21** F2
   CHSW S40 ...... **190** B3
   ST/HB/BR S6 ...... **120** C1 ▪
Hawthorn Gv *CONI* DN12 ...... **84** B3 ▪
Hawthorn Hl *STV/CWN* S43 ...... **175** D5
Hawthorn Rd *CHPT/GREN* S35 ...... **73** F4
   ECK/KIL S21 ...... **173** F1
   ST/HB/BR S6 ...... **107** F4
Hawthorn Wy *RCH* S42 ...... **182** A4
Haxby Cl *HAN/WDH* S13 ...... **138** C4
Haxby Pl *HAN/WDH* S13 ...... **138** C4
Haxby St *HAN/WDH* S13 ...... **138** C5
Haybrook Ct *TOT/DORE* S17 ...... **156** C3
Haydock Cl *MEX/SWTN* S64 ...... **58** C2 ▪
Hayes Cl *MOS* S20 ...... **164** C2
Hayes Cft *BSLY* S70 ...... **2** D6
Hayes Dr *MOS* S20 ...... **164** B2
Hayfield Cl *DRON* S18 ...... **168** B2 ▪
Hayfield Crs *HACK/IN* S12 ...... **150** B2 ▪
Hayfield Dr *HACK/IN* S12 ...... **150** A2
Hayfield Pl *HACK/IN* S12 ...... **150** B2
Hayfield Vw *ECK/KIL* S21 ...... **163** F5
Hayford Wy *STV/CWN* S43 ...... **181** F5
Hay Green La *BSLY* S70 ...... **50** A1
Hayland St *DARN/MH* S9 ...... **111** F2
Haymarket *SHEF* S1 ...... **9** F4
Haythorne Wy *MEX/SWTN* S64 ...... **81** E2
Haywood Av *STKB/PEN* S36 ...... **69** E2
Haywood Cl *RHAM/THRY* S65 ...... **105** D2
Haywood La *STKB/PEN* S36 ...... **69** E2
Hazel Av *ECK/KIL* S21 ...... **166** A3
Hazelbadge Crs *HACK/IN* S12 ...... **150** C2 ▪

Hazel Cl *DRON* S18 ...... **170** A3 ▪
Hazel Ct *DRON* S18 ...... **169** F3
Hazel Dr *CHSW* S40 ...... **189** E4
Hazel Gv *CHPT/GREN* S35 ...... **88** B2
   CONI DN12 ...... **84** C2
Hazel Rd *ECK/KIL* S21 ...... **174** A1 ▪
Hazelshaw *DOD/DAR* S75 ...... **20** B4 ▪
Hazelwood Cl *DRON* S18 ...... **168** A2 ▪
Hazelwood Dr *MEX/SWTN* S64 ...... **81** E3
Hazlebarrow Cl *SHEFS* S8 ...... **159** F5
Hazlebarrow Ct *SHEFS* S8 ...... **159** F1 ▪
Hazlebarrow Crs *SHEFS* S8 ...... **159** F1
Hazlebarrow Dr *SHEFS* S8 ...... **159** F1
Hazlebarrow Gv *SHEFS* S8 ...... **160** A1 ▪
Hazlebarrow Rd *SHEFS* S8 ...... **159** F2 ▪
Hazlehurst Av *CHNE* S41 ...... **11** F2
Hazlehurst La *CHNE* S41 ...... **11** F2
   SHEFS S8 ...... **161** D1
Headford Gdns *OWL* S3 ...... **122** A5
Headford Gv *OWL* S3 ...... **122** A5
Headford Ms *OWL* S3 ...... **122** A5 ▪
Headford St *OWL* S3 ...... **122** A5 ▪
Headingley Wy *CONI* DN12 ...... **62** A4
Headland Cl *STV/CWN* S43 ...... **185** F2
Headland Dr *FUL* S10 ...... **120** B4
Headland Rd *FUL* S10 ...... **120** B4
Headlands Rd *HOY* S74 ...... **51** E2
Heads La *STKB/PEN* S36 ...... **68** B5
Heath Av *ECK/KIL* S21 ...... **166** B3
Heath Bank Rd *WHHL* DN2 ...... **32** A2
Heathcote Dr *CHNE* S41 ...... **191** F4
Heathcote St *ATT* S4 ...... **110** B3 ▪
Heatherbank Rd *DONS/BSCR* DN4 .... **46** C5
Heather Cl *RHAM* S60 ...... **103** F5
Heather Gdns *CHNE* S41 ...... **191** F5 ▪
Heather Knowle *DOD/DAR* S75 ...... **20** B3 ▪
Heather Lea Av *TOT/DORE* S17 ...... **156** A1
Heather Lea Pl *TOT/DORE* S17 ...... **156** A1
Heather Rd *SHEFN* S5 ...... **110** C1
Heather Vale Cl *CHNE* S41 ...... **191** F5 ▪
Heather Vale Rd *CHNE* S41 ...... **191** F5 ▪
Heathfield Av *CHSW* S40 ...... **189** E1
Heathfield Cl *DRON* S18 ...... **169** D3 ▪
Heathfield Rd *HACK/IN* S12 ...... **150** B1
Heath Rd *ST/HB/BR* S6 ...... **97** E5
   STKB/PEN S36 ...... **69** E3
Heaton Cl *DRON* S18 ...... **168** B2
Heaton Gdns *CONI* DN12 ...... **62** A5
Heatons Bank *RAW* S62 ...... **80** B5
Heaton St *CHSW* S40 ...... **189** D2
Heavens Wk *DONS/BSCR* DN4 ...... **44** B3
Heavygate Av *FUL* S10 ...... **121** D1
   ST/HB/BR S6 ...... **121** D1
Heavygate Rd *ST/HB/BR* S6 ...... **121** D1
Hedley Dr *STV/CWN* S43 ...... **185** E1
Heeley Bank Rd *SHEF/MNR* S2 ..... **135** F3
Heeley Gn *SHEF/MNR* S2 ...... **135** F4
Heelis St *BSLY* S70 ...... **22** A2
Heighton Vw *AU/AST/KP* S26 ...... **142** B1
Helena Cl *RAW* S62 ...... **21** E2 ▪
Helena St *MEX/SWTN* S64 ...... **58** B5
Helensburgh Cl *DOD/DAR* S75 ...... **13** D5 ▪
Helliwell La *STKB/PEN* S36 ...... **69** F4
Helmsley Av *MOS* S20 ...... **164** B1
Helmsley Cl *AU/AST/KP* S26 ...... **142** A4 ▪
Helmton Dr *SHEFS* S8 ...... **147** E2
Helmton Rd *SHEFS* S8 ...... **147** D3
Helston Cl *CHNE* S41 ...... **190** C4
Helston Crs *BSLYN/ROY* S71 ...... **14** C4
Helston Ri *ABRD* S7 ...... **146** A1
Hemingfield Rd *WMB/DAR* S73 ...... **38** C4
Hemper Gv *SHEFS* S8 ...... **158** B2 ▪
Hemper La *SHEFS* S8 ...... **158** B2
Hemp Pits Rd *BTLY* DN5 ...... **17** E5
Hemsworth Rd *SHEFS* S8 ...... **148** A3
Hendon St *HAN/WDH* S13 ...... **139** D1
Hengist St *BTLY* DN5 ...... **43** D2 ▪
Henley Av *SHEFS* S8 ...... **147** F5
Henley Grove Rd *KIMB* S61 ...... **102** C2
Henley La *KIMB* S61 ...... **102** B1
Henley Ri *KIMB* S61 ...... **102** C2
Henley Rd *WHHL* DN2 ...... **32** A4
Henley Wy *KIMB* S61 ...... **102** B2
Hennings Cl *DONS/BSCR* DN4 ...... **45** F5
Henry La *NROS/TKH* DN11 ...... **66** B5
Henry Pl *MEX/SWTN* S64 ...... **59** D4 ▪
Henry Rd *DEARNE* S63 ...... **56** A2
Henry St *BSLY* S70 ...... **22** B5 ▪
   CHNE S41 ...... **184** C1
   CHPT/GREN S35 ...... **73** D4
   ECK/KIL S21 ...... **164** B5
   OWL S3 ...... **8** B2
   RAW S62 ...... **94** A3
   RHAM/THRY S65 ...... **6** D4
   WMB/DAR S73 ...... **40** A1
Henshall St *BSLY* S70 ...... **22** B3 ▪
Heppenstall La *DARN/MH* S9 ...... **124** A1 ▪
Heptinstall St *BSLY* S70 ...... **22** C5 ▪
Hepworth Dr *AU/AST/KP* S26 ...... **142** B3
Hepworth Rd *DONS/BSCR* DN4 ...... **43** D5 ▪
Herald Rd *ARMTH* DN3 ...... **19** F4
Herbert Rd *ABRD* S7 ...... **134** C4 ▪
   BTLY DN5 ...... **29** E4
Herbert St *KIMB* S61 ...... **101** F2
   MEX/SWTN S64 ...... **58** C3

Herdings Ct *HACK/IN* S12 .... **149** E2 🔲
Herdings Rd *HACK/IN* S12 .... **149** E2
Herdings Vw *HACK/IN* S12 .... **149** E2
Hereford Dr *STV/CWN* S43 .... **186** A1
Hereford Rd *WHHL* DN2.................... **31** F2
Hereford St *SHEF* S1 .... **135** E1 🔲
Hereward Ct *CONI* DN12 .... **85** F1
Hereward St *SHEFP/MNR* S2 ...... **135** D1 🔲
Hermitage St *SHEFP/MNR* S2 ...... **135** D1 🔲
Hermit Hl *CHPT/GREN* S35.............. **48** A2
Hermit La *DOD/DAR* S75 .... **12** A5
Heron Hl *AU/AST/KP* S26 .... **142** C4
Heron Mt *SHEFP/MNR* S2 .... **123** F5
Herons Wy *BSLY* S70.......................... **36** A5
Herrick Gdns *DONS/BSCR* DN4 ...... **64** A1
Herries Av *SHEFN* S5................... **109** E2
Herries Dr *SHEFN* S5 .... **109** E2
Herries Pl *SHEFN* S5 .... **109** E2
Herries Rd *SHEFN* S5 .... **108** C2
  SHEFN S5..................................... **109** F2
  ST/HB/BR S6 .... **108** A2
Herringthorpe Av
  RHAM/THRY S65............................ **104** C5
Herringthorpe Cl
  RHAM/THRY S65............................ **104** C4 🔲
Herringthorpe Gv
  RHAM/THRY S65............................ **105** D5
Herringthorpe La
  RHAM/THRY S65............................ **105** D4
Herringthorpe Valley Rd
  RHAM/THRY S65............................ **105** D1
  RHAM/THRY S65............................ **116** A1
Herriot Dr *CHSW* S40 .... **190** C5
Herschell Rd *SHEFS* S8 .... **135** D2 🔲
Hesley Bar *KIMB* S61 .... **89** F2
Hesley Ct *MEX/SWTN* S64 .... **81** D2 🔲
Hesley Gra *KIMB* S61 .... **90** C4
Hesley Gv *CHPT/GREN* S35 .... **89** D2
Hesley La *KIMB* S61 .... **89** F2
Hesley Rd *SHEFN* S5 .... **99** E2
Hesley Ter *SHEFN* S5 .... **99** E3
Heslow Gv *KIMB* S61....................... **89** F1
Hessey St *HAN/WDH* S13 .... **139** D4
Hessle Rd *ST/HB/BR* S6 .... **107** F2
Hewitt St *MEX/SWTN* S64 .... **59** D3
Hexthorpe Rd *DONS/BSCR* DN4 ...... **4** B5
Heyhouse Dr *CHPT/GREN* S35....... **74** B4
Heyhouse Wy *CHPT/GREN* S35....... **74** A4
Heysham Gn *BSLYN/ROY* S71 .... **15** E2
Heywood St *STV/CWN* S43 .... **185** F1
Hibberd Rd *ST/HB/BR* S6 .... **107** E4
Hickleton Ct *DEARNE* S63 .... **26** C4
Hickleton St *CONI* DN12.................. **84** D3
Hickmott Rd *ECC* S11 .... **134** B2 🔲
Hickson Dr *BSLYN/ROY* S71 .... **15** F3 🔲
Hicks St *OWL* S3............................ **122** B1
Hides St *DARN/MH* S9 .... **111** F4
High Alder Rd *DONS/BSCR* DN4 ...... **46** A4
Highbury Av *DONS/BSCR* DN4 .... **46** C4
Highbury Rd *CHNE* S41 .... **10** D2
Highcliffe Ct *MEX/SWTN* S64....... **57** F5
Highcliffe Dr *ECC* S11 .... **133** D3
  MEX/SWTN S64............................. **57** E5
Highcliffe Pl *ECC* S11 .... **133** D4
Highcliffe Rd *ECC* S11 .... **133** D3
High Cft *HOY* S74 .... **51** F3
Higher Albert St *CHNE* S41 .... **11** E3
Highfield Av *BSLY* S70 .... **22** A4 🔲
  BSLYN/ROY S71 .... **14** B1
  CHNE S41 .... **10** A1
Highfield Gv *DEARNE* S63 .... **54** B1
Highfield La *CHNE* S41 .... **183** F5
  HAN/WDH S13 .... **126** C5
  RHAM S60 .... **127** D1
Highfield Pl *SHEFP/MNR* S2 ...... **135** E2
Highfield Ri *ST/HB/BR* S6 .... **118** C2
Highfield Rd *CHNE* S41.................... **10** D2
  CONI DN12...................................... **5** F2
  DON S1 .... **5** F2
  KIMB S61 .... **93** D4
  MEX/SWTN S64............................. **56** C5
Highfields Crs *DRON* S18 .... **169** E3 🔲
High Field Spring *HAN/WDH* S13 ... **126** B3
Highfields Rd *DRON* S18 .... **169** E3
Highfield Vw *RHAM* S60................ **127** D1
High Fisher Ga *DON* DN1............... **5** F2
Highgate Cl *DARN/MH* S9 .... **112** C2
Highgate *DARN/MH* S9
  DEARNE S63 .... **40** C3
Highgate Dr *DRON* S18 .... **170** A4
Highgate La *DRON* S18 .... **170** A4
Highgreave *SHEFN* S5 .... **99** D3
High Greave Av *SHEFN* S5 .... **99** D3
High Greave Ct *SHEFN* S5 .... **98** C2
High Greave Pl *RHAM/THRY* S65 ... **105** D2
High Greave Rd *RHAM/THRY* S65 ... **105** D2
High Hazel Crs *RHAM* S60 .... **127** D1
High Hazels Cl *DARN/MH* S9 ...... **125** E3 🔲
High Hazels Md *DARN/MH* S9 ..... **125** E3 🔲
High House Farm Ct
  AU/AST/KP S26.............................. **155** F3
High House Ter *ST/HB/BR* S6 ...... **108** B5
Highland Rd *STV/CWN* S43 .... **179** E1
High La *HACK/IN* S12..................... **150** D3
Highlow Cl *CHSW* S40 .... **183** D4

Highlow Vw *RHAM* S60 .... **114** A3
High Matlock Av *ST/HB/BR* S6 .... **119** E1
High Matlock Rd *ST/HB/BR* S6 .... **119** F1 🔲
Highmill Av *MEX/SWTN* S64.......... **56** B5
Highnam Crescent Rd *FUL* S10 ... **121** D4 🔲
High Rdg *BSLY* S70 .... **22** A5
High Rd *DONS/BSCR* DN4............. **43** C5
  DONS/BSCR DN4 .... **62** A1
Highroyds *BSLY* S70 .... **22** A5
Highstone Av *BSLY* S70 .... **21** F3
Highstone Crs *BSLY* S70 .... **21** F3
Highstone La *BSLY* S70 .... **21** F3
Highstone Rd *BSLY* S70 .... **22** A3
Highstone V *BSLY* S70 .... **21** F3 🔲
High Storrs Cl *ECC* S11 .... **133** D4
High Storrs Crs *ECC* S11 .... **133** E3
High Storrs Dr *ECC* S11 .... **133** D3
High Storrs Ri *ECC* S11 .... **133** E3
High Storrs Rd *ECC* S11 .... **133** D4
High St *AU/AST/KP* S26 .... **142** A2
  BSLY S70 .... **2** B4
  BSLY S70 .... **22** C5
  BSLYN/ROY S71 .... **15** D3
  BTLY DN5 .... **7** E4
  BTLY DN5 .... **29** F1
  CHNE S41 .... **178** B4 🔲
  CHPT/GREN S35 .... **98** C1
  CHSW S40 .... **11** E6
  CONI DN12...................................... **85** D1
  DEARNE S63 .... **26** C4
  DEARNE S63 .... **58** B4
  DOD/DAR S75 .... **20** A3
  DON DN1 .... **4** D3
  DRON S18 .... **169** D1
  DRON S18 .... **171** E2
  ECK/KIL S21 .... **164** B5
  ECK/KIL S21 .... **166** B2
  HOY S74... **51** F2
  KIMB S61 .... **101** F2
  MEX/SWTN S64 .... **58** B4
  MOS S20 .... **153** E1
  MOS S20 .... **164** A1
  RAW S62 .... **94** A2
  RHAM S60 .... **6** D5
  RHAM S60 .... **115** F3
  SHEF S1 .... **9** F4
  STV/CWN S43 .... **179** E5
  STV/CWN S43 .... **181** F4
  STV/CWN S43 .... **186** A1
  TOT/DORE S17 .... **156** B1
  WMB/DAR S73 .... **39** E2
High Street La *SHEFP/MNR* S2 .... **9** H5
Highthorn Rd *MEX/SWTN* S64 ...... **81** E2
Highton St *FUL* S10...................... **121** D1
High Trees *TOT/DORE* S17 .... **156** B1
High View Cl *CHNE* S41 .... **191** E2
Highwood Pl *ECK/KIL* S21 .... **164** A5
Highwoods Crs *MEX/SWTN* S64 .... **57** F3 🔲
Highwoods Rd *MEX/SWTN* S64 ..... **57** F3
High Wray Cl *ECC* S11................... **145** F1
Hilary Wy *AU/AST/KP* S26 .... **142** B3
Hill Cl *RHAM/THRY* S65 .... **105** E5
  ST/HB/BR S6................................ **119** D1
Hillcote Cl *FUL* S10 .... **132** B1
Hillcote Dr *FUL* S10 .... **132** B1
Hillcote Ms *FUL* S10 .... **132** B1
Hillcote Ri *FUL* S10 .... **132** B1
Hillcrest *DEARNE* S63 .... **26** C4
Hill Crest *HOY* S74 .... **51** D3
Hillcrest Ri *STKB/PEN* S36 .... **70** A3
Hillcrest Rd *CHNE* S41 .... **191** E5
Hill Crest Rd *CHPT/GREN* S35 ...... **88** A1
  RHAM/THRY S65............................ **104** C2
Hillcrest Rd *STKB/PEN* S36 .... **70** A3
  WHHL DN2 .... **31** E5
Hill Farm Cl *DEARNE* S63 .... **26** B4 🔲
Hillfoot Rd *TOT/DORE* S17 .... **156** A3
Hill Gv *STV/CWN* S43 .... **180** C2
Hillman Dr *STV/CWN* S43 .... **187** D3
Hill Park Gv *DOD/DAR* S75 .... **20** A2
Hillsborough Pl *ST/HB/BR* S6 .... **108** A4 🔲
Hillsborough Rd *DONS/BSCR* DN4 ... **46** C4
  ST/HB/BR S6................................ **108** A4 🔲
Hills Cl *BTLY* DN5 .... **42** B2
Hillside *BSLYN/ROY* S71 .... **24** B2 🔲
  MOS S20 .... **164** A1
Hill Side *RHAM* S60 .... **115** F3
Hillside Av *DRON* S18 .... **169** E3
  SHEFN S5 .... **98** C3
Hillside Cl *KIMB* S61 .... **93** E5
Hillside Dr *CHSW* S40 .... **189** E3
  HOY S74.. **52** A3
Hills Rd *STKB/PEN* S36 .... **69** E2
Hill St *BSLYN/ROY* S71.................. **23** F2
  HOY S74.. **52** B3
  SHEFP/MNR S2 .... **135** D1
Hill Top Cl *KIMB* S61 .... **101** E3
  MOS S20 .... **113** E5
Hill Top Crs *MOS* S20 .... **152** B4
  WHHL DN2 .... **32** A2
Hilltop Gdns *CONI* DN12............... **84** A1
Hill Top La *CHPT/GREN* S35 .... **96** C1
  DOD/DAR S75 .... **12** C4
Hill Top Ri *CHPT/GREN* S35 .... **97** E2
Hill Top Rd *BSLY* S70 .... **36** A5

Hilltop Rd *CHNE* S41 .... **178** C4
Hill Top Rd *CHPT/GREN* S35 .... **97** E2
  CONI DN12...................................... **84** A2
Hilltop Rd *DRON* S18................... **169** E3
Hilltop Wy *DRON* S18.................. **169** E4
Hill Turrets Cl *ECC* S11 .... **145** D1
Hill Vw East *KIMB* S61 .... **101** E1 🔲
Hill View Rd *KIMB* S61 .... **101** E1
  STV/CWN S43 .... **185** F1
Hilton Dr *CHPT/GREN* S35 .... **98** C1
Hilton St *DOD/DAR* S75 .... **13** E5 🔲
Hindburn Cl *DONS/BSCR* DN4 ...... **46** A5
Hinde House Crs *ATT* S4 .... **110** C2
Hinde House Cft *ATT* S4 .... **110** C2
Hinde House La *ATT* S4 .... **110** B3
Hinde St *ATT* S4 .... **110** C3
Hindewood Cl *ATT* S4 .... **110** C2
Hindle St *BSLY* S70 .... **2** A6
Hind Rd *RHAM* S60 .... **116** A2
Hipley Cl *CHSW* S40 .... **182** C4
Hipper St *CHSW* S40 .... **190** B2
Hipper St South *CHSW* S40 .... **190** B2
Hipper St West *CHSW* S40 .... **189** F2
Hirst Common La *ST/HB/BR* S6 ...... **96** B3
Hirst Dr *RHAM/THRY* S65 .... **105** E2
Hirst Ga *MEX/SWTN* S64 .... **59** D3
Hobart St *ECC* S11........................ **135** D2
Hobson Av *ST/HB/BR* S6 .... **108** C5
Hobson Pl *ST/HB/BR* S6.............. **108** C5
Hodder Ct *CHPT/GREN* S35 .... **74** A5 🔲
Hodgson St *OWL* S3..................... **122** A5
Hoggarth Ri *DRON* S18 .... **169** D2
Holbeach Dr *CHSW* S40 .... **189** F4
Holbeck Cl *CHNE* S41 .... **11** C4
Holbein Cl *DRON* S18 .... **169** D3
Holberry Cl *FUL* S10 .... **121** F5 🔲
Holberry Gdns *FUL* S10 .... **121** F5 🔲
Holbourne Gv *CHPT/GREN* S35 .... **73** E2
Holbrook Av *MOS* S20 .... **153** D5
Holbrook Cl *CHSW* S40 .... **189** D4 🔲
Holbrook Dr *HAN/WDH* S13 ...... **137** F4 🔲
Holbrook Gn *MOS* S20 .... **153** D5
Holbrook Pl *STV/CWN* S43 .... **187** D2 🔲
Holbrook Ri *MOS* S20 .... **153** D4
Holbrook Rd *HAN/WDH* S13 ...... **137** F3
Holburn Av *DRON* S18 .... **169** E1
Holden Ct *BSLY* S70 .... **2** B6
Holderness Dr *AU/AST/KP* S26 .... **142** B2
Holdings Rd *SHEFP/MNR* S2 ...... **136** B1
Hole House La *STKB/PEN* S36 ...... **68** C1 🔲
Holgate *WMB/DAR* S73 .... **24** C5
Holgate Av *SHEFN* S5 .... **98** A3
Holgate Crs *SHEFN* S5 .... **98** B3
Holgate Dr *SHEFN* S5 .... **98** B3
Holgate Mt *BSLY* S70 .... **22** A4
Holgate Rd *SHEFN* S5 .... **98** B3
Holkham Ri *ECC* S11 .... **145** D3 🔲
Holland Cl *RAW* S62 .... **80** A4
Holland Pl *SHEFP/MNR* S2 .... **135** E2 🔲
Holland Rd *CHNE* S41................... **178** A4
  CHPT/GREN S35 .... **73** C4
  SHEFP/MNR S2 .... **135** E2
Holland St *SHEF* S1 .... **8** C5
Hollens Wy *RCH* S42 .... **182** A4 🔲
Hollies Cl *DRON* S18 .... **170** A3
Hollinberry La *CHPT/GREN* S35.... **72** C2
Hollin Busk La *STKB/PEN* S36 ...... **69** D4
Hollin Busk Rd *STKB/PEN* S36 ..... **69** D3
Hollin Cl *CHNE* S41 .... **183** D1
  NROS/TKH DN11............................ **67** F5
Hollin Cft *DOD/DAR* S75 .... **20** B2
Hollindale Dr *HACK/IN* S12......... **138** A5
Holling Cft *STKB/PEN* S36 .... **69** F2 🔲
Hollingwood Crs *STV/CWN* S43 ... **180** B5
Hollins Cl *ST/HB/BR* S6............... **120** A2
Hollins Dr *ST/HB/BR* S6 .... **120** A2
Hollinsend Av *HACK/IN* S12 .... **138** A5
Hollinsend Pl *HACK/IN* S12 .... **138** A5 🔲
Hollinsend Rd *HACK/IN* S12 .... **149** E1 🔲
Hollins La *ST/HB/BR* S6 .... **120** B1
Hollins Spring Av *DRON* S18 .... **169** E3
Hollins Spring Rd *DRON* S18 .... **169** E3
Hollis Cl *RAW* S62.......................... **79** D3
Hollis Cft *HAN/WDH* S13 .... **139** E4 🔲
  SHEF S1 .... **8** C4
Hollis La *CHNE* S41 .... **190** C2
Hollowdene *DOD/DAR* S75 .... **12** C4
Hollow Ga *BTLY* DN5.................... **55** D5
  CHPT/GREN S35 .... **87** E1
Hollowgate *RHAM* S60 .... **103** F4
Hollow Ga *RHAM* S60 .... **115** F3 🔲
Hollowgate *RHAM/THRY* S65 ...... **103** F4 🔲
Hollowgate Av *DEARNE* S63 .... **41** D5
Hollow La *MOS* S20 .... **164** B2
The Hollows *DONS/BSCR* DN4...... **66** C1
Holly Av *BTLY* DN5......................... **29** E2
Hollybank Av *HACK/IN* S12 .... **138** A4
Hollybank Cl *HACK/IN* S12 .... **138** B4
Hollybank Crs *HACK/IN* S12 .... **138** A4
Hollybank Dr *HACK/IN* S12 .... **138** B4
Hollybank Rd *HACK/IN* S12 .... **138** A5
Hollybank Wy *HACK/IN* S12 .... **138** B4
Holly Bush Dr *DEARNE* S63 .... **27** D3
Hollybush St *RAW* S62.................. **94** A3
Holly Cl *CHPT/GREN* S35............... **88** A2

MEX/SWTN S64	59 E3
RHAM S60	6 A4
Janson Av MOS S20	111 E4
Jardine CI DARN/MH S9	100 B5
Jardine St DARN/MH S9	100 C5
WMB/DAR S73	39 F1
Jarratt St DON DN1	5 F6
Jarrow Rd ECC S11	134 B2
Jasmine Av MOS S20	153 D2
Jasmine CI CONI DN12	85 E2
Jaunty Av HACK/IN S12	149 F2
Jaunty CI HACK/IN S12	149 F2
Jaunty Crs HACK/IN S12	149 F1
Jaunty Dr HACK/IN S12	149 F2
Jaunty La HACK/IN S12	149 F1
Jaunty Mt HACK/IN S12	150 A2
Jaunty PI HACK/IN S12	149 F2
Jaunty Rd HACK/IN S12	150 A2
Jaunty Vw HACK/IN S12	150 A2
Jaunty Wy HACK/IN S12	149 F1
Jay La AU/AST/KP S26	142 C1
Jebb Gdns CHSW S40	189 D2
Jedburgh Dr DARN/MH S9	100 B5
Jedburgh St DARN/MH S9	100 B5
Jeffcock Rd CHPT/GREN S35	73 F4
DARN/MH S9	125 D3
Jefferson Av WHHL DN2	19 E5
Jeffery Av STKB/PEN S36	69 E5
Jeffery St SHEFP/MNR S2	135 F4
Jenkin Av DARN/MH S9	111 E1
Jenkin CI DARN/MH S9	111 E1
Jenkin Dr DARN/MH S9	111 E2
Jenkin Rd DARN/MH S9	111 E1
Jennings CI RHAM/THRY S65	7 F2
Jepson Rd SHEFN S5	100 A5
Jericho St OWL S3	8 A3
Jermyn Av HACK/IN S12	150 C1
Jermyn CI HACK/IN S12	151 D2
Jermyn Crs HACK/IN S12	151 D2
Jermyn Cft DOD/DAR S75	20 A3
Jermyn Dr HACK/IN S12	151 D2
Jermyn Wy HACK/IN S12	150 C2
Jersey Rd SHEFP/MNR S2	135 E3
Jervis PI STV/CWN S43	186 C3
Jessamine Rd SHEFN S5	99 F5
Jessell St DARN/MH S9	124 A1
Jessop St SHEF S1	122 B5
Jewitt Rd KIMB S61	91 F4
Jockell Dr RAW S62	94 A1
John Calvert Rd HAN/WDH S13	140 B4
John Hibbard Av HAN/WDH S13	141 D3
John Hibbard CI HAN/WDH S13	140 C3
John Hibbard Crs HAN/WDH S13	140 C3
John Hibbard Ri HAN/WDH S13	140 C3
Johnson Ct CONI DN12	62 A4
Johnson La CHPT/GREN S35	88 C5
OWL S3	9 F3
Johnson St DOD/DAR S75	13 E5
OWL S3	9 F2
STKB/PEN S36	68 C2
Johnstone CI CHSW S40	190 A3
John St BSLY S70	22 A2
BSLY S70	22 B5
BSLY S70	36 B1
CHSW S40	10 A6
DEARNE S63	27 D5
ECC/KIL S21	164 B5
MEX/SWTN S64	58 B4
RHAM S60	6 A6
SHEFP/MNR S2	135 E1
STV/CWN S43	185 F1
WMB/DAR S73	39 D2
John Ward St HAN/WDH S13	140 B3
John West St STKB/PEN S36	68 C3
Joiner St OWL S3	9 F3
Jones Av WMB/DAR S73	38 C2
Jordan Crs KIMB S61	101 F4
Jordanthorpe Gn SHEFS S8	160 A2
Jordanthorpe Pkwy SHEFS S8	159 E3
Jordanthorpe Vw SHEFS S8	160 A1
Josephine Rd KIMB S61	102 B3
Joseph Rd FUL S10	121 D2
Joseph St BSLY S70	21 F2
ECC/KIL S21	164 B5
RHAM S60	6 A3
Joshua Rd ABRD S7	134 C3
Josselin Ct CHPT/GREN S35	88 A1
Jossey La BTLY DN5	28 E1
Jowitt Rd ECC S11	133 F4
Jubb CI RHAM/THRY S65	105 F3
Jubilee Crs ECK/KIL S21	166 C1
Jubilee Rd DARN/MH S9	124 C1
DON DN1	30 C4
Jubilee St RHAM S60	103 E5
Judith Rd AU/AST/KP S26	142 B4
Judy Rw BSLYN/ROY S71	15 D3
Julian Rd DARN/MH S9	111 F1
Julian Wy DARN/MH S9	111 F1
Jumble La KIMB S61	89 F4
Junction CI WMB/DAR S73	40 A4
Junction Rd ECC S11	134 A4
HAN/WDH S13	140 B3
Junction St BSLY S70	22 C2
WMB/DAR S73	40 A4
June Rd HAN/WDH S13	140 B4
Juniper Ri ECK/KIL S21	166 A3

K

Kashmir Gdns DARN/MH S9	124 C2
Kathleen Gv DEARNE S63	27 F5
Kay Crs RAW S62	79 D3
Kaye PI FUL S10	121 E3
Kay's Ter BSLY S70	23 F3
Kay St HOY S74	50 C3
Kearsley La CONI DN12	84 C3
Kearsley Rd SHEFP/MNR S2	135 E2
Keats Rd CHNE S41	184 A1
DONS/BSCR DN4	63 F1
ST/HB/BR S6	97 E3
Keble Martin Wy DEARNE S63	55 E2
Keepers CI NROS/TKH DN11	67 F5
Keeton's HI SHEFP/MNR S2	135 D1
Kelder Ct CHSW S40	189 D3
Keir PI RAW S62	80 C5
Keir St BSLY S70	2 A4
Keir Ter BSLY S70	2 A4
Kelburn Av CHSW S40	189 D3
Kelgate MOS S20	164 B2
Kelham Island OWL S3	8 D2
Kelham St DON DN1	44 A3
Kelsey Gdns DONS/BSCR DN4	66 C2
Kelsey Ter BSLY S70	22 A3
Kelso Dr DONS/BSCR DN4	42 B5
Kelvin Gv WMB/DAR S73	39 F3
Kelvin St MEX/SWTN S64	58 B3
RHAM/THRY S65	95 E5
Kemp CI ECK/KIL S21	166 A2
Kempton Gdns MEX/SWTN S64	59 D2
Kempton Park Rd BTLY DN5	28 B4
Kempwell Dr RAW S62	80 A3
Kenbourne Gv ABRD S7	134 C5
Kenbourne Rd ABRD S7	134 C3
Kendal Crs BSLY S70	36 B1
CONI DN12	85 E1
Kendal Dr DRON S18	168 C2
Kendal Green Rd BSLY S70	35 F1
Kendal Rd BSLYN/ROY S71	24 B2
Kendal Rd BTLY DN5	29 E2
CHNE S41	183 F1
ST/HB/BR S6	107 F4
Kendal V BSLY S70	36 B1
Kendray St BSLY S70	2 D5
Kenilworth Av BTLY DN5	28 B3
Kenilworth PI ECC S11	134 A2
Kenilworth Rd DONS/BSCR DN4	42 C5
Kenmare Crs WHHL DN2	31 E5
Kennedy Rd SHEFS S8	146 C3
Kenneth St RHAM/THRY S65	7 E3
Kennet V CHSW S40	183 E5
Kenning Hall CI SHEFP/MNR S2	136 B3
Kenninghall Dr SHEFP/MNR S2	136 B3
Kenninghall Mt SHEFP/MNR S2	136 B3
Kenninghall PI SHEFP/MNR S2	136 B3
Kenninghall Rd SHEFP/MNR S2	136 B3
Kennington Gv CONI DN12	62 A4
Kenrock CI BTLY DN5	17 F5
Kensington Rd DOD/DAR S75	13 E4
Kent Av RAW S62	79 F4
Kent CI CHNE S41	10 D2
Kent House CI HACK/IN S12	150 C5
Kentmere CI DRON S18	168 C2
Kent Rd DONS/BSCR DN4	63 F1
KIMB S61	91 F5
SHEFS S8	135 F4
Kent St CHNE S41	191 D4
Kenwell Dr TOT/DORE S17	157 F3
Kenwood Av ABRD S7	134 C3
Kenwood Bank ECC S11	134 B2
Kenwood CI BSLY S70	23 E2
Kenwood Park Rd ABRD S7	134 C3
Kenwood Rd ABRD S7	134 B3
ECC S11	134 C2
Kenworthy Rd BSLY S70	22 A3
STKB/PEN S36	68 C3
Kenyon Rd CHNE S41	191 F5
Kenyon St OWL S3	8 B4
Keppel Dr KIMB S61	90 C4
Keppel PI SHEFN S5	99 F3
Keppel Rd KIMB S61	90 C4
SHEFN S5	100 A3
Keppel View Rd KIMB S61	101 E1
Keresforth CI BSLY S70	21 D2
Keresforth Ct BSLY S70	21 D2
Keresforth Hall Rd BSLY S70	21 E3
Keresforth Hill Rd BSLY S70	21 D3
Keresforth Rd DOD/DAR S75	20 A4
Kerwin CI TOT/DORE S17	144 A5
Kerwin Dr TOT/DORE S17	144 A5
Kerwin Rd TOT/DORE S17	144 A5
Kestrel Av WHHL DN2	31 F5
Kestrel CI ECK/KIL S21	165 F1
Kestrel Dr ECK/KIL S21	163 F5
Kestrel Gn SHEFP/MNR S2	123 F3
Kestrel Ri BSLY S70	36 A5
Keswick BTLY DN5	29 E1
Keswick CI ST/HB/BR S6	106 C4
Keswick Crs RHAM S60	113 F5
Keswick Dr CHNE S41	183 D2
Keswick PI DRON S18	168 B2
Keswick Wk BSLYN/ROY S71	24 C2
Kettlebridge Rd DARN/MH S9	124 B4
Ketton Av SHEFS S8	147 E2
Ketton Wk DOD/DAR S75	13 D4
Kew Crs HACK/IN S12	149 D5
Key Av HOY S74	51 F2
Keyworth PI HAN/WDH S13	139 E4
Keyworth Rd ST/HB/BR S6	108 A3
Khartoum Rd ECC S11	134 B2
Kidsley CI CHSW S40	188 A2
Kilburn Rd DRON S18	168 A2
Kildale Gdns MOS S20	164 B1
Kildonan Gv HACK/IN S12	150 A2
Killamarsh La ECK/KIL S21	167 E2
Kilner Wy SHEFN S5	108 B1
Kilnhurst Rd CONI DN12	82 A4
RAW S62	80 B5
RHAM/THRY S65	82 B4
Kiln Rd KIMB S61	102 A1
Kilton HI OWL S3	122 C1
Kilton PI OWL S3	9 G1
Kilvington Av HAN/WDH S13	137 F3
Kilvington Crs HAN/WDH S13	137 F3
Kilvington Rd HAN/WDH S13	137 F3
Kimberley St DARN/MH S9	124 A1
Kimberworth Park Rd KIMB S61	91 F5
KIMB S61	102 A2
Kimberworth Rd KIMB S61	102 A2
Kinder Gdns SHEFN S5	98 C4
Kinder Rd STV/CWN S43	186 C3
King Egbert Rd TOT/DORE S17	156 C3
King Edward Rd DONS/BSCR DN4	43 F4
King Edward St BSLYN/ROY S71	15 E1
Kingfield Rd ECC S11	134 B3
Kingfisher CI WHHL DN2	31 F2
Kingfisher Ri KIMB S61	76 B5
King James St ST/HB/BR S6	121 E1
Kings Coppice TOT/DORE S17	156 B2
Kings Ct BSLY S70	37 D1
Kingscroft CI TOT/DORE S17	144 C5
Kingsley Av BTLY DN5	29 D5
CHSW S40	190 A4
Kingsley CI BSLYN/ROY S71	14 B1
Kingsley Crs ARMTH DN3	33 F3
Kingsley Park Av ABRD S7	145 F1
Kingsley Park Gv ECC S11	145 F1
Kingsmede Av CHSW S40	189 C5
Kings Ms ECK/KIL S21	164 C5
King's Rd DON DN1	5 G2
MEX/SWTN S64	58 C3
WMB/DAR S73	39 E3
Kingstone PI BSLY S70	21 E3
Kingston Rd WHHL DN2	31 F5
Kingston St ATT S4	110 A5
King St AU/AST/KP S26	142 A2
BSLY S70	22 A2
CHPT/GREN S35	74 B5
DEARNE S63	27 F4
DON DN1	5 F3
HOY S74	52 A2
MEX/SWTN S64	57 E5
SHEF S1	9 F4
STV/CWN S43	180 A5
King St North CHNE S41	184 B2
King St South CHSW S40	190 B5
Kings Wy RHAM S60	115 E2
Kingsway DEARNE S63	26 C3
WMB/DAR S73	39 E3
Kingsway Gv DEARNE S63	26 C3
Kingswood Av MOS S20	151 E3
Kingswood CI CHNE S41	183 E1
MOS S20	151 E3
Kingswood Crs HOY S74	51 F1
Kingswood Cft MOS S20	151 E3
Kingswood Gv MOS S20	151 E3
Kingwell Crs BSLY S70	22 A4
Kingwell Cft BSLY S70	22 B5
Kingwell Ms BSLY S70	22 B5
Kingwell Rd BSLY S70	22 B5
Kinharvie Rd SHEFN S5	109 D1
Kinnaird Av SHEFN S5	99 D4
Kinnaird PI SHEFN S5	99 D4
Kinnaird Rd SHEFN S5	99 D4
Kinsey Rd CHPT/GREN S35	73 D1
Kipling Av DONS/BSCR DN4	63 D1
Kipling CI DRON S18	170 A4
Kipling Rd CHNE S41	184 A1
Kirby La KIMB S61	75 E4
Kirby St MEX/SWTN S64	58 B3
Kirk Balk HOY S74	51 E2
Kirkby Av BTLY DN5	29 E3
HACK/IN S12	149 E1
Kirkby Dr HACK/IN S12	149 E1
Kirkby Rd HACK/IN S12	149 E1
Kirkby Vw HACK/IN S12	149 E2
Kirkcroft Av ECK/KIL S21	166 B1
KIMB S61	90 A1
Kirkcroft CI KIMB S61	90 A1
Kirkcroft Dr ECK/KIL S21	166 B2
Kirkcroft La ECK/KIL S21	166 B2
Kirkdale CI CHSW S40	190 C4
Kirkdale Crs HAN/WDH S13	139 F1
Kirkdale Dr HAN/WDH S13	139 F1
Kirkham CI BSLYN/ROY S71	15 D4
Kirklands Dr RAW S62	79 F5

Kirkstall Cl *BTLY* DN5 .... **28** B4
RHAM S60 .... **113** E3
Kirkstall Rd *ECC* S11 .... **134** A2
Kirkstead Abbey Ms *KIMB* S61 ..... **90** B3
Kirkstead Gdns *HAN/WDH* S13 ... **140** C3
Kirkstead Rd *KIMB* S61 .... **100** B2
Kirkstone Cl *BTLY* DN5 .... **29** E1
Kirkstone Rd *CHNE* S41 .... **183** D1
ST/HB/BR S6 .... **108** A5
Kirk St *ATT* S4 .... **123** C1
DONS/BSCR DN4 .... **4** A5
Kirk Wy *BSLYN/ROY* S71 .... **15** E4
Kirton Rd *ATT* S4 .... **110** A5
Kitchin Rd *WMB/DAR* S73 .... **38** C2
Kitson Dr *BSLYN/ROY* S71 .... **15** E4
Knab Cl *ECC* S11 .... **134** E1
Knab Cft *ECC* S11 .... **134** A5
Knab Ri *ECC* S11 .... **134** A5
Knab Rd *ECC* S11 .... **134** A5
Knapton Av *RAW* S62 .... **79** F5
Knaresboro Rd *ABRD* S7 .... **146** A2
Knaresborough Cl
AU/AST/KP S26 .... **142** A3
Knaresborough Rd *CONI* DN12 ... **84** A2
Knavesmire Gdns
DONS/BSCR DN4 .... **46** B2
Knifesmithgate *CHSW* S40 .... **11** E6
Knollbeck Av *WMB/DAR* S73 .... **40** B5
Knoll Beck Crs *WMB/DAR* S73 ..... **40** B5
Knollbeck La *WMB/DAR* S73 .... **40** B5
Knoll Cl *STKB/PEN* S36 .... **69** D2
The Knoll *CHSW* S40 .... **188** A2
DRON S18 .... **160** B5
Knowle Cl *ST/HB/BR* S6 .... **119** D1
Knowle Cft *ECC* S11 .... **133** E5
Knowle La *TOT/DORE* S17 .... **156** A1
Knowle La *ECC* S11 .... **133** D1
Knowle Rd *BSLY* S70 .... **22** C4
SHEFN S5 .... **98** C3
Knowles Av *STKB/PEN* S36 .... **69** E3
Knowle Top *MOS* S20 .... **164** C1
Knowsley St *BSLY* S70 .... **21** E3
Knutton Crs *SHEFN* S5 .... **97** F3
Knutton Ri *SHEFN* S5 .... **97** F2
Knutton Rd *SHEFN* S5 .... **97** F3
Kyle Cl *SHEFN* S5 .... **97** F5
Kyle Crs *SHEFN* S5 .... **97** F5
Kynance Crs *RHAM* S60 .... **113** F5

L

Laburnam *BSLY* S70 .... **36** C1
Laburnum Cl *CHPT/GREN* S35 ..... **88** B2
ECK/KIL S21 .... **166** A3
STKB/PEN S36 .... **68** C3
Laburnum Pl *BTLY* DN5 .... **16** C4
Laburnum Rd *DONS/BSCR* DN4 .... **63** D1
MEX/SWTN S64 .... **58** A2
Laburnum St *STV/CWN* S43 .... **180** C5
Laceby Ct *BSLY* S70 .... **21** D3
Ladies Spring Gv *TOT/DORE* S17 . **157** E1
Ladock Cl *BSLYN/ROY* S71 .... **3** H2
Ladybank Rd *MOS* S20 .... **164** B2
Ladybank Vw *ECK/KIL* S21 .... **164** B4
Ladybower La *STV/CWN* S43 ...... **187** E1
Lady Cft *DEARNE* S63 .... **55** F2
Lady Croft La *WMB/DAR* S73 ...... **53** D1
Ladycroft Rd *ARMTH* DN3 .... **33** F5
Lady Ida's Dr *ECK/KIL* S21 .... **163** E4
MOS S20 .... **164** A3
Lady Oak Rd *RHAM/THRY* S65 .... **95** D5
Lady's Br *OWL* S3 .... **9** F3
Ladysmith Av *ABRD* S7 .... **134** B4
Ladywood Dr *CHSW* S40 .... **183** D2
Laird Av *ST/HB/BR* S6 .... **107** E3
Laird Dr *ST/HB/BR* S6 .... **107** E3
Laird Rd *ST/HB/BR* S6 .... **107** E3
Laithe Cft *DOD/DAR* S75 .... **20** A3
Lakeen Rd *WHHL* DN2 .... **31** E1
Lakeside Bvd *DONS/BSCR* DN4 ... **45** F5
Lake View Av *CHSW* S40 .... **189** D4
Lambcroft Vw *HAN/WDH* S13 ..... **140** A4
Lamb Dr *SHEFN* S5 .... **108** B1
Lambert Fold *DOD/DAR* S75 ...... **20** B3
Lambert La *BSLY* S70 .... **23** D3
Lamberts La *RHAM/THRY* S65 ..... **95** F3
Lambert St *OWL* S3 .... **8** D4
Lambert Wk *BSLY* S70 .... **23** D2
Lambeth Rd *DONS/BSCR* DN4 ..... **43** F5
Lamb Hill Cl *HAN/WDH* S13 ...... **138** B3
Lamb La *BSLYN/ROY* S71 .... **15** D2
Lambra Rd *BSLY* S70 .... **3** E6
Lamb Rd *SHEFN* S5 .... **108** B1
Lanark Dr *MEX/SWTN* S64 .... **59** D1
Lanark Gdns *WHHL* DN2 .... **32** A4
Lancaster Av *WHHL* DN2 .... **32** A5
Lancaster Ga *BSLY* S70 .... **2** C6
Lancaster Rd *CHNE* S41 .... **183** F1
STKB/PEN S36 .... **68** C2
Lancaster St *BSLY* S70 .... **21** E3
DEARNE S63 .... **27** E4

Lancelot Cl *CHSW* S40 .... **189** E4
Lancing Rd *SHEFP/MNR* S2 .... **135** E2
SHEFP/MNR S2 .... **135** F1
SHEFP/MNR S2 .... **135** F2
Landsdowne Av *CHNE* S41 .... **183** F2
Landseer Cl *DRON* S18 .... **168** C3
SHEFS S8 .... **148** B5
Landseer Dr *SHEFS* S8 .... **148** B3
Landseer Pl *GLV* S14 .... **148** C3
Lane End *CHPT/GREN* S35 .... **74** A4
Lane End Rd *RHAM* S60 .... **115** E1
Laneham Cl *DONS/BSCR* DN4 ..... **66** B1
Lane Head Cl *RAW* S62 .... **80** B5
Lane Head Rd *TOT/DORE* S17 .... **156** A4
Laneside Cl *DONS/BSCR* DN4 ..... **43** E3
The Lanes *RHAM/THRY* S65 .... **104** C2
Lang Av *BSLYN/ROY* S71 .... **15** F5
Lang Crs *BSLYN/ROY* S71 .... **15** F5
Langdale Cl *RCH* S42 .... **182** A4
Langdale Dr *BTLY* DN5 .... **29** D1
DRON S18 .... **160** A5
Langdale Rd *BSLYN/ROY* S71 ..... **3** E6
SHEFS S8 .... **134** C5
Langdale Sq *STV/CWN* S43 .... **185** E1
Langdon Rd *KIMB* S61 .... **101** F1
Langdon St *ECC* S11 .... **135** D2
Langer Field Av *CHSW* S40 .... **190** B5
Langer St *DONS/BSCR* DN4 .... **43** E3
Langford Cl *DOD/DAR* S75 .... **20** A3
Langhurst Rd *CHSW* S40 .... **183** E5
Langley Cl *CHSW* S40 .... **182** B4
RHAM/THRY S65 .... **105** E2
Langsett Av *ST/HB/BR* S6 .... **107** E2
Langsett Cl *ST/HB/BR* S6 .... **108** B5
Langsett Crs *ST/HB/BR* S6 .... **108** B5
Langsett Gv *ST/HB/BR* S6 .... **121** E1
Langsett Ri *ST/HB/BR* S6 .... **121** E1
Langsett Rd *ST/HB/BR* S6 .... **108** A4
Langtree Av *CHNE* S41 .... **178** B5
Lansbury Av *CHPT/GREN* S35 ..... **88** A1
Lansbury Pl *RAW* S62 .... **81** D5
Lansbury Rd *ECK/KIL* S21 .... **164** B5
Lansdowne Cl *DEARNE* S63 .... **26** C4
Lansdowne Crs *MEX/SWTN* S64 .. **81** E1
Lansdowne Rd *STV/CWN* S43 ..... **32** A4
WHHL DN2 .... **32** A4
Lanyon Wy *BSLYN/ROY* S71 ...... **14** C4
Lapwater Rd *KIMB* S61 .... **92** A3
Lapwing V *KIMB* S61 .... **76** B3
Larch Av *ECK/KIL* S21 .... **166** A3
The Larches *MEX/SWTN* S64 ...... **81** D1
Larchfield Pl *BSLYN/ROY* S71 .... **15** E2
Larchfield Rd *DONS/BSCR* DN4 ... **43** D5
Larch Gv *CHPT/GREN* S35 .... **88** B2
CONI DN12 .... **84** B3
Larch Hl *DARN/MH* S9 .... **125** F4
Larch Pl *BSLY* S70 .... **23** E3
Larch Rd *ECK/KIL* S21 .... **173** F1
Larch Wy *CHSW* S40 .... **183** E4
Larkhill Cl *RAW* S62 .... **94** B3
Larkspur Cl *MEX/SWTN* S64 ...... **81** D3
Lark St *ST/HB/BR* S6 .... **120** C1
Larwood Gv *CONI* DN12 .... **62** A4
Latham Sq *ECC* S11 .... **132** C5
Lathe Rd *RHAM* S60 .... **116** A2
Lathkill Av *STV/CWN* S43 .... **186** C3
Lathkill Cl *HAN/WDH* S13 .... **138** A3
Lathkill Rd *HAN/WDH* S13 .... **138** A3
Latin Gdns *BTLY* DN5 .... **28** A2
Lauder Rd *BTLY* DN5 .... **28** B2
Lauder St *ATT* S4 .... **110** B3
Laudsdale Cl *RHAM/THRY* S65 ... **105** E2
Laudsdale Rd *RHAM/THRY* S65 ... **105** D1
Laughton Rd *DARN/MH* S9 .... **111** F2
DONS/BSCR DN4 .... **4** A5
Launce Rd *SHEFN* S5 .... **98** A5
Laurel Av *BSLY* S70 .... **23** E3
DRON S18 .... **28** C4
Laurel Cl *ECK/KIL* S21 .... **174** A1
Laurel Crs *STV/CWN* S43 .... **180** B5
Laurel Dr *ECK/KIL* S21 .... **166** A4
Laurel Garth Cl *CHNE* S41 .... **178** C3
Laurel Rd *ARMTH* DN3 .... **33** F2
Laurel Ter *DONS/BSCR* DN4 ...... **43** E5
Laurence Cl *CHNE* S41 .... **178** B4
Lavender Cl *CONI* DN12 .... **85** E2
Laverack St *HAN/WDH* S13 ...... **139** D1
Laverdene Av *TOT/DORE* S17 .... **157** D3
Laverdene Cl *TOT/DORE* S17 ..... **156** C4
Laverdene Dr *TOT/DORE* S17 .... **157** D3
Laverdene Rd *TOT/DORE* S17 .... **156** C4
Laverdene Wy *TOT/DORE* S17 ... **157** D3
Laverock Wy *SHEFN* S5 .... **99** E4
Lavinia Rd *CHPT/GREN* S35 ...... **97** E2
Lawn Av *DON* DN1 .... **5** G5
Lawn Garth *BTLY* DN5 .... **29** D2
Lawn Rd *DON* DN1 .... **5** G3
The Lawns *ECC* S11 .... **133** F4
The Lawn *DRON* S18 .... **169** F1
Lawrence Dr *MEX/SWTN* S64 ..... **81** D1
Lawson Rd *FUL* S10 .... **120** C5
Lawton La *RHAM* S60 .... **114** C1
Laxey Rd *ST/HB/BR* S6 .... **119** F2
Laxfield Cl *CHSW* S40 .... **189** D4

Laycock Av *AU/AST/KP* S26 ...... **142** C3
Layden Dr *BTLY* DN5 .... **28** A1
Layton Dr *CHNE* S41 .... **178** C5
Leabrook Rd *DRON* S18 .... **168** A2
Leach La *MEX/SWTN* S64 .... **58** B4
Leadbeater Dr *HACK/IN* S12 ..... **137** E5
Leadbeater Rd *HACK/IN* S12 ..... **137** D5
Leader Rd *ST/HB/BR* S6 .... **107** F3
Leadmill Rd *SHEF* S1 .... **122** C5
SHEFP/MNR S2 .... **135** F1
Leadmill St *SHEF* S1 .... **122** C5
Leake Rd *ST/HB/BR* S6 .... **108** A2
Leamington Gdns *WHHL* DN2 .... **32** A4
WHHL DN2 .... **32** A4
Leamington St *FUL* S10 .... **121** D3
Lea Rd *DRON* S18 .... **169** E2
Lease Gate Rd *RHAM* S60 .... **115** F2
The Leas *BTLY* DN5 .... **29** D4
The Lea *MEX/SWTN* S64 .... **80** C2
MOS S20 .... **152** B3
Leaton Cl *ST/HB/BR* S6 .... **106** B3
Leavy Greave *FUL* S10 .... **8** A6
Leavygreave Rd *OWL* S3 .... **8** A5
Leawood Pl *ST/HB/BR* S6 .... **119** E1
Ledbury Gdns *BTLY* DN5 .... **28** B4
Ledbury Rd *BSLYN/ROY* S71 ..... **14** A1
Ledsham St *HOY* S74 .... **52** C2
Ledsham Rd *RHAM/THRY* S65 ... **104** B5
Ledstone Rd *SHEFS* S8 .... **146** C1
Lee Av *STKB/PEN* S36 .... **69** E2
Lee Brook La *RAW* S62 .... **77** F1
Lee Cft *SHEF* S1 .... **8** D4
Leedham Cl *SHEFN* S5 .... **100** A5
Leedham Rd *RHAM/THRY* S65 ... **105** D3
SHEFN S5 .... **100** A5
Leeds Rd *DARN/MH* S9 .... **124** B1
Lee House La *STKB/PEN* S36 ..... **68** A3
Lee Rd *CHNE* S41 .... **191** F2
ST/HB/BR S6 .... **106** B3
Lees Hall Av *SHEFS* S8 .... **147** E1
Lees Hall Pl *SHEFS* S8 .... **135** F5
Lees Hall Rd *SHEFS* S8 .... **135** F5
Lees House Ct *SHEFS* S8 .... **147** E1
Leeswood Cl *CHNE* S41 .... **183** E1
Leger Wy *DONS/BSCR* DN4 ...... **32** A5
DONS/BSCR DN4 .... **45** E1
WHHL DN2 .... **32** A5
Legion Dr *AU/AST/KP* S26 .... **142** C3
Leicester Av *WHHL* DN2 .... **45** E1
Leigh St *DARN/MH* S9 .... **111** E5
Leighton Cl *BSLYN/ROY* S71 ..... **2** D2
Leighton Dr *GLV* S14 .... **149** D2
Leighton Pl *GLV* S14 .... **149** D2
Leighton Rd *GLV* S14 .... **136** C5
Leighton Vw *SHEFP/MNR* S2 .... **136** C5
Leinster Av *WHHL* DN2 .... **31** E4
Lemont Rd *TOT/DORE* S17 .... **156** C4
Lennox Rd *ST/HB/BR* S6 .... **107** F3
WHHL DN2 .... **31** F4
Lenton St *SHEFP/MNR* S2 .... **135** F1
Leonard Cl *SHEFP/MNR* S2 ...... **137** D3
Leopold St *BSLY* S70 .... **21** E2
SHEF S1 .... **8** D5
Leppings La *ST/HB/BR* S6 .... **108** A2
Lepton Gdns *BSLY* S70 .... **23** E4
Lescar La *ECC* S11 .... **134** A2
Leslie Av *CONI* DN12 .... **84** B3
Leslie Rd *BSLY* S70 .... **23** E3
ST/HB/BR S6 .... **107** E3
Letard Dr *RHAM* S60 .... **114** A3
Levens Wy *CHNE* S41 .... **183** F1
Leverick Dr *RAW* S62 .... **81** D4
Leverton Dr *ECC* S11 .... **135** D1
Leverton Gdns *SHEFP/MNR* S2 .. **135** D1
Leverton Wy *RHAM/THRY* S65 ... **95** F5
Leveson St *ATT* S4 .... **123** C2
Levet Rd *DONS/BSCR* DN4 .... **47** D3
Lewdendale *BSLY* S70 .... **36** B1
Lewes Rd *CONI* DN12 .... **84** C2
Lewis Rd *BSLYN/ROY* S71 .... **15** F3
HAN/WDH S13 .... **138** A3
Leybourne Rd *KIMB* S61 .... **91** F5
Leyburn Cl *CHSW* S40 .... **183** E4
DONS/BSCR DN4 .... **47** D5
Leyburn Dr *AU/AST/KP* S26 ..... **142** A3
Leyburn Gv *CHPT/GREN* S35 .... **74** B3
Leyburn Rd *SHEFS* S8 .... **135** D4
Ley End *BSLY* S70 .... **36** A1
Leyfield Rd *TOT/DORE* S17 ...... **156** B1
The Leylands *DOD/DAR* S75 ..... **12** B3
Leys Cl *DONS/BSCR* DN4 .... **63** D3
Liberty Cl *ST/HB/BR* S6 .... **119** F2
Liberty Dr *ST/HB/BR* S6 .... **119** F2
Liberty HI *ST/HB/BR* S6 .... **119** F2
Liberty La *ST/HB/BR* S6 .... **119** F2
Liberty Rd *ST/HB/BR* S6 .... **119** F2
Library Cl *KIMB* S61 .... **92** B3
Lichfield Rd *CHSW* S40 .... **189** D4
WHHL DN2 .... **31** D3
Lichfield Wy *RHAM* S60 .... **114** B3
Lichford Rd *SHEFP/MNR* S2 ..... **136** A4
Lidget Cl *DONS/BSCR* DN4 .... **46** C5
Lidget La *DEARNE* S63 .... **27** F4
Lidgett La *DOD/DAR* S75 .... **49** E3
Liffey Av *WHHL* DN2 .... **31** E4

Lifford Pl *HOY* S74.............................. 52 C3
Lifford Rd *WHHL* DN2........................ 31 D4
Lifford St *DARN/MH* S9 .... 112 C1
Lightowler Rd *ECK/KIL* S21 .... 172 C1
Lilac Av *STKB/PEN* S36 .... 68 C3
Lilac Gv *CONI* DN12 .... 84 B2
  DONS/BSCR DN4 .... 47 D4
  SHEFN S5 .... 110 C1
Lilac St *STV/CWN* S43 .... 180 B5
Lilian St South *RHAM/THRY* S65 ..... 103 F4
Limb La *TOT/DORE* S17 .... 144 B5
Limbreck Ct *BTLY* DN5 .... 16 B5
Limbrick Cl *ST/HB/BR* S6 .... 107 F5
Limbrick Rd *ST/HB/BR* S6 .... 108 A5
Lime Av *STV/CWN* S43 .... 181 F5
Lime Ct *BTLY* DN5 .... 42 B3 🔢
Lime Gv *CHPT/GREN* S35 .... 88 B2
  MEX/SWTN S64 .... 81 E2
Limegrove *RHAM* S60 .... 104 B5
Lime Gv *STKB/PEN* S36 .... 68 B5
Lime Rd *ECK/KIL* S21 .... 173 F2
Limes Av *DOD/DAR* S75 .... 12 C4
Limestone Cottage La
  ST/HB/BR S6 .... 96 C5
Lime St *MOS* S20 .... 153 D1
  ST/HB/BR S6 .... 121 F1
Limesway *DOD/DAR* S75 .... 12 C4
Lime Tree Av *ARMTH* DN3 .... 33 F2
  DONS/BSCR DN4 .... 5 H6
  ECK/KIL S21 .... 166 A3
Limetree Ct *STV/CWN* S43 .... 186 A4
Lime Tree Ct *DONS/BSCR* DN4 .... 45 D5
Lime Tree Crs *RAW* S62 .... 80 C5
Limpool Cl *DONS/BSCR* DN4 .... 47 D5
Limpsfield Rd *DARN/MH* S9 .... 111 E2
Linacre Rd *CHSW* S40 .... 182 B5
Linaker Rd *ST/HB/BR* S6 .... 120 C2
Linburn Rd *SHEFS* S8 .... 147 D3
Lincoln Rd *WHHL* DN2 .... 31 D3
Lincoln St *CHSW* S40 .... 190 B4
  DARN/MH S9 .... 111 F2 🔢
  RHAM S60 .... 6 C2
Lincroft Dr *RAW* S62 .... 94 A5
Linda Rd *CHNE* S41 .... 183 F1
The Lindales *DOD/DAR* S75 .... 13 D5 🔢
Linden Av *CHSW* S40 .... 188 C3
  DRON S18 .... 159 F5
  SHEFS S8 .... 146 C5
Linden Ct *CHPT/GREN* S35 .... 88 C5
Linden Crs *STKB/PEN* S36 .... 68 C2
Linden Park *CHSW* S40 .... 10 A5
Linden Rd *CHPT/GREN* S35 .... 88 C5
  DEARNE S63 .... 54 C2
Linden Wk *BTLY* DN5 .... 16 B2
Lindholme Dr *NROS/TKH* DN11...... 42 F1
Lindholme Gdns *MOS* S20 .... 152 A3 🔢
Lindisfarne Rd *DRON* S18 .... 169 F3 🔢
Lindley Crs *DEARNE* S63 .... 27 D4
Lindley Rd *SHEFS* S8 .... 110 B2 🔢
Lindley St *RHAM/THRY* S65 .... 7 E3
Lindrick Av *MEX/SWTN* S64 .... 81 F1
Lindrick Cl *DONS/BSCR* DN4 .... 66 A2
Lindrick Dr *ARMTH* DN3 .... 33 F4 🔢
Lindrick Gdns *CHSW* S40 .... 189 D4 🔢
Lindsay Av *SHEFN* S5 .... 98 C5
Lindsay Cl *SHEFN* S5 .... 98 C4
Lindsay Crs *SHEFN* S5 .... 98 C4
Lindsay Dr *SHEFN* S5 .... 98 C4
Lindsay Pl *AU/AST/KP* S26 .... 142 B3
Lindsay Rd *SHEFN* S5 .... 98 C4
Lindsey Cl *DONS/BSCR* DN4............... 66 B2
Lindum St *DEARNE* S63 .... 4 A6
Lingamore Leys *DEARNE* S63 .... 27 D2
Lingard Ct *DOD/DAR* S75 .... 2 A3 🔢
Lingard St *DOD/DAR* S75 .... 2 A2
Lingfield Dr *BTLY* DN5 .... 28 B4
Lingfoot Av *SHEFS* S8 .... 159 F2
Lingfoot Cl *SHEFS* S8 .... 159 F2 🔢
Lingfoot Crs *SHEFS* S8 .... 159 F2
Lingfoot Dr *SHEFS* S8 .... 160 A2 🔢
Lingfoot Pl *SHEFS* S8 .... 159 F2
Lingmoor Cl *DONS/BSCR* DN4 .... 62 C1
Ling Rd *SHEFS* S8 .... 189 E4
Lingthwaite *DOD/DAR* S75 .... 20 B3 🔢
Links Rd *DRON* S18 .... 169 F3
Linkswood Av *WHHL* DN2 .... 32 A2
The Link *DOD/DAR* S75 .... 20 B4
Linkway *WHHL* DN2 .... 31 F3
Linley La *HACK/IN* S12 .... 138 C5 🔢
Linnet Mt *KIMB* S61 .... 90 A1
Linscott Cl *CHNE* S41 .... 183 E2
Linscott Rd *SHEFS* S8 .... 146 C3
Linthwaite La *HOY* S74....................... 53 D3
  RAW S62 .... 53 D3
Linton Cl *BSLY* S70 .... 20 C2
Linton Rd *CHSW* S40 .... 189 D4
Lipp Av *ECK/KIL* S21 .... 166 A1
Lisle Rd *RHAM/THRY* S65 .... 104 B5
Lismore Rd *SHEFS* S8 .... 135 F5
Lister Av *DONS/BSCR* DN4.................. 43 F4
  HACK/IN S12 .... 149 F1
  RAW S62 .... 79 F4
Lister Cl *HACK/IN* S12 .... 149 F2 🔢

Lister Ct *WHHL* DN2 .... 31 E4
Lister Crs *HACK/IN* S12 .... 149 F2
Lister Dr *HACK/IN* S12 .... 149 F2
Lister La *OWL* S3 .... 8 B2
Lister Pl *HACK/IN* S12 .... 149 F2 🔢
Lister Rd *ST/HB/BR* S6 .... 121 D1
Lister St *RHAM/THRY* S65 .... 7 H6
Lister Wy *HACK/IN* S12 .... 149 F2
Little Brind Rd *CHSW* S40 .... 182 C2
Little Common La *ECC* S11 .... 145 D2
  KIMB S61 .... 101 E2
  RHAM S60 .... 116 C3
Littledale Rd *DARN/MH* S9 .... 124 C5
Littlefield La *WMB/DAR* S73 .... 39 E2
Little La *ATT* S4 .... 111 D3 🔢
  HACK/IN S12 .... 137 F4
  KIMB S61 .... 75 F5
  WHHL DN2 .... 19 D5
Little Leeds *HOY* S74......................... 51 F2 🔢
Little London Pl *SHEFS* S8 .... 135 D4 🔢
Little London Rd *SHEFS* S8 .... 134 C5
Little Matlock Gdns *ST/HB/BR* S6 .. 119 E1
Little Matlock Wy *ST/HB/BR* S6 .. 119 E1 🔢
Littlemoor *CHNE* S41 .... 183 E2
  CHNE S41 .... 183 F2 🔢
  ECK/KIL S21 .... 164 C4
Littlemoor Crs *CHNE* S41 .... 183 E2
Littlemoor La *DONS/BSCR* DN4........ 43 F3
Littlemoor St *DONS/BSCR* DN4 .... 43 F3 🔢
Little New Cl *DOD/DAR* S75 .... 12 C4 🔢
Little Norton Av *SHEFS* S8 .... 159 E1
Little Norton Dr *SHEFS* S8 .... 147 E5
Little Norton La *SHEFS* S8 .... 159 E1
Little Norton Wy *SHEFS* S8 .... 159 E1
Little Wood Dr *GLV* S14 .... 149 D2
Little Wood Rd *GLV* S14 .... 149 E2 🔢
Littlewood St *DONS/BSCR* DN4 .... 4 A6
Littleworth La *BSLYN/ROY* S71 .... 15 E4
Litton Cl *STV/CWN* S43 .... 187 D1
Liverpool Av *WHHL* DN2 .... 31 D3
Liverpool St *DARN/MH* S9 .... 111 D5
Livesey St *ST/HB/BR* S6 .... 108 B4
Livingstone Av *WHHL* DN2 .... 19 E5
Livingstone Crs *BSLYN/ROY* S71 .... 14 C2
Livingstone Rd *CHPT/GREN* S35 ...... 73 F5
Livingston Rd *DARN/MH* S9 .... 123 F1 🔢
Lloyd St *ATT* S4 .... 110 B3
  RAW S62 .... 94 A3
Loakfield Dr *SHEFN* S5 .... 98 A2
Lobwood *BSLY* S70 .... 22 B5
Lobwood La *BSLY* S70 .... 22 C5 🔢
Lockeaflash Crs *BSLY* S70 .... 23 E4
Locke Av *BSLY* S70 .... 21 F3
  BSLY S70 .... 22 A4 🔢
Locke Rd *DOD/DAR* S75 .... 20 B4
Lockesley Av *CONI* DN12 .... 84 B1
Locke St *BSLY* S70 .... 21 E3
Lock House Rd *DARN/MH* S9 .... 112 A5
Lock La *DARN/MH* S9 .... 112 C1
Lockoford La *CHNE* S41 .... 184 B3
Lock St *ST/HB/BR* S6 .... 121 F1
Lockton Cl *CHPT/GREN* S35 .... 73 D3
Lockwood Av *RHAM/THRY* S65 .... 105 D3
Lockwood La *BSLY* S70 .... 22 A3
Lockwood Rd *DEARNE* S63 .... 27 E5
  DON DN1 .... 30 C4
  RHAM/THRY S65.............................. 105 D3
Lodge Cl *STV/CWN* S43 .... 186 B5
Lodge Dr *RAW* S62 .... 75 E2
Lodge Farm Cl *CHSW* S40 .... 189 D5
Lodge Hill Dr *AU/AST/KP* S26 .... 155 F3
Lodge La *AU/AST/KP* S26 .... 142 B4
  CHPT/GREN S35 .... 118 B5
  FUL S10 .... 118 B5
  KIMB S61 .... 90 A3
Lodge Moor Rd *FUL* S10 .... 130 C2
Lodge Pl *STV/CWN* S43..................... 187 D3
Lodge Wy *RHAM* S60 .... 114 A3
Logan Rd *DARN/MH* S9 .... 125 E3
Loicher La *CHPT/GREN* S35 .... 89 E5
Lomas Cl *ST/HB/BR* S6 .... 106 A5
Lombard Cl *DOD/DAR* S75 .... 2 B1
Lombard Crs *WMB/DAR* S73 .... 25 F5
London Rd *SHEFP/MNR* S2 .... 135 D1
London Rd South *SHEFS* S8 .... 135 E3
London St *CHNE* S41 .... 179 E3
  CONI DN12 .... 89 F2
Longacre Cl *MOS* S20 .... 153 E4
Longacre Vw *MOS* S20 .... 153 E5
Longacre Wy *MOS* S20 .... 153 E5
Longcar La *BSLY* S70 .... 21 E2
Long Cswy *BSLYN/ROY* S71 .... 15 D4
Longcliff Wk *CHSW* S40 .... 183 D3 🔢
Long Cl *DONS/BSCR* DN4 .... 66 B2
Longcroft Crs *DRON* S18 .... 168 A1
Long Croft *DRON* S18 .... 168 A1
Longfellow Dr *RHAM/THRY* S65 ...... 104 C4
Longfellow Rd *DONS/BSCR* DN4 .... 64 A1
Longfield Cl *WMB/DAR* S73 .... 38 C1
Longfield Dr *DONS/BSCR* DN4 .... 66 B1
Longfield Rd *FUL* S10 .... 120 C2
Longfields Crs *HOY* S74...................... 51 E5
Longford Cl *TOT/DORE* S17 .... 157 E5 🔢
Longford Crs *TOT/DORE* S17............ 157 E3

Longford Dr *TOT/DORE* S17 .... 157 D4
Longford Rd *TOT/DORE* S17 .... 157 D4
Longford Spinney *TOT/DORE* S17 .. 157 D4
Long La *ECK/KIL* S21 .... 166 C2
  ECK/KIL S21 .... 172 A2
  FUL S10 .... 120 A3
  RHAM S60 .... 128 A1
  ST/HB/BR S6 .... 106 C3
  ST/HB/BR S6 .... 119 F2
Longley Av West *SHEFN* S5 .... 109 D2
Longley Cl *SHEFN* S5 .... 109 F1
Longley Crs *SHEFN* S5 .... 109 F1
Longley Dr *SHEFN* S5 .... 109 F2
Longley Farm Vw *SHEFN* S5 .... 109 F2
Longley Hall Gv *SHEFN* S5 .... 110 A3
Longley Hall Ri *SHEFN* S5 .... 109 F2
Longley Hall Rd *SHEFN* S5 .... 109 F2
Longley Hall Wy *SHEFN* S5 .... 110 A1
Longley La *SHEFN* S5 .... 109 F2
Long Line *ECC* S11 .... 144 A4
Longman Rd *BSLY* S70 .... 2 C2
Longridge Rd *BSLYN/ROY* S71 .... 15 E1 🔢
Long Shambles *CHSW* S40 .... 11 F6
Longshaw Cl *STV/CWN* S43 .... 187 E2
Longside Wy *DOD/DAR* S75 .... 12 B5
Longstone Crs *HACK/IN* S12 .... 150 B3
Lonsdale Av *BSLYN/ROY* S71 .... 24 C2
  WHHL DN2 .... 45 F1
Lonsdale Rd *ST/HB/BR* S6 .... 108 A5
Loosemore Dr *HACK/IN* S12 .... 137 D5
Lopham Cl *OWL* S3 .... 9 G1
Lopham St *OWL* S3 .... 122 C1 🔢
Lord Roberts Rd *CHSW* S40 .... 190 B3 🔢
Lords Cl *CONI* DN12 .... 62 A3
Lord's Head La *DONS/BSCR* DN4 ...... 62 B3
Lordsmill St *CHNE* S41 .... 190 C2
  CHSW S40 .... 11 G6
Lord St *BSLYN/ROY* S71 .... 15 D5
  RHAM/THRY S65.............................. 104 B2
Lorna Rd *MEX/SWTN* S64 .... 58 B5
Lorne Cl *DRON* S18 .... 168 B1
Lorne Rd *DEARNE* S63 .... 26 B3
Lothian Rd *WHHL* DN2 .... 32 A4
Louden Cl *KIMB* S61 .... 90 C4
Louden Rd *KIMB* S61 .... 90 C4
Lounde Cl *BTLY* DN5 .... 42 A3
Loundes Rd *DRON* S18 .... 170 C5
Loundes Wood Av *CHNE* S41 .... 183 D1
Lound Rd *DARN/MH* S9 .... 125 E4
Lound Side *CHPT/GREN* S35 .... 74 B5
Loundsley Green Rd *CHSW* S40 ..... 182 C5
Louth Rd *ECC* S11 .... 133 F3
Lovell St *ATT* S4 .... 123 E2
Loversall Cl *DONS/BSCR* DN4 .... 63 F2
Love St *OWL* S3 .... 9 E3
Lovetot Av *AU/AST/KP* S26 .... 142 B2
Lovetot Rd *DARN/MH* S9 .... 123 F2 🔢
  KIMB S61 .... 91 F4
Lowburn Rd *HAN/WDH* S13.............. 138 A3
Lowedges Crs *SHEFS* S8 .... 159 D2 🔢
Lowedges Dr *SHEFS* S8 .... 159 D2 🔢
Lowedges Pl *SHEFS* S8 .... 159 E2 🔢
Lowedges Rd *SHEFS* S8 .... 159 D5
Lowe La *DOD/DAR* S75........................ 34 A2
Lowell Av *DONS/BSCR* DN4 .... 63 F1 🔢
Lower Castlereagh St *BSLY* S70 .... 2 C6
Lower Dolcliffe Rd *MEX/SWTN* S64 .. 58 A3
Lower Grove Rd *CHSW* S40 .... 10 D6
Lower Malton Rd *BTLY* DN5 .... 28 C2
Lower Thomas St *BSLY* S70 .... 21 F2 🔢
Lower York St *WMB/DAR* S73 .... 39 E2 🔢
Lowfield Av *HACK/IN* S12 .... 150 C4
  KIMB S61 .... 93 D3
Lowfield Rd *WHHL* DN2 .... 32 A2
Low Fisher Ga *DON* DN1 .... 4 D2
Lowgate *BTLY* DN5 .... 28 C2
Low Grange Rd *DEARNE* S63 .... 26 C5
Low Grange Sq *DEARNE* S63 .... 26 C5
Lowhouse Rd *SHEFN* S5 .... 99 F2
Low Laithes Vw *WMB/DAR* S73 ...... 38 C1 🔢
Lowlands Cl *BSLYN/ROY* S71 .... 15 E2
  BTLY DN5 .... 16 C3
Low La *KIMB* S61 .... 102 B1 🔢
Low Pasture Cl *DOD/DAR* S75........... 20 B3
Low Pavement *CHSW* S40 .... 11 E6
Low Rd *CONI* DN12 .... 61 D5
  DONS/BSCR DN4 .... 43 E5
  ST/HB/BR S6 .... 120 B1
Low Rd East *DONS/BSCR* DN4 .... 62 B1
Low Rd West *DONS/BSCR* DN4 .... 62 A2
Lowry Dr *DRON* S18 .... 169 D2
Low St *DOD/DAR* S75 .... 20 C4
Lowther Rd *DON* DN1 .... 30 C4
  ST/HB/BR S6 .... 108 B3
Low Wood Cl *MEX/SWTN* S64 .... 81 D2 🔢
Loxley Av *WMB/DAR* S73 .... 39 D3
Loxley Cl *CHSW* S40 .... 188 C1
Loxley Rd *ST/HB/BR* S6 .... 106 C2
Loxley View Rd *FUL* S10 .... 120 C2
Loy Cl *KIMB* S61 .... 92 B3
Lucas Rd *CHNE* S41 .... 183 F1
Lucas St *ATT* S4 .... 110 A5 🔢
Ludham Cl *CHNE* S41 .... 184 A2
Lugano Gv *WMB/DAR* S73 .... 25 F4
Luke La *ST/HB/BR* S6 .... 107 D3

Lulworth Cl *BSLY* S70 .... 22 C2 ⊡
Lumley St *ATT* S4 .... 123 E3
⎿ *DARN/MH* S9 .... 124 A3 ⊡
Lump La *CHPT/GREN* S35 .... 87 D5
Lumsdale Rd *STV/CWN* S43 .... 187 D1
Luna Cft *HACK/IN* S12 .... 149 D3
Lunbreck Rd *DONS/BSCR* DN4 ...... 62 A2
Lundhill Cl *WMB/DAR* S73 .... 39 F4
Lundhill Rd *WMB/DAR* S73 .... 39 F5
Lundhill Rd *WMB/DAR* S73 .... 39 F5
Lundwood Cl *MOS* S20 .... 152 A3 ⊡
Lundwood Dr *MOS* S20 .... 152 A3
Lundwood Gv *MOS* S20 .... 152 A3
Lundy Rd *DRON* S18 .... 169 E3
Lupton Crs *SHEFS* S8 .... 159 D2
Lupton Dr *SHEFS* S8 .... 159 D2
Lupton Rd *SHEFS* S8 .... 159 D2
Luterel Dr *AU/AST/KP* S26 .... 142 B2
Lych Gate Cl *DONS/BSCR* DN4 ...... 47 E5 ⊡
Lydden St *STV/CWN* S43 .... 185 F1 ⊡
Lydford Av *CHNE* S41 .... 178 C5 ⊡
Lydgate Cl *FUL* S10 .... 120 C4
Lydgate Hall Crs *FUL* S10 .... 120 B4
Lydgate La *FUL* S10 .... 120 B4
Lyme St *RHAM* S60 .... 6 A6
Lyminster Rd *ST/HB/BR* S6 .... 97 D4
Lyminton La *RHAM* S60 .... 127 F3
Lymister Av *RHAM* S60 .... 115 D2
Lyncroft Cl *RHAM* S60 .... 114 B4 ⊡
Lyndale Av *ARMTH* DN3 .... 19 F5
Lyndhurst Cl *ECC* S11 .... 134 A4
Lyndhurst Crs *ARMTH* DN3 .... 19 F3
Lyndhurst Rd *ECC* S11 .... 134 A4 ⊡
Lynmouth Rd *ABRD* S7 .... 134 C5
Lynn Pl *DARN/MH* S9 .... 111 F4 ⊡
Lynton Av *RHAM* S60 .... 115 E1
Lynton Dr *ARMTH* DN3 .... 19 F3
Lynton Rd *ECC* S11 .... 134 B2 ⊡□
Lynwood Dr *DRON* S18 .... 168 B2 ⊡
Lynwood Dr *MEX/SWTN* S64 .... 58 A3
Lyons Cl *ATT* S4 .... 110 A3
Lyons St *ATT* S4 .... 110 A5 ⊡
Lytham Av *BSLYN/ROY* S71 .... 15 E2
Lytton Av *SHEFS* S5 .... 97 F5
Lytton Cl *DONS/BSCR* DN4 .... 63 F1
Lytton Crs *SHEFS* S5 .... 97 F4
Lytton Dr *SHEFN* S5 .... 97 F4
Lytton Rd *SHEFN* S5 .... 97 F4

M

Mabel St *RHAM/THRY* S65 .... 104 A4 ⊡
Machin St *RAW* S62 .... 79 D3
Machins Ct *DRON* S18 .... 169 E1 ⊡
Machon Bank *ABRD* S7 .... 134 C4
Machon Bank Rd *ECC* S11 .... 134 B4
Mackenzie Crs *CHPT/GREN* S35 .... 87 C2
⎿ *FUL* S10 .... 121 F5 ⊡
Mackenzie St *ECC* S11 .... 134 C2 ⊡
Macmanus Av *RAW* S62 .... 80 A3 ⊡
Macnaghten Rd *DOD/DAR* S75 ...... 50 A3 ⊡
Macro Rd *WMB/DAR* S73 .... 39 F4
Madehurst Gdns
⎿ *SHEFP/MNR* S2 .... 135 F3 ⊡
Madehurst Ri *SHEFP/MNR* S2 ...... 135 F3 ⊡
Madehurst Rd *SHEFP/MNR* S2 ...... 135 F3 ⊡
Madehurst Vw *SHEFP/MNR* S2 .... 135 F3 ⊡
Madin Dr *STV/CWN* S43 .... 186 C3
Madingley Cl *DONS/BSCR* DN4 .... 63 E2
Madin St *CHNE* S41 .... 11 E3
Mafeking Pl *CHPT/GREN* S35 .... 74 B5
Magna La *RHAM/THRY* S65 .... 95 E5
Magpie Gv *SHEFP/MNR* S2 .... 123 F5 ⊡
Mahon Av *RAW* S62 .... 80 A5
Maidstone Rd *ST/HB/BR* S6 .... 97 E5
Maidwell Wy *ARMTH* DN3 .... 19 F2
Main Av *TOT/DORE* S17 .... 156 C4 ⊡
Main Rd *DARN/MH* S9 .... 125 D2
⎿ *DARN/MH* S9 .... 125 D3 ⊡
⎿ *DRON* S18 .... 170 C4
⎿ *ECK/KIL* S21 .... 162 C5
⎿ *ECK/KIL* S21 .... 172 B4
⎿ *ECK/KIL* S21 .... 175 F2
⎿ *HACK/IN* S12 .... 162 C1
Main St *ARMTH* DN3 .... 47 F3
⎿ *AU/AST/KP* S26 .... 129 F3
⎿ *AU/AST/KP* S26 .... 142 A1
⎿ *AU/AST/KP* S26 .... 142 A3
⎿ *CHPT/GREN* S35 .... 97 D1
⎿ *HACK/IN* S12 .... 151 F1
⎿ *KIMB* S61 .... 93 D3
⎿ *MEX/SWTN* S64 .... 58 A4
⎿ *RAW* S62 .... 76 B2
⎿ *RAW* S62 .... 80 B5
⎿ *RHAM* S60 .... 6 B6
⎿ *RHAM* S60 .... 127 F3
⎿ *WMB/DAR* S73 .... 39 D2
Makin St *MEX/SWTN* S64 .... 59 D3
Malcolm Cl *BSLY* S70 .... 23 E2 ⊡
Malham Cl *CHSW* S40 .... 183 E4
Malham Gdns *MOS* S20 .... 164 B1

Malham Gv *MOS* S20 .... 164 C1
Malham Pl *CHPT/GREN* S35 .... 74 A5
Malham Tarn Cft
⎿ *DONS/BSCR* DN4 .... 45 F4 ⊡
Malia Rd *STV/CWN* S43 .... 185 D3
Malinda St *OWL* S3 .... 8 B2
Malin Rd *DARN/MH* S9 .... 105 E1
⎿ *ST/HB/BR* S6 .... 107 E5
Malkin St *CHNE* S41 .... 11 C5
Mallard Dr *ECK/KIL* S21 .... 165 F1 ⊡
⎿ *KIMB* S61 .... 90 B1
Mallard Cl *DONS/BSCR* DN4 .... 63 D1
Mallory Av *RAW* S62 .... 79 F5
Mallory Dr *MEX/SWTN* S64 .... 59 E2
Mallory Rd *RHAM/THRY* S65 .... 105 D1
Malson Wy *CHNE* S41 .... 184 A3
Maltby St *DARN/MH* S9 .... 111 G5
Malthouse Rd *BSLYN/ROY* S71 .... 3 E6 ⊡
Malting La *ATT* S4 .... 9 H3
The Maltings *RHAM* S60 .... 103 E4 ⊡
Maltkiln St *RHAM* S60 .... 103 E4
Malton Dr *AU/AST/KP* S26 .... 142 C3
Malton Rd *BTLY* DN5 .... 28 B2
⎿ *WHHL* DN2 .... 31 F4
Malton St *ATT* S4 .... 110 A5
Maltravers Cl *SHEFP/MNR* S2 ...... 123 F3
Maltravers Crs *SHEFP/MNR* S2 .... 123 E4
Maltravers Pl *SHEFP/MNR* S2 ...... 123 F3 ⊡
⎿ *SHEFP/MNR* S2 .... 123 F4 ⊡
Maltravers Rd *SHEFP/MNR* S2 .... 123 F4
Maltravers Ter *SHEFP/MNR* S2 .... 123 F5
Maltravers Wy *SHEFP/MNR* S2 .... 123 E4
Malvern Av *BTLY* DN5 .... 28 C4 ⊡
Malvern Cl *DOD/DAR* S75 .... 12 C5 ⊡
Malvern Rd *CHSW* S40 .... 190 A4
⎿ *DARN/MH* S9 .... 124 C2
⎿ *WHHL* DN2 .... 32 A5
Manchester St *FUL* S10 .... 119 F4
⎿ *STKB/PEN* S36 .... 68 A3
⎿ *STKB/PEN* S36 .... 70 B4
Mandeville St *DARN/MH* S9 .... 125 D2
Mangham Rd *KIMB* S61 .... 93 F5
Mangham Wy *KIMB* S61 .... 93 E5
Manifold Av *STV/CWN* S43 .... 187 E1
Manknell Rd *CHNE* S41 .... 184 B1
Mannering Rd *DONS/BSCR* DN4 .... 62 C1 ⊡
Manners St *OWL* S3 .... 122 A1
Manor Ap *KIMB* S61 .... 102 A2
Manor Av *STV/CWN* S43 .... 186 A2
Manor Cl *DEARNE* S63 .... 54 C1 ⊡
⎿ *RAW* S62 .... 79 D3
Manor Ct *RHAM/THRY* S65 .... 105 E3
Manor Crs *CHSW* S40 .... 189 E1
⎿ *DRON* S18 .... 169 D2
⎿ *RHAM* S60 .... 113 F4
Manor Dr *BTLY* DN5 .... 61 E3
⎿ *CHSW* S40 .... 189 E1
⎿ *RHAM* S60 .... 116 A3
⎿ *STV/CWN* S43 .... 186 A2
⎿ *WHHL* DN2 .... 45 D1
Manor End *BSLY* S70 .... 22 A5
Manor Est *BTLY* DN5 .... 16 A2
Manor Farm *AU/AST/KP* S26 .... 129 E5
Manor Farm Ct *MOS* S20 .... 153 E2
Manor Farm Dr *MEX/SWTN* S64 .... 81 D1
Manor Farm Ms *MOS* S20 .... 153 E2
Manor Flds *KIMB* S61 .... 101 F1
Manor Gdns *BSLYN/ROY* S71 .... 24 B2
Manor House Ct *BTLY* DN5 .... 51 F2
Manor House Ct *BTLY* DN5 .... 16 A5 ⊡
Manor House Rd *KIMB* S61 .... 101 F1
Manor Laith Rd *SHEFP/MNR* S2 .... 123 E5
Manor La *SHEFP/MNR* S2 .... 123 F3
Manor Oaks Cl *SHEFP/MNR* S2 .... 123 F4
Manor Oaks Dr *SHEFP/MNR* S2 .... 123 E4 ⊡
Manor Oaks Dr *SHEFP/MNR* S2 .... 123 D4 ⊡
Manor Oaks Gdns
⎿ *SHEFP/MNR* S2 .... 123 D4 ⊡
Manor Oaks Pl *SHEFP/MNR* S2 .... 123 F5
Manor Oaks Rd *SHEFP/MNR* S2 .... 123 E4
Manor Park Av *SHEFP/MNR* S2 .... 137 D1
Manor Park Centre
⎿ *SHEFP/MNR* S2 .... 124 B5 ⊡
Manor Park Cl *SHEFP/MNR* S2 .... 137 D1
Manor Park Cr *SHEFP/MNR* S2 .... 137 D1 ⊡
Manor Park Crs *SHEFP/MNR* S2 .... 137 D1
Manor Park Dr *SHEFP/MNR* S2 .... 137 D1
Manor Park Pl *SHEFP/MNR* S2 .... 124 A5
Manor Park Ri *SHEFP/MNR* S2 .... 124 A5
Manor Park Rd *SHEFP/MNR* S2 .... 124 A5
Manor Park Wy *SHEFP/MNR* S2 .... 137 D1
Manor Pl *RAW* S62 .... 94 B1 ⊡
Manor Rd *AU/AST/KP* S26 .... 155 F1 ⊡
⎿ *BTLY* DN5 .... 16 B2 ⊡
⎿ *CHSW* S40 .... 189 D1
⎿ *DEARNE* S63 .... 26 C3
⎿ *DEARNE* S63 .... 54 B1
⎿ *ECK/KIL* S21 .... 166 B3
⎿ *MEX/SWTN* S64 .... 81 E1
⎿ *RHAM* S60 .... 113 F4
⎿ *STV/CWN* S43 .... 186 A2
Manor Sq *DEARNE* S63 .... 26 B3
Manor Vw *MOS* S20 .... 164 C1 ⊡
Manor Wy *HOY* S74 .... 51 F2
⎿ *SHEFP/MNR* S2 .... 123 F4

Manse Cl *DONS/BSCR* DN4 .... 47 E4
Mansel Av *SHEFN* S5 .... 97 F3
Mansel Crs *SHEFN* S5 .... 97 F3
Mansel Rd *SHEFN* S5 .... 97 F3
Mansfeldt Crs *CHNE* S41 .... 183 F3
Mansfeldt Rd *CHNE* S41 .... 183 F3
Mansfield Crs *ARMTH* DN3 .... 33 D2
Mansfield Dr *HACK/IN* S12 .... 137 F4
Mansfield Rd *AU/AST/KP* S26 .... 142 B4
⎿ *AU/AST/KP* S26 .... 155 D2
⎿ *CHNE* S41 .... 191 E5
⎿ *DONS/BSCR* DN4 .... 83 F5
⎿ *ECK/KIL* S21 .... 167 D2
⎿ *HACK/IN* S12 .... 137 F4
Manton St *SHEFP/MNR* S2 .... 135 F1 ⊡
Manvers Cl *AU/AST/KP* S26 .... 142 B3 ⊡
Manvers Pk *DEARNE* S63 .... 57 D2
Manvers Rd *AU/AST/KP* S26 .... 142 B3
⎿ *MEX/SWTN* S64 .... 57 F3
⎿ *MOS* S20 .... 153 D1
⎿ *ST/HB/BR* S6 .... 108 A5
⎿ *STV/CWN* S43 .... 186 B5
Manvers Wy *DEARNE* S63 .... 81 E5
⎿ *DEARNE* S63 .... 56 C1
Maple Av *DONS/BSCR* DN4 .... 47 D4
Maplebeck Dr *DARN/MH* S9 .... 112 C3
Maplebeck Rd *DARN/MH* S9 .... 112 C3
Maple Cl *BSLY* S70 .... 22 C3
Maple Croft Crs *SHEFN* S5 .... 111 D1
Maple Croft Rd *SHEFN* S5 .... 111 D1
Maple Dr *ECK/KIL* S21 .... 166 A3 ⊡
Maple Gv *AU/AST/KP* S26 .... 143 D2
⎿ *CONI* DN12 .... 84 A3
⎿ *DARN/MH* S9 .... 68 C4
⎿ *STKB/PEN* S36 .... 68 C3
Maple Pl *CHPT/GREN* S35 .... 88 B2
Maple Rd *DOD/DAR* S75 .... 49 E5
⎿ *MEX/SWTN* S64 .... 58 A3
Maple St *STV/CWN* S43 .... 186 C1
Mapperley Rd *DRON* S18 .... 168 A2 ⊡
Mappin's Rd *RHAM* S60 .... 127 F2 ⊡
Mappin St *SHEF* S1 .... 8 B5
Mapplebeck Rd *CHPT/GREN* S35 .. 73 F4
Marcham Dr *MOS* S20 .... 153 E1 ⊡
March Ga *CONI* DN12 .... 85 D2
March St *CONI* DN12 .... 85 D1
⎿ *DARN/MH* S9 .... 111 F5
March Vale Ri *CONI* DN12 .... 84 C2
Marchwood Av *ST/HB/BR* S6 .... 119 F1
Marchwood Cl *CHSW* S40 .... 10 A1
Marchwood Dr *ST/HB/BR* S6 .... 106 C5
Marchwood Rd *ST/HB/BR* S6 .... 106 C5
Mardale Cl *CHNE* S41 .... 177 F5
Marden Rd *ABRD* S7 .... 134 C4 ⊡
Margaret Cl *AU/AST/KP* S26 .... 142 B4 ⊡
Margaret St *SHEF* S1 .... 135 E1
Margaret St *ATT* S4 .... 110 B4
Margetson Crs *SHEFS* S5 .... 98 A3
Margetson Dr *SHEFN* S5 .... 97 F3
Margetson Rd *SHEFN* S5 .... 98 A3
Marian Rd *ARMTH* DN3 .... 19 F4 ⊡
Marigold Cl *SHEFN* S5 .... 110 C1
Marina Ri *WMB/DAR* S73 .... 25 F5
Marion Rd *ST/HB/BR* S6 .... 107 F2
Markbrook Dr *CHPT/GREN* S35 .... 73 D3
Market Cl *BSLYN/ROY* S71 .... 3 F6
Market Hl *BSLY* S70 .... 2 C5
Market Pl *DON* DN1 .... 5 E3
Market Rd *DON* DN1 .... 5 E3
Market Sq *HAN/WDH* S13 .... 140 A4 ⊡
Market St *BSLY* S70 .... 2 C5
⎿ *CHPT/GREN* S35 .... 88 C1
⎿ *DEARNE* S63 .... 26 C3
⎿ *ECK/KIL* S21 .... 164 B5
⎿ *HAN/WDH* S13 .... 140 A4 ⊡
⎿ *HOY* S74 .... 51 F1
⎿ *MEX/SWTN* S64 .... 57 F5
⎿ *MEX/SWTN* S64 .... 58 B4 ⊡
⎿ *RHAM* S60 .... 6 C5
⎿ *STV/CWN* S43 .... 181 F4
Markham Av *ARMTH* DN3 .... 33 E2
⎿ *CONI* DN12 .... 84 B1
Markham Cr *CONI* DN12 .... 84 B1 ⊡
Markham Sq *CONI* DN12 .... 62 A5
Markham Ter *SHEFS* S8 .... 135 D4 ⊡
Mark La *FUL* S10 .... 131 E4
Mark St *BSLY* S70 .... 2 B6
Marlborough Av *BTLY* DN5 .... 43 D3
Marlborough Cl *DEARNE* S63 .... 26 C3 ⊡
Marlborough Ri *AU/AST/KP* S26 .... 142 C4
Marlborough Rd *FUL* S10 .... 121 D4
⎿ *WHHL* DN2 .... 31 D5
Marlcliffe Rd *ST/HB/BR* S6 .... 107 E2
Marley Rd *SHEFP/MNR* S2 .... 136 C1
Marlfield Cft *CHPT/GREN* S35 ...... 98 C1
Marlow Cl *WHHL* DN2 .... 32 A4 ⊡
Marlowe Dr *RHAM/THRY* S65 ...... 104 C4
Marlowe Rd *RHAM/THRY* S65 ...... 104 C4
Marlow Rd *WHHL* DN2 .... 32 A4
Marmion Rd *ECC* S11 .... 133 F5 ⊡
Marples Cl *SHEFS* S8 .... 135 D3 ⊡
Marples Dr *SHEFS* S8 .... 135 D3 ⊡□
Marrick Ct *CHPT/GREN* S35 .... 88 A1 ⊡
Marrion Rd *RAW* S62 .... 80 B5

Marriott La *SHEFS* S8 .... 146 B2
Marriott Pl *RAW* S62 .... 79 E4
Marriott Rd *MEX/SWTN* S64 .... 57 F4
  SHEFS S8 .... 146 B2
Marrison Dr *ECK/KIL* S21 .... 166 A2
Marr Ter *FUL* S10 .... 133 D1
Marsden La *OWL* S3 .... 8 B4
Marsden Rd *STKB/PEN* S36 ...... 69 D2 ▣
Marsden St *CHSW* S40 .... 11 E5
Marshall Av *DONS/BSCR* DN4 .... 43 E5 ▣
Marshall Cl *RAW* S62 .... 94 A2
Marshall Gv *DEARNE* S63 .... 56 A3 ▣
Marshall Rd *SHEFS* S8 .... 147 D5
Marsh Av *DRON* S18 .... 159 F5
Marsh Cl *MOS* S20 .... 164 A2
Marshfield *BSLY* S70 .... 36 A4 ▣
Marsh Ga *BTLY* DN5 .... 4 B1
Marsh House Rd *ECC* S11 .... 133 D5
Marsh La *BTLY* DN5 .... 17 D2
  FUL S10 .... 120 A4
Marsh Rd *BTLY* DN5 .... 29 F4
Marsh St *RHAM* S60 .... 103 D4
  STKB/PEN S36 .... 69 E2 ▣
  WMB/DAR S73 .... 39 E2
Marsh Vw *ECK/KIL* S21 .... 173 F1
Marston Cl *DRON* S18 .... 168 B3
Marston Crs *BSLYN/ROY* S71 ...... 14 A1
Marstone Crs *TOT/DORE* S17 .... 156 A1
Marston Rd *FUL* S10 .... 120 C3
Martin Cl *AU/AST/KP* S26 .... 142 A1
  BSLY S70 .... 36 A5
Martin Ct *ECK/KIL* S21 .... 164 A5
Martin Crs *SHEFN* S5 .... 98 C3
Martin La *HOY* S74 .... 37 E4
Martin Ri *ECK/KIL* S21 .... 164 A5
  KIMB S61 .... 76 B5
Martin's Rd *BSLYN/ROY* S71 ...... 15 F4
Martin St *ST/HB/BR* S6 .... 8 A2
  ST/HB/BR S6 .... 121 F3
Marton Rd *BTLY* DN5 .... 16 A1
Marvell Rd *BTLY* DN5 .... 28 B3 ▣
Mary Ann Cl *BSLYN/ROY* S71 ...... 15 E5
Mary Ann St *DRON* S18 .... 177 F2 ▣
Mary's Pl *DOD/DAR* S75 .... 12 C5 ▣
Mary St *ECK/KIL* S21 .... 164 B5
  RHAM S60 .... 6 B4
  SHEF S1 .... 135 C1
Masbrough St *RHAM* S60 .... 6 B5
  RHAM S60 .... 102 C3
Masefield Rd *DEARNE* S63 .... 55 D1 ▣
  HAN/WDH S13 .... 138 A3
  WHHL DN2 .... 32 A2
Masham Ct *DONS/BSCR* DN4 .... 46 C4 ▣
Mason Av *AU/AST/KP* S26 .... 142 B1
Mason Crs *HAN/WDH* S13 .... 138 B3
Mason Dr *AU/AST/KP* S26 .... 142 A1
Mason Gv *HAN/WDH* S13 .... 138 B4
Mason Lathe Rd *SHEFN* S5 .... 99 F4
Masons Wy *BSLY* S70 .... 23 D4
Mason Wy *HOY* S74 .... 51 E1
Massey Rd *HAN/WDH* S13 .... 140 B5
Masson Cl *CHSW* S40 .... 183 E4 ▣
Mastall La *BTLY* DN5 .... 17 F4
Masters Crs *SHEFN* S5 .... 98 C4
Masters Rd *SHEFN* S5 .... 98 C4
Mather Av *DARN/MH* S9 .... 124 C5
Mather Crs *DARN/MH* S9 .... 124 C5
Mather Dr *DARN/MH* S9 .... 124 C5
Mather Dr *DARN/MH* S9 .... 124 C5
Mather Rd *DARN/MH* S9 .... 124 C5
Matilda La *SHEF* S1 .... 122 C5
Matilda St *SHEF* S1 .... 122 B5
Matlock Dr *STV/CWN* S43 .... 187 D4
Matlock Rd *BSLYN/ROY* S71 .... 14 C1
  FUL S10 .... 121 D2
Mattersey Cl *DONS/BSCR* DN4 .. 66 C2 ▣
Matthews Av *DEARNE* S63 .... 55 E2
Matthews Cl *DEARNE* S63 .... 55 E3
Matthews Dr *MALT* S66 .... 117 F1 ▣
Matthews Fold *SHEFS* S8 .... 148 A4 ▣
Matthews La *SHEFS* S8 .... 148 A3
Matthew St *OWL* S3 .... 8 C3
Mauncer Crs *HAN/WDH* S13 .... 139 F3
Mauncer Dr *HAN/WDH* S13 ...... 139 F3
Mauncer La *HAN/WDH* S13 ...... 139 F3
Maun Wy *SHEFN* S5 .... 110 A1
Maurice St *RAW* S62 .... 94 A3
Mawfa Av *ST/HB/BR* S6 .... 148 B3
Mawfa Crs *SHEFS* S8 .... 148 B3 ▣
Mawfa Dr *SHEFS* S8 .... 148 B3
Mawfa Rd *SHEFS* S8 .... 148 B3 ▣
Mawfield Av *DOD/DAR* S75 .... 12 A3
Maxey Pl *SHEFS* S8 .... 135 E4 ▣
Maxfield Av *FUL* S10 .... 121 D4
Maxwell St *ATT* S4 .... 123 D1
Maxwell Wy *ATT* S4 .... 123 D1
May Av *CHNE* S41 .... 179 D3
  DONS/BSCR DN4 .... 63 E1
Maycock Av *KIMB* S61 .... 91 E4
May Day Gn *BSLY* S70 .... 2 D5
Mayfield Av *BSLYN/ROY* S71 ...... 14 C3
Mayfield Crs *BSLY* S70 .... 21 F4 ▣
Mayfield Rd *BTLY* DN5 .... 29 E4
  CHSW S40 .... 189 D2

  FUL S10 .... 131 E3
Mayflower Rd *DONS/BSCR* DN4 .... 62 A2
Maynard Rd *CHSW* S40 .... 190 A3
  RHAM S60 .... 116 A1
May Rd *ST/HB/BR* S6 .... 107 F4
May Ter *BSLY* S70 .... 21 D1
May Tree Cl *MOS* S20 .... 152 C4
Maytree Cl *RHAM* S60 .... 40 B1
May Tree Cft *MOS* S20 .... 152 C4 ▣
Mcintyre Rd *STKB/PEN* S36 .... 68 C3
Mclintock Wy *BSLY* S70 .... 2 A5
Mcmahon Av *STV/CWN* S43 .... 186 C3
Meaburn Cl *DONS/BSCR* DN4 .... 47 D5
Meadow Av *RAW* S62 .... 79 E4
Meadow Bank Av *ABRD* S7 ...... 134 B3 ▣
Meadowbank Cl *KIMB* S61 .... 102 B3 ▣
Meadow Bank La *ABRD* S7 .... 134 B3
  DARN/MH S9 .... 101 D3
  KIMB S61 .... 101 E4
Meadow Cl *CHNE* S41 .... 179 E4
  DRON S18 .... 160 A4 ▣
  RHAM/THRY S65 .... 95 F5
Meadowcourt *DARN/MH* S9 ...... 111 F2 ▣
Meadow Crs *MOS* S20 .... 163 F1 ▣
Meadow Cft *BTLY* DN5 .... 42 A4
  MEX/SWTN S64 .... 81 D3
Meadowcroft Cl *RHAM* S60 ...... 115 F4
Meadowcroft Gdns *MOS* S20 .... 152 C5
Meadowcroft Gld *MOS* S20 .... 152 C5 ▣
Meadowcroft Ri *MOS* S20 .... 152 C5 ▣
Meadow Dr *BSLYN/ROY* S71 ...... 15 E3
  CHPT/GREN S35 .... 87 F1
  MEX/SWTN S64 .... 81 D1
Meadowfield Dr *HOY* S74 .... 51 F4
Meadow Gate Av *MOS* S20 .... 153 F2
Meadow Gate Cl *MOS* S20 .... 153 F3 ▣
Meadow Gate La *MOS* S20 .... 153 F4
Meadow Gv *TOT/DORE* S17 ...... 156 C4
Meadow Grove Rd *TOT/DORE* S17 .. 156 B4
Meadowhall Rd *DARN/MH* S9 .... 111 F2
  KIMB S61 .... 101 E4
Meadowhall Wy *DARN/MH* S9 .. 112 A1
Meadowhead *SHEFS* S8 .... 159 E1 ▣
Meadow Head *SHEFS* S8 .... 158 C1
Meadow Head Dr *SHEFS* S8 .... 147 D5
Meadow House Dr *FUL* S10 .... 132 B5
Meadow La *MEX/SWTN* S64 .... 58 B5
  RAW S62 .... 79 E4
Meadow Ri *CHSW* S40 .... 182 A5
The Meadows *RCH* S42 .... 182 A4
Meadow St *BSLYN/ROY* S71 .... 3 E3
  KIMB S61 .... 102 B3
  OWL S3 .... 8 B3
Meadow Ter *ECC* S11 .... 134 A2 ▣
The Meadow *BTLY* DN5 .... 42 A3
Meadow Vw *BSLY* S70 .... 22 B5
  CHSW S40 .... 188 B4
Meadow View *HOY* S74 .... 51 E3
Meadow View Rd *MEX/SWTN* S64 .... 81 E3
  SHEFS S8 .... 147 D5
Meadow Wy *MEX/SWTN* S64 ...... 58 A5
The Meads *SHEFS* S8 .... 147 F5
The Meadway *TOT/DORE* S17 .... 156 B1
Meakin St *CHNE* S41 .... 191 E4
Medley Vw *CONI* DN12 .... 85 C2
Medlock Cl *HAN/WDH* S13 .... 126 B5
Medlock Crs *HAN/WDH* S13 ...... 126 B5
Medlock Cft *HAN/WDH* S13 ...... 126 B5
Medlock Dr *HAN/WDH* S13 ...... 139 E1
Medlock Rd *CHSW* S40 .... 189 D4
  HAN/WDH S13 .... 139 E1 ▣
Medlock Wy *HAN/WDH* S13 ...... 126 B5
Medway Cl *DOD/DAR* S75 .... 12 A2
Medford Dr *DONS/BSCR* DN4 ...... 63 E5
Medway Pl *WMB/DAR* S73 .... 40 A4 ▣
Meersbrook Av *SHEFS* S8 .... 135 D5
Meersbrook Park Rd *SHEFS* S8 .. 135 E4
Meersbrook Rd *SHEFS* S8 .... 135 F5
Meetinghouse Cft *HAN/WDH* S13 .. 140 A4
Meetinghouse La *HAN/WDH* S13 .. 140 A4
  SHEF S1 .... 9 E4
Melbeck Ct *CHPT/GREN* S35 .... 87 F1 ▣
Melbourne Av *AU/AST/KP* S26 .. 142 C2
  FUL S10 .... 121 D4
Melbourne Rd *DONS/BSCR* DN4 .. 62 C1
  STKB/PEN S36 .... 68 B2
Melbourn Rd *FUL* S10 .... 121 D2
Melford Dr *DONS/BSCR* DN4 ...... 63 E3
Melfort Cln *FUL* S10 .... 120 A4 ▣
Mell Av *HOY* S74 .... 51 E2
Melling Av *BTLY* DN5 .... 43 D1
Melling Cl *CHSW* S40 .... 190 A4
Melling Ct *CHSW* S40 .... 190 A4
Mellington Cl *SHEFS* S8 .... 148 A3
Mellor Lea Farm Cha
  CHPT/GREN S35 .... 88 C4
Mellor Lea Farm Dr
  CHPT/GREN S35 .... 88 C4
Mellor Lea Farm Garth
  CHPT/GREN S35 .... 88 C4
Mellor Rd *WMB/DAR* S73 .... 39 F3
Mellor Wy *CHSW* S40 .... 190 B5
Mellwood Gv *WMB/DAR* S73 .... 39 D5 ▣
Melrose Cl *CHSW* S40 .... 189 D1
  DONS/BSCR DN4 .... 42 C5

Melrose Gv *RHAM* S60 .... 115 E2
Melrose Rd *ATT* S4 .... 122 C1
Melton Av *BSLYN/ROY* S71 .... 15 E5
Meltham La *CHNE* S41 .... 184 C3
Melton Av *WMB/DAR* S73 .... 40 C5
Melton Gn *DEARNE* S63 .... 55 D2
Melton Gv *HACK/IN* S12 .... 151 E3
Melton High St *DEARNE* S63 ...... 55 D2
Melton Rd *BTLY* DN5 .... 42 B2
Melton St *MEX/SWTN* S64 .... 59 D4
  WMB/DAR S73 .... 40 C5 ▣
Melton Ter *BSLY* S70 .... 22 B5
Melville Crs *STV/CWN* S43 ...... 186 A5
Melville St *WMB/DAR* S73 .... 39 E2 ▣
Melvinia Crs *DOD/DAR* S75 .... 13 E3
Mendip Cl *BTLY* DN5 .... 28 C4 ▣
  DOD/DAR S75 .... 12 C5 ▣
Mendip Crs *CHSW* S40 .... 182 C5
Mendip Ri *RHAM* S60 .... 114 B4 ▣
Merbeck Dr *CHPT/GREN* S35 ...... 73 F2
Merbeck Gv *CHPT/GREN* S35 .... 73 F3 ▣
Mercaston Cl *CHSW* S40 .... 182 B4 ▣
Mercia Dr *TOT/DORE* S17 .... 156 C2
Meredith Crs *DONS/BSCR* DN4 .. 63 F1
Meredith Rd *ST/HB/BR* S6 .... 107 F4
Mere La *ARMTH* DN3 .... 33 E2
Merlin Cl *BSLY* S70 .... 36 A5
Merlin Wy *KIMB* S61 .... 76 B5
  SHEFN S5 .... 110 A1
Merrick Cl *CHSW* S40 .... 183 E4
Merrill Rd *DEARNE* S63 .... 26 C2
Merton La *DARN/MH* S9 .... 100 C5
Merton Rd *DARN/MH* S9 .... 100 C5
Merton Ri *DARN/MH* S9 .... 100 C5
  DARN/MH S9 .... 100 C5 ▣
Metcalfe Av *ECK/KIL* S21 .... 166 A2
Methley Cl *SHEFP/MNR* S2 ...... 137 D4
Meynell Av *CHSW* S40 .... 189 D2 ▣
Meynell Crs *SHEFN* S5 .... 97 E5
Meynell Rd *SHEFN* S5 .... 97 E5
Michael Cft *DEARNE* S63 .... 55 E2
Michael Rd *BSLYN/ROY* S71 .... 15 F5
Mickelden Wy *DOD/DAR* S75 ...... 20 B1 ▣
Micklebring Gv *CONI* DN12 .... 84 B3
Mickley La *TOT/DORE* S17 .... 157 D4
Middle Av *RAW* S62 .... 80 A5
Middle Bank *DONS/BSCR* DN4 .... 44 C4
Middleburn Cl *BSLY* S70 .... 22 E3
Middlecliff Cl *MOS* S20 .... 152 C4
Middlecliff Ct *MOS* S20 .... 152 C4 ▣
Middlecliff Ri *MOS* S20 .... 152 C4
Middlecroft Rd *STV/CWN* S43 .. 187 D2
Middle Dr *RHAM* S60 .... 115 D3
Middlefield Cl *TOT/DORE* S17 .. 156 A1
Middlefield Cft *TOT/DORE* S17 .. 156 A2
Middlefield Rd *DONS/BSCR* DN4 .. 46 B5
  RHAM S60 .... 115 E2
Middlefields Dr *RHAM* S60 ...... 116 A3
Middle Hay Cl *HACK/IN* S12 .... 136 C5
Middle Hay Pl *HACK/IN* S12 .... 136 C5
Middle Hay Ri *HACK/IN* S12 .... 136 C5
Middle Hay Vw *GLV* S14 .... 148 C1
Middle La *CHPT/GREN* S35 .... 86 C5
  RHAM/THRY S65 .... 7 H4
  ST/HB/BR S6 .... 120 B1 ▣
Middle La South *RHAM/THRY* S65 .. 104 B3
Middle Ox Cl *MOS* S20 .... 165 D2 ▣
Middle Ox Gdns *MOS* S20 .... 165 D2
Middle Pl *RHAM/THRY* S65 ...... 104 C2
Middlesex St *BSLY* S70 .... 22 A3
Middle Shambles *CHSW* S40 ...... 11 E6
Middleton Dr *STV/CWN* S43 ...... 186 C5
Middleton La *CHPT/GREN* S35 .... 97 E1
Middleton Rd *RHAM/THRY* S65 .... 7 H5
Middlewood Rd *ST/HB/BR* S6 .. 107 E1
Middlewood Rd North
  CHPT/GREN S35 .... 96 A4
Middlewoods *DOD/DAR* S75 ...... 20 B5 ▣
Midfield Rd *FUL* S10 .... 120 B3
Midhill Rd *SHEFP/MNR* S2 .... 135 F2
Midhope Wy *DOD/DAR* S75 .... 20 B1
Midhurst Rd *ST/HB/BR* S6 .... 96 C4
Midland Rd *KIMB* S61 .... 102 B3
  MEX/SWTN S64 .... 57 F5
Midland St *BSLY* S70 .... 2 D5
  RAW S62 .... 93 F4
  SHEF S1 .... 135 E1 ▣
Midvale Av *ST/HB/BR* S6 .... 121 F1
Midvale Cl *ST/HB/BR* S6 .... 121 F1
Milbanke St *DON* DN1 .... 5 F1
Milburn Ct *MOS* S20 .... 153 E4 ▣
Milburn Gv *MOS* S20 .... 153 E4
Milden Pl *BSLY* S70 .... 22 B3
Milden Rd *ST/HB/BR* S6 .... 107 E2
Mile Oak Rd *RHAM* S60 .... 115 D1
Miles Cl *SHEFN* S5 .... 109 E3
Miles Rd *CHPT/GREN* S35 .... 73 F4
  SHEFN S5 .... 109 D3
Milethorn La *DON* DN1 .... 30 B4
Milford Rd *STV/CWN* S43 .... 187 D4
Milford St *DARN/MH* S9 .... 111 F4
Milgrove Crs *CHPT/GREN* S35 .... 73 E3
Mill Cl *RHAM* S60 .... 103 D5
Mill Ct *BSLY* S70 .... 22 B5
Milldale Cl *CHSW* S40 .... 183 D4

Milldale Rd *TOT/DORE* S17 .... 157 D3
Milldyke Cl *RHAM* S60 .... 116 B3 🔲
Millennium Wy *CHNE* S41 .... 177 F5
Miller Cft *HAN/WDH* S13 .... 139 E4
Miller Dale Dr *RHAM* S60 .... 116 B5
Miller Rd *SHEFS* S8 .... 135 D3 🔲🔲
Millers Dl *BSLY* S70 .... 36 B1
Millfield Rd *BTLY* DN5 .... 30 A1
Mill Ga *BTLY* DN5 .... 29 F1
Mill Gn *STV/CWN* S43 .... 181 E4
Mill Hl *RHAM* S60 .... 116 A3
Mill Hill Cl *BTLY* DN5 .... 43 D1
Millhouses Ct *ECC* S11 .... 145 F1
Millhouses Gln *ECC* S11 .... 145 F1 🔲
Millhouses La *ABRD* S7 .... 146 A2
Millhouses St *HOY* S74 .... 51 F3
Mill La *CHSW* S40 .... 189 D4
   DEARNE S63 .... 55 D3
   DRON S18 .... 169 F2
   ECK/KIL S21 .... 175 E1
   RAW S62 .... 76 A1
   RHAM S60 .... 127 E3
   STKB/PEN S36 .... 70 A2
   TOT/DORE S17 .... 157 D3
Mill Meadow Gdns *WMB* S20 .... 153 F4
Millmoor La *RHAM* S60 .... 102 C3
Millmoor Rd *WMB/DAR* S73 .... 40 A1
Millmount Rd *HOY* S74 .... 52 A2
   SHEFS S8 .... 135 D5
Mill Rd *CHPT/GREN* S35 .... 88 C5
   ECK/KIL S21 .... 164 B4
   RHAM S60 .... 127 E3
Mill Road Cl *CHPT/GREN* S35 .... 88 B5
Millsands *OWL* S3 9
Millside Ct *BTLY* DN5 .... 29 F1 🔲
Millstone Cl *BSLY* S70 .... 168 B1 🔲
Millstone Dr *AU/AST/KP* S26 .... 142 B5
Millstream Cl *BTLY* DN5 .... 22 B3
Mill Stream Cl *CHSW* S40 .... 189 D4
Mill St *ARMTH* DN3 .... 33 F3
   CHNE S41 .... 11 G6
   KIMB S61 .... 92 C2
   RHAM S60 .... 103 E4
Millthorpe Rd *SHEFN* S5 .... 99 E5
Millwood Rd *DONS/BSCR* DN4 .... 63 D2 🔲
Mill Wood Vw *ST/HB/BR* S6 .... 106 A5
Milner Ga *CONI* DN12 .... 61 F5
Milner Gate Ct *CONI* DN12 .... 85 E1
Milner Rd *DONS/BSCR* DN4 .... 43 D5 🔲
Milnes St *BSLY* S70 .... 22 B2 🔲
Milnrow Crs *SHEFN* S5 .... 98 A3
Milnrow Dr *SHEFN* S5 .... 98 A3
Milnrow Rd *SHEFN* S5 .... 98 A3
Milton Av *BTLY* DN5 .... 29 D5
   HOY S74 .... 52 A1
   KIMB S61 .... 92 C2
Milton Cl *DEARNE* S63 .... 40 C5
   HOY S74 .... 51 F3
Milton Crs *CHSW* S40 .... 190 B4
   HOY S74 .... 51 F3
Milton Gv *ARMTH* DN3 .... 33 F3
   WMB/DAR S73 .... 39 F3
Milton La *SHEF* S1 .... 122 A5
Milton Rd *ABRD* S7 .... 134 C3
   CHPT/GREN S35 .... 87 E1
   HOY S74 .... 51 F2 🔲
   MEX/SWTN S64 .... 58 B3
   RHAM/THRY S65 .... 7 G2
Milton St *MEX/SWTN* S64 .... 57 D5
   OWL S3 .... 122 A5
   RHAM S60 .... 6 B2
Mitton Wk *DON* DN1 .... 4 D5
Minden Ct *BTLY* DN5 .... 29 F1 🔲
Minna Rd *OWL* S3 .... 109 F5
Minneymoor HI *CONI* DN12 .... 61 E5
Minneymoor La *CONI* DN12 .... 85 E1
Minster Cl *CHPT/GREN* S35 .... 99 D1
   DONS/BSCR DN4 .... 47 E5
Minster Rd *CHPT/GREN* S35 .... 98 C1
Minster Wy *BSLY/ROY* S71 .... 15 E4
Minto Rd *ST/HB/BR* S6 .... 107 F5
Miriam Av *RCH* S42 .... 188 B4
Mission Fld *WMB/DAR* S73 .... 40 B5
Mitchell Cl *BSLY* S70 .... 23 E5 🔲
Mitchell Rd *SHEFS* S8 .... 147 D5
   WMB/DAR S73 .... 25 F5
Mitchell's St *BSLY* S70 .... 23 E5
Mitchell St *OWL* S3 .... 8 A4
Mitchell Wy *STV/CWN* S43 .... 179 F3 🔲
Moat Cft *BTLY* DN5 .... 16 A5 🔲
Moat Hills Ct *BTLY* DN5 .... 16 B5
Modena Ct *WMB/DAR* S73 .... 25 F4
Moffat Gdns *WHHL* DN2 .... 19 E5
Moffatt Rd *SHEFP/MNR* S2 .... 135 F4
Molineaux Cl *SHEFN* S5 .... 99 E4 🔲
Molineaux Rd *SHEFN* S5 .... 99 D3
Molineux Av *STV/CWN* S43 .... 181 E5
Molloy Pl *SHEFS* S8 .... 135 E5 🔲
Molloy St *SHEFS* S8 .... 135 E4 🔲
Mona Av *FUL* S10 .... 121 D3
Mona Rd *DONS/BSCR* DN4 .... 43 D4
   FUL S10 .... 121 D2

Monckton Rd *SHEFN* S5 .... 111 D1
Moncrieffe Rd *ABRD* S7 .... 134 C4
Monks Cl *KIMB* S61 .... 91 D4
Monkspring *BSLY* S70 .... 23 D5
Monks Wy *BSLY/ROY* S71 .... 15 E4
Monkwood Rd *CHNE* S41 .... 183 E1
   RAW S62 .... 79 E4
Monmouth Rd *WHHL* DN2 .... 31 E3
Monmouth St *OWL* S3 .... 121 F5 🔲
Monsal Crs *STV/CWN* S43 .... 186 C3
Monsal St *DEARNE* S63 .... 26 C3
Montague Cl *CONI* DN12 .... 60 B5
Montague St *DON* DN1 .... 5 F1
   ECC S11 .... 134 C1
Montagu Rd *BTLY* DN5 .... 42 C2
Montagu St *MEX/SWTN* S64 .... 58 C4 🔲
Monteney Crs *SHEFN* S5 .... 98 B1
Monteney Gdns *SHEFN* S5 .... 98 B2
Monteney Rd *SHEFN* S5 .... 98 B2
Montfort Dr *OWL* S3 .... 122 C1
Montgomery Av *ABRD* S7 .... 134 C3
Montgomery Dr *ABRD* S7 .... 134 C3 🔲
Montgomery Rd *ABRD* S7 .... 134 C3
   DEARNE S63 .... 55 F2 🔲
Montgomery Terrace Rd *OWL* S3 .... 8 B2
Montrose Av *WHHL* DN2 .... 31 F4
Montrose Pl *DRON* S18 .... 168 B1
Montrose Rd *ECC* S11 .... 134 A5
Monyash Cl *STV/CWN* S43 .... 187 D2 🔲
Moonpenny Wy *DRON* S18 .... 169 E2
Moonshine La *SHEFN* S5 .... 109 F1
Moorbank Cl *DOD/DART* S75 .... 13 D5 🔲
   FUL S10 .... 119 E4
   WMB/DAR S73 .... 38 C1
Moorbank Dr *FUL* S10 .... 119 F4
Moorbank Rd *FUL* S10 .... 119 E4 🔲
   WMB/DAR S73 .... 24 C5
Moorbank Vw *WMB/DAR* S73 .... 24 C5
Moorbridge Crs *WMB/DAR* S73 .... 40 C4
Moor Crs *MOS* S20 .... 164 A1
Moorcroft Av *FUL* S10 .... 131 F2
Moorcroft Cl *FUL* S10 .... 131 F3
Moorcroft Dr *FUL* S10 .... 131 F3
Moorcroft Rd *FUL* S10 .... 131 F3 🔲
Moordale Vw *RAW* S62 .... 81 D4
Moor End Rd *FUL* S10 .... 121 D3
Moore St *SHEFP/MNR* S2 .... 122 A5
Moore Street Rbt *OWL* S3 .... 122 A5
Moor Farm Av *MOS* S20 .... 151 F5
Moor Farm Garth *MOS* S20 .... 152 A5 🔲
Moorfield Dr *ARMTH* DN3 .... 33 F4
Moorgate Av *FUL* S10 .... 121 E3
   RHAM S60 .... 103 F5
Moorgate Cha *RHAM* S60 .... 103 F4
Moorgate Crs *DRON* S18 .... 169 F3 🔲
Moorgate Gv *RHAM* S60 .... 103 F5
Moorgate La *RHAM* S60 .... 103 F5
Moorgate Rd *RHAM* S60 .... 103 F4 🔲
Moorgate St *RHAM* S60 .... 6 D5
Moor Green Cl *DOD/DART* S75 .... 12 B5
Moorhay Cl *CHSW* S40 .... 182 C2 🔲
Moor Head *SHEF* S1 .... 122 B5 🔲
Moorhouse Cl *RHAM* S60 .... 116 B3 🔲
Moorhouse La *RHAM* S60 .... 116 A3
Moorland Av *BSLY* S70 .... 20 C2
Moorland Ct *DEARNE* S63 .... 41 D5 🔲
Moorland Dr *STKB/PEN* S36 .... 68 B2
Moorland Gv *DONS/BSCR* DN4 .... 46 A3
Moorland Pl *ST/HB/BR* S6 .... 119 D1
Moorlands Cl *RHAM* S60 .... 116 A3
Moorland Vw *AU/AST/KP* S26 .... 142 C3
   DEARNE S63 .... 41 D5
   DRON S18 .... 171 E2 🔲
   HACK/IN S12 .... 149 E3
Moorland View Rd *CHSW* S40 .... 189 D5
Moor La *ARMTH* DN3 .... 19 F1
   BSLY S70 .... 50 A3
Moor Oaks Rd *FUL* S10 .... 121 D4
Moorpark Av *CHSW* S40 .... 189 D4
Moor Rd *DEARNE* S63 .... 56 A2 🔲
   RHAM/THRY S65 .... 104 C3
Moorside *FUL* S10 .... 131 E2
Moorside Cl *MOS* S20 .... 152 A5
Moorsyde Av *FUL* S10 .... 120 C2
Moorsyde Crs *FUL* S10 .... 120 C2
Moorthorpe Gdns *MOS* S20 .... 151 E3
Moorthorpe Gn *HACK/IN* S12 .... 151 D3
Moorthorpe Wy *HACK/IN* S12 .... 151 E3
   MOS S20 .... 152 A3
Moortop Rd *DRON* S18 .... 171 F2
Moor Va *MOS* S20 .... 151 D3
Moor Valley Cl *HACK/IN* S12 .... 151 E4
Moorview *KIMB* S61 .... 101 E3
Moorview Cl *STV/CWN* S43 .... 185 E2 🔲
Moor View Dr *SHEFS* S8 .... 146 C3 🔲
Moor View Rd *SHEFS* S8 .... 146 C3
Moor View Ter *ECC* S11 .... 132 C5 🔲
Moorwinstow Cft
   TOT/DORE S17 .... 156 C1 🔲
Moorwoods Av *CHPT/GREN* S35 .... 74 B5 🔲
Moorwoods La *CHPT/GREN* S35 .... 88 A1
Moray Pl *DRON* S18 .... 168 B1
Mordaunt Rd *SHEFP/MNR* S2 .... 137 D4

Morgan Av *SHEFN* S5 .... 108 C1
Morgan Cl *SHEFN* S5 .... 109 D1
Morgan Rd *SHEFN* S5 .... 108 C2
Morland Cl *GLV* S14 .... 149 D2
Morland Dr *GLV* S14 .... 149 D2
Morland Pl *GLV* S14 .... 149 D2
Morland Rd *GLV* S14 .... 148 C2
Morley Av *CHSW* S40 .... 183 D5
Morley Cl *DRON* S18 .... 168 A2
Morley Rd *KIMB* S61 .... 91 F5
   WHHL DN2 .... 30 C4
Morley St *RAW* S62 .... 94 A2
   ST/HB/BR S6 .... 107 F5
Morpeth St *OWL* S3 .... 8 B3
   RHAM/THRY S65 .... 7 E4 🔲
Morrall Rd *SHEFN* S5 .... 98 A2
Morris Av *CHNE* S41 .... 10 B1
   RAW S62 .... 80 A3
Morris Dr *CHNE* S41 .... 10 B1
Morris Rd *DONS/BSCR* DN4 .... 62 C1
Mortain Rd *RHAM* S60 .... 115 D3
Morthen Hall La *MALT* S66 .... 117 F5
Morthen La *MALT* S66 .... 117 E4
   RHAM S60 .... 129 E1
Morthen Rd *MALT* S66 .... 117 F1
Mortlake Rd *SHEFN* S5 .... 110 B2 🔲
Mortomley Cl *CHPT/GREN* S35 .... 73 F4
Mortomley La *CHPT/GREN* S35 .... 73 F4
Morton Cl *BSLY/ROY* S71 .... 15 E2 🔲
Morton La *ECK/KIL* S21 .... 172 A2
Morton Pl *CHPT/GREN* S35 .... 97 D1
Morton Rd *MEX/SWTN* S64 .... 58 C3
Mosborough Hall Dr *MOS* S20 .... 164 C3
Mosborough Moor *MOS* S20 .... 151 F5
Mosbrough Rd *HAN/WDH* S13 .... 137 F3
Mossdale Av *MOS* S20 .... 164 B1
Mossdale Cl *BTLY* DN5 .... 28 C2
Moss Dr *ECK/KIL* S21 .... 166 B3
Moss Gv *HACK/IN* S12 .... 152 B1
Moss Vw *MOS* S20 .... 163 F2
Moss Wy *HACK/IN* S12 .... 152 B2
   MOS S20 .... 164 B1
Motehall Dr *SHEFP/MNR* S2 .... 137 E1
Motehall Pl *SHEFP/MNR* S2 .... 137 F1
Motehall Rd *SHEFP/MNR* S2 .... 137 E1
Motehall Wy *SHEFP/MNR* S2 .... 137 E1 🔲
The Motte *KIMB* S61 .... 102 A1
Mottram St *BSLY/ROY* S71 .... 2 D4
Mound Rd *CHSW* S40 .... 190 B3
Mountbatten Dr *CHPT/GREN* S35 .... 97 D1
Mountcastle Cl *CHNE* S41 .... 184 A1
Mount Cl *BSLY* S70 .... 22 A3
Mount Crs *HOY* S74 .... 51 E2
Montenoy Rd *RHAM* S60 .... 103 E5
Mountford Cft *TOT/DORE* S17 .... 156 C3 🔲
Mount Pleasant *BSLY* S70 .... 36 C1 🔲
   DONS/BSCR DN4 .... 43 E5 🔲
Mount Pleasant Cl
   CHPT/GREN S35 .... 74 B5 🔲
Mount Pleasant Rd *DEARNE* S63 .... 56 A4
   KIMB S61 .... 102 C2
   SHEFP/MNR S2 .... 135 D2 🔲
Mount Rd *CHPT/GREN* S35 .... 73 F5
   OWL S3 .... 109 D5
Mount St *BSLY* S70 .... 22 A3
   BSLY/ROY S71 .... 24 A2
   ECC S11 .... 135 D1
   KIMB S61 .... 102 C2
Mount Ter *DEARNE* S63 .... 55 D2
   WMB/DAR S73 .... 39 D2
Mount Vernon Av *BSLY* S70 .... 22 A3
Mount Vernon Crs *BSLY* S70 .... 22 B4
Mount Vernon Rd *BSLY* S70 .... 22 A4
Mount View Av *SHEFS* S8 .... 147 E2
Mount View Gdns *SHEFS* S8 .... 147 E2 🔲
Mount View Rd *SHEFS* S8 .... 147 E3
Mousehole Cl *RHAM/THRY* S65 .... 95 F5
Mousehole La *RHAM/THRY* S65 .... 95 F5
Mouse Park Ga *CHPT/GREN* S35 .... 86 A5
Mowbray Gdns *RHAM/THRY* S65 .... 105 D1
Mowbray Pl *RHAM/THRY* S65 .... 105 D1
Mowbray St *OWL* S3 .... 8 D1
   RHAM/THRY S65 .... 104 C1
Moxon Cl *STKB/PEN* S36 .... 69 E3
Mucky La *BSLY/ROY* S71 .... 24 B1
   STKB/PEN S36 .... 68 A4
Muirfield Av *DONS/BSCR* DN4 .... 67 F1
   MEX/SWTN S64 .... 81 F1
Muirfield Cl *CHNE* S41 .... 184 C3
Mulberry Cl *BTLY* DN5 .... 28 B4
   RAW S62 .... 94 A3 🔲
Mulberry Rd *ECK/KIL* S21 .... 173 F1
Mulberry St *SHEF* S1 .... 9 F5 🔲
Mulberry Wy *ARMTH* DN3 .... 33 F5 🔲
   ECK/KIL S21 .... 165 F3 🔲
Mulehouse Rd *FUL* S10 .... 120 B3
Mundella Pl *SHEFS* S8 .... 147 E2
Munro Cl *ECK/KIL* S21 .... 166 B2
Munsbrough La *KIMB* S61 .... 92 B4
   KIMB S61 .... 93 D4
Munsbrough Ri *KIMB* S61 .... 92 C3
Murdock Rd *SHEFN* S5 .... 98 A5
Murrayfield Dr *MOS* S20 .... 164 C2 🔲
Murray Rd *ECC* S11 .... 133 F4

ECK/KIL S21 .... **166** C1 🔲
  RAW S62 .... **80** B5
Musard Pl *STV/CWN* S43 .... **181** E5
Musgrave Crs *SHEFN* S5 .... **109** E3
Musgrave Dr *SHEFN* S5 .... **109** E3
Musgrave Pl *SHEFN* S5 .... **109** E3
Musgrave Rd *SHEFN* S5 .... **109** D3
Mushroom La *FUL* S10 .... **121** E4
Muskoka Av *ECC* S11 .... **132** C5
Muskoka Dr *ECC* S11 .... **132** C4
Mutual St *DONS/BSCR* DN4 .... **4** A6
Myers Grove La *ST/HB/BR* S6 ...... **106** C5
  ST/HB/BR S6 .... **107** D5
Myers St *WMB/DAR* S73 .... **39** D1
Mylnhurst Rd *ECC* S11 .... **145** F1
Mylor Ct *STV/CWN* S43 .... **15** D4 🔲
Mylor Rd *ECC* S11 .... **133** E4
Myrtle Gv *STV/CWN* S43 .... **180** B5
Myrtle Rd *SHEFP/MNR* S2 .... **135** E2
  WMB/DAR S73 .... **39** D2
Myrtle Springs *HACK/IN* S12 ...... **137** D3
Myrtle St *DARN/MH* S9 .... **13** D5 🔲
Myton St *DARN/MH* S9 .... **124** B3

N

Nairn Dr *DRON* S18 .... **168** B2 🔲
Nairn St *FUL* S10 .... **120** C4
Nanny Hl *STKB/PEN* S36 .... **69** D2
Napier Mt *BSLY* S70 .... **22** A4
Napier St *ECC* S11 .... **134** C1
Naseby Av *BTLY* DN5 .... **28** B3
Naseby St *DARN/MH* S9 .... **111** E2
Nathan Ct *MOS* S20 .... **153** D4
Nathan Dr *MOS* S20 .... **153** D3
Nathan Gv *MOS* S20 .... **152** C3
Navan Rd *DONS/BSCR* DN4 .... **137** E3
Naylor Gv *WMB/DAR* S75 .... **20** A3
Naylor St *RAW* S62 .... **94** A3
Neale Bank *STV/CWN* S43 .... **185** E2
Neale Rd *WHHL* DN2 .... **31** F1
Nearcroft Rd *KIMB* S61 .... **102** A1
Nearfield Rd *DONS/BSCR* DN4 ...... **66** B1
Needham Wy *ECC* S11 .... **134** A5
Needlewood La *DOD/DAR* S75 .... **20** A4 🔲
Neepsend La *OWL* S3 .... **121** F1
Neild Rd *HOY* S74 .... **52** A2
Neill Rd *ECC* S11 .... **134** A2
Nelson Av *BSLYN/ROY* S71 .... **14** B3
Nelson Cl *RHAM* S60 .... **114** B4
Nelson Dr *CHPT/GREN* S35 .... **87** E1
Nelson Rd *ST/HB/BR* S6 .... **120** A1
Nelson St *BSLY* S70 .... **2** C6 🔲
  CHNE S41 .... **184** B3
  RHAM/THRY S65 .... **7** F1
Nesfield Cl *CHNE* S41 .... **183** E1
Nesfield Wy *SHEFN* S5 .... **99** E5
Nether *CHPT/GREN* S35 .... **87** B1
  ECK/KIL S21 .... **166** A2
Nether Cantley La *ARMTH* DN3 .... **47** E4
Nether Crs *CHPT/GREN* S35 .... **87** E5
Nether Croft *STV/CWN* S43 .... **185** F2
Netherdene Rd *DRON* S18 .... **169** E2
Nether Edge Rd *ABRD* S7 .... **134** C5
Netherfield Cl *STKB/PEN* S36 .... **70** A2 🔲
Netherfield La *RAW* S62 .... **94** A2
Netherfield Rd *CHSW* S40 .... **188** B4
  FUL S10 .... **120** C2
Netherfields Crs *DRON* S18 .... **169** E3
Netherfield Vw *RHAM/THRY* S65 ..... **105** E1
Nethergate *ST/HB/BR* S6 .... **118** C2
Nethergreen Av *ECK/KIL* S21 .... **166** B6
Nethergreen Ct *ECK/KIL* S21 ...... **166** B1 🔲
Nethergreen Gdns *ECK/KIL* S21 .. **166** B1 🔲
Nethergreen Rd *ECC* S11 .... **132** C2
Nether Hall Rd *DON* DN1 .... **5** E3
Netherleigh Rd *CHSW* S40 .... **188** C1
Nether Ley Av *CHPT/GREN* S35 ...... **88** B1
Nether Ley Ct *CHPT/GREN* S35 ...... **88** B1 🔲
Nether Ley Cft *CHPT/GREN* S35 ..... **88** B1 🔲
Nether Ley Gdns
  CHPT/GREN S35 .... **88** B1 🔲
Nethermoor Av *ECK/KIL* S21 .... **166** B1 🔲
Nethermoor Cl *ECK/KIL* S21 .... **166** B1 🔲
Nethermoor Dr *ECK/KIL* S21 .... **166** B1
Nethermoor La *ECK/KIL* S21 .... **166** B1
Nether Oak Cl *MOS* S20 .... **153** F3 🔲
Nether Oak Dr *MOS* S20 .... **153** F3
Nether Oak Vw *MOS* S20 .... **153** F3 🔲
Nether Shire La *SHEFN* S5 .... **99** D2
Netherthorpe La *ECK/KIL* S21 ..... **166** A2
Netherthorpe Pl *OWL* S3 .... **8** B2
Netherthorpe Rd *OWL* S3 .... **8** A4
Netherthorpe St *OWL* S3 .... **8** B3 🔲
Netherwood Rd *WMB/DAR* S73 ...... **25** E5
Nettleham Rd *SHEFS* S8 .... **147** D2
Neville Av *BSLY* S70 .... **23** D3
Neville Cl *BSLY* S70 .... **23** E3 🔲
  WMB/DAR S73 .... **38** C1
Neville Ct *WMB/DAR* S73 .... **38** C1
Neville Crs *BSLY* S70 .... **23** E3
Neville Dr *OWL* S3 .... **122** C1

Neville Rd *KIMB* S61 .... **92** A5
Neville St *RHAM* S60 .... **6** C4
Nevis Cl *CHSW* S40 .... **183** E5
Newark Rd *MEX/SWTN* S64 .... **57** F3
Newark St *DARN/MH* S9 .... **111** E5 🔲
New Beetwell St *CHSW* S40 .... **11** E6
Newbiggin Cl *RAW* S62 .... **93** F2
Newbiggin Dr *RAW* S62 .... **93** F2
Newbold Av *CHNE* S41 .... **183** F3
Newbold Back La *CHSW* S40 .... **183** E5
Newbold Dr *CHNE* S41 .... **183** F3
Newbold Rd *CHNE* S41 .... **10** D3
  CHNE S41 .... **182** C2
  RCH S42 .... **182** B1
Newbold Ter *BTLY* DN5 .... **29** D3
Newbould La *DONS/BSCR* DN4 .... **63** F1
Newbould Crs *MOS* S20 .... **153** E2
Newbridge Ct *CHNE* S41 .... **178** B5 🔲
Newbridge Dr *STV/CWN* S43 .... **185** E1
Newbridge Gv *CONI* DN12 .... **62** A5 🔲
Newbridge La *CHNE* S41 .... **178** C5
  STV/CWN S43 .... **185** D1
Newburn Dr *DARN/MH* S9 .... **112** C2
Newbury Rd *FUL* S10 .... **120** C3 🔲
Newbury Wy *BTLY* DN5 .... **28** B3 🔲
Newby Crs *DONS/BSCR* DN4 .... **63** E2
Newby Rd *CHNE* S41 .... **183** D1
Newcastle St *SHEF* S1 .... **8** C5
Newcomen Rd *BTLY* DN5 .... **29** D4
Newcroft Cl *MOS* S20 .... **153** F2
New Cross Dr *HAN/WDH* S13 .... **139** E4
New Cross Wy *HAN/WDH* S13 .... **139** E4
New Droppingwell Rd *KIMB* S61 ... **100** C3
Newent La *FUL* S10 .... **120** C3
Newfield Av *BSLYN/ROY* S71 .... **15** E3
Newfield Crs *DEARNE* S63 .... **55** F5
  TOT/DORE S17 .... **156** A1
Newfield Cft *TOT/DORE* S17 .... **144** A5
Newfield Farm Cl
  SHEFP/MNR S2 .... **136** C5 🔲
Newfield Green Rd
  SHEFP/MNR S2 .... **136** B4
Newfield La *TOT/DORE* S17 .... **156** A1
Newgate Cl *CHPT/GREN* S35 .... **73** E4
New Hall Crs *STKB/PEN* S36 .... **68** A1 🔲
Newhall Rd *ATT* S4 .... **110** C4
New Hall Rd *CHSW* S40 .... **189** D2
Newhall Rd *DARN/MH* S9 .... **111** D5
Newhaven Cl *CHSW* S40 .... **188** C3 🔲
New Hl *CONI* DN12 .... **85** D1
Newhill Rd *BSLYN/ROY* S71 .... **14** B2
  DEARNE S63 .... **55** E3
New Ings *ARMTH* DN3 .... **33** E3
Newington Dr *AU/AST/KP* S26 ...... **142** C3
Newington Rd *ECC* S11 .... **134** A2
Newland Dl *CHNE* S41 .... **11** F3
Newland Gdns *CHNE* S41 .... **10** B1
Newlands Av *CHSW* S40 .... **189** D1
  HACK/IN S12 .... **137** F4
Newlands Cl *DONS/BSCR* DN4 .... **67** D1
Newlands Dr *BTLY* DN5 .... **29** D4
  HACK/IN S12 .... **137** F4
Newlands Gv *HACK/IN* S12 .... **137** F4
Newlands Rd *HACK/IN* S12 .... **137** F4
Newlyn Dr *BSLYN/ROY* S71 .... **3** H2
Newlyn Pl *SHEFS* S8 .... **147** D2
Newlyn Rd *SHEFS* S8 .... **147** D2
Newman Cl *DARN/MH* S9 .... **100** C3 🔲
Newman Ct *RHAM* S60 .... **115** E2
Newman Dr *DARN/MH* S9 .... **100** B5
Newman Rd *DARN/MH* S9 .... **111** E1
  RHAM S60 .... **115** E2
Newmarch St *DARN/MH* S9 .... **112** C1
Newmarket Rd *DONS/BSCR* DN4 ..... **46** B2
New Mdw *RAW* S62 .... **79** E3
New Queen St *CHNE* S41 .... **10** D3
New St *DEARNE* S63 .... **56** A2
  DOD/DAR S75 .... **49** E3
  DOD/DAR S75 .... **50** A4
  DRON S18 .... **171** E2
  HOY S74 .... **53** E1
  KIMB S61 .... **100** C4
  STKB/PEN S36 .... **69** E2
Newsam Rd *MEX/SWTN* S64 .... **81** E2
Newsham Rd *SHEFS* S8 .... **135** F3
Newsome Av *WMB/DAR* S73 .... **38** C3
New Station Rd *MEX/SWTN* S64 ..... **57** F5
Newstead Av *HACK/IN* S12 .... **150** C3
Newstead Cl *DRON* S18 .... **168** A2 🔲
  HACK/IN S12 .... **150** C2 🔲
Newstead Dr *HACK/IN* S12 .... **150** C3
Newstead Gv *HACK/IN* S12 .... **150** C2 🔲
Newstead Pl *HACK/IN* S12 .... **150** C2
Newstead Ri *HACK/IN* S12 .... **150** C2
Newstead Rd *BTLY* DN5 .... **16** A5
  HACK/IN S12 .... **150** C2
Newstead Wy *HACK/IN* S12 .... **150** C3
New St *BSLY* S70 .... **2** D6
  BSLY S70 .... **21** F2
  BSLY S70 .... **36** B1 🔲
  BSLY S70 .... **37** D1
  BSLYN/ROY S71 .... **23** F2 🔲
  BTLY DN5 .... **29** E1
  CHPT/GREN S35 .... **73** E3

CHSW S40 .... **190** B2
DOD/DAR S75 .... **20** A4
DON DN1 .... **44** A3
KIMB S61 .... **90** A2
KIMB S61 .... **92** C2
MEX/SWTN S64 .... **59** E3
MOS S20 .... **153** E5
RAW S62 .... **94** A1
RHAM S60 .... **127** E1
SHEF S1 .... **9** E4
WMB/DAR S73 .... **39** F2 🔲
WMB/DAR S73 .... **52** C1
New Street Bus Link *MOS* S20 ..... **153** E5
New Street La *SHEFP/MNR* S2 .... **9** H4
Newton Av *STKB/PEN* S36 .... **68** A1
Newton Dr *BTLY* DN5 .... **43** D1
  RHAM/THRY S65 .... **104** B3
Newton La *BTLY* DN5 .... **122** B5 🔟
  STKB/PEN S36 .... **68** A1
Newton Pl *KIMB* S61 .... **90** A3
Newton Rd *CHPT/GREN* S35 .... **73** F5
Newton St *BSLY* S70 .... **2** A5
  RHAM/THRY S65 .... **104** B3
New Wortley Rd *KIMB* S61 .... **102** C2
Niagara Rd *ST/HB/BR* S6 .... **108** A1
Nicholas St *BSLY* S70 .... **2** A6 🔟
  CHNE S41 .... **191** E5 🔲
Nicholson Av *DEARNE* S63 .... **55** E3
Nicholson Pl *SHEFS* S8 .... **135** F4 🔟
Nicholson Rd *DONS/BSCR* DN4 ...... **43** E3
  SHEFS S8 .... **135** E4
Naylor Rd *ST/HB/BR* S6 .... **120** B2
Nickerwood Dr *AU/AST/KP* S26 .... **142** B4
Nidderdale Rd *KIMB* S61 .... **92** A3
Nidd Rd *DARN/MH* S9 .... **124** B2
Nidd Rd East *DARN/MH* S9 .... **124** B2
Nightingale Cl *RHAM* S60 .... **103** E4
Nightingale Ct *RHAM* S60 .... **103** E4
Nightingale Cft *KIMB* S61 .... **76** B5
Nightingale Rd *CHPT/GREN* S35 ..... **97** E1 🔲
Nile St *FUL* S10 .... **121** D5 🔟
Ninian Gv *DONS/BSCR* DN4 .... **46** C1
Noble St *HOY* S74 .... **52** A3
Noehill Rd *HAN/WDH* S13 .... **138** A5
Noehill Pl *SHEFP/MNR* S2 .... **137** F1 🔲
Noehill Rd *SHEFP/MNR* S2 .... **137** F1
Nook La *ST/HB/BR* S6 .... **119** D1
The Nook *FUL* S10 .... **121** E3
Nora St *DEARNE* S63 .... **27** F5
Norborough Rd *DARN/MH* S9 ...... **112** C2
  WHHL DN2 .... **31** D4
Norbreck Rd *DONS/BSCR* DN4 .... **62** A2
Norbrook Wy *RHAM* S60 .... **116** B3
Norburn Dr *ECK/KIL* S21 .... **166** B2
Norbury Cl *CHSW* S40 .... **182** C4
  DRON S18 .... **168** B2 🔲
Norcroft *BSLY* S70 .... **22** A4
Norfolk Cl *BSLYN/ROY* S71 .... **14** C3
  CHSW S40 .... **183** E5
Norfolk Hl *CHPT/GREN* S35 .... **87** D5
Norfolk La *SHEF* S1 .... **9** E6 🔟
Norfolk Park Av *SHEFP/MNR* S2 ... **136** B2
Norfolk Park Dr *SHEFP/MNR* S2 ... **136** A1
Norfolk Park Rd *SHEFP/MNR* S2 ... **136** A1
Norfolk Rd *DONS/BSCR* DN4 .... **63** F1 🔲
  SHEFP/MNR S2 .... **123** D5
Norfolk Rw *SHEF* S1 .... **9** E5
Norfolk St *RHAM/THRY* S65 .... **7** E4
  SHEF S1 .... **9** E6
Norfolk Wy *RHAM* S60 .... **115** E2
Norgreave Wy *MOS* S20 .... **164** C1
Norman Cl *BSLY* S70 .... **22** B5 🔲
  BSLYN/ROY S71 .... **15** D5 🔲
Norman St *BTLY* DN5 .... **28** B2
Normancroft Crs
  SHEFP/MNR S2 .... **138** A1 🔟
Normancroft Dr
  SHEFP/MNR S2 .... **137** F1 🔟
Normancroft Wy *SHEFP/MNR* S2 .. **137** F1
Normandale Av *ST/HB/BR* S6 ...... **106** B4
Normandale Rd *ST/HB/BR* S6 ...... **108** B5 🔲
Norman St *DARN/MH* S9 .... **111** E5
  DEARNE S63 .... **27** E3
Normanton Gdns *ATT* S4 .... **110** A5
Normanton Gv *HAN/WDH* S13 ...... **139** D4
Normanton Hl *HACK/IN* S12 .... **138** A4
Normanton Spring Ct
  HAN/WDH S13 .... **138** C4
Normanton Spring Rd
  HAN/WDH S13 .... **138** D5
Normanville Av *RHAM* S60 .... **113** F3
Norrel's Cft *RHAM* S60 .... **104** A5
Norris Rd *ST/HB/BR* S6 .... **107** F4
Norroy St *ATT* S4 .... **123** E1 🔟
Northampton Rd *WHHL* DN2 .... **32** A4 🔟
North Bridge Rd *BTLY* DN5 .... **4** B1
North Church St *SHEF* S1 .... **9** E4
North Cliff Rd *CONI* DN12 .... **60** C5
North Cl *DRON* S18 .... **170** C5
Northcote Av *SHEFS* S8 .... **135** F4
Northcote Rd *SHEFS* S8 .... **135** F4
North Crs *ECK/KIL* S21 .... **154** C5
  RHAM/THRY S65 .... **104** B3
North Dr *KIMB* S61 .... **6** C2

Northern Av *SHEFP/MNR* S2 .... 136 C3
Northern Common *DRON* S18 .... 157 F5
North Farm Ct *AU/AST/KP* S26 .... 143 D3
Northfield Av *FUL* S10 .... 120 C2
   RAW S62 .... 80 A4
Northfield Cl *FUL* S10 .... 121 D2 🔲
Northfield Rd *BTLY* DN5 .... 4 A2
   BTLY DN5 .... 29 E4
   FUL S10 .... 120 C3
   RHAM S60 .... 6 D3
Northgate *DOD/DAR* S75 .... 13 D4
North Ga *MEX/SWTN* S64 .... 59 D3
North Hill Rd *SHEFN* S5 .... 98 A5
Northlands Rd *SHEFN* S5 .... 98 A5
Northmoor Cl *STV/CWN* S43 .... 186 A2 🔲
North Moor Vw *STV/CWN* S43 .... 186 A2
North Pitt St *KIMB* S61 .... 102 A3
North Pl *DOD/DAR* S75 .... 12 C4
   RHAM/THRY S65 .... 104 B2
North Qd *SHEFN* S5 .... 99 E5
North Quarry *RHAM/THRY* S65 .... 104 C2
Northside Rd *DEARNE* S63 .... 56 A2
North St *CONI* DN12 .... 62 A5
   DONS/BSCR DN4 .... 44 B3
   KIMB S61 .... 6 A3
   MEX/SWTN S64 .... 57 F5
   RAW S62 .... 80 C4
North Swaithe Cl *BTLY* DN5 .... 16 B4
Northumberland Av *HOY* S74 .... 51 F1
   WHHL DN2 .... 31 F4
Northumberland Rd *FUL* S10 .... 121 D4
Northumberland Wy
   BSLYN/ROY S71 .... 24 A2
Norton Av *HACK/IN* S12 .... 149 D3
   RCH S42 .... 188 B4
   SHEFS S8 .... 148 B4
Norton Church Glebe *SHEFS* S8 .... 147 F4 🔲
Norton Church Rd *SHEFS* S8 .... 147 F4
Norton Green Cl *SHEFS* S8 .... 148 A4
Norton Hammer La *SHEFS* S8 .... 146 C1 🔲
Norton La *SHEFS* S8 .... 147 F5
   SHEFS S8 .... 159 E1
Norton Lees Cl *SHEFS* S8 .... 147 E2 🔲
Norton Lees Crs *SHEFS* S8 .... 147 E1
Norton Lees La *SHEFS* S8 .... 147 D1
Norton Lees Rd *SHEFS* S8 .... 135 D5
Norton Lees Sq *SHEFS* S8 .... 147 E1
Norton Ms *SHEFS* S8 .... 148 A4
Norton Park Av *SHEFS* S8 .... 147 F5 🔲
Norton Park Crs *SHEFS* S8 .... 147 E5
Norton Park Dr *SHEFS* S8 .... 147 E5
Norton Park Rd *SHEFS* S8 .... 159 E1
Norton Park Vw *SHEFS* S8 .... 147 E5
Norton Rd *DEARNE* S63 .... 55 E1
   SHEFS S8 .... 148 C3
   WHHL DN2 .... 31 F4 🔲
Norwich Rd *WHHL* DN2 .... 31 E2
Norwith Rd *DONS/BSCR* DN4 .... 66 B1
Norwood Av *CHNE* S41 .... 191 F5
   SHEFN S5 .... 109 F3
Norwood Cl *SHEFN* S5 .... 109 F3
Norwood Crs *ECK/KIL* S21 .... 167 D1
Norwood Dr *BTLY* DN5 .... 16 B3
   SHEFN S5 .... 109 F3
Norwood Grange Dr *SHEFN* S5 .... 109 F2
Norwood Rd *ECK/KIL* S21 .... 167 D1
Norwood Rd *CONI* DN12 .... 84 C1
   SHEFN S5 .... 109 F3
Norwood St *RHAM/THRY* S65 .... 95 E5
Nostell Fold *DOD/DAR* S75 .... 20 A4 🔲
Nostell Pl *DONS/BSCR* DN4 .... 66 B1
Nottingham Cliff *OWL* S3 .... 122 B1
Nottingham Cl *BSLYN/ROY* S71 .... 24 B3
   BTLY DN5 .... 28 B3 🔲
Nottingham St *OWL* S3 .... 109 F5
   RHAM/THRY S65 .... 7 E4
Nowill Ct *SHEFS* S8 .... 135 E4 🔲
Nowill Pl *SHEFS* S8 .... 135 E4 🔲
Nunnery Crs *RHAM* S60 .... 127 D1
Nunnery Dr *SHEFP/MNR* S2 .... 124 A3
Nunnery Ter *SHEFP/MNR* S2 .... 123 F4
Nursery Dr *CHPT/GREN* S35 .... 98 C1
   RHAM S60 .... 127 D1
Nursery Gdns *BSLY* S70 .... 23 F3 🔲
Nursery Gv *CHPT/GREN* S35 .... 98 C1
Nursery La *OWL* S3 .... 9 F2
Nursery Rd *AU/AST/KP* S26 .... 142 C2
Nursery St *BSLY* S70 .... 21 F2
   OWL S3 .... 9 E2
Nuttall Pl *SHEFP/MNR* S2 .... 123 E4
Nutwell Cl *DONS/BSCR* DN4 .... 66 C1
Nutwell La *ARMTH* DN3 .... 33 F3

O

Oak Av *DEARNE* S63 .... 56 B3
Oak Bank Av *CHNE* S41 .... 178 C3
Oakbank Cl *MEX/SWTN* S64 .... 81 E3
Oakbank Ct *TOT/DORE* S17 .... 156 C3 🔲
Oakbrook Rd *ECC* S11 .... 133 D2
Oak Cl *ECK/KIL* S21 .... 166 C4
   HOY S74 .... 51 D3

MEX/SWTN S64 .... 57 F3
   STV/CWN S43 .... 185 E2
Oak Ct *BTLY* DN5 .... 42 B3
   MEX/SWTN S64 .... 57 F3
Oakcrest *DONS/BSCR* DN4 .... 67 F3
Oakdale *BSLY* S70 .... 22 C5
Oakdale Pl *KIMB* S61 .... 102 A3
Oak Dale Rd *DONS/BSCR* DN4 .... 62 A3
Oakdale Rd *ECC* S11 .... 134 B4
   KIMB S61 .... 102 A4
Oakdell *DRON* S18 .... 160 B5
Oaken Wood Cl *KIMB* S61 .... 90 B1
Oaken Wood Rd *KIMB* S61 .... 90 A1
Oakes Gn *DARN/MH* S9 .... 124 A1
Oakes Park Vw *SHEFS* S8 .... 148 B4 🔲
Oakes St *DARN/MH* S9 .... 100 C5 🔲
Oakfern Gv *CHPT/GREN* S35 .... 73 E5
Oakfield Av *DRON* S18 .... 188 C3
Oakfield Wk *DOD/DAR* S75 .... 12 C5
Oak Gv *CONI* DN12 .... 84 C2
Oak Grove Gn *TOT/DORE* S17 .... 156 C4
Oakham Dr *OWL* S3 .... 122 A1
Oakham Pl *DOD/DAR* S75 .... 13 D4
Oakhill Rd *ABRD* S7 .... 134 B4
   DRON S18 .... 160 A5
   WHHL DN2 .... 31 F3
Oakholme Ms *ECC* S11 .... 134 A1 🔲
Oakholme Rd *ECC* S11 .... 134 A1
Oakland Rd *SHEFN* S5 .... 107 F4
Oaklands Av *BSLYN/ROY* S71 .... 15 E3
Oaklands Dr *DONS/BSCR* DN4 .... 46 B4
Oaklands Gdns *DONS/BSCR* DN4 .... 46 B5
Oaklands Pl *DEARNE* S63 .... 55 E1
Oak Lea *KIMB* S61 .... 92 C3
Oak Lea Av *DEARNE* S63 .... 55 D1
Oaklea Gv *BSLY* S70 .... 37 D1 🔲
Oakley Cl *CHSW* S40 .... 10 B4
Oakley Rd *HAN/WDH* S13 .... 125 F5
Oak Lodge Rd *CHPT/GREN* S35 .... 73 D4
Oak Pk *FUL* S10 .... 120 C5
Oak Rd *ARMTH* DN3 .... 33 E1
   DEARNE S63 .... 27 D3
   DEARNE S63 .... 56 B3
   HACK/IN S12 .... 149 E3
   MEX/SWTN S64 .... 57 F5
   MOS S20 .... 153 D1
Oaks Av *STKB/PEN* S36 .... 68 B2
Oaks Cl *DEARNE* S63 .... 56 B4
Oaks Crs *BSLY* S70 .... 23 D2
Oaks Fold *SHEFN* S5 .... 99 F3
Oaks Fold Av *SHEFN* S5 .... 99 F4
Oaks Fold Rd *SHEFN* S5 .... 99 F4
Oaks La *BSLY* S70 .... 23 D2
   BSLYN/ROY S71 .... 23 D1
   KIMB S61 .... 91 D5
   SHEFN S5 .... 99 F4
Oak St *BSLY* S70 .... 2 A6
   MOS S20 .... 152 A5
   SHEFS S8 .... 135 E3
   STV/CWN S43 .... 180 B5
Oak Ter *AU/AST/KP* S26 .... 141 F2
   DONS/BSCR DN4 .... 44 A3
Oak Well La *BSLY* S70 .... 22 B2
   BSLYN/ROY S71 .... 3 F6
Oakwell Ter *BSLYN/ROY* S71 .... 22 B2 🔲
Oakwell Vw *BSLYN/ROY* S71 .... 3 F6
Oakwood Av *SHEFN* S5 .... 98 A2
Oakwood Cl *BSLY* S70 .... 37 D1
Oakwood Crs *RAW* S62 .... 79 F4
Oakwood Dr *ARMTH* DN3 .... 33 E4
   RHAM S60 .... 115 F1
Oakwood Gv *RHAM* S60 .... 104 B5
Oakwood Rd *DONS/BSCR* DN4 .... 43 D5
Oakwood Rd East *RHAM* S60 .... 115 F1
Oakwood Rd West *RHAM* S60 .... 115 D1
Oakworth Cl *MOS* S20 .... 164 C2 🔲
Oakworth Dr *MOS* S20 .... 164 B2 🔲
Oakworth Gv *MOS* S20 .... 164 B2
Oakworth Vw *MOS* S20 .... 164 B2 🔲
Oates Av *RAW* S62 .... 94 B1
Oates Cl *KIMB* S61 .... 102 B2
Oates St *KIMB* S61 .... 102 B2
Oats Orch *MOS* S20 .... 164 B2 🔲
Occupation La *HACK/IN* S12 .... 151 D2
Occupation Rd *CHNE* S41 .... 184 A1
   RAW S62 .... 75 F2
   RAW S62 .... 93 F2
Ochre Dike Cl *MOS* S20 .... 152 C3 🔲
Ochre Dike La *MOS* S20 .... 152 B3
Octavia Cl *RHAM* S60 .... 114 A2 🔲
Odom Ct *SHEFS* S8 .... 135 F4
Ogden Rd *WHHL* DN2 .... 32 B1
Oil Mill Fold *RHAM* S60 .... 6 D6
Oldale Cl *HAN/WDH* S13 .... 140 A5
Oldale Ct *HAN/WDH* S13 .... 140 A4
Oldale Gv *HAN/WDH* S13 .... 140 A4
Old Bakery Cl *CHNE* S41 .... 178 B4 🔲
Old Cross La *DEARNE* S63 .... 56 A2
Old Farm Ct *MEX/SWTN* S64 .... 57 F2
Oldfield Av *CONI* DN12 .... 84 A1
   ST/HB/BR S6 .... 119 E1
Oldfield Cl *HOY* S74 .... 51 F2
Oldfield Gv *ST/HB/BR* S6 .... 119 E2
Oldfield Rd *RHAM/THRY* S65 .... 105 E2

ST/HB/BR S6 .... 119 E2
Old Fulwood Rd *ECC* S11 .... 132 B3
Old Garden Dr *RHAM/THRY* S65 .... 7 H3
Oldgate La *RHAM/THRY* S65 .... 95 F5
Old Hall Cl *BTLY* DN5 .... 42 A4
Old Hall Pl *BTLY* DN5 .... 29 F1
Old Hall Rd *BTLY* DN5 .... 29 F1
   CHSW S40 .... 189 E2
Oldhay Cl *TOT/DORE* S17 .... 156 B2
Old Hay Gdns *TOT/DORE* S17 .... 156 A2
Old Hay La *TOT/DORE* S17 .... 156 A2
Old Hexthorpe *DONS/BSCR* DN4 .... 43 E3 🔲
Old House Cl *WMB/DAR* S73 .... 55 D1 🔲
Old House Rd *CHSW* S40 .... 183 E3 🔲
Old La *MOS* S20 .... 165 E1
Old Mill Dr *RCH* S42 .... 182 B2
Old Mill La *BSLY* S70 .... 2 C5
   BSLYN/ROY S71 .... 3 F2
Old Mill Rd *CONI* DN12 .... 85 E2
Old Park Av *SHEFS* S8 .... 158 B1
Old Park Rd *SHEFS* S8 .... 158 B1
Old Quarry Av *AU/AST/KP* S26 .... 155 F2
The Old Railway Yd *SHEFS* S8 .... 146 B2
Old Retford Rd *HAN/WDH* S13 .... 140 A1
Oldridge Cl *CHSW* S40 .... 182 B3
Old Rd *BSLYN/ROY* S71 .... 14 B2
   CHSW S40 .... 188 B1
   CONI DN12 .... 85 E1
Old School La *HOY* S74 .... 51 F1 🔲
Old School La *RHAM* S60 .... 127 E1
Old Sheffield Rd *RHAM* S60 .... 103 D4
Old St *SHEFP/MNR* S2 .... 123 D3
Old Warren V *RAW* S62 .... 80 B4
Oldwell Cl *TOT/DORE* S17 .... 156 B4
Old Whittington La *DRON* S18 .... 170 C5
Old Wortley Rd *KIMB* S61 .... 101 F1
Olive Cl *AU/AST/KP* S26 .... 142 B3
Olive Crs *HACK/IN* S12 .... 149 E3
Olive Grove Rd *SHEFP/MNR* S2 .... 135 F2
Olive Rd *MOS* S20 .... 164 B1
   STKB/PEN S36 .... 68 C2 🔲
Oliver Rd *ABRD* S7 .... 146 A1
   DONS/BSCR DN4 .... 43 E5
Olivers Dr *DARN/MH* S9 .... 125 E3
Olivers Mt *DARN/MH* S9 .... 125 E3
Oliver St *MEX/SWTN* S64 .... 58 A3
Olivers Wy *RHAM* S60 .... 113 F5
Olivet Rd *SHEFS* S8 .... 147 D3
Onchan Rd *ST/HB/BR* S6 .... 119 F2 🔲
Onslow Rd *ECC* S11 .... 133 F3
Orange St *SHEF* S1 .... 8 C5
Orchard Cl *ARMTH* DN3 .... 19 F2 🔲
   BSLYN/ROY S71 .... 15 D2
   CHPT/GREN S35 .... 98 C2
   RHAM S60 .... 127 E1
Orchard Crs *SHEFN* S5 .... 98 C2
Orchard Cft *AU/AST/KP* S26 .... 155 F2
   DOD/DAR S75 .... 20 B4
Orchard Flatts Crs *KIMB* S61 .... 92 B4
Orchard La *AU/AST/KP* S26 .... 155 F2
   MOS S20 .... 153 D3
   SHEF S1 .... 8 D5
Orchard Lea Dr *AU/AST/KP* S26 .... 142 B3 🔲
Orchard Pl *DEARNE* S63 .... 55 E2
   ECK/KIL S21 .... 166 B2
   RHAM S60 .... 6 A5
Orchard Rd *ST/HB/BR* S6 .... 121 D1
Orchard Sq *DRON* S18 .... 168 B1
Orchard St *DONS/BSCR* DN4 .... 43 F3
   SHEF S1 .... 9 E5
   STKB/PEN S36 .... 70 A3 🔲
   WMB/DAR S73 .... 39 E2
Orchards Wy *CHSW* S40 .... 189 D3
Orchard View Rd *CHSW* S40 .... 183 D5
Orchard Wy *DEARNE* S63 .... 27 D3
   RHAM S60 .... 114 A5
Orgreave Dr *HAN/WDH* S13 .... 140 A1
Orgreave La *HAN/WDH* S13 .... 139 E1
Orgreave Pl *HAN/WDH* S13 .... 126 C5
Orgreave Rd *RHAM* S60 .... 127 D2
Orgreave Wy *HAN/WDH* S13 .... 140 A2
Oriel Rd *FUL* S10 .... 132 A3
Oriel Wy *BSLYN/ROY* S71 .... 15 E4
Ormesby Cl *DRON* S18 .... 168 A2 🔲
Ormesby Crs *BTLY* DN5 .... 28 C4
Ormes Meadow *MOS* S20 .... 152 A3
Ormond Cl *CHSW* S40 .... 188 C5 🔲
   SHEFS S8 .... 159 E1
Ormond Dr *SHEFS* S8 .... 159 F2
Ormond Rd *SHEFS* S8 .... 159 F2
Ormond Wy *SHEFS* S8 .... 159 F1
Ormsby Cl *DONS/BSCR* DN4 .... 63 E3
Ormsby Rd *CHNE* S41 .... 184 A2
Orpen Dr *SHEFS* S8 .... 148 C3
Orpen Wy *SHEFS* S8 .... 148 C3 🔲
Orwell Cl *WMB/DAR* S73 .... 40 A4
Osberton Pl *ECC* S11 .... 134 A2
Osberton St *RAW* S62 .... 80 C5
   RHAM/THRY S65 .... 95 D5
Osbert Rd *RHAM* S60 .... 115 F1
Osborne Av *AU/AST/KP* S26 .... 142 C2
Osborne Cl *ECC* S11 .... 134 A3 🔲
Osborne Ms *BSLY* S70 .... 22 B2 🔲
Osborne Rd *ECC* S11 .... 134 A3

WHHL DN2 .... 31 D5
Osborne St *BSLY* S70 .... 22 B2
Osgathorpe Cft *ATT* S4 .... 110 A4 ⊞
Osgathorpe Dr *ATT* S4 .... 110 A4
Osgathorpe Rd *ATT* S4 .... 110 A4
Osmaston Rd *SHEFS* S8 .... 147 D3 ⊞
Osmond Dr *BSLY* S70 .... 22 B5
Osmond Pl *BSLY* S70 .... 22 B5 ⑩
Osmond Wy *BSLY* S70 .... 22 B5 ⑪
Osmund Rd *ECK/KIL* S21 .... 163 F5
Osprey Av *BSLY* S70 .... 36 A5
Osprey Gdns *SHEFP/MNR* S2 .... 123 F5 ⑥
Osprey Rd *AU/AST/KP* S26 .... 142 C4 ⊞
Oswestry Rd *SHEFN* S5 .... 99 D5
Oswin Av *DONS/BSCR* DN4 .... 43 D4
Otley Cl *CONI* DN12 .... 85 E1
Otter St *DARN/MH* S9 .... 124 A1
Oughton Wy *ATT* S4 .... 110 B5
Oulton Ri *MEX/SWTN* S64 .... 59 E2
Ouseburn Cft *DARN/MH* S9 .... 124 B2
Ouseburn Rd *DARN/MH* S9 .... 124 B2
Ouseburn St *DARN/MH* S9 .... 124 B2 ⊞
Ouse Rd *DARN/MH* S9 .... 124 B2
Ouslethwaite Ct *BSLY* S70 .... 21 F4
Outram Rd *CHNE* S41 .... 184 A3
  SHEFP/MNR S2 .... 123 F5
Oval Rd *RHAM/THRY* S65 .... 104 C2
The Oval *CONI* DN12 .... 61 D5
  DONS/BSCR DN4 .... 46 A3
  SHEFN S5 .... 110 A1
Overcroft Ri *TOT/DORE* S17 .... 156 A4
Overdale Av *BSLY* S70 .... 22 C4
Overdale Gdns *TOT/DORE* S17 ...... 156 A4 ⊞
Overdale Ri *TOT/DORE* S17 .... 156 A2 ⊞
Overdale Rd *WMB/DAR* S73 .... 39 F4
Overend Cl *GLV* S14 .... 148 B1
Overend Dr *GLV* S14 .... 148 B1
Overend Rd *GLV* S14 .... 148 B1
Overend Wy *GLV* S14 .... 148 B1
Oversley Rd *WHHL* DN2 .... 31 D3
Oversley St *DARN/MH* S9 .... 112 C1
Overton Rd *ST/HB/BR* S6 .... 107 F2
Owen Cl *RHAM/THRY* S65 .... 7 F2
  ST/HB/BR S6 .... 97 E3
Owen Pl *ST/HB/BR* S6 .... 97 E3
Owler La *ATT* S4 .... 110 B3
Owler La *DRON* S18 .... 160 C4
  SHEFS S4 .... 160 C3
Owler La *ATT* S4 .... 110 B3
Owlings Pl *ST/HB/BR* S6 .... 107 E4
Owlings Rd *ST/HB/BR* S6 .... 107 E4
Owlthorpe Av *MOS* S20 .... 151 F5
Owlthorpe Cl *MOS* S20 .... 151 F5 ⊞
Owlthorpe Dr *MOS* S20 .... 151 F5
Owlthorpe Greenway *MOS* S20 ..... 152 C4
Owlthorpe Gv *MOS* S20 .... 151 F5
Owlthorpe La *MOS* S20 .... 151 F5
Owlthorpe Ri *MOS* S20 .... 151 F5
Ox Carr *ARMTH* DN3 .... 33 E3
Ox Close Av *KIMB* S61 .... 91 F5
  TOT/DORE S17 .... 157 E3
Oxclose Dr *DRON* S18 .... 168 A2 ⑩
Oxclose La *DRON* S18 .... 168 A2
Oxclose Park Rd *MOS* S20 .... 165 D1
Oxclose Park Rd North *MOS* S20 ... 165 D2
Oxford Cl *KIMB* S61 .... 93 D5 ⑤
  STV/CWN S43 .... 186 A1
Oxford Pl *BSLYN/ROY* S71 .... 23 F2 ⑥
Oxford Rd *STV/CWN* S43 .... 186 A1
Oxford St *BSLY* S70 .... 22 B3
  BSLYN/ROY S71 .... 23 F2
  MEX/SWTN S64 .... 57 F3
  RHAM/THRY S65 .... 104 B2
  ST/HB/BR S6 .... 121 E3
Ox Hi *MOS* S20 .... 165 E3
Oxley Cl *STKB/PEN* S36 .... 68 B2
Oxley Gv *RHAM* S60 .... 104 A5
Oxspring Bank *SHEFN* S5 .... 108 C3
Oxted Rd *DARN/MH* S9 .... 111 E2
Oxton Dr *DONS/BSCR* DN4 .... 62 B1

P

Packer's Rw *CHSW* S40 .... 11 F6
Pack Horse La *CHPT/GREN* S35 .... 73 F3
Packington Rd *DONS/BSCR* DN4 .... 47 E5
Packman Rd *DEARNE* S63 .... 54 C1
Packman Wy *DEARNE* S63 .... 54 C2
Paddock Cl *BTLY* DN5 .... 28 C4
Paddock Cft *MEX/SWTN* S64 .... 56 C5
The Paddocks *AU/AST/KP* S26 .... 142 C5
  BTLY DN5 .... 28 B4
  BTLY DN5 .... 61 E2 ⑥
The Paddock *KIMB* S61 .... 90 C2
  WMB/DAR S73 .... 39 D5
Paddock Wy *DRON* S18 .... 169 F1
Padley Wy *SHEFN* S5 .... 99 D5
Page Hall Rd *SHEFN* S5 .... 110 B3
Pagenall Dr *AU/AST/KP* S26 .... 142 B2
Paget St *DARN/MH* S9 .... 111 D4
Pagnall Av *DEARNE* S63 .... 26 B4
Paisley Cl *STV/CWN* S43 .... 187 D1 ⑥

Palgrave Crs *SHEFN* S5 .... 97 F5
Palgrave Rd *SHEFN* S5 .... 97 E5
Pall Ml *BSLY* S70 .... 2 C6
Palmer Crs *DRON* S18 .... 169 F2
Palmer Rd *DARN/MH* S9 .... 125 D1
Palmersgate *CHSW* S40 .... 11 F6
Palmerston Rd *FUL* S10 .... 121 E4 ⑥
Palmer St *DARN/MH* S9 .... 124 A2 ⊞
  DONS/BSCR DN4 .... 44 C3
Palm Gv *CONI* DN12 .... 84 B3
Palm La *ST/HB/BR* S6 .... 121 D1 ⊞
Palm St *DOD/DAR* S75 .... 13 D4
  ST/HB/BR S6 .... 121 D1
Pamela Dr *DONS/BSCR* DN4 .... 62 A1
Pangbourne Rd *DEARNE* S63 .... 26 C2
Pantry Gn *BSLY* S70 .... 37 D1 ⊞
Pantry Hl *BSLY* S70 .... 23 D5
Pantry Well *BSLY* S70 .... 37 D1 ⊞
Paper Mill Rd *SHEFN* S5 .... 99 E2
The Parade *RAW* S62 .... 79 F4 ⊞
Paradise La *SHEF* S1 .... 9 E4
Paradise Sq *SHEF* S1 .... 9 E4 ⊞
Parish Wy *BSLYN/ROY* S71 .... 15 E4
Park Av *ARMTH* DN3 .... 33 D2
  BSLY S70 .... 2 B6
  BTLY DN5 .... 42 A3
  CHPT/GREN S35 .... 88 A3
  CONI DN12 .... 85 D2
  DRON S18 .... 169 F1
  ECK/KIL S21 .... 133 F2
  MEX/SWTN S64 .... 58 B3
  RHAM S60 .... 116 A2
Park Ct *BTLY* DN5 .... 42 A3
  CHSW S40 .... 190 B5
  MEX/SWTN S64 .... 57 D5
Park Crs *CHPT/GREN* S35 .... 98 C1
  DONS/BSCR DN4 .... 62 A2
  FUL S10 .... 121 E5
Park Dr *RHAM/THRY* S65 .... 7 G6
Parkfield Ct *RAW* S62 .... 94 A3 ⊞
Parkfield Rd *RHAM/THRY* S65 .... 7 G6
Parkgate Av *CONI* DN12 .... 84 B3
Parkgate Cl *MOS* S20 .... 151 E5 ⊞
Parkgate Cft *MOS* S20 .... 151 E5 ⊞
Parkgate Dr *HACK/IN* S12 .... 151 E4
Parkgate La *ECK/KIL* S21 .... 179 F1
Park Grange Cl *SHEFP/MNR* S2 ...... 136 A2
Park Grange Ct *SHEFP/MNR* S2 ...... 136 A2
Park Grange Dr *SHEFP/MNR* S2 ...... 136 A2
Park Grange Mt *SHEFP/MNR* S2 ..... 136 A2
Park Grange Rd *SHEFP/MNR* S2 ...... 135 F1
Park Grange Vw *SHEFP/MNR* S2 ..... 136 A2
Park Gv *BSLY* S70 .... 21 F2
  RAW S62 .... 80 A4
  STKB/PEN S36 .... 68 C1 ⊞
Park Hall Av *CHSW* S40 .... 188 B4
Park Hall Cl *CHSW* S40 .... 188 C5
Park Hall Gdns *CHSW* S40 .... 188 C4
Parkhead Ct *ECC* S11 .... 145 D1
Parkhead Crs *ECC* S11 .... 145 D1
Parkhead Rd *ECC* S11 .... 145 D2
Park Hill *WMB/DAR* S73 .... 39 F2
Park Hollow *WMB/DAR* S73 .... 40 A3
Park House La *DARN/MH* S9 .... 113 D3
Park La *CHNE* S41 .... 184 A2
  CHPT/GREN S35 .... 69 E1
  DONS/BSCR DN4 .... 46 A2
  FUL S10 .... 121 E5
Park Mt *RHAM/THRY* S65 .... 7 F6
Park Nook *RHAM/THRY* S65 .... 95 F4
Park Rd *RHAM/THRY* S65 .... 104 C2
  BSLY S70 .... 21 F5
  BSLY S70 .... 36 B1
  BTLY DN5 .... 16 Ed ⊞
  BTLY DN5 .... 16 B5
  CHSW S40 .... 11 E6
  CONI DN12 .... 84 C2
  DEARNE S63 .... 27 F3
  DEARNE S63 .... 55 F3
  DON DN1 .... 4 E2
  MEX/SWTN S64 .... 58 B3
  MEX/SWTN S64 .... 80 C1
  RHAM/THRY S65 .... 104 B2
  ST/HB/BR S6 .... 120 A1
Parkside La *ST/HB/BR* S6 .... 119 E2
Parkside Ms *BSLY* S70 .... 22 E5 ⊞
Parkside Rd *HOY* S74 .... 50 C4
  ST/HB/BR S6 .... 108 A3
Parkson Rd *RHAM* S60 .... 115 F2
Park Spring Dr *SHEFP/MNR* S2 ...... 136 A2
Park Spring Gv *SHEFP/MNR* S2 ..... 136 A2

Park Spring Pl *SHEFP/MNR* S2 .... 136 A2
Park Spring Wy *SHEFP/MNR* S2 ..... 136 A2
Park Square Rbt *ATT* S4 .... 9 G5
Parkstone Delph *HACK/IN* S12 .... 149 E3
Parkstone Wy *WHHL* DN2 .... 32 A2 ⊞
Park St *AU/AST/KP* S26 .... 142 A3
  BSLY S70 .... 21 F2
  CHSW S40 .... 190 B5
  KIMB S61 .... 102 C2
  RAW S62 .... 80 A5
  WMB/DAR S73 .... 39 F3
Park Ter *CHPT/GREN* S35 .... 88 C2
  DON DN1 .... 5 E3
Parkview *BSLY* S70 .... 22 C5
Park Vw *CHNE* S41 .... 191 E5
  DOD/DAR S75 .... 20 A3
Park View Av *MOS* S20 .... 164 C1
Park View Rd *CHPT/GREN* S35 .... 88 B2
  KIMB S61 .... 101 D4
  ST/HB/BR S6 .... 109 D3
Parkway *ARMTH* DN3 .... 33 F4 ⊞
Parkway Av *DARN/MH* S9 .... 124 A3
Parkway Cl *DARN/MH* S9 .... 124 A3
Parkway Dr *DARN/MH* S9 .... 124 B3
Parkway North *WHHL* DN2 .... 31 D3
Parkway South *WHHL* DN2 .... 31 E3
Parkwood Rd *OWL* S3 .... 108 C5
Parkwood Rd North *SHEFN* S5 .... 109 D3
  ST/HB/BR S6 .... 109 D3
Parliament St *ECC* S11 .... 134 C1 ⊞
Parma Ri *WMB/DAR* S73 .... 25 F5
Parsley Hay Cl *HAN/WDH* S13 .... 139 D1
Parsley Hay Dr *HAN/WDH* S13 ...... 139 D1 ⊞
Parsley Hay Gdns *HAN/WDH* S13 .. 139 D1
Parsley Hay Rd *HAN/WDH* S13 ...... 139 D1
Parsonage Cl *MOS* S20 .... 164 B2 ⊞
Parsonage Crs *ST/HB/BR* S6 .... 121 D1
Parsonage St *ST/HB/BR* S6 .... 121 D1
Parson Cross Rd *ST/HB/BR* S6 .... 97 D5
Partridge Cl *ECK/KIL* S21 .... 163 F5
Partridge Flatt Rd
  DONS/BSCR DN4 .... 67 D1
Partridge Pl *AU/AST/KP* S26 .... 142 C4
Partridge Ri *DONS/BSCR* DN4 .... 67 D1
Partridge Vw *SHEFP/MNR* S2 .... 123 F5 ⊞
Parwich Cl *CHSW* S40 .... 182 B4 ⊞
Passhouses Rd *ATT* S4 .... 109 F4 ⊞
Pasture Cl *ARMTH* DN3 .... 33 E4
Pasture Gv *ECK/KIL* S21 .... 164 C5
Pasture La *BTLY* DN5 .... 60 C2
  DEARNE S63 .... 41 E1
Pastures Rd *MEX/SWTN* S64 .... 59 F3
Paternoster Rw *SHEF* S1 .... 122 C5
Paterson Cl *STKB/PEN* S36 .... 68 B1
Paterson Cres *STKB/PEN* S36 .... 68 B1 ⊞
Paterson Cft *STKB/PEN* S36 .... 68 B1 ⊞
Paterson Gdns *STKB/PEN* S36 .... 68 B1
Patmore Rd *SHEFN* S5 .... 99 E5
Paton Gv *STV/CWN* S43 .... 185 E1
Patrick Stirling Ct
  DONS/BSCR DN4 .... 43 E3 ⊞
Patterdale Cl *DRON* S18 .... 168 C2 ⊞
Pavilion La *RHAM* S60 .... 113 F2
Pavillion Cl *CONI* DN12 .... 62 A4
Paxton Crs *ARMTH* DN3 .... 33 D2
Paxton La *FUL* S10 .... 121 E5 ⊞
Paxton Rd *CHNE* S41 .... 185 D4
Payler Cl *SHEFP/MNR* S2 .... 137 E2
Payne Crs *RAW* S62 .... 79 F4
Peacock Cl *ECK/KIL* S21 .... 166 A2
  KIMB S61 .... 76 A5
Pea Fields La *CHPT/GREN* S35 .... 72 A1
Peakdale Crs *HACK/IN* S12 .... 138 C5
Peake Av *CONI* DN12 .... 84 B1
Peak Pl *STV/CWN* S43 .... 187 E2
Peaks Mt *MOS* S20 .... 152 C2
Peak View Rd *CHSW* S40 .... 183 E5
Pearce Rd *DARN/MH* S9 .... 125 D4
Pearce Wk *DARN/MH* S9 .... 125 D4
Pearl St *ECC* S11 .... 134 C2
Pea Royd La *STKB/PEN* S36 .... 69 D1
Pearson Crs *WMB/DAR* S73 .... 38 C1
Pearson's Cl *RHAM/THRY* S65 .... 105 D5
Pearson's Fld *WMB/DAR* S73 .... 39 E2
Pearson St *STKB/PEN* S36 .... 68 C1 ⊞
Pear St *ECC* S11 .... 134 C1
Peartree Av *DEARNE* S63 .... 26 C3
Pear Tree Cl *ECK/KIL* S21 .... 166 A3
  RHAM S60 .... 114 B4
  STV/CWN S43 .... 186 B1
Pear Tree Rd *SHEFN* S5 .... 99 E5
Pearwood Crs *DONS/BSCR* DN4 .... 63 D2
Peasehill Cl *BSLY* S70 .... 21 F2
Peashill St *RAW* S62 .... 94 A1
Peatfield Rd *ECK/KIL* S21 .... 167 D1
Peckham Rd *CHPT/GREN* S35 .... 74 A5 ⊞
Pedley Av *MOS* S20 .... 152 C4
Pedley Cl *MOS* S20 .... 152 C4 ⊞
Pedley Dr *MOS* S20 .... 152 C5 ⊞
Pedley Gv *MOS* S20 .... 152 C4
Peel De *BSLY* S70 .... 2 B5
Peel Pl *BSLYN/ROY* S71 .... 3 F1
Peel Sq *BSLY* S70 .... 2 C5

Peel St *BSLY* S70 .... 2 B5
FUL S10 .... 121 D5 🖸
Peil's Cl *DON* DN1 .... 4 D4 🖸
Pembrey Ct *MOS* S20 .... 153 E3
Pembroke Av *DONS/BSCR* DN4 .... 63 E1
Pembroke Cl *CHSW* S40 .... 189 D3 🖸
Pembroke Crs *CHPT/GREN* S35 ...... 73 E5
Pembroke Ri *BTLY* DN5 .... 28 B3
Pembroke Rd *DRON* S18 .... 169 E1
Pembroke St *ECC* S11 .... 134 C1 🖸
KIMB S61 .... 102 A3
Pendeen Rd *ECC* S11 .... 133 D2 🖸
Pendlebury Gv *HOY* S74 .... 51 D3 🖸
Pendle Cft *MOS* S20 .... 153 F4 🖸
Penistone Rd *CHPT/GREN* S35 ...... 87 E3
OWL S3 .... 8 B1
Penistone St *DON* DN1 .... 5 F2
Penley St *ECC* S11 .... 135 D2 🖸
Penmore Cl *CHNE* S41 .... 191 D3
Penmore Gdns *CHNE* S41 .... 191 D4
Penmore La *CHNE* S41 .... 191 D4
Penmore St *CHNE* S41 .... 191 D4
Pennine Vw *STKB/PEN* S36 .... 68 C4
Pennine Wy *CHSW* S40 .... 183 D4
DOD/DAR S75 .... 12 C5
Pen Nook Cl *STKB/PEN* S36 .... 69 E4
Pen Nook Ct *STKB/PEN* S36 .... 69 F4 🖸
Pen Nook Dr *STKB/PEN* S36 .... 69 F4
Pen Nook Gdns *STKB/PEN* S36 .... 69 F4
Penns Rd *SHEFP/MNR* S2 .... 136 A4
Penny Engine La *ECK/KIL* S21 .... 164 C4
Penny La *TOT/DORE* S17 .... 156 A3
Penrhyn Rd *ECC* S11 .... 134 A3
Penrhyn Wk *BSLYN/ROY* S71 .... 24 B2
Penrith Cl *SHEFN* S5 .... 108 C2
Penrith Crs *SHEFN* S5 .... 108 C2
Penrith Gv *BSLYN/ROY* S71 .... 24 A2
Penrith Rd *SHEFN* S5 .... 108 C2
Penrose Pl *HAN/WDH* S13 .... 139 E4
Penthorpe Cl *HACK/IN* S12 .... 137 F4 🖸
Pentland Cl *CHSW* S40 .... 183 D4 🖸
Pentland Gdns *MOS* S20 .... 152 B3
Pentland Rd *DRON* S18 .... 168 B2
Penton St *SHEF* S1 .... 8 D5 🖸
Penyghent Cl *CHPT/GREN* S35 .... 74 A5 🔟
Pepper Cl *KIMB* S61 .... 91 E3
Pepper St *HOY* S74 .... 37 F5
Percy St *OWL* S3 .... 8 C1
RHAM/THRY S65 .... 7 E5
Peregrine Dr *BSLY* S70 .... 36 A5
Perigree Rd *SHEF* S8 .... 146 C2
Periwood Av *SHEFS* S8 .... 146 B2
Periwood Cl *SHEFS* S8 .... 146 C2 🖸
Periwood Dr *SHEFS* S8 .... 146 C2 🖸
Periwood Gv *SHEFS* S8 .... 146 C2 🖸
Perkyn Rd *SHEFN* S5 .... 99 D2
Perkyn Ter *SHEFN* S5 .... 99 D2
Perran Gv *BTLY* DN5 .... 29 D4
Perseverance St *BSLY* S70 .... 21 E1 🖸
Perth Cl *MEX/SWTN* S64 .... 59 D2
Peterborough Cl *FUL* S10 .... 131 E2
Peterborough Dr *FUL* S10 .... 131 E1
Peterborough Rd *FUL* S10 .... 131 E1
Peterdale Cl *STV/CWN* S43 .... 185 F1
Peterdale Rd *STV/CWN* S43 .... 185 F1
Petersgate *BTLY* DN5 .... 29 D1
Peter St *KIMB* S61 .... 101 F2
Petre Dr *ATT* S4 .... 110 C4
Petre St *ATT* S4 .... 110 B5
Pettyclose La *CHNE* S41 .... 185 E4
Petworth Dr *ECC* S11 .... 145 D3
Pevensey Av *CHNE* S41 .... 183 F5
Peveril Rd *CHNE* S41 .... 184 A2 🔟
ECC S11 .... 133 F3
ECK/KIL S21 .... 164 C4
Pexton Rd *ATT* S4 .... 110 A4
Philadelphia Dr *ST/HB/BR* S6 .... 8 A1
Philadelphia Gdns *ST/HB/BR* S6 .... 8 A1
Philadelphia Gv *ST/HB/BR* S6 .... 8 A1
Philip Rd *BSLY* S70 .... 23 E3
Phillimore Rd *DARN/MH* S9 .... 124 C1
Phillips Rd *ST/HB/BR* S6 .... 106 B3
Phoenix Ct *HACK/IN* S12 .... 150 C4
Phoenix Gv *RHAM* S60 .... 113 F3
Phoenix La *DEARNE* S63 .... 27 E4
Phoenix Rd *DARN/MH* S9 .... 112 C1
HACK/IN S12 .... 150 C4
Piccadilly *BTLY* DN5 .... 29 E1
Piccadilly Rd *CHNE* S41 .... 190 C2
MEX/SWTN S64 .... 81 D2
Pickering Crs *AU/AST/KP* S26 .... 142 A4
Pickering Rd *BTLY* DN5 .... 16 E3
OWL S3 .... 109 D5
Pickering St *DARN/MH* S9 .... 111 F4 🖸
Pickhill's Av *DEARNE* S63 .... 27 F5
Pickmere Rd *FUL* S10 .... 108 C4
Pickton Cl *CHSW* S40 .... 189 E2 🖸
Pickup Crs *WMB/DAR* S73 .... 39 E4
Pickwick Dr *RHAM* S60 .... 126 C1
Piece End *CHPT/GREN* S35 .... 73 E3
Piece End Cl *CHPT/GREN* S35 .... 73 E3 🖸
The Pieces North *RHAM* S60 .... 115 F4
The Pieces South *RHAM* S60 .... 115 F4
Pighills La *DRON* S18 .... 159 F4
Pike Cl *CHSW* S40 .... 182 C4 🖸

Pike Rd *RHAM* S60 .... 114 A3
Pilgrim St *FUL* S10 .... 109 F5
Pilley Gn *DOD/DAR* S75 .... 49 E3
Pilley Hl *DOD/DAR* S75 .... 20 A4 🖸
Pilley La *DOD/DAR* S75 .... 49 E2
Pinchfield Ct *MALT* S66 .... 117 F1
Pinchfield Holt *MALT* S66 .... 117 F1
Pinchfield La *MALT* S66 .... 117 F1
Pinchmill Hollow *MALT* S66 .... 117 F2
Pinch Mill La *RHAM* S60 .... 116 C3
Pindale Av *STV/CWN* S43 .... 187 D2
Pindar Oaks Cottages *BSLY* S70 .. 22 C2 🖸
Pindar Oaks St *BSLY* S70 .... 22 B2
Pindar St *BSLY* S70 .... 22 C2 🖸
Pine Cl *BSLY* S70 .... 23 D4
ECK/KIL S21 .... 166 A3
HOY S74 .... 51 F5
Pine Crt *CHPT/GREN* S35 .... 88 B2
Pinecroft Wy *CHPT/GREN* S35 .... 88 B2
Pine Gv *CONI* DN12 .... 84 B3
Pinehall Dr *BSLYN/ROY* S71 .... 15 E3
Pinehurst Ri *MEX/SWTN* S64 .... 81 E1
Pine Rd *DONS/BSCR* DN4 .... 47 D4
The Pines *FUL* S10 .... 131 E2
Pine St *STV/CWN* S43 .... 186 B1
Pine Vw *CHSW* S40 .... 188 C1
Pine Wk *MEX/SWTN* S64 .... 81 E3
Pinewood Av *ARMTH* DN3 .... 33 F1
DONS/BSCR DN4 .... 62 C2 🖸
Pinfold Cl *BSLYN/ROY* S71 .... 23 F2 🖸
MEX/SWTN S64 .... 81 D1
Pinfold Hl *BSLY* S70 .... 22 B4
Pinfold Lands *MEX/SWTN* S64 .... 58 C4
Pinfold La *OWL* S3 .... 109 E5
RHAM/THRY S65 .... 7 F6 🖸
RHAM/THRY S65 .... 103 F4 🖸
Pinfold St *ECK/KIL* S21 .... 164 B5
Pingle Av *ABRD* S7 .... 146 A2
Pingle Gra *STV/CWN* S43 .... 185 F2
Pingle Rd *ABRD* S7 .... 146 A2
ECK/KIL S21 .... 166 C1
Pingles Crs *RHAM/THRY* S65 .... 95 F4
Pinner Rd *ECC* S11 .... 134 A3
Pipe House La *RAW* S62 .... 80 A4 🖸
Piper Cl *SHEFN* S5 .... 109 E1
Piper Ct *SHEFN* S5 .... 109 E1 🖸
Piper Crs *SHEFN* S5 .... 109 F1
Pipering La (East) *BTLY* DN5 .... 29 D2
Pipering La (West) *BTLY* DN5 .... 28 C2
Piper La *AU/AST/KP* S26 .... 143 D3
Piper Rd *SHEFN* S5 .... 109 F1
Pipeyard La *ECK/KIL* S21 .... 164 A5
Pipworth Gv *SHEFP/MNR* S2 .... 138 A1
Pipworth La *ECK/KIL* S21 .... 165 D4
Pisgah House Rd *FUL* S10 .... 121 D4 🖸
Pitchford La *FUL* S10 .... 132 B1
Pithouse La *AU/AST/KP* S26 .... 154 A2
Pit La *HAN/WDH* S13 .... 137 E4
KIMB S61 .... 90 A3
RHAM S60 .... 128 A3
Pitman Rd *CONI* DN12 .... 59 F5
Pitsmoor Rd *ATT* S4 .... 109 F5
OWL S3 .... 122 B1
Pittam Cl *ARMTH* DN3 .... 33 F3
Pitt Cl *SHEF* S1 .... 8 B6
Pitt La *SHEF* S1 .... 8 B6 🖸
Pitt St *BSLY* S70 .... 2 B6
ECK/KIL S21 .... 174 A1
KIMB S61 .... 102 A3
MEX/SWTN S64 .... 59 D3
SHEF S1 .... 8 B6
WMB/DAR S73 .... 25 F5
Pitt St West *BSLY* S70 .... 2 A6 🖸
Plank Ga *STKB/PEN* S36 .... 70 B4
Plantation Av *DONS/BSCR* DN4 .... 67 F3
Plantation Rd *SHEFS* S8 .... 135 E4 🔟
Plantin Ri *MOS* S20 .... 153 F4
The Plantin *MOS* S20 .... 164 C1
Platts Dr *MOS* S20 .... 153 E1
Platt St *OWL* S3 .... 122 B1
Pleasant Cl *HACK/IN* S12 .... 137 F4 🖸
Pleasant Rd *HACK/IN* S12 .... 137 F4
Pleasley Rd *RHAM* S60 .... 115 E3
Plover Ct *SHEFP/MNR* S2 .... 123 F5 🖸
Plover Cft *KIMB* S61 .... 76 B5
Plover Dr *BSLY* S70 .... 36 A5
Plowright Dr *SHEFP/MNR* S2 .... 136 B5
Plowright Mt *SHEFP/MNR* S2 .... 136 B5
Plowright Wy *SHEFP/MNR* S2 .... 136 B5 🖸
Plumber St *BSLY* S70 .... 2 A5
Plumbley Hall Ms *MOS* S20 .... 164 A2
Plumbley Hall Rd *MOS* S20 .... 164 A1 🖸
Plumbley La *MOS* S20 .... 163 F2
Plum La *OWL* S3 .... 9 E3
Plumper's Rd *DARN/MH* S9 .... 112 B2 🖸
Plumpton Av *MEX/SWTN* S64 .... 59 D2
Plumpton Gdns *DONS/BSCR* DN4 ..... 67 E1
Plumpton Park Rd
DONS/BSCR DN4 .... 67 E2
Plum St *OWL* S3 .... 9 E3
Plunket Rd *WHHL* DN2 .... 31 D5
Plymouth Rd *ABRD* S7 .... 134 C5
Pogmoor La *DOD/DAR* S75 .... 12 B5
Pogmoor Rd *DOD/DAR* S75 .... 20 C1
Pole Hl *SHEFS* S8 .... 147 E3

Polka Ct *OWL* S3 .... 122 B1
Pollard Av *SHEFN* S5 .... 108 C1
Pollard Crs *SHEFN* S5 .... 108 C1
Pollard Rd *SHEFN* S5 .... 108 C1
Pollard St *KIMB* S61 .... 101 F3
Pollitt St *DOD/DAR* S75 .... 2 A2
Pomona St *ECC* S11 .... 134 C1
Pond Cl *ST/HB/BR* S6 .... 119 E1
Pond Hl *SHEF* S1 .... 9 G5
Pond Rd *ST/HB/BR* S6 .... 119 E1
Pond St *BSLY* S70 .... 21 F2
CHSW S40 .... 190 B2
SHEF S1 .... 9 F5
Pondwell Dr *STV/CWN* S43 .... 186 A2
Pontefract Rd *BSLYN/ROY* S71 .... 3 F6
DEARNE S63 .... 54 C1
Pool Dr *DONS/BSCR* DN4 .... 67 F1
Poole Pl *DARN/MH* S9 .... 125 D3
Poole Rd *DARN/MH* S9 .... 125 D3
Pool's La *ECK/KIL* S21 .... 172 A4
Pool Sq *SHEF* S1 .... 9 E5
Pope Av *CONI* DN12 .... 84 A1
Poplar Av *CHSW* S40 .... 188 C3
MOS S20 .... 141 D5
RHAM/THRY S65 .... 95 F4
STKB/PEN S36 .... 68 C3
Poplar Cl *DRON* S18 .... 170 A4 🖸
ECK/KIL S21 .... 166 A3
MEX/SWTN S64 .... 58 A2
Poplar Dr *DEARNE* S63 .... 56 A4
RHAM S60 .... 113 F4
Poplar Gv *BSLYN/ROY* S71 .... 15 F3
CONI DN12 .... 84 C2
DONS/BSCR DN4 .... 62 A3
MEX/SWTN S64 .... 57 E5 🖸
Poplar Pl *ARMTH* DN3 .... 33 F3
Poplar Rd *ECK/KIL* S21 .... 174 A1
WMB/DAR S73 .... 39 F4
Poplars Rd *BSLY* S70 .... 22 C3
The Poplars *CONI* DN12 .... 84 C2
Poplar Ter *BTLY* DN5 .... 29 F1 🖸
Poplar Wy *RHAM* S60 .... 126 B2
Popple St *ATT* S4 .... 110 C3
Porter Brook Vw *ECC* S11 .... 134 B2
Porter St *STV/CWN* S43 .... 181 F4
Porter Ter *DOD/DAR* S75 .... 12 C5 🖸
Portland Av *AU/AST/KP* S26 .... 142 C3
Portland Ct *ST/HB/BR* S6 .... 121 F1
Portland La *SHEF* S1 .... 8 B6
Portland Pl *DON* DN1 .... 4 D5
Portland Rd *MOS* S20 .... 153 E5
Portland St *BSLY* S70 .... 22 C2
MEX/SWTN S64 .... 57 E5
ST/HB/BR S6 .... 8 A1
ST/HB/BR S6 .... 121 F2 🔟
Portobello *SHEF* S1 .... 8 B5
Portobello St *SHEF* S1 .... 8 C5
Portsea Rd *ST/HB/BR* S6 .... 107 F4
Pot House La *STKB/PEN* S36 .... 68 C3
Potterdyke Av *RAW* S62 .... 80 A3
Potter Hl *KIMB* S61 .... 93 D3
Potter Hill La *CHPT/GREN* S35 .... 73 D4
Potteric Carr Rd *DONS/BSCR* DN4 .... 44 C3
Potters Cl *CHNE* S41 .... 178 C4
Potters Ga *CHPT/GREN* S35 .... 73 D4
Pottery Cl *RAW* S62 .... 94 A1
Pottery La East *CHNE* S41 .... 184 C1
Pottery La West *CHNE* S41 .... 184 B2
Poucher St *KIMB* S61 .... 101 D3
Poulton St *BSLYN/ROY* S71 .... 15 E1
Powder Mill La *BSLY* S70 .... 37 D2
Powell Dr *ECK/KIL* S21 .... 166 A2
Powell St *BSLY* S70 .... 36 C1
OWL S3 .... 121 F3
Power Station Rd *BTLY* DN5 .... 4 A1
Powley Rd *ST/HB/BR* S6 .... 97 D4
Poynton Av *AU/AST/KP* S26 .... 129 F4
Poynton Wy *AU/AST/KP* S26 .... 129 F4
Poynton Wood Crs
TOT/DORE S17 .... 157 E2 🖸
Poynton Wood Gld
TOT/DORE S17 .... 157 E2
Prescott Rd *ST/HB/BR* S6 .... 107 E2
President Wy *ATT* S4 .... 123 D2
Preston Av *HOY* S74 .... 52 B1
Preston St *SHEFP/MNR* S2 .... 135 E3 🖸
Preston Wy *BSLYN/ROY* S71 .... 15 E1
Prestwich St *DARN/MH* S9 .... 100 C3 🖸
Priestfield Gdns *CHSW* S40 .... 182 C2 🖸
Priestley Av *RAW* S62 .... 80 C4
Priestley Cl *DONS/BSCR* DN4 .... 63 D2
Priestley St *SHEFP/MNR* S2 .... 135 F1 🖸
Primrose Av *RHAM* S60 .... 114 B5 🖸
SHEFN S5 .... 99 F5
Primrose Cl *ECK/KIL* S21 .... 166 C1
Primrose Crs *MOS* S20 .... 153 D2 🖸
Primrose Dr *CHPT/GREN* S35 .... 98 C1
Primrose Hl *KIMB* S61 .... 6 B2
ST/HB/BR S6 .... 121 F1 🖸
Primrose La *ECK/KIL* S21 .... 154 C5
Primrose Wy *HOY* S74 .... 51 F4 🖸
Prince Arthur St *DOD/DAR* S75 .... 2 A3
Prince of Wales Rd *DARN/MH* S9 .... 125 D4
SHEFP/MNR S2 .... 137 F1 🖸
Prince's Rd *DONS/BSCR* DN4 .... 46 A3 🖸

Sellers St *SHEFS* S8 .... 135 D3 🔢
Selly Oak Cv *SHEFS* S8 .... 160 A2
Selly Oak Rd *SHEFS* S8 .... 160 A2 🔢
Selmer Ct *STV/CWN* S43 .... 185 E1 🔢
Selwyn St *RHAM/THRY* S65 .... 7 F2
Senior Rd *DARN/MH* S9 .... 125 D3
　DONS/BSCR DN4 .... 43 E2
Sennen Cft *BSLYN/ROY* S71 .... 14 C4 🔢
Setcup La *ECK/KIL* S21 .... 174 A1
Seth Ter *BSLY* S70 .... 22 B2 🔢
Sevenairs Rd *MOS* S20 .... 152 C2
Sevenfields Ct *ST/HB/BR* S6 .... 107 E3
Sevenfields La *ST/HB/BR* S6 .... 107 E3
Severn Ct *FUL* S10 .... 121 E4 🔢
Severn Rd *FUL* S10 .... 121 E4 🔢
Severnside Dr *HAN/WDH* S13 .... 139 E3
Severnside Gdns *HAN/WDH* S13 .... 139 E3
Severnside Pl *HAN/WDH* S13 .... 139 E3
Sewell Rd *MOS* S20 .... 165 D2
Seymore Rd *AU/AST/KP* S26 .... 142 B4
Shackleton St *WHHL* DN2 .... 19 E5
Shady Side *DONS/BSCR* DN4 .... 43 E3
Shaftesbury Av *CHSW* S40 .... 189 E1
　WHHL DN2 .... 45 F1
Shaftesbury Dr *HOY* S74 .... 51 E3
Shaftesbury St *BSLY* S70 .... 23 E2
Shaftholme Rd *BTLY* DN5 .... 17 E1
Shafton Rd *RHAM* S60 .... 115 F3
Shaftsbury Sq *RHAM/THRY* S65 .... 7 E3
Shakespeare Av *BTLY* DN5 .... 29 D5
Shakespeare Crs *DRON* S18 .... 170 A3
Shakespeare Rd *BTLY* DN5 .... 16 C5 🔢
　DEARNE S63 .... 55 E1
　RHAM/THRY S65 .... 7 H1
Shaldon Av *AU/AST/KP* S26 .... 142 B3
Shalesmoor *OWL* S3 .... 8 C2
Shambles St *BSLY* S70 .... 2 C5 🔢
Shap Cl *CHSW* S40 .... 183 D4
Shardlow Gdns *DONS/BSCR* DN4 .... 67 D1
Sharman Ct *DRON* S18 .... 171 E2
Sharpe Av *SHEFS* S8 .... 146 C5
Sharpfield Av *RAW* S62 .... 79 F3
Sharrard Cl *HACK/IN* S12 .... 137 F5
Sharrard Dr *HACK/IN* S12 .... 137 F5
Sharrard Gv *HACK/IN* S12 .... 137 F4
Sharrard Rd *HACK/IN* S12 .... 137 F5
Sharrow St *ECC* S11 .... 134 C2
Sharrow St *ECC* S11 .... 135 D2
Sharrow Vale Rd *ECC* S11 .... 134 A2
Sharrow Vw *ABRD* S7 .... 134 C2
Shawfield Rd *BSLYN/ROY* S71 .... 15 D1
Shaw La *BSLY* S70 .... 21 D1
　WHHL DN2 .... 32 B1
Shaw Rd *RHAM/THRY* S65 .... 104 B1
Shawsfield Rd *RHAM* S60 .... 115 D4
Shaw's Rw *CHSW* S40 .... 189 E2 🔢
Shaw St *BSLY* S70 .... 21 E2
　CHNE S41 .... 184 B1
Shaw Wood Wy *WHHL* DN2 .... 32 B2
Shay House La *STKB/PEN* S36 .... 68 C2
Shay Rd *STKB/PEN* S36 .... 68 C2
The Shay *DONS/BSCR* DN4 .... 46 C5
Sheaf Bank *SHEFP/MNR* S2 .... 135 E3 🔢
Sheaf Cl *CONI* DN12 .... 85 E2
Sheaf Ct *BSLY* S70 .... 23 E3
Sheaf Gdns *SHEFP/MNR* S2 .... 135 F1 🔢
Sheaf St *SHEF* S1 .... 9 G6
Sheards Cl *DRON* S18 .... 169 D2
Sheards Dr *DRON* S18 .... 168 C2 🔢
Sheards Wy *DRON* S18 .... 168 C2
Shearman Av *KIMB* S61 .... 91 F4
Shear Square Rbt *SHEF* S1 .... 122 C5
Shearwood Rd *FUL* S10 .... 121 E4 🔢
Sheep Bridge La *NROS/TKH* DN11 .... 67 F5
Sheepcote Rd *ECK/KIL* S21 .... 166 A2
Sheep Cote Rd *RHAM/THRY* S65 .... 116 B1
Sheffield Pkwy *HAN/WDH* S13 .... 125 F4
　SHEFP/MNR S2 .... 123 E3
　SHEFP/MNR S2 .... 125 E5
Sheffield Rd *BSLY* S70 .... 22 A2
　BSLY S70 .... 50 A1
　CHNE S41 .... 11 F1
　CHNE S41 .... 178 B5 🔢
　CHNE S41 .... 184 B1 🔢
　CONI DN12 .... 84 A3
　DARN/MH S9 .... 112 A3
　DONS/BSCR DN4 .... 62 A2
　DRON S18 .... 159 D5
　DRON S18 .... 177 F2
　ECK/KIL S21 .... 166 A1
　HACK/IN S12 .... 139 E4 🔢
　HAN/WDH S13 .... 141 E2
　MOS S20 .... 164 B3
　RHAM S60 .... 103 E4
Sheldon Av *CONI* DN12 .... 85 E2
Sheldon La *ST/HB/BR* S6 .... 119 D1 🔢
Sheldon Rd *ABRD* S7 .... 134 C4
　CHSW S40 .... 182 C4 🔢
　STKB/PEN S36 .... 68 C2
Sheldon Rw *ATT* S4 .... 9 G3
Sheldrake Cl *KIMB* S61 .... 90 A1
Shelley Av *DONS/BSCR* DN4 .... 63 F1

Shelley Dr *BSLYN/ROY* S71 .... 3 G1
　DRON S18 .... 170 A4
　RHAM/THRY S65 .... 104 C4
Shelley Gv *BTLY* DN5 .... 29 D5 🔢
Shelley Rd *RHAM/THRY* S65 .... 104 C3
Shelley Wy *DEARNE* S63 .... 55 D1 🔢
Shenstone Dr *RHAM/THRY* S65 .... 104 C4
Shenstone Rd *RHAM/THRY* S65 .... 104 C5
　ST/HB/BR S6 .... 107 F2
Shepcote La *DARN/MH* S9 .... 112 A5
Shepcote Wy *DARN/MH* S9 .... 112 A5
Shephard's Cl *CONI* DN12 .... 60 A5
Shepherd Dr *CHPT/GREN* S35 .... 73 F5 🔢
Shepherd La *DEARNE* S63 .... 27 D4
Shepherd St *OWL* S3 .... 8 C3
Shepley Cft *CHPT/GREN* S35 .... 73 F5 🔢
Shepley Rd *CHSW* S40 .... 189 E2
Sheppard Rd *DONS/BSCR* DN4 .... 43 E5
Shepperson Rd *ST/HB/BR* S6 .... 107 F3
Sherbourne Av *CHNE* S41 .... 183 F1
Sherburn Ga *CHPT/GREN* S35 .... 74 A5
Sherde Rd *ST/HB/BR* S6 .... 121 E1
Sheridan Av *DONS/BSCR* DN4 .... 64 A1
Sheridan Ct *BSLYN/ROY* S71 .... 3 H1
Sheridan Dr *RHAM/THRY* S65 .... 105 D5
Sheringham Cl *CHPT/GREN* S35 .... 73 E4
Sherwood Av *BTLY* DN5 .... 28 B3
　CONI DN12 .... 84 B2
Sherwood Crs *RHAM/THRY* S65 .... 7 E6
Sherwood Dr *DONS/BSCR* DN4 .... 62 C2
Sherwood Gln *SHEFS* S8 .... 145 F4
Sherwood Rd *DRON* S18 .... 168 B2
　ECK/KIL S21 .... 166 C1
Sherwood St *BSLYN/ROY* S71 .... 3 E5
　CHSW S40 .... 190 C3
Shetland Rd *DRON* S18 .... 169 F3
Shield Av *BSLY* S70 .... 22 A5
Shinwell Av *STV/CWN* S43 .... 186 C2
Ship Hl *RHAM* S60 .... 6 D6
Shipman Ct *MOS* S20 .... 164 B1 🔢
Shipton St *ST/HB/BR* S6 .... 121 F2 🔢
Shirburn Gdns *DONS/BSCR* DN4 .... 46 C3
Shirebrook Rd *SHEFS* S8 .... 135 E4
Shirecliffe Cl *OWL* S3 .... 109 E5
Shirecliffe La *OWL* S3 .... 109 E5
Shirecliffe Rd *SHEFN* S5 .... 109 E2
Shiregreen La *SHEFN* S5 .... 99 F5
Shiregreen Ter *SHEFN* S5 .... 99 E4
Shirehall La *SHEFN* S5 .... 99 E2
Shirehall Rd *SHEFN* S5 .... 99 E3
Shireoaks Rd *DRON* S18 .... 170 A1
Shirland Av *BSLYN/ROY* S71 .... 14 B1
Shirland Ct *DARN/MH* S9 .... 124 C3 🔢
Shirland La *DARN/MH* S9 .... 124 A1
Shirland Ms *DARN/MH* S9 .... 124 C2 🔢
Shirland Pl *DARN/MH* S9 .... 124 C3 🔢
Shirland St *CHNE* S41 .... 11 F3
Shirley Cl *CHSW* S40 .... 182 C4
Shirley Rd *DONS/BSCR* DN4 .... 43 E3 🔢
Shoreham Av *RHAM* S60 .... 115 D3
Shoreham Dr *RHAM* S60 .... 115 D3
Shoreham St *SHEF* S1 .... 122 C5
　SHEFP/MNR S2 .... 135 E2
Shore La *FUL* S10 .... 120 B5
Shortbrook Bank *MOS* S20 .... 152 C5 🔢
Shortbrook Cl *MOS* S20 .... 152 C5
Shortbrook Cft *MOS* S20 .... 153 D5 🔢
Shortbrook Dr *MOS* S20 .... 152 C5
Shortbrook Rd *MOS* S20 .... 152 C5
Shortbrook Wy *MOS* S20 .... 152 C5
Short La *DONS/BSCR* DN4 .... 45 F5
Shortridge St *DARN/MH* S9 .... 124 A1
Short Rd *WHHL* DN2 .... 32 A5
Short Wood Cl *BSLY* S70 .... 36 A4
Shrewsbury Cl *MEX/SWTN* S64 .... 58 A3 🔢
Shrewsbury Rd *SHEFP/MNR* S2 .... 122 C5
Shrewsbury Ter *KIMB* S61 .... 102 A3
Shrogswood Rd *RHAM/THRY* S65 .... 116 B1
Shubert Cl *HAN/WDH* S13 .... 139 F2
Shude Hl *SHEF* S1 .... 9 G5
Sicey Av *SHEFN* S5 .... 99 E1
Sicey La *SHEFN* S5 .... 99 E3
Sicklebrook La *DRON* S18 .... 160 C4
Siddall St *OWL* S3 .... 8 B5
Sidings Ct *DONS/BSCR* DN4 .... 44 C4
Sidlaw Cl *CHSW* S40 .... 183 D4 🔢
Sidney Rd *WHHL* DN2 .... 31 F5
Sidney St *MEX/SWTN* S64 .... 57 E5
　SHEF S1 .... 122 B5
Sidons Cl *KIMB* S61 .... 91 F4 🔢
Siemens Cl *DARN/MH* S9 .... 112 C2 🔢
Siena Cl *WMB/DAR* S73 .... 25 F4
Silkstone Cl *DOD/DAR* S75 .... 49 E3
　HACK/IN S12 .... 150 C1
Silkstone Crs *HACK/IN* S12 .... 150 C1
Silkstone Dr *HACK/IN* S12 .... 150 B1
Silkstone Pl *HACK/IN* S12 .... 150 C1
Silkstone Rd *HACK/IN* S12 .... 150 C1
Silkstone Vw *HOY* S74 .... 37 F5
Silver Birch Av *FUL* S10 .... 132 A3 🔢
Silverdale Cl *CHNE* S41 .... 177 F5
　ECC S11 .... 133 E5
Silverdale Crs *ECC* S11 .... 133 E5
Silverdale Cft *ECC* S11 .... 145 E1
Silverdale Dr *BSLYN/ROY* S71 .... 15 E2

Silverdale Gdns *ECC* S11 .... 145 F1 🔢
Silverdale Gld *ECC* S11 .... 145 E1 🔢
Silverdale Rd *ECC* S11 .... 145 E1
Silver Hill Rd *ECC* S11 .... 133 F5
Silver Jubilee Cl *WHHL* DN2 .... 32 A3
Silver Mill Rd *SHEFP/MNR* S2 .... 135 E2 🔢
Silver St *BSLY* S70 .... 21 F2
　DOD/DAR S75 .... 20 A4
　DON DN1 .... 5 E3
　RHAM/THRY S65 .... 95 F4
　SHEF S1 .... 9 E4
Silver Street Head *SHEF* S1 .... 8 D4
Simcrest Av *ECK/KIL* S21 .... 166 B3
Simmonite Rd *KIMB* S61 .... 92 A5
Simons Wy *WMB/DAR* S73 .... 24 C5
Simpson Pl *MEX/SWTN* S64 .... 58 A3
Sims Cft *CHNE* S41 .... 179 D3 🔢
Sims St *SHEF* S1 .... 8 D2
Singleton Crs *ST/HB/BR* S6 .... 108 A5 🔢
Singleton Gv *ST/HB/BR* S6 .... 108 A5 🔢
Singleton St *ST/HB/BR* S6 .... 108 A5
Sitwell Av *CHSW* S40 .... 190 A3
　STKB/PEN S36 .... 68 B2
Sitwell Dr *RHAM* S60 .... 115 E1
Sitwell Gv *MEX/SWTN* S64 .... 81 E1
　RHAM S60 .... 115 E2
Sitwell La *MALT* S66 .... 117 F1 🔢
Sitwell Park Rd *RHAM/THRY* S65 .... 116 B1
Sitwell Pl *SHEFP/MNR* S2 .... 135 D2 🔢
Sitwell Rd *ABRD* S7 .... 135 D2
Sitwell St *ECK/KIL* S21 .... 174 A1
Sitwell V *RHAM* S60 .... 115 D3
Sitwell Vw *RHAM* S60 .... 116 B3
Sivilla Rd *MEX/SWTN* S64 .... 81 E3
Skeldale Dr *CHSW* S40 .... 190 C4
Skelton Dr *HAN/WDH* S13 .... 139 F4
Skelton Gv *HAN/WDH* S13 .... 139 F4
Skelton La *HAN/WDH* S13 .... 139 F4
　MOS S20 .... 153 D2
Skelton Rd *SHEFS* S8 .... 135 E5
Skelwith Cl *ATT* S4 .... 111 D3
　CHNE S41 .... 183 F1 🔢
Skelwith Dr *ATT* S4 .... 111 D3
Skelwith Rd *ATT* S4 .... 111 D3
Skew Hill La *CHPT/GREN* S35 .... 96 C1
Skiddaw Cl *CHSW* S40 .... 183 E3
Skiers View Rd *HOY* S74 .... 51 D3
Skiers Wy *HOY* S74 .... 51 D3
Skimmerthorpe Rd *ATT* S4 .... 110 B3
Skipton Cl *CONI* DN12 .... 59 F5
Skipton Rd *ATT* S4 .... 110 A4
　AU/AST/KP S26 .... 142 A3
Skipwith Cl *NROS/TKH* DN11 .... 64 A5
Skye Edge Av *SHEFP/MNR* S2 .... 123 E5
Skye Edge Rd *SHEFP/MNR* S2 .... 123 E5
Slack La *CHSW* S40 .... 188 C1
Slade Rd *MEX/SWTN* S64 .... 81 D1
Slag La *ECK/KIL* S21 .... 172 B5
Slaidburn Av *CHPT/GREN* S35 .... 74 A5
Slate St *SHEFP/MNR* S2 .... 135 F3 🔢
Slayleigh Av *FUL* S10 .... 132 A2
Slayleigh Dr *FUL* S10 .... 132 A2
Slayleigh Delph *FUL* S10 .... 132 A2
Slayleigh Dr *FUL* S10 .... 132 B2
Slayleigh La *FUL* S10 .... 132 A2
Sleaford St *DARN/MH* S9 .... 124 A1 🔢
Sledgate Dr *MALT* S66 .... 117 D1
Sledgate La *MALT* S66 .... 117 D1
Sledmere Rd *BTLY* DN5 .... 28 C3
Slinn St *FUL* S10 .... 121 D3
Slitting Mill La *DARN/MH* S9 .... 124 A1 🔢
Sloade La *HACK/IN* S12 .... 162 B1
Smallage La *HAN/WDH* S13 .... 141 E1
Smalldale Rd *HACK/IN* S12 .... 150 B1
Smeaton St *ECC* S11 .... 135 D2 🔢
Smeckley Wood Cl *DRON* S18 .... 177 F5
Smelter Wood Av *HAN/WDH* S13 .... 138 C5
Smelter Wood Cl *HAN/WDH* S13 .... 138 C3 🔢
Smelter Wood Crs *HAN/WDH* S13 .... 139 D3
Smelter Wood Dr *HAN/WDH* S13 .... 138 C3
Smelter Wood La *HAN/WDH* S13 .... 138 C3
Smelter Wood Pl *HAN/WDH* S13 .... 139 D3
Smelter Wood Ri *HAN/WDH* S13 .... 139 D4
Smelter Wood Rd *HAN/WDH* S13 .... 138 C3
Smelter Wood Wy *HAN/WDH* S13 .... 138 C3
Smith Av *STV/CWN* S43 .... 186 C2
Smith Crs *CHNE* S41 .... 191 E3
Smithey Cl *CHPT/GREN* S35 .... 73 E5
Smithfield *OWL* S3 .... 8 D5
Smithfield Av *CHNE* S41 .... 191 D5
Smithfield Rd *HACK/IN* S12 .... 149 E3
Smithies La *BSLYN/ROY* S71 .... 13 F5
Smithies Rd *MEX/SWTN* S64 .... 57 D4
Smithies St *BSLYN/ROY* S71 .... 13 F5
Smithley La *WMB/DAR* S73 .... 38 B1
Smith Rd *STKB/PEN* S36 .... 68 B2
Smith Sq *DONS/BSCR* DN4 .... 43 D5
Smith St *CHPT/GREN* S35 .... 88 B1
　DONS/BSCR DN4 .... 43 D5
　WMB/DAR S73 .... 39 F2 🔢
Smithy Bridge La *WMB/DAR* S73 .... 53 E1
Smithy Carr Av *CHPT/GREN* S35 .... 88 A1
Smithy Carr Cl *CHPT/GREN* S35 .... 88 A1
Smithy Cl *KIMB* S61 .... 92 A5
Smithy Cft *DRON* S18 .... 168 A1
Smithy Fold La *CHPT/GREN* S35 .... 71 F4

Smithy Wood Crs *SHEFS* S8 ...... 147 D1 [E]
Smithy Wood La *DOD/DAR* S75 ...... 20 A4
Smithy Wood Rd *CHPT/GREN* S35 ...... 89 D2
  SHEFS S8 ...... 146 C1
Snail La *RHAM* S60 ...... 6 D6
Snaithing La *FUL* S10 ...... 132 C1
Snaithing Park Cl *FUL* S10 ...... 132 C1 [E]
Snaithing Park Rd *FUL* S10 ...... 132 C1
Snake La *CONI* DN12 ...... 85 E2
Snape HI *DRON* S18 ...... 169 E1
Snapehill Cl *DRON* S18 ...... 159 E5 [E]
Snapehill Crs *DRON* S18 ...... 159 E5
Snape Hill Dr *DRON* S18 ...... 159 F5 [E]
Snape Hill La *DRON* S18 ...... 169 E1
Snelston Cl *DRON* S18 ...... 168 A2 [E]
Sniq HI *SHEF* S1 ...... 9 F4
Snowberry Cl *MEX/SWTN* S64 ...... 81 D3
Snowden Ter *WMB/DAR* S73 ...... 39 E2
Snowdon La *ECK/KIL* S21 ...... 161 F5
Snowdon Wy *RHAM* S60 ...... 114 B5
Snow La *OWL* S3 ...... 8 D3
Soaper La *DRON* S18 ...... 169 E1
Soap House La *HAN/WDH* S13 ...... 140 C3
Sokell Av *WMB/DAR* S73 ...... 39 D3
Solly St *SHEF* S1 ...... 8 B4
Solway Ri *DRON* S18 ...... 168 D1
Somercotes Rd *HAN/WDH* S12 ...... 138 B5
Somersall Cl *CHSW* S40 ...... 188 B3
Somersall La *CHSW* S40 ...... 188 B3
Somersall Park Rd *CHSW* S40 ...... 188 B3 [E]
Somersall Willows *CHSW* S40 ...... 188 C1
Somersby Av *BTLY* DN5 ...... 29 D5
  CHSW S40 ...... 188 C5
Somerset Dr *STV/CWN* S43 ...... 186 A1
Somerset Rd *DON* DN1 ...... 5 F6
  OWL S3 ...... 122 C1
Somerset St *BSLY* S70 ...... 2 A4 [E]
  OWL S3 ...... 122 C1 [E]
Somerton Dr *DONS/BSCR* DN4 ...... 46 C5
Somerville Ter *ST/HB/BR* S6 ...... 121 E1
Sorby Rd *AU/AST/KP* S26 ...... 141 F3
Sorby St *ATT* S4 ...... 9 H1
Sorby Wy *MALT* S66 ...... 117 F1
Soresby St *CHSW* S40 ...... 11 E6
Sorrelsykes Cl *RHAM* S60 ...... 115 F4 [E]
Sothall Cl *MOS* S20 ...... 153 D2
Sothall Ct *MOS* S20 ...... 153 D2 [E]
Sothall Gn *MOS* S20 ...... 153 D2
Sothall Ms *MOS* S20 ...... 153 D2 [E]
Sough Hall Av *KIMB* S61 ...... 90 A1
Sough Hall Cl *KIMB* S61 ...... 90 A1
Sough Hall Crs *KIMB* S61 ...... 90 A1
Sough Hall Rd *KIMB* S61 ...... 90 A2
Soughley La *CHPT/GREN* S35 ...... 70 B1
  FUL S10 ...... 130 C2
Southall St *SHEFS* S8 ...... 135 E4 [E]
South Av *MEX/SWTN* S64 ...... 80 C1
Southbourne Rd *ECC* S11 ...... 121 D5
South Cl *DRON* S18 ...... 170 C5
Southcote Dr *DRON* S18 ...... 168 B2
South Crs *DOD/DAR* S75 ...... 20 A3
  ECK/KIL S21 ...... 166 C1
  RHAM/THRY S65 ...... 104 C2
Southcroft Gdns *SHEFS* S8 ...... 135 D4 [E]
Southdown Av *CHSW* S40 ...... 183 D5
Southend Pl *SHEFP/MNR* S2 ...... 136 C1 [E]
Southend Rd *SHEFP/MNR* S2 ...... 136 C1 [E]
Southey Av *SHEFN* S5 ...... 109 E4
Southey Cl *SHEFN* S5 ...... 109 D1 [E]
Southey Crs *SHEFN* S5 ...... 109 E1
Southey Dr *SHEFN* S5 ...... 109 E1
Southey Green Cl *SHEFN* S5 ...... 109 D1 [E]
Southey Green Rd *SHEFN* S5 ...... 97 E5
Southey Hall Dr *SHEFN* S5 ...... 109 D1
Southey Hall Rd *SHEFN* S5 ...... 97 F5
Southey Hi *SHEFN* S5 ...... 109 E1
Southey Pl *SHEFN* S5 ...... 109 D1
Southey Ri *SHEFN* S5 ...... 109 E1
Southfield Crs *DEARNE* S63 ...... 26 B4
Southfield Dr *DRON* S18 ...... 170 A3
Southfield La *DEARNE* S63 ...... 26 B4
Southfield Mt *DRON* S18 ...... 170 A3 [E]
Southgate *DOD/DAR* S75 ...... 13 D4
  ECK/KIL S21 ...... 164 C5
  HOY S74 ...... 51 F5
Southgate Ct *ECK/KIL* S21 ...... 164 C5
Southgate Wy *STV/CWN* S43 ...... 180 C2
South Grimesthorpe Rd *ATT* S4 .... 123 D1 [E]
Southgrove Rd *FUL* S10 ...... 134 B1
Southlands Wy *AU/AST/KP* S26 ...... 142 C3
South La *SHEF* S1 ...... 135 E1
Southlea Av *HOY* S74 ...... 52 A3
Southlea Cl *HOY* S74 ...... 52 A3 [E]
Southlea Dr *HOY* S74 ...... 51 F3
Southlea Rd *HOY* S74 ...... 51 F2
South Lodge Ct *CHSW* S40 ...... 188 C1
Southmoor Av *ARMTH* DN3 ...... 33 E4
Southmoor Cl *STV/CWN* S43 ...... 186 A5
Southmoor La *ARMTH* DN3 ...... 33 E4
South Pde *DON* DN1 ...... 5 G4
  OWL S3 ...... 8 D2
South Pl *CHSW* S40 ...... 190 B2 [E]
  DOD/DAR S75 ...... 12 C4
  WMB/DAR S73 ...... 38 C2 [E]

South Rd *CHPT/GREN* S35 ...... 73 E4
  DOD/DAR S75 ...... 20 A2
  KIMB S61 ...... 101 F2
  ST/HB/BR S6 ...... 121 D1
Southsea Rd *HAN/WDH* S13 ...... 139 E4
South St *BSLY* S70 ...... 21 D1 [E]
  DOD/DAR S75 ...... 20 A4
  DONS/BSCR DN4 ...... 44 B3
  KIMB S61 ...... 93 D3
  KIMB S61 ...... 101 F4
  MOS S20 ...... 164 B2
  RAW S62 ...... 80 B5
South St North *STV/CWN* S43 ...... 179 E2
South Street Pk *SHEFP/MNR* S2 ...... 9 H5
South Vw *MOS* S20 ...... 165 E1
South View Cl *ST/HB/BR* S6 ...... 106 C5
South View Crs *ABRD* S7 ...... 135 D5 [E]
South View Ri *ST/HB/BR* S6 ...... 106 C3
South View Rd *ECC* S11 ...... 135 D2
  HOY S74 ...... 51 E2
South View Ter *RHAM* S60 ...... 127 D2 [E]
Southwell Ri *MEX/SWTN* S64 ...... 58 C2 [E]
Southwell Rd *ATT* S4 ...... 111 D3 [E]
  RAW S62 ...... 80 C5
  WHHL DN2 ...... 31 D3
Southwell St *DOD/DAR* S75 ...... 13 E5 [E]
Southwood Av *DRON* S18 ...... 169 E4
Sowters Rw *CHSW* S40 ...... 11 E6
Spa Brooke Cl *HACK/IN* S12 ...... 151 D1
Spa Brooke Dr *HACK/IN* S12 ...... 139 D5
Spa La *CHNE* S41 ...... 11 G6
  HAN/WDH S13 ...... 140 A4
Spa Lane Cft *HAN/WDH* S13 ...... 140 A4
Spalton Rd *RAW* S62 ...... 94 A2
Spansyke St *DONS/BSCR* DN4 ...... 4 B5
Spa View Av *HACK/IN* S12 ...... 151 D2
Spa View Dr *HACK/IN* S12 ...... 151 D2
Spa View Pl *HACK/IN* S12 ...... 151 D2
Spa View Rd *HACK/IN* S12 ...... 151 D2
Spa View Ter *HACK/IN* S12 ...... 151 D2 [E]
Spa View Wy *HACK/IN* S12 ...... 151 D2
Spa Well Crs *RAW* S62 ...... 79 D5
Speeton Rd *ST/HB/BR* S6 ...... 108 A5 [E]
Spencer Gn *RHAM* S60 ...... 116 B3 [E]
Spencer Rd *SHEFP/MNR* S2 ...... 135 E3
Spencer St *BSLY* S70 ...... 21 F2
  CHSW S40 ...... 11 E4
  MEX/SWTN S64 ...... 57 F3
Spenser Rd *RHAM/THRY* S65 ...... 104 B4
Spilsby Ct *DONS/BSCR* DN4 ...... 67 E1
Spink Hall Cl *STKB/PEN* S36 ...... 69 D3 [E]
Spink Hall La *STKB/PEN* S36 ...... 68 C3
Spinkhill Av *HAN/WDH* S13 ...... 138 A2
Spinkhill Dr *HAN/WDH* S13 ...... 138 B2
Spinkhill Rd *ECK/KIL* S21 ...... 166 C4
  HAN/WDH S13 ...... 138 B3
Spinney Cl *RHAM* S60 ...... 115 E1
Spinneyfield *RHAM* S60 ...... 115 E2
The Spinney *DONS/BSCR* DN4 ...... 63 D2 [E]
Spital Brook Cl *CHNE* S41 ...... 191 D3
Spitalfields *OWL* S3 ...... 9 F2
Spital Gdns *CHNE* S41 ...... 191 D3
Spital HI *ATT* S4 ...... 9 H2
Spital La *CHNE* S41 ...... 190 C2
  OWL S3 ...... 9 H1
Spital St *OWL* S3 ...... 9 G1
Spofforth Rd *DARN/MH* S9 ...... 124 B3 [E]
Spooner Dr *ECK/KIL* S21 ...... 166 A2
Spooner Rd *FUL* S10 ...... 121 D4
Spoon Gld *ST/HB/BR* S6 ...... 119 D1 [E]
Spoonhill Rd *ST/HB/BR* S6 ...... 120 A1
Spoon La *ST/HB/BR* S6 ...... 118 B1
Spoon Ms *ST/HB/BR* S6 ...... 119 D1
Spoon Wy *ST/HB/BR* S6 ...... 119 D1
Spotswood Cl *GLV* S14 ...... 148 C1 [E]
Spotswood Dr *SHEFP/MNR* S2 ...... 136 C5 [E]
Spotswood Mt *GLV* S14 ...... 136 C5 [E]
Spotswood Pl *GLV* S14 ...... 148 B1
Spotswood Rd *SHEFS* S8 ...... 148 B1
Spout La *ST/HB/BR* S6 ...... 118 C1
Spout Spinney *ST/HB/BR* S6 ...... 118 C1
Spring Bank Rd *CHSW* S40 ...... 10 C5
  CONI DN12 ...... 84 C3
Spring Close Dell *GLV* S14 ...... 149 D1
Spring Close Mt *GLV* S14 ...... 149 D1
Spring Close Vw *GLV* S14 ...... 148 C1
  HACK/IN S12 ...... 137 F5
  SHEFP/MNR S2 ...... 135 E1
Spring Cft *KIMB* S61 ...... 92 A5
Springcroft Dr *BTLY* DN5 ...... 28 C1
Spring Dr *WMB/DAR* S73 ...... 40 B5
Springfield Av *CHSW* S40 ...... 189 E1
  ECC S11 ...... 134 A5
Springfield Cl *ABRD* S7 ...... 146 A1
  ECK/KIL S21 ...... 164 A5
  KIMB S61 ...... 93 E5
Springfield Ct *BTLY* DN5 ...... 28 C4 [E]
Springfield Crs *HOY* S74 ...... 51 D3
Springfield Gln *ECC* S11 ...... 145 F1
Springfield Pl *BSLY* S70 ...... 21 E1 [E]
Springfield Rd *ABRD* S7 ...... 146 A1
  CONI DN12 ...... 62 A5
  HOY S74 ...... 50 C3
  MEX/SWTN S64 ...... 81 F4
Springfield St *BSLY* S70 ...... 21 D1

Spring Gdns *BSLYN/ROY* S71 ...... 15 D3 [E]
  DON DN1 ...... 4 D4
  HOY S74 ...... 51 F2
Spring HI *FUL* S10 ...... 121 D3
Springhill Av *WMB/DAR* S73 ...... 40 B5
Spring Hill Rd *FUL* S10 ...... 121 D3
Spring House Cl *RCH* S42 ...... 182 A4
Spring House Rd *FUL* S10 ...... 121 D3 [E]
Spring La *SHEFP/MNR* S2 ...... 136 C2
Spring St *BSLY* S70 ...... 21 F2
  OWL S3 ...... 9 E3
  RHAM/THRY S65 ...... 7 F4
Spring Vale Av *BSLY* S70 ...... 36 A1 [E]
Springvale Rd *ST/HB/BR* S6 ...... 121 E5
Spring Vale Rd *STV/CWN* S43 ...... 185 F1
Spring View Rd *FUL* S10 ...... 121 D5 [E]
Spring Water Av *HACK/IN* S12 ...... 151 D2
Spring Water Cl *HACK/IN* S12 ...... 151 E2 [E]
Spring Water Dr *HACK/IN* S12 ...... 151 D1
Springwell Av *MOS* S20 ...... 152 C1
Springwell Crs *MOS* S20 ...... 152 C1
Springwell Dr *MOS* S20 ...... 152 C1
Springwell Gdns
  DONS/BSCR DN4 ...... 63 D1 [E]
Springwell Gv *MOS* S20 ...... 152 C1
Springwell La *DONS/BSCR* DN4 ...... 63 D2
  NROS/TKH DN11 ...... 63 E5
Springwood Av *AU/AST/KP* S26 ...... 142 A1
Spring Wood Cl *CHNE* S41 ...... 188 D3
Springwood La *CHPT/GREN* S35 ...... 73 D5
Springwood Rd *BTLY* DN5 ...... 28 C1
  HOY S74 ...... 51 D3
  SHEFS S8 ...... 135 E4 [E]
Sprotbrough Rd *BTLY* DN5 ...... 43 D3
Spruce Ri *ECK/KIL* S21 ...... 166 A3
Spurley Hey Gv *STKB/PEN* S36 ...... 69 D3
Spurr St *SHEFP/MNR* S2 ...... 135 F2
The Square *AU/AST/KP* S26 ...... 155 F3
  BSLY S70 ...... 21 E2
  RAW S62 ...... 75 E2
The Stables *MEX/SWTN* S64 ...... 56 C4
Stacey Dr *RHAM/THRY* S65 ...... 95 F3 [E]
Stacye Av *HAN/WDH* S13 ...... 140 B4
Stacye Ri *HAN/WDH* S13 ...... 140 B4
Stadium Ct *RAW* S62 ...... 93 F4
Stadium Wy *DARN/MH* S9 ...... 124 A2
  RHAM/THRY S65 ...... 94 A5
Stafford Cl *DRON* S18 ...... 168 A1 [E]
Stafford Crs *RHAM* S60 ...... 115 D3
Stafford Dr *RHAM* S60 ...... 115 D3
Stafford Gv *BSLY* S70 ...... 50 A3
Stafford La *SHEFP/MNR* S2 ...... 123 E5 [E]
Stafford Rd *SHEFP/MNR* S2 ...... 123 E5
Stafford St *SHEFP/MNR* S2 ...... 9 H6
Stafford Wy *CHPT/GREN* S35 ...... 88 A1 [E]
Stag Cl *RHAM* S60 ...... 116 A1
Stag Crs *RHAM/THRY* S65 ...... 116 A1
Stag La *RHAM* S60 ...... 115 F1
Stainborough Cl *DOD/DAR* S75 ...... 20 A4
Stainborough Rd *DOD/DAR* S75 ...... 20 A4
Stainborough Vw *BSLY* S70 ...... 22 A5 [E]
  DOD/DAR S75 ...... 20 A4
Staindrop Vw *CHPT/GREN* S35 ...... 74 B5
Stainley Cl *DOD/DAR* S75 ...... 12 C3 [E]
Stainmore Av *MOS* S20 ...... 153 E3
Stainton Cl *BSLYN/ROY* S71 ...... 13 F1
Stainton Rd *ECC* S11 ...... 133 F2
Stainton St *CONI* DN12 ...... 60 A5
Stair Rd *ATT* S4 ...... 110 A4
Stalker Lees Rd *ECC* S11 ...... 134 B2
Stamford St *DARN/MH* S9 ...... 111 D5 [E]
Stampers HI *DOD/DAR* S75 ...... 35 E3
Stanage Ri *HACK/IN* S12 ...... 138 B5
Stanage Wy *RCH* S42 ...... 182 A4 [E]
Stanbury Cl *DOD/DAR* S75 ...... 12 C4
Standish Av *SHEFN* S5 ...... 109 E4
Standish Cl *SHEFN* S5 ...... 109 E3
Standish Dr *SHEFN* S5 ...... 109 E3
Standish Gdns *SHEFN* S5 ...... 109 E3
Standish Rd *SHEFN* S5 ...... 109 E3
Standon Crs *DARN/MH* S9 ...... 100 A4
Standon Dr *DARN/MH* S9 ...... 100 A4
Standon Rd *DARN/MH* S9 ...... 100 B4
Stand Rd *CHNE* S41 ...... 184 A2
Staneford Ct *MOS* S20 ...... 152 B4
Stanford Rd *DRON* S18 ...... 168 A2 [E]
Stanhope Gdns *DOD/DAR* S75 ...... 13 D4
Stanhope Rd *DON* DN1 ...... 30 C4
  HACK/IN S12 ...... 138 A5
Staniforth Av *ECK/KIL* S21 ...... 165 F5
Staniforth Rd *DARN/MH* S9 ...... 124 B2
Stanley Av *STV/CWN* S43 ...... 186 C2
Stanley Gdns *DONS/BSCR* DN4 ...... 43 F3 [E]
Stanley Gv *AU/AST/KP* S26 ...... 143 D2 [E]
Stanley La *OWL* S3 ...... 9 F2
Stanley Rd *BSLY* S70 ...... 23 F2
  BTLY DN5 ...... 28 B2
  CHPT/GREN S35 ...... 73 F5
  SHEFS S8 ...... 135 F5
  STKB/PEN S36 ...... 69 D2 [E]
Stanley St *BSLY* S70 ...... 2 A5
  CHNE S41 ...... 190 C2
  ECK/KIL S21 ...... 166 B1
  OWL S3 ...... 9 F2
Stannington Gin *ST/HB/BR* S6 ...... 119 F1

Stannington Ri *ST/HB/BR* S6 ...... 107 E5 🔲
Stannington Rd *ST/HB/BR* S6 ...... 118 C1
Stannington View Rd *FUL* S10 ...... 120 B3
Stanton Crs *HACK/IN* S12 ...... 150 B1 🔲
Stanwell Av *DARN/MH* S9 ...... 100 B5
Stanwell Rd *DARN/MH* S9 ...... 100 B5
Stanwood Av *ST/HB/BR* S6 ...... 120 A1
Stanwood Crs *ST/HB/BR* S6 ...... 120 A1
Stanwood Dr *CHSW* S40 ...... 188 C4 🔲
  ST/HB/BR S6 ...... 120 A1 🔲
Stanwood Ms *ST/HB/BR* S6. ...... 120 A1 🔲
Stanwood Rd *ST/HB/BR* S6. ...... 120 A1
Stapleton Rd *DONS/BSCR* DN4 ...... 62 B2
Star La *BSLY* S70 ...... 2 B5
Starling Md *SHEFP/MNR* S2 ...... 123 F5 🔲
Starnhill Cl *CHPT/GREN* S35. ...... 89 D5
Station La *CHNE* S41 ...... 178 B4
  DARN/MH S9 ...... 111 E2
Station Rd *BSLY* S70 ...... 13 E5
  BSLY S70 ...... 37 D1
  BTLY DN5 ...... 17 E4
  CHNE S41 ...... 11 G6
  CHNE S41 ...... 184 B1
  CHPT/GREN S35 ...... 74 C5
  CHPT/GREN S35 ...... 89 D5
  CONI DN12 ...... 61 D5
  DARN/MH S9 ...... 125 D3 🔲
  DEARNE S63 ...... 27 D3
  DEARNE S63 ...... 56 A2
  ECK/KIL S21 ...... 164 C5
  ECK/KIL S21 ...... 165 F2
  ECK/KIL S21 ...... 175 D1
  HAN/WDH S13 ...... 140 B3
  MEX/SWTN S64 ...... 58 B4
  MOS S20 ...... 164 B1 🔲
  MOS S20 ...... 165 D1
  RHAM S60 ...... 102 C5
  RHAM S60 ...... 127 D1
  RHAM S60 ...... 127 F3
  STKB/PEN S36. ...... 70 B2
  STV/CWN S43 ...... 180 B1
  STV/CWN S43 ...... 180 C3
  STV/CWN S43 ...... 185 D1
  WMB/DAR S73 ...... 39 F2
Station St *MEX/SWTN* S64 ...... 57 F5
Staton Av *MOS* S20 ...... 153 E1
Staton La *DRON* S18 ...... 171 E2
The Statutes *RHAM* S60 ...... 6 B5
Staunton Rd *DONS/BSCR* DN4 ...... 47 E5
Staveley La *ECK/KIL* S21 ...... 173 E4
Staveley Rd *BSVR* S44 ...... 174 C3
  SHEFS S8 ...... 135 E3 🔲
  STV/CWN S43 ...... 179 F3
Steade Rd *ABRD* S7 ...... 135 D3
Steadfield Rd *HOY* S74 ...... 50 C4 🔲
The Steadlands *RAW* S62 ...... 79 E4 🔲
Stead La *HOY* S74 ...... 50 C3
Stead St *ECK/KIL* S21 ...... 164 B5
Steele Av *STV/CWN* S43 ...... 186 C3
Steele St *HOY* S74 ...... 50 B3
Steel Hl *CHPT/GREN* S35 ...... 97 D2
Steelhouse La *OWL* S3 ...... 9 E3 🔲
Steel Rd *ECC* S11 ...... 134 A4
Steel St *RHAM* S60 ...... 102 B4
Steeping Cl *STV/CWN* S43 ...... 185 F1
Steeton Ct *HOY* S74 ...... 52 B2
Stemp St *ECC* S11 ...... 135 D2 🔲🔲
Stenton Ct *SHEFS* S8 ...... 159 D1
Stephen Dr *CHPT/GREN* S35 ...... 96 C1
  FUL S10 ...... 120 A4
Stephen Hl *FUL* S10 ...... 120 A4
Stephen Hill Rd *FUL* S10 ...... 120 A4
Stephen La *CHPT/GREN* S35 ...... 96 C1
Stephenson Pl *CHNE* S41 ...... 11 F6 🔲
Stephenson St *SHEFS* S8 ...... 181 F5
Stepney St *SHEFP/MNR* S2 ...... 9 H4
Stepping La *CHPT/GREN* S35 ...... 86 C5
Sterland St *CHSW* S40 ...... 10 B6
Sterndale Rd *ABRD* S7 ...... 146 A2
Steven Cl *CHPT/GREN* S35 ...... 88 A2
Steven Crs *CHPT/GREN* S35 ...... 88 A1
Steven Pl *CHPT/GREN* S35 ...... 88 A2
Stevenson Dr *RHAM/THRY* S65 ...... 104 C4
Stevenson Rd *DARN/MH* S9 ...... 123 F1
  DONS/BSCR DN4 ...... 63 F1
Stevenson Wy *DARN/MH* S9 ...... 123 F1
Stevens Rd *DONS/BSCR* DN4 ...... 43 F3 🔲
Stewart Rd *ECC* S11 ...... 134 B2
Stewarts Rd *RAW* S62 ...... 80 B5
Stewart St *DON* DN1 ...... 4 C5
Sticking La *MEX/SWTN* S64 ...... 57 F1
Stillman Cl *CHNE* S41 ...... 191 D4
Stirling Cl *HOY* S74 ...... 52 B2 🔲
Stirling St *DON* DN1 ...... 4 D6
Stockarth Cl *CHPT/GREN* S35 ...... 96 A5
Stockbridge Av *BTLY* DN5 ...... 29 E2 🔲
Stockbridge La *BTLY* DN5 ...... 17 D4
Stockil Rd *DONS/BSCR* DN4 ...... 5 H6
Stock Rd *SHEFP/MNR* S2 ...... 136 C1
Stocks Green Ct *TOT/DORE* S17 ...... 156 A4
Stocks Green Dr *TOT/DORE* S17 ...... 156 B4 🔲
Stocks Hl *CHPT/GREN* S35 ...... 88 B5
Stock's La *DOD/DAR* S75 ...... 13 E5
  RAW S62 ...... 94 A1

Stockwell La *AU/AST/KP* S26. ...... 155 F4
Stoke St *DARN/MH* S9 ...... 123 F2
Stokewell Rd *DEARNE* S63 ...... 55 D1
Stoneacre Av *HACK/IN* S12 ...... 151 F2
Stoneacre Cl *HACK/IN* S12 ...... 151 F2 🔲
Stoneacre Ri *HACK/IN* S12 ...... 151 F3
Stoneacre Dr *HACK/IN* S12 ...... 151 F2
Stonecliffe Cl *SHEFF/MNR* S2 ...... 137 E1
Stonecliffe Dr *STKB/PEN* S36 ...... 68 C4
Stonecliffe Pl *SHEFP/MNR* S2 ...... 137 E1
Stonecliffe Rd *SHEFP/MNR* S2 ...... 137 E1
Stone Cl *DRON* S18 ...... 160 A5
Stone Close Av *DONS/BSCR* DN4 ...... 4 A6
Stonecroft Rd *TOT/DORE* S17 ...... 156 C3
Stonecross Gdns *DONS/BSCR* DN4.... 47 E4
Stonedale Cl *MOS* S20 ...... 164 B1 🔲
Stone Delf *FUL* S10 ...... 132 A1
Stone Font Gv *DONS/BSCR* DN4. ...... 47 D5
Stonegravels La *CHNE* S41 ...... 11 F1
Stonegravels Wy *MOS* S20 ...... 165 D2
Stone Gv *FUL* S10 ...... 121 E5
Stone Hill Dr *AU/AST/KP* S26. ...... 142 A3
Stonehill Ri *BTLY* DN5 ...... 28 C1 🔲
Stone La *HAN/WDH* S13 ...... 139 E5
  STV/CWN S43 ...... 179 E2
Stoneleigh Cft *BSLY* S70 ...... 22 A3 🔲
Stoneley Cl *HACK/IN* S12 ...... 149 E4
Stoneley Crs *HACK/IN* S12 ...... 149 F4
Stoneley Dell *HACK/IN* S12 ...... 149 F4
Stoneley Dr *HACK/IN* S12 ...... 149 E4
Stonelow Crs *DRON* S18 ...... 170 B1
Stonelow Rd *DRON* S18 ...... 169 F1
Stone Moor Rd *STKB/PEN* S36 ...... 68 B4
Stone Rd *DRON* S18 ...... 160 A4
Stone Rw *CHSW* S40 ...... 189 E2
Stone St *BSLYN/ROY* S71 ...... 13 F5
  MOS S20 ...... 164 B1
Stonewood Ct *FUL* S10 ...... 119 E5 🔲
Stonewood Gv *FUL* S10 ...... 119 E5
Stoney Ga *CHPT/GREN* S35 ...... 73 E5
Stonyford Rd *WMB/DAR* S73 ...... 40 A1
Stoops Cl *CHSW* S40 ...... 183 E5 🔲
Stoops Rd *DONS/BSCR* DN4 ...... 45 F3
Stoops Rd *DONS/BSCR* DN4 ...... 46 B5
Stopes Rd *DARN/MH* S9 ...... 110 B1
Store St *SHEFP/MNR* S2 ...... 135 F1
Storey's Ga *WMB/DAR* S73 ...... 38 C2
Storey St *MEX/SWTN* S64 ...... 57 D5
Storforth La *CHNE* S41 ...... 191 D5
  CHSW S40 ...... 190 B5
Storrs Hall Rd *ST/HB/BR* S6 ...... 120 C1
Storrs La *CHPT/GREN* S35 ...... 72 C1
Storrs Rd *CHSW* S40 ...... 188 C2
Storth Av *FUL* S10 ...... 132 C2
Storth La *FUL* S10 ...... 132 C1
Stortholme Ms *FUL* S10 ...... 133 D1 🔲
Stotfold Dr *DEARNE* S63 ...... 26 C3
Stothard Rd *FUL* S10 ...... 120 C3
Stour Cl *STV/CWN* S43 ...... 185 F1
Stour La *ST/HB/BR* S6 ...... 107 D2
Stovin Cl *DARN/MH* S9 ...... 124 C1
Stovin Dr *DARN/MH* S9 ...... 124 C1
Stovin Gdns *DARN/MH* S9 ...... 111 F5
Stow Bridge La *RHAM* S60 ...... 129 F1
Stow Av *ABRD* S7 ...... 146 A1
Stradbroke Av *HAN/WDH* S13 ...... 138 B3
Stradbroke Cl *HAN/WDH* S13 ...... 138 C3
Stradbroke Dr *HAN/WDH* S13 ...... 138 C3
Stradbroke Pl *HAN/WDH* S13 ...... 138 C3
Stradbroke Ri *HAN/WDH* S13 ...... 138 C3
Stradbroke Ri *CHSW* S40 ...... 189 D4
Stradbroke Rd *HAN/WDH* S13 ...... 138 B3
Stradbroke Wy *HAN/WDH* S13 ...... 138 C3
Strafford Av *BSLY* S70 ...... 22 A4
  HOY S74. ...... 52 B2
Strafford Pl *KIMB* S61 ...... 89 F1
Strafford Rd *KIMB* S61 ...... 91 F4
Strafford Wk *DOD/DAR* S75 ...... 20 A4
Strafford Rd *FUL* S10 ...... 132 B1
Strathmore Gv *DEARNE* S63 ...... 56 A2
Strathtay Rd *ECC* S11 ...... 133 F3
Strawberry Av *SHEFN* S5 ...... 98 C3
Streetfield Crs *MOS* S20 ...... 164 B2 🔲
Streetfields *MOS* S20 ...... 164 C2
Street La *RAW* S62 ...... 77 F1
Strelley Av *SHEFS* S8 ...... 146 C4
Strelley Rd *SHEFS* S8 ...... 146 B4
Stretton Cl *DONS/BSCR* DN4 ...... 47 E4
Stretton Rd *BSLYN/ROY* S71 ...... 14 B2
  ECC S11 ...... 134 A3
Stringers Cft *RHAM* S60 ...... 116 B3 🔲
Struan Rd *ECC* S11 ...... 134 A5
Strutt Rd *OWL* S3 ...... 109 E5
Stuart Cl *CHNE* S41 ...... 184 C3
Stuart Gv *CHPT/GREN* S35 ...... 88 B2
Stuart Rd *CHPT/GREN* S35 ...... 88 C2
Stuart St *DEARNE* S63 ...... 27 E3
Stubbin Cl *RAW* S62 ...... 79 E4
Stubbing House La
  CHPT/GREN S35 ...... 106 B1
Stubbing La *CHPT/GREN* S35 ...... 106 A1
Stubbing Rd *CHSW* S40 ...... 190 A5
Stubbin La *RAW* S62 ...... 79 E3
  SHEFN S5 ...... 99 D5
Stubbin Rd *RAW* S62. ...... 78 C4

Stubbs Crs *KIMB* S61 ...... 92 A5
Stubbs Rd *WMB/DAR* S73 ...... 39 D3
Stubley Cl *DRON* S18 ...... 168 C1
Stubley Cft *DRON* S18 ...... 168 B1
Stubley Dr *DRON* S18 ...... 168 C1
Stubley Hollow *DRON* S18. ...... 168 C1
Stubley La *DRON* S18 ...... 168 B1
Stubley Pl *DRON* S18 ...... 168 C1
Studfield Dr *ST/HB/BR* S6 ...... 107 D4
Studfield Dr *ST/HB/BR* S6 ...... 107 D4
Studfield Gv *ST/HB/BR* S6 ...... 107 D4
Studfield Hl *ST/HB/BR* S6 ...... 107 D3
Studfield Ri *ST/HB/BR* S6 ...... 107 D3
Studfield Rd *ST/HB/BR* S6 ...... 107 D4
Studley Ct *DARN/MH* S9 ...... 125 D3 🔲
Studmoor Rd *KIMB* S61 ...... 91 E4
Stump Cross Rd *DEARNE* S63 ...... 55 F3
Stumperlowe Av *FUL* S10 ...... 132 C2 🔲
Stumperlowe Cl *FUL* S10 ...... 132 C2 🔲
Stumperlowe Crescent Rd
  FUL S10 ...... 132 B2
Stumperlowe Cft *FUL* S10 ...... 132 B1
Stumperlowe Hall Cha *FUL* S10 .. 132 B1 🔲
Stumperlowe Hall Rd *FUL* S10 ...... 132 B3
Stumperlowe La *FUL* S10 ...... 132 B2
Stumperlowe Park Rd *FUL* S10 ...... 132 B2
Stumperlowe Vw *FUL* S10. ...... 132 B3
Stupton Rd *DARN/MH* S9 ...... 111 E2
Sturge Cft *SHEFP/MNR* S2 ...... 135 F4 🔲
Sturton Cl *DONS/BSCR* DN4 ...... 66 A1
Sturton Cft *RHAM/THRY* S65. ...... 95 F5
Sturton Rd *ATT* S4 ...... 110 A4
Sudbury Cl *CHSW* S40 ...... 182 C4
Sudbury Dr *AU/AST/KP* S26. ...... 142 C3
Sudbury St *OWL* S3 ...... 8 B2
Sudhall Cl *CHNE* S41 ...... 183 E1
Suffolk Rd *DONS/BSCR* DN4 ...... 63 F1 🔲🔲
  SHEFP/MNR S2 ...... 122 C5
Sulby Gv *BSLY* S70 ...... 23 E4
Summerfield *RHAM/THRY* S65 ...... 7 F5
Summerfield Crs *STV/CWN* S43 ...... 185 F1
  DRON S18 ...... 159 F5
Summerfield Rd *CHSW* S40 ...... 190 A3
  DRON S18 ...... 159 F5
Summerfield St *FUL* S10 ...... 134 C1
Summer La *TOT/DORE* S17 ...... 156 A4
  WMB/DAR S73 ...... 38 B3
Summerley Lower Rd *DRON* S18 ...... 170 C1
Summerley Rd *DRON* S18 ...... 170 C1
Summerskill Gn *STV/CWN* S43 ...... 187 D2
Summer St *BSLY* S70 ...... 2 A4
  OWL S3 ...... 121 F3
Summerwood La *DRON* S18 ...... 159 D5
Summerwood Pl *DRON* S18 ...... 169 D1
Summer Rd *RHAM/THRY* S65. ...... 7 G2
Sunderland St *ECC* S11 ...... 134 C1 🔲
Sunderland Ter *BSLY* S70 ...... 22 B2 🔲
Sundew Cft *CHPT/GREN* S35 ...... 73 E5 🔲
Sundew Gdns *CHPT/GREN* S35 ...... 73 E2
Sundown Pl *HAN/WDH* S13 ...... 139 D2
Sundown Rd *HAN/WDH* S13 ...... 139 D2
Sunningdale Cl *ARMTH* DN3 ...... 67 F1 🔲
  CHSW S40 ...... 189 F4 🔲
  MEX/SWTN S64 ...... 81 C2
Sunningdale Mt *ECC* S11 ...... 133 F5
Sunningdale Ri *RHAM* S60 ...... 114 A1 🔲
Sunningdale Rd *WHHL* DN2 ...... 31 E4 🔲
Sunny Bank *FUL* S10 ...... 134 C1
  HOY S74. ...... 52 A1
Sunnybank Crs *RHAM* S60 ...... 114 A4 🔲
Sunny Bank Ri *HOY* S74. ...... 52 B2 🔲
Sunny Bar *STKB/PEN* S36 ...... 69 D5
Sunny Bar *DON* DN1 ...... 5 E3
Sunnybrook Cl *HOY* S74. ...... 51 F4
Sunnyside *ARMTH* DN3 ...... 19 F4
Sunny Springs *CHNE* S41 ...... 11 F3
Sunnyvale Av *TOT/DORE* S17 ...... 156 B4
Sunnyvale Rd *TOT/DORE* S17 ...... 156 B4
Surbiton St *DARN/MH* S9. ...... 111 F4
Surrey Cl *BSLY* S70 ...... 22 A3
Surrey La *SHEF* S1 ...... 122 C5
Surrey Pl *SHEF* S1 ...... 9 F6 🔲
Surrey St *DONS/BSCR* DN4 ...... 43 F5
  SHEF S1 ...... 9 E6
Sussex Rd *ATT* S4 ...... 123 D1
  CHPT/GREN S35 ...... 88 B1
Sussex St *ATT* S4 ...... 123 D3
Suthard Cross Rd *FUL* S10 ...... 120 C3 🔲
Sutherland Rd *ATT* S4. ...... 123 D1
Sutherland St *ATT* S4 ...... 123 E2 🔲
Sutton Crs *STV/CWN* S43 ...... 187 D2
Sutton St *OWL* S3 ...... 8 B3
Swaddale Av *CHNE* S41 ...... 184 C3
Swaddale Cl *CHNE* S41 ...... 184 C3 🔲
Swaith Av *BTLY* DN5 ...... 29 D2
Swaithedale *BSLY* S70 ...... 23 D5
Swaithe Vw *BSLY* S70 ...... 23 E5
Swaledale Rd *ABRD* S7 ...... 134 B5
Swale Dr *CHPT/GREN* S35 ...... 73 E5
Swale Gdns *DARN/MH* S9 ...... 125 D3 🔲
Swale Rd *KIMB* S61 ...... 92 B3
Swallow Cl *BSLY* S70. ...... 36 A5
Swallow La *AU/AST/KP* S26. ...... 142 C4
Swallow Wood Ct *HAN/WDH* S13... 139 E4
Swamp Wk *ST/HB/BR* S6. ...... 108 B5
Swanbourne Pl *SHEFN* S5 ...... 99 D5 🔲

Swanbourne Rd *SHEFN* S5 .... 99 D4
Swanee Rd *BSLY* S70 .... 22 C4
Swannington Ct *DONS/BSCR* DN4 ... 47 E5
Swan Rd *AU/AST/KP* S26 .... 142 C4
Swan St *BTLY* DN5 .... 16 C5 **5**
RHAM S60 .... 103 E4
Swanwick St *CHNE* S41 .... 178 B4 **9**
Swarcliffe Rd *DARN/MH* S9 .... 124 B2
Sweyn Cft *BSLY* S70 .... 22 B5 **13**
Swifte Rd *RHAM* S60 .... 115 E1 **5**
Swift Ri *KIMB* S61 .... 76 B5
Swift Rd *CHPT/GREN* S35 .... 97 C1
Swift St *DOD/DAR* S75 .... 2 A3
Swift Wy *SHEFP/MNR* S2 .... 123 F5
Swinburne Av *DONS/BSCR* DN4 ... 63 F1 **11**
Swinburne Pl *RHAM/THRY* S65 ... 104 C3
Swinburne Rd *RHAM/THRY* S65 ... 104 C4
Swinscoe Wy *RCH* S42 .... 182 A4
Swinton Rd *MEX/SWTN* S64 .... 58 A4
Swinton St *OWL* S3 .... 9 E1
Sycamore Av *AU/AST/KP* S26 .... 155 F3
CHSW S40 .... 189 F3
DRON S18 .... 159 E5
Sycamore Crs *DEARNE* S63 .... 56 A3 **2**
Sycamore Dr *CHNE* S41 .... 191 E4
ECK/KIL S21 .... 166 A3
Sycamore Farm Cl *MALT* S66 .... 117 F1 **3**
Sycamore Gv *CONI* DN12 .... 84 B2 **1**
DONS/BSCR DN4 .... 47 D4
Sycamore House Rd *SHEFN* S5 .... 100 A3
Sycamore La *STV/CWN* S43 .... 180 B5
Sycamore Rd *CHPT/GREN* S35 .... 98 C1
MEX/SWTN S64 .... 57 F3
RHAM/THRY S65 .... 94 C5
STKB/PEN S36 .... 68 B3
STV/CWN S43 .... 180 A5
The Sycamores *BTLY* DN5 .... 28 A1
Sycamore St *DOD/DAR* S75 .... 13 D5 **4**
MOS S20 .... 152 A5
MOS S20 .... 153 D1 **6**
Sycamore Vw *BTLY* DN5 .... 42 B5
Sydney La *ST/HB/BR* S6 .... 121 E3
Sydney Rd *CHSW* S40 .... 10 A6
Sykes Av *DOD/DAR* S75 .... 2 A3
Sykes Ct *MEX/SWTN* S64 .... 81 E2
Sykes St *BSLY* S70 .... 21 E3
Sylvan Cl *CHNE* S41 .... 190 C3 **4**
Sylvester Av *DONS/BSCR* DN4 ... 44 A3
Sylvester Gdns *SHEF* S1 .... 122 B5
Sylvester St *SHEF* S1 .... 135 E1
Sylvia Cl *HAN/WDH* S13 .... 140 B3 **5**
Sylvia Rd *DRON* S18 .... 177 E1
Symes Gdns *DONS/BSCR* DN4 ... 47 D3
Symonds Av *RAW* S62 .... 79 D3
Symons Crs *SHEFN* S5 .... 98 A4

T

Tadcaster Cl *CONI* DN12 .... 83 F1
Tadcaster Crs *SHEFS* S8 .... 147 D1
Tadcaster Rd *SHEFS* S8 .... 147 D1
Tadcaster Wy *SHEFS* S8 .... 147 D1 **4**
Taddington Rd *CHSW* S40 .... 182 C4 **6**
Talbot Crs *CHNE* S41 .... 191 E5
SHEFP/MNR S2 .... 123 D5 **9**
Talbot Gdns *SHEFP/MNR* S2 .... 123 D5 **7**
Talbot Pl *SHEFP/MNR* S2 .... 123 D5 **8**
Talbot Rd *MEX/SWTN* S64 .... 58 A5
SHEFP/MNR S2 .... 123 D4 **0**
Talbot St *CHNE* S41 .... 191 E5
SHEFP/MNR S2 .... 123 D5
Talmont Rd *ECC* S11 .... 133 F4
Tanfield Rd *ST/HB/BR* S6 .... 108 B3
Tankersley La *HOY* S74 .... 50 A4
Tank Rw *BSLY* S70 .... 23 E1
Tannery Cl *HAN/WDH* S13 .... 139 F4
Tannery St *HAN/WDH* S13 .... 139 F4
Tansley Dr *CHSW* S40 .... 182 B4
DARN/MH S9 .... 100 C5
Tansley St *DARN/MH* S9 .... 100 C5
Tansley Wy *STV/CWN* S43 .... 187 D3
Tap La *CHSW* S40 .... 10 B6
Taplin Rd *ST/HB/BR* S6 .... 107 F4
Tapton Bank *FUL* S10 .... 120 B5 **1**
Tapton Crescent Rd *FUL* S10 .... 120 C5
Tapton Hill Rd *FUL* S10 .... 120 B4
Tapton House Rd *FUL* S10 .... 120 C5
Tapton La *CHNE* S41 .... 11 G5
Tapton Lock Hl *CHNE* S41 .... 184 C3
Tapton Ms *FUL* S10 .... 120 C4
Tapton Park Rd *FUL* S10 .... 133 D1
Tapton V *CHNE* S41 .... 185 D4
Tapton View Rd *CHNE* S41 .... 10 B2
Taptonville Crs *FUL* S10 .... 121 D5 **2**
Taptonville Rd *FUL* S10 .... 121 D4
Tapton Wy *STV/CWN* S43 .... 186 A5
Tasker Rd *FUL* S10 .... 120 C4
Tatenhill Gdns *DONS/BSCR* DN4 ... 67 E1
Taunton Av *DARN/MH* S9 .... 111 F1
Taunton Gdns *MEX/SWTN* S64 .... 59 B2
Taunton Gv *DARN/MH* S9 .... 111 F1 **1**
Taverner Cl *CHPT/GREN* S35 .... 73 E2

Taverner Cft *CHPT/GREN* S35 .... 73 F3 **3**
Taverner Wy *CHPT/GREN* S35 .... 73 F3
Tavistock Rd *SHEFS* S8 .... 135 D4
Tay Cl *DRON* S18 .... 168 B1
Taylor Crs *CHNE* S41 .... 191 E5
Taylor Rw *BSLY* S70 .... 22 A2 **12**
Taylors Av *RAW* S62 .... 93 F4
Taylors La *RAW* S62 .... 93 F3
Taylor St *CONI* DN12 .... 84 C3
T Benedict Ct *SHEFP/MNR* S2 ... 136 B2 **1**
Teesdale Rd *HACK/IN* S12 .... 151 D4
KIMB S61 .... 92 A3
Teeside Cl *BTLY* DN5 .... 28 B4
Telford Rd *BTLY* DN5 .... 29 C4
Telson Cl *MEX/SWTN* S64 .... 56 B5
Temperance St *MEX/SWTN* S64 ... 57 E5 **1**
Temple Gdns *DONS/BSCR* DN4 ... 47 D5
Temple Rd *RHAM* S60 .... 113 D1
Templestowe Ga *CONI* DN12 ... 85 F1 **1**
Temple Wy *BSLYN/ROY* S71 ... 15 E4 **1**
Ten Acre Rd *KIMB* S61 .... 102 A1
Tenby Gdns *DONS/BSCR* DN4 ... 43 E5
Tennyson Av *ARMTH* DN3 .... 33 F4
BTLY DN5 .... 29 D5
CHSW S40 .... 10 D5
MEX/SWTN S64 .... 58 C2
Tennyson Ri *DEARNE* S63 .... 55 D1
Tennyson Rd *BSLYN/ROY* S71 ... 3 H1
BTLY DN5 .... 29 D5
RHAM/THRY S65 .... 104 C3
ST/HB/BR S6 .... 121 E1
Ten Pound Wk *DONS/BSCR* DN4 ... 44 B4
Tenterden Rd *SHEFN* S5 .... 111 D1 **3**
Tenter La *DONS/BSCR* DN4 .... 62 A1
Tenter Rd *DONS/BSCR* DN4 .... 62 A1
Tenters Gn *BSLY* S70 .... 36 A1
Tenter St *RHAM* S60 .... 6 A3
SHEF S1 .... 8 D4
Terminus Rd *SHEFS* S8 .... 146 A2 **1**
Terrace Rd *RAW* S62 .... 94 A2
Terrey Rd *TOT/DORE* S17 .... 156 C3
Terry St *DARN/MH* S9 .... 111 F5
Tetney Rd *SHEFS* S10 .... 133 D1
Tewitt Rd *BTLY* DN5 .... 16 B2 **4**
Teynham Dr *SHEFN* S5 .... 109 D2
Teynham Rd *SHEFN* S5 .... 108 C2
Thackeray Av *RAW* S62 .... 80 C4
Thames St *RHAM* S60 .... 6 B4
Thealby Gdns *DONS/BSCR* DN4 ... 46 C5
Theatre La *BTLY* DN5 .... 11 C5 **1**
Thellusson Av *BTLY* DN5 .... 28 A3
Theobald Av *DONS/BSCR* DN4 ... 45 D2
Theobald Rd *DONS/BSCR* DN4 ... 44 C3 **1**
Thirlmere Dr *DRON* S18 .... 169 E1
Thirlmere Rd *BSLYN/ROY* S71 ... 3 F5
BSLYN/ROY S71 .... 3 F6
CHNE S41 .... 183 D2 **3**
CHNE S41 .... 183 D2
SHEFS S8 .... 134 C5 **3**
Thirlwall Av *CONI* DN12 .... 84 B1
Thirlwell Rd *SHEFS* S8 .... 135 E4
Thirsk Cl *CONI* DN12 .... 83 F1
Thomas St *BSLY* S70 .... 21 F2
BSLY S70 .... 36 B1 **6**
MEX/SWTN S64 .... 57 E5
MEX/SWTN S64 .... 81 F4
SHEF S1 .... 122 A5
Thompson Cl *CHNE* S41 .... 184 B1 **3**
RAW S62 .... 79 D3 **1**
Thompson Dr *MEX/SWTN* S64 ... 81 D2
Thompson Gdns
  CHPT/GREN S35 .... 73 D2 **3**
Thompson Hl *CHPT/GREN* S35 ... 73 D2 **3**
Thompson Rd *FUL* S10 .... 134 B1
  WMB/DAR S73 .... 39 E3
Thompson St *CHNE* S41 .... 184 B1
Thomson Av *DONS/BSCR* DN4 ... 43 D5
Thomson Cl *DEARNE* S63 .... 56 A2
Thoresby Av *BSLYN/ROY* S71 ... 14 C3
  DONS/BSCR DN4 .... 45 D3
Thoresby Cl *AU/AST/KP* S26 ... 143 D5
Thoresby Pl *STV/CWN* S43 .... 187 D3 **3**
Thoresby Rd *ST/HB/BR* S6 .... 108 A5
Thornborough Cl
  SHEFP/MNR S2 .... 136 A3 **1**
Thornborough Pl
  SHEFP/MNR S2 .... 136 A3 **2**
Thornborough Rd *SHEFP/MNR* S2 ... 135 F3 **3**
Thornbridge Av *HACK/IN* S12 ... 150 B2
Thornbridge Cl *HACK/IN* S12 ... 150 C2
Thornbridge Crs *HACK/IN* S12 ... 150 C2
Thornbridge Dr *HACK/IN* S12 ... 150 B2
Thornbridge Gv *HACK/IN* S12 ... 150 B2 **3**
Thornbridge La *HACK/IN* S12 ... 150 C2 **3**
Thornbridge Pl *HACK/IN* S12 ... 150 B2 **3**
Thornbridge Ri *HACK/IN* S12 ... 150 B2 **3**
Thornbridge Wy *HACK/IN* S12 ... 150 C2 **3**
Thornbrook Cl *CHPT/GREN* S35 ... 74 C5
Thornbrook Gdns *CHPT/GREN* S35 ... 74 B5
Thornbrook Ms *CHPT/GREN* S35 ... 74 B5 **3**
Thorncliffe La *CHPT/GREN* S35 ... 74 A4
Thorndale Ri *RHAM* S60 .... 114 B4
Thorndene Cl *CHNE* S41 .... 184 A3
Thorndon Wy *CHSW* S40 .... 189 D4

Thorne Cl *CHSW* S40 .... 182 A5 **5**
Thornely Av *DOD/DAR* S75 .... 20 A2
Thorne Rd *ABRD* S7 .... 134 C5 **5**
  ARMTH DN3 .... 19 F5
  DON DN1 .... 5 F3
Thornfield Av *CHSW* S40 .... 188 C3
Thorn Garth *BTLY* DN5 .... 29 E3
Thornham Cl *ARMTH* DN3 .... 33 F4 **3**
Thornhill Av *RHAM* S60 .... 113 F5
  WHHL DN2 .... 31 F3
Thornhill Edge *RHAM* S60 .... 6 A4
Thornhill Pl *DEARNE* S63 .... 55 F2 **3**
Thorn La *WHHL* DN2 .... 19 E4
Thornley Sq *DEARNE* S63 .... 26 B3 **3**
Thorn Rd *MEX/SWTN* S64 .... 81 E2
Thornsett Gdns *TOT/DORE* S17 ... 157 D1
Thornsett Rd *ECC* S11 .... 134 C2
Thorntondale Rd *BTLY* DN5 .... 28 B3
Thornton Pl *DRON* S18 .... 168 A2 **3**
Thornton Rd *BSLY* S70 .... 22 C3
Thornton St *KIMB* S61 .... 101 F4
Thornton Ter *BSLY* S70 .... 23 D3 **2**
Thorntree Cl *KIMB* S61 .... 90 A2 **3**
Thorntree La *DOD/DAR* S75 .... 13 E4 **3**
Thorntree Rd *KIMB* S61 .... 90 A3
Thornwell La *KIMB* S61 .... 76 A5
Thorogate *RAW* S62 .... 80 A4
Thorp Cl *SHEFP/MNR* S2 .... 135 E2
Thorpe Av *DRON* S18 .... 160 A4
Thorpe Cl *CHNE* S41 .... 184 A1 **5**
Thorpe Dr *MOS* S20 .... 152 C4
Thorpefield Cl *KIMB* S61 .... 90 A1
Thorpefield Dr *KIMB* S61 .... 90 A1
Thorpe Gn *MOS* S20 .... 152 B3 **4**
Thorpe House Av *SHEFS* S8 ... 147 E1
Thorpe House Ri *SHEFS* S8 ... 147 E1
Thorpe House Rd *SHEFS* S8 ... 147 E1
Thorpe St *KIMB* S61 .... 89 F1
Threshfield Wy *HACK/IN* S12 ... 151 F2 **3**
Thrush Av *RHAM* S60 .... 114 B4 **10**
Thrush St *ST/HB/BR* S6 .... 120 C1
Thrybergh Ct *CONI* DN12 .... 60 C5 **1**
Thrybergh Hall Rd *RAW* S62 ... 80 C5
Thundercliffe Rd *KIMB* S61 ... 100 C2
Thurnscoe Bridge La *DEARNE* S63 ... 27 D5
Thurstan Av *SHEFS* S8 .... 146 C5
Tiber Vw *RHAM* S60 .... 114 A2 **3**
Tickhill Rd *DONS/BSCR* DN4 ... 63 E1
Tickhill Sq *CONI* DN12 .... 60 A5
Tickhill St *CONI* DN12 .... 60 A4
Tideswell Cl *STV/CWN* S43 ... 186 C1
Tideswell Rd *SHEFN* S5 .... 99 E5
SHEFN S5 .... 110 A1
Tilford Rd *HAN/WDH* S13 .... 140 A4
Tillotson Cl *SHEFS* S8 .... 135 E4 **13**
Tillotson Ri *SHEFS* S8 .... 135 E4 **14**
Timothy Wood Av *BSLY* S70 ... 36 A5
Tingle Bridge Av *WMB/DAR* S73 ... 53 D1
Tingle Bridge Crs *WMB/DAR* S73 ... 53 D1 **3**
Tingle Bridge La *WMB/DAR* S73 ... 53 D1
Tingle Cl *WMB/DAR* S73 .... 53 D1
Tinker La *HOY* S74 .... 50 B2
  ST/HB/BR S6 .... 120 C2
Tinker Rd *RAW* S62 .... 80 B5
Tinsley Park Cl *DARN/MH* S9 ... 112 A5
Tinsley Park Rd *DARN/MH* S9 ... 111 F5
Tinsley Rd *HOY* S74 .... 51 E1
Tipton St *DARN/MH* S9 .... 111 E2
Tissington Cl *CHSW* S40 .... 182 C4
Tithe Barn Av *HAN/WDH* S13 ... 139 F3
Tithe Barn Cl *HAN/WDH* S13 ... 140 A3
Tithe Barn La *HAN/WDH* S13 ... 140 A4
Tithe Barn Wy *HAN/WDH* S13 ... 139 F3
Tithe Laithe *HOY* S74 .... 51 F2 **1**
Titterton Cl *DARN/MH* S9 .... 124 B1
Titterton St *DARN/MH* S9 .... 124 B1 **3**
Tiverton Cl *MEX/SWTN* S64 ... 81 E2 **3**
Tockwith Rd *DARN/MH* S9 ... 124 C2 **3**
Todmorden Cl *CONI* DN12 .... 59 F5
Todwick Rd *SHEFS* S8 .... 146 C4
Tofts La *ST/HB/BR* S6 .... 119 D3
Toftstead *ARMTH* DN3 .... 33 F4
Toftwood Av *FUL* S10 .... 120 B3 **1**
Toftwood Rd *FUL* S10 .... 120 C3
Togo St *DEARNE* S63 .... 26 C4 **1**
Toll Bar Av *HACK/IN* S12 ... 136 C5 **1**
Toll Bar Cl *HACK/IN* S12 .... 136 C5
Toll Bar Dr *HACK/IN* S12 .... 136 C5
Toll Bar Rd *MEX/SWTN* S64 ... 56 C5
  RHAM/THRY S65 .... 105 F5
Toll House Md *MOS* S20 .... 164 A1
Tom La *FUL* S10 .... 132 B1
Tomlinson Rd *HOY* S74 .... 52 A2
Tompson Hl *CHPT/GREN* S35 ... 72 C4
Tontine Rd *CHSW* S40 .... 190 B2 **4**
Tooker Rd *RHAM* S60 .... 103 F4
Topcliffe Rd *BSLYN/ROY* S71 ... 14 B2
Top Field La *RHAM/THRY* S65 ... 105 E1
Top Hall Rd *DONS/BSCR* DN4 ... 67 D2
Toppham Dr *SHEFS* S8 .... 159 D2
Toppham Rd *SHEFS* S8 .... 159 D2
Toppham Wy *SHEFS* S8 .... 159 D2
Top Pingle Ct *STV/CWN* S43 ... 185 F2
Top Side *CHPT/GREN* S35 .... 86 C5
Torbay Rd *ATT* S4 .... 110 B5

Tor Cl *BSLYN/ROY* S71 .... 14 B2
Torksey Cl *DONS/BSCR* DN4 .... 66 C2 🔢
Torksey Rd *DONS/BSCR* DN4 .... 99 E5
Torne Cl *DONS/BSCR* DN4 .... 67 E1
Torry Ct *HAN/WDH* S13 .... 140 A4
Torwood Dr *SHEFS* S8 .... 158 C1 🔢
Totley Brook Cl *TOT/DORE* S17 ... 156 B3 🔢
Totley Brook Cft *TOT/DORE* S17 .. 156 B3 🔢
Totley Brook Gln *TOT/DORE* S17 .... 156 B3 🔢
Totley Brook Gv *TOT/DORE* S17 .. 156 B3
Totley Brook Rd *TOT/DORE* S17 ... 156 B2
Totley Brook Wy *TOT/DORE* S17 .... 156 B3 🔢
Totley Grange Cl *TOT/DORE* S17 .. 156 B4 🔢
Totley Grange Rd *TOT/DORE* S17 .. 156 B4
Totley Hall La *TOT/DORE* S17 ...... 156 B4
Totley La *TOT/DORE* S17 .... 157 F3
Totley Mt *STV/CWN* S43 .... 185 E1
Towcester Wy *MEX/SWTN* S64 ..... 59 D2
Tower Cl *SHEFP/MNR* S2 .... 136 A2 🔢
Tower Dr *SHEFP/MNR* S2 .... 136 A2
Tower St *BSLY* S70 .... 21 F3
Town End *DRON* S18 .... 171 D2
Town End Av *AU/AST/KP* S26 ...... 142 B2
Townend Av *RHAM/THRY* S65 .... 95 F4
Townend Cl *RHAM* S60 .... 127 D3
Townend La *STKB/PEN* S36 .... 69 F4
Town End Rd *CHPT/GREN* S35 .... 98 A1
Townend St *FUL* S10 .... 121 D3
Town Fields Av *CHPT/GREN* S35 .... 98 C1
Townhead Rd *TOT/DORE* S17 .... 156 A2
Townhead Sd *SHEF* S1 .... 8 D5
Town La *KIMB* S61 .... 91 E4
Town Moor Mt *WHHL* DN2 .... 31 D5
Town St *DARN/MH* S9 .... 112 B1
RHAM S60 .... 103 E5
Toyne St *FUL* S10 .... 120 C3
Trafalgar Rd *ST/HB/BR* S6 .... 97 D5
Trafalgar St *SHEF* S1 .... 8 C6
Traffic Ter *STV/CWN* S43 .... 180 C2
Trafford Ct *DON* DN1 .... 4 C4 🔢
Trafford Wy *DON* DN1 .... 4 C4
Tranmoor Av *DONS/BSCR* DN4 ..... 46 C5
Tranmoor Ct *HOY* S74 .... 50 C3 🔢
Tranmoor La *ARMTH* DN3 .... 33 F4
Trans Pennine Trail *CONI* DN12 .... 60 D3
DARN/MH S9 .... 111 D5
ECK/KIL S21 .... 175 F2
HAN/WDH S13 .... 138 C1
KIMB S61 .... 102 A4
RAW S62 .... 51 E5
Trap La *ECC* S11 .... 132 C3
Travey Rd *SHEFP/MNR* S2 .... 137 E3 🔢
Travis Gdns *DONS/BSCR* DN4 .... 43 D3
Travis Pl *FUL* S10 .... 121 F5
Tredis Cl *BSLYN/ROY* S71 .... 3 H2
Treecrest Rd *DOD/DAR* S75 .... 13 F5
Treefield Cl *KIMB* S61 .... 92 B3
Treelands *DOD/DAR* S75 .... 12 C4
Treeneuk Cl *CHSW* S40 .... 188 C1 🔢
Tree Root Wk *FUL* S10 .... 121 E4 🔢
Treeton La *AU/AST/KP* S26 .... 128 C4
RHAM S60 .... 127 E2
Treetown Crs *RHAM* S60 .... 127 F2
Treherne Rd *RHAM/THRY* S65 ..... 104 A4
Trelawney Wk *BSLY* S70 .... 22 A5 🔢
Trent Cl *CONI* DN12 .... 62 A4
Trent Gv *DRON* S18 .... 159 F5
Trentham Cl *RHAM* S60 .... 114 B4 🔢
Trenton Cl *HAN/WDH* S13 .... 140 B4
Trenton Ri *HAN/WDH* S13 .... 140 B4
Trent St *DARN/MH* S9 .... 123 F1
Treswell Crs *ST/HB/BR* S6 .... 108 A4 🔢
Trewan Cl *BSLYN/ROY* S71 .... 14 C3 🔢
Tricket Rd *CHPT/GREN* S35 .... 73 C3
Trickett Rd *ST/HB/BR* S6 .... 108 A5
Trinity Cl *CHNE* S41 .... 10 D3
Trinity St *OWL* S3 .... 8 D3
Trippet La *SHEF* S1 .... 8 D5
Tristford Cl *RHAM* S60 .... 127 E1
Troon Cl *CHSW* S40 .... 189 D4
Troughbrook Rd *STV/CWN* S43 ... 180 C3
Troutbeck Cl *DEARNE* S63 .... 26 C4
Troutbeck Rd *SHEFS* S8 .... 146 C3
Trueman Ter *BSLYN/ROY* S71 ...... 15 F5 🔢
Truman Gv *STKB/PEN* S36 .... 70 A2 🔢
Truman St *BTLY* DN5 .... 16 B5
Truro Av *WHHL* DN2 .... 32 A1
Truro Ct *BSLYN/ROY* S71 .... 14 C4 🔢
Truswell Av *FUL* S10 .... 120 B3
Truswell Rd *FUL* S10 .... 120 B4
Tudor Rd *WHHL* DN2 .... 31 F5
Tudor St *DEARNE* S63 .... 27 E3
Tudor Wy *BSLY* S70 .... 22 B5
Tuffolds Cl *SHEFP/MNR* S2 .... 137 E3
Tulip Tree Cl *MOS* S20 .... 141 E5
Tullibardine Rd *ECC* S11 .... 133 F4
Tummon Rd *SHEFP/MNR* S2 .... 123 F5
Tummon St *KIMB* S61 .... 102 C3 🔢
Tune St *BSLY* S70 .... 22 B2
WMB/DAR S73 .... 39 D3
Tunstall Gn *CHSW* S40 .... 189 E3
Tunstall Wy *CHSW* S40 .... 189 E3

Tunwell Av *SHEFN* S5 .... 98 C2
Tunwell Dr *SHEFN* S5 .... 98 C2
Tunwell Greave *SHEFN* S5 .... 98 C2
Turie Av *SHEFN* S5 .... 98 B3
Turie Crs *SHEFN* S5 .... 98 B3
Turnberry Cl *CHSW* S40 .... 189 D4 🔢
Turnberry Ct *BTLY* DN5 .... 29 E1 🔢
Turner Av *WMB/DAR* S73 .... 38 C2
Turner Cl *DRON* S18 .... 169 D2 🔢
RAW S62 .... 94 B2
Turner Dr *STV/CWN* S43 .... 186 C2
Turner La *RHAM* S60 .... 115 F5
Turner's Cl *HOY* S74 .... 52 A1
Turners La *FUL* S10 .... 121 D5 🔢
Turner St *SHEFP/MNR* S2 .... 122 C5
Turnesc Gv *DEARNE* S63 .... 27 D4
Turnoaks La *CHSW* S40 .... 190 B5
Turnpike Cft *CHPT/GREN* S35 ...... 87 D5 🔢
Turnshaw Av *AU/AST/KP* S26 ..... 142 A1
Twibell St *BSLYN/ROY* S71 .... 3 F2
The Twenty Lands *RHAM* S60 ..... 127 F4
Twentywell Dr *TOT/DORE* S17 .... 157 F2 🔢
Twentywell La *TOT/DORE* S17 .... 157 F1
Twentywell Ri *TOT/DORE* S17 .... 157 F1
Twentywell Rd *TOT/DORE* S17 .... 157 F2
Twentywell Vw *TOT/DORE* S17 ... 157 F3
Twickenham Cl *MOS* S20 .... 164 C2 🔢
Twickenham Crs *MOS* S20 .... 164 C3
Twickenham Gld *MOS* S20 .... 164 C2 🔢
Twickenham Gln *MOS* S20 .... 165 D3 🔢
Twickenham Gv *MOS* S20 .... 164 C2 🔢
Twitchill Dr *HAN/WDH* S13 .... 139 F4
Twyford Cl *MEX/SWTN* S64 .... 56 B5
Tyas Pl *MEX/SWTN* S64 .... 58 C3 🔢
Tyas Rd *SHEFN* S5 .... 98 B2
Tye Rd *MOS* S20 .... 153 E2
Tyler St *DARN/MH* S9 .... 111 F1
Tyler Wy *DARN/MH* S9 .... 111 F1
Tylney Rd *CHSW* S40 .... 188 C5
SHEFP/MNR S2 .... 136 B1
Tynker Av *MOS* S20 .... 153 E2
Tyzack Rd *SHEFS* S8 .... 146 C3

U

Ulley Crs *HAN/WDH* S13 .... 137 F3
Ulley La *AU/AST/KP* S26 .... 129 F4
AU/AST/KP S26 .... 142 C2
Ulley Rd *HAN/WDH* S13 .... 137 F3
Ulley Vw *AU/AST/KP* S26 .... 129 E5
Ullswater Av *MOS* S20 .... 164 C4
Ullswater Cl *DRON* S18 .... 168 C1
MOS S20 .... 164 C2
Ullswater Dr *DRON* S18 .... 168 C2
Ullswater Pl *DRON* S18 .... 168 C2
Ullswater Rd *BSLYN/ROY* S71 ..... 24 C2 🔢
MEX/SWTN S64 .... 59 C2
SHEFS S8 .... 146 C1
Ulverston Rd *CHNE* S41 .... 183 E2
Underbank La *SHEFS* S8 .... 147 D1
Undercliffe Rd *ST/HB/BR* S6 ...... 120 A1 🔢
Underhill *BSLY* S70 .... 36 C1
Underhill La *ST/HB/BR* S6 .... 96 C4
Underwood Av *BSLY* S70 .... 22 C4
Underwood La *SHEFS* S8 .... 147 D1
Union Cl *BSLY* S70 .... 22 A2
Union La *SHEF* S1 .... 122 B5 🔢
Union Rd *ECC* S11 .... 134 B4
Union St *BSLY* S70 .... 22 A2
DON DN1 .... 4 D5
KIMB S61 .... 102 C3
SHEF S1 .... 122 B5 🔢
Unity Pl *RHAM* S60 .... 6 D6
Unstone-Dronfield By-pass
DRON S18 .... 159 D3
Unstone Hl *DRON* S18 .... 159 D3
Unstone Rd *DRON* S18 .... 170 B3
Unstone St *SHEFP/MNR* S2 .... 135 E1
Upland Ri *CHSW* S40 .... 189 E3
Uplands Rd *RAW* S62 .... 79 F5
Upper Albert Rd *SHEFS* S8 .... 135 F5
Upper Allen St *OWL* S3 .... 8 B4
Upper Clara St *KIMB* S61 .... 102 A3
Upper Croft Cl *STV/CWN* S43 ..... 185 F2
Upper Folderings *DOD/DAR* S75 ... 20 A3 🔢
Upper Gate Rd *ST/HB/BR* S6 ...... 118 C2
Upper Hanover St *OWL* S3 .... 8 A6
OWL S3 .... 121 F5 🔢
Upper Hoyland Rd *HOY* S74 .... 51 D1
Upper Ley Cft *CHPT/GREN* S35 ..... 88 B1 🔢
Upper Ley Dell *CHPT/GREN* S35 ... 88 B1 🔢
Upper Moor St *CHSW* S40 .... 188 C2 🔢
Upper Newbold Cl *CHSW* S40 ..... 182 C2 🔢
Upper New St *BSLY* S70 .... 22 A2 🔢
Upper Rye Cl *RHAM* S60 .... 116 B3
Upper School La *DRON* S18 .... 169 E3 🔢
DRON S18 .... 169 E3 🔢
Upper Sheffield Rd *BSLY* S70 ...... 22 B4
Upperthorpe *ST/HB/BR* S6 .... 121 E2
Upperthorpe Gln *ST/HB/BR* S6 ... 121 E2 🔢
Upperthorpe Rd *ECK/KIL* S21 .... 166 B3

ST/HB/BR S6 .... 8 A2
Upper Valley Rd *SHEFS* S8 .... 135 F5
Upper Whiston La *RHAM* S60 ..... 116 A5
Upperwood Rd *WMB/DAR* S73 ..... 25 F4
Upper Wortley Rd *KIMB* S61 .... 90 A3
Upton Cl *WMB/DAR* S73 .... 38 C1
Upwell Hl *ATT* S4 .... 110 C3
Upwell La *ATT* S4 .... 110 C3
Upwell St *ATT* S4 .... 110 C3
Upwood Cl *CHSW* S40 .... 182 B4 🔢
Upwood Rd *ST/HB/BR* S6 .... 107 F5
Urban Rd *DONS/BSCR* DN4 .... 43 F5
Urch Cl *CONI* DN12 .... 85 D2
Uttley Cl *DARN/MH* S9 .... 124 C1
Uttley Cft *DARN/MH* S9 .... 124 C1
Uttley Dr *DARN/MH* S9 .... 124 C1
Uttoxeter Av *MEX/SWTN* S64 ...... 59 D2

V

Vaal St *BSLY* S70 .... 22 C2
Vainor Rd *ST/HB/BR* S6 .... 107 E2
Vale Cl *DRON* S18 .... 169 F2 🔢
Vale Gv *ST/HB/BR* S6 .... 106 C4
Valentine Cl *SHEFN* S5 .... 99 D4
Valentine Crs *SHEFN* S5 .... 99 D4
Valentine Rd *SHEFN* S5 .... 99 D4
Vale Rd *OWL* S3 .... 109 D5
Valiant Gdns *BTLY* DN5 .... 42 C1
Valley Dr *DEARNE* S63 .... 55 E2
ECK/KIL S21 .... 166 B1 🔢
Valley Rd *CHNE* S41 .... 191 D2
CHPT/GREN S35 .... 73 F5
ECK/KIL S21 .... 166 B1
HACK/IN S12 .... 152 A3
MEX/SWTN S64 .... 80 C1
SHEFS S8 .... 135 E4
WMB/DAR S73 .... 25 F2
Valley View Cl *CHNE* S41 .... 191 F5
ECK/KIL S21 .... 174 A1 🔢
Valley Wy *HOY* S74 .... 51 F2
Varney Rd *DEARNE* S63 .... 55 F3
Vaughan Av *DON* DN1 .... 5 F2
Vaughan Rd *DOD/DAR* S75 .... 12 C4 🔢
Vaughton Hl *STKB/PEN* S36 .... 70 B2
Vauxhall Cl *DARN/MH* S9 .... 100 C5
Vauxhall Rd *DARN/MH* S9 .... 100 C5
Velvet Wood Cl *DOD/DAR* S75 ..... 12 B4
Ventnor Cl *DONS/BSCR* DN4 .... 43 D5 🔢
Ventnor Pl *ABRD* S7 .... 135 D2 🔢
Venture Wy *CHNE* S41 .... 178 A5
Venus Ct *RHAM* S60 .... 114 A2
Verdant Wy *SHEFN* S5 .... 99 E4
Vereist Av *AU/AST/KP* S26 .... 142 B1
Vere Rd *ST/HB/BR* S6 .... 108 A2
Vernon Av *BSLY* S70 .... 22 A3
Vernon Crs *BSLY* S70 .... 22 A5
Vernon Delph *FUL* S10 .... 120 A4
Vernon Dr *CHPT/GREN* S35 .... 74 A5
Vernon Rd *BSLY* S70 .... 22 A5
CHSW S40 .... 189 E1
RHAM/THRY S65 .... 115 F1
TOT/DORE S17 .... 156 C2
Vernon St *BSLY* S70 .... 50 A2
BSLYN/ROY S71 .... 3 E3
HOY S74 .... 51 D3
Vernon St North *BSLYN/ROY* S71 ... 3 E3
Vernon Ter *FUL* S10 .... 120 B5
Vernon Wy *DOD/DAR* S75 .... 12 C4
Vesey St *RAW* S62 .... 94 A2
Vicarage Crs *CHPT/GREN* S35 ...... 97 D1
DONS/BSCR DN4 .... 47 F5
HOY S74 .... 51 F2 🔢
MEX/SWTN S64 .... 59 D4
RHAM/THRY S65 .... 105 E1
Vicarage Cft *CHPT/GREN* S35 ...... 97 D1
Vicarage La *TOT/DORE* S17 .... 156 B1
Vicarage Rd *CHPT/GREN* S35 ...... 97 D1
DARN/MH S9 .... 111 D5
Vicarage Wy *BTLY* DN5 .... 11 F6
Vicar La *CHSW* S40 .... 11 F6
HAN/WDH S13 .... 139 F3
SHEF S1 .... 9 E4
Vicar Rd *DEARNE* S63 .... 55 E1
Vickers Dr *SHEFN* S5 .... 110 B1
Vickers Rd *CHPT/GREN* S35 .... 73 E4
SHEFN S5 .... 110 B2
Victoria Av *RHAM/THRY* S65 .... 7 H6
Victoria Cl *STKB/PEN* S36 .... 68 C2
Victoria Ct *BTLY* DN5 .... 16 C3
Victoria Crs *DOD/DAR* S75 .... 49 F1 🔢
DOD/DAR S75 .... 2 A3
Victoria Crs West *DOD/DAR* S75 .... 2 A4
Victoria Gv *STV/CWN* S43 .... 186 A4
Victorian Crs *WHHL* DN2 .... 31 D5
Victoria Park Rd *STV/CWN* S43 ... 186 A4
Victoria Rd *BSLY* S70 .... 2 B3
BTLY DN5 .... 16 C4
DEARNE S63 .... 55 E1
DONS/BSCR DN4 .... 43 F4
FUL S10 .... 134 C1
MEX/SWTN S64 .... 58 B3
MOS S20 .... 153 D1

RAW S62 .... **94** A2
STKB/PEN S36 .... **69** D2
WMB/DAR S73 .... **39** D2
Victoria Station Rd ATT S4 .... **9** C3
Victoria St BSLY S70
  BSLY S70 .... **23** E2
  CHNE S41 .... **11** E4
  DRON S18 .... **169** D1
  HOY S74 .... **52** A2
  MEX/SWTN S64 .... **57** F3
  MEX/SWTN S64 .... **81** F4
  OWL S3 .... **8** B6
  RHAM S60 .... **102** C3
  RHAM S60 .... **127** E1
  STKB/PEN S36 .... **68** C2
  STV/CWN S43 .... **180** A5
Victoria St North CHNE S41 .... **178** A4
Victoria St West CHSW S40 .... **189** D2
Victoria Ter BSLY S70 .... **22** B2 🔟
Victor Rd TOT/DORE S17 .... **157** D1
Victor St ST/HB/BR S6 .... **108** B5
View Rd RHAM/THRY S65 .... **104** B1
  SHEFS S8 .... **135** E3
Viewtree La RAW S62 .... **75** E2
Vikinglea Cl SHEFP/MNR S2 .... **137** F2 🔟
Vikinglea Dr SHEFP/MNR S2 .... **137** F2
Vikinglea Gld SHEFP/MNR S2 ... **137** F1 🔟
Vikinglea Rd SHEFP/MNR S2 .... **137** F1
Villa Gdns BTLY DN5 .... **16** B1
Villa Park Rd DONS/BSCR DN4 ..... **46** C4
Villiers Cl SHEFP/MNR S2 .... **136** C5
Villiers Dr SHEFP/MNR S2 .... **136** C4
Vincent Crs CHSW S40 .... **188** C2
Vincent La CHSW S40 .... **188** C2
Vincent Rd ECC S11 .... **135** D2
Vine Cl BSLYN/ROY S71 .... **15** D3
  RHAM S60 .... **6** A5
Viola Bank STKB/PEN S36 .... **69** D4
Violet Av MOS S20 .... **152** C2
Violet Bank Rd ABRD S7 ...... **134** C4 🔟
Vivian Rd SHEFN S5 .... **110** B2
Vizard Rd HOY S74 .... **52** A2
Vulcan Rd DARN/MH S9 .... **111** F3

W

Wadbrough Rd FUL S10 .... **134** B1
Waddington Rd DOD/DAR S75 ..... **12** C5
Wade Cl RHAM S60 .... **104** A5
Wade Meadow ST/HB/BR S6 ...... **107** E3 🔟
Wade St ATT S4 .... **110** C3 🔟
  DOD/DAR S75 .... **12** C5
Wadsley La ST/HB/BR S6 .... **107** E2 🔟
Wadsley Park Crs ST/HB/BR S6 ... **107** E2
Wadsworth Av HACK/IN S12 .... **38** C2 🔟
Wadsworth Cl HACK/IN S12 .... **138** B5 🔟
Wadsworth Dr HACK/IN S12 .... **138** B4
  RAW S62 .... **79** D3
Wadsworth Rd HACK/IN S12 .... **138** A5 🔟
Wadworth Ri RHAM/THRY S65 ..... **95** F5
Wadworth St CONI DN12 .... **60** B5
Wagon Rd KIMB S61 .... **92** C3
Waingate OWL S3 .... **9** F4
Wainwright Av HAN/WDH S13 ..... **138** B2
  WMB/DAR S73 .... **38** C2
Wainwright Crs HAN/WDH S13 .... **138** A2
Wainwright Pl WMB/DAR S73 ...... **38** C2 🔟
Wainwright Rd DONS/BSCR DN4 ... **5** H6
  KIMB S61 .... **92** A5 🔟
Wakefield Cl BSLYN/ROY S71 .... **14** A1
Wake Rd ABRD S7 .... **134** C3
Walbert Av DEARNE S63 .... **26** C4
Walbrook BSLY S70 .... **36** C1
Walden Rd SHEFP/MNR S2 .... **135** F3
Walders Av STKB/PEN S36 .... **107** E2
Walders La STKB/PEN S36 .... **69** D5
Wales Pl AU/AST/KP S26 .... **121** E1
Wales Rd AU/AST/KP S26 .... **155** F3
Waleswood Rd AU/AST/KP S26 ... **154** A1
Waleswood Vw AU/AST/KP S26 ... **142** B4
Walford Rd FUL/KIL S21 .... **166** A2
Walgrove Av CHSW S40 .... **189** E3
Walgrove Rd CHSW S40 .... **189** E2 🔟
Walker Cl CHPT/GREN S35 .... **97** D1
Walker La RHAM/THRY S65 .... **7** F5
  KIMB S61 .... **92** A5
Walker St MEX/SWTN S64 .... **57** F5
  OWL S3 .... **9** G2
  RAW S62 .... **80** C5
Walker Vw RAW S62 .... **80** C5
Walkley Bank Cl ST/HB/BR S6 .... **121** D1
Walkley Bank Rd ST/HB/BR S6 .... **120** C1
Walkley Crescent Rd
  ST/HB/BR S6 .... **120** C1
Walkley La ST/HB/BR S6 .... **108** A4
Walkley Rd ST/HB/BR S6 .... **121** D1
Walkley St ST/HB/BR S6 .... **121** E2
Walkley Ter ST/HB/BR S6 .... **120** B1
The Walk BSLY S70 .... **49** F2
Wallace Rd DONS/BSCR DN4 .... **62** C1

OWL S3 .... **122** A1
Waller Rd ST/HB/BR S6 .... **120** B2
Walling Cl DARN/MH S9 .... **111** F2
Walling Rd DARN/MH S9 .... **111** F2 🔟
Wall St BSLY S70 .... **21** F2
Walney Fold BSLYN/ROY S71 .... **15** E1 🔟
Walnut Dr ECK/KIL S21 .... **166** A3 🔟
Walnut Gv MEX/SWTN S64 .... **58** A2
Walnut Pl CHPT/GREN S35 .... **88** A2
Walpole Cl DONS/BSCR DN4 .... **63** D2
Walpole Gv AU/AST/KP S26 .... **142** B1
Walsham Dr BTLY DN5 .... **28** C4
Walter St RHAM S60 .... **6** A4
  ST/HB/BR S6 .... **108** B5 🔟
Waltham Gdns MOS S20 .... **153** E5 🔟
Waltham St BSLY S70 .... **22** A2
Waltheof Rd SHEFP/MNR S2 .... **137** D2
Walton Back La RCH S42 .... **188** A4
Walton Cl CHPT/GREN S35 .... **73** D3 🔟
  CHSW S40 .... **188** C4 🔟
  DRON S18 .... **168** A1
Walton Crs CHSW S40 .... **189** E3
Walton Dr CHSW S40 .... **189** E3
Walton Fields Rd CHSW S40 .... **189** E2
Walton Rd CHSW S40 .... **189** E3
  FUL S10 .... **134** B1
Walton St DOD/DAR S75 .... **13** D4
Walton St North DOD/DAR S75 .... **12** C4
Walton Wk CHSW S40 .... **189** F2
Wannop St RAW S62 .... **94** A3
Wansfell Rd ATT S4 .... **111** D3
The Wapping RHAM/THRY S65 ..... **85** E4
Warburton Cl SHEFP/MNR S2 ..... **136** A3 🔟
Warburton Gdns
  SHEFP/MNR S2 .... **136** A3 🔟
Warburton Rd SHEFP/MNR S2 .... **136** A3
Warde Av DONS/BSCR DN4 .... **63** D1
Warden Cl DONS/BSCR DN4 .... **47** E4
Warden St RHAM S60 .... **114** B1
Wardgate Wy CHSW S40 .... **182** B4
Ward La STV/CWN S43 .... **167** F5
Wardlow Cl CHSW S40 .... **190** A4
Wardlow Rd HACK/IN S12 .... **138** B5
Ward Pl SHEFP/MNR S2 .... **135** D2 🔟
Wardsend Rd SHEFN S5 .... **108** B3
Wardsend Rd North ST/HB/BR S6 ... **108** A1
Ward St OWL S3 .... **8** D2
Wareham Ct MOS S20 .... **153** E5 🔟
Wareham Gv DOD/DAR S75 .... **20** B2
Warehouse La DEARNE S63 .... **55** F2
Warminster Cl SHEFS S8 .... **147** F1
Warminster Crs SHEFS S8 .... **147** F1
Warminster Dr SHEFS S8 .... **147** F2 🔟
Warminster Pl SHEFS S8 .... **147** F3
Warminster Rd SHEFS S8 .... **147** E1
Warmsworth Rd DONS/BSCR DN4 ... **62** C1
Warner Av DOD/DAR S75 .... **12** C5
Warner Pl DOD/DAR S75 .... **13** D5
Warner Rd DOD/DAR S75 .... **12** C5
  ST/HB/BR S6 .... **107** F3
Warner St CHNE S41 .... **190** C3 🔟
Warnington Dr ARMTH DN3 .... **67** F3
  DONS/BSCR DN4 .... **67** E2
Warning Tongue La ARMTH DN3 ... **67** F4
Warren Av RAW S62 .... **79** F4
Warren Cl DONS/BSCR DN4 .... **62** A1
  WHHL DN2 .... **31** E5
Warren Crs BSLY S70 .... **22** A3
  ECK/KIL S21 .... **172** C1
Warren Dr KIMB S61 .... **102** A1
Warren Gdns CHPT/GREN S35 ...... **74** B3
Warren Hl KIMB S61 .... **102** A1
Warren La CHPT/GREN S35 .... **74** C3
  DONS/BSCR DN4 .... **67** D2
  HOY S74 .... **74** A2
Warren Mt KIMB S61 .... **102** A1
Warren Pl BSLY S70 .... **22** A3 🔟
Warren Quarry La BSLY S70 .... **22** A2
Warren Ri DRON S18 .... **160** A5
Warren St ATT S4 .... **123** E2
Warren V MEX/SWTN S64 .... **80** B2
  RAW S62 .... **80** B4
Warren Vale MEX/SWTN S64 .... **56** B5
Warren Vw HOY S74 .... **51** D4
Warrington Rd FUL S10 .... **121** E3 🔟
Warris Cl KIMB S61 .... **91** F5
Warris Pl SHEFP/MNR S2 .... **123** E4
Warwick Cl KIMB S61 .... **91** F5
Warwick Dr WHHL DN2 .... **31** F4
Warwick St CHSW S40 .... **190** C5
  FUL S10 .... **121** D3 🔟
  RHAM/THRY S65 .... **103** F4
Warwick Ter FUL S10 .... **121** D3 🔟
Wasdale Av MOS S20 .... **164** C2 🔟
Wasdale Cl MOS S20 .... **164** C2
Washfield Crs RHAM S60 .... **127** F3
Washfield La RHAM S60 .... **127** F4
Washford Rd DARN/MH S9 .... **123** F1
Wash House La CHSW S40 .... **189** D2
Washington Av CONI DN12 .... **84** A1
  WMB/DAR S73 .... **38** C3
Washington Gv BTLY DN5 .... **29** E2
Washington Rd CHPT/GREN S35 ... **88** C5
  ECC S11 .... **135** D2
Washington St MEX/SWTN S64 ..... **58** C3
Watch House La BTLY DN5 .... **29** D3

Watch St HAN/WDH S13 .... **140** B2
Waterdale DON DN1 .... **5** E5
Waterdale Cl BTLY DN5 .... **42** B4 🔟
Waterdale Rd BSLY S70 .... **36** A1
Waterfield Ms MOS S20 .... **152** C4 🔟
Waterfield Pl BSLYN/ROY S71 .... **23** F2 🔟
Waterford Rd OWL S3 .... **108** C5
Waterhouse Cl RHAM/THRY S65 ... **95** F5
Water La RAW S62 .... **52** B5
  RHAM S60 .... **103** E4
  TOT/DORE S17 .... **157** D1
Waterloo Rd BSLY S70 .... **2** A6
  BSLY S70 .... **21** E1 🔟
Waterloo Wk OWL S3 .... **8** C1
Watermeade ECK/KIL S21 .... **175** F1
Water Meadow La CHSW S40 ..... **182** C3
Water Royd Dr DOD/DAR S75 .... **20** A3
Water Slacks Cl HAN/WDH S13 ... **139** F4 🔟
Water Slacks Dr HAN/WDH S13 ... **139** F4
Water Slacks Rd HAN/WDH S13 ... **139** F4
Watersmeet Rd ST/HB/BR S6 ..... **107** F5
Water St OWL S3 .... **9** E3
  RHAM S60 .... **6** D4
Waterthorpe Cl MOS S20 .... **153** D5 🔟
Waterthorpe Crs MOS S20 .... **153** D5
Waterthorpe Gdns MOS S20 .... **152** C5
Waterthorpe Gln MOS S20 .... **153** D5 🔟
Waterthorpe Greenway MOS S20 ... **152** D2
Waterthorpe Ri MOS S20 .... **153** D5
Watery St OWL S3 .... **8** B2
Wath Rd ABRD S7 .... **134** C4
  HOY S74 .... **52** B4
  MEX/SWTN S64 .... **57** E2
  WMB/DAR S73 .... **40** A4
Wath Wood Bottom DEARNE S63 ... **55** F5
Wath Wood Dr DEARNE S63 .... **56** A5
Wath Wood Rd DEARNE S63 .... **56** A4
Watkinson Gdns MOS S20 .... **152** C5
Watson Cl KIMB S61 .... **102** A1
Watson Gln KIMB S61 .... **101** D1
Watson Rd FUL S10 .... **121** D5 🔟
  KIMB S61 .... **102** A1
Watson St HOY S74 .... **50** C3 🔟
Watt La FUL S10 .... **120** A5
Waverley Av CONI DN12 .... **85** D1
  DONS/BSCR DN4 .... **42** C5
Waverley Ct BTLY DN5 .... **16** B2
Waverley Rd DARN/MH S9 .... **125** D3 🔟
Waverley Vw RHAM S60 .... **127** D2
Wavecliffe BSLYN/ROY S71 .... **15** D3
Wayford Av CHNE S41 .... **190** C3 🔟
Wayland Av BSLY S70 .... **22** A5
Wayland Rd ECC S11 .... **134** B2
Wayside STV/CWN S43 .... **185** E1
Wayside Ct STV/CWN S43 .... **185** E1 🔟
Weakland Cl HACK/IN S12 .... **151** D3
Weakland Crs HACK/IN S12 .... **151** D3
Weakland Dr HACK/IN S12 .... **151** D2
Weakland Wy HACK/IN S12 .... **151** D2 🔟
Weavers Cl CHPT/GREN S35 .... **87** D5
Webb Av STKB/PEN S36 .... **69** F3
Webbs Av ST/HB/BR S6 .... **119** F1
Webster Cl KIMB S61 .... **101** E1 🔟
Webster Crs KIMB S61 .... **101** E1
Webster Cft CHNE S41 .... **178** C4 🔟
Wedgewood Cl RAW S62 .... **94** A1
Weedon St DARN/MH S9 .... **111** F2
Weetwood Dr ECC S11 .... **133** F5 🔟
Weetwood Rd RHAM S60 .... **115** D2
Weigh La SHEFP/MNR S2 .... **123** D4 🔟
Weir Head DARN/MH S9 .... **111** F3
Welbeck Cl DRON S18 .... **168** A1
  STV/CWN S43 .... **187** E3
Welbeck Dr AU/AST/KP S26 .... **143** D3
Welbeck Rd DONS/BSCR DN4 ...... **45** D2
Welbeck St DOD/DAR S75 .... **13** E5
Welbury Gdns MOS S20 .... **164** C2
Welby Pl SHEFS S8 .... **147** D1
Welfare Av CHSW S40 .... **189** E1
  CONI DN12 .... **84** B1
Welfare Rd DEARNE S63 .... **26** C3
Welham Dr RHAM S60 .... **103** F5
Welland Cl OWL S3 .... **122** A1
Welland Crs HOY S74 .... **52** B2
Wellbeck Rd ST/HB/BR S6 .... **120** C1
Wellcarr Rd SHEFS S8 .... **147** E3
Wellcroft Cl WHHL DN2 .... **32** A3
Wellesley Rd FUL S10 .... **121** E4
Wellfield Cl HACK/IN S12 .... **150** C4
  ST/HB/BR S6 .... **121** E2
Wellfield Rd DOD/DAR S75 .... **13** E4
  KIMB S61 .... **91** F4
  ST/HB/BR S6 .... **121** E2
Wellgate CONI DN12 .... **85** D1
  RHAM/THRY S65 .... **6** D5
Wellgate Mt RHAM/THRY S65 .... **7** E6
Well Green Rd ST/HB/BR S6 .... **118** C2
Wellhead Rd SHEFS S8 .... **135** E4 🔟
Wellington Cl BSLYN/ROY S71 ...... **14** C3
Wellington Crs BSLY S70 .... **23** D5
Wellington Gv BTLY DN5 .... **29** E2
Wellington Rd ST/HB/BR S6 .... **119** F2

Wellington St *BSLY* S70 .... **2** D6 🔢
   MEX/SWTN S64 .... **58** B3
   SHEF S1 .... **8** D6
   STV/CWN S43 .... **179** D1
Welling Wy *KIMB* S61 .... **101** F2
Well La *AU/AST/KP* S26 .... **129** D5
   BSLYN/ROY S71 .... **15** D2
   RHAM S60 .... **115** F3 🔢
   RHAM S60 .... **116** B5
   RHAM S60 .... **127** F3
   ST/HB/BR S6 .... **107** D2
Well Meadow Dr *OWL* S3 .... **8** B4
Well Meadow St *OWL* S3 .... **8** B3
Well St *SHEFS* S8 .... **135** E4 🔢
Well Rd *SHEFS* S8 .... **135** E4 🔢
Well Spring Cl *STV/CWN* S43 .... **185** F2 🔢
Wells Rd *WHHL* DN2 .... **31** D3
Well St *BSLY* S70 .... **2** A6
Well View Rd *KIMB* S61 .... **101** E1
Welney Pl *ST/HB/BR* S6 .... **97** D5
Welton Cl *DONS/BSCR* DN4 .... **66** A4
Welwyn Cl *DONS/BSCR* DN4 .... **189** E1
   HACK/IN S12 .... **149** F1 🔢
Welwyn Rd *HACK/IN* S12 .... **149** F1
Wembley Cl *CONI* DN12 .... **84** B1
Wembley Cl *WHHL* DN2 .... **32** A3 🔢
Wendel Gv *HOY* S74 .... **52** C2 🔢
Wenlock Cl *CHSW* S40 .... **183** E5
Wenlock Crs *CHSW* S40 .... **183** D5
Wenlock St *HAN/WDH* S13 .... **139** D1 🔢
Wensley Av *ATT* S4 .... **110** C3
Wensley Crs *DONS/BSCR* DN4 .... **47** D5
Wensley Cft *ATT* S4 .... **110** C2
Wensley Dale Dr *RHAM* S60 .... **114** B5
Wensleydale Rd *BTLY* DN5 .... **28** B2
   KIMB S61 .... **92** A3
Wensley Gdns *ATT* S4 .... **110** C2
Wensley Gn *ATT* S4 .... **110** C2
   DEARNE S63 .... **26** B3
Wensley Wy *STV/CWN* S43 .... **187** D1
Wentworth Av *AU/AST/KP* S26 .... **143** D4
   CHSW S40 .... **189** F4
   ECC S11 .... **145** D3
   ECC S11 .... **145** E3 🔢
Wentworth Cl *KIMB* S61 .... **89** F1
Wentworth Ct *RAW* S62 .... **92** C2
Wentworth Dr *RAW* S62 .... **94** A2
Wentworth Gdns *MEX/SWTN* S64 .... **81** D3
Wentworth Pl *KIMB* S61 .... **91** D4
Wentworth Rd *DRON* S18 .... **168** A2
   HOY S74 .... **37** E4
   HOY S74 .... **52** B4
   HOY S74 .... **52** B5
   KIMB S61 .... **90** A1
   RAW S62 .... **79** E3
   WHHL DN2 .... **30** C4
Wentworth St *BSLY* S70 .... **49** F1
   BSLYN/ROY S71 .... **2** C1
Wentworth Vw *HOY* S74 .... **52** A3 🔢
   WMB/DAR S73 .... **39** E4
Wentworth Wy *DOD/DAR* S75 .... **20** A4
   DOD/DAR S75 .... **49** E4
Wesley Av *AU/AST/KP* S26 .... **142** B2
Wesley Ct *KIMB* S61 .... **90** A1
Wesley La *FUL* S10 .... **120** C4
Wesley Rd *CHPT/GREN* S35 .... **73** D4
Wesley St *BSLY* S70 .... **2** D6
Wessenden Cl *DOD/DAR* S75 .... **20** B1 🔢
Wessex Gdns *TOT/DORE* S17 .... **156** B3
Wessington Dr *STV/CWN* S43 .... **187** D1
West Av *DONS/BSCR* DN4 .... **43** E5
   RAW S62 .... **80** A5
   WMB/DAR S73 .... **38** C2
Westbank Cl *DRON* S18 .... **159** F4
West Bar *SHEF* S1 .... **9** E4
West Bars *CHSW* S40 .... **10** D6
West Bawtry Rd *RHAM* S60 .... **114** B3
Westbourne Gdns
   DONS/BSCR DN4 .... **63** D1 🔢
Westbourne Gv *CHSW* S40 .... **188** C5 🔢
   DOD/DAR S75 .... **13** E4 🔢
Westbourne Rd *ECC* S11 .... **121** D5
Westbourne Ter *DOD/DAR* S75 .... **21** D1
Westbrook Bank *ECC* S11 .... **134** B2
Westbrook Cl *CHSW* S40 .... **188** A2
Westbrook Dr *CHSW* S40 .... **188** B3
Westbrook Rd *CHPT/GREN* S35 .... **88** B1
Westbury Av *CHPT/GREN* S35 .... **88** C3
Westbury Cl *DOD/DAR* S75 .... **12** C3
Westbury St *DARN/MH* S9 .... **124** A2
Westby Crs *RHAM* S60 .... **115** F3
West Cl *KIMB* S61 .... **101** F1
West Crs *STKB/PEN* S36 .... **68** B2
Westcroft Crs *MOS* S20 .... **152** C5
Westcroft Dr *MOS* S20 .... **152** C5
Westcroft Gdns *STV/CWN* S43 .... **186** C4
Westcroft Gdns *MOS* S20 .... **152** C5
Westcroft Gln *MOS* S20 .... **164** C1 🔢
Westcroft Gv *MOS* S20 .... **164** C1
West Don St *ST/HB/BR* S6 .... **121** D4
West End Av *MOS* S20 .... **29** E2
West End La *NROS/TKH* DN11 .... **66** B5
West End Rd *DEARNE* S63 .... **54** C2

West End Vw *ECK/KIL* S21 .... **174** A1
Westerdale Rd *BTLY* DN5 .... **28** B3
Western Bank *FUL* S10 .... **121** E4
   FUL S10 .... **121** F4 🔢
Western Rd *FUL* S10 .... **120** C3
   RHAM/THRY S65 .... **104** B2
Western St *BSLY* S70 .... **2** B3
Western Ter *WMB/DAR* S73 .... **39** D2
Westfield Av *AU/AST/KP* S26 .... **142** A1
   CHSW S40 .... **188** C3 🔢
   HACK/IN S12 .... **152** A2
Westfield Centre *MOS* S20 .... **152** C5
Westfield Cl *CHSW* S40 .... **188** C2
Westfield Crs *DEARNE* S63 .... **26** B3
   MOS S20 .... **152** B5
Westfield Gdns *CHSW* S40 .... **188** C2 🔢
Westfield Gv *HACK/IN* S12 .... **151** F2 🔢
Westfield La *ECK/KIL* S21 .... **172** B3
Westfield Northway *MOS* S20 .... **152** C5
Westfield Rd *ARMTH* DN3 .... **33** E3 🔢
   DEARNE S63 .... **54** B1 🔢
   DONS/BSCR DN4 .... **43** F3
   DRON S18 .... **170** A3
   ECK/KIL S21 .... **166** A3
   RAW S62 .... **93** F2
Westfields *BSLY* S70 .... **36** B1
Westfield Southway *MOS* S20 .... **152** C5
Westfield St *BSLY* S70 .... **21** E1 🔢
Westfield Ter *SHEF* S1 .... **8** C6
Westgate *BSLY* S70 .... **2** B5
   BSLYN/ROY S71 .... **14** C3
West Ga *MEX/SWTN* S64 .... **59** D3
Westgate *RHAM* S60 .... **6** D6
West Green Dr *ARMTH* DN3 .... **19** F2
West Gv *WHHL* DN2 .... **31** E4
West Hl *KIMB* S61 .... **101** D3
Westhill La *SHEF* S1 .... **8** B6
Westholme Rd *DONS/BSCR* DN4 .... **43** F3
West Laith Ga *DON* DN1 .... **4** D4
Westland Cl *MOS* S20 .... **152** C4
Westland Gdns *MOS* S20 .... **152** B5
Westland Gv *MOS* S20 .... **152** C5 🔢
Westland Rd *MOS* S20 .... **152** C4
West La *AU/AST/KP* S26 .... **141** F1
West Lea *CHSW* S40 .... **188** C2 🔢
Westleigh *CHSW* S40 .... **10** B5
Westminster Cl *FUL* S10 .... **131** F1 🔢
Westminster Crs *FUL* S10 .... **131** F1
   WHHL DN2 .... **32** A4 🔢
West Moor Crs *DOD/DAR* S75 .... **20** B3
Westmoor Rd *STV/CWN* S43 .... **186** A5
Westmoreland St *ST/HB/BR* S6 .... **121** F3 🔢
Westmorland St *DONS/BSCR* DN4 .... **63** F1
Westmount Av *DEARNE* S63 .... **41** D5 🔢
Westnall Rd *SHEFN* S5 .... **99** E2
Westnall Ter *SHEFN* S5 .... **99** E2
Weston Cl *CHSW* S40 .... **182** B3
Westongales Wy *BTLY* DN5 .... **29** E1 🔢
Weston Rd *DONS/BSCR* DN4 .... **63** F1
Weston St *OWL* S3 .... **8** A4
Westover Rd *FUL* S10 .... **119** F5
West Park Dr *AU/AST/KP* S26 .... **141** F3
Westpit Hl *DEARNE* S63 .... **54** B1
West Pl *BTLY* DN5 .... **16** C5
West Qd *SHEFN* S5 .... **110** B1
West Rd *DOD/DAR* S75 .... **12** C5
   MEX/SWTN S64 .... **58** A3
Westside Gra *DONS/BSCR* DN4 .... **43** E4 🔢
West St *BSLY* S70 .... **36** C1
   CHSW S40 .... **10** C4
   CONI DN12 .... **85** D1
   DEARNE S63 .... **27** E5 🔢
   DEARNE S63 .... **55** F2
   DON DN1 .... **4** C4
   DRON S18 .... **169** D1 🔢
   ECK/KIL S21 .... **174** A1
   HOY S74 .... **51** D2
   MEX/SWTN S64 .... **58** A4
   MOS S20 .... **153** D2
   SHEF S1 .... **8** C6
   WMB/DAR S73 .... **39** D2
West Street La *SHEF* S1 .... **8** D5
Westthorpe Fields Rd
   ECK/KIL S21 .... **166** A4
Westthorpe Rd *ECK/KIL* S21 .... **166** B3
West Vw *STV/CWN* S43 .... **181** E5
West View Cl *TOT/DORE* S17 .... **157** D2 🔢
West View La *TOT/DORE* S17 .... **157** D2 🔢
West View Rd *CHSW* S40 .... **183** F3
   KIMB S61 .... **101** D4
   MEX/SWTN S64 .... **58** A4
Westville Rd *DOD/DAR* S75 .... **13** E4
West Wy *BSLY* S70 .... **2** D6
Westwell Pl *MOS* S20 .... **164** B2
Westwick Crs *TOT/DORE* S17 .... **158** B2
Westwick Gv *SHEFS* S8 .... **158** B1
Westwick Rd *SHEFS* S8 .... **158** B1
Westwood Av *STV/CWN* S43 .... **187** D1
Westwood Cl *STV/CWN* S43 .... **187** D4 🔢
Westwood Ct *BSLY* S70 .... **23** B5
   CHPT/GREN S35 .... **73** E3
Westwood Dr *STV/CWN* S43 .... **186** C4
Westwood La *CHPT/GREN* S35 .... **48** C5
   STV/CWN S43 .... **186** A5
Westwood New Rd *DOD/DAR* S75 .... **49** E5

Westwood Rd *ECC* S11 .... **133** D2
   STV/CWN S43 .... **186** B5
Wetherby Cl *BTLY* DN5 .... **28** B4
Wetherby Ct *DARN/MH* S9 .... **125** D3
Wetherby Dr *AU/AST/KP* S26 .... **142** A3
   MEX/SWTN S64 .... **58** C2
Wetlands La *CHNE* S41 .... **185** F5
Wet Moor La *DEARNE* S63 .... **56** A4
Whaley Rd *DOD/DAR* S75 .... **12** A2
Wharf Cl *MEX/SWTN* S64 .... **57** F5 🔢
Wharfedale Dr *CHPT/GREN* S35 .... **87** F1
Wharfedale Rd *DOD/DAR* S75 .... **12** F4
Wharf La *CHNE* S41 .... **11** F3
Wharf Rd *DARN/MH* S9 .... **112** B1
   DON DN1 .... **30** B4
   MEX/SWTN S64 .... **81** F3
Wharf St *ATT* S4 .... **9** G4
   BSLYN/ROY S71 .... **3** F2
   MEX/SWTN S64 .... **57** F5
Wharncliffe Dr *DOD/DAR* S75 .... **20** B4 🔢
Wharncliffe Av *AU/AST/KP* S26 .... **142** C2 🔢
   DEARNE S63 .... **56** A2 🔢
Wharncliffe Cl *HOY* S74 .... **51** E4
   RAW S62 .... **79** E3 🔢
Wharncliffe Rd *CHPT/GREN* S35 .... **73** E4 🔢
   FUL S10 .... **121** F5
Wharncliffe St *BSLY* S70 .... **2** A5
   DONS/BSCR DN4 .... **43** E2
Wharton Av *AU/AST/KP* S26 .... **142** B1
Wheatacre Rd *STKB/PEN* S36 .... **69** D3
Wheata Dr *SHEFN* S5 .... **98** B2
Wheata Pl *SHEFN* S5 .... **98** B2
Wheata Rd *SHEFN* S5 .... **98** B3
Wheatbridge Rd *CHSW* S40 .... **10** B6
Wheat Cft *CONI* DN12 .... **85** F1
Wheatcroft Rd *RAW* S62 .... **80** C5
Wheathill Crs *SHEFN* S5 .... **99** E3
Wheatfield Dr *DEARNE* S63 .... **27** D4 🔢
Wheatfield Wy *RCH* S42 .... **182** A4 🔢
Wheathill Cl *CHSW* S40 .... **182** A4 🔢
   CHSW S40 .... **182** B4 🔢
   STV/CWN S43 .... **186** A5
Wheathill La *CHNE* S41 .... **185** F5
Wheathill St *RHAM* S60 .... **103** E4 🔢
Wheatley Cl *BSLYN/ROY* S71 .... **14** A3 🔢
Wheatley Gv *HAN/WDH* S13 .... **138** C1
Wheatley Hall Rd *WHHL* DN2 .... **19** E5
   WHHL DN2 .... **31** D3
Wheatley La *DON* DN1 .... **5** F1 🔢
Wheatley Pl *CONI* DN12 .... **60** A5 🔢
Wheatley Rd *BSLY* S70 .... **23** F3 🔢
   BTLY DN5 .... **16** B4
   KIMB S61 .... **91** F5
   MEX/SWTN S64 .... **81** F3
Wheeldon Crs *STV/CWN* S43 .... **185** E2
Wheeldon St *SHEF* S1 .... **8** B5
Wheel La *CHPT/GREN* S35 .... **97** E1
The Wheel *CHPT/GREN* S35 .... **97** F1
Weldrake Rd *SHEFN* S5 .... **110** B2
Wheelside Av *CHPT/GREN* S35 .... **74** A5 🔢
Whinacre Cl *SHEFS* S8 .... **159** F2 🔢
Whinacre Pl *SHEFS* S8 .... **159** F2
Whinby Cft *DOD/DAR* S75 .... **20** A3 🔢
Whinfell Ct *ECC* S11 .... **144** C3
Whin Gdns *DEARNE* S63 .... **27** D2
Whin Hill Rd *DONS/BSCR* DN4 .... **46** B3
Whinmoor Rd *CHPT/GREN* S35 .... **73** D4
   SHEFN S5 .... **111** D1 🔢
Whinside Crs *DEARNE* S63 .... **26** C2
The Whins *RAW* S62 .... **93** D1
Whiphill Cl *DONS/BSCR* DN4 .... **46** C5 🔢
Whirlow Court Rd *ECC* S11 .... **145** D3
Whirlowdale Cl *ECC* S11 .... **145** D3 🔢
Whirlowdale Crs *ECC* S11 .... **145** F2
Whirlowdale Ri *ECC* S11 .... **145** E3 🔢
Whirlowdale Rd *ABRD* S7 .... **145** E3
   ECC S11 .... **145** D3
Whirlow Gv *ECC* S11 .... **145** D2 🔢
Whirlow La *ECC* S11 .... **145** D2 🔢
Whirlow Ms *ECC* S11 .... **145** D2 🔢
Whirlow Park Rd *ABRD* S7 .... **145** D4
Whisperwood Dr *DONS/BSCR* DN4 .... **63** F3
Whiston Brook Vw *RHAM* S60 .... **116** A3
Whiston Gra *RHAM* S60 .... **115** E3 🔢
Whiston Gn *RHAM* S60 .... **115** F4 🔢
Whiston Grange *RHAM* S60 .... **104** A5
Whiston V *RHAM* S60 .... **115** F4
Whitbourne Cl *BSLYN/ROY* S71 .... **14** A2 🔢
Whitburn Rd *DON* DN1 .... **5** F6
Whitby Rd *DARN/MH* S9 .... **124** C3 🔢
   DARN/MH S9 .... **125** D2 🔢
Whitebank Cl *CHNE* S41 .... **190** C3
Whitecoats Pk *CHSW* S40 .... **190** A4
Whitecotes Cl *CHSW* S40 .... **189** F4
Whitecotes La *CHSW* S40 .... **189** F4
White Cft *SHEF* S1 .... **8** C4
Whitecroft Crs *RHAM* S60 .... **114** A4
White Cross La *BSLY* S70 .... **23** B5
White Cross Ri *BSLY* S70 .... **23** E5
White Edge Cl *CHSW* S40 .... **183** E4
Whitehall Rd *KIMB* S61 .... **92** A2
White Hill Av *STKB/PEN* S36 .... **69** E3
White Hill Av *BSLY* S70 .... **20** B1
Whitehill Av *RHAM* S60 .... **114** A4

Whitehill Dr *RHAM* S60............**114** A5
White Hill Gv *BSLY* S70............**20** C1 🔢
Whitehill La *RHAM* S60............**114** A3
Whitehill Rd *RHAM* S60............**114** A4
White Hill Ter *BSLY* S70............**20** B1 🔢
Whitehouse La *ST/HB/BR* S6............**121** E1
Whitehouse Rd *ST/HB/BR* S6............**121** E1
Whitehouses *CHNE* S41............**190** C3 🔢
White La *CHPT/GREN* S35............**74** C4
HACK/IN S12............**149** C4
Whitelea Rd *MEX/SWTN* S64............**58** A4
Whitelee Rd *MEX/SWTN* S64............**57** F4
Whiteley La *ECC* S11............**132** A3
Whiteley Wood Cl *ECC* S11............**132** C5
Whiteley Wood Rd *ECC* S11............**132** C4
White Rose Ct *BTLY* DN5............**17** D3
White Rose Wy *DONS/BSCR* DN4............**44** C4
DONS/BSCR DN4............**65** D1
White's La *SHEFP/MNR* S2............**123** E4
White Thorns Cl *SHEFS* S8............**159** F2 🔢
White Thorns Dr *SHEFS* S8............**159** F3
White Thorns Vw *SHEFS* S8............**159** F2
Whiteways *ATT* S4............**110** B4
Whiteways Gv *ATT* S4............**110** B4 🔢
Whiteways Gv *ATT* S4............**110** B4
Whitfield Rd *FUL* S10............**132** A3
RAW S62............**79** D3
Whiting St *SHEFS* S8............**135** E4 🔢
Whitley Carr *CHPT/GREN* S35............**87** F4
Whitley La *CHPT/GREN* S35............**87** E5
Whitley Vw *CHPT/GREN* S35............**88** A4
Whitley View Rd *KIMB* S61............**100** C4
Whitney Cl *DONS/BSCR* DN4............**62** C2 🔢
Whittier Rd *DONS/BSCR* DN4............**63** E1
Whittington Hl *CHNE* S41............**178** B5
Whittington La *DRON* S18............**178** A4
Whittington Rd *STV/CWN* S43............**179** F2
Whittington St *DON* DN1............**30** B4
Whitting Valley Rd *CHNE* S41............**178** B5
Whitton Cl *DONS/BSCR* DN4............**66** A1
Whitwell Crs *STKB/PEN* S36............**68** C1
Whitwell La *STKB/PEN* S36............**68** B3
Whitwell St *DARN/MH* S9............**125** E3
Whitworth La *DARN/MH* S9............**111** E5
Whitworth Rd *CHNE* S41............**184** A3 🔢
FUL S10............**132** C1
Whitworth Wy *DEARNE* S63............**56** C3 🔢
Whyn Vw *DEARNE* S63............**26** C5 🔢
Wicker *OWL* S3............**9** G2
Wicker La *OWL* S3............**9** G3
Wickersley Rd *RHAM/THRY* S65............**104** B5
Wicket Wy *CONI* DN12............**62** A4
Wickfield Cl *HACK/IN* S12............**139** D5
Wickfield Dr *HACK/IN* S12............**150** C1
Wickfield Gv *HACK/IN* S12............**138** C5
Wickfield Rd *HACK/IN* S12............**138** C5
Wickfield Rd *HACK/IN* S12............**151** D1
Wicklow La *WHHL* DN2............**31** E4
Widdop Cl *HAN/WDH* S13............**138** B2
Widdop Cft *HAN/WDH* S13............**138** B2
Wigfield Dr *BSLY* S70............**22** A5
Wigfull Rd *ECC* S11............**134** A1
Wigley Rd *STV/CWN* S43............**187** D3
Wikeley Wy *STV/CWN* S43............**185** E2
Wike Rd *BSLYN/ROY* S71............**15** F5
Wilberforce Rd *WHHL* DN2............**19** E5
Wilbrook Ri *DOD/DAR* S75............**12** B3
Wilby La *BSLY* S70............**22** B2 🔢
Wilcox Cl *ST/HB/BR* S6............**97** E4
Wilcox Rd *ST/HB/BR* S6............**97** D4
Wild Av *RAW* S62............**79** D4
Wildene Dr *MEX/SWTN* S64............**58** B2
Wilding Cl *KIMB* S61............**101** F1
Wilding Wy *KIMB* S61............**101** F1
Wilfred Cl *DARN/MH* S9............**124** D2 🔢
Wilfred Dr *DARN/MH* S9............**124** D2
Wilfred St *RHAM* S60............**6** D5
Wilfrid Rd *DARN/MH* S9............**124** B2
Wilkinson Dr *STV/CWN* S43............**186** C2
Wilkinson La *FUL* S10............**8** A6
Wilkinson Rd *HOY* S74............**52** B3
Wilkinson St *BSLY* S70............**22** A2 🔢
FUL S10............**121** F4
Willan Dr *RHAM* S60............**127** D2
Willbury Dr *HACK/IN* S12............**137** E4
Willey St *OWL* S3............**9** G3
William Cl *MOS* S20............**164** D2 🔢
William Crs *MOS* S20............**164** B1
Williamson Rd *ECC* S11............**134** B3
Williams Rd *BTLY* DN5............**29** D3
William St *BSLY* S70............**22** B5
CHNE S41............**184** B3 🔢
DEARNE S63............**56** A2
ECK/KIL S21............**164** B5
FUL S10............**121** F5
MEX/SWTN S64............**57** F5
RAW S62............**94** B2
RHAM/THRY S65............**7** F6
WMB/DAR S73............**39** D2 🔢
William St North *CHNE* S41............**178** A4
Willingham Cl *MOS* S20............**153** E4
Willingham Gdns *MOS* S20............**153** E4 🔢
Willington Rd *SHEFN* S5............**99** D5

Willis Rd *ST/HB/BR* S6............**107** F3
Willoughby St *ATT* S4............**110** B2
Willow Av *DONS/BSCR* DN4............**47** D4
RAW S62............**94** B1
Willow Bank *BSLYN/ROY* S71............**13** E5
Willow Cl *HOY* S74............**51** D3
RHAM S60............**114** B5
Willow Crs *CHPT/GREN* S35............**88** B2
Willowdale Cl *BTLY* DN5............**42** B4
Willow Dr *CONI* DN12............**62** A4
DARN/MH S9............**125** F4
MEX/SWTN S64............**58** A3
Willow Garth Av *RAW* S62............**80** B5
Willowgarth Av *RHAM* S60............**114** A5
Willow Garth Rd *CHNE* S41............**183** D1
Willow Gv *AU/AST/KP* S26............**143** D2 🔢
Willowlees Ct *DONS/BSCR* DN4............**46** C5 🔢
Willow Rd *DEARNE* S63............**27** D3
DEARNE S63............**56** B4
ECK/KIL S21............**166** A3
STKB/PEN S36............**68** C4
The Willows *KIMB* S61............**91** E4
Willow St *CONI* DN12............**85** E1
Willow Wk *BTLY* DN5............**16** E3 🔢
Wilmington Dr *DONS/BSCR* DN4............**45** D5
Wilsden Gv *DOD/DAR* S75............**12** C3 🔢
Wilson Av *RAW* S62............**79** F5
Wilson Dr *RHAM/THRY* S65............**95** F5
Wilson Gv *BSLYN/ROY* S71............**15** F3
Wilson Pl *SHEFS* S8............**135** E4 🔢
Wilson Rd *DRON* S18............**160** A4
ECC S11............**134** A2
STKB/PEN S36............**70** A3
Wilson St *DRON* S18............**169** E3 🔢
OWL S3............**122** B1
WMB/DAR S73............**38** C2
Wilthorpe Av *DOD/DAR* S75............**13** D3
Wilthorpe Crs *DOD/DAR* S75............**13** D3
Wilthorpe Farm Rd *DOD/DAR* S75............**13** D3
Wilthorpe Gdns *HACK/IN* S12............**151** E2 🔢
Wilthorpe Gn *DOD/DAR* S75............**13** D3 🔢
Wilthorpe La *DOD/DAR* S75............**12** C3
Wilthorpe Rd *DOD/DAR* S75............**12** B3
Wilton Cl *RAW* S62............**94** A1
Wilton Ct *KIMB* S61............**102** B2
Wilton Gdns *KIMB* S61............**102** B2
Wilton La *KIMB* S61............**102** B3
Wilton Pl *FUL* S10............**121** F5
Wiltshire Rd *WHHL* DN2............**32** A5
Wimborne Crs *CHNE* S41............**183** D1
Wincanton Cl *MEX/SWTN* S64............**58** C2
Winchester Av *FUL* S10............**131** F2
WHHL DN2............**31** E3
Winchester Crs *FUL* S10............**131** F2
Winchester Dr *FUL* S10............**131** F2 🔢
Winchester Rd *CHNE* S41............**183** F2
FUL S10............**131** F2
Winchester Wy *BSLYN/ROY* S71............**24** B3 🔢
BTLY DN5............**28** B3
RHAM S60............**113** E3
Wincobank Av *SHEFN* S5............**110** C1
Wincobank Cl *SHEFN* S5............**111** D1 🔢
Wincobank La *ATT* S4............**111** D3
Wincobank Rd *SHEFN* S5............**111** D1
Windermere Av *DRON* S18............**168** C2
WHHL DN2............**32** A4 🔢
Windermere Rd *BSLYN/ROY* S71............**3** F5
CHNE S41............**188** C5
SHEFS S8............**134** C5 🔢
Winders Pl *WMB/DAR* S73............**39** E3 🔢
Windgate Hl *CONI* DN12............**61** E5
Windham Cl *BSLYN/ROY* S71............**2** D2
Windhill Av *MEX/SWTN* S64............**59** D2
Windhill Crs *MEX/SWTN* S64............**59** D2
Windhill Ter *MEX/SWTN* S64............**59** D2
The Windings *DEARNE* S63............**27** E4
Windle Rd *DONS/BSCR* DN4............**43** E3
Windmill Greenway *MOS* S20............**164** C3
Windmill Hill La *CHPT/GREN* S35............**87** F2
Windmill La *DRON* S18............**171** E5
SHEFN S5............**110** C1
Windmill Rd *WMB/DAR* S73............**38** C3
Windsor Cl *CHSW* S40............**189** D3
Windsor Crs *BSLYN/ROY* S71............**3** H1
Windsor Dr *DOD/DAR* S75............**20** A3 🔢
DRON S18............**168** A2
MEX/SWTN S64............**59** D2
Windsor Rd *AU/AST/KP* S26............**142** C4
Windsor Rd *CONI* DN12............**60** C5 🔢
KIMB S61............**90** A2
SHEFS S8............**135** D4
WHHL DN2............**31** D5
Windsor Sq *DEARNE* S63............**27** E3
Windsor St *ATT* S4............**123** E1 🔢
DEARNE S63............**27** E3
HOY S74............**51** E1
Windsor Wk *BTLY* DN5............**28** C3
CHNE S41............**191** D3
Windy House La *SHEFP/MNR* S2............**137** D3
Windy Rdg *AU/AST/KP* S26............**142** A1
Winfield Rd *DEARNE* S63............**56** A3
Wingerworth Av *SHEFS* S8............**158** B1
Wingerworth Wy *CHSW* S40............**190** A5
Wingfield Cl *DRON* S18............**168** A3

KIMB S61............**92** B3
Wingfield Crs *HACK/IN* S12............**138** A5
Wingfield Rd *BSLYN/ROY* S71............**14** B1
KIMB S61............**91** F3
Winifred St *RHAM* S60............**6** A4
Winkley Ter *SHEFN* S5............**99** F5
Winlea Av *RHAM/THRY* S65............**105** F5
Winnat Pl *STV/CWN* S43............**187** D2
Winnats Cl *CHSW* S40............**183** D4 🔢
Winn Cl *ST/HB/BR* S6............**107** F1
Winn Dr *ST/HB/BR* S6............**107** F1
Winn Gdns *ST/HB/BR* S6............**107** F1
Winn Gv *ST/HB/BR* S6............**107** E1
Winnipeg Rd *BTLY* DN5............**16** C5
Winsford Rd *ST/HB/BR* S6............**97** D4
Winster Cl *BSLY* S70............**36** A5
Winster Rd *ST/HB/BR* S6............**108** A3
STV/CWN S43............**187** D1
Winston Av *STKB/PEN* S36............**68** A1
Winter Av *DOD/DAR* S75............**13** D5
Winter Hill La *KIMB* S61............**101** F2
Winterhill Rd *KIMB* S61............**101** E5
Winter Rd *DOD/DAR* S75............**13** D5
Winter St *OWL* S3............**121** F3
Winter Ter *DOD/DAR* S75............**13** D5
Winterton Cl *DONS/BSCR* DN4............**66** B1 🔢
Winterton Gdns *HACK/IN* S12............**152** A2
Winterwell Rd *DEARNE* S63............**55** D1
Winton Cl *BSLY* S70............**22** B3 🔢
Winton Rd *WHHL* DN2............**31** F5
Wisbech Cl *CHSW* S40............**189** F4
Wiseton Rd *ECC* S11............**134** A1
Wisewood Av *ST/HB/BR* S6............**107** E4
Wisewood La *ST/HB/BR* S6............**107** E4
Wisewood Pl *ST/HB/BR* S6............**107** E4
Wisewood Rd *ST/HB/BR* S6............**107** E4
Witham Cl *CHNE* S41............**185** D3 🔢
Witham Rd *FUL* S10............**121** D5
Withens Av *ST/HB/BR* S6............**107** E2
Witney St *SHEFP/MNR* S2............**135** E2 🔢
Wivelsfield Rd *DONS/BSCR* DN4............**42** B5
Woburn Cl *DONS/BSCR* DN4............**62** C2
Woburn Pl *DOD/DAR* S75............**20** A4 🔢
ECC S11............**145** D3
Wolfe Cl *CHSW* S40............**189** E3
Wolfe Dr *ST/HB/BR* S6............**97** E4 🔢
Wolfe Rd *ST/HB/BR* S6............**97** E4
Wollaton Av *TOT/DORE* S17............**157** E5
Wollaton Dr *TOT/DORE* S17............**157** E3 🔢
Wollaton Rd *TOT/DORE* S17............**157** D4
Wolseley Rd *SHEFS* S8............**135** D3
Wolsey Av *WHHL* DN2............**31** F5
Wolverley Rd *HAN/WDH* S13............**139** E4
Wombwell Av *DEARNE* S63............**55** E3 🔢
Wombwell La *BSLY* S70............**24** A3
WMB/DAR S73............**37** E3
Wombwell Rd *HOY* S74............**51** F1
Wood Acres *DOD/DAR* S75............**12** B3
Woodall Rd *ECK/KIL* S21............**167** D3
RHAM/THRY S65............**105** D4
Woodall Rd South
RHAM/THRY S65............**105** D4
Woodbank Crs *SHEFS* S8............**135** D4
Woodbank Rd *ST/HB/BR* S6............**118** A3
Woodbine Rd *DARN/MH* S9............**111** D5
Woodbourn Hl *DARN/MH* S9............**124** A3
Woodbourn Rd *DARN/MH* S9............**124** A3
Woodburn Dr *CHPT/GREN* S35............**88** C1
Woodbury Cl *DARN/MH* S9............**100** B4
Woodbury Rd *DARN/MH* S9............**100** B4
Wood Cliffe *ECC* S11............**131** F4
Wood Cl *CHPT/GREN* S35............**89** D2
RAW S62............**79** F4
Wood Close Cobnar *DRON* S18............**176** C3
Woodcock Cl *KIMB* S61............**92** A4
Woodcock Pl *SHEFP/MNR* S2............**123** E4
Woodcock Rd *HOY* S74............**51** E1
Wood Cft *KIMB* S61............**92** A5
Woodcross Av *DONS/BSCR* DN4............**47** E5
Woodend Cl *ST/HB/BR* S6............**107** E5
Woodend Dr *ST/HB/BR* S6............**107** E5
Woodfarm Av *ST/HB/BR* S6............**120** A1
Woodfarm Cl *ST/HB/BR* S6............**119** F1
Woodfarm Dr *ST/HB/BR* S6............**119** F1
Woodfarm Pl *ST/HB/BR* S6............**119** F1
Woodfield Av *MEX/SWTN* S64............**58** C3
Woodfield Rd *DEARNE* S63............**54** C2
DONS/BSCR DN4............**63** F1
DONS/BSCR DN4............**64** A1
FUL S10............**120** C3
Wood Fold *OWL* S3............**109** E5
Woodfoot Rd *RHAM* S60............**115** D3
Woodgrove Rd *DARN/MH* S9............**100** C4
RHAM/THRY S65............**105** D2
Woodhall Ri *MEX/SWTN* S64............**81** E3 🔢
Woodhead Dr *HOY* S74............**37** E4
Woodhead La *HOY* S74............**37** F4
Woodhead Rd *CHPT/GREN* S35............**71** E2
SHEFP/MNR S2............**135** E2
Woodholm Pl *SHEFS* S11............**133** F5 🔢
Woodholm Rd *ECC* S11............**133** F5
Woodhouse Av *MOS* S20............**153** D1
Woodhouse Cl *RAW* S62............**79** E3 🔢
Woodhouse Ct *MOS* S20............**140** C5
Woodhouse Crs *MOS* S20............**153** D1

Woodhouse La MOS S20 .... 140 C5
  MOS S20 .... 141 D5
Woodhouse Rd HACK/IN S12 .... 137 F4
  HOY S74 .... 51 E3
  WHHL DN2 .... 30 C3
Woodland Cl MALT S66 .... 117 F1
  RHAM S60 .... 126 C2
Woodland Dr BSLY S70 .... 20 C2
  HACK/IN S12 .... 149 F3 🔟
Woodland Gv DEARNE S63 .... 56 A4
Woodland Pl TOT/DORE S17 .... 157 D3
Woodland Rd DEARNE S63 .... 56 A4
  SHEFS S8 .... 147 F2
Woodlands STV/CWN S43 .... 185 E2
Woodlands Av MOS S20 .... 141 D5
Woodlands Cl AU/AST/KP S26 ...... 142 B1 🔟
Woodlands Crs MEX/SWTN S64 .... 80 B1
Woodlands Rd HOY S74 .... 37 F5
Woodlands Vw HOY S74 .... 51 F1
  WMB/DAR S73 .... 38 B5
Woodland Vw HACK/IN S12 .... 149 F3
  MEX/SWTN S64 .... 59 D4 🔟
Woodland View Rd
  ST/HB/BR S6 .... 120 B1 🔟
Woodland Wk RCH S42 .... 182 A4
Woodland Wy RHAM/THRY S65 ...... 105 D5
Wood La NROS/TKH DN11 .... 63 D5
  RHAM S60 .... 113 E5
  RHAM S60 .... 128 A4
  ST/HB/BR S6 .... 120 A1
Wood Lane Cl ST/HB/BR S6 .... 119 F1
Woodlea Gdns DONS/BSCR DN4 ...... 47 D5
Woodlea Gv ARMTH DN3 .... 33 F3
Woodlea Wy WHHL DN2 .... 32 A2 🔟
Woodleigh Cl RCH S42 .... 182 A4 🔟
Woodleys Av RHAM S62 .... 79 F3
Woodman Dr MEX/SWTN S64 .... 80 B1
Woodnook Cl MOS S20 .... 182 A5
Woodnook Gv ECK/KIL S21 .... 172 C1
Woodnook Wy CHSW S40 .... 182 A5
Woodpecker Cl AU/AST/KP S26 ...... 142 C4
Wood Rd KIMB S61 .... 92 A5
  ST/HB/BR S6 .... 107 F4
Woodrove Av HAN/WDH S13 .... 137 F3
Woodrove Cl HAN/WDH S13 .... 137 F3
Wood Royd Rd STKB/PEN S36 .... 69 E2
Wood Seats CHPT/GREN S35 .... 87 E3
Woodseats Cl SHEFS S8 .... 146 C1
Woodseats House Rd SHEFS S8 ...... 147 D3
Woodseats Rd SHEFS S8 .... 146 C1
Woodsett Wk CONI DN12 .... 61 F5
Woodside Av DEARNE S63 .... 56 A3
  ECK/KIL S21 .... 167 D1
Woodside Cl CHSW S40 .... 182 C5 🔟
Woodside La CHPT/GREN S35 .... 87 D5
  OWL S3 .... 122 B1 🔟
Woodside Rd BTLY DN5 .... 28 C1
Woodside Wk KIMB S61 .... 92 B4
Wood Spring Ct ATT S4 .... 110 C4
Wood's Riding DONS/BSCR DN4 .... 32 B5
Woodstock Dr CHNE S41 .... 191 D4
Woodstock Ri CHNE S41 .... 191 D4 🔟
Woodstock Rd ABRD S7 .... 134 C4
  DOD/DAR S75 .... 13 E3
  DONS/BSCR DN4 .... 62 C1
  ST/HB/BR S6 .... 106 C3
Wood St BSLY S70 .... 22 A2
  DON DN1 .... 5 E4
  MEX/SWTN S64 .... 57 F5
  MEX/SWTN S64 .... 58 A3
  RHAM/THRY S65 .... 95 F4
  ST/HB/BR S6 .... 121 F1
  WMB/DAR S73 .... 39 D3
Wood Syke DOD/DAR S75 .... 20 B3
Wood Ter RHAM S60 .... 114 B1
Woodthorpe Cl SHEFP/MNR S2 ...... 137 E2

Woodthorpe Crs HAN/WDH S13 .. 138 A2 🔟
Woodthorpe Rd HAN/WDH S13 ...... 138 A3
Woodvale Cl CHSW S40 .... 188 B4
Woodvale Rd ECC S11 .... 133 F1
Wood Vw CONI DN12 .... 62 A4
  CONI DN12 .... 85 F2
  HOY S74 .... 37 F5
Woodview La DOD/DAR S75 .... 12 C4 🔟
Wood View Pl RHAM S60 .... 114 B1
Woodview Rd ST/HB/BR S6 .... 108 A5
Woodview Ter ECC S11 .... 132 C2 🔟
Wood Wk HOY S74 .... 37 F5
  MEX/SWTN S64 .... 58 A2
  WMB/DAR S73 .... 38 B5
Woofindin Av ECC S11 .... 132 C3
Woofindin Rd ECC S11 .... 132 B3
Wooldale Cl MOS S20 .... 151 E3
Wooldale Cft MOS S20 .... 151 E3
Wooldale Dr MOS S20 .... 151 E3
Wooldale Gdns MOS S20 .... 151 E3
Wooley Av WMB/DAR S73 .... 39 D3
Woolley Rd STKB/PEN S36 .... 68 B2
Woolley Wood Rd SHEFN S5 .... 99 F2
Wootton Ct RHAM/THRY S65 .... 95 F4 🔟
Worcester Av WHHL DN2 .... 31 D2
Worcester Cl FUL S10 .... 131 F1 🔟
Worcester Dr FUL S10 .... 131 F1
Worcester Rd FUL S10 .... 131 F1
Wordsworth Av DONS/BSCR DN4 .... 63 F1
  SHEFN S5 .... 98 A3
  SHEFN S5 .... 108 C1
Wordsworth Cl SHEFN S5 .... 97 F3
Wordsworth Crs SHEFN S5 .... 97 F5
Wordsworth Dr BTLY DN5 .... 29 D5
  RHAM/THRY S65 .... 104 B3
  SHEFN S5 .... 97 F3
Wordsworth Pl DRON S18 .... 170 A4
Wordsworth Rd BSLYN/ROY S71 ...... 14 C3
  CHNE S41 .... 184 A1
  DEARNE S63 .... 55 D1
Workhouse La OWL S3 .... 9 E3
Worksop Rd AU/AST/KP S26 .... 142 B3
  DARN/MH S9 .... 124 B1
Works Rd STV/CWN S43 .... 180 C3
Worral Av RHAM S60 .... 127 F5
Worral Cl BSLY S70 .... 22 A4
Worrall Rd CHPT/GREN S35 .... 73 F5
Worry Goose La RHAM S60 .... 116 A2
Worsborough Vw DOD/DAR S75 ...... 49 E2
Worsbrough Rd BSLY S70 .... 36 A5
  HOY S74 .... 37 E4
Worsley Cl BSLY S70 .... 22 C4
Worthing Crs CONI DN12 .... 85 E1
Worthing Rd DARN/MH S9 .... 123 F3
Wortley Av MEX/SWTN S64 .... 81 E1
  WMB/DAR S73 .... 38 C1
Wortley Ms KIMB S61 .... 89 F2
Wortley Rd CHPT/GREN S35 .... 70 B1
  CHPT/GREN S35 .... 73 D3
  KIMB S61 .... 101 F1
  KIMB S61 .... 102 B2 🔟
  STKB/PEN S36 .... 70 A2
Wortley St BSLY S70 .... 2 C6
Wortley Vw HOY S74 .... 37 E4
Wostenholm Rd ABRD S7 .... 135 D3
Wragby Rd ECC S11 .... 133 E2
Wragg La AU/AST/KP S26 .... 141 F5
Wragg Rd SHEFP/MNR S2 .... 123 F5
Wreakes La DRON S18 .... 169 D1
Wren Bank SHEFP/MNR S2 .... 123 F5 🔟
Wren Park Cl CHSW S40 .... 190 A5
  HACK/IN S12 .... 150 C5
Wrens Wy BSLY S70 .... 36 A5
Wright Crs WMB/DAR S73 .... 39 E3
Wright's Hl SHEFP/MNR S2 .... 135 D1
Wrightson Av DONS/BSCR DN4 .... 62 A2

Wrightson Ter BTLY DN5 .... 29 F3 🔟
Wroxham Wy BTLY DN5 .... 28 C4
Wulfric Cl SHEFP/MNR S2 .... 137 D2
Wulfric Pl SHEFP/MNR S2 .... 137 D2
Wulfric Rd ECK/KIL S21 .... 164 A5
  SHEFP/MNR S2 .... 137 D3
Wyatt Av ECC S11 .... 134 A4
Wybourn House Rd
  SHEFP/MNR S2 .... 123 F4 🔟
Wybourn Ter SHEFP/MNR S2 .... 123 F4 🔟
Wychwood Cl DONS/BSCR DN4 .... 63 D3
Wychwood Cft MOS S20 .... 153 E3 🔟
Wychwood Gln MOS S20 .... 153 E3 🔟
Wychwood Gv MOS S20 .... 153 E3 🔟
Wycombe St BSLYN/ROY S71 .... 15 F5 🔟
Wyedale Cft MOS S20 .... 153 D1
The Wynd ECK/KIL S21 .... 175 F4
Wyn Gv WMB/DAR S73 .... 54 B1
Wynmoor Crs WMB/DAR S73 .... 40 B5
Wynyard Rd ST/HB/BR S6 .... 107 F3
Wythburn Rd CHNE S41 .... 183 D2
Wyvern Gdns TOT/DORE S17 .... 156 C2

Y

Yarborough Ter BTLY DN5 .... 29 F4
Yardley Sq OWL S3 .... 121 F3 🔟
Yarmouth St DARN/MH S9 .... 111 F5 🔟
Yarncliff Cl CHSW S40 .... 183 E4
Yates Cl MALT S66 .... 117 E1
Yearling Cha MEX/SWTN S64 .... 56 C5
Yeldersley Cl CHSW S40 .... 182 C4
Yeomans Rd ST/HB/BR S6 .... 121 F2 🔟
Yewdale BSLY S70 .... 22 C5
Yew Greave Crs SHEFN S5 .... 98 A2
Yewdale BSLY S70 .... 22 C5
  SHEFN S5 .... 98 A2
Yews Av BSLY S70 .... 22 C5
Yews La BSLY S70 .... 22 C4
Yews Pl BSLY S70 .... 22 C5
Yew Tree Crs NROS/TKH DN11 .... 67 E5
Yew Tree Dr DARN/MH S9 .... 113 D3
  ECK/KIL S21 .... 166 A3 🔟
  RCH S42 .... 188 B4
Yoredale Av CHPT/GREN S35 .... 74 A5
York Gdns DONS/BSCR DN4 .... 46 B3
York La MALT S66 .... 117 F5
York Ri AU/AST/KP S26 .... 142 A3
York Rd BTLY DN5 .... 28 B1
  DARN/MH S9 .... 125 D2
  RHAM/THRY S65 .... 7 F3
  STKB/PEN S36 .... 68 C2 🔟
York St BSLY S70 .... 2 B6
  CHNE S41 .... 191 D5
  DEARNE S63 .... 27 E2
  HOY S74 .... 51 F1
  MEX/SWTN S64 .... 58 A3
  NROS/TKH DN11 .... 66 C5
  SHEF S1 .... 9 E4
  WMB/DAR S73 .... 39 E2
Youlgreave Dr HACK/IN S12 .... 138 B5
Young St DON DN1 .... 5 E4
  SHEF S1 .... 122 A5
Yvonne Gv WMB/DAR S73 .... 38 C2

Z

Zetland Rd HOY S74 .... 52 C3
  WHHL DN2 .... 31 D5
Zion Pl DARN/MH S9 .... 124 A1

Abbeydale Grange School
ABRD S7 .... **146** B1

Abbeydale Park Sports Club
TOT/DORE S17 .... **157** E1

Abbeydale Primary School
ABRD S7 .... **135** D4

Abbey Lane Primary School
SHEFS S8 .... **146** C3

Abbey School
KIMB S61 .... **101** E2

Abercrombie Primary School
CHNE S41 .... **11** E3

A C E Business Centre
ATT S4 .... **9** G3

Acorn Business Park
SHEFS S8 .... **146** C1

Acres Hill Primary School
DARN/MH S9 .... **124** C4

Adwick Road Surgery
MEX/SWTN S64 .... **58** C3

Akwaaba Surgery
CHPT/GREN S35 .... **88** C2

The Alhambra Shopping Centre
BSLY S70 .... **2** D6

All Saints RC School
SHEFP/MNR S2 .... **136** A1

Amber Business Centre
RHAM S60 .... **6** D3

Ambergate Clinics
KIMB S61 .... **102** C3

Ambler Junior School
DONS/BSCR DN4 .... **63** D1

Anchorage School
BTLY DN5 .... **28** C3

Anns Grove Primary School
SHEFS S8 .... **135** E3

Apperknowle County Primary School
DRON S18 .... **171** D2

Arbourthorne Junior School
SHEFP/MNR S2 .... **136** B4

Ardsley Oaks Junior & Infant School
BSLY S70 .... **24** A2

Arksey County Junior & Infant School
BTLY DN5 .... **17** E4

Armthorpe High School
ARMTH DN3 .... **33** E2

Armthorpe Southfield Infant & Junior School
ARMTH DN3 .... **33** F4

The Armthorpe Surgery
ARMTH DN3 .... **33** E3

Art Gallery & Museum
RHAM/THRY S65 .... **7** G5

Ashdell Preparatory School
FUL S10 .... **120** C5

Ashley Industrial Estate
RHAM S60 .... **6** D2

Ash Lodge Medical Centre
CHSW S40 .... **189** E2

Ashville Medical Centre
BSLY S70 .... **23** E2

Ashwood Road Junior & Infant School
RAW S62 .... **94** A3

Asian Mosque Centre
SHEFP/MNR S2 .... **135** E3

Askern CP School
BTLY DN5 .... **16** B1

Aston Comprehensive School
AU/AST/KP S26 .... **142** A1

Aston Fence Junior & Infant School
HAN/WDH S13 .... **141** E2

Aston Hall Cricket Club
AU/AST/KP S26 .... **143** E3

Aston Lodge School
AU/AST/KP S26 .... **142** C4

Aston Springwood Junior School
AU/AST/KP S26 .... **142** C2

Aston Swallownest Junior & Infant School
AU/AST/KP S26 .... **141** F2

Athron Industrial Estate
DON DN1 .... **5** F1

Atlas Business Park
CHPT/GREN S35 .... **89** D5

Aughton Junior & Infant School
AU/AST/KP S26 .... **142** B1

Avenue House Surgery
CHSW S40 .... **10** D5

The Avenue Medical Practice
SHEFS S8 .... **158** B1

Badsley Moor Lane Jmi School
RHAM/THRY S65 .... **104** C3

Balby Carr School
DONS/BSCR DN4 .... **64** A1

Balby Waverley First School
DONS/BSCR DN4 .... **62** C1

Ballifield Primary School
HAN/WDH S13 .... **139** E2

Bank End Junior & Infant School
BSLY S70 .... **23** D4

Bankwood Lane Industrial Estate
NROS/TKH DN11 .... **66** B5

Bankwood Primary School
SHEFS S8 .... **136** B5

Barnsley Borough Council
BSLY S70 .... **2** D5

Barnsley Christian School
BSLY S70 .... **2** C6

Barnsley College
BSLY S70 .... **2** C3

Barnsley College
DOD/DAR S75 .... **2** C2

Barnsley County Court
BSLY S70 .... **2** C4

Barnsley District General Hospital
DOD/DAR S75 .... **13** D4

Barnsley Football Club Ltd
BSLYN/ROY S71 .... **3** G5

Barnsley Magistrates Court
BSLY S70 .... **2** B4

Barnsley Metropolitan Borough Council
BSLY S70 .... **2** C4

Barnsley Metropolitan Borough Council
BSLY S70 .... **2** B3

Barnsley Metropolitan Borough Council
BSLY S70 .... **2** D3

Barnsley Metropolitan Borough Council
BSLY S70 .... **21** E3

Barnsley Metropolitan Borough Council
BSLY S70 .... **36** B1

Barnsley Metropolitan Borough Council
BSLYN/ROY S71 .... **3** E5

Barnsley Metropolitan Borough Council
BSLYN/ROY S71 .... **3** F2

Barnsley Metropolitan Borough Council
DOD/DAR S75 .... **49** D2

Barnsley Metropolitan Borough Council
WMB/DAR S73 .... **39** F2

Barnsley Metropolitan Borough Council
WMB/DAR S73 .... **40** A2

Barnsley Private Clinic
DOD/DAR S75 .... **2** B2

Barrow Hill Primary School
STV/CWN S43 .... **180** C3

The Basement Gallery
FUL S10 .... **132** A3

Baslow Road Surgery
TOT/DORE S17 .... **156** C3

Beauchief Golf Club House
SHEFS S8 .... **145** F4

Beevor Industrial Estate
BSLYN/ROY S71 .... **14** C5

Beighton Health Centre
MOS S20 .... **153** D1

Belgrave Medical Centre
SHEFP/MNR S2 .... **135** E2

Bentley Colliery Cricket Club
BTLY DN5 .... **16** C4

Bentley Health Centre
BTLY DN5 .... **16** B5

Bentley High Street Primary School
BTLY DN5 .... **29** F1

Bentley Sunnyfields Infant School
BTLY DN5 .... **28** C2

Bentley Sunnyfields Junior School
BTLY DN5 .... **29** D2

Bents Green Special School
ECC S11 .... **132** C5

Birdwell Health Centre
BSLY S70 .... **50** A2

Birdwell Primary School
BSLY S70 .... **50** A1

Birkdale Preparatory School
FUL S10 .... **134** B1

Birkdale School
ECC S11 .... **134** A1

Birkhill Primary School
ECK/KIL S21 .... **173** F1

Birley First School
HACK/IN S12 .... **150** B2

Birley Health Centre
HACK/IN S12 .... **150** B3

Birley Middle School
HACK/IN S12 .... **150** B2

Birley Primary School
HACK/IN S12 .... **150** B2

Birley Spa Primary School
HACK/IN S12 .... **151** D1

Blackburn County Junior Mixed School
KIMB S61 .... **100** C3

Bluebell Medical Centre
SHEFN S5 .... **111** D1

Bluestone Middle School
SHEFP/MNR S2 .... **136** B2

Bluestone Primary School
SHEFP/MNR S2 .... **136** B2

Bond's Picture Gallery
CHNE S41 .... **10** D4

Bracken Moor Sports Club
STKB/PEN S36 .... **69** D3

Bradmarsh Business Park
RHAM S60 .... **103** D4

Brampton Ellis Infant School
DEARNE S63 .... **55** D2

Brampton Health Centre
WMB/DAR S73 .... **40** B5

Brampton Junior & Infant School
CHSW S40 .... **10** A6

Brantwood Independent School for Girls
ABRD S7 .... **134** B2

Brimington Clinic
STV/CWN S43 .... **185** F1

Brimington Manor County Infant School
STV/CWN S43 .... **186** A4

Brinsworth Clinic
RHAM S60 .... **113** F3

Brinsworth Comprehensive School
RHAM S60 .... **113** E4

Brinsworth Medical Centre
RHAM S60 .... **113** E3

Brinsworth Whitehill Jm School
RHAM S60 .... **114** A5

Broad Elms School
ECC S11 .... **145** D1

Broadway School
BSLY S70 .... **20** C2

Brockwell Junior School
CHSW S40 .... **183** E5

Brookfield Community School
CHSW S40 .... **188** B2

Brook House Junior School
MOS S20 .... **153** F2

Broomhill Clinic
FUL S10 .... **121** D5

Broomhill Infant School
FUL S10 .... **121** D5

Broomhill Medical Centre
FUL S10 .... **121** E5

Broomhill Medical Surgery
FUL S10 .... **120** C5

Broom Lane Medical Centre
RHAM S60 .... **115** E1

Broom Valley Junior & Infant School
RHAM S60 .... **103** F5

Brunswick Primary School
HAN/WDH S13 .... **140** B3

Burncross Surgery
CHPT/GREN S35 .... **88** A1

Burns Medical Centre
DONS/BSCR DN4 .... **46** C4

The Burns Practice
WHHL DN2 .... **5** G4

Burton Road Junior & Infant School
BSLYN/ROY S71 .... **3** G1

The Business Centre
RHAM S60 .... **6** D5
The Business Centre
RHAM S60 .... **103** D5
Byron Wood Primary School
ATT S4 .... **109** F5
Camms Endowed C of E
Primary School
MOS S20 .... **164** B4
Canklow Meadows
Industrial Estate
RHAM S60 .... **114** B3
Canklow Woods Junior
& Infant School
RHAM S60 .... **114** B2
Cantley Hawthorn First School
DONS/BSCR DN4 .... **46** C3
Cantley Hawthorn Junior School
DONS/BSCR DN4 .... **46** C3
Cantley Health Centre
DONS/BSCR DN4 .... **47** D5
Carbrook Hall Industrial Estate
DARN/MH S9 .... **111** F3
Carfield Primary School
SHEFS S8 .... **135** E5
Caribbean Sports Club
CHPT/GREN S35 .... **99** D1
Carfield Medical Centre
SHEFP/MNR S2 .... **135** F4
Carterknowle & Dore
Medical Practice
ABRD S7 .... **134** C5
Carter Knowle Junior School
ABRD S7 .... **134** B5
Castle Market
ATT S4 .... **9** G4
Cathedral Church of
St Peter & St Paul
SHEF S1 .... **9** E4
Cavendish Junior School
CHNE S41 .... **184** A1
Cedar Special School
DONS/BSCR DN4 .... **63** D1
Central Business Park
RHAM S60 .... **6** B5
Central Sheffield
University Hospitals
FUL S10 .... **121** E4
Chapeltown Surgery
CHPT/GREN S35 .... **88** C2
Charnock Hall Primary School
HACK/IN S12 .... **149** F3
Charter Gallery Museum
CONI DN12 .... **84** C1
Chatsworth Surgery
CHSW S40 .... **188** C2
Chaucer School
SHEFN S5 .... **97** F4
Chesterfield Borough Council
CHNE S41 .... **184** B3
Chesterfield Borough Council
CHSW S40 .... **190** A3
Chesterfield Bowl
CHSW S40 .... **190** C5
Chesterfield Caravan &
Leisure Centre
DRON S18 .... **177** F3
Chesterfield College of
Technology & Arts
CHNE S41 .... **11** F4
Chesterfield Football Club Ltd
CHSW S40 .... **10** C5
Chesterfield Museum
CHNE S41 .... **11** G6
Chesterfield Rugby Club
CHNE S41 .... **11** F1
Chesterfield Small
Business Centre
CHNE S41 .... **184** B2
Childrens Hospital N H S Trust
FUL S10 .... **121** E4
Child Welfare & School Clinic
RHAM/THRY S65 .... **7** H2
Christ Church School
CHNE S41 .... **11** E1
Clifford C of E Grammar School
ECC S11 .... **134** B2
City Museum & Mappin
Art Gallery
FUL S10 .... **121** E4
Civic Building
RHAM/THRY S65 .... **6** D4
Civic Theatre
BSLY S70 .... **2** D5

Claremont Hospital
FUL S10 .... **119** E5
Claycliffe Business Park
DOD/DAR S75 .... **12** A2
Clayfield Industrial Estate
DONS/BSCR DN4 .... **63** E1
Clocktower Business Centre
STV/CWN S43 .... **180** B3
Clough House Medical Centre
SHEFP/MNR S2 .... **135** F1
Coit Primary School
CHPT/GREN S35 .... **88** B2
Coleridge Road Jmi School
RHAM/THRY S65 .... **104** B1
College of Technology
RHAM/THRY S65 .... **6** D5
Colonnades Centre
DON DN1 .... **4** D4
Concord Middle School
SHEFN S5 .... **99** F5
Conisbrough Castle
CONI DN12 .... **61** F2
Contour Health Centre
RHAM S60 .... **103** E4
Cooper Gallery
BSLY S70 .... **2** C4
Cope Street Surgery
BSLY S70 .... **22** B3
Coroners Court
DON DN1 .... **4** D5
Cortonwood County
Primary School
WMB/DAR S73 .... **40** B5
The Crookes Practice
FUL S10 .... **121** D3
Crown Court
DON DN1 .... **5** E5
Crown Court
OWL S3 .... **9** E3
Crucible Theatre
SHEF S1 .... **9** F6
The Culvert Gallery
ECC S11 .... **134** B2
Cupola Gallery
ST/HB/BR S6 .... **108** A2
Curlew Junior School
WHHL DN2 .... **19** E5
The Curtain Gallery
ECC S11 .... **134** B2
Cusworth Hall
BTLY DN5 .... **28** B5
Dalton Foljambe Infant School
RHAM/THRY S65 .... **95** F5
Dalton Health Centre
RHAM/THRY S65 .... **95** E5
Danum Grammar School
WHHL DN2 .... **32** B4
Darfield Valley Primary School
WMB/DAR S73 .... **40** A1
Darnall Health Centre
DARN/MH S9 .... **125** D2
Darnall Road Surgery
DARN/MH S9 .... **124** C2
Dead Earnest Theatre
ST/HB/BR S6 .... **121** D1
Deepcar Junior School
STKB/PEN S36 .... **69** F3
Deerlands Special School
SHEFN S5 .... **98** C4
Deer Park Surgery
ST/HB/BR S6 .... **119** F1
Denaby Lane Industrial Estate
CONI DN12 .... **59** F5
Derbyshire County Council
CHNE S41 .... **11** F4
Derbyshire County Council
CHNE S41 .... **184** A1
Derbyshire County Council
CHSW S40 .... **10** C5
Derbyshire County Council
ECK/KIL S21 .... **164** C5
Devonshire Green Medical Centre
SHEF S1 .... **8** C6
Dobcroft Infant School
ECC S11 .... **145** F1
Dobcroft Junior School
ECC S11 .... **145** F2
Dodworth Health Centre
DOD/DAR S75 .... **20** A3
Dodworth Junior School
DOD/DAR S75 .... **20** A3
Doncaster Area Health Authority
CONI DN12 .... **84** C1

Doncaster Area Health Authority
DON DN1 .... **5** F4
Doncaster Area Health Authority
MEX/SWTN S64 .... **58** C4
Doncaster Balby
Central First School
DONS/BSCR DN4 .... **43** F3
Doncaster Civic Theatre
DON DN1 .... **5** F4
Doncaster College
DON DN1 .... **4** D2
Doncaster Golf Course
DONS/BSCR DN4 .... **67** E3
Doncaster Health Authority
DONS/BSCR DN4 .... **44** B4
Doncaster Health Authority
DONS/BSCR DN4 .... **63** F2
Doncaster Magistrates Court
DON DN1 .... **4** D5
Doncaster Metropolitan Borough
Council
ARMTH DN3 .... **19** F4
Doncaster Metropolitan Borough
Council
BTLY DN5 .... **4** B1
Doncaster Metropolitan Borough
Council
CONI DN12 .... **85** D1
Doncaster Metropolitan Borough
Council
DON DN1 .... **4** D6
Doncaster Metropolitan Borough
Council
DON DN1 .... **4** D4
Doncaster Metropolitan Borough
Council
DON DN1 .... **5** F3
Doncaster Metropolitan Borough
Council
DON DN1 .... **5** C5
Doncaster Metropolitan Borough
Council
DONS/BSCR DN4 .... **46** C4
Doncaster Metropolitan Borough
Council
MEX/SWTN S64 .... **59** D3
Doncaster Museum & Art Gallery
DON DN1 .... **5** F4
Doncaster Road Infant School
MEX/SWTN S64 .... **59** D4
Doncaster Road Jmi School
RHAM/THRY S65 .... **104** B1
Doncaster Road Junior School
MEX/SWTN S64 .... **59** D4
Doncaster Road Primary School
BSLY S70 .... **22** B2
Doncaster Rovers Football Club
DONS/BSCR DN4 .... **45** E2
Doncaster Royal Infirmary
& Montagu Hospital N H S Trust
WHHL DN2 .... **31** D4
Doncaster & South Humber
Healthcare Nhs Trust
DONS/BSCR DN4 .... **63** F2
Doncaster Town Cricket Club
WHHL DN2 .... **5** H4
Don Valley High School
BTLY DN5 .... **28** B1
Dore Junior & Infant School
TOT/DORE S17 .... **156** B2
Dovercourt Surgery
SHEFP/MNR S2 .... **136** C1
Dr Chambers & Partners
CHPT/GREN S35 .... **73** E3
Dr John Bingham Junior
& Infant School
SHEFS S8 .... **159** E3
Dr John Worrall School
DARN/MH S9 .... **111** E5
Dronfield County Junior School
DRON S18 .... **169** E2
Dronfield Health Centre
DRON S18 .... **169** E2
Dronfield Infant School
DRON S18 .... **169** E2
The Dronfield School
DRON S18 .... **168** C1
Dronfield Sports Centre
DRON S18 .... **169** D2
Dunston Primary School
CHNE S41 .... **183** E1
Dunston Trading Estate
CHNE S41 .... **177** F4

Dykeshall Medical Centre
ST/HB/BR S6.................................. **107** F3
Eastwood Trading Estate
RHAM/THRY S65....................... **94** B5
Ecclesall Infant School
ECC S11 .... **133** D4
Ecclesall Medical Centre
ECC S11 .... **133** E5
Ecclesfield Comprehensive
School
CHPT/GREN S35.................... **88** B3
Ecclesfield Health Centre
CHPT/GREN S35.................... **88** C5
Ecclesfield Parish Council
CHPT/GREN S35.................... **73** F4
Eckington Health Centre
ECK/KIL S21............................ **164** C5
Eckington Junior School
ECK/KIL S21............................ **164** B5
Eckington School
ECK/KIL S21............................ **163** E5
Edward Sheerien School
BSLYN/ROY S71 .... **14** C1
Ellers Middle School
DONS/BSCR DN4 .... **45** F4
Ellesmere Teaching School
ATT S4 .... **123** D1
Emmett Carr Surgery
ECK/KIL S21............................ **175** F3
Eppic Theatre
CHPT/GREN S35.................... **87** D5
Fairfield School of Art
BSLY S70 .... **2** B4
Falkland House Surgery
ECC S11 .... **133** E4
Far Lane Medical Centre
ST/HB/BR S6.............................. **107** F3
Ferham House Clinic
KIMB S61 .... **102** B3
Fernham Junior & Infant School
KIMB S61 .... **102** B3
Fire Police Museum
OWL S3 .... **8** D4
Firs Hill Junior School
ATT S4 .... **109** F4
Firth Park Medical Centre
SHEFN S5 .... **110** B1
Firth Park School
SHEFN S5 .... **110** A1
Foxhill Medical Centre
ST/HB/BR S6.............................. **97** E3
Fox Hill Primary School
ST/HB/BR S6.............................. **97** E3
Frame Gallery
RHAM S60 .... **6** D4
Frenchgate Centre
DON DN1 .... **4** D3
Fullerton House School
CONI DN12.................................. **60** A5
The Gables School
WMB/DAR S73 .... **39** E3
The Gallery
DON DN1 .... **5** E3
Gawber Junior & Infant School
DOD/DAR S75 .... **12** B4
Gilbert Heathcote Infant School
CHNE S41...................................... **184** A1
Gladys Buxton School
DRON S18 .... **170** A1
Gleadless Clinic
HACK/IN S12 .... **149** F2
Gleadless Primary School
HACK/IN S12 .... **137** F5
Globe Business Centre
OWL S3 .... **8** C1
Goldthorpe RC Jmi School
DEARNE S63.............................. **27** E5
Gooseacre Primary School
DEARNE S63.............................. **26** C2
Grange Gate Junior School
BSLYN/ROY S71 .... **15** F5
Grange Lane Industrial Estate
BSLYN/ROY S71 .... **23** F2
Graves Art Gallery
SHEF S1 .... **9** F6
Greasborough Health Centre
KIMB S61 .... **92** C3
Greasborough Junior & Infant School
KIMB S61 .... **92** C3
Greengate Lane Primary School
CHPT/GREN S35.................... **73** F4
Greenhill Health Centre
SHEFS S8 .... **158** C2

Greenhill Primary School
SHEFS S8 .... **158** C1
Greenlands Junior School
DARN/MH S9........................... **125** D3
Greenside Surgery
KIMB S61 .... **92** C3
Greenway Natural Health Centre
TOT/DORE S17 .... **156** B4
Grenoside Primary School
CHPT/GREN S35.................... **87** D5
Greystones First School
ECC S11 .... **133** E3
Greystones Medical Centre
ECC S11 .... **133** F3
Greystones Primary School
ECC S11 .... **133** F3
Grove Street Junior & Infant
School
BSLYN/ROY S71 .... **3** F5
Guildhall Industrial Estate
ARMTH DN3 .... **19** F3
Hackenthorpe Medical Centre
HACK/IN S12 .... **151** E2
Hady School
CHNE S41...................................... **191** E2
Halfway Infant School
MOS S20 .... **164** C1
Halfway Junior School
MOS S20 .... **164** C1
Hallam Primary School
FUL S10 .... **132** A1
Hallamshire Business Park
FUL S10 .... **134** C1
The Hallamshire Gallery
ECC S11 .... **133** F3
Hallamshire Natural
Health Centre
ECC S11 .... **134** A2
Hall Cross Comprehensive
School
DON DN1 .... **5** G3
Handsworth Branch Clinic
HAN/WDH S13 .... **139** D1
Handsworth Road
Medical Centre
HAN/WDH S13 .... **139** D1
Hanover Medical Centre
FUL S10 .... **121** F5
Hartington Industrial Estate
STV/CWN S43 .... **181** F2
Hasland Hall Community School
CHNE S41...................................... **191** E5
Hasland Primary Infant School
CHNE S41...................................... **191** D4
Hasland Primary Junior School
CHNE S41...................................... **191** D5
Hatfield Primary School
SHEFN S5 .... **99** E4
Healthcare Surgery
SHEFN S5 .... **97** E5
Heeley Business Centre
SHEFP/MNR S2........................ **135** E2
Heeley Green Surgery
SHEFP/MNR S2........................ **135** F4
Heeley Retail Park
SHEFS S8 .... **147** D2
Hemingfield Ellis C of E
Junior & Infant School
WMB/DAR S73 .... **39** D5
Hemsworth Primary School
GLV S14 .... **148** B3
Henry Bradley County
Infant School
STV/CWN S43 .... **186** A1
Herdings Primary School
GLV S14 .... **148** C3
Herries School
SHEFN S5 .... **108** C2
Herringthorpe Junior
& Infant School
RHAM/THRY S65................... **104** C5
Hexthorpe First School
DONS/BSCR DN4 .... **43** E2
Hexthorpe Primary School
DONS/BSCR DN4 .... **43** E3
Highfields Junior School
WMB/DAR S73 .... **39** D2
High Greave Jmi School
RHAM/THRY S65................... **105** D1
High Green Health Centre
CHPT/GREN S35.................... **73** E3
High Green Primary School
CHPT/GREN S35.................... **73** E3

High Storrs School
ECC S11 .... **133** D4
High Street Medical Centre
STV/CWN S43 .... **181** F4
Highwoods Infant School
MEX/SWTN S64...................... **57** F2
Hill House Preparatory School
DON DN1 .... **5** H2
Hill Primary School
DEARNE S63.............................. **27** F2
Hillsborough Health Centre
ST/HB/BR S6.............................. **108** A5
Hillsborough Primary School
ST/HB/BR S6.............................. **108** A3
Hinde House School
SHEFN S5 .... **99** F5
Hm Prison
BTLY DN5...................................... **4** B3
Holgate School
BSLY S70 .... **21** D1
Hollies Medical Centre
ECC S11 .... **134** B3
Hollingwood Junior
& Infant School
STV/CWN S43 .... **180** B5
Hollis Hospital
TOT/DORE S17 .... **144** C3
Holly House School
CHNE S41...................................... **178** B3
Hollywood Bowling
DARN/MH S9........................... **112** A4
Holme Hall Primary School
CHSW S40 .... **182** C4
Holt House Infant School
ABRD S7 .... **146** B1
Holy Cross Deanery C of E Junior
& Infant School
BSLYN/ROY S71 .... **14** C1
Holyrood RC Junior
& Infant School
BSLY S70 .... **21** E2
Howarth Junior & Infant School
RHAM S60 .... **114** A5
Hoyland Common
Primary School
HOY S74.. **50** B3
Hoyland Elsecar C of E Junior
& Infant School
HOY S74.. **52** C3
Hoyland Greenfield Junior
& Infant School
HOY S74.. **52** A2
Hoyland St Helens RC Junior
& Infant School
HOY S74.. **51** E2
Hoyland Sports Centre
HOY S74.. **51** D2
H S B C Sports Club
TOT/DORE S17 .... **144** B4
Hucklow Primary School
SHEFN S5 .... **110** A2
Hunloke Secondary School
CHSW S40 .... **190** B5
Hunningley Junior
& Infant School
BSLY S70 .... **23** F3
Hunters Bar Junior
& Infant School
ECC S11 .... **134** A2
Industrial Centre
MEX/SWTN S64...................... **58** B4
Inkersall Primary School
STV/CWN S43 .... **187** D2
Intake High School
WHHL DN2.................................... **32** B4
Intake Junior & Infant School
HACK/IN S12 .... **137** F4
Ironbridge Industrial Estate
HAN/WDH S13 .... **140** A2
Ivanhoe Junior & Infant School
CONI DN12.................................. **84** B2
Jamiyat Tablig Ul Islam Mosque
DARN/MH S9........................... **124** B1
Jaunty Springs Health Centre
HACK/IN S12 .... **149** F1
Jessop Hospital for Women
OWL S3 .... **8** A5
Jordanthorpe Health Centre
SHEFS S8 .... **159** F2
Junction 34 Industrial Estate
DARN/MH S9........................... **112** B3
Keir House Surgery
BSLY S70 .... **2** A3

Kelham Island Museum
  OWL S3 .... 8 D2
Kelvin Grove Surgery
  WMB/DAR S73 .... 39 F3
Kendray Hospital
  BSLY S70 .... 23 D2
Kendray Infant School
  BSLY S70 .... 23 D3
Kendray Primary School
  BSLY S70 .... 22 C3
Keresforth Primary School
  DOD/DAR S75 .... 20 B4
Killamarsh County Junior
  & Infant School
  ECK/KIL S21 .... 166 C1
Killamarsh Leisure Centre
  ECK/KIL S21 .... 166 B1
Killamarsh Medical Centre
  ECK/KIL S21 .... 166 A1
Kilnhurst Business Park
  MEX/SWTN S64 .... 81 F5
Kilnhurst Junior & Infants School
  MEX/SWTN S64 .... 82 A4
Kimberworth
  Comprehensive School
  KIMB S61 .... 102 A3
Kimberworth Infants School
  KIMB S61 .... 102 A2
Kimberworth Park Clinic
  KIMB S61 .... 91 F5
Kimberworth Park Medical Centre
  KIMB S61 .... 101 F1
King Ecgbert Secondary School
  TOT/DORE S17 .... 156 B2
King Edward Vii School
  FUL S10 .... 121 E5
Kingfisher First School
  WHHL DN2 .... 31 E2
Kingthorne Group Practice
  DON DN1 .... 5 G2
Kirk Balk School
  HOY S74 .... 51 D2
Kirkby Avenue Primary School
  BTLY DN5 .... 29 E3
Kitchen Gallery
  RHAM S60 .... 6 D6
Lakeside First School
  DONS/BSCR DN4 .... 45 D3
Lantern Theatre
  ABRD S7 .... 134 C2
Lecture Theatre
  SHEF S1 .... 8 B5
Lenthall School
  DRON S18 .... 159 F5
Limpsfield Junior School
  DARN/MH S9 .... 111 E2
Listerdale Shopping Centre
  RHAM/THRY S65 .... 105 F5
The Little Gallery
  RAW S62 .... 76 C2
Little Theatre
  DEARNE S63 .... 26 C4
Littleworth Lane Infant School
  BSLYN/ROY S71 .... 15 E4
Lobwood Junior & Infant School
  BSLY S70 .... 22 B5
Lodge Moor Medical Centre
  FUL S10 .... 131 E1
Longcar Junior & Infant School
  BSLY S70 .... 21 E2
Lound Infant School
  CHPT/GREN S35 .... 74 A5
Lound Junior School
  CHPT/GREN S35 .... 74 B5
Lowedges Primary School
  SHEFS S8 .... 159 D2
Loxley Primary School
  ST/HB/BR S6 .... 106 B3
Lundwood Medical Centre
  BSLYN/ROY S71 .... 15 E5
The Lyceum Theatre
  SHEF S1 .... 9 F6
Lydgate Infant School
  FUL S10 .... 120 B4
Lydgate Junior School
  FUL S10 .... 120 B4
Makki Mosque
  SHEFS S8 .... 135 E4
Malin Bridge Primary School
  ST/HB/BR S6 .... 107 F4
Manor Clinic
  SHEFP/MNR S2 .... 137 D4
Manor Lodge Middle School
  SHEFP/MNR S2 .... 136 C1

Manor Lodge Primary School
  SHEFP/MNR S2 .... 136 C1
Manor Park Medical Centre
  SHEFP/MNR S2 .... 124 B5
Manor Top Medical Centre
  HACK/IN S12 .... 137 E4
Market Hall
  DON DN1 .... 5 E2
Market Junior School
  HOY S74 .... 51 F1
Marlcliffe Primary School
  ST/HB/BR S6 .... 107 F2
Marshgate Industrial Estate
  BTLY DN5 .... 4 B2
Marsh Lane Primary School
  ECK/KIL S21 .... 162 C5
Mary Swanick Primary School
  CHNE S41 .... 178 D3
The Mcauley School
  DONS/BSCR DN4 .... 47 E4
Meadow Bank Industrial Estate
  KIMB S61 .... 102 A3
Meadowhall Centre
  DARN/MH S9 .... 112 A1
Meadowhall Junior School
  KIMB S61 .... 101 F3
Meadowhall Retail Park
  DARN/MH S9 .... 112 A4
Meadowhead School
  SHEFS S8 .... 159 E1
Meadows Community School
  CHNE S41 .... 178 C3
Meersbrook Bank
  Primary School
  SHEFS S8 .... 135 D5
Melrose Surgery
  OWL S3 .... 122 C1
Merlin Theatre
  ABRD S7 .... 134 B3
Merlin Theatre
  ST/HB/BR S6 .... 106 C3
Metrodome sports
  & Leisure complex
  BSLYN/ROY S71 .... 3 F4
Mexborough Business Centre
  MEX/SWTN S64 .... 58 C3
Mexborough Comprehensive
  School
  MEX/SWTN S64 .... 58 A2
Mexborough Windhill
  Junior & Infant School
  MEX/SWTN S64 .... 59 D2
Middlecroft Leisure Centre
  STV/CWN S43 .... 187 E2
Mill Road Surgery
  CHPT/GREN S35 .... 88 C5
Mill Trading Estate
  BSLYN/ROY S71 .... 22 C1
Monk Bretton Health Centre
  BSLYN/ROY S71 .... 15 D3
Monkwood Health Centre
  RAW S62 .... 79 F4
Montagu Hospital
  MEX/SWTN S64 .... 58 B2
Monteney Middle
  & Primary School
  SHEFN S5 .... 98 B2
Montgomery House
  Medical Centre
  ST/HB/BR S6 .... 8 B1
Montgomery Theatre
  SHEF S1 .... 9 E5
Monument
  DON DN1 .... 5 G4
Moorgate Business Centre
  RHAM S60 .... 7 E6
Moorgate Mosque &
  Community Centre
  RHAM S60 .... 6 D6
Morley Place Junior School
  CONI DN12 .... 84 B1
Mosborough Medical Centre
  MOS S20 .... 164 A1
Mosborough Primary School
  MOS S20 .... 164 B1
Mosque
  OWL S3 .... 122 C1
Mosque
  RHAM S60 .... 6 A5
Mossbrook Special School
  SHEFS S8 .... 148 A5
The Mount Group Practice
  DON DN1 .... 5 H2

Mount Osborne Industrial Park
  BSLYN/ROY S71 .... 3 H
Mount Vernon Hospital
  BSLY S70 .... 22 A
Museum
  ECC S11 .... 134 A
Myers Grove School
  ST/HB/BR S6 .... 107 E
National Music Centre
  SHEF S1 .... 122 C
The Nelson Practice
  BTLY DN5 .... 28 C
Nether Edge Hospital
  ECC S11 .... 134 B
Nether Green Infant School
  FUL S10 .... 132 B
Nether Green Junior School
  FUL S10 .... 132 C
Netherthorpe Primary School
  OWL S3 .... 8 B
Newbold C of E School
  CHNE S41 .... 183 F2
Newbold Community School
  CHNE S41 .... 183 F3
Newbold Community School
  CHSW S40 .... 183 E5
Newfield School
  SHEFS S8 .... 148 A2
Newman Special School
  RHAM S60 .... 115 E5
New Street Health Centre
  BSLY S70 .... 21 F2
New Surgery
  MEX/SWTN S64 .... 58 C4
Newton Business Centre
  BTLY DN5 .... 43 D1
New Village Primary School
  BTLY DN5 .... 16 C4
New Whittington Infant School
  STV/CWN S43 .... 179 E2
New Whittington Primary
  Junior School
  CHNE S41 .... 179 E3
Nightingale Primary School
  DONS/BSCR DN4 .... 62 C1
Nook Lane Junior School
  ST/HB/BR S6 .... 106 A5
Norfolk Middle School
  SHEFP/MNR S2 .... 136 C2
Norfolk Park Health Centre
  SHEFP/MNR S2 .... 136 A2
Northcliffe School
  CONI DN12 .... 60 B5
North Derbyshire
  Health Authority
  CHSW S40 .... 11 E4
North East Derbyshire
  District Council
  CHSW S40 .... 10 D5
North East Derbyshire
  District Council
  DRON S18 .... 169 E2
North East Derbyshire
  District Council
  DRON S18 .... 169 F2
Northfield Junior School
  DRON S18 .... 160 A5
Northlands Community
  Health Centre
  SHEFN S5 .... 98 A5
Norton Free Primary School
  SHEFS S8 .... 148 A4
Norton Oakes Cricket Club
  SHEFS S8 .... 148 B4
Notre Dame School
  FUL S10 .... 133 E1
Oakes Park Special School
  SHEFS S8 .... 148 A3
Oakfield Junior School
  WMB/DAR S73 .... 39 E3
Oakwell Business Centre
  BSLYN/ROY S71 .... 3 H6
Oakwood Surgery
  DONS/BSCR DN4 .... 46 C5
Oakwood Swimming Baths
  RHAM S60 .... 115 D1
Odeon Cinema
  BSLY S70 .... 2 D4
Odeon Cinema
  DON DN1 .... 5 F4
Odeon Cinema
  SHEF S1 .... 9 F5
Old College of Technology
  BSLY S70 .... 2 C4

Old Forge Business Park
SHEFP/MNR S2 .... 135 E3
Old Hall Comprehensive School
KIMB S61 .... 101 F2
Ora Gallery
ECC S11 .... 134 B2
Our Lady of Sorrows RC School
ARMTH DN3 .... 33 E2
Our Lady RC Primary School
BTLY DN5 .... 16 C5
Our Ladys & St Josephs
RC JMI School
DEARNE S63 .... 56 A2
Owlthorpe Surgery
MOS S20 .... 151 E3
Parkgate Business Park
RAW S62 .... 94 A4
Parkgate Medical Centre
RAW S62 .... 94 A2
Park Health Centre
SHEFP/MNR S2 .... 9 H6
Park Hill Primary School
SHEFP/MNR S2 .... 9 H6
Park Infant School
WHHL DN2 .... 31 D3
Park Primary School
WHHL DN2 .... 31 D3
Park Road Infant School
MEX/SWTN S64 .... 58 B2
Parkside Community School
CHSW S40 .... 190 A2
Park Street Junior
& Infant School
WMB/DAR S73 .... 39 F3
Parson Cross C of E
Primary School
ST/HB/BR S6 .... 97 E5
Peacock Trading Estate
ST/HB/BR S6 .... 108 C4
Pearsons Trading Estate
CHNE S41 .... 178 C5
The Petersgate Medical Centre
BTLY DN5 .... 28 C1
Peveril School of Art
ECC S11 .... 133 F2
Phillimore Park Primary School
DARN/MH S9 .... 124 C1
Phoenix Surgery
DON DN1 .... 5 F4
Pipworth Junior School
SHEFP/MNR S2 .... 137 F1
Pitsmoor Dental Health Centre
ATT S4 .... 109 F5
Pitsmoor Surgery
OWL S3 .... 109 E5
Platts Common Industrial Estate
HOY S74 .... 51 E1
Plumb Estates
ARMTH DN3 .... 19 E4
Pomegranate Theatre
CHNE S41 .... 11 G6
Ponds Forge International
Sports Centre
SHEF S1 .... 9 G5
Porter Croft School
ECC S11 .... 134 C1
Portland Business Park
HAN/WDH S13 .... 138 C1
Prince Edward Middle School
SHEFP/MNR S2 .... 137 E3
Prince Edward Primary School
SHEFP/MNR S2 .... 137 E3
Prince of Wales Road
Medical Centre
DARN/MH S9 .... 125 D4
Priory School
DONS/BSCR DN4 .... 46 C5
Public Baths
DEARNE S63 .... 56 A2
Public Baths
ST/HB/BR S6 .... 121 F2
Public Swimming Baths
ECK/KIL S21 .... 164 C5
Pye Bank Trinity C of E
Junior School
OWL S3 .... 122 C1
Queens Road Clinic
BSLYN/ROY S71 .... 3 E5
Queen Street Junior
& Infant School
MEX/SWTN S64 .... 57 E5
Ragged School
CHSW S40 .... 190 B2

Railway Staff Social
& Sports Club
STV/CWN S43 .... 180 A5
Rawmarsh Leisure Centre
RAW S62 .... 94 B2
Rawmarsh Monkwood
Jmi School
RAW S62 .... 79 F4
Rawmarsh Thorogate
Junior & Infant School
RAW S62 .... 80 A4
Redbrook Business Park
DOD/DAR S75 .... 12 C2
Redscope Junior & Infant School
KIMB S61 .... 91 F5
Reflex Theatre
SHEFS S8 .... 135 E4
Regent Square Group Practice
DON DN1 .... 5 G3
Register Office
DON DN1 .... 5 G5
Reignhead Primary School
MOS S20 .... 153 D2
Renishaw Primary School
ECK/KIL S21 .... 175 F3
Revolution House
CHNE S41 .... 178 B3
The Richmond Fellowship
MEX/SWTN S64 .... 57 E5
Richmond Hill Junior
& Infant School
BTLY DN5 .... 42 C1
Richmond Medical Centre
HAN/WDH S13 .... 138 B3
Ridgeway Medical Centre
RHAM/THRY S65 .... 105 D2
Ridgeway Primary School
HACK/IN S12 .... 150 C5
Ridgewood Comprehensive
School
BTLY DN5 .... 28 A3
Rivelin Primary School
ST/HB/BR S6 .... 107 F5
Rockingham Business Park
BSLY S70 .... 50 A2
Rockingham College of Further
Education
DEARNE S63 .... 55 F2
Rockingham Junior
& Infant School
KIMB S61 .... 92 A3
Rockley Mount School
BSLY S70 .... 21 D3
Rosedale Middle School
BTLY DN5 .... 28 B2
Rosedale Road Infant School
BTLY DN5 .... 28 B2
Rossington Swimming Pool
NROS/TKH DN11 .... 67 D5
Rother County Junior School
CHSW S40 .... 190 B4
Rotherham Civic Theatre
RHAM/THRY S65 .... 7 E5
Rotherham College of Arts
& Technology
RHAM/THRY S65 .... 7 E4
Rotherham County Court
RHAM S60 .... 7 E6
Rotherham District
General Hospital
RHAM S60 .... 115 D2
Rotherham Health Authority
RHAM S60 .... 114 C2
Rotherham Health Authority
RHAM/THRY S65 .... 104 B3
Rotherham Magistrates Court
RHAM S60 .... 6 C5
Rotherham Metropolitan
Borough Council
RAW S62 .... 93 F1
Rotherham Metropolitan
Borough Council
RHAM S60 .... 6 D6
Rotherham Metropolitan
Borough Council
RHAM S60 .... 6 C3
Rotherham Metropolitan
Borough Council
RHAM/THRY S65 .... 7 E5
Rotherham Metropolitan
Borough Council
RHAM/THRY S65 .... 7 E3
Rotherham Priority Health Trust
RHAM/THRY S65 .... 7 E5

Rotherham Road Medical Centre
BSLYN/ROY S71 .... 14 B1
Rotherham Rugby Club
RHAM/THRY S65 .... 104 A4
Rotherham Town Cricket Club
RHAM/THRY S65 .... 104 A4
Rotherham Town Hall
RHAM S60 .... 6 D6
Rotherham United Football Club
RHAM S60 .... 102 C4
Rotunda Business Centre
CHPT/GREN S35 .... 74 A4
Roughwood Junior School
KIMB S61 .... 91 F4
Rowan School
TOT/DORE S17 .... 156 C2
Rowena Infant School
CONI DN12 .... 84 C1
Royal Hallamshire Hospital
FUL S10 .... 121 E5
Rudston Preparatory School
RHAM/THRY S65 .... 104 A4
Ruskin Gallery
SHEF S1 .... 9 E6
Rustlings Road Medical Centre
ECC S11 .... 133 E2
Rutland Business Park
OWL S3 .... 122 A1
Ryecroft Infant School
RAW S62 .... 80 B5
Sacred Heart R C Primary School
ST/HB/BR S6 .... 108 A5
St Albans RC School
CONI DN12 .... 60 B5
St Andrews C of E
Methodist Aided School
DRON S18 .... 168 B2
St Anns Medical Centre
RHAM/THRY S65 .... 6 D3
St Anns Surgery
KIMB S61 .... 91 F5
St Bedes Primary School
KIMB S61 .... 101 F1
St Bernards RC School
RHAM/THRY S65 .... 105 D1
St Catherines RC
Primary School
OWL S3 .... 109 E4
St Francis Xavier RC School
DONS/BSCR DN4 .... 44 A3
St Georges Church
SHEF S1 .... 8 B5
St Georges Hospital
ST/HB/BR S6 .... 121 E3
St Giles C of E (aided)
Primary School
ECK/KIL S21 .... 166 A2
St Helens Junior & Infant School
BSLYN/ROY S71 .... 15 E2
St James Swimming Pool
DON DN1 .... 5 E5
St John Fisher RC Junior
& Infants School
HACK/IN S12 .... 151 E2
St Johns Business Centre
CHNE S41 .... 184 A1
St Johns C of E (Park)
Primary School
SHEFP/MNR S2 .... 123 E4
St Johns C of E School
MEX/SWTN S64 .... 58 C2
St Josephs Convent School
CHSW S40 .... 10 D4
St Josephs Junior
& Infants School
RAW S62 .... 94 A1
St Josephs RC Primary School
STV/CWN S43 .... 181 E5
St Maries R C Primary School
FUL S10 .... 133 E1
St Mary School
FUL S10 .... 121 D2
St Marys C of E Junior
& Infant School
DOD/DAR S75 .... 13 D5
St Marys C of E Junior
& Infant School
RAW S62 .... 94 A1
St Marys C of E Primary School
ST/HB/BR S6 .... 121 E1
St Marys High Green
RC Primary School
CHPT/GREN S35 .... 73 F3

St Marys RC High School
CHSW S40 .... **183** D2
St Marys RC Primary School
CHSW S40 .... **10** D4
St Marys RC School
RHAM/THRY S65 .... **105** D3
St Marys School
DONS/BSCR DN4 .... **46** B4
St Marys School
DRON S18 .... **171** D3
St Matthews Infant School
DOD/DAR S73 .... **13** D5
St Michaels RC Junior
& Infant School
WMB/DAR S73 .... **40** A1
St Oswalds RC Primary School
SHEFP/MNR S2 .... **123** F5
St Patricks RC School
SHEFN S5 .... **99** D5
St Peter & St Paul School
CHNE S41 .... **191** D2
St Peters RC Primary School
DONS/BSCR DN4 .... **45** E3
St Peters & St Pauls School
CHNE S41 .... **191** D4
St Theresas School
SHEFP/MNR S2 .... **137** F3
St Thomas More R C
Primary School
CHPT/GREN S35 .... **97** E2
St Thomas of Canterbury R C
Primary School
SHEFS S8 .... **147** D5
Saint Vincent Medical Centre
DON DN1 .... **5** G2
St Wilfrids RC Primary School
ABRD S7 .... **146** A1
Saltergate Health Centre
CHSW S40 .... **11** E5
Sandall Wood School
WHHL DN2 .... **32** B4
Sandhill J M I School
RAW S62 .... **81** D5
The Sandringham Practice
WHHL DN2 .... **31** F4
Scawsby College
BTLY DN5 .... **28** A3
Scawsby Health Centre
BTLY DN5 .... **28** C3
Scawthorpe Clinic
BTLY DN5 .... **28** C2
Shardlows Sports Club
CHPT/GREN S35 .... **88** C4
Sharrow Junior School
ECC S11 .... **135** D2
Shaw Lane Industrial Estate
WHHL DN2 .... **32** C1
Shaw Wood Junior
& Infant School
ARMTH DN3 .... **33** E1
Sheaf Heaf Gardens
Industrial Estate
SHEFP/MNR S2 .... **135** F1
Sheaf Market
SHEF S1 .... **9** G4
Sheepbridge Business Centre
CHNE S41 .... **177** F4
Sheffffield Area Health
Authority Sports & Social Club
ECC S11 .... **132** B3
Sheffield Area Health Authority
(Teaching)
FUL S10 .... **121** F4
Sheffield City Council
ATT S4 .... **9** H1
Sheffield City Council
ATT S4 .... **109** F5
Sheffield City Council
ATT S4 .... **110** A4
Sheffield City Council
CHPT/GREN S35 .... **97** E2
Sheffield City Council
DARN/MH S9 .... **112** A3
Sheffield City Council
DARN/MH S9 .... **125** D3
Sheffield City Council
HACK/IN S12 .... **150** C2
Sheffield City Council
HAN/WDH S13 .... **139** F4
Sheffield City Council
MOS S20 .... **152** C3
Sheffield City Council
OWL S3 .... **8** B5

Sheffield City Council
OWL S3 .... **122** B1
Sheffield City Council
SHEF S1 .... **9** F4
Sheffield City Council
SHEF S1 .... **9** E5
Sheffield City Council
SHEFN S5 .... **99** F2
Sheffield City Council
SHEFP/MNR S2 .... **9** H5
Sheffield City Council
SHEFP/MNR S2 .... **123** F4
Sheffield City Council
SHEFP/MNR S2 .... **135** F2
Sheffield City Council
SHEFP/MNR S2 .... **136** B5
Sheffield City Council
SHEFP/MNR S2 .... **137** E3
Sheffield City Council
SHEFS S8 .... **135** E5
Sheffield City Council
SHEFS S8 .... **158** C2
Sheffield City Council
ST/HB/BR S6 .... **8** A2
Sheffield City Council
ST/HB/BR S6 .... **108** A4
The Sheffield College
MOS S20 .... **153** D5
The Sheffield College
SHEFN S5 .... **98** A2
The Sheffield College
SHEFP/MNR S2 .... **135** F1
The Sheffield College
SHEFS S8 .... **159** F1
Sheffield Eagles R L F C Ltd
DARN/MH S9 .... **124** B1
Sheffield Hallam University
FUL S10 .... **121** E5
Sheffield Hallam University
SHEF S1 .... **9** F6
Sheffield Health Authority
FUL S10 .... **121** F4
Sheffield Health Authority
SHEFN S5 .... **99** E5
Sheffield High School
ECC S11 .... **121** D5
Sheffield Magistrates Court
SHEF S1 .... **9** F4
Sheffield Medical Centre
OWL S3 .... **9** G1
Sheffield Natural Health Centre
SHEFS S8 .... **135** D3
Sheffield Sports Stadium Ltd
ST/HB/BR S6 .... **108** B3
Sheffield Technology Park
DARN/MH S9 .... **124** A1
Sheffield United AFC
SHEFP/MNR S2 .... **135** E1
Sheffield United Cricket Club
DARN/MH S9 .... **113** D3
Sheffield Wednesday
Football Club Plc
ST/HB/BR S6 .... **108** A2
Shirecliffe Junior School
SHEFN S5 .... **108** C2
Shire Green Medical Centre
SHEFN S5 .... **99** F3
Shooters Grove Primary School
ST/HB/BR S6 .... **107** D5
Shopping Centre
BSLY S70 .... **2** D5
Shopping Centre
CHSW S40 .... **183** D4
Shopping Centre
RAW S62 .... **93** F1
Shortbrook Primary School
MOS S20 .... **153** D5
Shrewsbury Hospital
SHEFP/MNR S2 .... **123** D5
Sikh Temple
ATT S4 .... **110** A5
Sikh Temple
DON DN1 .... **5** E5
Silverdale School
ECC S11 .... **132** C5
Sir Harold Jackson
Primary School
TOT/DORE S17 .... **157** F3
Sitwell Junior & Infants School
RHAM S60 .... **115** F1
The Sloan Practice
SHEFS S8 .... **148** B3
Sothall Medical Centre
MOS S20 .... **153** D3

Sothall Snooker & Leisure Centre
MOS S20 .... **153** D2
South Cantley Middle School
DONS/BSCR DN4 .... **67** D1
Southey Green Medical Centre
SHEFN S5 .... **109** D1
Southey Hill Surgery
SHEFN S5 .... **98** A5
South Yorkshire
Business Centre
RAW S62 .... **93** F4
Speedwell County
Infants School
STV/CWN S43 .... **181** F5
Springfield Primary School
OWL S3 .... **122** A5
Springwell Community School
STV/CWN S43 .... **187** E2
Springwood Junior
& Infant School
HOY S74 .... **51** E3
Sprotbrough Health Centre
BTLY DN5 .... **42** C2
Stag Medical Centre
RHAM/THRY S65 .... **116** A1
Stairfoot Health Centre
BSLY S70 .... **23** E3
Stannington Health Centre
ST/HB/BR S6 .... **119** D1
Stannington Infant School
ST/HB/BR S6 .... **119** D1
Station Lane Industrial Estate
CHNE S41 .... **178** C4
Station Road Industrial Estate
WMB/DAR S73 .... **39** F2
Station Road Junior
& Infant School
CONI DN12 .... **61** D5
Staveley Council Office
STV/CWN S43 .... **181** F4
Staveley Health Clinic
STV/CWN S43 .... **181** F5
Staveley Junior School
STV/CWN S43 .... **181** E5
Staveley Urban District Council
STV/CWN S43 .... **181** F5
Stirling First School
DON DN1 .... **4** D6
Stirling Junior School
DON DN1 .... **5** E6
Stocksbridge Golf Club
STKB/PEN S36 .... **69** E4
Stocksbridge High School
STKB/PEN S36 .... **68** C2
Stocksbridge Junior School
STKB/PEN S36 .... **68** C3
Stocksbridge Leisure Centre
STKB/PEN S36 .... **68** B2
Stocksbridge Rugby Club
STKB/PEN S36 .... **68** C1
Stonelow Junior School
DRON S18 .... **169** F1
Storm House School
DEARNE S63 .... **57** D1
Stradbroke Primary School
HAN/WDH S13 .... **138** B3
Sunday School
DEARNE S63 .... **26** B3
Superbowl Two Thousand
KIMB S61 .... **101** F1
Superintendent Swimming Baths
CHPT/GREN S35 .... **88** B1
Swallownest Health Centre
AU/AST/KP S26 .... **142** B3
Swinton Brookfield
Primary School
MEX/SWTN S64 .... **81** E1
Swinton Comprehensive School
MEX/SWTN S64 .... **81** D1
Swinton Fitzwilliam
Infants School
MEX/SWTN S64 .... **80** C1
Swinton Meadows Business Park
MEX/SWTN S64 .... **58** A5
Swinton Meadows
Industrial Estate
MEX/SWTN S64 .... **58** A5
Swinton Milton Special School
MEX/SWTN S64 .... **57** D5
Swinton Swimming Pool
MEX/SWTN S64 .... **57** E5
Sycamore Hall Preparatory
School
DONS/BSCR DN4 .... **43** E5

Tapton Golf Course
CHNE S41 .... **185** D4
Tapton Secondary School
FUL S10 .... **120** B5
Tates Gallery
DARN/MH S9 .... **125** D3
Tates Gallery
ST/HB/BR S6 .... **108** A4
Templeborough Business Centre
RHAM S60 .... **103** D5
Tertiary College
ECK/KIL S21 .... **164** B5
Thomas Rotherham College
RHAM S60 .... **103** F5
Thornbridge School
HACK/IN S12 .... **150** B3
Thornhill Industrial Estate
KIMB S61 .... **6** B2
Thornhill Jmi School
RHAM S60 .... **6** A4
Thorpe Hesley Clinic
KIMB S61 .... **90** A2
Thorpe Hesley Infant School
KIMB S61 .... **89** F2
Thorpe Hesley Junior School
KIMB S61 .... **90** A2
Thrybergh St Gerards RC M
& I School
RHAM/THRY S65 .... **95** E4
Thurnscoe Business Centre
DEARNE S63 .... **27** E4
Thurnscoe Business Park
DEARNE S63 .... **27** E4
Thurnscoe Gooseacre J M School
DEARNE S63 .... **26** C2
Tinsley Junior School
DARN/MH S9 .... **112** C2
Totley All Saints C of E
Primary School
TOT/DORE S17 .... **156** A4
Totley Primary School
TOT/DORE S17 .... **156** B4
Town Fields Primary School
WHHL DN2 .... **5** H2
Trafalgar House Medical Centre
ST/HB/BR S6 .... **97** E5
Tramways Medical Centre
ST/HB/BR S6 .... **108** A4
Treeton C of E Junior
& Infant School
RHAM S60 .... **127** F3
U C I Cinema
MOS S20 .... **152** C2
University of Sheffield
ECC S11 .... **133** F1
University of Sheffield
FUL S10 .... **121** D4
University of Sheffield
OWL S3 .... **121** F4
University of Sheffield
SHEF S1 .... **8** C5
Unstone Junior School
DRON S18 .... **170** C4
Untitled Gallery
SHEF S1 .... **122** C5
Valley Medical Centre
STKB/PEN S36 .... **68** C1
Vanguard Trading Estate
CHSW S40 .... **190** B5
Verdon Recreation Centre
OWL S3 .... **9** F1
Victoria Primary School
DEARNE S63 .... **56** B2
Wales Junior & Infant School
AU/AST/KP S26 .... **155** F3
Walkley Medical Centre
FUL S10 .... **121** D1
Walk Talk Galleries
ECC S11 .... **133** F2
Waltheof School
SHEFP/MNR S2 .... **124** C5
Walton Hospital
CHSW S40 .... **189** F5
Ward Green Junior School
BSLY S70 .... **22** A5
Warmsworth Primary School
DONS/BSCR DN4 .... **62** A1
Warren House Surgery
BSLY S70 .... **22** A2
Warwick Street Industrial Estate
CHSW S40 .... **190** C5
Watergate Centre
DON DN1 .... **5** E4

Wath C of E JMI School
DEARNE S63 .... **55** F1
Wath Park Infant School
DEARNE S63 .... **55** F3
Wath Pope Pius R C
Secondary School
DEARNE S63 .... **56** B4
Wath R U F C
DEARNE S63 .... **56** A1
Wath Upon Dearne
Comprehensive School
DEARNE S63 .... **56** A3
Wath West Industrial Estate
DEARNE S63 .... **41** D5
Waverley Junior School
DONS/BSCR DN4 .... **62** C1
Welfare Clinic
ECK/KIL S21 .... **164** B5
Wentworth Castle College
of Education
DOD/DAR S75 .... **34** A2
Wentworth C of E School
RAW S62 .... **76** B2
Westfield Health Centre
MOS S20 .... **152** C5
Westfield Infant School
CHSW S40 .... **188** C2
West Melton J & I School
DEARNE S63 .... **55** D1
Weston Park Hospital
N H S Trust
FUL S10 .... **121** E4
Westside Gallery
FUL S10 .... **134** B1
Westways Middle
Primary School
FUL S10 .... **121** D3
Wheatley Hall Business Centre
WHHL DN2 .... **31** E2
Whiston Grange School
RHAM S60 .... **115** E3
Whiston Junior & Infant School
RHAM S60 .... **115** F3
Whiston Worry Goose
Jmi School
RHAM S60 .... **116** B3
Whitecotes Primary School
CHSW S40 .... **190** A4
White House Surgery
SHEFP/MNR S2 .... **137** F2
Whitelea Grove Trading Estate
MEX/SWTN S64 .... **57** F4
Whiteley Wood Clinic
ECC S11 .... **132** C3
Whiteways Junior School
ATT S4 .... **110** B4
Whitley Hall Cricket Club
CHPT/GREN S35 .... **87** F5
Whittington Medical Centre
CHNE S41 .... **178** B3
Whittington Moor Surgery
CHNE S41 .... **184** B1
Whittington Moor Surgery
CHNE S41 .... **184** C2
William Levick Infant School
DRON S18 .... **168** A1
William Levick Primary School
DRON S18 .... **168** A1
William Rhodes Primary School
CHSW S40 .... **189** F2
Wilthorpe Junior School
DOD/DAR S75 .... **13** D3
Wincobank Surgery
DARN/MH S9 .... **100** C5
Windermere Surgery
CHNE S41 .... **183** E2
Windmill Hill Primary School
CHPT/GREN S35 .... **88** A2
Wingfield Comprehensive School
KIMB S61 .... **92** B4
Wisewood Secondary School
ST/HB/BR S6 .... **107** D3
Wombwell Aldham Junior
& Infant School
WMB/DAR S73 .... **38** B2
Wombwell Clinic
WMB/DAR S73 .... **39** D2
Wombwell Cricket Club
WMB/DAR S73 .... **38** C3
Wombwell High School
WMB/DAR S73 .... **39** F4
Wombwell Jump Junior
& Infant School
HOY S74 .... **52** A1

Wombwell Public Baths
WMB/DAR S73 .... **39** E3
Woodfield First School
DONS/BSCR DN4 .... **63** F1
Woodgrove Surgery
DEARNE S63 .... **56** A2
Woodhouse Clinic
HAN/WDH S13 .... **139** F4
Woodhouse Medical Centre
HAN/WDH S13 .... **139** F4
Woodseats Medical Centre
SHEFS S8 .... **147** D3
Woodseats Primary School
SHEFS S8 .... **147** D2
Woodstock Bower Group Practice
KIMB S61 .... **102** B3
Woodthorpe Community
Primary School
HAN/WDH S13 .... **138** A3
Works
ARMTH DN3 .... **19** E2
Works
CHSW S40 .... **190** C2
Works
RHAM/THRY S65 .... **95** D3
Worsbrough Bridge RC School
BSLY S70 .... **22** C5
Worsbrough C of E Junior
& Infant School
BSLY S70 .... **36** A4
Worsbrough Common County
Primary School
BSLY S70 .... **22** A4
Worsbrough Health Centre
BSLY S70 .... **22** C5
Worsbrough High School
BSLY S70 .... **37** E1
Worsbrough Mill Museum
BSLY S70 .... **36** B2
Wybourn Primary School
SHEFP/MNR S2 .... **123** E4
Yewlands School
CHPT/GREN S35 .... **97** F2
York House Medical Centre
SHEFP/MNR S2 .... **137** D2

Page 13

F5
1 Aireton Rd
2 Churchfield
3 Church La
4 Church St
5 Eastgate
6 Lancaster Ga
7 Rosehill Ct
8 Sadler Ga
9 St Mary's Ga
10 St Mary's Pl
11 Victoria St
12 Westwood Ct

Page 22

A1
1 Burleigh Ct
2 Burlington Ar
3 Cheapside
4 Freemans Yd
5 Hayes Cft
6 Malthouse Rd
7 May Day Gn
8 Midland St
9 Pall Mall
10 Sherwood St
11 Wesley St

A2
1 Britannia Cl
2 Buckley Ct
3 Copper Cl
4 Denison Ct
5 Duke Crs
6 Duke St
7 Freeman St
8 Providence Ct
9 Quarry St
10 Rebecca Ms
11 Rosebery Ter
12 Taylor Rw
13 Upper New St
14 Wilkinson St

A3
1 California Crs
2 Chestnut Ct
3 Dickinson Pl
4 Dickinson Rd
5 Essex Rd
6 Frederic Pl
7 Hornby St
8 Howard St
9 Kelsey Ter
10 Kenworthy Rd
11 Stoneleigh Cft
12 Warren Pl

B2
1 Clifton St
2 Gold Cft
3 Henshall St
4 Milnes St
5 Oakwell Ter
6 Osborne Ms
7 St Peter's Ter
8 Seth Ter
9 Sunderland Ter
10 Victoria Ter
11 Wilby La

B5
1 Blackburn St
2 Brockfield Cl
3 Croft St
4 Henry St
5 John St
6 Kingwell Cft
7 Kingwell Ms
8 Mill Ct
9 Norman Cl
10 Osmond Pl
11 Osmond Wy
12 Parkside Ms
13 Sweyn Cft

Page 103

E3
1 College St
2 The Crofts
3 Domine La
4 Down's Rw
5 Quarry Hl
6 Snail Hl
7 Stanley St
8 The Statutes
9 Unity Pl

F3
1 Catherine St
2 Chatham St
3 Doncaster Ga
4 Douglas St
5 Morpeth St
6 Percy St
7 Summerfield
8 Whybourne Gv

Page 121

D3
1 Ainsley Rd
2 Clementson Rd
3 Cobden Pl
4 Conduit La
5 Leamington St
6 Romsdal Rd
7 Spring House Rd
8 Spring View Rd
9 Warwick St
10 Warwick Ter

Page 122

A2
1 Bedford St
2 Dixon St
3 Downing La
4 Dun Flds
5 Dun La
6 Henry St
7 Infirmary Rd
8 Lancaster St
9 Lister La
10 Matthew St
11 Montgomery Terrace Rd
12 Percy St
13 St Philip's Rd
14 Sudbury St
15 Waterloo Wk

A3
1 Blue Boy St
2 Brocco St
3 Brownell St
4 Burnt Tree La
5 Craven St
6 Ellison St
7 Morpeth St
8 Netherthorpe St
9 Queen's Rw
10 Well Meadow Dr
11 Well Meadow St

A4
1 Abney St
2 Boden La
3 Broad Lane Ct
4 Canning St
5 Charlotte La
6 Chester St
7 Congress St
8 Convent Pl
9 Devonshire La
10 Devonshire St
11 Orange St
12 Pitt Cl
13 Pitt La
14 Portland La
15 Red Hl
16 Regent St
17 St George's Ter
18 St Thomas St
19 Siddall St
20 Westhill La
21 Wheeldon St

D5
1 Ashdell
2 Ashdell La
3 Ashgate La
4 Caxton Rd
5 Chandos St
6 Hoole La
7 Nile St
8 Peel St
9 Taptonville Crs
10 Turners La
11 Watson Rd

E3
1 Barber Crs
2 Barber Pl
3 The Coach Houses
4 Crookesmoor Dr
5 Elliot Rd
6 Ivy Dr
7 Ivy Gv
8 Moorgate Av
9 Warrington Rd

E4
1 Claremont Crs
2 Damer St
3 Harcourt Crs
4 Palmerston Rd
5 Severn Ct
6 Severn Rd
7 Shearwood Rd
8 Tree Root Wk

F2
1 Blake Grove Rd
2 Brandreth Rd
3 Brandreth Cl
4 Burlington Ct
5 Carnarvon St
6 Daniel Hill Ter
7 Gilpin La
8 Philadelphia Dr
9 Philadelphia Gv
10 Portland St
11 Shipton St
12 Straw La
13 Westmoreland St
14 Yeomans Rd

F3
1 St Stephen's Wk
2 Yardley Sq

F4
1 Brightmore Dr
2 Conway St
3 Durham Rd
4 Favell Rd
5 Hounsfield La
6 Hounsfield Rd
7 Leavygreave Rd
8 Western Bank
9 Wilkinson La
10 Wilkinson St

F5
1 Broomspring Cl
2 Broomspring La
3 Exeter Wy
4 Gloucester Crs
5 Hanover St
6 Holberry Cl
7 Holberry Gdns
8 Mackenzie Crs
9 Monmouth St
10 Ruth Sq
11 Upper Hanover St

B3
1 Bower Spring
2 Cupola
3 Lee Cft
4 North Church St
5 Paradise La
6 Paradise Sq
7 Paradise St
8 Plum La
9 St Peter's Cl
10 Silver Street Head
11 Water St
12 Workhouse La

B4
1 Barker's Pool
2 Bells Sq
3 Cambridge St
4 Chapel Wk
5 Charles La
6 Cross Burgess St
7 East Pde
8 Fargate
9 Holly La
10 Norfolk La
11 Orchard La
12 Orchard St
13 Penton St
14 Pool Sq
15 St James' St
16 Wellington St
17 West Street La

B5
1 Cambridge St
2 Clay La
3 Cumberland Wy
4 Duke La
5 Froggatt La
6 Hallam La
7 Jessop St
8 Matilda Wy
9 Moor Head
10 Newton La
11 Rockingham Cl
12 Rockingham Ga
13 Rockingham Wy
14 Union La
15 Union St

C3
1 Castle Gn
2 Harts Head
3 Haymarket
4 Johnson La
5 Joiner St
6 Lady's Dr
7 Meetinghouse La
8 Shude Hl
9 Waingate
10 Wharf St
11 Willey St

C5
1 Brittain St
2 Cross Turner St
3 Furnival St
4 Granville St
5 Leadmill Rd

Page 123

D4
1 Anson St
2 Blackwell Cl
3 Blackwell Ct
4 Crown Pl
5 High Street La
6 Manor Oaks Dr
7 Manor Oaks Gdns
8 Rhodes St
9 Talbot Rd
10 Weigh La

D5
1 Coates St
2 Glencoe Dr
3 Glencoe Pl
4 Robinson Rd
5 Samson St
6 Talbot Crs
7 Talbot Gdns
8 Talbot Pl

F5
1 Kestrel Gn
2 Magpie Gv
3 Maltravers Cl
4 Osprey Gdns
5 Partridge Vw
6 Plover Ct
7 Quail Ri
8 Starling Mead
9 Wren Bank

Page 124

B2
1 Bray St
2 Cattal St
3 Chinley St
4 Faranden Rd
5 Fearnehough St
6 Garth Cl
7 Harry Firth Cl
8 Ouseburn St
9 Spofforth Rd
10 Wilfred Cl

Page 134

B2
1 Ashford Rd
2 Berresford Rd
3 Bruce Rd
4 Dyson Pl
5 Eastwood Rd
6 Gordon Rd
7 Harefield Rd
8 Hickmott Rd
9 Jarrow Rd
10 Lynton Rd
11 Rosedale Gdns
12 Rosedale Rd

C4
1 Archibald Rd
2 Gatefield Rd
3 Herbert Rd
4 Marden Rd
5 Violet Bank Rd

Page 135

D2
1 Asher Rd
2 Bennett St
3 Crowther Pl
4 Croydon St
5 Grosvenor Sq
6 Mount Pleasant Rd
7 Penley St
8 Salmon St
9 Sitwell Pl
10 Smeaton St
11 Stemp St
12 Ventnor Pl
13 Ward Pl

D3
1 Ainsty Rd
2 Aizlewood Rd
3 Alcester Rd
4 Brookfield Rd
5 Cutts Ter
6 Dalton Ct
7 Farrar Rd
8 Herschell Rd
9 Marples Cl
10 Marples Dr
11 Miller Rd
12 Rampton Rd
13 Sellers St
14 South View Crs

E2
1 Alderson Rd North
2 Atkin Pl
3 Batt St
4 Belgrave Sq
5 Harrington Rd
6 Holland Pl
7 St Barnabas La
8 Silver Mill Rd
9 Witney St

E3
1 Alderney Rd
2 Fieldhead Rd
3 Gifford Rd
4 Glover Rd
5 Guernsey Rd
6 Jersey Rd
7 Preston St
8 Sark Rd
9 Sheaf Bank
10 Staveley Rd

E4
1 Arthington St
2 Bradbury St
3 Gleadless Rd
4 Goodwin Rd
5 Gregory Rd
6 Maxey Pl
7 Molloy St
8 Nowill Cl
9 Nowill Pl
10 Plantation Rd
11 Southall St
12 Springwood Rd
13 Tillotson Cl
14 Tillotson Ri
15 Wellhead Rd
16 Well Pl
17 Well Rd
18 Whiting St
19 Wilson Pl

F4
1 Farish Pl
2 Gerard Pl
3 Gleadless Ct
4 Jeffery St
5 Nicholson Rd
6 Richards Rd
7 Romney Gdns
8 Sturge Cft

Page 136

B4
1 East Bank Cl
2 East Bank Vw
3 East Bank Wy
4 Gleadless Rd
5 Hartopp Dr

Page 137

F4
1 Applegarth Cl
2 Bagshaw's Rd
3 Holbrook Gv
4 Penthorpe Cl
5 Pleasant Rd

Page 152

C5
1 Birchwood Cl
2 Birchwood Gdns
3 Birchwood Ri
4 Birchwood Wy
5 Challoner Gn
6 Garland Mt
7 Meadowcroft Gld
8 Meadowcroft Ri
9 Pedley Dr
10 Shortbrook Bank
11 Westland Gv

Page 153

E3
1 Byron Rd
2 Charnwood Cl
3 Grizedale Cl
4 Hartland Av
5 Hartland Ct
6 Ringwood Rd
7 Rothbury Cl
8 Rothbury Ct
9 Rufford Ct
10 Waltham Gdns
11 Wareham Ct
12 Willingham Gdns
13 Wychwood Cl
14 Wychwood Cft
15 Wychwood Gv

Page 164

C2
1 Ambleside Cl
2 Borrowdale Av
3 Borrowdale Cl
4 Ennerdale Av
5 Ennerdale Dr
6 Murrayfield Dr
7 Oakworth Cl
8 Ralston Cft
9 Twickenham Av
10 Twickenham Cl
11 Twickenham Gld
12 Twickenham Gv
13 Wasdale Av

Page 182

A4
1 Briardene Cl
2 Easedale Cl
3 Foxbrook Cl
4 Hollens Wy
5 Langdale Cl
6 Stanage Wy
7 Wheatfield Wy
8 Wheathill Cl
9 Woodleigh Cl

B4
1 Ashbourne Cl
2 Bretton Cl
3 Butterton Dr
4 Cauldon Dr
5 Cornfield Cl
6 Harvest Wy
7 Langley Cl
8 Mercaston Cl
9 Parwich Cl
10 Quorn Dr
11 Ravenswood Rd
12 Rednall Cl
13 Upwood Cl
14 Wheathill Cl

Notes

Notes

Notes

Notes